International Rare
Book Prices

EARLY PRINTED
BOOKS

Series Editor: Michael Cole

1991

The Clique

International Rare Book Prices – Early Printed Books

ISBN 1 870773 22 5

North America

Spoon River Press, P.O. Box 3676
Peoria, Illinois 61614, U.S.A.

Typesetting by Maxiprint, York, England
Printed and bound by Biddles Ltd., Guildford, England

Contents

Introduction and Notes

Early Printed Books (being books published prior to 1800) is the second title in the annual series *International Rare Book Prices*. The other titles in the series are *The Arts & Architecture, Modern First Editions, Science & Medicine, Voyages, Travel & Exploration, Literature*.

The series, generally referred to as *IRBP*, provides annual records of the pricing levels of out-of-print, rare or antiquarian books within a number of specialty subject areas and gives likely sources and suppliers for such books in Britain and the United States of America. It is intended to be used by both the experienced bookman and the newcomer to book-collecting.

Sources of information:
The books recorded each year in the various subject volumes of *IRBP* have been selected from catalogues of books for sale issued during the previous year by numerous bookselling firms in Britain and the United States. These firms, listed at the end of this volume, range in nature from the highly specialized, handling books solely with closely defined subject areas, through to large concerns with expertise across a broad spectrum of interests.

Extent of coverage:
IRBP concentrates exclusively on books published in the English language and, throughout the series as a whole, encompasses books published between the 16th century and the 1970s.

The 30,000 or so separate titles recorded in the annual volumes of *IRBP* vary greatly from year to year although naturally there is a degree of overlap, particularly of the more frequently found titles. Consecutive annual volumes do not, therefore, merely update pricings from earlier years; they give substantially different listings of books on each occasion. The value of the *IRBP* volumes lies in providing records of an ever-increasing range of individual titles which have appeared for sale on the antiquarian or rare book market.

Emphasis is placed throughout on books falling within the lower to middle range of the pricing scale (£10 - £250; $20 - $500) rather than restricting selection to the unusually fine or expensive. In so doing, *IRBP* provides a realistic overview of the norm, rather than the exception, within the booktrade.

Authorship and cross-references:
Authors are listed alphabetically by surname.

Whenever possible, the works of each author are grouped together under a single form of name irrespective of the various combinations of initials, forenames and surnames by which the author is known.

Works published anonymously, or where the name of the author is not recorded on the title-page, are suitably cross-referenced by providing the main entry under the name of the author (when mentioned by the bookseller) with a corresponding entry under the first appropriate word of the title. In cases of unknown, or unmentioned, authorship, entry is made solely under the title.

Full-titles:

Editorial policy is to eschew, whenever possible, short-title records in favour of full-, or at least more complete and explanatory, titles. Short-title listings do little to convey the flavour, or even the content, of many books - particularly those published prior to the nineteenth century.

Descriptions:

Books are listed alphabetically, using the first word of the title ignoring, for alphabetical purposes, the definite and indefinite articles *the, a* and *an.* Within this alphabetical grouping of titles, variant editions are not necessarily arranged in chronological order, i.e., a 2nd, 3rd or 4th edition might well be listed prior to an earlier edition.

Subject to restrictions of space and to the provisos set out below, the substance of each catalogue entry giving details of the particular copy offered for sale has been recorded in full.

The listings have been made so as to conform to a uniform order of presentation, viz: Title; place of publication; publisher or printer; date; edition; size; collation; elements of content worthy of note; description of contents including faults, if any; description and condition of binding; bookseller; price; approximate price conversion from dollars to sterling or vice versa.

Abbreviations of description customary within the booktrade have generally been used. A list of these abbreviations will be found on page *x.*

Collations:

Collations, when provided by the bookseller, are repeated in toto although it should be borne in mind that booksellers employ differing practices in this respect; some by providing complete collations and others by indicating merely the number of pages in the main body of the work concerned. The same edition of the same title catalogued by two booksellers could therefore have two apparently different collations and care should be taken not to regard any collation recorded in *IRBP* as being a definitive or absolute record of total content.

Currency conversion:

IRBP lists books offered for sale priced in either pounds sterling (£) or United States dollars ($). For the benefit of readers unaccustomed to one or other of these currencies, an approximate conversion figure in the alternative currency has been provided in parentheses after each entry, as, for example, "**£100 [≃ $191]**", or, "**$60 [≃ £31]**". The conversion is based upon an exchange rate of £1 sterling ≃ US $1.91 (US $1 ≃ £0.525 sterling), the approximate rate applicable at the date of going to press.

It must be stressed that the conversion figures in parentheses are provided merely as an indication of the approximate pricing level in the currency with which the reader may be most familiar and that fluctuations in exchange rates will make these approximations inaccurate to a greater or lesser degree.

Acknowledgements:

We are indebted to those booksellers who have provided their catalogues during 1990 for the purposes of *IRBP*. A list of the contributing booksellers forms an appendix at the rear of this volume.

This appendix forms a handy reference of contacts in Britain and the United States with proven experience of handling books within the individual specialist fields encompassed by the series. The booksellers listed therein are able, between them, to offer advice on any aspect of the rare and antiquarian booktrade.

Many of the listed books will still, at the time of publication, be available for purchase. Readers with a possible interest in acquiring any of the items may well find it worth their while communicating with the booksellers concerned to obtain further and complete details.

Caveat:

Whilst the greatest care has been taken in transcribing entries from catalogues, it should be understood that it is inevitable that an occasional error will have passed unnoticed. Obvious mistakes, usually typographical in nature, observed in catalogues have been corrected. We have not questioned the accuracy in bibliographical matters of the cataloguers concerned.

The Clique

Abbreviations

advt(s)	advertisement(s)	intl	initial
addtn(s)	addition(s)	iss	issue
a.e.g.	all edges gilt	jnt(s)	joint(s)
ALS	autograph letter signed	lge	large
altrtns	alterations	lea	leather
Amer	American	lib	library
bibliog(s)	bibliography(ies)	ltd	limited
b/w	black & white	litho(s)	lithograph(s)
bndg	binding	marg(s)	margin(s)
bd(s)	board(s)	ms(s)	manuscript(s)
b'plate	bookplate	mrbld	marbled
ctlg(s)	catalogue(s)	mod	modern
chromolitho(s)	chromo-lithograph(s)	mor	morocco
ca	circa	mtd	mounted
cold	coloured	n.d.	no date
coll	collected	n.p.	no place
contemp	contemporary	num	numerous
crnr(s)	corner(s)	obl	oblong
crrctd	corrected	occas	occasional(ly)
cvr(s)	cover(s)	orig	original
dec	decorated	p (pp)	page(s)
detchd	detached	perf	perforated
diag(s)	diagram(s)	pict	pictorial
dw(s)	dust wrapper(s)	port(s)	portrait(s)
edn(s)	edition(s)	pres	presentation
elab	elaborate	ptd	printed
engv(s)	engraving(s)	qtr	quarter
engvd	engraved	rebnd	rebind/rebound
enlgd	enlarged	rec	recent
esp	especially	repr(d)	repair(ed)
ex lib	ex library	rvsd	revised
f (ff)	leaf(ves)	roy	royal
f.e.p.	free end paper	sep	separate
facs	facsimile	sev	several
fig(s)	figure(s)	sgnd	signed
fldg	folding	sgntr	signature
ft	foot	sl	slight/slightly
frontis	frontispiece	sm	small
hand-cold	hand-coloured	t.e.g.	top edge gilt
hd	head	TLS	typed letter signed
ill(s)	illustration(s)	unif	uniform
illust	illustrated	v	very
imp	impression	vell	vellum
imprvd	improved	vol(s)	volume(s)
inc	including	w'engvd	wood-engraved
inscrbd	inscribed	w'cut(s)	woodcut(s)
inscrptn	inscription	wrap(s)	wrapper(s)

Books published prior to 1800
1990 Catalogue Prices

A., D., Gent.
- The Whole Art of Converse: containing Necessary Instructions for all Persons ... London: for Joseph Hindmarsh, 1683. 12mo. [xii], 128 pp. Marg wormhole in 1st 20 ff. Short tear in D4. Old calf, worn. Wing A3A.
(Hollett) **£175 [≈ $335]**

A., T.
- A Funeral Handkerchief ... see Allestree, Thomas.

Abel, Thomas
- Subtensial Plain Trigonometry, wrought with a Sliding-Rule, with Gunter's Lines: and also Arithmetically, in a Very Concise Manner ... Phila: 1761. 12mo. [2], 86 pp (6 pp misnumbered). 7 fldg plates. Sm lib stamp. Foxed, sm repr to 1 plate. Mod three qtr calf.
(Reese) **$900 [≈ £468]**

Abercrombie, John
- The Garden Mushroom: Its Nature and Cultivation. A Treatise exhibiting Full and Plain Directions ... London: Lockyer Davies, 1780. 54 pp,advt leaf. Contemp qtr calf, mrbld bds, mor label.
(C.R. Johnson) **£320 [≈ $614]**

Account ...
- An Account of Denmark ... see Molesworth, Robert.
- An Account of the Conduct of the Dowager Dutchess of Marlborough ... see Hooke, Nathaniel.
- An Account of the Expedition to Carthagena ... see Knowles, Charles.
- An Account of the Late Establishment of Presbyterian Government by the Parliament of Scotland ... see Sage, John.
- An Account of the Life of Mr. Richard Savage ... see Johnson, Samuel.

- An Account of the Province of Carolina in America ... see Wilson, Samuel.
- An Account of the Tenia ... see Simmons, S.F.

The Actor ...
- See Hill, "Sir" John.

Acts of Parliament
- An Act prohibiting Trade with the Barbada's [sic], Virginia, Bermuda's and Antego. London: 1650. Sm folio. [ii], 1027-1034 pp. Browned. Later calf by Morley of Oxford.
(Bookpress) **$3,750 [≈ £1,953]**
- An Act to Settle the Trade to Africa. London: Charles Bill, 1698. Title,17 pp. New qtr calf.
(Young's) **£55 [≈ $105]**
- An Act for Enabling the South-Sea Company to increase their Present Capital Stock and Fund ... London: 1720. 4to. Title, pp 131-222. Tanned, some foxing. Mod half cloth.
(Reese) **$500 [≈ £260]**
- An Act for Making Several Provisions to restore the Publick Credit, which Suffers by the Frauds and Mismanagements of the late Directors of the South-Sea Company, and Others. London: 1721. Folio. 14,[1] pp. Tanned. Mod half cloth.
(Reese) **$200 [≈ £104]**
- An Act for Granting Liberty to carry Rice from His Majesty's Province of Carolina in America, directly to any Part of Europe Southward of Cape Finisterre ... London: 1730. Folio. Pp 559-64.
(Reese) **$150 [≈ £78]**
- An Act to Prohibit All Trade and Intercourse with the Colonies ... London: 1776. Folio. Pp 215-44. Title vignette. Sl foxing. Later wraps.
(Reese) **$400 [≈ £208]**

Adair, James
- The History of the American Indians ... also

an Appendix containing a description of the Floridas, and the Mississippi Lands ... London: 1775. [12],464 pp. Frontis, fldg map. Contemp calf backed mrbld bds, sl rubbed.   *(Reese)* **$2,500 [≃ £1,302]**

- The History of the American Indians; Particularly those Nations adjoining to the Missisippi [sic], East and West Florida, Georgia, South and North Carolina, and Virginia ... London: Dilly, 1775. 1st edn. 4to. 464 pp. Half-title. Fldg map. Early 19th c calf.   *(Chapel Hill)* **$2,750 [≃ £1,432]**

Adam, Alexander

- Roman Antiquities: or, an Account of the Manners and Customs of the Romans ... Second Edition, considerably enlarged. London: 1792. 608 pp. Contemp tree calf, red label. The William Downes copy.
          (C.R. Johnson) **£110 [≃ $211]**
- Roman Antiquities: or, an Account of the Manners and Customs of the Romans ... Second Edition, considerably enlarged. Edinburgh: for A. Strahan ..., 1792. 8vo. xvi,608 pp. Contemp calf, rehinged.
          (Young's) **£30 [≃ $57]**

Adam, Melchior

- The Life and Death of Dr Martin Lvther. London: Stafford, 1641. 1st edn of this translation. 4to. Frontis port, engvd title with vignette. calf, rubbed. Wing A.505.
          (Rostenberg & Stern) **$525 [≃ £273]**

Adams, G.

- Astronomical and Geographical Essays. London: the author, 1790. 8vo. xix,599,15 advt pp. 21 fldg plates. New half leather.
          (Gemmary) **$600 [≃ £312]**
- An Essay on Electricity. London: R. Hindmarch for the author, 1787. 8vo. lxxxvi, 473 pp. 10 fldg plates. Leather, rebacked.
          (Gemmary) **$750 [≃ £390]**

Adams, Hannah

- A Summary History of New-England, from the First Settlement at Plymouth, to the Acceptance of the Federal Constitution ... Dedham: for the author, by H. Mann & J.H. Adams, 1799. 1st edn. Lge 8vo. 513,[3] pp. Contemp calf, gilt label, spine ends chipped.
          (Karmiole) **$200 [≃ £104]**

Adams, John

- Index Villaris: or, an Alphabetical Table of all the Cities, Market-Towns, Parishes, Villages, and Private Seats, in England and Wales ...

London: 1680. 1st edn. Folio. [xii], 412 pp. Margs sl browned, minor worm in 1st 3 ff. Contemp mor gilt, sl worn. Wing A.479.
          (Pickering) **$1,200 [≃ £625]**

Adams, John

- An Address of the Convention, for Framing a New Constitution of Government, for the State of Massachusetts-Bay, to their Constituents. Boston: 1780. 18 pp. Some foxing & darkening, blank marg sl gnawed on 1 leaf. Mod half mor. *(Reese)* **$600 [≃ £312]**

Adams, Revd John

- The Flowers of Modern Travels ... intended chiefly for Young People of both Sexes. Boston: John West, 1797. 1st Amer edn. 2 vols. 8vo. 324; 312 pp. Some browning. Contemp sheep, rubbed & scuffed, jnts cracked but secure.   *(Clark)* **£85 [≃ $163]**

Adanson, Michel

- A Voyage to Senegal, in the Isle of Goree, and the River Gambia. Translated ... with Notes ... London: for J. Nourse ..., 1759. 1st edn in English. 8vo. Fldg map. Sl browning. Contemp calf, gilt spine (sl worn).
          (Ximenes) **$650 [≃ £338]**
- A Voyage to Senegal, the Isle of Goree and the River Gambia, translated from the French. London: 1759. 8vo. [xiv],337,[1] pp. Title margs browned. Calf, jnts cracked.
          (Wheldon & Wesley) **£320 [≃ $614]**

Addison, Joseph

- The Free-Holder, or Political Essays. London: for D. Midwinter ..., 1716. 1st edn. 12mo. [xii],311,[1 errata] pp. Half-title. Old calf, rebacked. Anon. *(Young's)* **£55 [≃ $105]**
- The Free-Holder. Or Political Essays. The Third Edition. London: for D. Midwinter, 1723. 12mo. [xii],311 pp. Half-title. Frontis. Period calf, sl surface worming. Anon.
          (Rankin) **£45 [≃ $86]**
- The Miscellaneous Works ... With some Account of the Life and Writings of the Author. By Mr. Tickell. London: Tonson, 1765. 4 vols. 8vo. Port frontis, 3 plates. Contemp calf, mor labels, sl worn.
          (Sotheran's) **£285 [≃ $547]**
- Remarks on Several Parts of Italy, &c. In the Years 1701, 1702, 1703. London: Tonson, 1705. 1st edn. 8vo. Num text ills. Calf, gilt spine. *(Rostenberg & Stern)* **$375 [≃ £195]**
- Remarks on Several Parts of Italy, &c. In the Years 1701 ... 1703. The Fifth Edition.

London: Tonson, 1736. Lge 12mo. 304,[8] pp. Contemp calf gilt, numbered Vol 4 on spine, sl worn. *(Fenning)* **£24.50 [≈ $47]**
- Remarks on Several Parts of Italy, &c. In the Years 1701, 1702, 1703. London: Tonson, 1761. 12mo. Contemp speckled calf, red label, hinges cracked. *(Jarndyce)* **£48 [≈ $92]**
- The Works. London: Tonson, 1721. 1st coll edn. 4 vols. 4to. Frontis in vol 1. Contemp Cambridge style calf, red mor labels.
  (Waterfield's) **£235 [≈ $451]**
- The Works ... London: Tonson, 1721. 4 vols. 4to. Port. Contemp calf, sometime reprd, sl worn. *(Stewart)* **£225 [≈ $431]**
- The Works. Dublin: George Grierson, 1722-23. 1st Irish edn. 4 vols in 2. 8vo. Contemp calf, sl rubbed.
  (Ximenes) **$350 [≈ £182]**

Addison, Joseph & Steele, Richard
- The Spectator. London: for J. & R. Tonson & S. Draper, 1749. 8 vols. Frontises, engvd titles. Contemp calf, gilt borders, rubbed, most labels chipped or missing. Anon.
  (Jarndyce) **£65 [≈ $124]**
- The Spectator. London: for John Donaldson ..., 1776. 8 vols. Sm 8vo. Rubberstamp on sev pp, underscoring in pencil on sev pp. Contemp calf, rubbed & somewhat worn.
  (Heritage) **$200 [≈ £104]**

Addison, Joseph, et al.
- The Guardian. London: for J. & R. Tonson ..., 1740. 7th edn. 2 vols. 8vo. Vol 1 misdated MCCDXL. Contemp speckled calf, 1 headpiece defective. Anon.
  (Young's) **£40 [≈ $76]**

Addison, Lancelot
- West Barbary, or, A Short Narrative of the Revolutions of the Kingdoms of Fez and Morocco. With an Account of the Present Customs ... Oxford: at the Theater ..., 1671. Intl leaf with vertical half-title. Sm hole in 1 leaf. Contemp sheep, sm split hd of spine. Wing A.532. *(Jarndyce)* **£650 [≈ $1,247]**

Additions to the Diaboliad ...
- See Combe, William.

Address ...
- An Address of Thanks to the Broad-Bottoms, for the Good Things they have done, and the Evil Things they have not done, since their Elevation ... London: for M. Cooper, 1745. Frontis. Rebound in half calf.

(Jarndyce) **£250 [≈ $479]**

The Advantages of Deliberation ...
- The Advantages of Deliberation; or, the Folly of Indiscretion. London: for Robertson & Roberts, 1772. 1st edn. 2 vols. 12mo. Half-titles. Sl browning. Contemp sheep, gilt spines, rubbed, jnts cracked, 1 cvr detached.
  (Ximenes) **$750 [≈ £390]**

Adventures ...
- The Adventures of David Simple ... see Fielding, Sarah.
- The Adventures of Ferdinand Count Fathom ... see Smollett, Tobias.
- The Adventures of Roderick Random ... see Smollett, Tobias.

Advice ...
- Advice from a Lady of Quality to her Children; in the last Stage of a Lingering Illness. Translated from the French, By Samuel Glasse, D.D., F.R.S. The Second Edition. London: Rivington, 1779. Early 19th c straight grain mor.
  (C.R. Johnson) **£140 [≈ $268]**
- Advice to a Son ... see Osborne, Francis.

Aesop
- Fables of Aesop and other Eminent Mythologists: with Morals and Reflections. By Sir Roger L'Estrange. The Second Edition Corrected and Amended. London: for R. Sare ..., 1694. 2 parts in one vol. Folio. Port, plate. Contemp calf, spine rubbed, split in hinge. Wing A.707. *(Jarndyce)* **£350 [≈ $671]**

Aglionby, William
- Painting Illustrated in Three Diallogues ... Together with the Lives of the most Eminent Painters ... London: John Gain for the author, 1685. 1st edn. Red & black title. 17 ff,'375" (ie 388) pp. Old calf, worn. Wing A.764. Anon *(Ars Artis)* **£500 [≈ $959]**
- Painting Illustrated in Three Diallogues ... London: Gain for Author, 1685. 1st edn. 4to. Red & black title. Calf, rebacked, recrnrd, scuffed. Wing A.764. Anon.
  (Rostenberg & Stern) **$1,750 [≈ £911]**
- Painting Illustrated in Three Diallogues ... London: John Gain for the author, 1685. 1st edn. 4to. [xxxviii],375 pp. Usual pagination errors. Red & black title. 3 top margs reprd. Near contemp calf gilt, rebacked. Wing A.764. Anon. *(Young's)* **£320 [≈ $614]**

Agricola, Georg Andreas
- A Philosophical Treatise of Husbandry and Gardening ... Revised ... with a Preface ... by Richard Bradley. London: 1721. 1st edn. Lge 4to. [xxii],300,[4] pp. Frontis, 32 plates. Occas sl marg damp stains, 2 faint marg blind stamps. Rec half calf gilt.
(Hollett) **£650 [≈ $1,247]**

Aikin, Anna Laetitia
- Poems. The Fifth Edition Corrected. London: Joseph Johnson, 1786. Fcap 8vo. vi, 138 pp. Top blank crnr of 1 leaf torn with loss. Contemp qtr calf, vellum crnrs, spine ends chipped.   *(Spelman)* **£30 [≈ $57]**
- Poems. By Mrs Barbauld. London: J. Johnson, 1773. 1st edn. 4to. vi,138 pp. A few spots & some sl marg dampstains. Old half calf, lib reback.   *(Hollett)* **£140 [≈ $268]**

Aikin, John
- A Description of the Country from Thirty to Forty Miles round Manchester. London: for John Stockdale, 1795. Lge 4to. xvi,[8 subscribers], 624 pp. 2 lge fldg linen backed maps, 71 plates. 2 sm blind stamps, free endpapers sl soiled. Mod half mor gilt extra.
(Hollett) **£495 [≈ $950]**
- Essays on Song-Writing ... London: Joseph Johnson, [1772]. 1st edn. Sm 8vo. Stain on some ff near hd of spine. Anon.
(Bookpress) **$375 [≈ £195]**
- A View of the Character and Public Services of the late John Howard, Esq. London: J. Johnson, 1792. 248 pp. frontis port. Contemp calf, hinges weakening, sm section of calf defective on 1 hinge.
(C.R. Johnson) **£145 [≈ $278]**

Aitken, James
- A Genuine Account of the Life, Transactions, Confession, and Execution, of James Aitken, alias John Hill, commonly called John the Painter ... setting fire to His Majesty's Dockyard at Portsmouth. London: Turner, 1777. 1st edn. 12mo. Frontis. Old wraps.
(Ximenes) **$2,250 [≈ £1,171]**

Aix, Pierre
- A Defence of the Brief History of the Unitarians against Dr. Sherlock's Answer in his Vindication of the Holy Trinity. London: 1791. 4to. Disbound.   *(Gage)* **£15 [≈ $28]**

A Kempis, Thomas
- Of the Imitation of Christ ... Now newlie

corrected, translated ... and illustrated by Thomas Rogers. London: Peter Short, 1602. 12mo. Frontis, ills. Some pale blue stains on upper outside crnrs of some ff. Early vellum. STC 23981.   *(Wreden)* **$850 [≈ £442]**

Akenside, Mark
- An Epistle to Curio. London: Dodsley ..., 1744. 4to. Half-title,27 pp. Disbound. Anon.
(C.R. Johnson) **£125 [≈ $239]**
- Odes on Several Subjects. London: Dodsley ..., 1745. Half-title,54 pp. Disbound. Anon.
(C.R. Johnson) **£125 [≈ $239]**
- The Pleasures of Imagination, and Other poems ... London: for J. Dodsley ..., 1788. 1st edn thus. 8vo. xii,401 pp. Old calf, rebacked.
(Young's) **£60 [≈ $115]**

Alberti, L.
- The Architecture ... in Ten Books ... translated ... into English ... by James Leoni ... London: T. Edlin, 1726. 1st edn in English. 3 vols. 297 ff. 103 plates. Lacks 1 Italian title, 1 text leaf & 4 plates. Half cloth.
(Ars Artis) **£150 [≈ $287]**

Albin, E.
- A Natural History of English Insects ... London: 1720. 1st edn. 4to. 100 hand cold plates. Calf, rebacked.
(Wheldon & Wesley) **£1,650 [≈ $3,167]**

Alchorne, William
- A Sermon Preached at the Funeral of that eminently   Vertuous,   and   Pious Gentlewoman, Mrs. Elizabeth Atwood ... London: William Godbid, 1674. Disbound. Wing A.885.   *(Waterfield's)* **£25 [≈ $47]**

Alciphron or the Minute Philosopher ...
- See Berkeley, George.

Alderson, John
- Some Useful Observations and Advices taken from the mouth of John Alderson deceased: with a Short Account of him ... London: Luke Hinde, 1765. Orig wraps.
(Waterfield's) **£45 [≈ $86]**

Alexander's   Expedition   down   the Hydaspes ...
- See Beddoes, Thomas.

Alexander, William, Earl of Stirling
- Recreations with the Muses. London: Tho. Harper, 1637. 1st coll edn. Folio. W'cut title

mtd & reprd at outer marg, few other v sl reprs. Lacks Al (blank). Late 18th c calf, mor label. STC 347. *(Waterfield's)* **£250 [≈ $479]**
- Recreations with the Mvses ... London: Tho. Harper, 1637. 1st coll edn. Folio. [x], 253,[i], [iv],326 pp. W'cut title border, 2 sep divisional titles. Final blank. Lacks Al (blank). Early ff sl frayed. Contemp calf, sometime rebacked, crnrs bumped. STC 347.
(Finch) **£380 [≈ $729]**

Alfred's Letters ...
- See Burges, Sir James Bland.

Algarotti, Francesco, Count
- An Essay on Painting ... London: L. Davis & C. Reymers, 1764. vii,186 pp, 2 advt ff. Leather, sl worn. *(Ars Artis)* **£150 [≈ $287]**
- Letters Military and Practical ... London: for T. Egerton ..., 1783. 2nd edn. 8vo. xxviii, 319 pp. Half-title. Sm marg paper flaw in 2 ff. Contemp calf, rebacked.
(Young's) **£60 [≈ $115]**

Alison, Archibald
- Essays on the Nature and Principles of Taste. Edinburgh: for Robinson ..., 1790. 4to. 415 pp. Contemp calf, hd of spine reprd.
(C.R. Johnson) **£850 [≈ $1,631]**

Alleine, Joseph
- An Alarm to Unconverted Sinners ... Boston: S. Kneeland, 1764. 2 parts in one. 12mo. xxii,198; 90 pp. Contemp calf, spine extremities chipped, crnrs worn, lacks free endpapers. *(Karmiole)* **$250 [≈ £130]**

Alleine, Richard
- The Godly Mans Portion and Sanctuary Opened in two Sermons Preached Aug 17 1662. London: (1663). 8vo. [6],175 pp. Title & 2 ff recrnrd. Some worming. New half calf. Wing A.989. *(Humber)* **£45 [≈ $86]**
- The World Conquered; or a Believers Victory over the World. Laid open in several Sermons on I John 5.4. London: for Peter Parker, 1676. Cr 8vo. End ff sl soiled. New cloth. Wing A.1010. *(Stewart)* **£45 [≈ $86]**

Allen, John
- Synopsis Medicinae: or, A Summary View of the Whole Practice of Physick ... London: W. Innys ..., 1749. 3rd edn. 2 vols. 8vo. [viii], 400; [iv],356,[43],[1] pp. Contemp calf, hinges & spines cracked.
(Bookpress) **$285 [≈ £148]**

Allestree, Richard
- The Art of Contentment. Oxford: The Theater, 1675. viii,214 pp. Frontis. Prelims soiled, damp stained, title torn. Lacks front bd. *(Gage)* **£22 [≈ $42]**
- The Art of Contentment. By the Author of The Whole Duty of Man ... Oxford: at the Theater, 1675. 1st edn. 8vo. Engvd frontis. Orig calf, mor label, gilt faded, hd of spine sl damaged. Wing A. 1085. Anon.
(Vanbrugh) **£155 [≈ $297]**
- Forty Sermons, whereof Twenty One are now first Published ... Prefixt, an Account of the Author's Life. Oxford; the Theater; London: for R. Scott ..., 1684. 1st coll edn. 2 vols in one. Folio. Errata leaf. Port. Orig calf, lacks label, hinges cracked. Wing P.3917.
(Vanbrugh) **£185 [≈ $355]**
- The Ladies Calling. In Two Parts. By the Author of The Whole Duty of Man ... Oxford: at the Theater, 1673. 1st edn. 8vo. [xxiv], 141, [iii],'104" [ie 96] pp. Engvd frontis (in 1st state). 1 sm marg repr. Orig calf, rebacked. Wing A.1140. Anon.
(Vanbrugh) **£285 [≈ $547]**
- The Ladies Calling in Two Parts. By the Author of the Whole Duty of Man &c. The Eleventh Impression. Oxford: at the Theater, 1720. 8vo in 4s. Frontis, title vignette. Contemp Cambridge panelled calf, jnts cracking. Anon. *(Sanders)* **£20 [≈ $38]**
- The Lively Oracles Given to Us ... Oxford: At the Theater, 1678. 1st edn. [12],226,[2] pp. Imprimatur leaf. Engvd frontis, title vignette. Contemp calf, elab gilt spine, spine extremities sl chipped, front outer hinge starting. Wing A.1149. Anon.
(Karmiole) **$150 [≈ £78]**
- The Lively Oracles given to Us, or the Christian's Birth-Right and Duty in the Custody and Use of the Holy Scripture. By the Author of The Whole Duty of Man. Oxford: 1682. 12mo. vii,136 pp. Title loose. Disbound. *(Gage)* **£16 [≈ $30]**
- A Sermon Preached before the King at Whitehall on Sunday Nov. 17. 1667. London: 1667. 1st edn. Sm 4to. 38 pp. Some marks. Stabbed as issued, lower crnrs sl frayed. Wing A.1167. *(Bow Windows)* **£48 [≈ $92]**
- The Whole Duty of Man ... New Edition. London: R. Norton for Robert Pawlet, 1675. 8vo. [xvi],503,[504-512] pp. Frontis, addtnl engvd title. Orig calf gilt, rebacked. Wing A.1179. Anon. *(Vanbrugh)* **£125 [≈ $239]**
- The Whole Duty of Man. London: Rivington, 1794. Frontis, addtnl engvd title.

Later roan. Anon. *(Waterfield's)* **£20** [≈ **$38**]

Allestree, Thomas
- A Funeral Handkerchief in Two Parts ... By T.A. Rector of Ashow in the C. of Warwick. London: for the author, 1671. Thick 8vo. [16], 300,86 pp. New qtr calf. Wing A.1197 (& 1196). *(Humber)* **£75** [≈ **$143**]

Almoran and Hamet: an Oriental Tale ...
- See Hawkesworth, John.

Altieri, Ferdinando
- A New Grammar, Italian-English, and English-Italian ... London: for William Innys, 1728. 1st edn. 8vo. [viii],416 pp. Contemp calf, sm cracks in jnts.
(Burmester) **£150** [≈ **$287**]

Alves, Robert
- Poems. Edinburgh: for the author, sold by William Creech ... & Cadell, London, 1782. Half-title. Orig bds, uncut.
(C.R. Johnson) **£245** [≈ **$470**]

Ambrose, Isaac
- Prima, Media & Ultima: The First, Middle, and Last Things: in Three Treatises ... London: T.R. & E.M. for Webb & Grantham, 1654. 2nd combined edn. 4to. [x],72,[iv],70, [xxviii], 576, [xii],228 pp. Worn, marked. Contemp calf, worn. Wing A.2962. *(Clark)* **£140** [≈ **$268**]

America, an Ode ...
- America, an Ode. To the People of England. London: for J. Almon, 1776. Only edn. 4to. [ii], 10 pp. Mod half mor.
(Georges) **£500** [≈ **$959**]

The American Latin Grammar ...
- See Ross, Robert.

Ames, Joseph
- A Catalogue of English Heads; or, An Account of about Two Thousand Prints. London: the editor, 1748. 1st edn. 8vo. 182,[1] pp. Calf. *(Bookpress)* **$235** [≈ **£122**]

Amhurst, Nicholas
- Oculus Britanniae: an Heroi-Panegyrical Poem on the University of Oxford illustrated with divers beautiful similes and useful digressions. London: for R. Francklin, 1724. Title sl dusty. Disbound. Anon.
(Waterfield's) **£60** [≈ **$115**]

- Terrae-Filius: or, The Secret History of the University of Oxford; in Several Essays ... London: for R. Francklin, 1726. 1st edn in book form. 2 vols in one. 12mo. xxiii,354 pp. Frontis by Hogarth. Orig calf, rubbed, lacks label. Anon. *(Bickersteth)* **£65** [≈ **$124**]
- Terrae-Filius; or, the Secret History of the University of Oxford; in several Essays ... London: for R. Francklin, 1754. 3rd edn. Cr 8vo. Contemp calf (rather marked), panelled spine gilt. *(Stewart)* **£30** [≈ **$57**]

Ammianus Marcellinus
- The Roman Historie ... Now translated ... by Philemon Holland ... London: Adam Islip, 1609. 1st edn of Holland's transl. Folio. [iv], 432,[lxxvi] pp. Contemp calf, mor label, red edges, spine ends worn. STC 17311.
(Finch) **£750** [≈ **$1,439**]

Amory, Thomas
- The Character and Blessedness of those to whom to live is Christ ... A Sermon ... May 25, 1738 ... London: Hett, 1739. 8vo. Black bordered title (sm loss in blank area lower left). Disbound. *(Waterfield's)* **£25** [≈ **$47**]

Anderson, Adam
- An Historical and Chronological Deduction of the Origin of Commerce, from the Earliest Accounts ... London: A. Millar ..., 1764. 1st edn. 2 vols. Folio. x,xxxiv,[iv],500; [ii], 433, [1 errata], [126],[4], 111,[5] pp. 3 maps. Contemp calf, sl worn & scuffed.
(Pickering) **$2,000** [≈ **£1,041**]
- An Historical and Chronological Deduction of the Origin of Commerce, from the Earliest Accounts ... London: J. Walter, Logographic Press, 1787. 4 vols. Demy 4to. Frontis, maps. Contemp calf gilt, restored, a few signs of age & use. Anon. *(Ash)* **£750** [≈ **$1,439**]

Anderson, Robert
- The Life of Samuel Johnson, LL.D. with Critical Observations on his Works. London: for J. & A. Arch, & for Bell & Bradfute, & J. Mundell, Edinburgh, 1795. 1st edn. Some browning, few marg marks. Faint lib stamps. Rebound in half calf.
(Jarndyce) **£160** [≈ **$307**]

Andrewes, Lancelot
- The Pattern of Cathechistical Doctrine at large: or a Learned and Pious Exposition of the Ten Commandments ... London: Roger Norton ... 1650. 1st folio edn. [xxxiv],530 pp. Port frontis. Rec period style calf. Wing

A.3147.   *(Sotheran's)* **£168 [≈ $322]**

Andrews, James Pettit
- The History of Great Britain connected with the Chronology of Europe. London: Cadell, 1794. 2 vols in one. 4to. Engvd title vignettes, 4 fldg tables. Mod qtr calf.
          (Waterfield's) **£120 [≈ $230]**

Andrews, John
- A Comparative View of the French and English Nations, in their Manners, Politics, and Literature. London: Longman & Robinson, 1785. 488 pp. Orig calf, spine rubbed, lacks label.
          (C.R. Johnson) **£125 [≈ $239]**
- History of the War with America, France, Spain, and Holland: commencing in 1775 and ending in 1783. London: 1785-86. 4 vols. [4], 448; [2],445; [2],445; [2],416,[60] pp & subscribers. 31 plates & maps. Three qtr mor, some rubbing.   *(Reese)* **$1,000 [≈ £520]**
- Letters to his Excellency the Count de Welderen, on the Present Situation of Affairs between Great Britain and the United Provinces. London: 1781. 8vo. 76 pp. Disbound.   *(Robertshaw)* **£25 [≈ $47]**
- Remarks on the French and English Ladies, in a Series of Letters ... London: Longman & Robinson, 1783. Half-title,360 pp. Contemp calf, spine rubbed, lacks label.
          (C.R. Johnson) **£150 [≈ $287]**
- A Review of the Characters of the Principal Nations in Europe. London: Cadell, 1770. 2 vols. Contemp calf, red & green labels. The Cator copy. Anon.
          (C.R. Johnson) **£285 [≈ $547]**

Andrews, Miles Peter
- Better Late than Never A Comedy. London: for J. Ridgway ..., 1790. 1st edn. 8vo. vi, 3-70, [2],4 advt pp. Half-title. Disbound.
          (Young's) **£25 [≈ $47]**

Andry, Nicholas
- An Account of the Breeding of Worms in Human Bodies ... London: H. Rhodes, 1701. 1st edn. 8vo. xl,[iv],120 pp, 121-176 ff, 177-266, [xxvi] pp. 5 plates. Later sheep.
          (Bookpress) **$600 [≈ £312]**

Andry, Nicolas
- Orthopaedia: or the Art of Correcting and Preventing Deformities in Children ... Translated from the French. London: 1743. 1st English edn. 2 vols. 8vo. viii,230,[8]; vi,

310 pp. 16 (of 21) plates. Lacks frontis. Title browned & mtd. Mod half calf gilt.
          (Hemlock) **$475 [≈ £247]**

Anecdotes ...
- Anecdotes of Some Distinguished Persons ... see Seward, William.

Angelus, Johannes
- [Greek title: Esoptron Astrologicon]. Astrological Opticks, Wherein are represented the Faces of every Sign ... Compiled at Venice by ... Johann. Regiomontanus and Johannes Angelus. London: [1655]. 1st English edn. 8vo. [xvi],184,[2 advt] pp. Contemp sheep, rubbed. Wing E.737.
          (Finch) **£750 [≈ $1,439]**

Annet, Peter
- The Resurrection of Jesus Considered; in Answer to the Tryal of the Witnesses ... London: for M. Cooper ..., 1744. 3rd edn. 8vo. 92 pp. Closed tear in title. Stitched as issued. Anon.   *(Young's)* **£30 [≈ $57]**

The Annual Register ...
- The Annual Register, or a View of the History, Politics, and Literature for the Year 1776. London: Dodsley, 1777. iv,192, 113-270, 259,[9] pp. Orig calf backed bds, spine worn. Half mor box. Inc 1st printing in an English book of the Declaration of Independence.   *(Reese)* **$1,500 [≈ £781]**

Anson, George
- A Voyage round the World. In the Years MDCCXL, I, II, III, IV ... Compiled ... by Richard Walter ... London: for the author, by John & Paul Knapton, 1748. 1st edn. 4to. [xxiv], 417,[iii] pp. 42 fldg plates. Some wear & tear. Contemp calf, rebacked.
          (Clark) **£500 [≈ $959]**
- A Voyage round the World, In the Years MDCCXL, I, II, III, IV ... Compiled ... by Richard Walter ... London: Knapton, 1748. 3rd edn. 3 fldg maps. Contemp polished calf, gilt spine.   *(Parmer)* **$650 [≈ £338]**
- A Voyage round the World. In the Years MDCCXL, I, II, III, IV ... Compiled ... by Richard Walter ... Ninth Edition. London: D. Browne ..., 1756. 4to. [xx],417,[ii] pp. 43 fldg plates. Contemp calf, rebacked.
          (Frew Mackenzie) **£460 [≈ $883]**

Anstey, Christopher
- An Election Ball in Poetical Letters in the

Zomerzetshire Dialect from Mr. Inkle a Freeman of Bath to his Wife at Gloucester ... Dublin: George Bonham, 1776. 1st Irish edn. Mod wraps. Anon.
(Waterfield's) **£65 [≈ $124]**

- An Election Ball in Poetical Letters from Mr Inkle at Bath to his Wife at Glocester ... Second Edition, with considerable Additions. Bath: for the author by S. Hazard, 1776. 4to. Frontis. Sl damage blank crnr of title. Disbound. Anon.   *(Waterfield's)* **£40 [≈ $76]**

- The New Bath Guide: Or Memoirs of the B-n-r-d Family. In a Series of Poetical Epistles ... London: Dodsley, 1784. 12th edn. 8vo. viii,175 pp. Frontis. Occas spotting. Calf backed bds. Anon.   *(Young's)* **£25 [≈ $47]**

- The New Bath Guide ... A New Edition. London: Dodsley, 1788. 8vo. Contemp tree calf, red label. Anon.
(Waterfield's) **£45 [≈ $86]**

Anthing, Frederick
- History of the Campaigns of Count Alexander Suworow Rymnikski ... London: for J. Wright, 1799. 1st edn in English. 2 vols. 8vo. Half-titles. Port. Contemp half calf, gilt spines, by Wood of Rochdale.
(Ximenes) **$225 [≈ £117]**

The Anti-Jacobin ...
- See Canning, George, et al.

Antient ...
- Antient and Modern Scotish Songs ... see Herd, David (ed.).
- The Antient and Present State of the County of Down ... see Harris, Walter & Smith, J.; Smith, C.

Apology ...
- An Apology for the Conduct of a late celebrated second-rate Minister ... see Winnington, Thomas.
- The Apology of Benjamin Ben Mordecai ... see Taylor, Henry.

Appian
- The History of Appian of Alexandria, in Two Parts ... Made English by J.D. [John Dancer]. London: for John Amery, 1679. 1st edn of this translation. 2 parts in one. 4to. [xiv],251, 273,[i advt] pp. Sm hole in 2 ff. Rec qtr calf. Wing A.3579.   *(Sotheran's)* **£285 [≈ $547]**

The Arabian Nights
- The Thousand One Days: Persian Tales.

Translated from the French. By Mr Phillips. The Third Edition. London: Tonson, 1722. 3 vols. 12mo. 3 frontis. Vol 1 rebacked.
(Bickersteth) **£220 [≈ $422]**

- The Persian and Turkish Tales, Compleat. Translated ... by M. Petis de la Croix ... and now into English ... by the late learned Dr. King, and several Other Hands ... Fifth Edition. London: 1767. 2 vols. 12mo. [viii], 434; [vi],404 pp. Orig calf, hd of spine vol 1 sl worn.   *(Bickersteth)* **£185 [≈ $355]**

- Persian Tales, or the Thousand and One Days. London: for W. Lane, 1789. 3 parts in 2 vols. 12mo. [2],339, iv,360 pp. 5 plates. Occas tears, sl foxed & stained. Contemp calf, worn, hinges broken, labels chipped.
(Worldwide) **$195 [≈ £101]**

Aram, Eugene
- The Genuine Account of the Trial of Eugene Aram, for the Murder of Daniel Clark. Eighth Edition. Knaresborough: for E. Hargrove, 1792. 12mo. 83 pp. Later three qtr calf.
(Meyer Boswell) **$275 [≈ £143]**

Arbuthnot, John
- The Miscellaneous Works. The Second Edition, with Additions. Glasgow: for James Carlisle, 1751. 2 vols. Supplement bound in vol 2. 8vo. Advt leaf before each title. Contemp reversed calf, spines chipped.
(Sanders) **£150 [≈ $287]**

- Tables of Grecian, Roman and Jewish Measures, Weights and Coins. Reduc'd to English Standard ... London: for Richard Smith, [1705?]. 1st edn. 8vo. Dble-page engvd title, 13 dble-page engvd ff containing 29 tables. Orig calf, rebacked.
(Bickersteth) **£148 [≈ $284]**

Arcana Aulica: or, Walsingham's Manual ...
- See Du Refuge, Eustache.

Archaeologia
- Archaeologia. Or Miscellaneous Tracts relating to Antiquity. London: 1770-1986. Vols 1-108 & General Index 1-100. Lge 4to. New cloth.   *(Ars Libri)* **$10,000 [≈ £5,208]**

Arderne, James
- A Sermon Preached at the Visitation of the Right Reverend Father in God, John Lord Bishop of Chester, at Chester ... London: for H. Brome ..., 1677. 1st edn. 4to. [iv],19 pp. Disbound. Wing A.3625.
(Young's) **£50 [≈ $95]**

Ariosto, Ludovico
- Orlando Furioso: Translated from the Italian. London: the translator [John Hoole], 1783. 1st edn of this translation. 5 vols. 8vo. Vol 3 frontis by William Blake. Contemp tree calf, 3 upper hinges cracking, spines darkened.
(Bookpress) **$425 [≈ £221]**

Aristophanes
- The Frogs. A Comedy. Translated from the Greek by C.D. [Charles Dunster]. Oxford: for J. & J. Fletcher, [1785]. Disbound.
(Waterfield's) **£100 [≈ $191]**

Aristotle (pseud.)
- The Works of Aristotle. In Four Parts. London: 1798. 407 pp. Leather.
(Fye) **$100 [≈ £52]**

Armstrong, John, engineer, of Minorca
- The History of the Island of Minorca. London: for C. Davis, 1752. 1st edn. 8vo. Fldg map, 2 fldg plates. Clean tear in 1 leaf. Contemp calf, trifle rubbed.
(Ximenes) **$325 [≈ £169]**

Armstrong, John, physician and poet
- Miscellanies. London: for T. Cadell, 1770. 1st edn. 2 vols. Sm 8vo. Leaf 07 in vol 1 is a cancel. Contemp polished calf.
(Hannas) **£110 [≈ $211]**
- Of Benevolence: an Epistle to Eumenes. London: for A. Millar, 1751. Folio. Half-title. New bds. *(C.R. Johnson)* **£160 [≈ $307]**

Arnauld, Antoine & Nicole, Pierre
- Logic; or, The Art of Thinking ... Done from the new French Edition. By Mr. Ozell. London: for William Taylor, 1717. 12mo. 4 advt pp. frontis (edges browned). Contemp calf, sl worn. Anon. *(Jarndyce)* **£120 [≈ $230]**
- Logic; or, the Art of Thinking ... Done from the new French Edition. By Mr. Ozell. London: for William Taylor, 1717. 1st edn of this translation. 12mo. [xii],215,240-452,[4 advt] pp. Frontis. Rec qtr calf. Anon.
(Burmester) **£140 [≈ $268]**

Arne, Thomas A.
- Artaxerxes. An English Opera. London: Tonson, 1764. 8vo. Sl browning. Later wraps. *(Dramatis Personae)* **$40 [≈ £20]**

Arnold, John
- The Complete Psalmodist: or the Organist's, Parish-Clerk's, and Psalm-Singer's

Companion ... Seventh Edition ... London: C. Bigg ..., 1779. 8vo. [iv],xiv, [ii], 419,[v] pp. Occas sl foxing, v sl worm. Rec qtr calf.
(Clark) **£90 [≈ $172]**

Arnot, Hugo
- A Collection and Abridgement of Celebrated Criminal Trials in Scotland, from A.D. 1536, to 1784. With Historical and Critical Remarks. Edinburgh: for the author by William Smellie, 1785. 4to. 400 pp. Contemp calf, red label. *(C.R. Johnson)* **£135 [≈ $259]**
- A Collection and Abridgement of Celebrated Criminal Trials in Scotland, from A.D. 1536, to 1784. With Historical and Critical Remarks. Edinburgh: William Smellie, 1785. 1st edn. 4to. Some browning & foxing, some pp dusty & chipped. Rec calf & bds.
(Meyer Boswell) **$350 [≈ £182]**

Arpasia ...
- Arpasia; or, The Wanderer. A Novel. By the Author of The Nabob. London: for William Lane, 1786. 3 vols. 12mo. Vol 1 prelims sl damp stained, sm marg reprs 1 leaf vol 3. Contemp half calf, mrbld bds, rubbed, sm reprs. *(Jarndyce)* **£1,250 [≈ $2,399]**

Arrowsmith, Joseph
- The Reformation: A Comedy ... London: for Wm. Cademan, 1673. 1st edn. State with triangular w'cut ornament on title. Sm 4to. Browned. Mod cloth. Anon.
(Dramatis Personae) **$200 [≈ £104]**

Art ...
- The Art of Contentment ...see Allestree, Richard.
- Art of Drawing and Painting in Water-Colours ... A New Edition, corrected, and ... Illustrated with Copper-Plates. London: G. Keith, 1763. Earliest recorded edn. Sm 8vo. iv,[1],6-96 pp. 4 fldg plates. Loosely bound in later paper bds. Thomas Phillipps copy.
(Spelman) **£250 [≈ $479]**
- The Art of Drawing and Painting in Water-Colours ... A New Edition, Corrected ... Dublin: J. Potts, 1778 (sep title to 'The Art of Drawing in Perspective' dated 1777). 2 parts in one vol, continuously paginated. 12mo. 4 plates. Contemp calf, sl worn.
(Jarndyce) **£80 [≈ $153]**
- The Art of Drawing, and Painting in Water Colours ... see also Peele, J.
- The Art of Joking; or, an Essay on Witticism; in the Manner of Mr. Pope's Essay on

Criticism ... added the Laws of Laughing ... London: for Joseph Deveulle, [1774?]. 1st edn. 12mo. [iv],7-63 pp. Later half mor.
(Burmester) **£450 [≈ $863]**

- The Art of Speaking ... see Lamy, Bernard.

- The Art of Tanning and Currying Leather ... see Vallancey, Charles.

Ascham, Roger

- The Scholemaster ... Now revised a Second Time, and much improved, by James Upton. London: for W. Innys, 1743. 8vo. xxii,274 pp. Contemp calf, rebacked, sides sl rubbed.
(Burmester) **£120 [≈ $230]**

- Toxophilus, The Schole, or Partitions, of Shooting ... To which is added, a Dedication and Preface by John Walters. Wrexham: R. Marsh, 1788. 12mo. xxii,230,[2] pp. Frontis. Some marg water stains. Rebound in calf & mrbld bds.
(Karmiole) **$125 [≈ £65]**

Asgill, John

- An Argument proving, that according to the Covenant of Eternal Life revealed in the Scriptures, Man may be translated from hence into Eternal Life, without passing through Death. London: 1715. 8vo. Damp stained. Disbound.
(Sanders) **£45 [≈ $86]**

- An Essay on a Registry for Title of Lands. London: ptd in the year, 1698. 34 pp. rec wraps. Wing A.3927.
(C.R. Johnson) **£125 [≈ $239]**

- An Essay on a Registry, for Titles of Lands. London: ptd in the year 1698. 1st edn. 8vo in 4s. [iv],34 pp. Browned & dusty, lib stamp on title verso. Disbound, stitching broken. Wing A.3927.
(Clark) **£45 [≈ $86]**

- The Succession of the House of Hannover Vindicated, against the Pretender's Second Declaration ... The Second Edition. London: for J. Roberts, 1714. 8vo. 75 pp. Disbound.
(Bickersteth) **£35 [≈ $67]**

Ash, John

- The Easiest Introduction to Dr. Lowth's English Grammar, designed for the use of Children under Ten Years of Age ... New Edition, Improved. London: Dilly, 1768. 24mo. 4 advt pp. Contemp sheep, 1 crnr worn, rebacked.
(Jarndyce) **£150 [≈ $287]**

- Grammatical Institutes: or, An Easy Introduction to Dr. Lowth's English Grammar: Designed for the Use of Schools ... New Edition ... enlarged. London: Dilly, 1786. 12mo. 6 advt pp. Sl browned at ends. Rebound in calf.
(Jarndyce) **£180 [≈ $345]**

Ashdowne, William

- The Unitarian, Arian, and Trinitarian Opinions concerning Christ, examined and tryed by Scripture Evidence alone. Canterbury: ptd by J. Grove, 1789. Disbound.
(Waterfield's) **£40 [≈ $76]**

Ashworth, Caleb

- Reflections on the Fall of a Great Man: a Sermon ... on occasion of the Death of the late Reverend Isaac Watts. London: J. Waugh ..., 1749. Disbound.
(Waterfield's) **£40 [≈ $76]**

The Asiatic Miscellany ...

- The Asiatic Miscellany ... By W. Chambers Esq. and Sir W. Jones ... and other Literary Gentlemen, now resident in India. Calcutta, printed. London: reptd for J. Wallis ..., 1787. 1st edn thus. 8vo. [iv],196 pp. Contemp tree calf gilt, spine worn, jnt cracking.
(Finch) **£95 [≈ $182]**

Astell, Mary

- An Enquiry after Wit ... Second Edition. London: for John Bateman, 1722. Sm 8vo. [6], 176 pp. Rebound in calf & mrbld bds. Anon.
(Karmiole) **$100 [≈ £52]**

Astle, Thomas

- The Origin and Progress of Writing ... Illustrated by Engravings. London: for the author; sold by T. Payne & Son ..., 1784. 1st edn. 4to. Half-title. Rebound in half calf.
(Jarndyce) **£450 [≈ $863]**

Astruc, Jean

- A General and Compleat Treatise on all the Diseases incident to Children ... London: John Nourse, 1746. 1st English edn. 8vo. [x], 229, [1] pp. Edges on 2 ff reinforced. Contemp calf, rebacked.
(Bookpress) **$750 [≈ £390]**

Atkins, William

- A Discourse Shewing the Nature of the Gout ... London: for Tho. Fabian ... & the author, 1694. xvi,128 pp. Port frontis. Browned, few sm tears & flaws not affecting text. Old sheep, worn. Wing A.4125. *(Clark)* **£750 [≈ $1,439]**

The Attorney's Compleat Pocket-Book ...

- The Attorney's Compleat Pocket-Book: or, New Magazine of Law for Clerks, and Universal Conveyancer. Dublin: Elizabeth Lynch, 1791. 2nd edn. 12mo. Some foxing. Contemp sheep, rubbed, hd of jnts sl cracked.
(Meyer Boswell) **$250 [≈ £130]**

Aubin, Nicholas
- The Cheats and Illusions of Romish Priests and Exorcists. Discover'd in the History of the Devils of Loudun ... London: for W. Turner, & R. Bassett, 1703. Only edn in English. 8vo. [viii],331,[v] pp. Some browning. Victorian speckled calf, jnts rubbed. Anon. *(Sotheran's)* **£185 [≈ $355]**

Aubrey, John
- Miscellanies. London: for Edward Castle, 1696. 1st edn. Intl blank A1. Occas diags in text. Cambridge panelled calf, rebacked, sm crnr repr. Wing A.4188.
(Sanders) **£650 [≈ $1,247]**
- Miscellanies ... The Second Edition, with large Additions ... London: for A. Bettesworth ..., 1721. 8vo. [ii],x,[iv],236 pp. 1 copperplate. Contemp speckled sheep, red speckled edges, jnts cracked, hd of backstrip absent. *(Sotheran's)* **£325 [≈ $623]**
- Miscellanies upon Various Subjects. A New Edition, with ... some Account of his Life. London: for W. Ottridge, 1784. 8vo. [ii],xiv, 292,[iv] pp. Occas foxing. Mod qtr pigskin.
(Rankin) **£75 [≈ $143]**

The Auction; A Town Eclogue ...
- See Combe, William.

Augustine, Saint
- Saint Augustines Confessions Translated with Some Marginal Notes ... By William Wats. London: for Abel Roper, 1650. 12mo. [12],513, 3 pp. Frontis. Few v sm marg worm holes. Early calf, rubbed & scuffed. Wing A.4206. *(Humber)* **£58 [≈ $111]**

Aurelius Antoninus, Marcus
- The Meditations ... Translated ... With Notes: By meric Casaubon ... The Fifth Edition. To which is added, The Life of Antoninus ... London: 1692. 8vo. [ii],xxxii, 127, [xvii],243, [i],67,[ix],102 pp. Port. Contemp calf, jnt cracked, crnrs knocked. Wing A.4230. *(Finch)* **£45 [≈ $86]**

Austen, James (? & Jane)
- The Loiterer, a Periodical Work, first published at Oxford in the Years 1789 and 1790. Dublin: William Porter, 1792. 1st Irish edn. 368 pp. Contemp tree calf, red label. Anon. *(C.R. Johnson)* **£750 [≈ $1,439]**

Ayloffe, Sir Joseph
- An Historical Description of an Ancient Picture in Windsor Castle, representing the Interview between King Henry VIII and the French King Francis I ... London: Society of Antiquaries, 1773. 4to. 45 pp. Some spotting. Lib stamp on title verso. Contemp qtr calf, worn. *(Hollett)* **£95 [≈ $182]**

Ayres, Philip
- Emblems of Love in Four Languages, Dedicated to the Ladys. London: for John Wren, [1683]. 1st or 2nd edn. Engvd title, 44 engvd plates, each with leaf of text. Faint lib stamp on title verso. Mod calf gilt. Wing A.4309. *(Hollett)* **£350 [≈ $671]**

B., J.
- The Epitome of the Art of Husbandry ... see Blagrave, Joseph.

B., W.
- A Treatise of Fornication ... see Barlow, William.

Babington, Gervaise
- A Profitable Exposition of the Lords Prayer, by way of Questions and Answers ... London: R. Robinson for Thomas Charde, 1596. 8vo. W'cut device on title, w'cut intls. Some damp staining throughout. Mod calf. STC 1091.
(Robertshaw) **£165 [≈ $316]**

Bacon, Anthony
- A Short Address to the Government, the Merchants, Manufacturers, and the Colonists in America, and the Sugar Islands, On the Present State of Affairs. By a Member of Parliament. London: G. Robinson, 1775. Half-title, 40 pp. Disbound. Anon.
(C.R. Johnson) **£220 [≈ $422]**

Bacon, Sir Francis, Lord Verulam
- Baconiana. Or certain Genuine Remains ... London: J.D. for Richard Chiswell, 1679. 1st edn. Issue with imprimatur on B4v. 8vo. Engvd & ptd titles, [viii],104,270 pp. Divisional title B1. Contemp calf, upper jnt split but holding. Wing B.269..
(Gaskell) **£350 [≈ $671]**
- A Brief Discourse of the Happy Union of the Kingdoms of England and Scotland ... London: B. Griffin, & H. Newman, 1700. 4to. 20 pp. Sm holes in title without loss of text. Disbound. Wing B.271. Anon.
(C.R. Johnson) **£95 [≈ $182]**
- The Elements of the Common Lawes of England, Branched into a double Tract ... London: Assignes of Iohn More, 1639. 4to.

Some browning. 2 sm marg reprs. New panelled calf gilt. STC 1136.
(Meyer Boswell) **$750** [≈ £390]
- The Essayes or, Counsels, Civil and Morall. London: John Beale, 1639. 4th edn. Sm 4to. [vi],340,[4],[38] pp. A1 blank. Later calf, a.e.g.   *(Bookpress)* **$650** [≈ £338]
- The Essays ... With a Table of the Colours of Good and Evil. And a Discourse of the Wisdom of the Ancients ... The Character of Queen Elizabeth ... London: E. Holt for Sam. Smith & Benj. Walford, 1701. Few stains. Contemp calf, rubbed, sl scarred.
(Jarndyce) **£70** [≈ $134]
- The History of Henry VII of England ... London: for the editor at the Logographic Press, 1786. 1st edn thus. 8vo. iv,288,4 pp. Rec half calf.   *(Young's)* **£42** [≈ $80]
- Letters ... Now Collected and Augmented ... London: for Benj. Tooke, 1702. Final errata & advt leaf. Lacks first f.e.p. The 2 dedic ff cancelled. Contemp calf, crnrs sl rubbed, sm splits at ends of hinges.
(Jarndyce) **£120** [≈ $230]
- Of the Advancement and Proficiencie of Learning ... Interpreted by Gilbert Wats. London: for Thomas Williams, 1674. Folio. Final printer's note. Frontis port. Lib stamps. Rebound in calf. Wing B.312.
(Jarndyce) **£250** [≈ $479]
- The Two Bookes of Sr Francis Bacon, of the Proficience and Advancement of Learning, Divine and Humane. Oxford: L.L. for Thomas Huggins, 1633. 4to. [ii],1-166,169-335,[i] pp. Last few ff creased. Mod half calf. STC 1166.
(Clark) **£285** [≈ $547]

Bacon, Nathaniel
- An Historical and Political Discourse of the Laws and Government of England ... London: for D. Browne ..., 1760. 5th edn, crrctd. 4to. xix,203,185 pp. Last few ff sl soiled. Old cloth.   *(Young's)* **£60** [≈ $115]

Bacon, Roger
- The Cure of Old Age ... Translated out of Latin; with Annotations ... Account of his Life ... By Richard Browne ... also A Physical Account of the Tree of Life ... London: 1683. 1st edn in English. [xl],156, [vi], 108,[8] pp. 19th c mor gilt, a.e.g., sl rubbed. Wing B.372   *(Clark)* **£480** [≈ $921]

Badger, John
- A Collection of Remarkable Cures of the King's Evil, Perfected by the Royal Touch.

Collected from the Writings of many Eminent Physicians and Surgeons ... London: Cooper, 1748. 8vo. Half-title,64 pp. Some foxing & early underlining. Antique style bds.
(Goodrich) **$135** [≈ £70]

Bagley; a Descriptive Poem ...
- See Schomberg, A.C.

Bailey, Nathaniel
- An Universal Etymological English Dictionary ... Fifth Edition, with considerable improvements. London: for J. & J. Knapton ..., 1731. 8vo. Rebound in half calf.   *(Jarndyce)* **£100** [≈ $191]
- An Universal Etymological English Dictionary ... The Four and Twentieth Edition, carefully enlarged and corrected by Edward Harwood. London: Buckland, Strahan ..., 1782. 8vo. Sheep, spine ends worn, hinges weakening.
(Jarndyce) **£75** [≈ $143]
- An Universal· Etymological English Dictionary ... The Four-and-Twentieth Edition, carefully enlarged and corrected By Edward Harwood. London: J. Buckland ..., 1782. 8vo. Crnrs of 1st few ff sl frayed, occas sl foxing. Rec half calf. *(Clark)* **£85** [≈ $163]

Bailey, Thomas
- The Life and Death of the Renowned John Fisher, Bishop of Rochester, who was beheaded on Tower-Hill, the 22d of June, 1535. London: 1740. 3rd edn. 12mo. Port. Contemp calf, worn.
(Robertshaw) **£18** [≈ $34]

Baker, Charles
- Charles Baker's Treatise for the preventing of the Smut in Wheat. Bristol: John Rose for the author, 1797. 31 pp. Authenticating sgntr of the author. Rebound in qtr calf.
(C.R. Johnson) **£160** [≈ $307]

Baker, David Erskine [& Reed, Isaac]
- Biographia Dramatica or A Companion to the Playhouse ... New Edition. London: Rivington, 1782. Rvsd edn. 2 vols. 8vo. New qtr leather & bds, hinges reinforced.
(Dramatis Personae) **$175** [≈ £91]

Baker, David Erskine, et al.
- The Companion to the Playhouse ... London: T. Becket ..., 1764. 1st edn. 2 vols. 12mo. Closed tear vol 1 title. Sm embossed marks on titles. Mod half calf. Anon.
(Dramatis Personae) **$285** [≈ £148]

Baker, H.
- Of Microscopes and the Discoveries made thereby. Vol. I. The Microscope Made Easy. London: Dodsley, 1785. 2nd edn. 8vo. xxiii, 324 pp. 14 plates. New leather.
(Gemmary) **$325** [≈ £169]
- The Well-Spring of Sciences ... London: 1650. Sm 8vo. [4],312,[21] pp. Lacks last leaf of index. Sm crnr torn from 1 leaf affecting text. Later half leather, sl worn, front hinge cracked. *(Whitehart)* £135 [≈ $259]

Baker, Henry
- Medulla Poetarum Romanorum: or, the most beautiful and instructive Passages of the Roman Poets ... London: printed in the year 1737. 1st edn. Large Paper. 2 vols in one. 8vo. Contemp calf gilt, spine ends trifle rubbed. *(Ximenes)* **$350** [≈ £182]

Baker, Revd J.
- The History of the Inquisition as it subsists in the Kingdoms of Spain, Portugal, &c. and in both the Indies to this day. London: Marshall, Davies, Spencer, 1734. 4to. 4 plates. Blank strip cut from hd of title. Contemp calf, rebacked.
(Waterfield's) £145 [≈ $278]
- The History of the Inquisition, as it subsists in the Kingdoms of Spain, Portugal, &c. and in both the Indies, to this Day ... London: Joseph Marshall ..., 1734. 4to. Frontis, 6 plates. Occas browning. Contemp calf, rebacked. *(Frew Mackenzie)* £300 [≈ $575]

Baker, Sir Richard
- A Chronicle of the Kings of England ... London: for H. Sawbridge ..., 1684. 8th edn. Folio. [xlviii],750,42 pp. Addtnl engvd title (sl edge worn). Old calf, rebacked. Wing B.509. *(Young's)* £85 [≈ $163]
- A Chronicle of the Kings of England ... With a Continuation ... Second Continuation ... London: 1733. Folio. [xxii],919,[1 blank, 10 index] pp. Addtnl engvd title. Sl browning & dust marks. Contemp calf, worn, scraped, jnts cracking, spine ends chipped.
(Bow Windows) £195 [≈ $374]
- Meditations and Disquisitions upon the One and Fiftieth Psalme of David. London: Anne Bowler, 1638. 4to. vi,75 pp. Browning. Mod qtr leather. Not in Wing. *(Gage)* £30 [≈ $57]
- Meditations and Motives for Prayer upon the Seven Dayes of the Weeke ... London: Royston & Eglesfield, 1642. 1st edn. 12mo. [xiv], 166 pp. Addtnl engvd title, 7 full page

engvs. Intl blank. Old calf, later reback, rubbed, crnrs sl worn. Wing B.511.
(Clark) £275 [≈ $527]

Baker, Thomas
- Reflections upon Learning, wherein is shewn the Insufficiency thereof ... In order to evince the Usefulness and Necessity of Revelation. The Second Edition, Corrected. London: for A. Bosvile, 1700. 8vo. [xvi],240 pp. Orig calf, spine rubbed, 1 jnt cracked. Anon.
(Bickersteth) £175 [≈ $335]
- Reflections upon Learning ... London: for J. Knapton ..., 1715. 5th edn. 8vo. [xvi],288 pp. Sm stain on title. Rec contemp style half calf. Anon. *(Young's)* £120 [≈ $230]
- Tunbridge-Walks: or, the Yeoman of Kent. A Comedy. London: Lintott, 1703. 1st edn. Sm 4to. Half-title. Some foxing & browning. Rec bds. Anon. *(Ximenes)* **$300** [≈ £156]

Bale, John
- A Brefe Cronycle Concerning the Examynacyon and Death of the Blessed Martyr of Christ Sir John Oldecastell, the Lorde Cobham ... London: for C. Davis, 1729. 8vo. Addtnl engvd title. Mod half mor.
(Dramatis Personae) **$125** [≈ £65]

Balfour, Sir Andrew
- Letters written to a Friend ... containing excellent directions and advices for travelling thro' France and Italy ... Edinburgh: [Michael Balfour], 1700. 12mo. 6 ff, x, 274 pp. Orig sheep, rebacked.
(Frew Mackenzie) £280 [≈ $537]

Balguy, Thomas
- Divine Benevolence Asserted; and Vindicated from the Objections of Ancient and Modern Sceptics. London: for Lockyer Davis, 1781. Disbound. *(Waterfield's)* £65 [≈ $124]

Balzac, Jean Louis Guez, Sieur de
- The Letters of Movnsevr de Balzac. Translated into English ... by W.T. [William Tirwhyt] ... London: 1638. 2nd English edn.. 4to. [xxiv],406,[iv] pp. Sm stain on top blank marg 1st 3 ff. Orig calf, sm repr to spine ends. STC 12453. *(Vanbrugh)* £155 [≈ $297]

Bancks, John
- See Banks, John.

Bancroft, E.
- An Essay on the Natural History of Guiana,

in South America ... London: 1769. 8vo. iv,
402, [2] pp. Frontis. Lib blind stamp on title.
Contemp calf, rebacked. Anon.
(Wheldon & Wesley) **£300 [≈ $575]**

Banks, John

- Cyrus the Great ... London: Bentley, 1696.
1st edn. 8vo. Sheets B & C in Bowers' (*)
setting. A few headlines shaved. Mod bds.
(Waterfield's) **£90 [≈ $172]**

- The History of the Life and Reign of the Czar
Peter the Great, Emperor of all Russia ...
Faithfully abridged from the best Historians,
by J. Bancks ... London: J. Hodges, 1740. 2nd
edn. 12mo. [iv],346,[14] pp. Port. V sl marg
stain at end. Contemp calf.
(Burmester) **£60 [≈ $115]**

- A Short Critical Review of the Political Life
of Oliver Cromwell ... The Second Edition,
carefully revised, and greatly enlarged ...
London: Osborn ..., 1742. 12mo.
[vi],359,[xix] pp. Port frontis. Some foxing.
Contemp calf, sometime rebacked, used.
Anon.   *(Sotheran's)* **£98 [≈ $188]**

- A Short Critical Review of the Political Life
of Oliver Cromwell ... By a Gentleman of the
Middle-Temple. The Fifth Edition, carefully
revised, and greatly enlarged. Glasgow: James
Knox, 1763. Half title. Contemp sheep,
rubbed, splits in hinges. Anon.
(Jarndyce) **£35 [≈ $67]**

Banks, John

- A Treatise on Mills. London: W. Richardson,
1795. 1st edn. 8vo. xxiv,172,[4] pp. 10 pp
subscribers. 3 fldg plates. Later half calf.
(Bookpress) **$585 [≈ £304]**

Barbauld, Anna Laetitia

- See Aikin, Anna Laetitia.

Barbette, Paul

- The Practice of the most successful Physitian
Paul Barbette, Doctour of Physick. With the
Notes and Observations of Frederick Deckers
... London: 1675. [xvi],272 pp. frontis. Last
page in facs on old paper. Cambridge style
calf antique.   *(Whitehart)* **£380 [≈ $729]**

Barbour, John

- The Bruce ... The First Genuine Edition ...
With Notes and a Glossary by J. Pinkerton.
London: H. Hughs for R. Nicol, 1790. 3 vols
in one. 8vo. Half-titles. Title vignettes,
vignette of Bruce, facs leaf. Later half calf,
jnts cracked but firm. *(Rankin)* **£85 [≈ $163]**

Barbut, J.

- The Genera Vermium exemplified by various
Specimens of the Animals contained in the
Orders of the Intestina et Mollusca Linnaei
[Part 1, only]. London: 1783. 4to. [ii],xx, ii,
101 pp. Engvd title, 11 hand cold plates (sl
offset). Qtr calf, rebacked.
(Wheldon & Wesley) **£160 [≈ $307]**

Barckley, Sir Richard

- A Discourse of the Felicitie of Man ...
London: for William Ponsonby, 1603. 2nd
edn. 4to. Upper outer edge of title & preface
sl frayed, 2 sm marg reprs. Contemp polished
calf gilt, rebacked. STC 1382.
(Stewart) **£550 [≈ $1,055]**

Barclay, John

- Barclay His Argenis: or, the Loves of
Poliarchus and Argenis. Faithfully
Translated ... by Kingsmill Long. London:
1625. 1st edn. Folio. [vi],404 pp. 2 sm lib
stamps. Sl mark & worm 1st few ff. Old calf,
rubbed, spine hd sl chipped. STC 1392.
(Clark) **£220 [≈ $422]**

- Barclay His Argenis. Or, the Loves of
Polyarchus and Argenis. Faithfully
Translated ... by Kingsmill Long ... Second
Edition ... London: 1636. 2nd edn. 4to.
[xxxvi],719 pp. Engvd title, port, 23 plates.
Text sl browned. Orig sheep, rebacked. STC
1395.   *(Vanbrugh)* **£395 [≈ $758]**

Barclay, Robert

- The Anarchy of the Ranters, and other
Libertines, the Hierarchy of the Romanists ...
Refuted, in a Two-fold Apology for the ...
Quakers ... London: Mary Hinde, 1771. 8vo.
viii,113,3 advt pp. Old qtr calf, rebacked.
(Young's) **£40 [≈ $76]**

- An Apology for the True Christian Divinity,
as the same is Held Forth, and Preached, by
the People, called Quakers ... London: T.
Sowle, 1703. 8vo. [xiv],574,[xxvi] pp.
Contemp black gilt panelled mor, a.e.g., sm
area of wear on lower bd.
(Sotheran's) **£138 [≈ $264]**

- An Apology for the True Christian Divinity,
as the Same is held Forth, and Preached, by
the People, called in Scorn, Quakers.
Newport, RI: 1729. [10],524,index pp. Some
dampstains, some soiling & sm tears.
Contemp calf, bds nearly detached, spine
chipped.   *(Reese)* **£400 [≈ $208]**

- Truth Triumphant through the Spiritual
Warfare ... of ... Robert Barclay. London: for
Thomas Northcott, 1692. 1st edn. Sm folio.

[28],[16], 908,[16] pp. Sm pieces missing from flyleaves & 1st page of text with sl loss. Contemp sheep, crnrs rubbed.
(Chapel Hill) **$200 [≈ £104]**

Baretti, Giuseppe (Joseph)
- A Dictionary of the English and Italian Languages ... Italian and English Grammar. A New Edition. Corrected and Improved, by Peter Ricci Roca. London: Rivington, Newbery, 1790. 2 vols in one. 4to. Early 19th c calf, spine rubbed, sm crack in jnt.
(Burmester) **£90 [≈ $172]**
- A Journey from London to Genoa, through England, Portugal, Spain, and France. London: for T. Davies & L. Davis, 1770. 1st 8vo edn. 4 vols. 8vo. Contemp calf, gilt spines, minor rubbing.
(Ximenes) **$400 [≈ £208]**
- A Journey from London to Genoa, through England, Portugal, Spain, and France. London: T. Davies ..., 1770. 4 vols. 19th c half calf, black & green labels, sl scuffed.
(Frew Mackenzie) **£350 [≈ $671]**
- Tolondron. Speeches to John Bowle about his Edition of Don Quixote; together with some Account of Spanish Literature. London: for R. Faulder, 1786. 1st edn. 8vo. iv,338 pp. Half-title. Contemp calf, sm cracks in jnts, sl wear on lower cvr. *(Burmester)* **£350 [≈ $671]**

Barlow, Joel
- Advice to the Privileged Orders in the Several States of Europe, resulting from the Necessity and Propriety of a General Revolution in the Principle of Government ... London: for J. Johnson ..., 1792. 2nd edn. 8vo. 156 pp. Title sl creased. New bds. *(Young's)* **£45 [≈ $86]**

Barlow, Thomas
- A Letter concerning Invocation of Saints and Adoration of the Cross wrote Ten Years since to John Evelyn of Deptford Esq. London: John Macock for John Martyn, 1679. 4to. Disbound. Wing B.834.
(Waterfield's) **£25 [≈ $47]**

Barlow, William
- A Treatise of Fornication ... By W.B. London: for John Dunton, 1690. Stained. 2 foredge margs scorched. Rebound in half calf. Wing B.848. *(Jarndyce)* **£150 [≈ $287]**

Barnard, E.
- Virtue the Source of Pleasure. London: ptd by John Oliver, sold by Buckland & Ward, 1757. 1st edn. 8vo. vii,319 pp. Sm reprs. Orig

calf, rebacked. Anon.
(Bickersteth) **£120 [≈ $230]**

Barnard, James
- The Life of the Venerable and Right Reverend Richard Challoner, D.D. ... London: ptd by J.P. Coghlan ..., 1784. 1st edn. 8vo. xii, 284 pp. Contemp calf, gilt ruled spine, black label. *(Young's)* **£55 [≈ $105]**

Barnard, Thomas
- An Historical Character relating to the Holy and Exemplary Life of ... Elizabeth Hastings. Leedes: ptd by James Lister, for John Swales ..., London ... Leicester, 1742. 1st edn. 12mo. Ink stain on title. Contemp red mor, a.e.g., upper jnt broken. *(Hannas)* **£90 [≈ $172]**

Barnes, Joshua
- The History of that most Victorious Monarch Edward IIId ... Cambridge: John Hayes for the author, 1688. Lge folio. [xvi],911 pp. Port frontis & 4 other ports. Contemp calf, upper hinge cracked. Wing B.871.
(Vanbrugh) **£475 [≈ $911]**
- A New Discovery of a Little Sort of People, Anciently Discoursed of, called Pygmies ... London: for R. Griffiths, 1750. 2nd edn of 'Gerania'. 8vo. Final "Epitaph" leaf (gutter sl reprd). Sm ink stain on title. Contemp calf.
(Georges) **£350 [≈ $671]**

Barrett, William
- The History and Antiquities of the City of Bristol ... Bristol: William Pine, [1789]. 4to. Subscribers. 30 plates. Mod qtr calf.
(Waterfield's) **£200 [≈ $383]**

Barrington, Daines
- Additional Instances of Navigators, who have reached High Northern Latitudes ... London: 1775. 1st issue. [91]-112 pp. Lib stamps. Half leather & bds. *(Reese)* **$300 [≈ £156]**
- Miscellanies ... London: 1781. 4to. iv, viii, 557 pp. 2 maps (1 fldg), tables. Blind stamp on title. Antique calf & mrbld bds, untrimmed. *(Reese)* **$1,000 [≈ £520]**
- The Naturalist's Journal. London: for Benjamin White, 1775. Oblong 4to. Contemp half calf, spine sl rubbed, hd of spine trifle worn. Anon. *(Ximenes)* **$450 [≈ £234]**

Barrow, Isaac
- Of the Love of God and our Neighbour, in Several Sermons. London: Miles Flesher for Brab. Aylmer, 1680. 8vo. [8],317,[2] pp. Port.

18th c dark blue calf elab gilt, a.e.g. Wing B.949.   *(Humber)* £78 [≈$149]
- A Treatise of the Popes Supremacy ... London: M. Flesher for Brab. Aylmer, 1680. 4to. [8],428,[1],49 pp. Sm marg hole in 1 leaf. 18th c calf, rubbed, jnts & crnrs worn. Wing B.961.   *(Humber)* £65 [≈$124]
- The Usefullness of Mathematical Learning Explained and Demonstrated ... London: 1734. 1st edn. xxxii,440,[23] pp. Frontis port, fldg plate. Contemp calf, rebacked, crnrs worn.   *(Whitehart)* £150 [≈$287]
- The Works (being All his English Works) in Three Volumes, Published by his Grace Dr. John Tillotson. London: Brabazon Aylmer, 1700. 3rd edn. 3 vols. 668; 476; 477,index pp. Leather, some bds detached. 'Treatise of the Pope's Supremacy' in vol 1.
(Gage) £70 [≈$134]

Barruel, Augustin
- Memoirs, illustrating the History of Jacobinism ... Translated ... by the Hon. Robert Clifford. Second Edition, revised and corrected. London: for the translator, by T. Burton, 1798. 4 vols. Fldg chart vol 4. Contemp calf, orig backstrips sometime relaid.   *(Jarndyce)* £180 [≈$345]

Bartram, William
- Travels through North and South Carolina, Georgia, East & West Florida ... London: 1792. 1st British edn. [24],520,[12] pp. Map, 8 plates. Antique half calf & mrbld bds.
(Reese) $1,250 [≈£651]

Barwick, John
- Querela Cantabrigiensis: or, A Remonstrance by way of Apologie, for the Banished Members of the late Flourishing University of Cambridge. By Some of the Said Sufferers. London: 1647. 2nd edn. Sm 8vo. [xii], 36 pp. Rec half calf. Wing B.1010. Anon.
(Vanbrugh) £75 [≈$143]

Barwick, Peter
- The Life of the Reverend Dr. John Barwick, D.D. ... London: 1724. London: 1724. [28], 552, [38] pp. 2 frontis ports. Some pp dusty, last index page remargd with v sl loss of text. New three qtr leather.
(Whitehart) £50 [≈$95]
- The Life of the Reverend Dr. John Barwick, D.D. ... London: J. Bettenham, 1724. 1st edn in English. 8vo. xxiv,552,2,[38] pp. 18th c diced calf, label chipped.
(Young's) £50 [≈$95]

Basnage, Jacques
- The History of the Jews ... Being a Supplement and Continuation of the History of Josephus. Translated ... by Thomas Taylor. London: J. Beaver ..., 1708. Folio. xvi,760 pp. Red & black title (sl soiled). Contemp calf, rebacked, outer front hinge cracked.   *(Karmiole)* $250 [≈£130]

The Batchelor's Directory ...
- The Batchelor's Directory: being a Treatise of the Excellence of Marriage ... London: for Richard Cumberland & Benjamin Bragg, 1694. 1st edn. 12mo. Title,2 advt ff, 253 pp, 2 advt ff. Few margs strengthened. Polished calf antique by Hatchards, t.e.g. Wing B.260.
(Bickersteth) £550 [≈$1,055]

Bate, George
- A Compendious Narrative of the late Troubles in England. or, Elenchus Englished ... London: 1652. 1st edn in English. 12mo. [xii], 192, 217-300 pp. Blank before title. Cropped at hd & side. Contemp calf, rebacked, extremities worn. Wing B.1978. Anon.   *(Clark)* £120 [≈$230]

Bate, Henry
- The Flitch of Bacon; A Comic Opera ... London: for T. Evans, 1779. 1st edn. 8vo. vi,28 pp. Disbound.   *(Young's)* £25 [≈$47]

Bates, William
- Considerations of the Existence of God and the Immortality of the Soul ... London: J.D. for Brab. Aylmer, 1676. 1st edn. 8vo. [16], 292, [12] pp. Edges sl browned. 19th c half calf. Wing B.1101.   *(Humber)* £65 [≈$124]

Bath Anecdotes ...
- Bath Anecdotes and Characters: By The Genius Loci. London: Dodsley, Dilly, & Shrimpton, Bath, 1782. 1st edn. Sm 8vo. Advt leaf at end. Some contemp MS notes (mostly shaved). Rec calf.
(Georges) £180 [≈$345]

Baudier, Michel
- The History of the Imperiall Estate of the Grand Seigneurs ... Translated out of French by E.G[rimeston]. London: 1635. 1st edn in English. 2 parts in one vol. Sm 4to. [viii], 248 pp. Gen title & 2 sep titles. Rec mor, a.e.g. STC 1593. Anon.
(Bow Windows) £375 [≈$719]

Baxter, Richard

- The Practical Works of the late Reverend and Pious Mr Richard Baxter. London: Parkhurst, Robinson & Laurence, 1707. 4 vols. Lge folio. Port, frontis. New half mor.
(Humber) **£290 [≈$556]**
- The Reasons of the Christian Religion. The First Part, of Godliness ... The Second Part, of Christianity ... London: R. White, for Fran. Titon, 1667. 1st edn. 4to. [xxxvi],604 pp. Port frontis. Few edges chipped, occas sl marks. Rec calf. Wing B.1367.
(Clark) **£125 [≈$239]**
- The Saints Everlasting Rest ... Phila: Henry Tuckniss, 1794. 12mo. 400 pp. Title soiled. Contemp calf, worn, spine extremities a bit chipped. *(Karmiole)* **$75 [≈£39]**
- A Treatise of Self-Denyall ... London: Robert White, for Nevil Simmons Bookseller in Kederminster, 1660. 1st edn. 4to. lxviii,329, [8] pp. Old calf, rubbed. Wing B.1430.
(Young's) **£120 [≈$230]**

Bayly, Anselm

- A Practical Treatise on Singing and Playing with Just Expression and Real Elegance ... London: for J. Ridley, 1771. 99 pp. Contemp sheep, red label.
(C.R. Johnson) **£450 [≈$863]**

Bayne, David, alias Kinneir

- A New Essay on the Nerves and the Doctrine of the Animal Spirits ... London: Innys & Manby, 1738. 1st edn. 4to. vi,167,19 advt pp. A few stains. Sm hole affecting 1 letter. Contemp calf, rebacked.
(Rootenberg) **$400 [≈£208]**

Bazin, Gilles Auguste

- The Natural History of Bees ... Translated from the French. London: Knapton, 1744. 1st English edn. 8vo. xvi,452,16 pp. 12 plates. Contemp calf, sl rubbed.
(Young's) **£325 [≈$623]**
- The Natural History of Bees ... Translated from the French. London: Knapton, Vaillant, 1744. 1st edn in English. 8vo. [xvi],542, [xvi] pp. 12 fldg plates. Orig calf, rebacked. Anon.
(Bickersteth) **£280 [≈$537]**

Beach, William Wither

- Abradates and Panthea: a Tale extracted from Xenophon. Salisbury: ptd by S. Collins for James Fletcher, London, 1765. 4to. Half-title. Disbound. *(Waterfield's)* **£60 [≈$115]**

Bearcroft, Philip

- An Historical Account of Thomas Sutton Esq; and his Foundation in Charter-House ... London: ptd by E. Owen, sold by F. Gyles, 1737. 1st edn. 8vo. xvi,276 pp. Last page is errata. Port frontis, 2 fldg plates. Orig panelled calf, v sl worn.
(Vanbrugh) **£115 [≈$220]**
- An Historical Account of Thomas Sutton Esq., and his Foundation in Charter-House. London: E. Owen ..., 1737. 8vo. xvi,275 pp. Frontis port, fldg view, 1 other plate. 19th c polished calf gilt, trifle rubbed.
(Hollett) **£75 [≈$143]**

Beatniffe, Richard

- The Norfolk Tour: Or the Travellers Pocket Companion ... Fourth Edition greatly enlarged and improved ... Norwich: 1786. Tall 12mo. [viii], 240, 129-136, 37*-44* pp. Half calf, gilt spine, uncut.
(Lamb) **£60 [≈$115]**

Beattie, James

- An Essay on the Nature and Immutability of Truth, in Opposition to Sophistry and Scepticism. London: Dilly, 1774. 5th edn. 8vo. 518 pp. Orig bds, uncut, rebacked, new endpapers. *(Young's)* **£140 [≈$268]**
- Essays: on Poetry and Music, as they affect the Mind; on Laughter, and Ludicrous Compositions; on the Utility of Classical Learning. Edinburgh: Edward & Charles Dilly, 1778. 555 pp. Contemp calf, rebacked.
(C.R. Johnson) **£265 [≈$508]**
- The Minstrel: or the Progress of Genius. A Poem. The First Book ... The Fourth Edition ... [With] The Minstrel ... The Second Book. London: for Edward & Charles Dilly, 1774. 1st edn of Book 2. 4to. Half-titles. Disbound.
(Waterfield's) **£65 [≈$124]**

Beaumont, Joseph

- Psyche, or Love's Mystery, In XXIV. Cantos ... Second Edition, With Corrections ... and Four New Cantos ... Cambridge: UP for Tho. Bennet, London, 1702. Folio. [xvi],370,[2 advt] pp. Port. Contemp calf, jnt just cracking, crnrs bumped.
(Finch) **£240 [≈$460]**

Beauties ...

- The Beauties of Poetry Display'd. Containing Observations on the Different Species of Poetry ... Dublin: J. & J. Hoey, 1757. 1st Dublin edn. 2 vols. 12mo. xxxiv, 324; [ii],324 pp. Contemp calf, minor scrape to 1 spine.

(Burmester) **£175 [≈ $335]**

Beauty, a Poetical Essay ...
- See Pye, Henry James.

Beawes, Wyndham
- Lex Mercatoria Rediviva: or, the Merchant's Directory. Being a Complete Guide to all Men in Business ... Third Edition, with Large Additions. London: Rivington ..., 1771. Folio. [ii],vii,[iii], 898,[xx] pp. Occas spotting & soiling. Rec half calf.
(Clark) **£250 [≈ $479]**

Beccaria, Cesare
- An Essay on Crimes and Punishments. Translated from the Italian; with a Commentary, Attributed to Mons. De Voltaire. Translated from the French. London: Almon, 1767. 1st English edn. 8vo. xii,179,lxxix pp. Sl foxing & browning, sl marg damp stain. Mod qtr calf.
(Meyer Boswell) **$1,250 [≈ £651]**

Beckford, Peter
- Thoughts on Hunting. Sarum [Salisbury]: E. Easton, 1781. 1st edn. Fcap 4to. [viii],334 pp. Frontis, 2 plates. Contemp calf gilt, v sl rubbed & chipped. Syston Park book label. Anon.
(Ash) **£750 [≈ $1,439]**

Beckford, William
- An Arabian Tale from an unpublished Manuscript: with Notes Critical and Explanatory. London: for J. Johnson, 1786. 1st edn in English, ordinary paper issue. 8vo. viii,334 pp. Lacks blank Y8 as often. Sl spotting. Contemp half calf, gilt spine reprd at ends.
(Finch) **£550 [≈ $1,055]**

Beckingham, Charles
- Scipio Africanus: A Tragedy ... London: for W. Mears ..., 1718. 1st edn. 8vo. [x],56 pp. frontis. New bds.
(Young's) **£65 [≈ $124]**

Beddoes, Thomas
- Alexander's Expedition down the Hydaspes and the Indus to the Indian Ocean. London [Madeley ptd]: sold by Murray & Phillips, 1792. 1st edn. 4to. W'engvd frontis (foxed), 6 other w'cuts. Title dusty. Contemp half calf, rather rubbed, later label. Anon.
(Ximenes) **$750 [≈ £390]**

Bedford, Arthur
- The Evil and Danger of Stage-Plays ... London: W. Bonny, Henry Mortlock, 1706.

[xii], 227,[5 errata & advt] pp. 1st few ff washed.
(Hollett) **£260 [≈ $499]**
- The Scripture Chronology demonstrated by Astronomical Calculations ... London: Knapton ..., 1730. 1st edn. Large Paper. Folio. [iv], vi, [ii], 774,[24] pp. 2 pp subscribers. 13 maps, 10 plates, num tables. Minor marg worm. Some browning. Contemp calf, sl worn.
(Clark) **£200 [≈ $383]**

The Bee ...
- The Bee, a Selection of Poetry from the Best Authors. A New Edition. Dublin: John Gough, 1796. 1st Dublin edn. 12mo. 11,[iii], 191 pp. Engvd title. Contemp tree calf.
(Burmester) **£60 [≈ $115]**

Behn, Aphra
- All the Histories and Novels ... Entire in One Volume ... Together with the History of the Life and Memoirs of Mrs. Behn. By One of the Fair Sex ... Fifth Edition, Corrected ... London: for R. Wellington, 1705. Intl advt leaf, 6 advt pp. Sl worm. Contemp calf, sl worn.
(Jarndyce) **£220 [≈ $422]**
- The City Heiress: or Sir Timothy Treat-all. A Comedy. London: Brown, Benskin, Rhodes, 1682. 1st edn. 4to. [viii],61,[3] pp. Browned, outer ff dusty. Epilogue leaf detached. Occas staining. Lib stamp on title verso. Wing B.1719.
(Clark) **£110 [≈ $211]**
- The Second Part of the Rover ... London: Tonson, 1681. 1st edn. 4to. [viii],85,[iii] pp. Browned, occas staining, some crnrs frayed, 1 marg tear. Lib stamp title verso. Disbound. Wing B.1765.
(Clark) **£75 [≈ $143]**

Behrens, George Henning
- The Natural History of Hartz-Forest, in His Majesty King George's German Dominions. Translated by John Andree. London: W. Pearson for T. Osborne, 1730. 1st English edn. 8vo. [16], 164,[12] pp, inc errata & advts. Contemp calf, jnts sl worn.
(Rootenberg) **$350 [≈ £182]**

Bell, Benjamin
- A System of Surgery. Phila: 1791. 1st Amer edn. 570,xxx pp. Leather, inner hinges taped, front outer hinge cracked, half backstrip missing.
(Fye) **$200 [≈ £104]**
- A System of Surgery. Worcester, Mass.: 1791. 1st Amer edn. 4 vols. 100 w'cut ills. Foxed. Leather, scuffed & worn, hinges cracked.
(Fye) **$300 [≈ £156]**

Belsham, Thomas

- A Review of Mr. Wilberforce's Treatise, Entitled A Practical View of the Prevailing Religious System of Professed Christians ... London: for J. Johnson, 1798. 1st edn. 8vo. Contemp calf gilt, sm pieces missing from spine ends. *(Sanders)* £35 [≈ $67]

Belsham, William

- Essays, Philosophical, Historical and Literary. Dublin: J. Moore, 1790-91. Contemp tree calf, red & green labels. *(C.R. Johnson)* £285 [≈ $547]
- Memoirs of the Reign of George III, to the Session of Parliament ending A.D. 1793. London: Robinson, 1795. 4 vols. Contemp calf. *(Peter Taylor)* £87.50 [≈ $168]
- Memoirs of the Reign of George III, to the Session of Parliament ending A.D. 1793. Second Edition. London: G.G. & J. Robinson, 1795. 4 vols. Some browning & spotting. Contemp speckled calf, worn. *(Clark)* £32 [≈ $61]

Benezet, Anthony

- The Case of our Fellow-Creatures, the Oppressed Africans, respectfully recommended to the Serious Consideration of the Legislature of Great-Britain. By the People called Quakers. London: James Phillips, 1783. 16 pp. Disbound. Anon. *(C.R. Johnson)* £200 [≈ $383]
- A Caution to Great Britain and her Colonies, in a short Representation of the Calamitous State of the enslaved Negroes in the British Dominions. Philadelphia Printed. London: reprinted, 1767. 46 pp. Disbound. *(C.R. Johnson)* £160 [≈ $307]
- Observations on the Inslaving, Importing and Purchasing of Negroes. Germantown: Sower, 1760. 2nd edn. 8vo. Stitched. Anon. *(Rostenberg & Stern)* $250 [≈ £130]
- Some Historical Account of Guinea, its Situation, Produce, and ... Inhabitants. With an Inquiry into the Rise and Progress of the Slave Trade ... New Edition. London: 1788. xv, 131,[1 advt] pp. Title vignette. Some soiling to title. Later half mor. *(Reese)* $100 [≈ £52]

Bennet, Thomas

- A Confutation of Popery in Three Parts ... Cambridge: UP, 1706. 8vo. xii,355,iv pp. Panelled calf. *(Gage)* £20 [≈ $38]
- The Nonjurors Separation from the Public Assemblys of the Church of England Examin'd and Prov'd to be Schismatical, upon their own Principles. London: for W. Innys ..., 1716. 2nd edn. 8vo. [vi],62 pp. Marg hole. Disbound. *(Young's)* £35 [≈ $67]

Bennett, Agnes Maria

- Anna; or Memoirs of a Welch Heiress. Interspersed with Anecdotes of a Nabob ... Fourth Edition. Dublin: Luke White, 1786. 2 vols. 296; 307 pp. Half-titles. Contemp tree calf, spines sl rubbed & lacking numbering labels. Anon. *(C.R. Johnson)* £325 [≈ $623]

Bennett, John

- Letters to a Young Lady, on a Variety of Useful and Interesting Subjects, calculated to improve the Heart, to form the Manners, and enlighten the Understanding. The Second Edition. London: Cadell & Davies, 1795. 244; 270, advt pp. Half-titles. Contemp qtr calf. *(C.R. Johnson)* £120 [≈ $230]

Benoist, Elie

- The History of the Famous Edict of Nantes ... London: for John Dunton, 1694. 1st English edn. 2 vols. 4to. [18],lxxxiv,[iv], 567,[1],[16]; xxxv,561,[15] pp. Lacks imprimatur leaf. Old calf, rebacked. *(Young's)* £140 [≈ $268]

Bentham, Edward

- A Letter to a Young Gentleman of Oxford ... The Second Edition. London: for S. Birt & M. Senex, 1749. Disbound. *(Waterfield's)* £25 [≈ $47]

Bentham, James

- The History and Antiquities of the Conventual and Cathedral Church of Ely. Illustrated with Copper Plates. Cambridge: at the UP by J. Bentham, 1770-71. 2 vols in one. Roy 4to. [viii],224; [ii],[iv], 225-292, 70* pp. Plates. Contemp calf, rebacked. *(Lamb)* £200 [≈ $383]

Bentham, Jeremy

- Defence of Usury ... Dublin: for Williams, Colles ..., 1788. 1st Dublin edn. 12mo. [viii], 232 pp. Contemp qtr calf, loss of leather from spine ends, partial loss of label. *(Finch)* £850 [≈ $1,631]
- Defence of Usury ... with a Letter to Adam Smith ... Dublin: D. Williams ..., 1788. 1st Irish edn. 12mo. [6],232 pp. Lacks half-title & blank flyleaves. Sm wormhole in blank marg. Contemp calf. *(Fenning)* £485 [≈ $931]
- Rhyme and Reason; or, a Fresh Stating of the Arguments against an Opening through the

Wall of Queen's Square, Westminster. By A. Knight [pseud.] ... London: R. Faulder, 1780. 4to. 24 pp. Rebound in red qtr mor.
(C.R. Johnson) £650 [≈ $1,247]

Bentivoglio, Guido
- The History of the Warrs of Flanders ... Englished by ... Henry Earl of Monmouth ... London: for D. Newman ..., 1678. 1st edn. Folio. [viii],1-387,[388-406], 56 pp. Fldg map, num engvd ports in text. Contemp panelled sheep, rebacked. Wing B.1912.
(Vanbrugh) £255 [≈ $489]

Bentley, John
- Halifax, and its Gibbet-Law Placed in a True Light. Together with a Description of the Town ... Halifax: P. Darby, for John Bentley ... [1761]. 1st edn. [ii],95 pp. Engvd frontis. Mod half calf gilt.   *(Hollett)* £120 [≈ $230]

Bentley, Richard
- A Confutation of Atheism from the Origin and Frame of the World. Part I ... Being the Sixth of the Lectures Founded by the Honourable Robert Boyle. London: for Henry Mortlock, 1692. 1st edn. 4to. Disbound.   *(Sanders)* £20 [≈ $38]

Berenger, Richard
- The History and Art of Horsemanship. London: Davies & Cadell, 1771. 1st edn. 2 vols. 4to. vii,319,[iv]; 264,[iv] pp. 2 frontises (1 mezzotint), 15 plates, title vignettes. Orig bds, uncut, rebacked, bds soiled.
(Frew Mackenzie) £375 [≈ $719]

Bergier, Nicolas
- The General History of the Highways, In all Parts of the World, more particularly in Great Britain ... London: D. Brown, W. Innis ..., 1712. 1st English edn. All published. 8vo. xii,164 pp. Browned. Single marg wormhole. Mod half calf. Anon. *(Finch)* £100 [≈ $191]

Bergman, Torbern Olof
- A Dissertation on Elective Attractions ... Translated from the Latin by the Translator of Spallanzani's Dissertations [Thomas Beddoes]. London: Murray, 1785. 1st edn in English. 8vo. xiv,[2],382,[2] pp. 4 fldg plates, 3 fldg tables. Few marg water stains Half calf.
(Rootenberg) $500 [≈ £260]

Berington, Joseph
- The Memoirs of Gregorio Panzani ... Birmingham: Swinney & Walker, 1793. 1st

edn. 8vo. xliii,473,[1],2 advt pp. Orig bds, uncut.   *(Young's)* £78 [≈ $149]

Berington, Simon
- A Modest Enquiry how far Catholics are Guilty of the Horrid Tenets laid to their Charge. By S.B. London: 1740. 1st edn. 8vo in 4s. Browned, early ff sl stained. Contemp sheep, worn, jnts cracked. Ducal b'plate.
(Sanders) £85 [≈ $163]

Berkeley, George
- Alciphron: or, the Minute Philosopher ... London: Tonson, 1732. 1st edn. 2 vols. 8vo. [xii], 350; viii, 358 pp. Contemp sprinkled calf, vol 2 rebacked. Pres copy inscrbd 'Given by the Author'.   *(Finch)* £500 [≈ $959]
- Alciphron or the Minute Philosopher ... Second Edition. London: Tonson, 1732. 2 vols. Contemp calf, rebacked, crnrs reprd. Anon.   *(Waterfield's)* £260 [≈ $499]
- Alciphron, or The Minute Philosopher ... Dublin: Risk, 1732. 1st Dublin edn. 2 parts in one vol. 8vo. Portion of title replaced in facs at hd. Contemp calf, rebacked.
(Emerald Isle) £185 [≈ $355]
- The Medicinal Virtues of Tar Water fully explained ... Dublin Printed. London: reprinted for the proprietors of the Tar Water Warehouse, & sold by M. Cooper, 1744. 8vo. Sm tear on 2 ff (no loss). Sewn as issued, uncut.   *(Waterfield's)* £235 [≈ $451]

Berkeley, George Monck
- Literary Relics: containing Original Letters from King Charles II, King James II ... Swift ... prefixed, an Enquiry into the Life of Dean Swift. London: Kay; Edinburgh: Elliot, 1789. 1st edn. 8vo. lvi,415 pp. Half-title. Contemp calf, gilt spine sl rubbed.
(Burmester) £200 [≈ $383]

Berkenhout, J.
- Clavis Anglica Linguae Botanicae; or, a Botanical Lexicon; in which the Terms of Botany, particularly those ... of Linnaeus ... are explained. London: 1764. Sm 8vo. xii, [215] pp. Lib b'plate. Contemp sheep.
(Wheldon & Wesley) £35 [≈ $67]

Berkley, Sir John
- Memoirs of Sir John Berkley, containing an Account of his Negotiation with Lieut. General Cromwel ... and other Officers of the Army, for restoring King Charles the First ... London: 1702. 2nd edn. 8vo. Sl damp staining. Later half calf, crnrs sl rubbed.

(Robertshaw) **£50 [≈ $95]**

Bernard, John
- The Anatomie of the Common Prayer-Book, wherein is remonstrated the Unlawfulness of it ... By Dwalphintramis. [London:] ptd in the year, 1661. 1st edn. Sm 4to. [iv],68 pp. Sl browned. Dampstaining last few ff. Wraps. Wing B.1996. *(Burmester)* **£65 [≈ $124]**

Bernard, N. & Walker, G.
- The Whole Proceedings of the Siege of Drogheda, to which is added a True Account of the Siege of Londonderry. Dublin: Reilly, 1726. Sm 4to. Some staining of 1st 2 ff. 19th c half leather. *(Emerald Isle)* **£175 [≈ $335]**

Bernard, Nicholas
- The Life and Death of the Most Rev. Dr. James Usher, Late Archbishop of Armagh. London: Tyler, 1656. 1st edn. Port. Calf, rebacked. *(Emerald Isle)* **£95 [≈ $182]**

Berquin, Arnaud
- The Looking Glass for the Mind ... Translated from ... L'Ami des Infants, or, the Children's Friend. London: for E. Newbery, 1787. 8vo. Engvd title. Sm loss to 1 leaf. Contemp roan, scuffed, jnt cracked. Anon. *(Waterfield's)* **£85 [≈ $163]**

Berrow, Capel
- A Pre-Existent Lapse of Human Souls. Demonstrated from Reason ... London: J. Whiston & B. White, 1762. 8vo. [8],156 pp. Later wraps. *(Karmiole)* **$200 [≈ £104]**

Besongne, Nicholas
- Galliae Notitia: or, The Present State of France ... Translated from the last Edition of the French ... By R.W. ... London: John Taylor, 1691. 12mo. [xii],516,[16] pp. Licence leaf. 3 pp errata. Old calf, rubbed, jnts cracked but firm. Wing B.2052. Anon. *(Clark)* **£160 [≈ $307]**

Besse, Joseph
- A Brief Account of many of the Prosecutions of the People call'd Quakers in the Exchequer, Ecclesiastical and other Courts ... humbly submitted to the Consideration of the Members of both Houses of Parliament. London: assigns of J. Sowle, 1736. Wraps. Anon. *(Waterfield's)* **£50 [≈ $95]**
- A Confutation of the Charge of Deism ... Orthodox Sentiments of William Penn are fully demonstrated ... London: assigns of J.

Sowle, 1734. 1st edn. 8vo. xii,172,[8 advt] pp. Contemp sheep, rebacked, recrnrd, some scrapes. *(Sotheran's)* **£135 [≈ $259]**
- A Vindication of a Book, Intituled, A Brief Account of the Prosecutions of the People call'd Quakers ... London: assigns of J. Sowle, 1737. 1st edn. 8vo. 138 pp. New contemp style half calf. Anon. *(Young's)* **£50 [≈ $95]**

Best, William
- An Essay upon the Service of the Church of England, Considered as a Daily Service ... London: J. Oliver, 1746. 1st edn. vii,99,[1 advt] pp. Contemp calf gilt, front bd loose, spine ends chipped. *(Wreden)* **$45 [≈ £23]**

Betterton, Thomas
- The History of the English Stage ... London: for E. curll, 1741. 1st edn. 8vo. Sep title & pagination to "Memoirs of Mrs. Oldfield". Port frontis, 5 ports in text. Contemp calf, rebacked. *(Dramatis Personae)* **$400 [≈ £208]**

Beveridge, William
- A Sermon concerning the Excellency and Usefulness of the Common Prayer ... Seventh Edition. London: T. James for Richard Northcott, 1684. 4to. Disbound. Wing B.2105. *(Waterfield's)* **£20 [≈ $38]**

Bewick, Thomas
- History of British Birds. London: 1797-1804. 1st edn. 2 vols. xxx,335; xx,400 pp. 218 figs, 227 vignettes & tailpieces. Contemp calf, jnts sl weak. Roscoe 14d & 17d, both variant B; the indelicate vignette p 289 is in the inked state, before the bar. *(Henly)* **£285 [≈ $547]**
- A General History of Quadrupeds ... Third Edition. Newcastle upon Tyne, 1792. 8vo. x, 483 pp. Occas sl spotting & browning. W'engvs. Rebound in half mor gilt. *(Frew Mackenzie)* **£125 [≈ $239]**

Bewick, Thomas & John
- Emblems of Mortality; Representing in upwards of Fifty Cuts, Death Seizing all Ranks and Degrees of People. ... London: for T. Hodgson, 1789. 12mo. Frontis & 51 text ills. Later (ca 1840) publisher's cloth, spine sl frayed. *(Sanders)* **£225 [≈ $431]**

Bibliotheca Americana ...
- Bibliotheca Americana; or, A Chronological Catalogue of the Most Curious and Interesting Books, Pamphlets, State Papers, etc. upon the subject of North and South America ... London: J. Debrett, 1789. 4to.

271 pp,errata. Contemp tree calf, rebacked.
(*C.R. Johnson*) **£750 [≈ $1,439]**

Bickham, George
- Deliciae Britannicae; or, the Curiosities of Kensington, Hampton Court, and Windsor Castle, Delineated ... Second Edition. London: E. Owen, [?1755]. 8vo. viii,184 pp. 10 plates. Orig bds, half calf.
(*Sotheran's*) **£195 [≈ $374]**

Bicknell, Alexander
- The Life of Alfred the Great, King of the Anglo-Saxons. London: for J. Bew ..., 1777. 1st edn. 8vo. xv,404 pp. Port frontis. Contemp calf gilt, yellow edges, jnts rubbed, chip at ft of spine. (*Sotheran's*) **£135 [≈ $259]**

Bigland, Ralph
- Observations on Marriages, Baptisms, and Burials, as preserved in Parochial Registers ... London: Richardson, Clark ..., 1764. 1st edn. 4to. Final advt leaf. Calf, gilt spine, red label.
(*Georges*) **£75 [≈ $143]**

Les Bijoux Indiscrets ...
- See Diderot, Denis.

Billings, William
- Music in Miniature. Containing a Collection of Psalm Tunes of Various Metres. Set in Score by W. Billings. Boston: the author, engvd by B. Johnston, 1779. 1st edn. 12mo. Contemp bds, sheep spine (worn), loose.
(*Ximenes*) **$5,000 [≈ £2,604]**

Biographical ...
- Biographical Anecdotes of William Hogarth ... see Nichols, John.

Birch, Thomas
- Heads of Illustrious Persons of Great Britain, engraven by Houbraken and Vertue, with their Lives and Characters by Thomas Birch. London: 1747-52. 2 vols in one. Folio. 80 + 28 ports. Lacks vol 2 title. Contemp calf, rebacked. (*Lamb*) **£400 [≈ $767]**
- An Historical View of the Negotiations. London: for A. Millar, 1749. 1st edn. Post 8vo. xxiv,[530] pp. A few ff remargd with loss of a few words. Old calf. Hugh Trevor-Roper b'plate. (*Ash*) **£100 [≈ $191]**
- The Life of the Honourable Robert Boyle. London: A. Millar, 1744. 1st edn. 8vo. [ii], [iv], 458,[14],[2] pp. Frontis. Contemp calf, hinges starting, sl worn. Contains a port not

called for by Fulton.
(*Bookpress*) **$185 [≈ £96]**
- Memoirs of the Reign of Queen Elizabeth ... London: for A. Millar, 1754. 1st edn. 2 vols. 4to. [iv],491; [iv],516,[xxx] pp. Contemp calf, dec gilt spines with contrasting labels, jnts cracked but firm. (*Sotheran's*) **£185 [≈ $355]**

Bisset, Robert
- The Life of Edmund Burke ... London: George Cawthorn, 1798. 1st edn. 8vo. xvi,592 pp. Frontis port (damp stained). Stain to lower margs of end ff. Mod cloth, uncut.
(*Rankin*) **£75 [≈ $143]**
- Sketch of Democracy. Dublin: S. Watson, 1798. 1st Dublin edn. 8vo. 19th c purple half calf, spine faded. (*Jarndyce*) **£80 [≈ $153]**

Blackall, Ofspring
- The Works ... With a Preface giving some Account of the Author ... London: Thomas Ward, 1723. 1st coll edn. 2 vols. Folio. [xx], 561,[i]; [xii],609-1187, [35] pp. Port frontis. Contemp panelled calf, extremities sl worn, lacks labels, jnts cracked & tender.
(*Clark*) **£95 [≈ $182]**

Blackerby, Samuel & Nathaniel
- The Justice of the Peace his Companion, or a Summary of all the Acts of Parliament, whereby ... Justices of the Peace are authorised to act ... London: 1723. 12mo. [xxx], 439,[i] pp. Some damp stains & sm reprs. Contemp sheep, rebacked, crnrs worn.
(*Clark*) **£65 [≈ $124]**

Blacklock, Thomas
- Poems on Several Occasions ... Edinburgh: Hamilton, Balfour & Neill, 1754. 2nd edn. 8vo. xvi,181 pp. 4 ff with sm marg tears. Contemp calf, mor label, front jnt sl tender. Anon. (*Finch*) **£100 [≈ $191]**

Blackmore, Sir Richard
- Creation. A Philosophical Poem, Demonstrating the Existence and Providence of God ... London: A. Bettesworth, 1718. 4th edn. 8vo. lxvi,[iv],237,3 advt pp. Rec calf.
(*Young's*) **£45 [≈ $86]**
- Essays upon Several Subjects. London: for E. Curll & J. Pemberton, 1716. [With] Vol. II. London: W. Wilkins, for A. Bettesworth & J. Pemberton, 1717. 1st edn. 2 vols. 8vo. Sm marg worm hole. Orig calf, spine ends chipped. (*Bickersteth*) **£145 [≈ $278]**

Blackstone, Sir William
- The Case of the late Election for the County of Middlesex, considered on the Principles of the Constitution and the Authorities of Law. London: Cadell, 1769. 4to. Half-title,48 pp. Rec wraps. Anon.
(C.R. Johnson) **£380 [≈ $729]**
- Commentaries on the Laws of England. Fifth Edition. Oxford: Clarendon Press ..., 1773. 1st authorized 8vo edn. 4 vols. 8vo. Contemp polished calf, v sl worn.
(Meyer Boswell) **$1,500 [≈ £781]**
- A Discourse on the Study of the Law; being an Introductory Lecture, read in the Public Schools, October 25, 1758 ... Oxford: Clarendon Press, 1758. 1st edn. 4to. [ii],40, [1 advt] pp. Stitched as issued, in loose contemp mrbld wraps, crnrs frayed, dusty.
(Pickering) **$3,250 [≈ £1,692]**
- The Great Charter and Charter of the Forest, with Other Authentic Instruments: to which is Prefixed an Introductory Discourse ... Oxford: Clarendon Press, 1759. 1st edn. Folio. Blank before title. Contemp calf, showing wear, rebacked. "Ex dono authoris".
(Meyer Boswell) **$2,250 [≈ £1,171]**

Blackwall, Anthony
- An Introduction to the Classics ... Second Edition, with additions and an index. London: for George Mortlock ..., 1719. 12mo. Contemp calf, sl rubbed, sm patch of wear on front cvr. *(Waterfield's)* **£50 [≈ $95]**

Blackwell, Thomas
- Letters concerning Mythology. London: printed in the year 1748. 8vo. [xvi],426 pp, advt leaf. Occas sl browning. Period calf gilt, sm split hd of jnts. Anon.
(Rankin) **£100 [≈ $191]**

Blagrave, Joseph
- Blagrave's Astrological Practice of Physick ... London: for Obadiah Blagrave, 1689. 2nd edn. 8vo. [xvi],139,[5 advt] pp. Upper marg trimmed close. Mod half calf antique. Wing B.3114. *(Bickersteth)* **£300 [≈ $575]**
- The Epitome of the Art of Husbandry. Comprising all necessary directions for the improvement of it ... By J.B. Gent. London: for Ben. Billingsley, 1669. 1st edn. Engvd title, ptd title, 306, 6 advt pp. V sl browning. Contemp sheep, rebacked. Wing B.3115.
(C.R. Johnson) **£1,500 [≈ $2,879]**

Blair, Hugh
- A Critical Dissertation on the Poems of Ossian, the Son of Fingal. London: for Becket & De Hondt, 1763. 4to. Sl marg worm hole. Disbound. *(Waterfield's)* **£125 [≈ $239]**
- Lectures on Rhetoric and Belles Lettres. Phila: Robert Aitken, 1784. 1st Amer edn. 4to. viii,454,[12] pp. Minor worm & old marg water stains. Contemp calf, gilt label, crnrs & lower spine chipped, cvrs rubbed.
(Karmiole) **$250 [≈ £130]**

Blair, Robert
- The Grave. A Poem with a Life of the Author ... added Gray's Elegy written in a Country Church Yard. Perth: James Morison, 1799. Vignette title,34 pp. Frontis. Disbound.
(C.R. Johnson) **£65 [≈ $124]**

Blancard or Blankaart, Steven
- The Physical Dictionary. Wherein the Terms of Anatomy, the Names and Causes of Diseases, Chyrurgical Instruments ... are accurately described ... London: 1708. 5th edn, enlgd. 8vo. [iv],318,[2 advt] pp. Plate. Sl foxed at ends. Rec qtr calf.
(Burmester) **£85 [≈ $163]**
- The Physical Dictionary. Wherein the Terms of Anatomy, the Names and Causes of Diseases, Chirurgical Instruments ... are accurately described ... London: 1726. 7th edn. [iv],370 pp. Marg damp stain to prelims. Orig leather, v worn.
(Whitehart) **£120 [≈ $230]**

Blane, William
- Cynegetica; or, Essays on Sporting ... London: Stockdale, 1788. New edn. 8vo. Frontis, engvd title. Orig bds, unopened, backstrip worn. *(Ximenes)* **$325 [≈ £169]**

Bligh, William
- A Voyage to the South Sea ... in His Majesty's Ship the Bounty ... including an Account of the Mutiny. London: George Nicol, 1792. 1st edn. 4to. 264 pp. 8 plates (sl offset). Sl foxing. Mod black mor. *(Parmer)* **$3,000 [≈ £1,562]**

The Blind Child ...
- See Pinchard, Elizabeth.

Blondel, David
- A Treatise of the Sibyls. London: T.R. for Author, 1661. 1st English edn. Sm folio. Edges of title frayed. Qtr calf. Wing B.3220.
(Rostenberg & Stern) **$450 [≈ £234]**

Blossoms of Morality ...
- See Johnson, Richard.

Blount, Thomas
- Glossographia: or, A Dictionary, interpreting the hard words of whatsoever Language, now used in our refined English Tongue ... The Fourth Edition, with many Additions. London: 1674. Final errata leaf. Sm repr title marg. Sl later calf, hinges cracking. Wing B.3337.   *(Jarndyce)* **£480 [≈ $921]**

Boccaccio, Giovanni
- The Novels and Tales ... Fifth Edition, much corrected and amended. London: for Awnsham Churchill, 1684. Folio. Port. Title stained & sl trimmed at 2 edges. Sl spotting & water staining. Later calf, sl rubbed, hinge weakening. Wing B.3378.
        (Jarndyce) **£250 [≈ $479]**

Boemus, Joannes
- The Manners, Lawes and Customs of All Nations ... Newly translated into English, by Ed. Aston. London: Eld for Burton, 1611. 1st edn of this translation. 4to. Title soiled, lib stamp on verso, minor stains elsewhere. Early calf, rebacked. STC 3198.
        (Hannas) **£750 [≈ $1,439]**

Bohun, Edmund
- A Geographical Dictionary ... London: for Charles Brome, 1688. 1st edn. 8vo. [xiv],822 pp. Addtnl engvd title. Prelims sl wormed. Orig bndg, rebacked. Wing B.3452.
        (Vanbrugh) **£155 [≈ $297]**
- A Geographical Dictionary ... Enlarged ... Fourth Edition ... London: Charles Brome, 1695. Folio. [viii],4,[xx], 23,[i],16, 437, [i] pp. Occas soiling, marg fraying at ends, some marg worm at beginning. Rec bds. Wing B.3455.   *(Clark)* **£160 [≈ $307]**

Bohun, William
- A Brief View of the Ecclesiastical Jurisdiction, as it is this Day Practised in England ... London: for J. Peele, 1733. 31 pp. Disbound.   *(Jarndyce)* **£25 [≈ $47]**

Bolingbroke, Henry St. John, 1st Viscount
- The Craftsman Extraordinary ... By John Trot, Yeoman [pseud.]. Published by Caleb D'Anvers, Esq. London: Richard Francklin, 1729. 1st edn. 8vo. Half-title. Errata leaf. Sewn as issued, uncut.
        (Ximenes) **$150 [≈ £78]**

- A Dissertation upon Parties; In Several Letters to Caleb D'Anvers Esq; ... London: H. Haines, 1735. 2nd edn. 8vo. xxxi, 246, [1 erratum] pp. Old speckled calf, rebacked.
        (Young's) **£40 [≈ $76]**
- A Final Answer to the Remarks on the Craftsman's Vindication ... London: for R. Francklin, 1731. 1st edn. 8vo. 32 pp. New wraps. Anon.   *(Young's)* **£48 [≈ $92]**
- A Letter to Sir William Windham. II. Some Reflections on the Present State of the Nation. III. A Letter to Mr. Pope. London: for A. Millar, 1753. 1st edn. 8vo. Half-title. Port frontis. Contemp gilt-ruled calf, backstrip sometime relaid, upper jnt cracked.   *(Sanders)* **£30 [≈ $57]**
- A Letter to Sir William Windham. II. Some Reflections on the Present State of the Nation. III. A Letter to Mr. Pope. Dublin: J. Smith, 1753. 12mo. Contemp calf, red label.
        (Robertshaw) **£50 [≈ $95]**
- Letters on the Spirit of Patriotism, on the Idea of a Patriot King: and on the State of Parties ... London: for A. Millar, 1752. 8vo. 280 pp. Marg repr to title. Period calf gilt, headcap sl rubbed.   *(Rankin)* **£45 [≈ $86]**
- Letters on the Study and Use of History. London: for A. Millar, 1752. 1st published edn. 2 vols. 8vo. Half-titles. Contemp sheep backed bds, vellum tips, entirely uncut, hd of spines sl chipped, mrbld paper on bds sl worn, vol 1 upper jnt cracked.
        (Sanders) **£185 [≈ $355]**
- Letters on the Study and Use of History ... Dublin: for John Smith ..., (1752). 1st Dublin edn. 2 vols. 12mo. [vi],268; [iv],224 pp. Contemp calf, red & black labels.
        (Young's) **£140 [≈ $268]**
- Letters on the Study and Use of History ... A New Edition, Corrected. Edinburgh: for Charles Elliot, 1777. Blind stamp on title. Lib buckram.   *(Waterfield's)* **£40 [≈ $76]**
- Remarks on the History of England. From the Minutes of Henry Oldcastle, Esq. London: for R. Francklin, 1743. 1st edn. 8vo. Contemp gilt-ruled calf, jnts cracked, extremities rubbed.   *(Sanders)* **£65 [≈ $124]**
- Remarks on the History of England. A New Edition. London: Cadell, [1780?]. 8vo. xvi, 330, [6] pp. Rec bds.
        (Fenning) **£24.50 [≈ $47]**
- The Works ... Published by David Mallet. London: ptd in the year, 1754. 1st coll edn. 5 vols. 4to. Contemp calf, gilt ruled spines, labels, minor reprs to crnrs.
        (Fenning) **£185 [≈ $355]**

Bolton, Robert

- An Answer to the Question, Where are your Arguments against what you call, Lewdness, if you make no use of the Bible? London: Dodsley, 1755. viii,48 pp. Disbound. Anon.
(C.R. Johnson) £225 [≈ $431]

- Letters and Tracts on the Choice of Company and other Subjects. London: Whiston, White, Dodsley, 1762. 2nd edn. 8vo. [ii], xxxii, 304 pp. Inserted leaf of errata & advts. Contemp calf, gilt spine, sl rubbed. Anon.
(Burmester) £180 [≈ $345]

Bolton, S.

- The Extinct Peerage of England. London: Rivington: 1769. [viii],315,index pp. Hand cold marg armorials by a previous owner. Calf, sl rubbed. *(Peter Taylor)* £25 [≈ $47]

Bond, Thomas

- A Digest of Foreign Exchanges ... Dublin: Alex. Stewart, 1795. 1st edn. 8vo. "xxvii" [ie xxvi], 289 pp. Subscribers. Some spotting. Doodle on title. Contemp calf, rubbed, upper jnt cracked but firm.
(Burmester) £75 [≈ $143]

Bonner, James

- A New Plan for Speedily increasing the Number of Bee-Hives in Scotland. Edinburgh: 1795. 8vo. xx,260 pp. Crude plain cloth.
(Wheldon & Wesley) £80 [≈ $153]

- A New Plan for Speedily Increasing the Number of Bee-Hives in Scotland; and which may be extracted, with equal Success, to England, Ireland, America ... Edinburgh: J. Moir, 1795. Half-title,258,[1] pp. Advt, errata leaf. Qtr calf, rebacked.
(C.R. Johnson) £225 [≈ $431]

Bonneval, Claudius Alexander de

- A Complete History of the Wars in Italy ... Translated from the Original French ... London: for W. Mears, 1734. 8vo. [xvi],376 pp. Fldg map. Contemp calf, hd of spine worn. *(Lloyd-Roberts)* £55 [≈ $105]

- Memoirs of the Bashaw Count Bonneval ... Written by himself, and collected from his Papers. London: Withers & Woodfall, 1750. 8vo. x,326 pp. Port frontis. Contemp calf, rebacked, crnrs sl rubbed.
(Clark) £125 [≈ $239]

Booker, Luke

- Malvern, a descriptive and Historical Poem

... Dudley: ptd by J. Rann ..., 1798. x,[2], 124, [2 advt] pp. Orig bds, uncut, spine worn.
(C.R. Johnson) £225 [≈ $431]

Borlase, Edmond

- The History of the Execrable Irish Rebellion ... to Grand Eruption, 23 Oct. 1641 and thence pursued to the Act of Settlement, 1662. London: Brome, 1680. Folio. Old calf, rebacked. *(Emerald Isle)* £250 [≈ $479]

Borlase, William

- The Natural History of Cornwall ... Oxford: for the author, by W. Jackson ..., 1758. 1st edn. Folio. xix,[i],326,[ii] pp. Fldg map, 28 plates. Occas spotting. 19th c diced russia, rebacked to style, edges rubbed.
(Finch) £380 [≈ $729]

- The Natural History of Cornwall. Oxford: 1758. Folio. xix,326,[2] pp. Dble-page map, 28 engvd plates. Minor foxing. Sm tears in map, 1 plate rprd. Occas MS notes. Contemp calf, rebacked.
(Wheldon & Wesley) £300 [≈ $575]

Born, Ignaz von

- New Process of Amalgamation of Gold and Silver Ores, and Other Metallic Mixtures ... Translated into English by R.E. Raspe. London: Cadell, 1791. 1st edn in English. 4to. xxxiv,256 pp. 22 plates. A few marg stains. Contemp calf, rebacked.
(Rootenberg) $750 [≈ £390]

Borthwick, George

- A Treatise upon the Extraction of the Crystalline Lens. Edinburgh: for Charles Elliot, 1775. 1st edn. 4to. viii,30 pp. Thick paper. Half mor, mrbld bds, mor label.
(Rootenberg) $500 [≈ £260]

Bossuet, Jacques Benigne

- An Exposition of the Doctrine of the Catholic Church in Matters of Controversie. London: 1685. 4to. 24,52,16 pp. Disbound. Wing B.3783. *(Robertshaw)* £28 [≈ $53]

Boswell, James

- An Account of Corsica, the Journal of a Tour to that Island; and Memoirs of Pascal Paoli. London: Robert & Andrew Foulis for Edward & Charles Dilly, 1768. 1st edn. Demy 8vo. Engvd title vignette, fldg map (sl used). Old half calf, upper jnt splitting.
(Ash) £250 [≈ $479]

- An Account of Corsica, the Journal of a Tour to that Island, and Memoirs of Pascal Paoli.

The Third Edition. Dublin: for J. Exshaw ...,
1768. 12mo. Contemp sheep, lib marks on
spine, hinge cracked. *(Jarndyce)* £85 [≈ $163]
- An Account of Corsica ... London: for
Edward & Charles Dilly, 1769. 3rd edn,
crrctd. 8vo. Fldg map, engvd title vignette,
inserted port frontis. Contemp polished calf,
backstrip relaid.   *(Horowitz)* $400 [≈ £208]
- The Journal of a Tour to the Hebrides, with
Samuel Johnson ... London: Henry Baldwin,
for Charles Dilly, 1785. 1st edn. Final errata
leaf. Lacks half-title. Title mtd on linen (sl
stained). Lib stamps. A few spots. Rebound in
half calf.   *(Jarndyce)* £140 [≈ $268]
- The Journal of a Tour to the Hebrides ...
London: Baldwin for Dilly, 1785. 1st edn.
2nd state, with the readings on pp 121, 237,
& 299 crrctd. 8vo. Half-title & errata slip in
2nd state. Sl foxing. Contemp three qtr calf,
backstrip relaid.   *(Horowitz)* $650 [≈ £338]
- The Life of Samuel Johnson. London: 1791.
1st edn. Issue with "give" at line 10, p 135,
vol 1. 2 vols. 4to. Large, uncut copy. Cancel
ff & stubs in vol 2. Port frontis (mtd, some ink
marks on verso), plate of Round Robin & facs
plate. Rec half calf gilt.
    (Spelman) £2,000 [≈ $3,839]
- The Life of Samuel Johnson ... London:
Henry Baldwin, for Charles Dilly, 1791. 1st
edn. 2 vols. 4to. With the spelling 'give' on
S4r. Frontis vol 1 (causing spotting on title),
Round-Robin & Facsimile plates vol 2. Few
spots. Contemp tree calf, rebacked.
    (Jarndyce) £2,400 [≈ $4,607]
- The Life of Samuel Johnson. London: for
Charles Dilly, 1793. 2nd (1st 8vo) edn, rvsd.
3 vols. Demy 8vo. Port frontis. Occas sl
browning. Contemp calf, rebacked & reprd.
    (Ash) £500 [≈ $959]
- The Life of Samuel Johnson ... London:
Henry Baldwin ..., 1793. 2nd (1st 8vo) edn. 3
vols. 8vo. Port, round robin, plate of facs.
19th c half calf, sl rubbed, new labels.
    (Young's) £350 [≈ $671]

The Botanist's Calendar ...
- The Botanist's Calendar, and Pocket Flora:
arranged according to the Linnaean System ...
London: Bensley for B. & J. White, 1797. 1st
edn. 2 vols. Sm 8vo. vi,[ii],264; [iv], 265-396,
[92] pp. Half-titles. Sm reprs to titles. 19th c
half cloth, hd of spines v sl frayed.
    (Burmester) £90 [≈ $172]

Bougainville, Louis Antoine
- A Voyage round the World. Performed by

order of His Most Christian Majesty, in the
Years 1766, 1767, 1768, and 1769. London:
1772. 1st English edn. 4to. xxviii,476 pp. 5
fldg maps, dble-page plate. Lib stamp. Occas
v sl foxing. Contemp calf, gilt spine, reprd.
    (Reese) $3,750 [≈ £1,953]

Bouhours, Dominic
- The Life of St. Ignatius, Founder of the
Society of Jesus ... Translated into English by
a Person of Quality ... London: Henry Hills,
1686. 1st edn in English. 8vo. [viii], 407,[3]
pp. 3 advt pp at end. Some ff sl dusty.
Contemp calf, rubbed. Wing B.3826.
    (Clark) £95 [≈ $182]
- The Life of St. Ignatius, Founder of the
Society of Jesus ... Translated into English by
a Person of Quality [John Dryden] ... London:
Henry Hills, 1686. 1st English edn. 8vo.
[viii],407,[3 advt] pp. Sl marks, sm reprs to
title. Later calf gilt. Anon.
    (Young's) £150 [≈ $287]

Boulainvilliers, Henri, Comte de
- An Historical Account of the Ancient
Parliaments of France, or States General of
the Kingdom ... translated ... by Charles
Forman, Esq. London: Brindley, 1739. 1st
edn in English. 2 vols. 8vo. 2 pp sl worn.
Contemp calf, rubbed, spine ends sl worn,
jnts cracked.   *(Bickersteth)* £85 [≈ $163]

Boulter, Hugh
- Letters ... to several Ministers of State in
England, and some others. [Collected by
Ambrose Philips]. Containing, an Account of
... Transactions which passed in Ireland from
1724 to 1738. Dublin: 1770. 1st Irish edn. 2
vols in one. 8vo. Rec qtr calf.
    (Fenning) £85 [≈ $163]

Bourignon, Antonia
- An Abridgement of the Light of the World ...
Preface ... by Joseph Whittingham Salmon.
London: R. Hindmarsh, 1786. 8vo. [xvi],464
pp. Port frontis. Minor spotting. Old cloth
backed bds, crnrs worn, jnts frayed.
    (Clark) £75 [≈ $143]

Bourne, Vincent
- Miscellaneous Poems ... London: for W.
Ginger ..., 1772. 1st edn. 4to. Contemp calf,
gilt spine, sl worn, upper jnt cracked but firm.
    (Ximenes) $175 [≈ £91]
- Poems consisting of Originals and
Translations. London: for W. Ginger ...,
1772. 4to. xvi,352 pp. Sl marg stain to 1

gathering. 19th c tree calf, gilt spine, extremities sl rubbed, sm split in 1 jnt.
(Frew Mackenzie) £75 [≃ $143]

Bourrit, Marc Theodore
- Relation of a Journey to the Glaciers, in the Dutchy of Savoy: translated ... by C. and F. Davy. Norwich: Richard Beatniffe, 1775. 1st edn in English. 8vo. [xxx], [xvi subscribers], xxi,264,[2] pp. Engvd dedic leaf, 3 plates. Mod cloth, mor label.
(Bickersteth) £130 [≃ $249]
- Relation of a Journey to the Glaciers ... The Second Edition. Norwich: Richard Beatniffe, 1776. 2nd edn in English. 8vo. [xxx], [xx subscribers],xxxi,266,[2] pp. Engvd dedic leaf, 3 plates. Orig calf, hd of spine sl worn.
(Bickersteth) £145 [≃ $278]

Boutcher, William
- A Treatise on Forest-Trees ... Edinburgh: ptd by R. Fleming, & sold by the author, J. Murray, London ..., 1775. 1st edn. Lge 4to. Half-title. Subscribers. Orig tree calf, gilt dec spine sl worn, front hinge cracked but firm.
(Vanbrugh) £175 [≃ $335]
- A Treatise on Forest-Trees ... Dublin: Wilson & Exshaw, 1776. 1st Dublin edn. 8vo. xvi, [iv],311 pp. Plate. Occas marg staining. Contemp calf, v worn, lacks label.
(Finch) £45 [≃ $86]
- A Treatise on Forest-Trees ... Dublin: for William Wilson ..., 1784. 3rd edn. 8vo. xxviii, [4],307 pp. Old calf, rebacked.
(Young's) £90 [≃ $172]

Bowdler, John
- Reform or Run; Take Your Choice! In which the Conduct of the King ... is considered ... Third Edition. Dublin: John Milliken, 1798. 32 pp. Rebound in bds. Anon.
(C.R. Johnson) £38 [≃ $72]

Bowen, Emanuel
- Atlas Minimus ... see Gibson, John.
- A Complete Atlas, or Distinct View of the Known World; exhibited in Sixty Eight Maps. London: 1752. 1st edn. Folio. 69 maps cold in outline. Sl used, occas crease or sl foxing. 1 map sl trimmed, 2 with sm splits at fold. Contemp leather, worn.
(Parmer) $7,500 [≃ £3,906]

Bowles, Carington
- Bowles's Compleat Drawing Book. London: Carington Bowles, [ca 1773]. 1st edn. Sm 4to.

[ii],4 pp. 100 plates. Contemp pencil drawing on verso of a few plates. Contemp qtr calf, worn.
(Bookpress) $1,350 [≃ £703]
- The Whole Art of Painting in Water-Colours; exemplified in Landscapes, Flowers, &c. ... By the Author of the Artists Assistant. London: T. Kitchin, 1773. Presumed 1st edn. Sm 8vo. [6],72 pp. Half-title. 1 plate of a painter's box. Orig mrbld paper wraps.
(Spelman) £300 [≃ $575]

Bowles, John
- A Protest against T. Paine's 'Rights of Man' ... London: for T. Longman, G. Nicol & W. Richardson, 1792. Errata slip pasted to D3. Lib number on A2. Disbound. Anon.
(Waterfield's) £100 [≃ $191]
- A Protest against T. Paine's 'Rights of Man' ... Fourth Edition, with Corrections and Additions. London: Longman ..., 1792. 8vo. xiv, 38 pp. Sl marked. Rec wraps. Anon.
(Bow Windows) £105 [≃ $201]

Bowlker, Charles
- The Art of Angling; or, Compleat Fly-Fisher ... Birmingham: Swinney & Walker ..., 1792. 12mo. xi,118,[2 advt] pp. Frontis. Sm grease stain on inner upper marg of title & frontis. Rec wraps.
(Fenning) £95 [≃ $182]

Bownas, Samuel
- An Account of the Life, Travels, and Christian Experiences in the Work of the Ministry of Samuel Bownas. London: Luke Hinde, 1756. 1st edn. 8vo. Final advt leaf. Some browning. Calf, recased.
(Stewart) £75 [≃ $143]
- A Description of the Qualifications necessary to a Gospel Minister ... London: Luke Hinde, 1750. 8vo. End ff browned. Contemp calf, sl worn.
(Stewart) £45 [≃ $86]

Bowyer, William & Nichols, John (eds.)
- The Origin of Printing. In Two Essays ... Second Edition: With Improvements. London: for W. Bowyer & J. Nichols, 1776. 8vo. viii, 176 pp. Mod lib cloth, spine ends sl rubbed. Anon.
(Finch) £300 [≃ $575]

Boyer, Abel
- The Complete French Master for Ladies and Gentlemen ... The Twentieth Edition, carefully corrected ... London: for E. Ballard, 1764. 8vo. A few pp proud. Lacks rear free endpaper. Contemp sheep, rubbed & scarred, sl worm ft of spine. *(Jarndyce)* £55 [≃ $105]

Boyle, John, Earl of Cork and Orrery

- The First Ode of the First Book of Horace Imitated and Inscribed to the Earl of Chesterfield. London: C. Bathurst, & G. Hawkins, 1741. Folio. New wraps. Anon.
 (C.R. Johnson) **£245 [≈ $470]**

- Remarks on the Life and Writings of Jonathan Swift ... Second Edition, corrected. London: for A. Millar, 1752. 8vo. [2],214,[8] pp. Port. Contemp calf, sl worn, lacks label, upper jnt cracked but firm.
 (Fenning) **£35 [≈ $67]**

- Remarks on the Life and Writings of Dr. Jonathan Swift ... in a Series of Letters from John Earl of Orrery ... Second Edition, corrected. London: A. Millar, 1752. 8vo. 214, [8] pp. Port. Contemp calf, rebacked.
 (Frew Mackenzie) **£45 [≈ $86]**

- Remarks on the Life and Writings of Dr Jonathan Swift ... Dublin: 1783. 12mo. [2], 204, [12] pp. Contemp calf, rubbed.
 (Claude Cox) **£28 [≈ $53]**

Boyle, Hon. Robert

- A Free Discourse against Customary Swearing and a Dissuasive from Cursing ... published by John Williams. London: R.R. for Thomas Cockerill, 1695. Engvd frontis. Title a cancel (as usual). Contemp panelled calf, rebacked. Wing B.3978.
 (Waterfield's) **£375 [≈ $719]**

- The Martyrdom of Theodora, and of Didymus. By a Person of Honour. London: H. Clark, for John Taylor & Christopher Skegnes, 1687. 1st edn. Contemp calf, elab gilt spine, red label. Wing B.3986. Anon.
 (Jarndyce) **£1,100 [≈ $2,111]**

- New Experiments and Observations touching Cold ... London: 1683. [xlii],325,20,29 pp. 2 plates in facs. Contemp leather, rubbed, hinges cracked, casing sl torn, torn patch on front inner cvr.   *(Whitehart)* **£400 [≈ $767]**

- Some Considerations about the Reconcileableness of Reason and Religion. By T.E. a Lay-man ... annex'd ... a Discourse of Mr. Boyle ... London: 11675. 1st edn. 12mo. [iv], xviii,[ii errata],126,[2 blank], [vi], [ii],39 pp. Contemp calf, spine reprd. Wing B.4024.
 (Burmester) **£250 [≈ $479]**

- Some Motives and Incentives to the Love of God ... Third Edition much corrected. London: for Henry Herringman, 1663. Sl marg stain at foredge. Crnr cut from final fe.p. Contemp calf gilt, sl rubbed, spine ends chipped. Wing B.4034.
 (Jarndyce) **£450 [≈ $863]**

Bradbury, Thomas

- Winning Christ, and being found in him, considered: in Two Sermons on the Death of the Reverend Mr Robert Bragge ... London: for J. Oswald & J. Buckland, 1737. Disbound.
 (Waterfield's) **£20 [≈ $38]**

Bradley, Richard

- A Complete Body of Husbandry ... London: Woodman & Lyon, 1727. 1st edn. 8vo. [iv],xi, 372,[4] pp. 4 plates. Contemp calf, respined. Fitzwilliam b'plate.
 (Bookpress) **£385 [≈ £200]**

- A Philosophical Account of the Works of Nature .... London: 1721. 4to. [xix],194,[1] pp. 28 hand cold engvd plates. Inscrptn & blind stamp on title. Some offsetting (12 plates seriously affected), minor foxing. Sm marg worm at end. Contemp calf, rebacked, trifle worn.
 (Wheldon & Wesley) **£220 [≈ $422]**

- A Philosophical Account of the Works of Nature. London: W. Mears, 1721. 1st edn. 4to. [20],194 pp, advt leaf. 8 pp subscribers. Red & black title. 28 full page ills (many hand cold, 1 fldg) by James Cole. Sl browning of prelims. Contemp calf, rebacked.
 (Rootenberg) **£800 [≈ £416]**

- The Plague at Marseilles consider'd; with Remarks upon the Plague in general ... London: for W. Mears, 1721. 1st edn. 8vo. [16], 60,[6 advt] pp. Title stained, minor spotting. Calf backed mrbld bds, mor label.
 (Rootenberg) **£900 [≈ £468]**

- The Science of Good Husbandry: or, the Oeconomics of Xenophon ... Translated from the Greek. London: Tho. Corbet, 1727. 131 pp. Disbound. *(C.R. Johnson)* **£180 [≈ $345]**

Bragge, Francis

- A Full and Impartial Account of the Discovery of Sorcery and Witchcraft, practis'd by Jane Wenham of Walkerne in Hertfordshire ... Fourth Edition. London: for E. Curll, 1712. 8vo. [iv],36 pp. Period style panelled calf by Middleton. Anon.
 (Sotheran's) **£265 [≈ $508]**

Bragge, Robert

- A Cry for Labourers in Gods Harvest: being a Sermon ... Funeral of ... Ralph Venning ... London: John Hancock, 1674. Disbound. Wing B.4202.   *(Waterfield's)* **£25 [≈ $47]**

Bramston, William

- A Sermon; preach'd at the Opening of the

Lecture at Maldon in Essex lately established ... London: for R. Clavell, 1697. 4to. 1 sheet loose. Disbound. Wing B.4243.

(Waterfield's) **£25 [≈ $47]**

Branch, Thomas

- Thoughts on Dreaming ... Occasioned by an Essay on the Phenomenon of Dreaming, in a Book, entitled, An Enquiry into the Nature of the Human Soul ... London: Dodsley, 1738. 96 pp. Disbound.

(C.R. Johnson) **£350 [≈ $671]**

Bransby, John

- The Use of Globes, containing an Introduction to Astronomy & Geography ... Ipswich: 1791. 8vo. x,216 pp. 2 fldg plates. Mod buckram gilt. *(Lamb)* **£30 [≈ $57]**

Brathwaite, Richard

- Drunken Barnaby's Four Journeys to the North of England. In Latin and English Verse ... London: for S. Illidge ..., 1716. 2nd edn. Sm 8vo. [viii],151,[viii] pp. Frontis, 1 plate. Orig sheep, rebacked. Anon.

(Bickersteth) **£145 [≈ $278]**

- A Svrvey of History: or, A Nursery for Gentry ... London: I. Okes, for Iasper Emery, 1638. Sm 4to. [xxvi],415,[i] pp. Addtnl engvd title (v sm reprs). Paper flaw at N1. Late Victorian dark blue half mor, a.e.g.

(Sotheran's) **£368 [≈ $706]**

Breton, John Le

- See Britton, John Le.

Breton, Nicholas

- Englands Selected Characters, describing the Good and Bad Worthies of this Age ... London: for T.S., 1643. 1st edn under this title. Sm 4to. Title sl browned. Mor gilt, uncut, by Sangorski & Sutcliffe. Wing B.4384. Anon. *(Ximenes)* **$1,750 [≈ £911]**

Brett, Thomas

- A Collection of the Principal Liturgies, used by the Christian Church ... Translated into English ... London: for Richard King, 1720. 1st edn. 8vo. xvi,[8],160, 437, [1 errata], [2 advt] pp. Sl foxing. Mod cloth.

(Fenning) **£55 [≈ $105]**

Brevint, Daniel

- Saul and Samuel at Endor, or the new Waies of Salvation and Service, which usually tent Men to Rome ... refuted ... Oxford: at the Theater, 1674. 1st edn. 8vo. [xiv],413,[1

errata] pp. Frontis. Old calf, rebacked. Wing B.4423. *(Young's)* **£45 [≈ $86]**

Brickell, John

- The Natural History of North Carolina ... Dublin: for the author, 1743. 2nd edn. 8vo. 408 pp. Contemp calf, rebacked.

(Chapel Hill) **$2,000 [≈ £1,041]**

Bridge, William

- Babylons Downfall. A Sermon ... London: I.N. for John Rothwell, 1641. 1st edn. 4to. [vi], 34 pp. Some staining, lib stamp on title verso. Later wraps. Wing B.4448.

(Clark) **£30 [≈ $57]**

Bridle, John

- A Letter to the Reverend Dr. Lowth, Prebendary of Durham in Vindication of the Conduct of the Fellows of New College in Oxford in their late Election of a Warden of Winchester. London: for R. Baldwin, 1758. Disbound. Anon. *(Waterfield's)* **£25 [≈ $47]**

A Brief Journal ...

- A Brief Journal of the Life ... of ... Thomas Wilson ... see Stoddart, John.

Brierley, Roger

- A Bundle of Soul Convincing, Directing and Comforting truths ... Edinburgh: James Brown, 1670. Sm 8vo. [8],238,92 pp. Sl wear to title border, index leaf defective. Early calf, rebacked. Wing B.4658.

(Humber) **£125 [≈ $239]**

Brightman, Thomas

- The Works ... London: John Field for Samuel Cartright, 1644. Thick 4to. [10],1088 pp. Port mtd. Engvd frontis. Occas sl browning & blemishes. New half calf. Wing B.4679.

(Humber) **£150 [≈ $287]**

Brissot de Warville, Jacques Pierre

- The Life of J.P. Brissot, Deputy from Eure and Loire, to the National Convention. Written by himself. Translated from the French. London: for J. Debrett, 1794. Half-title. 4 advt pp. Frontis. Rec imitation calf.

(Jarndyce) **£55 [≈ $105]**

- New Travels in the United States of America: including the Commerce of America with Europe. London: Jordan, 1794. 2 vols. 8vo. Engvd port, fldg table. Qtr calf. Anon.

(Rostenberg & Stern) **$425 [≈ £221]**

Bristow, James
- A Narrative of the Sufferings of James Bristow ... during Ten Years Captivity with Hyder Ally and Tippoo Saheb. Second Edition. Calcutta Printed. London: re-printed for J. Murray, 1794. Contemp tree calf, hd of spine sl worn.   *(Jarndyce)* £180 [≈ $345]

Britain's Remembrancer ...
- See Burgh, James.

British ...
- The British Hero in Captivity ... see Puddicomb, J.N.
- The British Jewel, or Complete Housewife's best Companion ... London: J. Miller, 1782. New edn. 8vo. 112 pp. Frontis defective, some soiling. Contemp wraps, wear ft of spine.   *(Chapel Hill)* $175 [≈ £91]
- The British Librarian ... see Oldys, William.
- British Public Characters of 1798. [Edited by Alexander Stevens]. London: for R. Phillips, [ca 1798]. 1st edn. 8vo. Fldg port frontis. Contemp half calf, worn, hd of spine defective.   *(Dramatis Personae)* $95 [≈ £49]

Britton, John Le
- Britton [on the Laws of England]. The Second Edition. Faithfully corrected according to divers ancient Manuscripts of the same Booke. London: assigned of John Moore, 1640. 2nd edn. 8vo. Occas browning. Contemp vellum, untrimmed, sl worn, lacks ties. STC 3804.
        (Meyer Boswell) $750 [≈ £390]

Brome, Alexander
- A Congratulatory Poem, on the Miraculous, and Glorious Return of that unparallel'd King Charls [sic] the II. May 29, 1660. L; for Henry Brome, 1660. 1st edn. Sm 4to. Disbound. Wing B.4849.
        (Ximenes) $750 [≈ £390]
- Songs and Other Poems. London: Henry Brome, 1661. 1st edn. Sm 8vo. [24],302 pp. Frontis port (laid down). Margs closely trimmed, affecting some catchwords & headings. Green mor (ca 1920), a.e.g., extremities rubbed. Wing B.4852.
        (Karmiole) $375 [≈ £195]

Brome, James
- An Historical Account of Mr. Brome's Three Years Travels over England, Scotland and Wales ... London: for Abel Roper ..., 1700. 1st authorized edn. 8vo. Contemp calf, v sl

wear to jnts. Wing B.4848A.
        (Ximenes) $750 [≈ £390]

Bromley, Henry
- A Catalogue of Engraved British Portraits from Egbert the Great to the Present Time ... London: T. Payne ..., 1793. 4to. xvi,479,56, [78] pp. Some old marks. Rebound in cloth, uncut.   *(Karmiole)* $125 [≈ £65]

Bromley, William
- Several Years Travels through Portugal, Spain, Italy, Germany ... Performed by a Gentleman. London: for A. Roper ..., 1702. 1st edn. 8vo. Interleaved. Contemp calf, spine ends reprd. Anon.   *(Hannas)* £240 [≈ $460]

Brooke, Frances, nee Moore
- The History of Lady Julia Mandeville. By the Translator of Lady Catesby's Letters. London: Dodsley, 1763. 1st edn. 2 vols. 8vo. Half-titles. Sl foxing. Period tree calf, contrasting labels, gilt spines, hd of spines v sl chipped. Anon.   *(Rankin)* £125 [≈ $239]

Brooke, Henry
- The Fool of Quality, or the History of the Earl of Moreland ... Second Edition. London: for W. Johnstone, 1767-69. 4 vols. Contemp calf, rather battered but sound.
        (Waterfield's) £100 [≈ $191]

Brookes, R.
- An Introduction to Physic and Surgery ... London: 1754. viii,536 pp. Top marg of title & some ff discold. Contemp leather, rebacked.   *(Whitehart)* £185 [≈ $355]
- A New and Accurate System of Natural History; containing the History of Quadrupeds, Birds, Fishes and Serpents, Insects, Waters, Earths, Stones, Fossils, Minerals and Vegetables. London: 1763. 6 vols. 12mo. 144 plates. Contemp calf, jnts weak.   *(Wheldon & Wesley)* £200 [≈ $383]

Brooks, Thomas
- Heaven on Earth, or a Serious Discourse touching a well-grounded Assurance of Mens Everlasting Happiness and Blessedness ... [With his] A Believer's Last Day is his Best Day ... London: Hancock, 1657. liv,552; 33,1 pp. Leather, lacks backstrip.
        (Gage) £50 [≈ $95]

Broughton, Hugh
- An Advertisement of Corruption in Our Handling of Religion. To the Kings Majestie.

[Middelburg: R. Schild,] 1604. 4to. 111 pp. A few side notes cropped. STC 3843 variant.
(Humber) £55 [≈ $105]
- A Letter to a Friend Touching Mardochai His Age. London: William White, 1612. 4to. [4],12 pp. Engvd title. Upper headlines & side notes cropped. Disbound. STC 3869.
(Humber) £35 [≈ $67]
- Principal Positions for Grounds of the Holy Bible ... London: W. White, 1609. 4to. 31 pp. Upper headlines cropped. Disbound, minor wear. STC 3880.
(Humber) £35 [≈ $67]
- The Works of the Great Albionean Divine ... London: Nath. Ekins, 1662. Folio. [20], 732,[12] pp. Contemp calf, rebacked, recrnrd. Wing B.4997.
(Humber) £175 [≈ $335]

Brouzet, Pierre
- An Essay on the Medicinal Education of Children; and the Treatment of their Diseases. London: for Thomas Field, 1755. 1st edn in English. 8vo. xxi,[5],364,3 advt pp. Sl browned. Contemp calf, rebacked.
(Rootenberg) $1,500 [≈ £781]

Brown, George
- Arithmetica Infinita or The Accurate Accomptant's Best Companion Contriv'd and Calculated ... London: for the author, 1717/18. 1st edn. Oblong 12mo. [iii],14,126, 10 pp. Engvd throughout. Port frontis. Sl damp stained. Contemp calf, rubbed, rebacked.
(Pickering) $450 [≈ £234]

Brown, George
- The New, Complete, and Universal English Letter-Writer ... A New Edition, carefully corrected and improved ... London: for Alex. Hogg, [ca 1795]. 12mo. Frontis. Contemp sheep, v rubbed, hinges splitting, spine defective at hd.
(Jarndyce) £45 [≈ $86]

Brown, John
- An Estimate of the Manners and Principles of the Times ... The Third Edition. London: Davis & Reymers, 1757. 8vo. Red & black title. Contemp calf, ft of spine chipped, jnts cracked. Anon.
(Waterfield's) £75 [≈ $143]
- Sermons on Various Subjects. London: Davies & Reymers, 1764. 1st edn. 8vo. Title-page in this copy does not appear to be a cancel. Contemp calf, sl rubbed.
(Waterfield's) £80 [≈ $153]

Brown, John, Philomath
- The Practical Gauger, Arithmetical and

Instrumental ... London: J.D. for John Brown, 1678. [10],12,127,[5] pp. Fldg plate. Ft of title trimmed close touching 2 letters on date. Sm section of blank marg of 2nd leaf missing. 18th c mrbld bds. Wing B.5042A.
(C.R. Johnson) £750 [≈ $1,439]

Brown, Thomas, 1663-1704
- Amusements Serious and Comical, Calculated from the Meridian of London. London: for John Nutt, 1700. 1st edn. 8vo. Sm crnr of title singed. Mod calf.
(Dramatis Personae) $400 [≈ £208]
- Letters from the Dead to the Living ... London: ptd in the Year, 1703. 3rd edn. 8vo. xvi,264 pp. Title edges sl frayed. Contemp calf, front jnt weak. *(Young's)* £55 [≈ $105]

Browne, Isaac Hawkins
- Poems upon Various Subjects, Latin and English ... Published by his Son. London: for J. Nourse, 1768. 1st coll edn. 8vo. [x],160. Port frontis. Contemp calf, rebacked. Anon.
(Young's) £87 [≈ $167]

Browne, Moses
- Angling Sports: in Nine Piscatory Eclogues ... Third Edition, Corrected ... London: Dilly, 1773. Post 8vo. xxxvii,[ii],136 pp. Frontis. Some foxing. Victorian green half mor, dec gilt spine.
(Sotheran's) £198 [≈ $380]

Browne, Peter
- Things Divine and Supernatural conceived by Analogy with Things Natural and Human. London: Innys & Manby, 1733. 8vo. Perf lib stamp on title. Rebound in half calf.
(Stewart) £275 [≈ $527]
- Things Divine and Supernatural conceived by Analogy with Things Natural and Human. London: Innys & Manby, 1733. 8vo. B6 cancelled as usual. Sm lib perf on title. Marg water stain 1st 2 sheets. Mod qtr calf.
(Waterfield's) £200 [≈ $383]
- Things Divine and Supernatural conceived by Analogy with Things Natural and Human. By the Author of The Procedure, Extent and Limits of Human Understanding. London: Innys & Manby, 1733. 1st edn. 8vo. [iv],554,16 ctlg pp. Orig calf, sl rubbed. Anon.
(Bickersteth) £220 [≈ $422]

Browne, Sir Thomas
- Certain Miscellany Tracts ... London: for Charles Mearne, & sold by Henry Bonwick, 1684. 1st edn, 2nd issue. 8vo. [viii],215,[i

blank],[vi] pp. Port frontis. Sl browned. Mod qtr calf. Wing B.5152.

(Frew Mackenzie) **£175 [≈ $335]**

- Certain Miscellany Tracts. London: Charles Mearne, 1684. 1st edn. 8vo. viii,215,[6] pp. Frontis (chipped). Later bds. Wing B.5152.

(Bookpress) **$350 [≈ £182]**

- Christian Morals ... The Second Edition. With a Life of the Author, by Samuel Johnson ... London: Richard Hett, for J. Payne, 1756. Sm 8vo. [iv],lxi,[ii blank],136 pp. Half-title & medial blank. Late 18th c calf gilt, sometime rebacked.   *(Sotheran's)* **£585 [≈ $1,123]**

- Pseudodoxia Epidemica ... London: T.H. for Edward Dod, 1646. 1st edn. Folio. [xviii],386 pp. Lacks imprimatur leaf. Few sm reprs, minor damp stain at ends, title sl browned. Rec half calf. Wing B.5159.

(Clark) **£280 [≈ $537]**

- Pseudodoxia Epidemica; or, Enquiries into very many received Tenets, and commonly presumed Truths. The Second Edition, Corrected and much enlarged by the Author. London: 1650. Sm folio. [8],329,[5] pp. Sl browning. Later calf, a.e.g., gilt dentelles. Wing B.5160.   *(Goodrich)* **$795 [≈ £414]**

- Pseudodoxia Epidemica ... Fourth Edition ... added Two Discourses ... London: for Edward Dod, & sould [sic] by Andrew Crook, 1658. 4to. [xvi],468,[xvi], [x],73,[iii] pp. 3 copperplates (1 in text). Lacks longitudinal label leaf. Contemp calf, sometime rebacked.Wing B.5162.

(Sotheran's) **£285 [≈ $547]**

- Pseudodoxia Epidemica ... Whereunto is added Religio Medici. London: Nath. Ekins, 1659. Folio. [xii],326,[10], [iv],64 pp. Calf.

(Bookpress) **$450 [≈ £234]**

Browne, Thomas, of St. John's College, Cambridge
- The Story of the Ordination of our First Bishops in Queen Elizabeth's Reign at the Nag's-Head Tavern in Cheapside ... proved to be a ... Fable. London: for William Innys, 1731. 1st edn. 8vo. Contemp calf, crudely rebacked & recrnrd.   *(Sanders)* **£42 [≈ $80]**

Browne, William
- The Works ... With Notes and Observations by the Rev. W. Thompson ... With the Life of the Author ... London: for T. Davies ..., 1772. 1st coll edn. 3 vols. 8vo. Contemp calf, rebacked.   *(Young's)* **£115 [≈ $220]**

Brownrigg, William
- The Art of Making Common Salt, as now

Practised ... London: Davis, Millar, Dodsley, 1748. 1st edn. 8vo. xxiv,295 pp, errata leaf. 6 fldg plates. Orig calf, rebacked.

(Bickersteth) **£320 [≈ $614]**

Bruce, Peter Henry
- Memoirs of Peter Henry Bruce, Esq., a Military Officer ... Containing an Account of his Travels in Germany, Russia ... London: for the author's widow, sold by T. Payne, 1782. 1st edn. 4to. Contemp calf, ducal monogram on cvr, spine worn, lacks label.

(Hannas) **£250 [≈ $479]**

Brucker, Johann Jakob
- The History of Philosophy, from the Earliest Times to the Beginning of the Present Century; drawn up from Brucker's Historia Critica Philosophiae. By William Enfield. London: for J. Johnson, 1791. 1st edn in English. 2 vols. 8vo. Fldg table. Orig calf, reprd.   *(Bickersteth)* **£240 [≈ $460]**

Bruckner, John
- Criticisms of the Diversions of Purley. In a Letter to Horne Tooke, Esq., by 'I. Cassander'. London: Cadell, 1790. Cr 8vo. Some ff cropped. New wraps.

(Stewart) **£30 [≈ $57]**

Bruel, Walter
- Praxis Medicinae, or, The Physicians Practice. London: William Sheares, 1632. 1st edn. Sm 4to. [iv],407,[4] pp. Later endpapers. Royal College of Physicians' stamp & b'plate. Contemp calf. *(Bookpress)* **$1,250 [≈ £651]**

Bryan, Matthew
- St. Paul's Triumph in his Sufferings for Christ. London: for the author, 1692. Sole edn. 4to. Rec wraps. Wing B.5248.

(Sanders) **£28 [≈ $53]**

Bryant, Jacob
- Observations upon the Plagues inflicted upon the Egyptians ... prefixed, a Prefatory Discourse concerning the Grecian Colonies from Egypt. London: for the author, 1794. 1st edn. 8vo. viii,441 pp. Sl foxed. Mor, worn, spine chipped, front bd detached.

(Worldwide) **$125 [≈ £65]**

- A Treatise upon the Authenticity of the Scriptures, and the Truth of the Christian Religion. London: Cadell, Elmsly, 1792. 1st edn. 8vo. xv,278 pp. Orig tree calf, gilt spine, sl wear at hd of spine.

(Bickersteth) **£38 [≈ $72]**

Brydone, Patrick
- A Tour through Sicily and Malta ... Second Edition, corrected. London: Strahan & Cadell, 1774. 2 vols. 8vo. Half-titles. 3 advt pp vol 1. A few gatherings sl sprung vol 1. Contemp calf, spine ends sl worn.
(Jarndyce) **£65 [≈ $124]**

Buchan, David Steuart Erskine, 11th Earl of
- Discourse delivered ... at a Meeting for the Purpose of promoting the Institution of a Society for the Investigation of the History of Scotland, and its Antiquities, November 14, 1780. 31 pp. Stabbed pamphlet, as issued.
(C.R. Johnson) **£55 [≈ $105]**

Buchan, William
- Domestic Medicine; or, the Family Physician. Edinburgh: Balfour, Auld, & Smellie, 1769. 1st edn. 8vo. xv,[i],624 pp. Browned. Later bds.
(Bookpress) **$400 [≈ £208]**
- Domestic Medicine ... London: for W. Strahan ..., 1772. 2nd edn, enlgd. 8vo. 2 ctlg pp. 2 ff sl soiled. New cloth.
(Stewart) **£125 [≈ $239]**
- Domestic Medicine ... Second Edition, with considerable additions. London: 1772. 8vo. xxxvi, 758 pp. Contemp half calf, worn.
(Goodrich) **$250 [≈ £130]**
- A Letter to the Patentee, concerning the Medical Properties of the Fleecy Hosiery ... Second American Edition, with Additional Notes and Observations. Providence: Carter & Wilkenson ..., 1795. 8vo. 34,[1] pp. Sl browned. Mod qtr calf.
(Hemlock) **$175 [≈ £91]**

Buchanan, Robert
- Poems on Several Occasions. Edinburgh: J. Moir for the author, 1797. vi,7-12, 345,[3] pp. Contemp calf, jnt broken.
(C.R. Johnson) **£250 [≈ $479]**

Buchius, Paulus
- The Divine Being and its Attributes philosophically demonstrated from the Holy Scriptures and Original Nature of Things according to the Principles of F.N.B. of Helmont. London: Randal Taylor, 1693. 8vo. With a1 (blank). 18th c calf. Wing B.5299.
(Waterfield's) **£200 [≈ $383]**

Buckingham, George Villiers, Duke of
- A Short Discourse upon the Reasonableness of Men's having a Religion, or Worship of God. London: John Leake, for Luke Meredith, 1685. 1st edn. 4to. [viii],21,[3] pp. Blank before title, final advt leaf. Dusty, some staining, lib stamp on title verso. Unbound. Wing B.5329.
(Clark) **£55 [≈ $105]**

Buckingham, John Sheffield, Duke of
- Plays. Glasgow: Robert Urie, 1751. 12mo. Some foxing. Period calf, lacks label, hinges sl cracked.
(Rankin) **£30 [≈ $57]**
- Poems on Several Occasions. To which are added, the Tragedies of Julius Caesar, and Marcus Brutus. Glasgow: Robert & Andrew Foulis, 1752. 1st edn. 8vo. viii,280 pp. Contemp calf, label chipped, front inner hinge cracked but firm. *(Finch)* **£70 [≈ $134]**

Buckler, Benjamin
- Stemmata Chicheleana: or, a Genealogical Account of Some of the Families derived from Thomas Chichele ... Oxford: Clarendon Press, 1765. 1st edn. 4to. [4],xiv,160,[8] pp. 2 plates. Mrbld bds, uncut, sometime rebacked in cloth, edges worn. Anon.
(Claude Cox) **£45 [≈ $86]**

Budgell, Eustace
- A Letter to Cleomenes King of Sparta ... London: for A. Moore ..., 1731. 2nd edn. 8vo. xvi, 154, 272, lxxxiii pp. Frontis. Contemp calf, jnts worn. *(Young's)* **£55 [≈ $105]**
- Memoirs of the Life and Character of the late Earl of Orrery and the Family of Boyles. London: W. Mears, 1732. 2nd edn. 8vo. xl,258, [2] pp. Frontis. Later calf.
(Bookpress) **$150 [≈ £78]**
- Verres and his Scribblers; a Satire in Three Cantos. To which is added an Examen of the Piece, and a Key to the Characters ... London: C. Browne, 1732. 70 pp. New wraps. Anon. *(C.R. Johnson)* **£125 [≈ $239]**

Buffon, Georges-Louis Leclerc, Comte de
- The History of Singing Birds containing an Exact Description of their Habits and Customs ... Edinburgh: for Silvester Doig, 1791. 1st edn. 12mo. 192 pp. Engvd half-title & title, plates. Orig calf, hinges cracking.
(Chapel Hill) **$150 [≈ £78]**
- Natural History ... Occasional Notes and Observations by the Translator (William Smellie). Edinburgh: Creech, 1780. 1st edn thus. 8 vols. 8vo. 299 engvs. Contemp three qtr leather & mrbld bds, hd of spines & some bds sl rubbed. *(Schoyer)* **$1,000 [≈ £520]**
- Natural History, General and Particular.

London: 1785. 2nd edn. 9 vols. Num engvs. Contemp calf, hinges weak, lacks labels.
(Grayling) £150 [≈ $287]
- Natural History. London: 1792. 2 vols. 8vo. Frontis, 2 engvd titles with vignettes, 107 plates. Sm water stains on 4 plates. Calf backed bds, jnts starting to crack.
(Henly) £45 [≈ $86]

Bugg, Francis
- Some of the Quakers Principles and Doctrines, Laws & Orders, &c. Reprinted for the sake of such as have not as yet seen them ... London: John Gwillim, 1693. Only edn. [ii], 17,[i] pp. Lib stamp title verso. Disbound. Wing B.5395. Anon.
(Clark) £65 [≈ $124]

Bulkeley, John & Cummins, John
- A Voyage to the South Seas, in the Years 1740-41. Phila: James Chattin, for the author, 1757. 1st Amer edn, enlgd. 8vo. 306 pp. Half mor, gilt spine, t.e.g., by Bradstreet's.
(Chapel Hill) $2,500 [≈ £1,302]

Bull, Roger
- Grobianus; or the Complete Booby. An Ironical Poem. Done into English, from the Original Latin of Frederick Dedekindus ... London: for T. Cooper, 1739. 1st edn. 8vo. xiii, [iii],276, [12] pp. Contemp calf.
(Burmester) £450 [≈ $863]

Bullingbrooke, Edward
- The Duty and Authority of Justices of the Peace and Parish-Officers for Ireland ... Dublin: Boulter Grierson, 1766. 1st edn. 4to. xviii,816 pp. No free endpapers, minor soiling. Contemp calf, some wear to edges & extremities.
(Clark) £130 [≈ $249]

Bunbury, Henry W.
- Annals of Horsemanship ... Communicated by Various Correspondents to Geoffrey Gambado, Esq. ... Dublin: for William Jones, 1792. 2nd edn. Sm 4to. [2],xviii,96 pp. 17 plates. Old qtr vellum & mrbld bds, sl rubbed.
(Karmiole) $250 [≈ £130]

Bunyan, John
- Grace Abounding to the Chief of Sinners ... To which is added Dying Sayings ... A New Edition. Leeds: J. Binns, 1798. Tall 12mo. 144 pp. Some wear. Old calf, worn.
(Humber) £35 [≈ $67]
- The Pilgrims Progress ... Compleat in Two Parts ... The Three and Twentieth Edition

Adorned with Curious Sculptures by J. Sturt. London: J. Clarke, 1741. 8vo. [16],213, [14], 196,[2] pp. Frontis (blank crnr torn). Sl marks, sl shaken. Early calf, worn.
(Humber) £55 [≈ $105]
- The Pilgrim's Progress ... Compleat in Two Parts. Thirtieth Edition. London: for W. Johnston, 1760. 8vo. xvi,196,[ii] pp. 22 plates. Contemp speckled calf gilt, lacks label.
(Hollett) £120 [≈ $230]
- The Pilgrims Progress ... In Two Parts ... The 31st Edition Adorned with Sculptures. London: W. Johnston, 1766. Tall 8vo. [16], 213, [14],196,[2] pp. Few sections sl pulled. Old calf, worn, jnts weak.
(Humber) £45 [≈ $86]

Burbury, John
- A Relation of a Journey of the Right Honourable My Lord Henry Howard, from London to Vienna, and thence to Constantinople ... London: 1671. 12mo. [x],225,[29] pp, inc blank A & 2 final blanks. Edges occas sl browned. Old calf, later mor reback. Wing B.5611.
(Hollett) £250 [≈ $479]

Burges, Sir James Bland
- Alfred's Letters; or, A Review of the Political State of Europe to the End of the Summer 1792 ... London: B. Millan for J. Debrett, (1793). Contemp half calf, hinges splitting. Anon.
(Jarndyce) £40 [≈ $76]

Burgess, Anthony
- Vindiciae Legis or a Vindication of the Moral Law and the Covenants from the Errors of Papists ... Antinomians ... Second Edition Corrected and Augmented. London: James Young for Thomas Underhill, 1647. 4to. [12],283,[7] pp. Some wear & tear. New half calf. Wing B.5667. *(Humber)* £185 [≈ $355]

Burgess, Thomas
- An Essay on the Study of Antiquities. The Second Edition, Corrected and Enlarged. Oxford: sold by D. Prince, 1782. 142 pp. Rec wraps. Anon. *(C.R. Johnson)* £65 [≈ $124]
- See also under Schomberg, A.C.

Burgh, James
- Britain's Remembrancer ... London: for G. Freer, J. Highmore, M. Cooper, 1747. 4th edn. 8vo. 48 pp. Old wraps. Anon.
(Burmester) £30 [≈ $57]

Burgher, Gottfried Augustus
- Leonora. Translated ... by W.R. Spencer, with Designs by Lady Diana Beauclerc. London: T. Bensley ..., 1796. Folio. [8],35 pp. 4 plates, 4 vignettes. Occas soil or fox mark. Early mrbld bds & calf crnrs, worn, mod reback of black mor gilt.
(Beech) **£45 [≈ $86]**

Burgoyne, John
- A Letter from Lieut. Gen. Burgoyne to his Constituents, upon his late Resignation ... London: for J. Almon, 1779. 37 pp. Disbound. *(Jarndyce)* **£65 [≈ $124]**
- A State of the Expedition of Canada, as laid before the House of Commons ... London: Almon, 1780. 2nd edn. 8vo. (192),109 pp. 6 fldg maps (some with an overlay, 1 with a tear reprd). Contemp calf, rebacked.
(Respess) **$1,250 [≈ £651]**

Burke, Edmund
- An Appeal from the New to the Old Whigs, in consequence of some late Discussions in Parliament, relative to the Reflections on the French Revolution. Dublin: M. Mills, 1791. 1st Irish edn. 141 pp. Disbound. Anon.
(C.R. Johnson) **£65 [≈ $124]**
- An Authentic Copy of Mr. Pitt's Letter to his Royal Highness the Prince of Wales, with his Answer. London: for John Stockdale ..., 1789. 1st sep authorised edn (?). 8vo. 12,4 advt pp. Disbound. Anon.
(Young's) **£90 [≈ $172]**
- The History of American Taxation ... London: ptd by J. Dodsley; Dublin: for John Exshaw ..., 1775. 3rd edn, rvsd & crrctd with addtns. 8vo. 98 pp. Half-title sl dusty. Disbound. Todd 24m. *(Young's)* **£35 [≈ $67]**
- A Letter ... to Sir Hercules Langrishe, Bart., M.P. on the subject of Roman Catholics of Ireland ... London: for J. Debrett, 1792. 1st London edn, 1st imp. 88 pp. Ink underlining at end. Disbound. Todd 59c.
(Jarndyce) **£35 [≈ $67]**
- A Philosophical Enquiry into the Origin of Our Ideas of the Sublime and Beautiful. London: Dodsley, 1757. 1st edn. 8vo. viii, [viii],184 pp. Lacks half-title. Sl foxing. Early 19th c blue polished half calf gilt, a.e.g.
(Claude Cox) **£450 [≈ $863]**
- Speech ... On presenting to the House of Commons (on the 11th of February, 1780) a Plan for the better Security of the Independence of Parliament ... London: Dodsley, 1780. 1st authorised edn. 95 pp.

Stained at end. Disbound. Todd 33b.
(Jarndyce) **£40 [≈ $76]**
- The Sublime and Beautiful. With an Introductory Discourse concerning Taste, and other Additions. Oxford: 1796. 1st English reprint with Burke's name on title. 8vo. vi, [iv],194 pp. Contemp tree calf, rebacked. *(Burmester)* **£58 [≈ $111]**
- Substance of the Speeches made in the House of Commons, on Wednesday, the 15th of December, 1779 ... London: J. Almon, 1779. 1st edn. 17 pp. Stabbed as issued, unopened. Todd 31. *(C.R. Johnson)* **£65 [≈ $124]**

Burlamaqui, Jean Jacques
- The Principles of Moral Law ... Translated into English by Mr. Nugent. London: for J. Nourse, 1752. 2nd edn in English. 8vo. xvi, [xxiv], 312 pp. Contemp calf, rebacked.
(Burmester) **£110 [≈ $211]**

Burn, A.
- Geodosia Improved; or, a New and Correct Method of Surveying ... In Two Parts ... London: T. Evans, 1775. 1st edn. 8vo. x,355 pp. 5 fldg plates. Some browning. Contemp calf, edges sl rubbed. *(Gough)* **£65 [≈ $124]**

Burn, Richard
- Ecclesiastical Law. London: Woodfall & Strahan for A. Millar, 1767. 2nd edn. 4 vols. Leather, rather worn. *(Gage)* **£30 [≈ $57]**
- The Justice of the Peace, and Parish Officer. London: Lintot for Millar, 1755. 1st edn. 2 vols. 8vo. Occas sl browning, few margs torn. Contemp calf, worn, rebacked.
(Meyer Boswell) **$1,250 [≈ £651]**

Burnaby, Andrew
- Travels through the Middle Settlements in North-America. In the Years 1759 and 1760. With Observations upon the State of the Colonies. London: for T. Payne, 1775. 2nd edn. 8vo. 198,[1] pp. Contemp calf, jnts weak but holding. *(Chapel Hill)* **$375 [≈ £195]**
- Travels through the Middle Settlements in North America, in the Years 1759 and 1760; with Observations upon the State of the Colonies. London: 1798. 3rd edn. Lge 4to. xix, 209 pp, inc 2 fldg tables. Fldg map, 2 plates. Occas damp stains. Contemp three qtr calf, sl worn. *(Reese)* **$950 [≈ £494]**

Burnet, Elizabeth
- A Method of Devotion: or, Rules for Holy & Devout Living, with Prayers ... London: for

Joseph Downing, 1709. 2nd edn. 8vo. Port. Lacks endpapers. Contemp calf, sl worn.
(Stewart) **£30 [≈ $57]**

Burnet, Gilbert

- The Bishop of Salisbury, his Speech in the House of Lords, on the First Article of the Impeachment of Dr. henry Sacheverell. London, Printed. Edinburgh: reptd by James Watson, 1710. 16 pp. Sl browned. Disbound.
(Wreden) **$35 [≈ £18]**

- An Essay on the Memory of the late Queen. The Second Edition. London: Chiswell, 1696. 197,advt pp. Contemp calf, rebacked. Wing B.5786. *(C.R. Johnson)* **£65 [≈ $124]**

- An Exposition of the Thirty Nine Articles of the Church of England. The Second Edition Corrected. London: R. Roberts for Richard Chiswell, 1700. Folio. iv,xxiv,396 pp. Sl marg worming. Half leather, worn, spine defective. *(Gage)* **£32 [≈ $61]**

- Bishop Burnet's History of his Own Time ... To which is added the Author's Life by the Editor. London: for Thomas Ward, 1724; for J. Downing, 1734. 1st edn. 2 vols. Folio. Contemp calf gilt, rebacked.
(Lloyd-Roberts) **£225 [≈ $431]**

- The Life and Death of Sir Matthew Hale, Kt. ... London: for William Shrowsbery, 1682. 2nd edn. 8vo. Port. New calf, gilt spine, mor label. Wing B.5828.
(Meyer Boswell) **$225 [≈ £117]**

- The Memoires of the Lives and Actions of James and William, Dukes of Hamilton and Castle Herald, &c. ... London: for R. Royston, 1678. Sm folio. 436,[12] pp. Port frontis, full-page engvd port. Orig calf, rubbed spots on spine & cvrs.
(Chapel Hill) **$325 [≈ £169]**

- News from France: in a Letter Giving a Relation of the Present State of the Difference between the French King and the Court of Rome. London: for Richard Chiswel, 1682. 4to. Disbound. Wing B.5839. Anon.
(Sanders) **£25 [≈ $47]**

- Reflections on Mr. Varillas's History of the Revolutions ... Amsterdam: ptd in the year 1686. 12mo. 96 pp. Minor soiling, marg burn scars on 2 ff. Disbound. Wing B.5825A.
(Clark) **£35 [≈ $67]**

- Some Letters containing an Account of what seemed most remarkable in Switzerland, Italy, &c. Printed in the Year, 1687. 12mo. [ii], "225" [ie 244] pp. Some soiling & damp staining. Old calf, later reback. Wing B.5917.
(Clark) **£55 [≈ $105]**

- Some Passages in the Life and Death of the Right Honourable John Earl of Rochester ... London: Chiswel, 1680. 1st edn. 2nd issue, with no errata on A8v. 8vo. [xiv],182,[8 advt] pp. Port (sl browned, sm repr). Occas marg marks. Old calf, rebacked, crnrs sl worn. Wing B.5922.
(Clark) **£85 [≈ $163]**

- Three Letters Concerning the Present State of Italy ... Being a Sequel to Dr. Burnet's Letters. London: ptd in the year 1688. 1st edn. 8vo. [xvi],191,[i] pp. Minor marg worm. Sl marking. Contemp calf, extremities worn, jnts cracked but firm. Wing B.5931. Anon.
(Clark) **£85 [≈ $163]**

- A Vindication of the Bishop of Salisbury and Passive Obedience, with Some Remarks upon a Speech which goes under his Lordship's Name, and a Postscript ... London: ptd in the year 1710. 1st edn. 8vo. 16 pp. Soiled. Disbound. Anon. *(Young's)* **£75 [≈ $143]**

Burney, Charles

- An Account of the Musical Performances in Westminster-Abbey, and the Pantheon, May 26th ... 1784, in commemoration of Handel. Dublin: Moncrieffe, Jenkin, White ..., 1785. Contemp calf, gilt spine, 1 hinge weakening.
(C.R. Johnson) **£385 [≈ $739]**

Burney, Frances (Fanny)

- Camilla: or, A Picture of Youth, by the Author of Evelina and Cecilia ... Dublin: William Porter ..., 1796. 1st Dublin edn. 3 vols. 8vo. Occas spotting, foxing or browning. Contemp half calf, worn, spine extremities defective. Anon. *(Finch)* **£45 [≈ $86]**

Burns, John

- An Historical and Chronological Remembrancer of all remarkable Occurrences, from the Creation to this Present Year of Our Lord, 1775 ... Dublin: for the author, 1775. 1st edn. 8vo. 504,[8] pp. Subscribers. Contemp calf, new label.
(Young's) **£85 [≈ $163]**

Burns, Robert

- Poems chiefly in the Scottish Dialect. Edinburgh: for the author, 1787. 1st Edinburgh edn. Issue with "Skinking" on p 263. Port. Lacks half-title. 19th c qtr calf, gilt spine, red label. *(C.R. Johnson)* **£185 [≈ $355]**

- Poems, chiefly in the Scottish Dialect. A New Edition, considerably enlarged. Edinburgh: 1798. 2 vols in one. 8vo. xii,237, [i],[2 blank] [4],287 pp. Minor foxing. 19th c cloth.
(Spelman) **£65 [≈ $124]**

Burrough, Edward

- The Memorable Works of a Son of Thunder and Consolation ... Who Died a Prisoner for the Word of God, in the City of London ... London: 1672. 1st coll edn. Folio. [lii],896, [viii] pp. No free endpapers, end ff sl frayed & loose. Contemp calf, extremities worn. Wing B.5980.   *(Clark)* **£135 [≈ $259]**

Burroughs, Jeremiah

- Gospel Remission or a Treatise showing that True Blessedness Consists in Pardon of Sin. London: Dor. Newman, 1674. 2nd edn. 4to. [8],220,[12] pp. Minor marks & browning. 18th c qtr calf, bds worn, jnts cracked. Wing B.6082.   *(Humber)* **£85 [≈ $163]**

- Gospel Worship or the Right Manner of Sanctifying the Name of God in general ... London: Peter Cole, 1653. 4to. [10],120, 161-297, [13] pp. Minor blemishes. 19th c half calf, crnrs worn. Wing B.6085.
          (Humber) **£85 [≈ $163]**

- The Popish Doctrine of Auricular Confession and Priestly Absolution Considered: a Sermon ... Third Edition. London: for J. Noon & J. Gray, 1735. Mod wraps.
          (Waterfield's) **£40 [≈ $76]**

Burton, John

- Lectures on Female Education and Manners. The Third Edition. Dublin: ptd by J. Milliken, 1794. 430 pp. Contemp tree calf, red label, hd of spine v sl chipped.
          (C.R. Johnson) **£260 [≈ $499]**

- Monasticon   Eboracense: and   the Ecclesiastical History of Yorkshire ... London: for the author by N. Nickson ..., 1758. 1st edn. Vol 1, all published. Folio. xii,448,[35] pp. Fldg map, 2 fldg plans, complete. Contemp diced calf gilt, upper hinge tender.   *(Hollett)* **£250 [≈ $479]**

Burton, Robert

- The Anatomy of Melancholy ... The Eighth Edition, corrected and augmented. London: Peter Parker, 1676. Folio. Sl foxing. Later calf.   *(Goodrich)* **$495 [≈ £257]**

Burton, William

- A Commentary on Antoninus His Itinerary, or Journies of the Roman Empire ... London: Roycroft ..., 1658. 1st edn. Folio. [xxii], 266,[11] pp. Port frontis, dble-page map. Rebound in qtr calf. Wing B.6185.
          (Vanbrugh) **£355 [≈ $681]**

Bushell, Seth

- The Believers Groan for Heaven: In a Sermon at the Funeral of the Honourable Sir Richard Hoghton, of Hoghton ... Feb.14 1677 ... London: Tho. Sawbridge ..., 1678. Only edn. 4to. [vi],29 pp. Disbound. Wing B.6236.   *(Young's)* **£80 [≈ $153]**

Butler, John

- A Consultation on the Subject of a Standing Army held at the King's Arms Tavern on the Twenty-Eighth Day of February 1763. London: for G. Kearsly, [1763?]. 4to. Half-title. Disbound. Anon.
          (Waterfield's) **£65 [≈ $124]**

Butler, Joseph

- Fifteen Sermons Preached at the Rolls Chapel. London: W. Botham for James & John Knapton, 1726. 1st edn. 8vo. Contemp panelled calf, front jnt cracked but sound.
          (Waterfield's) **£110 [≈ $211]**

Butler, Samuel, author of Hudibras

- The Genuine Remains in Verse & Prose ... with Notes by R. Thyer ... London: Tonson, 1759. 1st edn. 2 vols. 8vo. [xl],429; [viii], 512 pp. 25 pp subscribers. Contemp half calf, some wear to spine ends, hinges cracked.
          (Claude Cox) **£60 [≈ $115]**

- The Posthumous Works ... Third Edition, corrected. London: R. Reilly, 1730. Tall 12mo. viii,312 pp. Contemp panelled calf, spine rubbed.   *(Lloyd-Roberts)* **£50 [≈ $95]**

- The Posthumous Works ... Third Edition, Corrected. London: R. Reilly, 1730. 12mo. Contemp calf, jnts cracked, label defective.
          (Waterfield's) **£40 [≈ $76]**

Butler, Weedon

- Memoirs of Mark Hildesley, D.D. Lord Bishop of Sodor and Mann ... under whose auspices the Holy Scriptures were translated into the Manx Language. London: J. Nichols, 1799. 691 pp. Contemp qtr calf, hinges weakening.   *(C.R. Johnson)* **£65 [≈ $124]**

Butter, William

- An Improved Method of Opening the Temporal Artery. Also, a New Proposal for extracting the Cataract. London: for J. Robson, 1783. 1st edn. 8vo. viii,213,[1] pp,advt leaf. Fldg plate. Half calf, mrbld bds. Anon.   *(Rootenberg)* **$500 [≈ £260]**

Button, Edward (translator)
- A New Translation of The Persian Tales;
from an Original Version of the Indian
Comedies of Mocles ... for the Service and
Amusement of the British Ladies. London:
for W. Owen, 1754. 1st edn. 12mo. xii,324
pp. Occas sm stamp. Contemp sheep,
rebacked in mor, crnrs reprd.
(Burmester) **£160 [≈ $307]**

Byfield, Timothy
- Some Plain Directions for the Use of our Sal
Oleosum Volatile. [London: ca 1710?]. Sm
8vo. 8 pp. Stitched, as issued.
(Burmester) **£250 [≈ $479]**

Byng, John
- The Trial of the Honourable Admiral John
Byng at a Court Martial ... London: for R.
Manby ... & W. Faden, 1757. 1st edn. Folio.
1-36,37*, 38*,37-76, 73*-76*, 77-130,19 pp.
Sl browning & spotting. Sm piece torn from
1 marg. Old cloth, worn.
(Bow Windows) **£140 [≈ $268]**

Byrom, John
- Miscellaneous Poems. Manchester: J.
Harrop, 1773. 2 vols. 8vo. Contemp tree calf,
rebacked. *(Waterfield's)* **£200 [≈ $383]**

Byron, John
- The Narrative of the Honourable John Byron
... containing an Account of the Great
Distresses suffered by himself and his
Companions on the Coast of Patagonia ...
London: 1768. 1st edn. 8vo. viii,257 pp.
Half-title. Frontis. Contemp calf, rebacked,
extremities rubbed *(Zwisohn)* **$350 [≈ £182]**
- The Narrative of the Honourable John Byron
... London: 1768. 1st edn. 8vo. viii,257 pp.
Half-title. Frontis. Occas sl foxing. Rebound
in mrbld bds. *(Zwisohn)* **$300 [≈ £156]**

Bysshe, Edward
- The British Parnassus: or, A compleat
Common- Place- Book of English Poetry ...
Dictionary of Rhymes ... London: ptd by J.
Nutt ..., 1714. Only edn. 2 vols. 12mo. Red
& black titles with lib marks on verso.
Rebound in half calf.
(Jarndyce) **£125 [≈ $239]**

C., Sir R.
- See Cotton, Sir Robert Bruce.

Cabala ...
- Cabala, Mysteries of State, in Letters of the
Great Ministers of K. James and K. Charles
... London: for Bedell & Collins, 1654. 1st
edn. 4to. [14],347,[12],[7 advt] pp. Few sm
marg reprs. Edges & margs sl browned. Mod
half mor. Wing C.183.
(Claude Cox) **£110 [≈ $211]**
- Cabala, sive Scrinia Sacra: Mysteries of State
and Government, in Letters of Illustrious
Persons ... To which is added in the Third
Edition, A Second Part ... London:
Sawbridge ..., 1691. Folio. Rec half calf.
Wing C.186. *(Vanbrugh)* **£175 [≈ $335]**

The Cabinet of Genius ...
- The Cabinet of Genius containing
Frontispieces and Characters adapted to the
most Popular Poems, &c. ... London: Taylor,
1787. 4to. 6,6,6,10, 2,4,2,6, 2,2,6,6, 2,12,
14,4, 6,[ii] pp. Engvd title, 26 stipple & 3
copper engvd plates. Sl used. Contemp calf, sl
worn. *(Clark)* **£125 [≈ $239]**

Calamy, Benjamin
- Sermons preached upon several Occasions.
London: John Darby, 1700. 3rd edn, crrctd.
Cr 8vo. Port. Contemp panelled calf, upper
jnt reprd. Wing C.223. *(Stewart)* **£40 [≈ $76]**

Calamy, Edmund
- The Nonconformist's Memorial ... Now
abridged and corrected ... by Samuel Palmer.
London: for W. Harris, 1775. 1st edn thus. 2
vols. 8vo. 14 pp subscribers. 26 ports. 19th c
half mor gilt, t.e.g.. *(Ximenes)* **$225 [≈ £117]**

Calcott, Wellins
- A Candid Disquisition of the Principles and
Practices of the most Ancient and Honourable
Society of Free and Accepted Masons ...
London: for the author, by Brother James
Dixwell, 1769. 1st edn. 8vo. [iv], xxxii, 243.
Calf backed bds, worn. *(Finch)* **£145 [≈ $278]**
- A Candid Disquisition of the Principles and
Practices of the most Antient and Honourable
Society of Free and Accepted Masons ...
Boston: 1772. 1st Amer edn. 8vo.
[iv],xiv,[ii],256 pp. 14 pp subscribers. Minor
browning. Contemp sheep, sl rubbed.
(Clark) **£225 [≈ $431]**

Caldwell, Sir James
- Debates Relative to the Affairs of Ireland; In
the Years 1763 and 1764. Taken by a Military
Officer ... London: 1766. 1st edn. 2 vols. 8vo.
[iv],x,iii,[i],404; [ii], [405]-853 pp. Contemp

calf, mor labels, spines worn at hd, sides sl stripped. Anon.   *(Finch)* £240 [≈ $460]

Callieres, Francois de
- The Knowledge of the World, and the Attainments useful in the Conduct of Life. Translated from the French ... London: for the translator, (1770). 2nd edn. 8vo. xviii, 179 pp. V occas spotting. Orig calf backed bds, uncut.   *(Young's)* £150 [≈ $287]

Calonne, Charles Alexandre de
- The Political State of Europe at the Beginning of 1796 ... Translated from the French MS. by D. St. Quentin. London: Debrett ..., 1796. Contemp tree calf, hinges cracking.   *(Jarndyce)* £58 [≈ $111]

Calvin, John
- Sermons of Maister John Calvin, Upon the Booke of Job. Translated out of the French by Arthur Golding. London: 1580. Sm folio. [36], 752 pp. Engvd title. Few sm marg tears & stains. Early calf. STC 4446.
      (Humber) £350 [≈ $671]

Cambridge, Richard Owen
- The Fable of Jotham: to the Borough-Hunters. London: for R. & J. Dodsley, sold by M. Cooper, 1754. 1st edn. Folio. 7 pp. Rec wraps. Anon.   *(C.R. Johnson)* £80 [≈ $153]

Camden, William
- Britannia, Newly Translated into English ... Published by Edmund Gibson. London: 1695. 1st Gibson edn. Folio. cxcv,1116, [18],[24], [2] pp. Engvd port & title, 50 maps by Morden, 8 plates of coins, 65 text ills. Few sm tears. Contemp calf, rebacked.
      (Henly) £1,600 [≈ $3,071]
- Britannia Abridg'd; with Improvements, and Continuations, to this Present Time ... London: Joseph Wild, 1701. 1st edn thus. 2 vols. 8vo. xxxvi,466; [iv],467-822, [ii],103, [2],[4] pp. 60 maps. Contemp calf, rebacked.
      (Bookpress) $1,350 [≈ £703]
- Remaines concerning Britaine ... The fifth Impression with many rare Antiquities never before imprinted ... by John Philipot ... London: Harper for Waterson, 1636. 5th edn. 4to. Port frontis. 19th c half mor, sm lib stamp on spine. STC 4524.
      (Vanbrugh) £155 [≈ $297]

Cameron, John
- The Messiah. In Nine Books. Belfast: James Magee, 1768. 1st edn. 12mo. [ii],xxiii, [i],

3-299 pp. Subscribers. Contemp calf, jnts reprd.   *(Burmester)* £50 [≈ $95]

Cameron, William
- Poetical Dialogues on Religion in the Scots Dialect, between Two Gentlemen and Two Ploughmen. Edinburgh: Peter Hill, 1788. New bds. Anon.
      (C.R. Johnson) £165 [≈ $316]

Camilla ...
- See Burney, Frances (Fanny).

Camoens, Luis de
- The Lusiad ... Translated ... By William Julius Mickle. The Second Edition. Oxford: Jackson & Lister, for J. Bew ..., 1778. 4to. [iv],ccxxxvi,496 pp. Frontis, fldg map. Orig calf, mor label.   *(Bickersteth)* £125 [≈ $239]

Campbell, George
- Poems on Several Occasions. Kilmarnock: John Wilson, 1787. 19th c half calf.
      (C.R. Johnson) £225 [≈ $431]

Campbell, John
- A Political Survey of Britain ... London: for the author, & sold by Richardson & Urquhart ..., 1774. 2 vols. 4to. Rec half calf. *(Lloyd-Roberts)* £180 [≈ $345]
- A Political Survey of Britain ... London: for the author, & sold by Richardson & Urquhart ..., 1774. 2 vols. 4to. Rec cloth backed bds.
      (Lloyd-Roberts) £150 [≈ $287]
- A Political Survey of Britain ... London: for the author, & sold by Richardson & Urquhart ..., 1774. 1st edn. 2 vols. 4to. [iv],vi,726; [iv],739,[i] pp. Half-titles. Without Index sometimes found. Contemp calf, gilt dec spines, jnts cracked but holding.
      (Clark) £125 [≈ $239]

Campe, J.H.
- Elementary Dialogues, or the Improvement of Youth, translated by Mr Seymour ... London: for Hookham & Carpenter, 1792. 1st edn in English. 8vo. [viii],196 pp. 16 plates. Rec half calf.   *(Bickersteth)* £140 [≈ $268]
- Pizarro; or, the Conquest of Peru ... Designed for the Instruction of Youth. Translated ... by Elizabeth Helme. London: Sampson Low ..., 1799. 1st edn in English. 2 vols in one. Sm 8vo. 136; 136 pp. Fldg map (2 sm tears). Contemp calf, spine sl rubbed.
      (Burmester) £175 [≈ $335]

A Candid Inquiry ...
- A Candid Inquiry into the Present State of the Laws relative to the Game in Scotland. By an Admirer of Truth. Edinburgh: Robert Mundell, 1772. 28 pp. Disbound.
(C.R. Johnson) **£55 [≈ $105]**

Canning, George
- Horace's First Satire Modernised and Addressed to Jacob Henriques. London: J. Cooke, 1762. 4to. 27 pp. New wraps. Anon.
(C.R. Johnson) **£125 [≈ $239]**

Canning, George, et al.
- The Microcosm, a Periodical Work, by Geoffrey Griffin, of the College of Eton. Windsor: for C. Knight ..., 1787. 1st edn in book form. 8vo. xvi,455 pp. Addtnl engvd title. Divisional title to each part. Occas v sl browning. Contemp calf, rebacked.
(Finch) **£90 [≈ $172]**
- The Microcosm, a Periodical Work, by Geoffrey Griffin, of the College of Eton. The Second Edition. Windsor: for C. Knight ..., 1788. Engvd title (dated 1787). Piece cut from endpaper. Contemp sheep, hinge splitting.
(Jarndyce) **£60 [≈ $115]**
- Poetry of the Anti-Jacobin. London: for J. Wright, 1799. 1st edn. Half-title. Rebound in half calf. Anon. By Canning, William Gifford, Frere and Ellis.
(Jarndyce) **£58 [≈ $111]**

The Canons of Criticism ...
- See Edwards, Thomas.

Capel, Arthur, Earl of Essex
- Letters written ... in the Year 1675 ... Life, and deplorable Death in the Tower of London. Dublin: Boulter Grierson, 1770. 1st Irish edn. 8vo. xxxix,367 pp. Contemp calf, worn, lacks label, jnts cracked.
(Fenning) **£75 [≈ $143]**

Capell, Edward (ed.)
- Prolusions; or, select Pieces of Antient Poetry ... in Three Parts ... London: Tonson, 1760. 8vo. [iv],xii,256 pp. Some foxing. Period calf, later reback, inner jnts strengthened. Anon.
(Rankin) **£75 [≈ $143]**

Caractacus, a Dramatic Poem ...
- See Mason, William.

Cardale, Paul
- The True Doctrine of the New Testament concerning Jesus Christ, considered ... London: for J. Johnson, 1771. iii,418,index pp. Lib stamp. Half leather, lib label, spine damaged.
(Gage) **£25 [≈ $47]**

Care, Henry
- An Answer to a Paper importing a Petition of the Archbishop of Canterbury, and Six Other Bishops ... London: Henry Hills, 1688. 4to. 31 pp. Disbound. Anon.
(Jarndyce) **£40 [≈ $76]**
- English Liberties: or, the Free-Born Subject's Inheritance, Containing 1. Magna Charta ... London: Larkin for Harris, [?1680]. 12mo. [xii],228 pp. Contemp calf, crnrs reprd. Wing C.515 (8vo). Anon.
(Claude Cox) **£120 [≈ $230]**
- English Liberties, or the Free-Born Subject's Inheritance. Containing Magna Charta ... The Habeas Corpus Act, and Several Other Statutes; with Comments ... The Sixth Edition ... Providence: John Carter ..., 1774. viii,350,subscribers pp.
(Reese) **$750 [≈ £390]**

Carew, Bampfylde-Moore
- The Life and Adventures of Bampfylde-Moore Carew, commonly called King of the Beggars ... Dictionary of the Cant Language ... London: for Buckland, Bathurst, Davies, 1793. 12mo. 235,[5] pp. Contemp bds, spine sl worn. Sometimes attrib to Robert Goadby.
(Burmester) **£45 [≈ $86]**

Carlisle, Isabella Byron Howard, Countess
- Thoughts in the Form of Maxims addressed to Young Ladies, on their First Establishment in the World. London: for T. Cornell, 1789. 249, errata pp. 1 sm repr. Contemp sheep, rebacked.
(C.R. Johnson) **£145 [≈ $278]**

Carlyle, Alexander
- The Question relating to a Scots Militia considered. In a Letter to the Lords and Gentlemen ... By a Freeholder. Edinburgh: Hamilton, Balfour, 1760. 1st edn. 8vo. [ii], 45 pp. Disbound. Anon.
(Burmester) **£45 [≈ $86]**

Carr, William
- An Accurate Description of the United Netherlands ... Written by an English Gentleman. London: for Timothy Childe, 1691. 1st edn. 2 parts in one. Sm 8vo. 5 fldg plates. Half calf, rebacked, crnrs worn. Wing C.632 & A.438. Anon.
(Hannas) **£160 [≈ $307]**

Carter, Francis
- An Account of the Various Systems of Medicine ... London: for the author ... particularly from the Works of John Brown, M.D. ... 1788. 1st edn. 2 vols in one. 8vo. vi, 200; 239 pp, errata leaf. Orig half calf, jnts cracked, spine ends worn.

(Bickersteth) £185 [≈ $355]

Carter, John
- Specimens of the Ancient Sculpture and Painting ... to the Reign of Henry ye VIII ... London: Carter, 1780-87. 1st edn. 2 vols. Folio. 60; 70 pp. 2 frontis, engvd titles, 57 + 57 plates. Clean tear in 1 plate. Orig half calf, rubbed, 2 hinges cracked.

(Chapel Hill) $350 [≈ £182]
- Specimens of the Ancient Sculpture and Painting now remaining in this Kingdom ... London: 1780-87-(94). 1st edn. 2 vols in one. Folio. iv,1-8,7*, 8*,9-60; iv,70 pp. Engvd titles & frontises, 114 plates (31 cold or partly cold). Russia gilt, a.e.g., rebacked.

(Bow Windows) £700 [≈ $1,343]

Carter, Matthew
- Honor Redivivus or an Analysis of Honor and Armory. London: E. Coates, 1655. 1st edn. Variant issue with regular collation of 2nd gathering F. Fcap 8vo. [viii],88,[172] pp. Sl used & marked, some head rules shaved. Later half calf, rebacked, bds rubbed.

(Ash) £400 [≈ $767]
- Honor Redivivus: or, the Analysis of Honor and Armory ... Third Edition ... London: Hen. Herringman, 1673. 8vo. [iv],351,[i] pp. Engvd frontis & addtnl title, 9 plates, num text w'cuts. Minor spotting. Old calf, rebacked, crnrs worn. Wing C.660.

(Clark) £85 [≈ $163]
- Honor Redivivus or an Analysis of Honor and Armory ... Third Edition ... London: Hen. Herringman, 1673. 8vo. [iv],351 pp. Addtnl engvd title, 8 engvd plates, num text w'cuts. 19th c half calf, gilt spine. Wing C.660.

(Vanbrugh) £155 [≈ $297]

Carter, William
- The Disbanded Subaltern. A Poem. [London:] for the author, [1780?]. 1st edn. 17 pp. Rec wraps. Anon.

(C.R. Johnson) £180 [≈ $345]

Cartwright, William
- The Royall Slave. A Tragi-Comedy. The Third Edition. London: for T.R. & Humphrey Moseley, 1651. 16mo. Epilogue

soiled. Lower foredge damp stained. Disbound. *(Dramatis Personae)* $45 [≈ £23]

Cary, John
- Cary's New Map of England and Wales with part of Scotland ... London: publish'd June 11th 1794 by J. Cary. 1st edn. Lge 4to (310 x 245 mm). 85 index, 3 subscribers pp. 81 hand cold engvd maps. Contemp (orig?) sheep, rebacked. *(Claude Cox)* £200 [≈ $383]
- Cary's Traveller's Companion ... London: John Cary, 1791. Sm 8vo. 3 engvd ff (title, advt, contents), 43 maps (inc general map & fldg map of Yorkshire), 6 pp list of towns, 2 advt pp. Contemp calf, gilt spine.

(Beech) £225 [≈ $431]

Casaubon, Meric
- Of Credulity and Incredulity in Things Divine & Spiritual ... as also the Business of Witches and Witchcraft ... London: T.N. for Samuel Lowndes, 1670. 8vo. Sm hole in 1 leaf. 19th c calf, sl rubbed, front jnt cracked. Wing C.806. *(Waterfield's)* £200 [≈ $383]

Case ...
- The Case of Impropriations ... see Kennett, White.
- The Case of Orphans Consider'd, from Antiquity ... London: for J. Peele, 1725. Only edn. 8vo. iv,64 pp. Title sl browned. New qtr calf. *(Meyer Boswell)* $450 [≈ £234]
- The Case of the Sinking Fund and the Right of the Publick Creditors to it considered ... London: ptd by H. Haines, at R. Francklin's, 1735. 8vo. Mod mrbld bds.

(Waterfield's) £75 [≈ $143]

Casley, David
- A Catalogue of the Manuscripts of the King's Library: An Appendix to the Cottonian Library ... London: for the author, 1734. 1st edn. 4to. 16 plates (1 fldg). Contemp calf, sl rubbed, sl surface damage.

(Georges) £250 [≈ $479]

Caslon, William
- A Specimen of Printing Types, by William Caslon, Letter-Founder to his Majesty. N.p.: [1785]. 8 pp. Folio. Later qtr mor.

(Spelman) £180 [≈ $345]

Castiglione, Baldassare
- The Courtier. In Four Books ... Translated from the Original [by Robert Samber]. London: Bettesworth, 1724. 1st edn of this

translation. 8vo. xxi,[i],336,[8] pp. Some foxing. Contemp calf, jnts cracked towards hd of spine.   *(Spelman)* **£120 [≈ $230]**
- Il Cortegiano, or The Courtier ... and a New Version of the same into English ... prefix'd the Life of the Author by A.P. Castiglione ... London: Bowyer, for the editor, 1727. 1st edn of this trans. 4to. [lxii], 480, 475-508 pp. Subscribers. Port. Contemp calf, reprd.
    (Burmester) **£225 [≈ $431]**

The Castle of Otranto ...
- See Walpole, Horace.

Catalogue ...
- Catalogue of Five Hundred Celebrated Authors of Great Britain, now Living ... London: R. Faulder ..., 1788. Only edn. 8vo. viii,[276] pp. Contemp half sheep, uncut, worn.   *(Bookpress)* **$550 [≈ £286]**

Caussin, Nicolas
- A Voice from the Dead: or the Speech of an Old Noble Peer: Being the Excellent Oration of the Learned and Famous Boethius, to the Emperor Theodoricus. London: Janeway, 1681. 1st edn. Sm 4to. 8 pp. Sl wear. 19th c qtr mor, sl worn. Wing C.1551C. Anon.
    (Finch) **£50 [≈ $95]**

Cave, Jane
- Poems on Various Subjects, Entertaining, Elegiac, and Religious. Winchester: J. Sadler, 1783. 150,26 subscribers pp. Port frontis. Contemp qtr calf, rebacked.
    (C.R. Johnson) **£180 [≈ $345]**

Cave, William
- Apostolici: or, the History of the Lives ... of those who were contemporary with ... the Apostles ... London: 1682. 2nd edn & 1st edn. 2 vols. Folio. [xxxv],xxxii, 335; [lii], lxxi, 543,59 pp. Addtnl engvd title vol 1, frontis vol 2. Contemp calf, jnts split. Wing C.1591/96.   *(Young's)* **£85 [≈ $163]**
- Apostolici: or the History of the Lives ... of those who were contemporary with ... the Apostles ... also the most Eminent of the Primitive Fathers ... London: B.W. for Richard Chiswell, 1687. 3rd edn. Folio. [xxxii], 336 pp. Frontis, 23 plates. Contemp calf. Wing C.1592.
    (Lloyd-Roberts) **£100 [≈ $191]**
- Apostolici ... London: W.D. for J. Walthoe ..., 1716. 4th edn. Folio. [xxiv],738 pp. Contemp panelled calf, rebacked, crnrs sl worn.   *(Lloyd-Roberts)* **£125 [≈ $239]**

- See also Taylor, Jeremy.

Cavendish, George
- The Negotiations of Thomas Woolsey, The great Cardinall of England, Containing his Life and Death ... London: for William Sheares, 1641. 1st edn. Sm 4to. xii,118 pp. Engvd plate. Occas staining. 18th c polished calf gilt. Wing C.1619. *(Finch)* **£500 [≈ $959]**

Cawley, John
- The Case of Founders Kinsmen: with relation to the Statutes of [All Souls] College in the University of [Oxford]. London: for J. Whitlock, [1694]. 4to. Water stained. Disbound. Wing C.1649.
    (Waterfield's) **£30 [≈ $57]**

Cellini, Benvenuto
- The Life ... Translated from the Original by Thomas Nugent. London: T. Davies, 1771. 1st English edn. 2 vols. x,512; 404 pp, 22 ff. Port. Leather.   *(Ars Artis)* **£150 [≈ $287]**

Cerdan, Jean Paul, Comte de
- The Kingdom of Sweden restored to its True Interest. A Political Discourse. London: M. Flesher, for Joanna Brome, 1682. 1st English edn. 4to. [4],32 pp. Title & final page dust soiled. Disbound. Old Wing K.581; not in New Wing.   *(Hannas)* **£35 [≈ $67]**

Cervantes Saavedra, Miguel de
- The History and Adventures of the Renowned Don Quixote. Translated from the Spanish ... Some Account of the Author's Life, by T. Smollett. London: Strahan ..., 1782. 5th edn. 4 vols. 8vo. Plates by Hayman. Contemp calf gilt, sl rubbed, 1 crnr bumped.
    (Bromer) **$250 [≈ £130]**
- Persiles and Sigismunda: a Celebrated Novel ... London: for Ward & Chandler, & Wood & Woodward, 1741. 1st edn of this transl. 2 vols. 12mo. Intl advt leaf in vol 2. Port in vol 1. Contemp calf, rebacked, scuffed, crnrs rubbed.   *(Ximenes)* **$750 [≈ £390]**

Chalmers, George
- The Life of Thomas Ruddiman, the Keeper ... of the Library belonging to the Faculty of Advocates of Edinburgh ... . London: Stockdale, 1794. Frontis port. 2 pp of facs (1 fldg). Later calf, spine rubbed, lacks label.
    (Waterfield's) **£85 [≈ $163]**
- The Life of Thomas Ruddiman. London: Stockdale, 1794. Frontis port. Contemp speckled calf.   *(C.R. Johnson)* **£225 [≈ $431]**

- Opinions on Interesting Subjects of Public Law and Commercial Policy arising from American Independence. London: Debrett, 1784. Half-title,195 pp. Disbound.
  (C.R. Johnson) **£180 [≈ $345]**

Chambaud, Louis
- A Grammar of the French Tongue ... Sixth Edition, Revised and Corrected. London: C. Bathurst, 1775. Fcap 8vo. xxvi,[10],434 pp, advt leaf. Fldg table. Contemp calf, some wear. *(Spelman)* **£45 [≈ $86]**
- A Grammar of the French Tongue ... London: Rivington ..., 1787. 9th edn. 8vo. xxvi,[10], 434, [2 advt] pp. Fldg table. Contemp half calf. *(Burmester)* **£55 [≈ $105]**

Chamberlayne, John
- The Arguments of the Books and Chapters of the New Testament with Practical Observations, Translated from the Original Manuscript of Mr Ostervald. London: J. Downe, 1718. 8vo. [6],522 pp. 19th c tree calf, rear jnt reprd. *(Humber)* **£35 [≈ $67]**

Chambers, William
- A Dissertation on Oriental Gardening. London: W. Griffin, 1772. 1st edn. 4to. Engvd title & dedic, x,94 pp, errata leaf. Contemp calf, backstrip relaid.
  (Spelman) **£750 [≈ $1,439]**

Chambray, Roland Freart, Sieur de
- An Idea of the Perfection of Painting ... rendred English by J.E. [John Evelyn] ... London: for Henry Herringman, 1668. Only edn in English. [xl],136 pp. Some browning. Sl cropped. Crayon underlinings on a few ff. Old calf, rebacked, crnrs sl worn. Wing F.1922. *(Clark)* **£320 [≈ $614]**

Chandler, Richard
- Travels in Greece: or An Account of a Tour made at the Expense of the Society of Dilettanti. Oxford: Clarendon Press, 1776. 1st edn. 4to. xiv,[ii],304 pp. 7 maps & plans (some spotting & browning). Contemp qtr calf, spine reprd & rubbed.
  (Frew Mackenzie) **£450 [≈ $863]**
- Travels in Greece: or an Account of a Tour made at the Expense of the Society of Dilettanti. Oxford: Clarendon Press, 1776. 1st edn. 4to. 4,[xiv], [ii],304 pp. 7 maps & plans. Title sl foxed, occas sl offsetting. Contemp calf, sometime rebacked.
  (Frew Mackenzie) **£450 [≈ $863]**

Chandler, Samuel
- A Paraphrase and Critical Commentary on the Book of Joel. London: for J. Noon, R. Hett, J. Gray, 1735. 4to. Mod qtr calf, vellum tips. *(Waterfield's)* **£65 [≈ $124]**

Chapman, George
- A Treatise on Education. With a Sketch of the Author's Method. Edinburgh: for Kincaid & Creech, 1773. 1st edn. 256 pp. Contemp calf, hinges weakening, some wear.
  (C.R. Johnson) **£400 [≈ $767]**

Chapone, Hester
- Letters on the Improvement of the Mind ... New Edition. London: for J. Walter, 1787. 8vo. viii,238 pp. Period calf, sl cracking upper jnt. *(Rankin)* **£45 [≈ $86]**

Chaptal, M.I.A.
- Elements of Chemistry. Translated from the French. Phila: 1796. 3 vols in one. 8vo. 673 pp. Title mtd. Lib stamp. Old calf, rebacked.
  (Goodrich) **$195 [≈ £101]**

Charles I, King of England
- The Pourtraicture of His Sacred Majesty in His Solitudes and Sufferings. Together with His Majesties Praiers delivered ... before His Death ... [London]: 1649. 8vo. [viii], 278, [2] pp. Fldg frontis (with explanation). Orig sheep, old reback. *(Vanbrugh)* **£155 [≈ $297]**
- Reliquiae Sacrae Carolinae. Or the Works of that Great Monarch and Glorious Martyr ... The Hague: Samuel Browne, 1650. 8vo. [xvi], 280, 12,[iv],361 pp. Port frontis. Sep title to Eikon Basilike. Contemp sheep, lacks label, spine ends sl worn. Wing C.2072.
  (Vanbrugh) **£195 [≈ $374]**
- Reliquiae Sacrae Carolinae. Or the Works of that Great Monarch and Glorious Martyr ... The Hague: Samuel Browne, 1651. 8vo. [xvi], 276, [vi],268, 10,149-324 pp. 2 ports, fldg frontis to Eikon Basilike. Contemp calf, rebacked. Wing C.2073.
  (Clark) **£150 [≈ $287]**
- The Works of King Charles the Martyr ... Second Edition. London: R. Chiswell, 1687. Lge folio. [viii],720,[4] pp. Frontis, addtnl engvd title, 2 dble-page engvs. Orig calf, Victorian reback, 2 sm cracks. Wing C.2076.
  (Vanbrugh) **£295 [≈ $566]**

Charlevoix, Pierre Francis Xavier de
- The History of Paraguay ... Written Originally in French ... London: Lockyer

Davis, 1769. 1st edn in English. 2 vols. 8vo. vii,[i],463; viii,415 pp. Contemp dark calf, elab gilt spine, mor labels, spines sl worn, gilt faded, jnts cracked but firm.
(Finch) **£240 [≈ $460]**

- A Voyage to North America ... Containing the Geographical Description and Natural History of Canada and Louisiana ... Dublin: 1766. 2 vols. 228; 336 pp. 8 maps, 2 plates. Later three qtr calf, mrbld bds, jnts sl rubbed.
(Reese) **$2,000 [≈ £1,041]**

- A Voyage to North America ... Containing the Geographical Description and Natural History of Canada and Louisiana ... Dublin: Exshaw & Potts, 1766. 2 vols in one. Sm 8vo. 8 maps (1 partly lined with paper), 2 port frontises. Contemp calf, rebacked, tips reprd.
(Bookpress) **$1,650 [≈ £859]**

Charlton, Jasper
- The Ladies Astronomy and Chronology, in Four Parts ... and the Machine called the Assimilo, explained. London: Thomas Gardner, for the author ..., 1735. 1st edn. 8vo. Errata leaf. 9 fldg plates. Contemp calf gilt.
(Ximenes) **$300 [≈ £156]**

Chastellux, Francois Jean
- Travels in North-America, in the Years 1780, 1781, and 1782. London: Robinson, 1787. 1st edn in English. 2 vols. 8vo. xv,462; xii, 432 pp. 2 maps, 2 plates. Sl foxing. Contemp qtr calf, hinges reprd. *(Bookpress)* **$850 [≈ £442]**
- Travels in North-America, in the Years 1780, 1781, and 1782. Dublin: Colles ..., 1787. 1st Dublin edn. 2 vols. [xvi],462; [xvi], 430 pp. 2 fldg maps, 3 plates. Contemp calf, gilt spines, contrasting labels. *(Bookpress)* **$750 [≈ £390]**

Chatterton, Thomas
- Miscellanies in Prose and Verse ... London: for Fielding & Walker, 1778. 1st edn. 8vo. xxxii,245,[iii] pp. Frontis, 1 plate. Contemp calf, elab gilt spine, mor label, extremities worn, jnts cracked but firm.
(Finch) **£100 [≈ $191]**

Chaucer, Geoffrey
- The Works ... London: 1687. 684 pp. Frontis port. Polished calf gilt, sometime rebacked with elab gilt spine. Wing C.3736.
(C.R. Johnson) **£850 [≈ $1,631]**
- The Works ... London: 1687. Roy 4to. [ii], 660, [xxiv] pp. Lacks the port, A4 & a-c4 (ie the prelims but for title). Sl spotting & soiling. Old panelled calf, sometime rebacked. Wing C.3736. *(Sotheran's)* **£325 [≈ $623]**

- The Works ... [edited] by John Urry ... London: Lintot, 1721. Folio. [52],626,81,[1] pp. 2 ports, engvd head-pieces. Single worm cut in inner marg of 1st few ff. Contemp calf, rebacked. *(Claude Cox)* **£220 [≈ $422]**

Cheats ...
- The Cheats and Illusions of Romish Priests ... see Aubin, Nicholas.

Chelsum, James
- Remarks on the last Two Chapters of Mr Gibbon's History of the Decline and Fall of the Roman Empire, in a Letter to a Friend. London: for T. Payne & Son, & J. Robson & Co, 1776. 1st edn. [iv],94,[2 blank] pp. Half-title. Wraps. Anon.
(C.R. Johnson) **£120 [≈ $230]**

Cheselden, William
- The Anatomy of the Human Body. London: Knapton, 1726. 3rd edn. 8vo. [xvi],376 pp. 34 plates. Contemp calf, jnts reprd.
(Bookpress) **$325 [≈ £169]**
- The Anatomy of the Human Body. London: 1750. 7th edn. [vi],334,[16] pp. Frontis, 40 plates (1 reprd). Orig leather, sl worn & marked, backstrip relaid.
(Whitehart) **£120 [≈ $230]**

The Chester Miscellany ...
- The Chester Miscellany. Being a Collection of Several Pieces, both in Prose and Verse, which were in the Chester Counrant from January 1745, to May 1750. Chester: Eliz. Adams ..., 1750. Only edn. 12mo. Sl later half calf, sl worn. *(Sanders)* **£100 [≈ $191]**

Chesterfield, Philip Dormer Stanhope, Earl of
- Letters written ... to his Son ... Published by Mrs. Eugenia Stanhope, from the Originals ... Second Edition. London: Dodsley, 1774. 4 vols. 8vo. Port frontis. Occas sl spotting. Contemp half sheep, smooth spines, red labels, sl rubbed, 1 jnt cracked but firm.
(Finch) **£120 [≈ $230]**
- Letters written ... to his Son ... Tenth Edition ... London: Dodsley, 1792. 4 vols. 8vo. Half-title. Port. Contemp tree calf, pale calf spines gilt, contrasting labels.
(Burmester) **£130 [≈ $249]**

Cheyne, George
- The English Malady: or, A Treatise of Nervous Disorders of all Kinds; as Spleen, Vapours,   Lowness   of   Spirits,

Hypochondriacal and Hysterical Distempers ... Fourth Edition. London: Strahan, 1734. 8vo. xxxi,370,advt pp. Some foxing. Contemp calf, jnts cracked.
(Goodrich) **$195 [≈ £101]**

- An Essay on Health and Long Life. London: 1724. 1st edn. 8vo. Contemp calf, jnts cracked. *(Goodrich)* **$195 [≈ £101]**

- An Essay on Health and Long Life. London: 1725. 4th edn. 232 pp. Title wrinkled & stained, with old repr. Rec qtr leather.
(Fye) **$150 [≈ £78]**

- An Essay on Health and Long Life. London: 1725. 5th edn. xx,[xxiv],232 pp. Bottom marg of title reprd. New leather backed bds.
(Whitehart) **£150 [≈ $287]**

- An Essay on Regimen. Together with Five Discourses, Medical, Moral, and Philosophical ... London: 1740. 1st edn. 344 pp. Rec qtr leather. *(Fye)* **$300 [≈ £156]**

Child, Sir Josiah
- A New Discourse of Trade ... London: T. Sowle ..., 1698. 12mo. [xlviii],238,[2 blank] pp. Minor marg worm in gatherings L-O affecting sev letters of text. Contemp calf, jnts & edges sl rubbed, hand-lettered foredge label (detached). Wing C.3862.
(Pickering) **$1,250 [≈ £651]**

Chippendale, Thomas
- The Gentleman and Cabinet-Maker's Director ... Third Edition. London: for the author ..., 1762. Folio. Preface leaf, 20 pp. Engvd dedic & 200 plates. Occas sl spotting. 2 index ff supplied from shorter copy. Contemp calf, reprd.
(Frew Mackenzie) **£2,500 [≈ $4,799]**

Chisholm, Colin
- An Essay on the Malignant Pestilential Fever introduced into the West Indian Islands from Boullam, on the Coast of Guinea ... Phila: Thomas Dobson, 1799. 8vo. xvi,308 pp. Some browning & spotting. Contemp calf, crnrs worn, front hinge split.
(Hemlock) **$275 [≈ £143]**

Chishull, Edmund
- Travels in Turkey and back to England ... London: Bowyer, 1747. Only edn. Folio. viii, 192 pp. Later olive half mor, upper jnt rubbed. *(Frew Mackenzie)* **£400 [≈ $767]**

The Christmas Treat ...
- The Christmas Treat: or Gay Companion.

Being a Collection of Epigrams, Ancient and Modern ... With an Essay on that Species of Composition. Dublin: for Will. Whitestone, 1767. 1st edn. 8vo. xxxviii,192 pp. Repr to 1 leaf. Orig wraps, uncut, lacks backstrip.
(Burmester) **£300 [≈ $575]**

A Chronological Series of Engravers ...
- See Martyn, Thomas.

Churchill, Charles
- The Author. London: for W. Flexney ... J. Coote ..., 1763. 1st edn. Fcap folio. Lib stamp & label. Later half calf. *(Ash)* **£75 [≈ $143]**
- The Candidate. A Poem. London: for the author, 1764. 1st edn. 4to. [ii],38 pp. Three qtr calf, lib book label. *(Young's)* **£32 [≈ $61]**
- The Conference. A Poem. London: for G. Kearsley, 1763. 1st edn. 4to. [ii],19 pp. Sm flaw in last leaf. Three qtr calf, lib book label.
(Young's) **£32 [≈ $61]**
- The Prophecy of Famine. A Scots Pastoral ... Dublin: for Wilson & Exshaw, 1763. 1st Irish edn. 8vo. Half-title. Disbound.
(Ximenes) **$125 [≈ £65]**
- The Times. A Poem. London: for the author ..., 1764. 1st edn. 4to. Half-title. As usual sgnd by the author on title. Sl foxed. Rec wraps. Anon. *(Sanders)* **£28 [≈ $53]**

Churchill, Sir Winston
- Divi Britannici being a remark upon the Lives of all the Kings of this Isle from the Year of the World 2855 Unto the Year of Grace 1660. London: Roycroft, 1675. Folio. [vi], 362, [iv] pp. 3 pp reprd without loss. Orig calf, rebacked, crnrs reprd. Wing C.4275. *(Lamb)* **£65 [≈ $124]**

Churchman, John, of Nottingham, Pennsylvania
- An Account of the Gospel Labours, and Christian Experiences of a Faithful Minister of Christ, John Churchman ... added, a Short Memorial of ... Joseph White. Philadelphia & London: James Phillips, 1781. vii,351 pp. Few pp loose. Disbound. *(Gage)* **£25 [≈ $47]**
- An Account of the Gospel Labours, and Christian Experiences of ... John Churchman ... added, a Short Memorial of ... Joseph White. Philadelphia, Printed. London: reprinted, 1781. 1st English edn. 8vo. vii, 351 pp. Old calf, jnts weak. *(Young's)* **£30 [≈ $57]**

Churchman, John, surveyor
- An Explanation of the Magnetic Atlas, or

Variation Chart ... Phila: James & Johnson, 1790. 1st edn. 8vo. 2 lge fldg tables. Some foxing. Lacks chart as usual. Sewn as issued, uncut.   *(Ximenes)* **$850 [≈ £442]**

Cibber, Colley

- An Apology for the Life of Mr Colley Cibber ... The Fourth Edition. Dublin: George Faulkner, 1740. Orig calf, brown label.
(C.R. Johnson) **£65 [≈ $124]**

- A Letter from Mr Cibber to Mr Pope, inquiring into the motives that might induce him in his satyrical works, to be so frequently fond of Mr. Cibber's name. The Second Edition. London: W. Lewis, 1742. 66 pp. Half-title. Rebound in bds.
(C.R. Johnson) **£65 [≈ $124]**

- Plays Written by Mr. Colley Cibber. London: Tonson ..., 1721. 1st edn. 2 vols in one. Sm folio. Contemp calf, rubbed & worn, cvrs detached, lacks label.
(Dramatis Personae) **$125 [≈ £65]**

Cibber, Colley & Vanbrugh, John

- The Provok'd Husband, or a Journey to London. A Comedy ... London: for J. Watts ..., 1728. 1st edn. 8vo. Disbound. This edn does not carry the press figures to B2v & C8v.
(Dramatis Personae) **$65 [≈ £33]**

Cibber, Theophilus

- The Lives and Characters of the most Eminent Actors and Actresses of Great Britain and Ireland ... Part I ... London: for R. Griffiths, 1753. 1st edn. 8vo. Orig grey bds, uncut & unopened, extremities sl rubbed. Boxed.
(Dramatis Personae) **$550 [≈ £286]**

Cicero, Marcus Tullius

- Cato: or, an Essay on Old Age ... With Remarks [by William Melmoth]. London: Dodsley, 1733. 8vo. [vi],319 pp. Port vignette on title. Contemp sprinkled calf, label, gilt spine, spine ends sl chipped.
(Rankin) **£35 [≈ $67]**

- M.T. Cicero's Cato Major, or his Discourse of Old-Age: with Explanatory Notes, by Benj. Franklin ... London: for Fielding & Walker, 1778. [2],163 pp. Port of Franklin. Contemp calf, scuffed, outer hinges worn but cords sound.   *(Reese)* **$400 [≈ £208]**

- M.T. Cicero's Cato Major, or Discourse on Old-Age ... With Explanatory Notes by Benj. Franklin ... Philadelphia, printed ... London: Re-printed ..., 1788. 8vo. [iv],163 pp. Port of Franklin. Some stains. Old bds, crnrs worn,

backstrip relaid.
(Bow Windows) **£165 [≈ $316]**

- The Orations ... Translated into English, with Notes ... by the Translator [William Guthrie]. London: for T. Waller, 1741. 1st edn. 2 vols. 8vo. Contemp calf, spines trifle worn.   *(Young's)* **£55 [≈ $105]**

The Citizen of the World ...

- See Goldsmith, Oliver.

Claiborne, John

- An Inaugural Essay on Scurvy ... Phila: Stephen C. Ustick, 1798. 1st edn. 8vo. [viii], 35 pp. Disbound.   *(Bookpress)* **$185 [≈ £96]**

Clarendon, Edward Hyde, Earl of

- A Brief View and Survey of the Dangerous and Pernicious Errors to Church and State, In Mr. Hobbes's Book, Entitled Leviathan ... The second Impression. Oxford: at the Theater, 1676. 4to. [viii],322 pp. Pale early water stains. Contemp calf, jnts worn. Wing C.4421.   *(Finch)* **£150 [≈ $287]**

- The Life ... Oxford: Clarendon Printing House, 1760. 2nd 8vo edn. 2 vols. 8vo. [x], 512; 525,[28] pp. Contemp calf, rebacked.
(Young's) **£56 [≈ $107]**

Clarendon, R.V.

- A Sketch of the Revenue and Finances of Ireland and of the appropriated Funds, Loans and Debt of the Nation ... London: for Lowndes & Debrett, & P. Byrne, Dublin, 1791. 4to. 2 advt pp. Charts, tables. Contemp tree calf, spine rubbed, sm splits in hinges.
(Jarndyce) **£580 [≈ $1,113]**

Claridge, John

- The Shepherd of Banbury's Rules to Judge of the Changes of the Weather ... London: W. Bickerton, 1744. 64 pp. Rec wraps.
(C.R. Johnson) **£95 [≈ $182]**

- The Shepherd of Banbury's Rules to Judge of the Changes of the Weather ... Second Edition, Corrected. London: T. Waller, 1748. 54 pp. Rec wraps.
(C.R. Johnson) **£75 [≈ $143]**

- The Shepherd of Banbury's Rules to judge of the Changes of the Weather ... Second Edition, Corrected [by John Campbell]. London: for T. Waller, 1748. 8vo. x,54 pp. Sl used. Mod bds.   *(Hannas)* **£20 [≈ $38]**

Clark, Ewan

- Miscellaneous Poems. Whitehaven: J. Ware

& Son, 1779. 8vo. List of subscribers pp vii-xxii. B'plate imperfectly removed. Contemp half calf, uncut, mrbld bds sl rubbed.
(Jarndyce) **£240 [≈ $460]**

Clark, Hugh & Wormull, Thomas, engravers
- A Short and Easy Introduction to Heraldry ... The Second Edition, much enlarged ... London: for G. Kearsley, 1776. Sm 8vo. [iv], 100 pp. 16 pp of engvd arms. Contemp gilt ruled sheep, hinges tender but firm.
(Rankin) **£50 [≈ $95]**

Clark, John, of Trowbridge
- Poems on Several Subjects, and Occasions ... Trowbridge: for the author, by T. Long ..., 1799. 1st edn. 8vo. [ii],188 pp. Addtnl engvd port. Contemp sheep, rebacked.
(Burmester) **£300 [≈ $575]**

Clarke, Alured
- An Essay Towards the Character of Her Late Majesty Caroline, Queen-Consort of Britain, &c. London: Knapton, 1738. 2nd edn. 8vo. [iv], 46 pp. Half-title. Stitched as issued. Anon.
(Young's) **£38 [≈ $72]**

Clarke, James
- A Survey of the Lakes of Cumberland, Westmorland, and Lancashire ... London: for the author, 1787. 2nd edn. tall folio. xlii, 194 pp. 11 lge fldg plans or maps, 2 plates. Occas sl spotting, few sm reprs to plans. Old half calf gilt.
(Hollett) **£875 [≈ $1,679]**

Clarke, John
- An Essay upon Study ... London: Bettesworth, 1731. vi,350 pp. Contemp calf, spine ends reprd, new label.
(C.R. Johnson) **£350 [≈ $671]**
- An Essay upon the Education of Youth in Grammar-Schools ... The Second Edition. With very large Additions. London: for Arthur Bettesworth, 1730. 222 pp, advt leaf. Contemp calf, rebacked.
(C.R. Johnson) **£350 [≈ $671]**
- A New Grammar of the Latin Tongue ... annexed, a Dissertation upon Language. The Fourth Edition. London: for W. Clarke ..., 1754. 173 pp. Contemp sheep, worn, hinges cracked.
(C.R. Johnson) **£75 [≈ $143]**

Clarkson, David
- The Practical Divinity of the Papists Discovered to be destructive of Christianity and Mens Souls ... London: Parkhurst,

Ponder ..., 1676. 1st edn. 4to. [xxxvi],413,[1 errata] pp. Usual mispagination from p 210. Old calf. Wing C.4575. Anon.
(Young's) **£120 [≈ $230]**

Clarkson, Thomas
- An Essay on the Impolicy of the African Slave Trade ... London: J. Phillips, 1788. Orig blue bds, paper spine, uncut.
(C.R. Johnson) **£320 [≈ $614]**

Clavering, Robert
- An Essay on the Construction and Building of Chimneys ... London: for I. Taylor, 1779. 1st edn. 8vo. 2 advt ff at end. Fldg frontis, fldg table. New half calf, padded with blanks at end.
(Georges) **£400 [≈ $767]**
- An Essay on the Construction and Building of Chimneys ... London: for I. Taylor, 1779. 1st edn. 8vo. Fldg frontis, fldg table. 2 advt ff at end. New half calf. *(Georges)* **£300 [≈ $575]**

Cleeve, Bourchier
- A Scheme for Preventing a Further Increase of the National Debt, and for reducing the same. Inscribed to the ... Earl of Chesterfield. London: Dodsley, 1756. 1st edn. 4to. Disbound. Cloth case. Anon.
(Ximenes) **$350 [≈ £182]**

Clement, S.
- Faults on Both Sides: or, An Essay upon the Original Cause, Progress, and Mischievous Consequences of the Factions in this Nation ... London: the booksellers, 1710. 2nd edn. 8vo. 56 pp. Title soiled. Anon.
(Young's) **£45 [≈ $86]**

The Clergyman's Vade-Mecum ...
- See Johnson, John.

Clerke, William
- The Triall of Bastardie ... London: Adam Islip, 1594. 1st edn. Sm 4to. 2 (of 4) fldg plates. Title spotted. 19th c half mor, extremities rubbed. STC 5411.
(Stewart) **£250 [≈ $479]**

Clery, Jean Baptiste Cant Hanet
- A Journal of the Occurrences at the Temple, during the Confinement of Louis XVI ... Translated ... by R.C. Dallas. London: ptd by Baylis, sold by the author, 1798. 1st edn in English. 8vo. Plate, facs. Half-title. 16pp subscribers. Some marg dampstain. Disbound.
(Clark) **£25 [≈ $47]**

Clube, William
- The Omnium: containing the Journal of a late Three Days Tour into France; Curious and Extraordinary Anecdotes ... Ipswich: George Jermyn, 1798. 158 pp. Orig pink bds, uncut. *(C.R. Johnson)* **£110 [≈ $211]**

Cobden, Edward
- A Persuasive to Chastity: A Sermon Preached before the King at St. James's on the 11th of December, 1748 ... London: for J. Lodge ..., 1749. 1st edn. 4to. [iv],20 pp. Title sl soiled. Stitched as issued.   *(Young's)* **£40 [≈ $76]**
- A Persuasive to Chastity: A Sermon Preached before the King at St. James's, on the 11th of December, 1748 ... London: for J. Lodge ..., 1749. 2nd edn. 8vo. iv,24 pp. Disbound.   *(Young's)* **£20 [≈ $38]**
- Poems on Several Occasions ... London: for the Benefit of a Clergyman's Widow ..., 1748. 1st edn. 8vo. x,352,[vi] pp. Contemp calf, rebacked, endpapers renewed, worn.   *(Finch)* **£125 [≈ $239]**

Cockburn, W.
- The Symptoms, Nature, Cause and Cure of a Gonorrhoea. London: Strahan, 1728. 4th edn. 8vo. [xxxvi],332 pp. Contemp calf, spine sl worn.   *(Bookpress)* **$350 [≈ £182]**

Cocker, Edward
- Cocker's Arithmetic ... Perused and published by John Hawkins. London: for Eben. Tracy, 1710. 28th edn. Sm 8vo. Port frontis. Few minor stains, crnrs of last 4 ff frayed. Contemp sheep, sl worn.   *(Stewart)* **£100 [≈ $191]**
- Cocker's Arithmetic ... published by John Hawkins ... Forty Third Edition ... amended by George Fisher. London: Edw. Midwinter, [ca 1725]. 12mo. vi,183,[1 advt] pp. Frontis port. Contemp sheep.   *(Spelman)* **£140 [≈ $268]**
- Cocker's Decimal Arithmetic ... London: 1695. [16],436 pp. Foxed. Sm marg repr. New leather.   *(Whitehart)* **£120 [≈ $230]**
- The Young Clerks Tutor enlarged: Being a most useful Collection of the best Presidents of Recognizances, Obligations, Conditions ... Sixth Edition. London: for Thomas Bassett, 1670. 208 pp. 4 plates (sl marg wear). Some early notes. Rebound in calf.   *(C.R. Johnson)* **£265 [≈ $508]**

A Code of Gentoo Laws ...
- A Code of Gentoo Laws, or, Ordinations of

the Pundits. From a Persian Translation, made from the Original written in the Shanscrit Language. London: ptd in the year 1781. 8vo. cxx, 284 pp, 2 advt ff. 8 plates. V sl marg worm. Orig calf, lower jnt cracked.   *(Bickersteth)* **£140 [≈ $268]**

Coetlogon, C.E. de
- The Test of Truth, Piety and Allegiance: a Sermon delivered on the Day of Sacramental Qualification for the Chief Magistracy of the City of London. London: Rivington, 1790. 4to. Disbound.   *(Waterfield's)* **£40 [≈ $76]**

Cole, Benjamin, engraver
- Select Tales and Fables with Prudential Maxims and other Little Lessons of Morality in Prose and Verse ... London: for F. Wingrave ..., [ca 1780]. 2 vols in one. 12mo. iv,80; iv,80 pp. Engvd titles & frontises, 60 engvd ills. 19th c half calf, rebacked.   *(Burmester)* **£225 [≈ $431]**

Cole, Christian (ed.)
- Memoirs of Affairs of State: containing Letters written by Ministers employed in Foreign Transactions, from the Year 1697 ... 1708 ... London: for the editor ..., 1732. 1st edn. Folio. [ii],xii,559,[i] pp. Intl licence leaf. 4 pp subscribers. Rec half mor.   *(Clark)* **£125 [≈ $239]**

Cole, William
- A Rod for the Lawyers: Who are hereby declared to be the grand Robbers & Deceivers of the Nation ... London: for Giles Calvert ..., 1659. 4to. Browned, few edges chipped & frayed. New calf. Wing C.5039A.   *(Meyer Boswell)* **$600 [≈ £312]**

Coleridge, Samuel Taylor
- Poems on Various Subjects. London: for G.G. & J. Robinsons, & J. Cottle, Bristol, 1796. 1st edn. Sm 8vo. [iii]-xvi,188,[iv] pp. Lacks half-title. Contemp sprinkled calf gilt, spine ends sl worn, 1 jnt beginning to crack at ft, crnrs bumped.   *(Finch)* **£875 [≈ $1,679]**
- Poems ... Second Edition. To which are now added Poems by Charles Lamb and Charles Lloyd. London: N. Biggs, for J. Cottle, Bristol, & Robinsons, London, 1797. Sm 8vo. xx, 278 pp. Contemp half calf, rebacked & recrnrd.   *(Finch)* **£400 [≈ $767]**
- Poems ... Second Edition. To which are now added Poems by Charles Lamb and Charles Lloyd. London: N. Biggs, for J. Cottle, Bristol, & Messrs. Robinson, London, 1797.

Sm 8vo. Lacks errata slip (as always). Blue crushed mor. *(Hannas)* £480 [≈ $921]
- See also J., S. (ed.).

Coles, Elisha
- An English Dictionary ... London: for Samuel Crouch, 1676. 1st edn. Last leaf sl creased. Contemp panelled calf, old reback, leading hinge weakening, spine rubbed & sl chipped at hd, scar on front bd. Wing C.5070.
(Jarndyce) £200 [≈ $383]
- An English Dictionary ... London: for Peter Parker, 1692. Contemp calf, rubbed & marked, split in hinge, spine ends reprd, new label. Wing C.5074.
(Jarndyce) £200 [≈ $383]
- An English Dictionary ... London: Peter Parker, 1701. 12mo. Ink scribbles on front endpapers. Contemp calf, rebacked, rear endpapers renewed.
(Jarndyce) £150 [≈ $287]

Collard, John
- A Epitome of Logic. By N. Dralloc. London: for the author, sold by J. Johnson, 1795. 1st edn. 12mo. [iii]-xvi,180 pp. Title spotted. Old half calf, worn, jnts cracked, backstrip defective. *(Clark)* £200 [≈ $383]

Collection of Epigrams ...
- See Oldys, William.

College of Physicians
- Medical Transactions published by the College of Physicians in London. Volume the First. London: 1785. xv,474 pp. Title sl marked. Later bds. *(Whitehart)* £60 [≈ $115]

Collier, Jane
- An Essay on the Art of Ingeniously Tormenting ... Second Edition, Corrected. London: A. Millar, 1757. 8vo. iii,234 pp. Frontis. Occas sl foxing. Contemp calf, scuffed, rebacked. Anon.
(Gough) £135 [≈ $259]

Collier, Jeremy
- A Defence of the Reasons for Restoring some Prayers and Directions of King Edward the Sixth's First Liturgy ... London: for John Morphew, 1718. Disbound. Anon.
(Waterfield's) £50 [≈ $95]
- A Defence of the Short View of the Profaneness and Immorality of the English Stage ... London: for S. Keble ..., 1699. 1st edn. 12mo. 1st gathering browned. Later calf.

Wing C.5248.
(Dramatis Personae) $200 [≈ £104]
- An Ecclesiastical History of Great Britain chiefly of England ... With a Brief Account of the Affairs of Religion in Ireland ... London: for Samuel Keble ..., 1708-14. 1st edn. 2 vols. Folio. Frontis. Contemp panelled calf, rebacked. *(Lloyd-Roberts)* £150 [≈ $287]
- An Essay upon Gaming, In a Dialogue between Callimachus and Dolomedes. London: for J. Morphew, 1713. 1st edn. Sm 4to. Half-title & final blank dusty. Top edge trimmed with loss of a few page numbers. Stitched as issued, lower & outer edges uncut. Boxed. *(Dramatis Personae)* $450 [≈ £234]
- The Great Historical, Geographical, Genealogical and Poetical Dictionary ... Second Edition revised ... London: 1701. 2 vols. [With] A Supplement ... Second Edition. London: 1727. [With] An Appendix. London: 1721. Together 4 vols in 3. Folio. Contemp polished & reversed calf.
(Lloyd-Roberts) £200 [≈ $383]
- Mr. Collier's Dissuasive from the Play-House; in a Letter to a Person of Quality. Occasioned by the late Calamity of the Tempest ... London: Richard Sare, 1704. 32 pp. Disbound, untrimmed.
(C.R. Johnson) £125 [≈ $239]
- A Short View of the Immorality and Profaneness of the English Stage ... Third Edition. London: for S. Keble ..., 1698. 8vo. Contemp panelled calf, mor label, some chipping at ft of spine. Wing C.5263.
(Waterfield's) £90 [≈ $172]
- A Short View of the Profaneness and Immorality of the English Stage, etc. With Several Defences of the Same ... London: G. Strahan, 1728. 437,3 advt pp. Foredge of 1st few ff sl defective. Disbound.
(C.R. Johnson) £75 [≈ $143]

Collier, Joel (ie John Laurens Bicknell)
- Musical Travels through England. By the late Joel Collier, Licentiate in Music. With an Appendix ... Third Edition. London: G. Kearsly ..., 1775. Disbound.
(C.R. Johnson) £110 [≈ $211]

Collins, Samuel
- Paradise Retriev'd: plainly and fully demonstrating the most beautiful, durable, and beneficial Method of managing and improving Fruit-Trees ... London: John Collins, Seedsman, 1717. 8vo. [2],v,[5],6-106 pp. 2 fldg plates. 1 tear reprd. Contemp calf, rebacked. *(Spelman)* £180 [≈ $345]

Collins, William
- Persian Eclogues. Written originally for the Entertainment of the Ladies of Tauris. And now first translated, &c. London: for J. Anon.
(Georges) £3,500 [≈ $6,719]

Colman, George, the elder
- The Spleen, or Islington Spa. London: for T. Becket, 1776. 1st edn. Fcap 4to. Sm hole in last leaf with loss of a few letters from advt. Later wraps. *(Ash) £100 [≈ $191]*
- T. Harris Dissected. London: T. Becket, 1768. 4to. 36 pp. Rec wraps.
(C.R. Johnson) £245 [≈ $470]

Columella ...
- See Graves, Richard.

Colville, Samuel
- The Whig's Supplication; Or, the Scots Hudibras. A Mock Poem in Two Parts. St. Andrews: James Morison, 1796. 12mo. 152 pp. Plates called for on title but none ever bound in this copy. Contemp qtr calf, rebacked. *(Gough) £30 [≈ $57]*

Comazzi, Giovanni Battista, Count
- The Morals of Princes: or, An Abstract of the most Remarkable Passages Contain'd in the History of all the Emperors who reign'd in Rome ... Done into English by William Hatchett ... London: Worrall, 1729. 1st English translation. 8vo. xvi,391,[i] pp. Frontis. Contemp calf, sl worn.
(Finch) £30 [≈ $57]
- The Morals of Princes ... With a Moral Reflection Drawn from each Quotation ... Done into English by William Hatchett ... London: for T. Worrall ..., 1729. 1st edn. 8vo. xvi, 391,[1 advt] pp. Subscribers. Frontis. Red & black title. Contemp calf, rebacked. *(Young's) £75 [≈ $143]*

Combe, William
- Additions to the Diaboliad: a Poem dedicated to the Worst Man in his Majesty's Dominions. By the Same Author. London: for G. Kearsley, "1677" [ie 1777]. 4to. Half-title. Contemp MS identifications. Disbound. Anon. *(Waterfield's) £125 [≈ $239]*
- The Auction; A Town Eclogue. By the Honourable Mr. ***. London: J. Bew, 1780. 4th edn. 4to. ix,[1],12-25 pp. Minor marg staining. Later wraps. Anon.
(Bookpress) $65 [≈ £33]
- The Diaboliad, A Poem. Dedicated to the

Worst Man in His Majesty's Dominions ... London: for G. Kearsly ..., 1677 [ie 1777]. 2nd edn. [iv],iv,24 pp. Disbound. Anon.
(Young's) £20 [≈ $38]
- The Diaboliad, A Poem. Dedicated to the Worst Man in His Majesty's Dominions ... London: for G. Kearsley ..., 1777. New edn. 4to. [iv],24 pp. Half-title. New bds. Anon.
(Young's) £45 [≈ $86]
- The First of April: or, The Triumphs of Folly: A Poem. Dedicated to a Celebrated Duchess ... London: for J. Bew, 1777. 1st edn. 4to. iv,38 pp. New bds. Anon.
(Young's) £45 [≈ $86]
- The First of April: or, The Triumphs of Folly: A Poem. Dedicated to a Celebrated Duchess. By the Author of the Diaboliad. Dublin: J. Mehain, 1777. 1st Dublin edn. 8vo. 36 pp. Disbound. Anon.
(Young's) £95 [≈ $182]
- Letters supposed to have been written by Yorick and Eliza. London: for J. Bew, 1779. 1st edn. 2 vols. [ii],176; [ii],180 pp. Possibly lacks half-titles. Polished calf, gilt spines, contrasting labels, hd of 1 spine v sl chipped. Anon. *(Burmester) £180 [≈ $345]*
- The Royal Interview: a Fragment. London: Logographic Press, 1789. 61,1 advt pp. Disbound. Anon. *(C.R. Johnson) £45 [≈ $86]*

Comber, Thomas
- Friendly and Seasonable Advice to the Roman Catholics of England. The Third Edition enlarg'd ... By a Charitable Hand. London: for Henry Brome, 1677. 12mo. [xvi],152,4 advt pp. Imprimatur leaf. Red & black title. Orig calf, label sl damaged. Wing C.5468. Anon. *(Vanbrugh) £155 [≈ $297]*
- The Occasional Offices of Matrimony, Visitation of the Sick, Burial of the Dead ... explained ... London: M.C. for Brome & Clavel, 1679. xiv,580 pp. Foxed. Leather, damaged, rebacked, crnrs bumped.
(Gage) £30 [≈ $57]

Combrune, Michael
- An Essay on Brewing. With a View of Establishing the Principles of the Art. London: Dodsley, 1758. 214 pp. Half-title, vignette title. Contemp calf, red label. Anon.
(C.R. Johnson) £280 [≈ $537]

Comines, Philippe de, Seigneur d'Argenton
- The Historie of Philip De Commines Knight, Lord of Argenton. London: Hatfield for

Norton, 1601. 2nd edn. Sm folio. [xvi],364 pp. W'cut title & tables. Contemp sheep. STC 5603. *(Vanbrugh)* **£295 [≈ $566]**

- The Historie of Philip De Commines Knight, Lord of Argenton. London: [Eliot's Court Press,] for Iohn Bill, 1614. 3rd edn of Danett's transl. Folio. [viii],366 pp. Title foredge marg sl frayed, 2 ff singed in marg. Contemp calf, rebacked, crnrs worn. STC.5604. *(Finch)* **£150 [≈ $287]**

The Companion to the Playhouse ...
- See Baker, David Erskine, et al.

A Comparative View ...
- A Comparative View of the State and Faculties of Man ... see Gregory, John.

Compleat ...
- A Compleat Collection of Devotions ... see Deacon, Thomas.
- A Compleat History of Europe ... see Jones, David.
- The Compleat Justice: being an exact and compendious Collection out of such as have treated of the Peace ... Now amplified ... London: for John Streater, 1667. 3rd recorded edn. 430 pp. V sl traces of damp in some ff. Contemp vellum. Wing C.5645. *(C.R. Johnson)* **£385 [≈ $739]**
- The Compleat Letter Writer: or, New and Polite English Secretary ... The Third Edition improved. London: Crowder & Woodgate, 1756. 12mo. Rebound in half calf. *(Jarndyce)* **£75 [≈ $143]**
- The Compleat Parish-Officer ... see Jacob, Giles.

Complete ...
- A Complete Collection of State-Trials, and Proceedings for High- Treason, and other Crimes ... from the Reign of King Richard II ... Second Edition, with great Additions. London: for J. Walthoe ..., 1730. 6 vols. Folio. Contemp calf, worn, jnts cracked (1 broken). *(Waterfield's)* **£300 [≈ $575]**
- The Complete English Dictionary ... By a Lover of Good English and Common Sense ... see Wesley, John.
- The Complete English Farmer ... see Henry, David.
- The Complete Family-Piece: and, Country Gentleman, and Farmer's Best Guide ... Physick and Surgery; Cookery ... Hunting ... Fishing ... Gardens ... Improving of Land ...

London: J. Roberts, 1736. 1st edn. 12mo. Contemp calf, hinges splitting. *(Jarndyce)* **£380 [≈ $729]**

- The Complete Farmer: or, a General Dictionary of Husbandry, in all its Branches ... By a Society of Gentlemen. Fourth Edition, considerable improved ... London: Longman, [1793]. Folio. Engvd frontis, 34 plates. Final leaf creased. Contemp mor, backstrip relaid. *(Spelman)* **£200 [≈ $383]**
- The Complete Grazier: or, Gentleman and Farmer's Directory ... London: for J. Almon, 1767. 1st edn. 12mo. [iii]-xii,252,[ii] pp. Intl advt leaf bound in at end. 1 w'cut in text. Contemp calf, mor label, extremities worn, jnts cracked but firm. *(Finch)* **£130 [≈ $249]**

Conciliatory Address ...
- Conciliatory Address to the People of Great Britain and of the Colonies, on the Present Important Crisis. London: for J. Wilkie, 1775. Half-title, 56 pp. Disbound. *(C.R. Johnson)* **£220 [≈ $422]**

Concise ...
- A Concise and Accurate Description of the University, Town, and County of Cambridge ... Cambridge: [1790]. 12mo. A few contemp marg ink annotations. New leather spine, contemp leather crnrs & mrbld bds. *(Whitehart)* **£48 [≈ $92]**

Confucius
- The Morals of Confucius ... Translated by Father Prospero Intorcetta. London: for Randal Taylor, 1691. 1st edn. 12mo. 183 pp. Orig calf, sl rubbed, worn spot. *(Chapel Hill)* **$450 [≈ £234]**

Congreve, William
- Amendments of Mr. Collier's False and Imperfect Citations ... London: Tonson, 1698. 1st edn. Issue with "Supposition" crrctly ptd p 44. 8vo. Top third of half-title lacking, hd of title trimmed. Contemp calf, extremities worn. Wing C.5844. Anon. *(Dramatis Personae)* **$125 [≈ £65]**
- The Works. London: for the editor, 1778. 2 vols. 8vo. Frontis to each play (some offsetting from plates). Later half calf. *(Dramatis Personae)* **$95 [≈ £49]**

Consett, Matthew
- A Tour through Sweden, Swedish-Lapland, Finland and Denmark ... London: J. Johnson, 1789. 1st edn. 4to. [xvi],157 pp. 8 copper engvs by Thomas Bewick. Orig bds,

extremities rubbed, rebacked to style.
(Bromer) **$1,200 [≈ £625]**

Considerations ...
- Considerations on the Propriety of Imposing Taxes in the British Colonies ... see Dulaney, Daniel.
- Considerations upon a Printed Sheet ... see L'Estrange, Sir Roger.
- Considerations upon the American Enquiry ... see Dallas, Robert.

The Consolidator ...
- See Defoe, Daniel.

The Contest ...
- The Contest. A Poem. London: for J. Almon, 1764. 4to. 20 pp. 2 letters blocked out in ink. Disbound.   *(C.R. Johnson)* **£85 [≈ $163]**

Conti, Armand de Bourbon, Prince de
- The Works of the most Illustrious and Pious Armand de Bourbon, Prince of Conti ... Account of His Life ... added some other Pieces ... London: for W. Bray, 1711. 1st edn. 8vo. Port. Contemp calf, rebacked.
(Dramatis Personae) **$175 [≈ £91]**

Conybeare, John
- Calumny Refuted: or, an Answer to the Personal Slanders published by Dr. Richard Newton in his Letter to Dr. Holmes ... London: Knapton, 1735. Sewn as issued.
(Waterfield's) **£40 [≈ $76]**

Cook, Captain James & King, James
- A Voyage to the Pacific Ocean. London: Stockdale, Scatcherd & Whitaker ..., 1784. 1st 8vo edn. 4 vols. demy 8vo. Fldg maps, num plates (2 supplied from another copy). Contemp tree calf, rebacked, gilt spines.
(Ash) **£1,000 [≈ $1,919]**

Cook, Moses
- The Manner of Raising, Ordering, and Improving Forest-Trees ... Second Edition, very much Corrected. London: for Daniel Browne ..., 1717. 8vo. [iii]-xix,[i],276 pp. Frontis, 4 fldg plates (1 sl defective). Sl damp stain throughout. Contemp calf, sl worn.
(Finch) **£55 [≈ $105]**
- The Manner of Raising, Ordering, and Improving Forest-Trees ... Second Edition, very much Corrected. London: 1717. 8vo. xix, [i],276 pp, inc frontis. 4 fldg diags. Contemp Cambridge style calf, rebacked,

crnrs worn.   *(Bow Windows)* **£205 [≈ $393]**

Cooke, Edward
- A Voyage to the South Sea and Around the World performed in the Years 1708-11 by the Ships "Duke" and "Duchess" of Bristol. London: 1712. 2 vols. 8vo. [xxii],432, [10]; xxiv, 328, [8] pp. 2 charts, 20 plates in vol 1, lacks vol 2 plates. Mod qtr calf.
(Lewis) **£320 [≈ $614]**

Cooke, Thomas
- The Elements of Dramatic Criticism ... London: G. Kearsley, 1775. Half-title, 216 pp. Contemp calf, sl worn.
(C.R. Johnson) **£225 [≈ $431]**
- The Letters of Atticus. As Printed in the London Journal, in the Years 1729 and 1730, on Various Subjects ... London: J. Crichley, 1731. 1st edn. 8vo. 71 pp. Title sl soiled. Stitched as issued. Anon.
(Young's) **£70 [≈ $134]**
- The Universal Letter-Writer ... London: for Osborne & Griffin, & H. Mozley, Gainsborough, 1788. 240 pp. Frontis. Contemp sheep, rebacked.
(C.R. Johnson) **£125 [≈ $239]**

Cooke, William, Rector of Oldbury
- An Enquiry into the Patriarchal and Druidical Religion ... Second Edition, with additions. London: Lockyer Davis, 1755. Sm 4to. Title (loose),ix,[i],75 pp. 5 plates (3 fldg). Mod half calf.
(Frew Mackenzie) **£100 [≈ $191]**

Cooke, William, barrister
- The Life of Samuel Johnson, LL.D ... Dublin: R. Montcrieffe ..., 1785. Half-title, 240 pp. Contemp calf, gilt spine.
(C.R. Johnson) **£380 [≈ $729]**

Cooper, Revd. Mr.
- A New History of England ... London: for E. Newbery, 1791. 8th edn, with addtns. Frontis, 5 plates. Calf backed mrbld bds.
(Stewart) **£40 [≈ $76]**

Cooper, John Gilbert
- The Life of Socrates. Collected from the Memorabilia of Xenophon and the Dialogues of Plato ... Third Edition. London: Dodsley, 1750. 8vo. 180 pp. Frontis, 5 engvd head-pieces. Contemp calf, rubbed, spine extremities sl chipped.
(Karmiole) **$125 [≈ £65]**

- Poems on several Subjects ... By the Author of the Life of Socrates. London: Dodsley, 1764. 1st edn. 12mo. [iv],140 pp. Fldg frontis. End ff sl browned. Contemp calf. Anon. *(Finch)* £165 [≃ $316]

Copywell, J. (pseudonym)
- The Shrubs of Parnassus ... see Woty, William.

Cordiner, Charles
- Antiquities and Scenery of the North of Scotland, in a Series of Letters to Thomas Pennant, Esq. London: 1780. 1st edn. 4to. 173,[1] pp. Illust title, 21 plates. Orig half calf, sl worn. *(Chapel Hill)* $200 [≃ £104]

Cornaro, Luigi (Lewis)
- Discourses on a Sober and Temperate Life. London: Benjamin White, 1768. 8vo. 281 pp. Contemp calf, elab gilt spine, split upper hinge. *(Hemlock)* $125 [≃ £65]
- The Temperate Man, or the Way of Preserving Life and Health. London: John Starkey, 1678. 12mo. [xxxvi],168 pp. Contemp sheep. Anon.
(Bookpress) $450 [≃ £234]

Cornwallis, Charles
- The Life and Death of Our Late Most Incomparable and Heroique Prince, Henry, Prince of Wales ... London: Nathanael Butter, 1641. 1st edn. Sm 8vo. [iv],106 pp. Mod mor by Riviere. Wing C.6330.
(Bookpress) $300 [≃ £156]

Corrie, Edgar
- Letters on the Subject of the Scotch Distillery Laws. Liverpool: J. McCreery, 1796. Half-title, 23 pp. Rec wraps. Author's pres inscrptn. *(C.R. Johnson)* £165 [≃ $316]

Coryate, Thomas
- Thomas Coriate Traueller for the English VVits: Greeting. From the Court of the Great Mogvl ... London: Iaggard & Featherston, "1616" [type facsimile ca 1760]. 4to. [ii],56 pp. W'cut on title & in text. Disbound.
(Vanbrugh) £225 [≃ $431]

Cosin, John
- A Scholastic History of the Canon of the Holy Scriptures ... London: E. Tyler & R. Holt for Robert Pawlett, 1683. 4to. [36],224, 48 pp. Old panelled calf, worn. Wing C.6363.
(Humber) £45 [≃ $86]

Cotes, R.
- Hydrostatical and Pneumatical Lectures ... Published from the Author's Original Manuscript, with Notes by Robert Smith. London: 1775. 3rd edn. 8vo. [xvi],288,[8] pp. Fldg plates. Occas sl foxing. Half mor gilt, uncut. *(Whitehart)* £150 [≃ $287]

Cotton, John
- The Churches Resurrection, or the Opening of the First and Sixth Verses of the 20th Chap. of the Revelation. London: Henry Overton, 1642. Sm 4to. 30 pp. Later wraps, soiled. Wing C.6419. *(Reese)* $400 [≃ £208]

Cotton, Nathaniel
- Visions in Verse, for the Entertainment and Instruction of Younger Minds ... London: Dodsley, 1776. 9th edn. 12mo. 141,[2] pp. Frontis. Early calf, gilt spine, red label, front jnt partially worn. Anon. *(Young's)* £28 [≃ $53]
- Visions in Verse, for the Entertainment and Instruction of Younger Minds. A New Edition. London: Joseph Wenman, 1781. 12mo. 79,[i] pp, 2 advt ff. Frontis. Minor soiling. Contemp calf. *(Spelman)* £25 [≃ $47]

Cotton, Sir Robert Bruce
- The Forme of Government of the Kingdome of England ... London: for Tho. Bankes, 1642. 1st edn. Sm 4to. 19,[1 blank] pp. Old calf, rebacked, new endpapers. Wing C.6492. Anon. *(Bow Windows)* £150 [≃ $287]
- Seriovs Considerations for repressing of the Increase of Jesvites, Priests, and Papists, without shedding of blood. Written by Sir R.C. ... [London]: 1641. 1st edn. 4to. [ii],52 pp. 1st leaf blank. Some sgntrs & catchwords shaved. Disbound. Wing C.6497.
(Vanbrugh) £175 [≃ $335]

Courtenay, John
- Philosophical Reflections on the late Revolution in France, and the Conduct of the Dissenters in England; in a Letter to the Rev. Dr. Priestley. London: T. Becket, 1790. Half-title, 94 pp. Stabbed pamphlet as issued, uncut. *(C.R. Johnson)* £90 [≃ $172]

Courtilz de Sandras, Gatien de (supposed author)
- The Memoirs of the Marquess de Langallerie ... The Second Edition. Translated from the French ... London: J. Round, N. Cliff, 1710. 8vo. [xvi],416 pp. Contemp calf, rebacked, spine ends worn, jnts cracked.
(Burmester) £225 [≃ $431]

Coventry, Francis

- The History of Pompey the Little. Or, the Life and Adventures of a Lap-Dog. Dublin: George Faulkner, 1751. 1st Dublin edn. 12mo. vii,176 pp. Port frontis (frayed at edges, strengthened at foredge). Contemp calf rebacked. Anon. *(Sotheran's)* **£228** [≈ **$437**]

Cowell, John

- The Curious and Profitable Gardener ... London: Weaver Bickerton, 1730. 1st edn. 8vo. iv, [iv],126, [ii],67,[1] pp. Frontis, fldg plate. Contemp sheep, worn.
  (Bookpress) **$650** [≈ **£338**]

Cowley, Abraham

- Poems: viz. 1. Miscellanies ... IV. Davideis ... London: for Humphrey Moseley, 1656. Folio. Sm repr to title. Mod red pigskin to a cottage roof design, black leather inlays. Wing C.6682.   *(Waterfield's)* **£425** [≈ **$815**]
- Select Works; With a Preface and Notes by the Editor [Richard Hurd]. The Third Edition. London: Cadell, 1773. 3 vols. 8vo. Title vignettes. Contemp calf, 1 backstrip relaid.   *(Bickersteth)* **£55** [≈ **$105**]
- The Works ... London: J.M. for Henry Herringman, 1668. 1st coll edn. Sm folio. Port frontis (sl defective). Lacks final blank. 2 ff reprd. Final text leaf creased. Contemp panelled calf. Wing C.6649.
  (Stewart) **£75** [≈ **$143**]
- The Works ... Third Edition. London: J.M. for Henry herringman, 1672. Folio. Port. Sl marg worm. Contemp speckled calf, crnrs & spine ends worn, splits in 1 hinge. Wing C.6651.   *(Jarndyce)* **£90** [≈ **$172**]
- The Works ... London: J.M. for Henry Herringman ..., 1678. 5th edn. Folio. xlii, 42,80, 70,154,24,148 pp. Port frontis. Old calf, sometime rebacked, sl worn. Wing C.6653.   *(Young's)* **£85** [≈ **$163**]
- The Works ... The Tenth Edition. [With] The Third and Last Volume of the Works. London: Tonson, 1707, & Charles Harper, 1708. 3 vols. 8vo. 27 engvd ills. Occas browning. Contemp calf.
  (Frew Mackenzie) **£135** [≈ **$259**]

Cowley, Hannah

- The Maid of Aragon. A Tale. Part 1 [all published in quarto]. London: T. Spilsbury, 1780. 4to. Some spotting of title. New bds.
  (C.R. Johnson) **£95** [≈ **$182**]

Cowper, John

- An Essay proving that Inclosing Commons, and Common-field-lands, is contrary to the Interest of the Nation ... London: E. Nutt, 1732. Half-title, 24 pp, advt leaf. Dusty at ends. Sewn as issued, uncut. Anon.
  (C.R. Johnson) **£225** [≈ **$431**]

Cowper, Maria Frances Cecilia

- Original Poems, On Various Occasions. By a Lady. Revised by William Cowper ... London: Deighton, Mathews, Faulder, 1792. 1st edn. Sm 8vo. viii,115 pp. Contemp tree calf gilt, mor label, mrbld edges, jnts sl rubbed. Anon.   *(Finch)* **£240** [≈ **$460**]

Cowper, William

- Poems. The Third Edition. London: for J. Johnson, 1787. 2 vols. 8vo. Orig calf, gilt spines, rubbed, crnrs sl worn, sl wear to spines & jnts.   *(Bickersteth)* **£30** [≈ **$57**]
- Poems. In Two Volumes. The Fourth Edition. Dublin: John Jones, 1787. 2 vols. 12mo. Final advt leaf vol 2. 2 gatherings sl proud. Contemp calf, dble red & olive labels.
  (Sanders) **£90** [≈ **$172**]
- Poems ... The Fourth Edition. London: for J. Johnson, 1788. 2 vols. 8vo. Contemp tree calf gilt, dble mor labels, crnrs worn, upper hinges broken but cvrs secure.
  (Claude Cox) **£30** [≈ **$57**]
- Poems. London: for J. Johnson, 1788. 4th edn. 2 vols. 8vo. 367; 359 pp. Contemp speckled calf, jnts worn, labels chipped.
  (Young's) **£28** [≈ **$53**]
- Poems. In Two Volumes. The Sixth Edition. London: J. Johnson, 1794/5. 2 vols. 8vo. xii, 367; [8],389,[3 advt & blank] pp. Contemp tree calf, elab gilt spines, contrasting labels, lemon edges.   *(Claude Cox)* **£150** [≈ **$287**]

Coxe, William

- Sketches of the Natural, Civil, and Political State of Swisserland; in a Series of Letters to William Melmoth. London: Dodsley, 1779. 1st edn. 8vo. viii,532,[1] pp. Old mrbld bds, calf crnrs, rebacked in cloth.
  (Bickersteth) **£200** [≈ **$383**]
- Sketches of the Natural, Civil, and Political State of Swisserland; in a Series of Letters to William Melmoth. London: Dodsley, 1779. 1st edn. Final leaf of Postscript. Contemp calf, later rebacked, new endpapers.
  (Jarndyce) **£70** [≈ **$134**]
- Sketches of the Natural, Civil, and Political State of Swisserland; in a Series of Letters to

William Melmoth, Esq. Dublin: George Bonham, 1779. 1st Dublin edn. 8vo. viii,478,[1] pp. Orig tree calf, mor label, jnts cracked but firm. *(Bickersteth)* **£110** [≈ **$211**]

Crabbe, George
- The Village: a Poem. London: Dodsley, 1783. 1st edn. 4to. [2],38 pp. Title guarded & sl soiled. Partly deleted inscrptns. Mod qtr calf. *(Claude Cox)* **£160** [≈ **$307**]
- The Village: a Poem. In Two Books. London: Dodsley, 1783. 4to. Half mor & bds. *(C.R. Johnson)* **£300** [≈ **$575**]

Cradock, Samuel
- The Harmony of the Four Evangelists, and their Text Methodiz'd ... London: for Samuel Thompson ..., 1668. 1st edn. Folio. [xxxviii], 287,[1],[1 errata] pp. Rec calf. Wing C.6748. *(Young's)* **£75** [≈ **$143**]

Cradock, Z.
- A Sermon Preached before the King, February 10th 1677/78 ... London: for Richard Royston ..., 1678. 2nd edn. 4to. 43 pp. Disbound. Wing C.6766. *(Young's)* **£40** [≈ **$76**]

Cramer, Johann Andreas
- Elements of the Art of Assaying Metals ... Translated from the Latin ... With an Appendix ... London: Woodward, Davis, 1741. 1st edn in English. 8vo. [xii],208, 201-470, [8] pp. 6 fldg plates. Sl waterstain. 19th c half calf, rubbed. *(Burmester)* **£250** [≈ **$479**]

Cranmer, Thomas
- An Avnsvvere ... vnto a craftie and Sophisticall cauillation, deuised by Stephen Gardiner ... Reuised and corrected ... London: Iohn Daye, 1580. 2nd edn, rvsd. Folio. [xxviii],428,[iv] pp. 2 fldg w'cut plates. Sl marks. New bds. STC.5992. *(Sotheran's)* **£598** [≈ **$1,148**]

Crantz, David
- The History of Greenland ... Translated from the High-Dutch ... London: 1767. 1st edn. 2 vols. 8vo. Fldg map, 8 plates. Orig calf, Victorian reback. *(Vanbrugh)* **£195** [≈ **$374**]

Craufurd, Quintin
- Sketches chiefly relating to the History ... of the Hindoos. London: Cadell, 1790. 1st edn. Demy 8vo. [viii],422,[2] pp, irregular collation but complete. Fldg plate. Sl wear & tear. Mod qtr calf gilt. Anon.

(Ash) **£200** [≈ **$383**]

Crawford, William
- A History of Ireland from the Earliest Period to the Present Time ... Strabane: John Bellew, 1783. 2 vols. 8vo. 350; 387 pp. Contemp calf. *(Emerald Isle)* **£220** [≈ **$422**]

Cressy, Hugh Paulinus or Serenus
- The Church-History of Brittany, from the Beginning of Christianity to the Norman Conquest ... By R.F.S. [sic] Cressy ... [Rouen]: printed in the year 1668. 1st edn. Lge folio. [xxii],1002,[17] pp. Orig sheep, gilt spine (faded), spine ends sl damaged. Wing C.6890. *(Vanbrugh)* **£295** [≈ **$566**]

Crisp, Stephen
- A Memorable Account of the Christian Experiences, Gospel Labours, Travels and Sufferings of that Ancient Servant of Christ Stephen Crisp ... London: T. Sowle, 1694. 1st edn. 4to. xxx,544 pp. Contemp calf, sometime rebacked. Wing C.6921. *(Young's)* **£75** [≈ **$143**]

Critical Observations ...
- Critical Observations on the Buildings and Improvements of London ... see Stuart, James.

Croft, Herbert
- The Abbey of Kilkhampton; or, Monumental Records for the Year 1980. London: G. Kearsley, 1780. 7th edn part 1, 1st edn part 2. 4to. 141 pp. 2 ff reprd. Rec qtr calf. *(Spelman)* **£60** [≈ **$115**]

Croft, Herbert
- The Legacy of ... Herbert Lord Bishop of Hereford to his Diocese ... London: for Charles Harper, 1679. Imprimatur leaf. Disbound. Wing C.6966. *(Waterfield's)* **£40** [≈ **$76**]
- A Short Discourse concerning the Reading His Majesties late Declaration in the Churches. London: for Charles Harper, Randal Taylor, 1688. 4to. 15 pp. Pencil marks. Disbound. Wing C.6976. *(Jarndyce)* **£30** [≈ **$57**]
- A Short Narrative of the Discovery of a College of Jesuits, at a Place called Come, in the County of Hereford ... London: T.N. for Charles Harper, 1679. 1st edn. Sm 4to. [ii], 18 pp. Lacks licence leaf & final blank. Sl browned. Rec half calf. Wing C.6977. Anon. *(Georges)* **£65** [≈ **$124**]

Croker, Richard
- Travels through Several Provinces of Spain and Portugal &c. London: for the author, 1799. Minor spotting on early ff. Mod half calf.   *(Waterfield's)* **£135 [≈ $259]**

Croker, Temple Henry
- Experimental Magnetism, or the Truth of Mr. Mason's Discoveries ... Proved and Ascertained. London: for J. Coote, 1761. Only edn. 8vo. Half-title, title, iii-x,72 pp. Frontis, fldg plate. Rec wraps.
        (Gaskell) **£325 [≈ $623]**

Crook, John
- The Design of Christianity ... Prefixed, a Short Account of his Life written by himself. London: James Phillips, 1791. 8vo. End ff spotted. Contemp calf. *(Stewart)* **£35 [≈ $67]**

Crouch, William
- Posthuma Christiana; or, a Collection of some Papers ... London: J. Sowle, 1712. 1st edn. Sm 8vo. 34,[2],xii,224 pp. Occas sl foxing. Contemp sheep.   *(Fenning)* **£45 [≈ $86]**

Crowe, William
- Lewesdon Hill. A Poem. Oxford: Clarendon Press, 1788. 4to. New bds. Anon.
        (C.R. Johnson) **£125 [≈ $239]**

Crowne, John
- Darius, King of Persia. A Tragedy ... London: for R. Bentley, 1688. 1st edn. Sm 4to. Title shaved at foredge. Some browning. Rec wraps. *(Dramatis Personae)* **$250 [≈ £130]**
- The Misery of Civil-War. A Tragedy ... London: Bentley & Magnes, 1680. 1st edn. 4to. [iv],71,[i] pp. Browned, minor staining. Lib stamp on title verso. Later wraps (frayed). Wing C.7395.   *(Clark)* **£110 [≈ $211]**

Crunden, John
- Convenient and Ornamental Architecture, Consisting of Original Designs ... New Edition. London: for I. Taylor, 1785. 4to. viii, 26 pp. 70 plates. Contemp calf, backstrip relaid.   *(Bookpress)* **$1,350 [≈ £703]**

Cullen, William
- First Lines of the Practice of Physic ... New York: Samuel Campbell, 1793. 2 vols. 8vo. 438,[2]; vi,(9)-410,21 pp. Contemp calf.
        (Bookpress) **$225 [≈ £117]**
- A Treatise on the Materia Medica. Dublin: Luke White, 1789. 2 vols. 8vo. xxiii,351; viii,

511 pp. Contemp calf, dull, hinges cracked but holding. Amer inscrptn dated 1800.
        (Hemlock) **$700 [≈ £364]**

Culpeper, Nicholas
- Culpeper's English Physician and Complete Herbal ... Illustrated with Notes ... by E. Sibly ... London: for the author ..., [1793]. 4to. xvi,396,256 pp. Port, 29 hand cold (v occas sl spotting) & 13 sepia (damp marked) plates. Contemp calf, rebacked.
        (Gough) **£325 [≈ $623]**
- The English Physician Enlarged, with 369 Medicines made of English Herbs. London: 1788. 12mo. xii,371 pp. Antique style calf.
        (Henly) **£90 [≈ $172]**
- Pharmacopoeia Londinensis: or the London Dispensatory. London: for Peter Cole, 1653. 1st edn, 4th imp. Tall 4to. [x],325,[15] pp. Port frontis, 2 title-pages (worn, soiled, laid down). Lacks S2. Rec polished calf gilt.
        (Hollett) **£650 [≈ $1,247]**
- Pharmacopoeia Londinensis: or the London Dispensatory ... London: Peter Cole, 1655. [With] A Key to Galen's Method of Physick. London: Peter Cole, 1654. 6th edn. 8vo. [xxiv], 294 (paginated 1-106,106, 191-377), [32] pp. Port frontis. Sl used. Contemp sheep, rebacked. Wing C.7528.
        (Sotheran's) **£1,250 [≈ $2,399]**

Cumberland, Richard, Bishop of Peterborough
- Origines Gentium Antiquissimae; or, Attempts for discovering the Times of the first Planting of Nations ... London: for R. Wilkin, 1724. 1st edn. 8vo. xxxiii,[vii], 480, [viii] pp. Contemp calf, rebacked, crnrs sl worn.   *(Clark)* **£85 [≈ $163]**

Cumberland, Richard
- The Brothers, a Comedy. London: for W. Griffin, 1770. 1st edn. Engvd title. Mod wraps.   *(Waterfield's)* **£20 [≈ $38]**
- The Observer. Dublin: for L. White, P. Byrne ..., 1785. 1st Dublin edn. 12mo. [iv], 304 pp. Half-title. Contemp calf, sl worm damage along jnts. Anon.
        (Burmester) **£45 [≈ $86]**
- Odes. Dublin: for S. Price ..., 1776. 1st Irish edn. 12mo. 30,[2 blank] pp. Rec wraps.
        (Fenning) **£55 [≈ $105]**
- The West Indian: A Comedy ... London: for W. Griffin, 1771. New edn. 8vo. [vi],77,[2] pp. Title vignette. Disbound. Anon.
        (Young's) **£24 [≈ $46]**

Cunningham, John
- Poems Chiefly Pastoral. London: for the author, 1766. 1st edn. 8vo. Subscribers. Frontis. Contemp calf, rebacked.
(Waterfield's) **£225 [≈ $431]**
- Poems, Chiefly Pastoral ... Newcastle: by T. Slack, for the author ..., 1766. 1st edn (?). 8vo. xvi,240 pp. Lacks frontis (?). Old calf, rebacked.
(Young's) **£60 [≈ $115]**
- Poems, Chiefly Pastoral ... London: for the author, & sold by J. Dodsley, J. Almon ... & T. Slack, in Newcastle, 1766. 1st coll edn, reissue. 12 pp subscribers. Frontis. Contemp calf, orig backstrip relaid.
(Jarndyce) **£85 [≈ $163]**
- Poems, Chiefly Pastoral ... Second Edition. With the Addition of several Pastorals, and other Pieces. Newcastle: by T. Slack ..., 1771. 8vo. iv,259 pp. Frontis (just trimmed). Contemp sheep, mor label, yellow edges, some sl stripping of sides.
(Finch) **£130 [≈ $249]**
- Poems, Chiefly Pastoral. Newcastle: by T. Slack ..., 1771. 2nd edn. 8vo. iv,259 pp. Frontis. Contemp calf gilt, sl worn.
(Young's) **£85 [≈ $163]**

Cunningham, Timothy
- A New Treatise on the Laws concerning Tithes ... Second Edition. London: for W. Griffin ..., 1766. 8vo. Blank, half-title, title, 298 pp, 4 ff, 2 blanks. Sm piece torn from hd of title. Contemp calf, v sl rubbed. Anon.
(Meyer Boswell) **$225 [≈ £117]**

Curious ...
- Curious Enquiries. Being six Brief Discourses ... London: Randal Taylor, 1688. Only edn. 4to. [vi],24 pp. BM duplicate stamp on title verso. Outer ff dusty. Disbound, stitching broken. Wing C.7678.
(Clark) **£200 [≈ $383]**
- A Curious Hieroglyphick Bible; or Select Passages in the Old and New Testaments, represented with Emblematical Figures, for the Amusement of Youth. Seventh Edition. London: T. Hodgson, 1789. 12mo. [6],136 pp. Frontis, num ills. Orig ptd bds, v rubbed, rebacked.
(Spelman) **£65 [≈ $124]**

Cursory Remarks on Tragedy ...
- See Richardson, William.

D'Urfey, Thomas
- New Opera's, with Comical Stories and Poems, on several Occasions, never before printed. London: William Chetwood, 1721. 1st edn. 8vo. [x],88,[ii], 89-349, 348-382 pp. 8 parts with sep titles. Occas browning. Contemp calf, sl worn, jnts cracked.
(Clark) **£160 [≈ $307]**

Da Costa, Emanuel Mendes
- Elements of Conchology; or, an Introduction to the Knowledge of Shells. London: Benjamin White, 1776. 1st edn. vi, 318, [i errata,i advt] pp. 7 fldg hand cold plates. Occas v sl spotting. 19th c green half calf.
(Gough) **£225 [≈ $431]**
- A Natural History of Fossils. Volume 1 Part 1. London: 1757. All published. 4to. viii,294 pp. Plate. Old blind stamp on title, occas sl foxing. New half calf, antique style.
(Wheldon & Wesley) **£200 [≈ $383]**

Daille, John
- A Treatise Concerning the Right Use of the Fathers in the Decisions of the Controversies that are this Day in Religion. London: John Martin, 1651. 4to. [14],163,196 pp. Contemp diced calf, gilt spine. Wing D.118.
(Humber) **£88 [≈ $168]**

Dallas, Robert
- Considerations Upon the American Enquiry. London: 1779. 55 pp. Half-title. Lib stamp. Occas sl foxing. Mod cloth. Anon.
(Reese) **$250 [≈ £130]**

Dallaway, James
- Constantinople Ancient and Modern, with Excursions to the Shores and Islands of the Archipelago and the Troad. London: Bensley for Cadell & Davies, 1797. 1st edn. 4to. [ii], xi,[i], 415,[ix] pp. Engvd title, 9 plates, map. Sl used. Contemp half calf, backstrip relaid.
(Clark) **£360 [≈ $691]**

Dalrymple, David
- Annals of Scotland ... Edinburgh: Balfour & Smellie, for J. Murray, London, 1776-79. 1st edn. 2 vols. 4to. [viii],401; [vi],397 pp. Half-titles. Sl later diced russia, gilt spines, jnts of vol 1 reprd. Currer b'plate.
(Burmester) **£350 [≈ $671]**

Dalton, Michael
- Officium Vicecomitum. The Office and Authoritie of Sherifs ... London: Companie of Stationers, 1623. 1st edn. Folio. V sl foxing & browning. Contemp reversed calf, minor reprs. STC 6212.
(Meyer Boswell) **$1,000 [≈ £520]**

Danby, Earl of, later Duke of Leeds
- Copies of some Letters Written to and from The Earl of Danby (now Duke of Leeds) in the Years 1676, 1677, and 1678. London: for John Nicholson ..., 1710. 1st edn. 8vo. [xv],364,4 advt pp. Lacks 1st blank or half-title. Title marg reprd. Sl browned. Rec calf.
(Young's) **£60 [≈ $115]**

Danet, Pierre
- A Complete Dictionary of the Greek and Roman Antiquities ... Made English ... London: 1700. 1st edn in English. 4to. Approbation leaf before title, final advt leaf. 4 fldg maps. Contemp calf, gilt spine, extremities worn, jnts cracked but firm. Wing D.171.   *(Clark)* **£75 [≈ $143]**

Dangerous Connections ...
- See Laclos, P.A.F. Choderlos de.

Darby, Charles
- Bacchanalia: or a Description of a Drunken Club. A Poem. London: for Robert Boulter, 1680. 1st edn. Folio. [ii],14 pp. Sl browned. 19th c half calf, rebacked. Wing D.243. Anon.   *(Burmester)* **£150 [≈ $287]**

Darrell, William
- The Gentleman Instructed, in the Conduct of a Virtuous and Happy Life. In Three Parts ... added, A Word to the Ladies ... The Fifth Edition. London: J. Heptinstall for E. Smith ..., 1713. Contemp calf, hinges cracking, sm chip hd of spine. Anon.
(Jarndyce) **£130 [≈ $249]**
- The Gentleman Instructed, in the Conduct of a Virtuous and Happy Life. To which is added, A Word to the Ladies ... Sixth Edition. London: J. Heptinstall, 1716. 8vo. [22], 584,[16 advt] pp. Contemp calf, rebacked.
(Spelman) **£110 [≈ $211]**
- See also Hickes, George.

Darwin, Erasmus
- A Plan for the Conduct of Female Education, in Boarding Schools. Derby: for J. Drewry ... & J. Johnson (London), 1797. 1st edn. 4to. Half-title. frontis (sl foxed). Contemp calf, rebacked to style. *(Ximenes)* **$1,750 [≈ £911]**

Darwin, R.W.
- Principia Botanica: or, a Concise and Easy Introduction to the Sexual Botany of Linnaeus. Newark: 1787. 1st edn. 8vo. vii, 280, [1] pp. Contemp calf, lower jnt

beginning to crack but sound.
(Wheldon & Wesley) **£180 [≈ $345]**

Daubeny, Charles
- The Fall of Papal Rome: Recommended to the Consideration of England: In a Discourse on Isaiah xlvi,9,10 ... London: Cadell ..., 1798. 1st edn. 8vo. Half-title. Disbound.
(Young's) **£28 [≈ $53]**

Dauncey, John
- A Compendious Chronicle of the Kingdom of Portugal ... with a Cosmographical Description ... London: 1661. 1st edn. 12mo. [xvi],216,[4 advt] pp. Frontis. Some cropping, marg tears, title soiled, browned. 18th c calf, backstrip relaid. Family copy. Wing D.289.
(Burmester) **£80 [≈ $153]**

Davanzati, Bernardo
- A Discourse upon Coins ... Translated out of Italian by John Toland. London: J.D. for Awnsham & John Churchill, 1696. 1st edn in English. 4to. vi,7-26 pp. Occas sl marg staining. Mod half mor. Wing D.301.
(Pickering) **$3,000 [≈ £1,562]**

D'Avenant, Sir William
- Gondibert: An heroic Poem. London: for John Holden, 1651. 3rd edn. Sm 8vo. [iv],243, [6] pp. Errata leaf. Text of V7 repeated on V8. Orig vellum, label sl worn. Wing D.326.   *(Vanbrugh)* **£325 [≈ $623]**
- The Works ... London: for Henry Herringman, 1673. 1st edn. Folio. Sm tear title marg. Lacks port. Contemp calf, worn, rebacked, crnrs reprd.
(Dramatis Personae) **$250 [≈ £130]**

Davies, Edward
- Aphtharte, the Genius of Britain. A Poem ... Bath: R. Crutwell ... , 1784. 1st edn. 4to. 32 pp. 2 sm stamps. Old wraps, uncut.
(C.R. Johnson) **£225 [≈ $431]**

Davies, Thomas
- Memoirs of the Life of David Garrick, Esq. ... Dublin, Joseph Hill, for J. Williams ..., 1780. 1st Dublin edn. 2 vols. 12mo. Frontis port vol 1. Contemp calf, gilt spines, red & green labels, vol 2 spine ends damaged.
(Jarndyce) **£60 [≈ $115]**
- Memoirs of the Life of David Garrick, Esq ... London: for the author ..., 1784. 4th edn. 2 vols. 8vo. [xvi],368; [xiv],471 pp. Occas spotting. Calf, rebacked, 1 bd replaced.
(Young's) **£50 [≈ $95]**

Davies, William
- Plays Written for a Private Theatre ... London: for R. Faulder, 1786. Only edn. 8vo. Lacks half-title. Contemp half calf, foredges rubbed, dec spine gilt, mor label. Westport House b'plate.
(Dramatis Personae) **$185 [≈ £96]**

Davila, Henry Caterino
- The Historie of the Civill Warres of France, Written in Italian ... Translated out of the Original. London: R. Raworth ..., 1647. 1st English edn. Folio. [iv],1478,[2 errata] pp. Contemp calf, mor label, top of lower jnt sl damaged. Wing D.413.
(Finch) **£350 [≈ $671]**

Davis, Henry Edwards
- An Examination of the Fifteenth and Sixteenth Chapters of Mr. Gibbon's History of the Decline and Fall of the Roman Empire ... London: Dodsley, 1778. 1st edn. 8vo. [viii], iv, 284 pp. Contemp sprinkled calf gilt, mor label, hd of spine sl worn.
(Finch) **£120 [≈ $230]**

Davys, John
- An Essay on the Art of Decyphering. In which is inserted a Discourse of Dr. Wallis. Now first publish'd ... London: Gilliver & Clarke, 1737. 4to. Half-title,58,[1 advt] pp. Disbound. *(C.R. Johnson)* **£380 [≈ $729]**

Day, Thomas
- The History of Sandford and Merton ... London: for John Stockdale, 1795. 12mo. 5 advt pp vol 3. 3 frontis. Early 19th c green roan-backed bds, spines a little worn. Anon.
(Sanders) **£45 [≈ $86]**

Day, Thomas & Bicknell, John
- The Dying Negro, a Poem. To which is added a Fragment of a Letter on the Slavery of Negroes by Thomas Day ... London: Stockdale, 1793. Half-title,82 pp. Frontis. Lacks final advt leaf. Sl traces of damp on last leaf. Disbound.
(C.R. Johnson) **£125 [≈ $239]**

Deacon, Thomas
- A Compleat Collection of Devotions, both Publick and Private ... In Two Parts ... added an Appendix ... London: for the author, 1734. 1st edn. xxxi,341,[3], 119,[8],6 pp, errata leaf. Pp 337-40 in contemp MS. 19th c calf, orig cvrs laid down. Anon.
(Wreden) **$250 [≈ £130]**

- The Doctrine of the Church of Rome concerning Purgatory proved to be contrary to Catholick Tradition ... London: for Richard King, 1718. 12mo. Contemp calf, rebacked. *(Waterfield's)* **£80 [≈ $153]**

Deans, Archibald
- An Account of the Last Words of Christian Kerr, who died at Edinburgh, the 4th of Feb. 1702 in the 11th year of her Age ... Glasgow: 1773. 1st edn. 12mo. 16 pp. Disbound, uncut. *(Burmester)* **£85 [≈ $163]**

D'Arnay, M.
- The Private Life of the Romans ... Edinburgh: Donaldson, Reid ..., 1764. 2nd edn. 8vo. v,306 pp. Contemp calf, sl rubbed.
(Young's) **£40 [≈ $76]**

Debates ...
- Debates relative to the Affairs of Ireland ... see Caldwell, Sir James.

Declaration ...
- The Declaration of the Rebels now at Arms in the West of Scotland. [Edinburgh: 1679]. Folio. 4 pp. Wing D.761.
(C.R. Johnson) **£55 [≈ $105]**

Defence ...
- A Defence of the Dissertation on the Validity of the English Ordination ... see Le Courayer, P.F.

De Fleury, Maria
- Divine Poems and Essays on Various Subjects ... London: for the author ..., 1791. 1st edn. 8vo. xii,244 pp. Duplicates of pp 241-244 bound with prelims. Contemp sheep, jnts reprd. *(Burmester)* **£90 [≈ $172]**

Defoe, Daniel
- The Consolidator: or, Memoirs of Sundry Transactions from the World in the Moon. Translated from the Lunar Language. London: Bragg, 1705. 1st edn. 8vo. [iv],360 pp. Half-title. Some browning & minor defects. Contemp calf, extremities worn. Anon. *(Clark)* **£300 [≈ $575]**
- Eleven Opinions about Mr. H[arle]y; with Observations. London: J. Baker, 1711. 1st edn. 8vo. 89,[5 advt] pp. 3 sm holes, title dusty. 19th c blind stamped mor, old mrbld wraps bound in, rubbed, spine ends sl worn. Anon. *(Clark)* **£85 [≈ $163]**
- The History of the Devil ... Second Edition.

London: for T. Warner, 1727. Contemp calf, hinges sl rubbed. Anon.
(Jarndyce) **£120 [≈ $230]**

- The History of the Great Plague in London ... By a Citizen, who lived the whole time in London ... London: F. & J. Noble, 1754. 2nd edn, with the "Journal of the Plague at Marseilles". 8vo. [4],376 pp. Advt leaf after title. Rec qtr calf. Anon.
(Fenning) **£225 [≈ $431]**

- The Layman's Vindication of the Church of England, as well against Mr. Howell's Charge of Schism, as against Dr. Bennett's Pretended Answer to it. London: for A. & W. Bell, 1716. 1st edn. 8vo. [iv],79,5 advt pp. Half-title. Disbound. Anon.
(Young's) **£140 [≈ $268]**

- A Letter from a Gentleman in Scotland to his Friend at London. London: ptd in the year 1712. 1st edn. 8vo. 16 pp. Qtr calf. Anon.
(Burmester) **£1,250 [≈ $2,399]**

- A Letter from a Member of the House of Commons to his Friend in the Country, relating to the Bill of Commerce ... London: J. Baker ..., 1713. 1st edn. Issue with comma after 'printed' on title & w'cut ornament on A1r. 8vo. [2],46 pp. Sl soiled. Mod bds. Anon.
(Pickering) **£400 [≈ £208]**

- Memoirs of a Cavalier ... Written Threescore Years ago by an English Gentleman ... London: A. Bell ..., [1720]. 1st edn. 8vo. [viii],338 pp. Title dusty with 2 sm reprs. 19th c half calf, jnts & crnrs rubbed. Anon.
(Clark) **£200 [≈ $383]**

- Minutes of the Negotiations of Monsr. Mesnager at the Court of England, towards the Close of the last Reign ... Written by himself. Done out of the French. London: for S. Baker, 1717. 1st edn. 8vo. 326 pp. Old calf, rebacked.
(Bickersteth) **£180 [≈ $345]**

- Minutes of the Negotiations of Monsr. Mesnager at the Court of England during the last four Years of the Reign of her late Majesty Q. Anne ... Written by himself ... The Second Edition. London: for J. Roberts, 1736. 8vo. Contemp calf, rebacked.
(Waterfield's) **£90 [≈ $172]**

- The Scotch Medal Decipher'd, and the New Hereditary-Right Men display'd ... London: for S. Popping, 1711. 1st edn. 12mo. 24 pp. Rec bds. Anon. *(Burmester)* **£850 [≈ $1,631]**

- A Seasonable Warning and Caution against the Insinuations of Papists and Jacobites in favour of the Pretender. being a Letter from an Englishman at the Court of Hanover. London: for J. Baker, 1712. 1st edn. 12mo. [ii], 24 pp. Intl advt leaf. Outer ff sl soiled.

Anon.   *(Burmester)* **£350 [≈ $671]**
- A Tour Thro' the Whole Island of Great Britain ... By a Gentleman. The Fifth Edition with very great additions and corrections ... London: S. Birt ..., 1753. 4 vols. Tall 12mo. viii,388,[xii]; iv,418,[xvii]; iv,312, [xviii]; iv,371,[xx] pp. Contemp calf, lacks 1 label.
(Lamb) **£200 [≈ $383]**

- A True Collection of the Writings of the Author of The True Born English-man. Corrected by himself. London: the booksellers, 1703. 1st authorised collection. Frontis port (reprd). Some spotting & marks. Rebound in half calf. Anon.
(Jarndyce) **£180 [≈ $345]**

De la Court, Pieter

- The True Interest and Political Maxims of the Republick of Holland and West-Friesland. In Three Parts ... Written by John de Witt, and other Great Men in Holland ... London: 1702. 1st edn in English. 8vo. lvi,492 pp. Port. Sl browned. Mod calf.
(Pickering) **$350 [≈ £182]**

Delamayne, Thomas Hallie

- The Senators: or, a Candid Examination into the Merits of the Principal Performers of St. Stephen's Chapel. The Second Edition, with Alterations and Additions. London: for G. Kearsly, 1772. Title vignette. Lacks half-title. Disbound. Anon. *(Waterfield's)* **£45 [≈ $86]**
- The Senators ... The Third Edition, with Alterations and Additions. London: for G. Kearsly, 1772. 4to. Tear on title reprd. Disbound. Anon. *(Waterfield's)* **£40 [≈ $76]**

Delany, Patrick

- Observations upon Lord Orrery's Remarks on the Life and Writings of Dr. Jonathan Swift ... London: sold by W. Reeve, 1754. 1st edn. 8vo. [xvi],310 pp. Old calf, rebacked. Anon.
(Young's) **£110 [≈ $211]**

- Reflections upon Polygamy and the Encouragement given to that Practice in the Scriptures of the Old Testament ... By By Phileleutherus Dubliniensis. The Second Edition, with a Preface ... London: 1739. 8vo. Lacks half-title. Rebound in half calf.
(Jarndyce) **£150 [≈ $287]**

Delille, Jacques

- The Garden; or, the Art of Laying out Grounds. Translated from the French of the Abbe de Lille. London: Cadell, 1789. 1st edn in English. 8vo. vii,[i],188 pp. Contemp calf, jnts tender.   *(Burmester)* **£120 [≈ $230]**

- The Garden; or, the Art of Laying Out Grounds. London: Cadell, 1789. 1st edn in English. 8vo. [iii]-vii,188 pp. Contemp half calf, hinges weak. *(Bookpress)* **$375 [≈£195]**

Dellon, Charles
- The History of the Inquisition, as it is exercised at Goa ... Translated into English [by Henry Wharton]. London: Printed ... Dublin: reptd for Robert Owen, 1732. Sm 8vo. 142,[2] pp. Occas sl soiling. Contemp calf, rebacked. *(Fenning)* **£85 [≈$163]**

De Lolme, Jean Louis
- The Constitution of England ... London: T. Spilsbury, sold by G. Kearsley, 1775. 1st English edn. 8vo. Contemp speckled calf, crnrs rubbed, rear bd chipped, rebacked. *(Jarndyce)* **£200 [≈$383]**
- The Constitution of England ... London: T. Spilsbury, sold by G. Kearsley, 1775. 1st edn in English. 8vo. vii,[1],448 pp. Contemp mottled calf, extremities of jnts cracked, spine ends rubbed, edges & crnrs rubbed. *(Pickering)* **$350 [≈£182]**
- The Constitution of England ... Fourth Edition, corrected and enlarged. London: 1784. 8vo. [8],xvi,540,[20] pp. Port. Contemp calf gilt. *(Fenning)* **£35 [≈$67]**
- The Constitution of England ... New Edition, corrected. London: 1789. 8vo. Port. Contemp tree calf, red label, sl rubbed, spine sl faded. *(Robertshaw)* **£36 [≈$69]**

Delpino, Joseph Giral
- A Dictionary, Spanish and English, and English and Spanish ... London: for A. Millar, 1763. 1st edn. Folio. Some damp staining to prelims. Minor holing at end. Cloth backed bds. *(Young's)* **£75 [≈$143]**

De Moivre, Abraham
- Annuities upon Lives ... The Second Edition, corrected. London Printed. Dublin: reprinted by Samuel Fuller, 1731. 1st Irish edn. 8vo. 6,viii,122 pp. Contemp calf, new label, sl marked. *(Fenning)* **£350 [≈$671]**
- The Doctrine of Chances: or, a Method of Calculating the Probability of Events in Play. London: W. Pearson, for the author, 1718. 1st edn. 4to. [6],[xiv],175 pp. Num blanks bound in at end. Contemp calf, backstrip relaid. *(Rootenberg)* **$1,500 [≈£781]**

Denham, John
- Poems and Translations, with the Sophy ...

London: Herringman, 1668. 1st edn. 8vo. [viii], 186,[viii],97,[i] pp. Contemp calf, sometime rebacked, endpapers renewed, sides rubbed. Wing D.1005. *(Finch)* **£110 [≈$211]**

Dennis, John
- The Comical Gallant: or the Amours of Sir John Falstaffe. A Comedy ... London: A. Baldwin, 1702. 1st edn. Sm 4to. [50] pp. Rec qtr mor. *(Georges)* **£250 [≈$479]**
- Liberty Assured. A Tragedy ... London: for George Strahan & Bernard Lintott, 1704. 1st edn. Sm 4to. Cropped at ft cutting into sev catchwords. Lacks half-title. New bds. *(Dramatis Personae)* **$600 [≈£312]**
- A Proposal for Putting a Speedy End to the War, by ruining the Commerce of the French and Spaniards ... London: for Daniel brown, 1703. 1st edn. 4to. viii,5-28 pp. New mor backed bds. Anon. *(Pickering)* **$1,000 [≈£520]**
- The Usefulness of the Stage to Religion and to Government ... London: for Thomas Harper, 1738. 2nd edn. Sm 8vo. Mod wraps. Anon. *(Dramatis Personae)* **$200 [≈£104]**

Denon, Vivant
- Travels in Sicily and Malta: Translated from the French. London: Robinson, 1789. 8vo. Contemp tree calf, red mor label, sprinkled edges, fine. *(Book Block)* **$425 [≈£221]**

Dent, John
- Too Civil by Half, a Farce in Two Acts ... London: Stockdale, 1783. 1st edn. 8vo. [viii], 39 pp. Disbound. *(Bickersteth)* **£25 [≈$47]**

D'Orleans, F.J.
- The History of the Revolutions in England under the Family of the Stuarts from the Year 1603, to 1690. London: 1722. 2nd edn. 8vo. Contemp panelled calf, upper jnt cracked, title label chipped. *(Robertshaw)* **£28 [≈$53]**

The Deportment of a Married Life ...
- See Stanhope, Eugenia.

Derham, W.
- Astro-Theology; or a Demonstration of the Being and Attributes of God from a Survey of the Heavens ... Third Edition Improv'd. London: Innys, 1719. 8vo. [xvi],lvi,[viii], 246,[x] pp. 3 fldg plates. Contemp calf. *(Lloyd-Roberts)* **£90 [≈$172]**

Derrick, Samuel
- The Battle of Lora.˙A Poem. With Some Fragments written in the Erse, or Irish Language, by Ossian, the Son of Fingal. Translated into English Verse. London: Gardner ..., 1762. 1st edn. 4to. Sl foxing. Disbound..   *(Ximenes)* **$350 [≈£182]**

De St. Marthe, Scevole
- Paedotrophia, or the Art of Nursing and Rearing Children. London: the author, 1797. 1st edn in English. 8vo. [cxcii],224 pp. Later calf. Translated by H.W. Tytler.
        (Bookpress) **$425 [≈£221]**

Description ...
- A Description of Killarney. London: Dodsley, 1776. 4to. Half-title, 50 pp. Title-page with engvd map, vignette illust at end. Rebound in qtr mor.
        (C.R. Johnson) **£325 [≈$623]**
- A Description of Killarney ... see also Dunn, ----.
- A Description of South Carolina ... see Glenn, James.

Des Maizeaux, I.
- An Historical and Critical Account of the Life & Writings of William Chillingworth ... London: for Woodward & Peele, 1725. v,372,xx pp. Contemp calf, spine worn.
        (Gage) **£30 [≈$57]**

Deveil, Sir Thomas
- Memoirs of the Life and Times of ... One of His Majesty's Justices of the Peace, for the Counties of Middlesex, Essex, Surry ... London: M. Cooper ..., 1748. Only edn. 8vo. [ii], 83 pp. Half-title. Disbound.
        (Young's) **£120 [≈$230]**

Devonshire, Georgiana Cavendish, Duchess of
- The Sylph; a Novel. Dublin: for S. Price, J. Williams ..., 1779. 12mo. Sl worm in endpapers with 1 text marg hole. Contemp Irish (?) mottled calf, hinges sl cracked, sl scars back bd. Anon.
        (Jarndyce) **£950 [≈$1,823]**

De Witt, John
- See De la Court, Pieter.

The Diaboliad ...
- See Combe, William.

Dialogues ...
- Dialogues concerning Education ... see Fordyce, David.
- Dialogues of the Dead ... see Fontenelle, B. le B. de; Lyttelton, George, 1st Lord Lyttelton.
- Dialogues on the Uses of Foreign Travel ... see Hurd, Richard.

Dibdin, Charles, the elder
- The Musical Tour of Mr. Dibdin; in which
- previous to his Embarkation for India - he left his career as a Public Character. Sheffield: for the author by J. Gales, 1788. 1st edn. 4to. 4 pp subscribers. 19 engvd pp of music. Rec half mor, uncut.   *(Georges)* **£550 [≈$1,055]**

Dickinson, John
- Letters from a Farmer in Pennsylvania, to the Inhabitants of the British Colonies. Philadelphia printed. London: re-printed, 1774. 136 pp. Half-title. Foxing. Mod cloth. Anon.   *(Reese)* **$400 [≈£208]**

Dickinson, Jonathan
- Familiar Letters to a Gentleman, upon a Variety of Seasonable and Important Subjects in Religion. Dundee: ptd in the year, 1772. 12mo. Contemp calf gilt, upper jnt just held by cords.   *(Sanders)* **£45 [≈$86]**
- Familiar Letters to a Gentleman upon a Variety of Seasonable and Important Subjects in Religion ... Third Edition. Edinburgh: R. Fleming, 1757. 12mo. Front endpaper reprd. Contemp sheep rubbed, front jnt cracked.
        (Waterfield's) **£50 [≈$95]**

Dictionary ...
- A Dictionary of the Bible; or, An Explanation of the Proper Names and Difficult Words in the Old and New Testament ... Second Edition, corrected and enlarged. London: Robinson, Goldsmith ..., 1792. 6 advt pp. Sl worm in prelims. Contemp calf, sl rubbed.
        (Jarndyce) **£25 [≈$47]**
- A Dictionary of the English Language ... prefixed a comprehensive View of English Grammar. The Fifth Edition ... London: W. Peacock, 1797. 12mo in 6s. Contemp mor, a.e.g., rubbed, crnrs worn.
        (Clark) **£48 [≈$92]**
- A Dictionary of the English Language ... prefixed ... English Grammar. The Fifth Edition, with considerable additions and improvements. London: W. Peacock, 1797. 12mo. Contemp tree calf gilt, red label, v sm reprs to spine ends. *(Jarndyce)* **£150 [≈$287]**

Diderot, Denis
- Les Bijoux Indiscrets. or, The Indiscreet Toys. Translated from the Congese Language ... Tobago [ie London]: Re-printed for Pierre Ragout ..., 1749. 1st edn in English. 2 vols. vi,276; ii,316 pp. 8 plates. Contemp calf, old reback. Anon.
(C.R. Johnson) **£2,800 [≈ $5,375]**

Difference ...
- The Difference between Words, esteemed Synonymous ... see Trusler, John.

Digby, Sir Kenelm
- Letters between The Ld. George Digby, and Kenelm Digby Kt. Concerning Religion. London: for Humphrey Moseley, 1651. Setting with final letter misdated March 39. Sm 8vo. Occas sl soiling. New qtr calf. Wing B.4768.
(Sanders) **£100 [≈ $191]**
- Letters between The Ld. George Digby, and Kenelm Digby Kt. Concerning Religion. London: for Humphrey Moseley, 1651. Setting with final letter dated March 30. Sm 8vo. New qtr calf. Wing B.4768.
(Sanders) **£100 [≈ $191]**
- Two Treatises: in the One of which, The Nature of Bodies; In the Other The Nature of Mans Soul, is Looked Into. London: Williams, 1658. 4to. Text diags. Panelled calf. Wing D.1450.
(Rostenberg & Stern) **$675 [≈ £351]**

Digges, Dudley
- The Compleat Ambassador. London: Newcomb for Bedell & Collins, 1655. 1st edn. Folio. Addtnl engvd title by Faithorne. Calf. Wing D.1453.
(Rostenberg & Stern) **$385 [≈ £200]**

Dillenius, John James
- Historia Muscorum: a General History of Land and Water & Mosses and Corals ... London: J. Millan, 1768. 4to. [ii],13,10 pp. 85 plates. Some marg pencil notes. Contemp tree calf, rebacked. *(Bookpress)* **£425 [≈ £221]**

Dillingham, William
- A Sermon at the Funeral of the Lady Elizabeth Alston ... Septemb. 10 1677. London: for Jonathan Robinson, 1678. Disbound. Wing D.1487.
(Waterfield's) **£20 [≈ $38]**

Dilworth, Thomas
- The Schoolmasters Assistant: being a

Compendium of Arithmetic, both Practical and Theoretical. Second Edition. London: Henry Kent, 1744. 8vo. xv,[9],168 pp. Frontis, fldg tables, num tables in text. Contemp calf, jnts cracked, spine ends worn, crnrs bumped.   *(Spelman)* **£50 [≈ $95]**
- The Schoolmasters Assistant: being a Compendium of Arithmetic, both Practical and Theoretical ... Twentieth Edition. London: Causton, 1780. Frontis. Few ink scrawls. Lacks free endpaper. Contemp sheep, rubbed, wear to spine ends.
(Jarndyce) **£40 [≈ $76]**

Dilworth, W.H.
- The Life and Heroic Actions of Frederick III. King of Prussia ... Published for the Entertainment and Improvement of the British Youth of both Sexes. London: G. Wright, 1758. 1st edn. 12mo. 168 pp. Port. Contemp sheep, spine sl worn.
(Burmester) **£50 [≈ $95]**
- The Life of Alexander Pope, Esq; with a View of his Writings ... London: for Woodgate, Brooks, 1760. 12mo. [iv],151 pp. Half-title. Bottom edge trimmed touching a catchword. Rebound in half calf.
(Burmester) **£200 [≈ $383]**

Dinarbas; a Tale ...
- See Knight, Cornelia.

Dirom, Major
- A Narrative of the Campaign in India which terminated the War with Tippoo Sultan in 1792. London: 1793. 296 pp. 9 maps, plates, plans & views. Orig bds, new gilt spine, crnrs sl bumped.   *(Trophy Room)* **$450 [≈ £234]**

Discourse(s) ...
- A Discourse against Transubstantiation ... see Tillotson, John.
- A Discourse concerning the Successe of Former Parliaments ... see May, Thomas.
- A Discourse of Ecclesiastical Politie ... see Parker, Samuel.
- A Discourse on the Emigration of British Birds ... see Edwards, George.
- Discourses concerning the Truth of the Christian Religion ... see Jortin, John.

The Dispensary, A Poem ...
- See Garth, Samuel.

D'Israeli, Isaac
- Curiosities of Literature. London: for H. Murray ..., 1795. 4th edn. 2 vols. 8vo. Contemp calf, rebacked. Anon.
(Young's) **£75 [≈ $143]**
- Miscellanies; or, Literary Recreations. London: Cadell & Davies, 1796. 1st edn. 8vo. xxiv,432,[2 errata] pp. Sl stain on a few ff, 2 sm marg tears. Contemp calf backed mrbld bds, uncut, rubbed, lacks label.
(Burmester) **£90 [≈ $172]**

Diston, John
- The Seaman's Guide, chiefly the Experience of the Author; the Other Parts taken from the latest and best Surveys of the English, French, Dutch, and Danes ... Liverpool: for the author ..., [178-]. Oblong 8vo. [2],51, [4], 4-20 pp. Endpapers browned. Contemp sheep.
(C.R. Johnson) **£300 [≈ $575]**

Dixon, George A.
- A Voyage round the World ... London: George Goulding, 1789. 1st edn. 4to. 22 plates & maps. Lacks half-title. Title reprd. Occas sl offsetting. Later vellum backed bds.
(Parmer) **$1,500 [≈ £781]**

Dobson, Matthew
- A Medical Commentary on Fixed Air ... Chester: ptd by J. Monk, 1779. 1st edn. 198 pp. Half-title, dedic leaf. Occas spotting or browning. Old mrbld bds, edges darkened & worn, sometime rebacked in calf, few sm worm holes, jnts cracking.
(Hollett) **£140 [≈ $268]**

Dodd, William
- The Hymns of Callimachus, translated from the Greek into English Verse, with Explanatory Notes ... L; for the translator, & sold by T. Waller & J. Ward, 1755. 4to. 7 pp subscribers. Port on title, ills. Contemp qtr calf, hinges weak. *(Jarndyce)* **£150 [≈ $287]**
- Poems. London: Dryden Leach, for the author, 1767. 1st edn. 8vo. Contemp calf, gilt spine (upper cvr sl scraped).
(Ximenes) **$650 [≈ £338]**
- The Sisters; or, the History of Lucy and Caroline Sanson ... New Edition. London: T. Wilkins, for T. Jones, 1791. 3 vols. 12mo. Half-titles. Contemp calf, spines sl worn.
(Burmester) **£380 [≈ $729]**
- The Sisters; or, the History of Lucy and Caroline Sanson, entrusted to a false Friend ... London: by T. Wilkins, for T. Jones, 1791.

New edn. 3 vols. Half-titles. Contemp calf, spines sl worn. *(C.R. Johnson)* **£380 [≈ $729]**
- Thoughts in Prison: in Five Parts ... added, His Last Prayer ... and Other Miscellaneous Pieces. London: Dilly, Kearsley, 1777. 1st edn. Final advt leaf. Occas sl staining. Rebound in half calf.
(Jarndyce) **£380 [≈ $729]**
- Thoughts in Prison. In Five Parts ... added, His Last Prayer ... and Other Miscellaneous Pieces. Dublin: for S. Price ..., 1778. 12mo. 251 pp. Contemp Irish sheep, sl worn.
(Rankin) **£150 [≈ $287]**

Doddridge, Philip
- Letters to and from the Rev Philip Doddridge D.D. With Notes ... by Thomas Stedman ... Shrewsbury: Eddowes, 1790. Tall 8vo. [16],472 pp. Sm piece cut from blank marg of 1st 2 ff. 19th c half calf, scuffed, worn in places. *(Humber)* **£28 [≈ $53]**
- Meditations on the Tears of Jesus over the Grave of Lazarus. A Funeral Sermon ... Death of the late Reverend Samuel Clark, D.D. London: James Wright, 1751. Disbound. *(Waterfield's)* **£25 [≈ $47]**
- The Rise and Progress of Religion in the Soul ... Twelfth Edition to which is added a Sermon on the Care of the Soul. London: J. Buckland ..., 1789. Sm 8vo. [2],336,4 pp. Minor wear. Contemp calf, cloth on spine, front bd detached. *(Humber)* **£25 [≈ $47]**
- Some Remarkable Passages in the Life of the Honourable Col. James Gardiner who was slain at the Battle of Preston-Pans ... London: for the booksellers, [1747]. 1st edn. ix,10-262 pp. Few sections sl shaken. Old mottled calf.
(Hollett) **£220 [≈ $422]**
- Some Remarkable Passages in the Life of the Honourable Col. James Gardiner, who was slain at the Battle of Preston-Pans ... London: for James Buckland ..., 1747. 1st edn. Sm 4to. [xiv],260 pp. Blank outer crnr pp 3-12 sl ragged. *(Young's)* **£80 [≈ $153]**
- Some Remarkable Passages in the Life of the Honourable Col. James Gardiner, who was slain at the Battle of Preston-Pans ... Third Edition. Boston: D. henchman, 1748. 8vo. 157, [2] pp. Lacks pp 139-142. Orig wraps, sl worn. *(Bookpress)* **$135 [≈ £70]**
- Some Remarkable Passages in the Life of the Honourable Col. James Gardiner who was slain at the Battle of Prestonpans ... London: J. Buckland ..., 1772. 5th edn. 8vo. [14],272,[4] pp. Port. New half calf.
(Humber) **£35 [≈ $67]**

- Some Remarkable Passages in the Life of the Honourable Col. James Gardiner, who was slain at the Battle of Preston-Pans ... Wigan: W. Bancks, 1782. 8vo. [x],263 pp. Port. Half-title. Rec half calf. *(Young's)* £60 [≈ $115]
- Some Remarkable Passages in the Life of the Honourable Col. James Gardiner who was slain at the Battle of Preston-Pans ... London: for Crowder & Rivington, 1791. 8vo. xii, 13-280 pp. Tree calf gilt.
(Hollett) £35 [≈ $67]

Dodington, George Bubb
- The Diary ... With an Appendix ... Now first Published from his Lordship's Original Manuscripts. By Henry Penruddocke Wyndham. Salisbury: E. Easton ..., 1784. 1st edn. 8vo. Contemp calf gilt.
(Ximenes) $150 [≈ £78]
- The Diary ... With an Appendix ... By Henry Penruddocke Wyndham. Dublin: William Porter, 1784. 1st Dublin edn. 12mo. xiv,346 pp. Half-title bound at end. Old calf, a little worn. *(Young's)* £45 [≈ $86]
- The Diary ... With an Appendix ... A New Edition. By Henry Penruddocke Wyndham. Salisbury: by E. Easton; Wilkie, London, 1784. 8vo. xv,[i blank],506 pp. Lacks half-title. Early 19th c half calf, mor label, top edges trimmed, others uncut, rubbed.
(Finch) £35 [≈ $67]

Dodsley, Robert
- A Collection of Poems in Six Volumes by Several Hands. London: J. Hughes for J. Dodsley, 1766. 6 vols. 8vo. Contemp speckled calf, red mor labels.
(Waterfield's) £235 [≈ $451]
- The Modern Reasoners: an Epistle to a Friend. London: for Lawton Gilliver, 1734. 1st edn. Folio. Disbound. Anon.
(Ximenes) $225 [≈ £117]
- The Oeconomy of Human Life. Translated from an Indian Manuscript, Written by an Ancient Bramin ... London: for M. Cooper, 1751. 1st edn, with 'spiritless' without interrogation mark at p 27 line 14. Sm 8vo. xxxii,111 pp. Frontis. Occas v sl spot. Contemp calf, rebacked. Anon
(Finch) £140 [≈ $268]
- The Oeconomy of Human Life. Translated from an Indian Manuscript, Written by an Ancient Bramin ... Dublin: George Faulkner, 1751. 8vo. 58 pp. Frontis. Lib stamps on back of frontis & title. Rec lib cloth. Anon.
(Clark) £35 [≈ $67]

- The Oeconomy of Human Life, Complete in Two Parts: Translated from an Indian Manuscript, Written by an Ancient Bramin ... New York: William Durell, 1793. 2 parts in one. 12mo. 130 pp. Some old waterstains. Contemp calf over paper cvrd wood bds, rubbed, chipped. *(Karmiole)* $125 [≈ £65]
- The Oeconomy of Human Life. Translated from an Indian Manuscript, Written by an Ancient Bramin ... London: Rickaby, for S. & E. Harding, 1795. Lge 12mo. 22,[2],119 pp. 49 text engvs by Harding. Orig calf, rubbed. Anon. *(Bickersteth)* £48 [≈ $92]
- The Preceptor: containing a General Course of Education ... The Sixth Edition, with additions and improvements. London: for J. Dodsley, 1775. 2 vols. 8vo. 3 advt pp vol 1. 2 frontis, fldg plates. Contemp calf, hinges splitting but sound. Anon.
(Jarndyce) £140 [≈ $268]
- Trifles. London: at Tully's Head in Pall Mall, 1745. 1st edn. 8vo. Contemp calf, sl rubbed, jnts cracked.
(Waterfield's) £80 [≈ $153]

Dodsley, Robert (ed.)
- A Select Collection of Old Plays. London: for R. Dodsley, 1744. 12 vols. 8vo. List of subscribers. Contemp mottled calf, orange labels, 1 jnt cracking, some rubbing on spines & wear to extremities.
(Waterfield's) £450 [≈ $863]

Dodson, J.
- The Mathematical Repository containing Analytical Solutions of near Five Hundred Questions ... London: 1775. 2nd edn. ix,336 pp. V sl tear in 1st few pp reprd. Contemp leather, v worn with large piece missing from front cvr, front hinge weak.
(Whitehart) £120 [≈ $230]

Dodwell, William
- The Sick Man's Companion: or, the Clergyman's Assistant in Visiting the Sick ... London: for B. White ..., 1768. 2nd edn. 8vo. xlvii,48-260 pp. Old sheep, jnts partly cracked. *(Young's)* £65 [≈ $124]

Dolce, L. Aretin
- A Dialogue on Painting. London: for P. Elmsley, 1770. 1st English edn. 8,xix,262 pp. Contemp leather, jnts cracked.
(Ars Artis) £195 [≈ $374]

Donne, John
- [Greek title: Biathanatos]. A Declaration of

that Paradox, or Thesis, that Self-Homicide is not so naturally Sin, that it may never be Otherwise ... London: in the year, 1700. 2nd edn. 8vo. [xxxii],190 pp. Contemp calf, jnt cracking at hd, sm surface wear. Wing D.1860.   *(Finch)* **£475 [≈$911]**

- The Poetical Works ... With the Life of the Author, by J.W. Edinburgh: Apollo Press, 1779. 3 vols in one. Orig three qtr calf, uncut, worn..   *(Limestone Hills)* **$60 [≈£31]**

- Six Sermons upon severall Occasions, preached before the King, and elsewhere. Cambridge: 1634. 1st edn. Sm 4to. With A1 (blank except for ornament). Few sl stains. Contemp calf, jnts partly split, sm reprs to spine. STC 7056. John Hayward's label.
            (Ximenes) **$2,000 [≈£1,041]**

Dorchester, Henry Pierpoint, Marquess of
- Two Speeches spoken in the House of the Lords, by the Lord Viscount Newarke ... May 21 [24] 1641 ... London: ptd 1641. Sm 4to. 10 pp. Title sl soiled. Disbound. Wing D.1921.
            (Bickersteth) **£20 [≈$38]**

Dornford, Josiah
- The Motives and Consequences of the Present War Impartially Considered. London: for J. Pridden, 1792. 8vo. Mod qtr calf. Inscrbd "From the Author". Anon.
            (Waterfield's) **£60 [≈$115]**

Dossie, Robert
- The Elaboratory Laid Open, or the Secrets of Modern Chemistry and Pharmacy revealed ... London: Nourse, 1758. 1st edn. 8vo. xi,[3], 375, [9] pp. Old lib stamp. Contemp calf gilt, rebacked, crnrs rubbed. Anon.
            (Rootenberg) **$750 [≈£390]**

Douglas, James
- Travelling Anecdotes through various Parts of Europe. London: for J. Debrett, 1785. 2nd edn. 8vo. 7 plates. Half calf, uncut.
            (Ximenes) **$300 [≈£156]**

Douglas, John
- A Letter addressed to Two Great Men, on the Prospect of Peace ... London: for A. Millar, 1760. 2nd edn, rvsd. 8vo. Half-title (clean tear). Sewn as issued, uncut. Anon.
            (Ximenes) **$125 [≈£65]**

- A Serious Defence of some late Measures of the Administration ... with regard to the Introduction and Establishment of Foreign Troops. London: J. Morgan, 1756. 54 pp. Anon.   *(C.R. Johnson)* **£40 [≈$76]**

Dove, Henry
- A Sermon preached before the Right Honorable the Lord Mayor of the City of London ... on the Feast of St. Michael 1682 ... London: for Benj. Tooke, 1682. Licence leaf. Disbound. Wing D.2049.
            (Waterfield's) **£20 [≈$38]**

Downes, Samuel
- The Lives of the Compilers of the Liturgy ... The Second Edition, Corrected and Improved. London: Rivington, 1722. 8vo. Frontis (sm marg repr). Lacks rear free endpaper. Contemp calf, lacks label.
            (Waterfield's) **£65 [≈$124]**

Downing, Clement
- A Compendious History of the Indian Wars with an Account of the Rise, Progress, Strength and Forces of Angria the Pyrate. London: for T. Cooper, 1737. 1st edn. 12mo. Contemp calf, dble gilt rule, green spine label, hinges cracking but sound.
            (Blakeney) **£550 [≈$1,055]**

Downman, Hugh
- The Land of the Muses: a Poem, in the manner of Spenser. With Poems on Several Occasions. Edinburgh: for the author, 1768. 4to. Half-title, 84 pp. Disbound.
            (C.R. Johnson) **£165 [≈$316]**

- Poems to Thespia. Exeter: W. Grigg, 1781. 1st edn. 8vo. 112 pp. Title sl dusty. Contemp calf. Anon.   *(Burmester)* **£250 [≈$479]**

- Tragedies. Exeter: ptd by E. Grigg; for Robinson, Wilkie, Kearsley, London; Bell, Edinburgh, 1792. 1st coll edn. 8vo in 4s. Half calf, gilt spine, worn, jnts cracked, lacks label.
            (Sanders) **£45 [≈$86]**

Doyne, Philip
- Irene, a Canto, on the Peace; written in the Stanza of Spencer. Dublin: for W. Ross, 1763. 30 pp. Disbound.
            (C.R. Johnson) **£125 [≈$239]**

- The Triumph of Parnassus, a Poem. On the Birth of His Royal Highness the Prince of Wales. Dublin: for W. Ross, 1763. 56 pp. Disbound.   *(C.R. Johnson)* **£125 [≈$239]**

Drake, Nathan
- Literary Hours, or Sketches Critical and Narrative ... Sudbury: J. Burkitt ..., 1798. 1st edn. 8vo. [iv],viii,[iv],529,[ii] pp. Half-title bound as fly-title Front free endpaper cut away. Contemp tree calf, smooth spine, gilt

bands, red mor label, sl rubbed.
(Finch) £75 [≈ $143]

Dralloc, N.
- An Epitome of Logic ... see Collard, John.

Dramatic Dialogues ...
- See Pinchard, Elizabeth.

Drayton, Michael
- Poems ... newly corrected. London: for John Smethwick, 1637. 12mo. Engvd title. Sl marg soil. 19th c mor gilt, a.e.g., minor rubbing. STC 7225. (Ximenes) $500 [≈ £260]

The Dream of Alcibiades ...
- See Pic, Jean.

Drexelius, Hieremias
- The Considerations of Drexelius upon Eternity, made English from the Latin of S. Dunster. London: J. Rawlins & J. Pickard ..., 1710. 8vo. Port frontis, 9 plates. Contemp Cambridge style panelled calf, rebacked. (Waterfield's) £55 [≈ $105]
- The Considerations of Drexelius upon Eternity. Made English from the Latin by S. Dunster. London: D. Brown, 1710. xvi,231,i pp. Port frontis, 9 plates. Leather, rebacked. (Gage) £35 [≈ $67]

Drinkwater, John
- A History of the late Siege of Gibraltar ... Third Edition. London: J. Johnson ..., 1786. 4to. xxiv,356 pp. 10 fldg plates. Contemp calf, gilt spine, a.e.g., hd of spine reprd. (Frew Mackenzie) £450 [≈ $863]

Drummond, Thomas, LL.D.
- Poems Sacred to Religion and Virtue. London: D. Wilson & T. Durham, 1756. Half-title, 175 pp. Contemp speckled calf, leading hinge weakening, spine rubbed. (C.R. Johnson) £180 [≈ $345]

Drunken Barnaby's Four Journeys ...
- See Brathwaite, Richard.

Dryden, John
- Absalom and Achitophel. London: for J.T. ..., 1681. 2nd London edn. 4to. 32 pp. Few spots, final leaf sl soiled. Rec polished calf gilt. Wing D.2217. (Hollett) £220 [≈ $422]
- Britannia Rediviva: a Poem on the Birth of the Prince. London: Tonson, '1688' [actually 1691]. 4to. [ii],20,[ii] pp. Final advt leaf.

Browned, minor spotting. Rec wraps. Wing D.2253. (Clark) £38 [≈ $72]
- Don Sebastian, King of Portugal: a Tragedy. London: Jo. Hindmarsh, 1692. 2nd edn. 4to. [xvi],109,[iii] pp. Outer ff dusty & sl dogeared. Paper browned. Disbound. Wing D.2263. (Clark) £40 [≈ $76]
- The Dramatic Works. London: Tonson, 1735 [-53]. 6 vols. 12mo. Frontis port vol 1, plates. Contemp speckled calf gilt, sl rubbed, 1 label chipped. (Jarndyce) £80 [≈ $153]
- Eleonora: A Panegyrical Poem ... London: Tonson, 1692. 1st edn. 4to. [viii],24 pp. Browned, few pp edges chipped. Rec wraps. Wing D.2270. (Clark) £90 [≈ $172]
- Fables Ancient and Modern; Translated into verse ... With Original Poems. London: Tonson, 1713. 1st 8vo edn. Frontis. Few marg damp stains. Rebound in calf. (Jarndyce) £90 [≈ $172]
- Fables Ancient & Modern; Translated into Verse ... with Original Poems. Glasgow: Foulis, 1752. The issue on better quality paper. 2 vols. Sm 8vo. Titles & last ff sl browned. Contemp calf gilt, labels. (Georges) £125 [≈ $239]
- The Fables, Ornamented with Engravings from the Pencil of Lady Diana Beauclerc. London: T. Bensley for J. Edwards & E. Harding, 1797. Folio. Half-title. Plates with sl offsetting. Contemp straight grained green mor gilt, a.e.g., sl marking. (Jarndyce) £450 [≈ $863]
- The Fables ... Ornamented with Engravings from the Pencil of Lady Diana Beauclerc. London: Bensley, 1797. 1st edn. Folio. xviii, 241 pp. 8 plates, num engvd head- & tailpieces. Occas marg spotting to plates. Contemp straight grain red mor gilt. (Gough) £395 [≈ $758]
- The Hind and the Panther. A Poem, in Three Parts. The Third Edition. London: Tonson, 1687. Sm 4to. [viii],145 pp. Sl paper flaw in 1 leaf. New period style calf by Middleton. Wing D.2285. Anon. (Sotheran's) £225 [≈ $431]
- Love Triumphant; or, Nature will Prevail. A Tragi-Comedy ... London: Tonson, 1694. 1st edn. 4to. [x],82,[2] pp. Marg wormholes, occas sl spotting. Mor by Sangorski & Sutcliffe. Wing D.2302. (Finch) £150 [≈ $287]
- Love Triumphant; or, Nature Will Prevail. A Tragi-Comedy. London: for Jacob Tonson, 1694. 1st edn. Sm 4to. Half-title, final blank. Mod wraps. Wing D.2302.

(Dramatis Personae) **$250 [≈ £130]**
- Lucretius: a Poem against the Fear of Death. With an Ode in Memory of ... Mrs. Ann Killigrew ... London: H. Hills, 1709. 1st sep edn. Sl stained. Disbound.
(Jarndyce) **£20 [≈ $38]**
- The Medal. A Satyr against Sedition. By the Author of Absalom and Achitophel. London: ptd & sold by H. Hills, 1709. Sl spotting. Disbound. Anon. *(Jarndyce)* **£15 [≈ $28]**
- Original Poems and Translations. Edinburgh: Churnside & Wilson, 1777. 2 vols. 12mo. Contemp sheep, red mor labels.
(Waterfield's) **£50 [≈ $95]**
- Original Poems. Glasgow: Foulis, 1756. The issue on better quality paper. 2 vols. Sm 8vo. Half-title crrctly in vol 1 only. Vol 1 lacks final blank. 1st & final ff sl browned. Contemp calf gilt, labels.
(Georges) **£125 [≈ $239]**
- A Poem upon the Death of His Late Highness, Oliver, Lord Protector of England, Scotland, & Ireland. London: William Wilson, "1659" [actually ca 1691]. 4to. 12 pp. Sl browned, few sm marg reprs. Rec wraps. Wing D.2330. *(Clark)* **£45 [≈ $86]**
- Poems and Fables. Now first published together. To which is prefix'd, an Account of his Life and Writings. Dublin: A. Reilly for William Smith, 1753. 2 vols. 12mo. Frontises. 1 stain vol 2. Contemp calf, gilt spines, red & black labels, vol 2 front bd rubbed. *(Jarndyce)* **£110 [≈ $211]**
- Religio Laici or a Layman's Faith. A Poem. London: Tonson, 1683. 3rd edn. 4to. [xvi],28 pp. Minor browning, some early page edges sl chipped. 1 sm repr. Rec wraps. Wing D.2345.
(Clark) **£35 [≈ $67]**
- The Rival Ladies. A Tragi-Comedy. London: for Henry Herringman, 1675. 3rd edn. Sm 4to. Disbound.
(Dramatis Personae) **$200 [≈ £104]**
- The Second Part of Absalom and Achitophel. A Poem ... London: Tonson, 1682. 1st edn. Folio. 34 pp. New bds. Wing D.2350.
(Young's) **£75 [≈ $143]**
- Threnodia Augustalis ... London: Tonson, 1685. 1st edn. MacDonald's 1st issue. 4to. [ii], 25,[i] pp. Sl browned, localised stain in upper marg. Rec wraps. Wing D.2383.
(Clark) **£85 [≈ $163]**
- The Vindication ... London: Tonson, 1683. 1st edn. Sm 4to. Occas spotting & sl darkening. Disbound. Wing D.2398.
(Dramatis Personae) **$275 [≈ £143]**

Dryden, John & Lee, Nathaniel
- Oedipus: a Tragedy ... The Third Edition. London: Bentley, 1687. 4to. [vi],71,[3] pp. Browned, few marg tears. Disbound. Wing D.2324. *(Clark)* **£32 [≈ $61]**

Du Bartas, Guillaume de Salluste
- Dv Bartas His deuine Weekes and Workes Translated by Josuah Syluester. Now fourthly corr: & Augm: ... London: 1613. Thick 8vo. [xxxii], 819, [xlvi],87,[viii] pp. Engvd title, w'cuts in text. Sl marking, sm reprs to title. New period style calf. STC 21652.
(Sotheran's) **£285 [≈ $547]**

Dubreuil, Jean
- The Practice of Perspective ... By a Jesuit of Paris ... Translated ... by E. Chambers. The Third Edition. London: Bowles, 1743 [sic]. 4to. xviii,150 pp. 2 fldg & 150 full page plates. Text pasted to versos of Aa1 & Aa3. Period calf, sl worn. Anon.
(Rankin) **£225 [≈ $431]**
- The Practice of Perspective ... By a Jesuit of Paris ... Translated ... by E. Chambers. London: Tho. & John Bowles, 1749. "Third Edition" of this translation. 4to. 2 fldg plates (1 reprd), 150 full page engvs, each with facing text. Contemp calf gilt. Anon.
(Ximenes) **$800 [≈ £416]**
- The Practice of Perspective ... By a Jesuit of Paris. London: 1749. 3rd edn of the Chambers version. 4to. xvi,16 pp. 2 fldg plates (1 reprd), 150 plates (1 loose), each plate with facing text. Contemp calf, rebacked. Anon. *(Bernett)* **$950 [≈ £494]**

Duck, Stephen
- The Vision. A Poem of the Death of Her most gracious Majesty Queen Caroline. London: for J. Roberts & J. Jackson, 1737, 1st edn. Folio. Half-title. Disbound.
(Ximenes) **$650 [≈ £338]**

Du Fresnoy, C.A.
- The Art of Painting. London: Lintot, 1750. 3rd edn of Dryden's translation. Cr 8vo. [18], [lxx],[404] pp. Frontis. Occas sl marks. Contemp calf gilt, rebacked & restored.
(Ash) **£100 [≈ $191]**

Dugdale, Sir William
- The Antient Usage in bearing such Ensigns of Honour as are commonly call'd Arms ... Oxford: at the Theater ..., 1682. 1st edn, 2nd issue. Sm 8vo. [viii],210 pp. Advt on 1st leaf, 17 ctlg pp at end. Title marg trimmed.

Contemp calf, spine worn. Wing D.2477A.
(Vanbrugh) **£125 [≈ $239]**
- The Antient Usage in bearing such Ensigns of Honour as are commonly call'd Arms. With a Catalogue of the present Nobility of England ... Oxford: 1682. 2nd edn. Sm 8vo. [viii],210 pp. Intl advt leaf, 17 pp ctlg. 1 gathering sprung. Contemp calf, spine worn.
(Vanbrugh) **£65 [≈ $124]**
- Monasticon Anglicanum, or, the History of the Ancient Abbies ... in England and Wales ... London: Sam. Keble, 1693. Folio. [xii], 331, [xiii] pp. 15 plates. Later calf, hinges cracked but firm, mod endpapers.
(Bookpress) **$350 [≈ £182]**

Dulaney, Daniel
- Considerations on the Propriety of Imposing Taxes in the British Colonies, for the Purpose of Raising a Revenue, by Act of Parliament. North America [ie Boston: William McAlpine for John Mein, 1766]. Title, ii, [5]-47 pp. Errata slip. Old wraps, used & worn.
(Reese) **$1,250 [≈ £651]**

Du Mont, Sieur
- A New Voyage to the Levant ... Done into English, and Adorned with Figures. London: for T. Goodwin, 1702. 3rd edn. Sm 8vo. [xxii], 416 pp. 8 fldg plates. Sl foxed. Half mor. *(Worldwide)* **$275 [≈ £143]**

Du Moulin, Louis
- Moral Reflections upon the Number of the Elect ... London: for Richard Janeway, 1680. 1st edn. Sm 4to. [vi],32 pp. Disbound. Wing D.2543. *(Finch)* **£95 [≈ $182]**
- A Short and True Account of the Several Advances the Church of England Hath Made towards Rome. London: ptd in the year, 1680. Disbound. Wing D.2553.
(Waterfield's) **£35 [≈ $67]**

Dumourier, C.F.D.
- Memoirs of General Dumourier, written by himself ... Phila: 1794. 1st Amer edn. 2 parts in one. 260,advt pp. Title margs reprd. Occas foxing & staining. Mod cloth.
(Reese) **$225 [≈ £117]**

The Dunciad ...
- See Pope, Alexander.

Dunn, ----
- A Description of Killarney. London: for J. Dodsley, 1776. 1st edn. Lge 4to. [4],50,[2

blank] pp. Vignette map on title, lge vignette view at end. Lacks half-title. Green mor, gilt label on upper bd. Anon.
(Fenning) **£185 [≈ $355]**

Dunton, John
- The Young Students Library ... London: for John Dunton, 1692. Folio. [iv],479,[16] pp. Fldg frontis reprd. Marg wormtracks in 1st few ff reprd. Rec half calf gilt. Wing D.2635.
(Hollett) **£150 [≈ $287]**

Du Refuge, Eustache
- Arcana Aulica: or, Walsingham's Manual of Prudential Maxims for the States-Man and the Courtier. London: 1655. 12mo. [xxiv],153,[3] pp. Intl & final blank ff. Contemp sheep, sl worn. Wing D.2685. Anon. *(Clark)* **£130 [≈ $249]**
- Arcana Aulica: or, Walsingham's Manual ... added Fragmenta Regalia ... by Sir Robert Naunton. London: 1694. 12mo. [xxiv],247,[5 advt] pp. Frontis. Sep title to 2nd part. Contemp calf, sl rubbed, sm split in jnt. Wing D.2686. Anon. *(Clark)* **£120 [≈ $230]**

Durfey, Thomas
- A Commonwealth of Women. A Play. London: for R. Bentley, & J. Hindmarsh, 1686. 1st edn. Sm 4to. Sl chipping of blank margs at ends. Disbound. Wing D.2715.
(Ximenes) **$400 [≈ £208]**

Durham, James
- Clavis Cantici; or an Exposition of the Song of Solomon. Glasgow: John Bryce, 1767. Contemp sheep, worn, jnts cracked.
(Waterfield's) **£60 [≈ $115]**

Du Val, Claude
- A Geographical Dictionary ... Third Edition corrected. London: ptd by M.C. for Henry Brome, 1678. 132,7 ctlg pp. Fldg map (sm repr without loss). Contemp sheep. Wing D.2920C. Anon.
(C.R. Johnson) **£350 [≈ $671]**

Dwalphintramis (pseud.)
- See Bernard, John.

Dyche, Thomas & Pardon, William
- A New General English Dictionary ... together with a Supplement. The Third Edition, with Additions ... London: for Richard Ware, 1740. 8vo. Marg worm at front sl affecting text but not sense. Contemp calf, hd of spine sl worn, lacks f.e.ps.

(Jarndyce) **£80 [≈ $153]**
- A New General English Dictionary ... Fourth Edition ... London: for Richard Ware, 1744. 8vo. Names & scrawls on endpapers. Contemp calf, spine ends & crnrs worn, splits in hinges.   *(Jarndyce)* **£110 [≈ $211]**
- A New General English Dictionary ... Twelfth Edition ... London: Catherine & Richard Ware, 1765. 8vo. Rebound in half calf.   *(Jarndyce)* **£95 [≈ $182]**
- A New General English Dictionary ... Fourteenth Edition ... London: C. & R. Ware, J. Beecroft ..., 1771. 8vo. Contemp calf gilt, rebacked.   *(Jarndyce)* **£85 [≈ $163]**

Dyde, William
- The History and Antiquities of Tewkesbury. Tewkesbury: ptd by the editor, & sold by G. Wilkie, 1798. 2nd edn, with addtns. 8vo. 10 pp subscribers. Frontis, map, 3 plates. Orig pale blue bds, drab backstrip, paper label, sm hole in upper cvr. *(Ximenes)* **$200 [≈ £104]**

Dyer, John
- Poems ... London: John Hughs, for Dodsley, 1761. 1st coll edn. 8vo. 188 pp. 3 engvd ills. Orig calf, spine reprd.
    (Vanbrugh) **£165 [≈ $316]**
- Poems. Viz. I. Grongar Hill. II. The Ruins of Rome. III. The Fleece ... London: John Hughes for Dodsley, 1761. 1st edn. 8vo. 188 pp. 3 plates. Orig calf, rebacked.
    (Bickersteth) **£85 [≈ $163]**

Eachard, John
- The Grounds and Occasions of the Contempt of the Clergy and Religion enquired into; in a Letter to R.L. ... London: for T. Davies, 1772. New edn. 2 vols. 8vo. iv,296; x,228 pp. 18th c tree calf gilt, sl worn, 1 jnt cracked.
    (Young's) **£38 [≈ $72]**
- Some Opinions of Mr. Hobbs considered in a Second Dialogue between Philautus and Timothy. By the same Author. London: J. Macock for Walter Kettilby, 1673. A few gatherings sl stained at foredge. Lacks A1 (half-title?). Rebound in calf. Wing E.64. Anon.   *(Jarndyce)* **£200 [≈ $383]**
- A Vindication of the Clergy, from the Contempt imposed upon them by the Author of the Contempt of the Clergy and Religion ... London: Andr. Clark, for Hen. Brome ..., 1672. 1st edn. 8vo. xvi,135 pp. Rec contemp style calf. Wing E.65. *(Young's)* **£95 [≈ $182]**

Eachard, Laurence
- See Echard, Laurence.

Earle, Jabez
- A Funeral Sermon occasioned by the Death of the late reverend John Cumming ... Minister of the Scots Church in London. London: for J. Gray, 1729. Disbound.
    (Waterfield's) **£20 [≈ $38]**

Earle, John
- Microcosmography: or, a Piece of the World Discover'd. in Essays and Characters. London: E. Say, 1732. 12mo. [ii],ii,iv,[iv],164 pp. Contemp calf, rebacked & recrnrd.
    (Sotheran's) **£235 [≈ $451]**

Eastcott, Richard
- Sketches of the Origin, Progress and Effects of Music ... Bath: S. Hazard, 1793. Orig bds, uncut. Sgnd by the author on title.
    (C.R. Johnson) **£185 [≈ $355]**

Easton, James
- Human Longevity ... Salisbury: James Easton, 1799. 1st edn. 8vo. xxxii,[lx],292 pp. Occas sl spotting. Orig bds, paper label, uncut, spine sl rubbed.
    (Pickering) **$500 [≈ £260]**

Eaton, Richard
- A Book of Rates, Inwards and Outwards ... The Method of making Entries Inwards and Outwards ... New and useful Tables ... Second Edition. Dublin: Boulter Greirson, 1767. 8vo. [iv], xxiv,279 pp. Contemp calf, red mor label.   *(Finch)* **£320 [≈ $614]**

Echard, Laurence
- The Gazetteer's: or, Newsman's Interpreter; being a Geographical Index of all the Considerable Cities ... in Europe ... London: for Tho. Salusbury, 1693. 2nd edn. 12mo. Contemp calf, gilt spine, sl rubbed, sm crack 1 jnt. Wing E.145. *(Young's)* **£120 [≈ $230]**
- The Gazetteer's; or, Newsman's Interpreter. Being a Geographical Index of all the Considerable Cities ... London: Knapton, Robinson, Ballard, 1724. 2 parts in one vol. 12th edn, 5th edn. 12mo. Contemp calf, sl rubbed, sm split in hinge.
    (Jarndyce) **£85 [≈ $163]**
- The Gazetteer's, or, Newsman's Interpreter. being a Geographical Index of all the Considerable Provinces, Cities ... in Europe ... Asia, Africa and America ... London: for S.

Ballard ..., 1741. 15th & 8th edns. 2 parts in one vol. 8vo. Old calf. *(Young's)* £46 [≈ $88]
- A General Ecclesiastical History from the Nativity of our Blessed Saviour to the first Establishment of Christianity ... Fifth Edition. London: Tonson, 1719. Folio. [xiv], 472,[34] pp. Frontis, dble-page map. Contemp calf, sl worn. *(Clark)* £40 [≈ $76]
- The History of England ... London: Tonson, 1707-18. 1st edn. 3 vols. Folio. Port, 3 frontis. Contemp calf, gilt dec backstrips relaid, minor wear. *(Clark)* £180 [≈ $345]

Ecton, John
- Liber Valorum et Decimarum; Being an Account of the Valuation and Yearly Tenths of all such Ecclesiastical Benefices in England and Wales ... London: Harrison, 1711. 8vo. [viii], 396,[xii] pp. Contemp calf, rebacked. *(Lamb)* £30 [≈ $57]
- Thesaurus Rerum Ecclesiasticarum being an Account of the Valuation of All the Ecclesiastical Benefices in the Several Dioceses of England and Wales ... Second Edition ... by Browne Willis. London: Knapton ..., 1754. 4to. xl,704 pp. Mod half mor. *(Lamb)* £50 [≈ $95]

Edgeworth, Maria
- Letters for Literary Ladies ... Second Edition, Corrected and much Enlarged ... London: for J. Johnson, 1799. 8vo. v,[iii], 240 pp. Contemp tree calf, sl rubbed, minor cracking in jnts. *(Burmester)* £175 [≈ $335]

Edmondson, Joseph
- An Historical and Genealogical Account of the Noble Family of Greville ... London: 1766. 8vo. [iv],108 pp. 9 fldg pedigrees, plans, plates &c., num text w'cuts. Some browning & spotting. Half calf gilt, worn, piece missing from spine.
(Hollett) £38 [≈ $72]

Edwards, George
- A Discourse on the Emigration of British Birds ... By a Naturalist. The Second Edition. London: for Stanley Crowder; & B.C. Collins, Salisbury, [1781]. 2nd edn. 8vo. [ii], ix,[i],45 pp, advt leaf. Half-title sl browned & frayed. Old wraps. Anon.
(Burmester) £65 [≈ $124]

Edwards, Jonathan
- A Faithful Narrative of the Surprising Work of God in the Conversion of many Hundred Souls in Northampton ... in New-England ...

Edinburgh: reptd for J. Oswald, London ..., 1737. Sm 8vo. xvi,132 pp. Contemp sheep, rebacked, recrnrd. *(Sotheran's)* £285 [≈ $547]

Edwards, Thomas
- The Canons of Criticism, and Glossary, being a Supplement to Mr. Warburton's Edition of Shakespear ... London: for C. Bathurst, 1758. 6th edn. 8vo. [vi],325,[16],1 advt pp. Old calf, rebacked. Anon. *(Young's)* £65 [≈ $124]

Egerton, Thomas & John
- Egerton's Theatrical Remembrancer ... London: for T. & J. Egerton, 1788. 1st edn. 12mo. Sm hole not affecting legibility. Mod qtr cloth. *(Dramatis Personae)* $175 [≈ £91]

Eginardus (pseud.)
- Memoirs of Europe ... see Manley, Mary Delariviere.

Eighty-Nine Fugitive Fables ...
- Eighty-Nine Fugitive Fables, in Verse ... London: Murray, 1792. half-title, viii,232 pp. Orig wraps, uncut, sl worn.
(C.R. Johnson) £125 [≈ $239]

The Elaboratory Laid Open ...
- See Dossie, Robert.

An Election Ball ...
- See Anstey, Christopher.

An Elegy Written in a Country Church Yard ...
- See Gray, Thomas.

Eleven Opinions about Mr. H----y ...
- See Defoe, Daniel.

Elliot, John
- An Account of the Nature and Medicinal Virtues of the Principal Mineral Waters of Great Britain and Ireland ... Second Edition, Corrected and Enlarged. London: for J. Johnson, 1789. 8vo. Fldg plate. Contemp calf, gilt spine. *(Waterfield's)* £200 [≈ $383]

Ellis, Clement
- The Vanity of Scoffing: or A Letter to a Witty Gentleman ... London: for R. Royston, 1674. 1st edn. 38 pp. Title sl stained, faint BM duplicate stamp on verso. Wing E.576. Anon.
(Hollett) £75 [≈ $143]

Ellis, Henry
- Voyage to Hudson's-Bay. By the Dobbs Galley and California, in the Years 1746 and 1747. For Discovering a North West Passage ... London: Whitridge, 1748. 1st edn. Sm 8vo. xxviii, 336 pp. Fldg map, 9 plates. Few sm marg reprs, sl stains. Rec mor gilt.
(Terramedia) **$1,500 [≈ £781]**

Ellis, William
- New Experiments in Husbandry, for the Month of April ... London: for the author, sold by Fox, Meadows, Astley, Bickerton, 1736. 1st edn. 8vo. [viii],124,[4] pp. Plate (backed). Contemp underlining & notes. Rec bds.
(Burmester) **£85 [≈ $163]**

Elstob, Elizabeth (ed.)
- An English-Saxon Homily on the Birthday of St Gregory ... Translated into Modern English, with Notes, &c. by Eliz. Elstob. London: W. Bowyer, 1709. 1st edn. 8vo. [x], lx, [ii], 44,[iv],11, [ii], [6 subscribers] pp. Frontis. Orig calf, rubbed, jnts cracked.
(Bickersteth) **£385 [≈ $739]**

Elsynge, Henry
- The Ancient Method and Manner of holding Parliaments in England. The Third Edition enlarged. London: for S.S. & sold by Tho. Dring, 1675. 371 pp. Rebound in qtr sheep. Wing E.654A. *(C.R. Johnson)* **£160 [≈ $307]**
- The Ancient Method and Manner of Holding Parliaments in England ... Third Edition Enlarged. London: for S.S. & sold by Thomas dring, 1675. Lge 12mo. [xii],371 pp. V sl damp stain 1st 7 ff. Contemp calf, gilt spine, lacks label. Wing E.645A.
(Vanbrugh) **£125 [≈ $239]**

Emblems of Mortality ...
- See Bewick, Thomas & John (illust.).

Emerson, William
- The Mathematical Principles of Geography ... [with] Dialling, or the Art of Drawing Dials. London: 1770. 2 parts in one vol. 8vo. [ii],viii,ii,172; iv,164 pp. 4 + 18 fldg plates. Orig tree calf, spine ends chipped.
(Vanbrugh) **£175 [≈ $335]**

Emiliane, Gabriel d' (Antonio Gavin)
- Observations on the Journy [sic] to Naples ... By the Author of ... The Frauds of Romish Monks and Priests. London: Samuel Roycroft, for Robert Clavell, 1691. 3 advt pp. Lib stamp on title. Contemp calf, crnrs worn,

inner hinge strengthened. Wing G.393.
(Jarndyce) **£110 [≈ $211]**

Enfield, William
- Institutes of Natural Philosophy, Theoretical and Experimental. Second Edition, with Corrections and Considerable Additions ... London: J. Johnson, 1799. 4to. xvi,428 pp. 13 plates. Minor spotting. Orig bds, untrimmed, rebacked, crnrs sl worn.
(Clark) **£160 [≈ $307]**

England ...
- England's Petition to their King. Or an humble Petition of the Distressed and almost Destroyed Subjects of England ... [London]: Printed on the Day of Jacobs Trouble ..., May 5, 1643. 4to. [2],6 pp. Some underlining. Disbound. Wing E.3013.
(Jarndyce) **£120 [≈ $230]**
- England's Remembrancer: Setting forth the Beginning of Papal Tyrannies, Bloody Persecutions, Plots, and Inhuman Butcheries ... London: for E. Smith, 1682. 173 pp. Contemp calf, rebacked. Wing E.3036.
(C.R. Johnson) **£110 [≈ $211]**

English ...
- The English Garden ... see Mason, William.
- English Irish Dictionary ... see O'Begley, Conor.
- English Liberties ... see Care, Henry.
- The English Topographer ... see Rawlinson, Richard.

Enquiry ...
- An Enquiry after Wit ... see Astell, Mary.
- An Enquiry into the Causes of the Decay of the Dissenting Interest ... see Gough, Strickland.
- An Enquiry into the Conduct of our Domestic Affairs ... see Pulteney, William.

Entertaining Account ...
- An Entertaining Account of all the Countries of the Known World Describing the different Religions, Habits, Tempers, Customs, Traffick, and Manufactures, of their Inhabitants ... London: for R. Goadby, Sherborne, 1752. 3rd edn. 8vo. 261,8 pp. 6 plates. Contemp calf, rebacked
(Young's) **£120 [≈ $230]**

Entick, John
- Entick's New Spelling Dictionary ... New

Edition. revised, corrected, and enlarged ... added, A Catalogue ... by William Crakelt. London: Charles Dilly, 1788. Oblong 8vo. Contemp sheep, crnrs rubbed, spine partly defective.   *(Jarndyce)* **£120 [≈ $230]**
- Entick's New Spelling Dictionary ... by William Crakelt. London: C. Dilly ..., 1796. Sq 12mo. Title cropped at hd, some soiling & browning, pen-trials. Contemp sheep, rec reback, crnrs worn.   *(Clark)* **£68 [≈ $130]**

An Epistle to the Fair-Sex ...
- An Epistle to the Fair-Sex, on the Subject of Drinking ... Dublin: G. Faulkner, 1744. 55 pp, advt leaf. Rebound in bds.
                    (C.R. Johnson) **£550 [≈ $1,055]**

Equiano, Olaudah
- See Vassa, Gustavus.

Erasmus, Desiderius
- All the Familiar Colloquies ... Translated ... by N[athan] Bailey. London: for J. Darby ..., 1725. 1st of this edn. 8vo. [iv],608 pp. Pagination jumps from 288 to 305. Lacks final advt leaf. Sl foxing. Rec period style calf.
                    (Sotheran's) **£135 [≈ $259]**
- All the Familiar Colloquies ... Translated ... by N. Bailey. London: Knapton ..., 1733. 2nd edn. 19th c calf, sl rubbed.
                    (Bell) **£75 [≈ $143]**
- Moriae Encomium: or, A Panegyrick upon Folly ... Illustrated with above Fifty Curious Cuts, design'd and Drawn by Hans Holbeine ... London: J. Woodward, 1709. 8vo. Port frontis, 29 plates. Contemp calf.
                    (Vanbrugh) **£255 [≈ $489]**

Erskine, Thomas
- A View of the Causes and Consequences of the Present War with France. London: for J. Debrett, 1797. 17th edn. 8vo. [iv],138,2 advt pp. Half-title. Stitched as issued, uncut.
                    (Young's) **£35 [≈ $67]**
- A View of the Causes and Consequences of the Present War with France. The Eighteenth Edition. London: for J. Debrett, 1797. 8vo. Rec binder's cloth.   *(Jarndyce)* **£15 [≈ $28]**

Espagnet, Jean d'
- Enchyridion Physicae Restitutae, or, the Summary of Physicks recovered. London: 1651. 1st edn in English. 12mo. [xx],167,[1] pp. Lacks A1 (blank except for sgntr) & A12 as usual. Dust soiling & dampstains, a few headlines just shaved. Contemp mor gilt,

rebacked. Wing E.3276A.
                    (Gaskell) **£800 [≈ $1,535]**

Esprit, Jacques
- Discourse on the deceitfulness of Humane Virtues. Done out of the French by William Beauvoir ... added, The Duke de la Rochefoucaut's Moral Reflections. London: Bell, Smith, Round, 1706. 8vo. [xvi],432, [iv], xiv,95,[viii] pp. Orig calf, sl worn.
                    (Bickersteth) **£48 [≈ $72]**

Essay(s) ...
- An Essay on Brewing ... see Combrune, Michael.
- An Essay on Crimes and Punishments ... see Beccaria, Cesare.
- An Essay on Design in Gardening ... see Mason, George.
- An Essay on Hunting. By A Country Squire. London: for J. Roberts, 1733. 92 pp. Rebound in qtr mor. Contemp MS attribution to 'The Rev. Mr. Squire, A.M., Chancellor of Wells".
                    (C.R. Johnson) **£350 [≈ $671]**
- An Essay on Political Lying. The Second Edition. London: S. Hooper, 1757. 28 pp. Disbound.   *(C.R. Johnson)* **£35 [≈ $67]**
- An Essay on Punctuation ... see Robertson, Joseph.
- An Essay on Reason ... see Harte, William.
- An Essay on the Antiquity of the Irish Language ... see Vallancey, Charles.
- An Essay on the Art of Ingeniously Tormenting ... see Collier, Jane.
- An Essay on the Different Stiles of Poetry ... see Parnell, Thomas.
- An Essay on the Dramatic Character of Sir John Falstaff ... see Morgann, Maurice.
- An Essay on the Landscape Painting ... see Pott, Joseph Holden.
- Essay on the Life and Character of Petrarch ... see Tytler, Alexander Fraser.
- An Essay on the Natural History of Guiana ... see Bancroft, E.
- An Essay on the Nature, Design, and Origin, of Sacrifices ... see Sykes, Arthur Ashley.
- An Essay on the Study on the Study of Antiquities ... see Burgess, Thomas.
- An Essay toward the Proof of a Separate State of Souls ... see Watts, Isaac.
- An Essay upon the Harmony of Language ... see Mitford, William.

- Essays Moral, Philosophical, and Political ...
  see Mills, John (d. 1784?).
- Essays on Song-Writing ... see Aikin, John.
- Essays, Philosophical, Historical and Literary
  ... see Belsham, William.

Este, Charles
- A Journey in 1793, through Flanders,
  Brabant, and Germany, to Switzerland ...
  London: for J. Debrett, 1795. 1st edn. 8vo.
  [iv],381,[i blank],[x] pp. Orig bds, uncut, MS
  label, spine darkened.   *(Finch)* **£70 [≈ $134]**
- A Journey in the Year 1793, through
  Flanders, Brabant, and Germany, to
  Switzerland. London: for J. Debrett ..., 1795.
  1st edn. 8vo. [iv],381,[x] pp. Contemp half
  calf, rebacked.   *(Young's)* **£70 [≈ $134]**

**An Estimate of the Manners and
Principles of the Times ...**
- See Brown, John.

Euclid
- Euclid's Elements ... from the Latin ... of
  Commandine ... Preface ... by John Keill ...
  Revised ... by Samuel Cunn. The Eleventh
  Edition ... London: Strahan ..., 1772. 8vo.
  [16], 399,[1 advt] pp. 14 fldg plates (1 with 5
  onlays). Rec bds.   *(Fenning)* **£85 [≈ $163]**

Euphrosyne ...
- See Graves, Richard.

Eusebius, Pamphili
- The Auncient Ecclesiastical Histories ...
  Faithfully translated by Meredith Hanmer.
  London: Vautrollier, 1585. 2nd edn. Folio. 5
  parts in 1 vol, each with sep title. Few damp
  stains. 1st title laid down & sl soiled. Lacks
  blanks 2Y4 & 3D6. 19th c half calf. STC
  10573.   *(Robertshaw)* **£175 [≈ $335]**
- The History of the Church ... Cambridge:
  John Hayes, 1683. Folio. Longitudinal title,
  red & black title, [40],700,[22] pp. Few sl
  marks. Sm persistent marg worm hole. Old
  calf, jnts cracked, spine ends & crnr tips
  worn. Wing E.3423.
       (Bow Windows) **£230 [≈ $441]**
- The History of the Church ... Cambridge:
  John Hayes for Nathaniel Rolls, 1692. Folio.
  [xlii],700,[22] pp. Old style half calf. Wing
  E.3424.   *(Lloyd-Roberts)* **£150 [≈ $287]**

Eustace, John Chetwood
- An Elegy to the Memory of the Right
  Honourable Edmund Burke. London:

Rivington, 1798. 4to. 15 pp. Orig blue wraps,
unopened.   *(C.R. Johnson)* **£125 [≈ $239]**

Euthelius (pseudonym)
- Religion represented in a true Light. Oxford:
  Clarendon Printing House, 1761. 4to. List of
  subscribers. Mrbld wraps, uncut, backstrip
  defective.   *(Waterfield's)* **£135 [≈ $259]**

Evans, Abel
- The Apparition. A Poem ... London: ptd in
  the year 1710. 1st edn. 8vo. 38 pp. Mrbld
  wraps. Anon.   *(Young's)* **£75 [≈ $143]**
- Vertumnus. An Epistle of Mr Jacob Bobart,
  Botany Professor to the University of Oxford
  and Keeper of the Physick-Garden. By the
  Author of The Apparition. Oxford: L.L. for
  Stephen Fletcher, London, 1713. New bds.
  Anon.   *(C.R. Johnson)* **£175 [≈ $335]**

Evans, Revd Evan
- Some Specimens of the Poetry of the Antient
  Welsh Bards. Translated into English. With
  Explanatory Notes ... London: Dodsley,
  1764. 1st edn. 4to. viii,vi,[i], [7]-162,[i] pp.
  Title rather dusty, some spotting to later
  gatherings, sm hole in last leaf. Half calf
  antique.   *(Finch)* **£120 [≈ $230]**
- Some Specimens of the Poetry of the Antient
  Welsh Bards, translated into English, with
  Explanatory Notes ... London: Dodsley,
  1764. Sm 4to. Mod linen backed bds.
       (Emerald Isle) **£65 [≈ $124]**

Evans, John
- The Case of Kneeling at the Holy Sacrament
  Stated and Resolved. London: for T. Basset,
  D. Took & F. Gardiner, 1683. 2 parts. 4to.
  Disbound. Wing E.3445, 3448. Anon.
       (Waterfield's) **£45 [≈ $86]**

Evelyn, John
- Acetaria, a Discourse of Sallets. London:
  1706. 2nd edn. 8vo. [xl],190,[49] pp. Fldg
  table. Pp 33 to end foxed. Mod half calf gilt.
       (Wheldon & Wesley) **£200 [≈ $383]**
- Fumifugium: or, the Inconvenience of the
  Aer [sic], and Smoake of London Dissipated.
  Together with some Remedies humbly
  proposed by J.E. ... London: for B. White,
  1772. 4to. Advt leaf at end. New bds.
       (Georges) **£150 [≈ $287]**
- Kalendarium Hortense: or, the Gard'ners
  Almanac, directing what he is to do monthly
  throughout the year ... London: 1673. 5th
  edn. Sm 8vo. 127,[8] pp. Lacks half-title.

Blind stamp on title. New calf.
(Wheldon & Wesley) **£90 [≈ $172]**
- Kalendarium Hortense: or, the Gard'ners Almanac. London: 1706. 10th edn. 8vo. [vi],x, [xiv], 170,[14] pp. Frontis, plates. Mod half calf. *(Wheldon & Wesley)* **£80 [≈ $153]**
- Sculptura. London: Murray, 1755. 2nd edn. 8vo. [iv],xxvi,140 pp. Frontis, 2 plates (inc fldg mezzotint). Speckled calf, sl rubbed.
(Bookpress) **$425 [≈ £221]**
- Sylva: or A Discourse of Forest Trees and the Propagation of Timber in His Majesty's Dominions. London: 1776. 1st Hunter edn. 4to. liv, 649,ix pp. Fldg table, 40 plates. Contemp calf, backstrip relaid.
(Henly) **£245 [≈ $470]**

Evelyn, John
- Sylva, or a Discourse of Forest Trees. London: 1670. 2nd edn, enlgd. Folio. [xlviii], 247,[iv], 67,33, [2] pp. Imprimatur leaf (mtd, old notes on reverse), errata leaf, insert *Z. 5 engvs. Mod calf.
(Wheldon & Wesley) **£200 [≈ $383]**

Ewing, Alexander
- Practical Astronomy ... Edinburgh: 1797. Only edn. 8vo. xi,268,143 pp. Fldg plate. Orig tree calf, spine sl rubbed.
(Bickersteth) **£55 [≈ $105]**

Exempla Moralia ...
- Exempla Moralia or Third Book of new English Examples to be rendered into Latin ... lately printed for the use of Youth. A New Edition, revised. Eton: T. Pote, 1789. 8vo. Lacks rear free endpaper. Contemp sheep.
(Waterfield's) **£45 [≈ $86]**

Expediency ...
- The Expediency and Necessity of revising and improving the Publick Liturgy humbly represented, being the Substance of an Essay for a Review of the Book of Common Prayer ... London: for R. Griffiths, 1749. 8vo. Disbound. *(Waterfield's)* **£60 [≈ $115]**

Exquemeling, Alexandre Olivier
- The History of the Bucaniers of America ... London: for T. Evans, 1774. 5th edn. 2 vols. 8vo. [iv],318; [ii],360,[12] pp. Rec calf. Anon.
(Young's) **£240 [≈ $460]**

F., J.
- Cryptomenysis Patefacta ... see Falconer, John.

F., L.M.D.
- Memoirs and Reflections ... see La Fare, Charles Augustus de.

Fairfax, Thomas
- The Complete Sportsman; or Country Gentleman's Recreation ... London: for J. Cooke, 1765. 12mo. Contemp speckled sheep gilt, red label. *(Jarndyce)* **£125 [≈ $239]**

Faith ...
- The Faith of One God, who is only the Father; and of one Mediator between God and Men ... Asserted and Defended, in Several Tracts. London: printed in the Year, 1691. 8vo. Sm tear general title. Contemp calf, rubbed, jnts cracked, crnrs worn. Wing F.258B. *(Waterfield's)* **£105 [≈ $201]**

Falconer, John
- Cryptomenysis Patefacta: Or the Art of Secret Information Disclosed without a Key ... Rules for Decyphering all Manner of Secret Writing ... By J.F. London: 1685. 1st edn. [xxiv],180 pp. Blank before title. Sl wear. Contemp sheep, rebacked, recrnrd. Wing F.296. *(Clark)* **£285 [≈ $547]**

Falconer, William
- An Account of the Efficacy of the Aqua Mephitica Alkalina ... London: Cadell, 1792. 4th edn. 8vo. iv,208 pp. Half calf, upper bd loose. *(Hemlock)* **$275 [≈ £143]**
- A Dissertation on the Influence of the Passions upon Disorders of the Body ... London: for C. Dilly, 1791. 2nd edn. Sm 8vo. iv, 148 pp. Port. Sl dampstain. Rec bds.
(Burmester) **£175 [≈ $335]**
- Observations respecting the Pulse ... London: Cadell & Davies, 1796. 1st edn. Sm 8vo. [ii],158 pp. Lacks half-title. Tables. 2 sm marg tears. Rec bds.
(Burmester) **£250 [≈ $479]**

Fanshawe, Sir Richard
- Il Pastor Fido: The Faithful Shepherd [of Guarini]. With the Addition of Divers Other Poems ... London: for Henry Herringman, 1676. 8vo. [xxii],321 pp. W'cut before text of Pastor Fido. Prelims sl browned. Early 18th c sheep, gilt spine. Wing G.2177.
(Vanbrugh) **£145 [≈ $278]**

Farley, John
- The London Art of Cookery. London: for John Fielding ..., 1783. 1st edn. Demy 8vo.

[xx],[460] pp. Port frontis, 12 plates. Rec mor gilt. *(Ash)* **£400 [≈$767]**

The Farmer's Guide to Hiring and Stocking Farms ...
- See Young, Arthur.

Farmer, Richard
- An Essay on the Learning of Shakespeare: addressed to Joseph Cradock, Esq. Cambridge: J. Archdeacon, 1767. 50 pp. Rebound in qtr calf, mrbld bds.
(C.R. Johnson) **£185 [≈$355]**

Farquhar, George
- The Works ... The Eighth Edition. London: Knapton ..., 1742. 2 vols. 12mo. Contemp mottled calf, lacks 1 label.
(Waterfield's) **£50 [≈$95]**
- The Works ... Tenth Edition ... added, some Memoirs of the Author, never before Published. London: Rivington, 1772. 2 vols. 8vo. Orig calf, hinges tender but firm.
(Limestone Hills) **$110 [≈£57]**
- The Works ... Tenth Edition ... added some Memoirs of the Author ... London: Rivington ..., 1772. 2 vols. 12mo. 4 advt pp vol 1, 4 pp ctlg vol 2. Contemp calf, labels.
(Jarndyce) **£140 [≈$268]**

Farringdon, Anthony
- LXXX Sermons ... the 2nd Edition in Two Volumes ... With a Large Table to Both. London: 1672. Folio. 3 vols in 2. 34,548, 8,547-1129, [36],15,562 pp. Lacks vol 3 title. Few sm marg wormholes. 2 ff dusty. rebound in half mor. Wing F.429A & F432.
(Humber) **£150 [≈$287]**

A Father's Legacy to his Daughters ...
- See Gregory, John.

Fauquier, Francis
- An Essay on Ways and Means for Raising Money for the Support of the Present War, without Increasing the Public Debts ... London: 1756. 2nd edn, enlgd. iv,58 pp. Half-title. Mod cloth. *(Reese)* **$600 [≈£312]**

Fawcett, Benjamin
- Murther Lamented and Improved. A Sermon preached at Kidderminster June 16 1771. On the Occasion of the Death of John Child ... Shrewsbury: J. Eddowes, 1771. Half-title,35 pp. Rebound in bds.
(C.R. Johnson) **£40 [≈$76]**

- Observations on the Nature, Causes and Cure of Melancholy: especially of that which is called Religious Melancholy. Shrewsbury: J. Eddowes, 1780. Contemp qtr calf, mrbld bds.
(C.R. Johnson) **£225 [≈$431]**

Fawcett, William
- Rules and Regulations for the Sword Exercise of the Cavalry. London: The War Office, 1796. 1st edn. 8vo. xii,98,[1] pp. 29 plates. Orig mrbld bds. Anon.
(Bookpress) **$575 [≈£299]**

Fawkes, Francis
- Original Poems and Translations. London: for the author ..., 1761. 1st edn. 8vo. Subscribers. Lacks errata slip. Tiny marg worm holes. Remains of b'plate. Contemp calf gilt. *(Hannas)* **£130 [≈$249]**
- Original Poems and Translations. London: for the author ..., 1761. 1st edn. Fine Paper issue, with the preface to the subscribers. 20 pp subscribers. Title vignette. Damp staining. Early bds, uncut, 19th c cloth spine, lib labels. *(Jarndyce)* **£120 [≈$230]**
- Original Poems and Translations. London: for the author ..., 1761. 1st edn. 8vo. Subscribers. Errata slip. Faint waterstains in upper marg. Mod qtr mor.
(Hannas) **£100 [≈$191]**

The Fears of the Nation Quieted ...
- The Fears of the Nation Quieted; in a Letter to a Whig-Gentleman. London: for J. Roberts ..., 1714. 1st edn. 8vo. 54 pp. Title soiled. Inner marg tear reprd.
(Young's) **£55 [≈$105]**

Fellows, John
- An Elegiac Poem in Blank Verse on the Death of the Rev. Mr. A.M. Toplady, A.B. late Vicar of Broad Hembury, Devon. London: J. Mathews & G. Keith, 1778. Half-title, 28 pp. Disbound. *(C.R. Johnson)* **£90 [≈$172]**

Feltham, John
- The English Enchiridion ... Bath: R. Cruttwell ..., 1799. 1st edn. 8vo. viii,125 pp. Frontis. 1 leaf cleanly torn. Parchment cvrd bds, backstrip split, sl loose.
(Young's) **£18 [≈$34]**
- A Tour through the Isle of Mann, in 1797 and 1798 ... Bath: R. Cruttwell, 1798. 1st edn. 8vo. [viii],294,[ii] pp. Fldg map, 3 plates, fldg table, vignettes. Map offset onto title. Contemp calf, rebacked.
(Clark) **£110 [≈$211]**

Feltham, Owen
- A Brief Character of the Low-Countries under the States. Being Three Weeks Observations of the Vices and Vertues of the Inhabitants. London: 1660. 2nd authorised edn. 16mo. [vi],100 pp. Lacks A1 (blank). Sl foxed & browned. 19th c calf, sl worn. Wing F.650. Anon.   *(Burmester)* **£160 [≈ $307]**

Felton, Henry
- A Dissertation on Reading the Classics, and forming a Just Style ... Third Edition corrected. London: for Jonah Bowyer, 1718. 12mo. [ii],xx,[xii],230 pp. Lacks f.e.p. Contemp calf, lacks label, extremities worn, upper jnt cracked but firm.
          (Finch) **£48 [≈ $92]**
- A Dissertation on Reading the Classics, and Forming a Just Style ... London: for Richard Baldwin ..., 1753. 5th edn. 12mo. xvi, [xxii],240 pp. Contemp calf, v sl rubbed.
          (Young's) **£55 [≈ $105]**

The Female Jockey Club ...
- See Pigott, Charles.

Fenelon, Francois de Salignac de la Mothe
- Instructions for the Education of a Daughter ... added a Small Tract of Instructions for the Conduct of Young Ladies ... Done into English and Revised by Dr. George Hickes. Edinburgh: James Reid, 1750. 12mo. [xii],283 pp. Frontis. Contemp sheep, sl worn. Anon   *(Burmester)* **£85 [≈ $163]**
- Twenty Seven Moral Tales and Fables, French and English ... for the Use of Schools ... prefix'd An Essay on the Nature of Fable ... London: for J. Wilcox ..., 1729. 1st edn. 8vo. [viii], xxxiv, 207 pp. Advt leaf. Old calf, backstrip relaid. Anon.
          (Young's) **£90 [≈ $172]**

Fenn, Lady
- A Short History of Insects ... A Pocket Companion for those who visit the Leverian Museum. Norwich: [1797]. Sm 8vo. xxiv,107 pp. 8 cold plates. Outer crnr of 1st few margs stained. Contemp half calf. Anon.
          (Wheldon & Wesley) **£100 [≈ $191]**

Fenn, Eleanor
- School Occurrences: supposed to have arisen among a Set of Young Ladies, under the Tuition of Mrs. Teachwell ... London: John Marshall, [ca 1785]. 3rd edn. Cr 8vo. Contemp calf backed mrbld bds (crnrs worn). Anon.   *(Stewart)* **£75 [≈ $143]**

Fenning, Daniel
- The British Youth's Instructor: or, A New and Easy Guide to Practical Arithmetic ... The Eighth Edition ... London: for S. Crowder, 1775. 12mo. Contemp sheep, sm splits in hinges.   *(Jarndyce)* **£90 [≈ $172]**
- The Ready Reckoner; or, Trader's most useful Assistant ... Ninth Edition. With Additions ... Corrected by Joseph Moon. London: for S. Crowder; & B.C. Collins, Salisbury, 1788. 12mo. Staining. Early coarse brown cloth.   *(Jarndyce)* **£35 [≈ $67]**
- The Royal English Dictionary ... London: for S. Crowder, "1741" [ie 1761]. 1st edn. 8vo. Unpaginated. Lower margs shaved, 2 outer margs trimmed. Minor marg repr to intl licence leaf. 19th c half calf, sl scuffed.
          (Burmester) **£80 [≈ $153]**
- The Royal English Dictionary ... Third Edition improved. London: Baldwin, Hawes, Caslon ..., 1768. Thick 8vo. Unnumbered pp. Occas v sl signs of use. Sl loss to 1 leaf. Rec cloth.   *(Fenning)* **£48.50 [≈ $94]**
- The Royal English Dictionary ... The Fourth Edition, improved ... London: for L. Hawes, T. Caslon ..., 1771. 8vo. Intl licence leaf. Contemp sheep, sl rubbed & scarred, splitting at hinges.   *(Jarndyce)* **£180 [≈ $345]**
- The Universal Spelling Book; or, A New and Easy Guide to the English Language ... Twenty-Second Edition, with Additions. London & Salisbury: 1776. Lge 12mo. vi,[iii],152,[4] pp. W'cut frontis, 8 w'cut text ills. Orig sheep. *(Bickersteth)* **£180 [≈ $345]**
- The Young Man's Book of Knowledge: being a proper Supplement to the Young Man's Companion in Six Parts. The Fourth Edition, revised ... London: S. Crowder & B.C. Collins, 1786. 12mo. xiv, 381, errata pp. Diag, fldg tables. Contemp calf, rebacked.
          (Lamb) **£35 [≈ $67]**

Fenton, Elijah
- Poems on Several Occasions. London: Lintot, 1717. 1st edn. 8vo. [viii],224,[8 advt] pp. Frontis. Contemp panelled calf, rebacked. Anon.   *(Burmester)* **£75 [≈ $143]**
- Poems on Several Occasions. London: Lintot, 1717. 8vo. Sheet Q (advts) present. Frontis. Minute wormhole in some lower marg of some ff. Contemp calf, minor splits in jnts.
          (Waterfield's) **£180 [≈ $345]**

Fenton, Richard
- Poems. London: for E. & T. William, 1790. 168; 166,errata pp. Half-titles. Orig green

paper wraps, uncut, paper label.
(*C.R. Johnson*) £180 [≈$345]

Ferguson, Adam
- An Essay on the History of Civil Society ... A New Edition. Basil: ptd by J.J. Tourneisen, 1789. 1st Basle edn. 8vo. vi,424 pp. Sl foxing, sl marg damp stain to 1st 20 pp. Contemp half mor, jnts reprd.   (*Pickering*) $750 [≈ £390]

Ferguson, James, 1710-1776
- The Art of Drawing in Perspective made easy to those who have no previous knowledge of the Mathematics. London: Strahan & Cadell, 1775. 1st edn. 12mo. xii,123,[1 advt] pp. 9 fldg plates. Contemp calf, rebacked.
(*Gaskell*) £385 [≈ $739]
- The Art of Drawing in Perspective made easy to those who have no previous knowledge of the Mathematics. London: Strahan, 1775. 1st edn. 8vo. xii,123,[1 advt] pp. 9 fldg plates. Lacks half-title. Sl browning, 1 sm repr. Rec bds.   (*Fenning*) £125 [≈ $239]
- Astronomy Explained upon Sir Isaac Newton's Principles ... London: Rivington ..., 1790. 8th edn. 8vo. viii,503,xvi pp. 17 fldg plates. Crnr of pp damp stained. Leather, crnrs worn.   (*Gemmary*) $175 [≈ £91]
- An Easy Introduction to Mechanics, Geometry, Plane Trigonometry ... Optics, Astronomy. To which is prefixed, an Essay [by John Ryland] ... London: Dilly, 1768. Only edn. 12mo. [ii],lii,161,[1] pp. 12 plates. 2 tears reprd. Contemp sheep, rebacked, crnrs reprd, stained.   (*Burmester*) £350 [≈ $671]
- Lectures on Select Subjects in Mechanics, Hydrostatics, Pneumatics, and Optics ... London: for A. Millar, 1760. 1st edn. 8vo. [viii], 418, [vi] pp. 23 plates. Occas sl browning. Contemp calf, new label, inner jnts strengthened, spine ends sl chipped.
(*Rankin*) £150 [≈ $287]
- Tables and Tracts, relative to Several Arts and Sciences. London: Millar & Cadell, 1767. 1st edn. 8vo. xvi,328 pp. 3 plates. Contemp polished sprinkled calf, citron mor label, fine.
(*Gaskell*) £550 [≈ $1,055]

Fergusson, Robert
- Poems. Edinburgh: Ruddiman, 1773. [Bound with his] Poems on Various Subjects ... Part II. Edinburgh: 1779. 1st edns. 2 vols in one. 8vo. [ii],iv,132; viii,152 pp. Engvd title vol 1. Occas browning. Rebound in calf.
(*Rankin*) £1,250 [≈ $2,399]

Ferne, John
- The Blazon of Gentrie ... London: John Windet for Toby Cooke, 1586. 1st edn. Sm 4to. [xx],341,[ii],130 pp. Errata. Blank Z present. W'cut ills. Rec calf & mrbld paper bds. STC 10824.
(*Vanbrugh*) £655 [≈ $1,257]

Field, Richard
- Of the Church. Five Bookes. The Third Edition. Oxford: William Turner, 1635. Folio. [xvi],906 pp. Occas marks & sl marg worm. Contemp calf, crnrs worn, jnts split at ends. STC 10859.   (*Clark*) £90 [≈ $172]

Fielding, Henry
- Amelia ... London: for A. Millar, 1752. 1st edn. 4 vols. 12mo. Lacks final blank vol 1. V sm hole in 1 leaf. Antique mottled calf, red & green labels, a.e.g., probably 19th c by Riviere, spines sl rubbed.
(*Finch*) £375 [≈ $719]
- An Enquiry into the Causes of the late Increase of Robbers ... London: for A. Millar ..., 1751. 1st edn. 8vo. xv,127 pp. Later qtr calf, sl rubbed.
(*Meyer Boswell*) $1,250 [≈ £651]
- The History of the Adventures of Joseph Andrews, and of his Friend Mr. Abraham Adams. London: for A. Millar, 1742. 1st edn. 2 vols. 12mo. Lacks advt ff. A few minor tears, not affecting text. Late 19th c mottled calf gilt. Anon.   (*Hannas*) £580 [≈ $1,113]
- The History of the Adventures of Joseph Andrews ... Third Edition, illustrated with Cuts. London: A. Millar, 1743. 2 vols. 12mo. [xx],226,[ii]; [vi],226 pp. Final advt leaf vol 1. 12 plates. Occas sl soiling, few gatherings advanced. Contemp calf.
(*Clark*) £75 [≈ $143]
- The History of the Adventures of Joseph Andrews, and his Friend Mr. Abraham Adams ... Eighth Edition ... London: A. Millar for T. Cadell, 1768. 2 vols. 8vo. [xx],226; [vi],226 pp. 12 plates. Browned. Contemp calf, rubbed, 2 jnts tender.
(*Clark*) £35 [≈ $67]
- The History of the Adventures of Joseph Andrews ... Tenth Edition, Illustrated with Cuts. London: Strahan, Rivington ..., 1781. 2 vols. 12mo. Engvd plates (dated 1742/3). Contemp calf, red labels.
(*Jarndyce*) £160 [≈ $307]
- The Journal of a Voyage to Lisbon. London: A. Millar, 1755. 1st edn, 1st issue. "228' [ie 276] pp. Half-title. Contemp calf, rebacked.

(C.R. Johnson) £380 [≈ $729]
- The Journal of a Voyage to Lisbon ... London: for A. Millar, 1755. 1st published edn. 12mo. [iv],iv,xvii, [ii],20-240,193-228 pp. Antique mottled calf, red & green labels, a.e.g., probably 19th c by Riviere, spine sl rubbed. *(Finch)* £285 [≈ $547]
- The Journal of a Voyage to Lisbon. London: for A. Millar, 1755. 1st published edn. 12mo. Half-title. Monogram stamp on title. Polished calf gilt, a.e.g., by Riviere, jnts chafed.
(Hannas) £180 [≈ $345]
- The Lottery. A Farce. With the Musick Prefix'd to Each Song. London: for J. Watts, 1732. 1st edn. 8vo. W'cut music in text. Later wraps. Anon.
(Dramatis Personae) $450 [≈ £234]
- Pasquin. A Dramatick Satire on the Times ... London: Ed. Cook ..., 1737. 10th edn. 8vo. 62,1 pp. Lacks half-title. Disbound.
(Young's) £12 [≈ $23]
- The History of Tom Jones, a Foundling. London: for Andrew Millar, 1749. 1st edn. 2nd issue, with errata crrctd, & ptd on heavier paper. 6 vols. 12mo. Few sl signs of age. Old half calf gilt, sl rubbed, spines v sl creased.
(Ash) £1,250 [≈ $2,399]
- The History of Tom Jones, a Foundling. London: for A. Millar, 1749. 2nd edn. 6 vols. 12mo. Orig final blanks in vols 1 & 3. Contemp sprinkled calf, mor labels, spines worn at hd, ft of vol 2 spine chipped, 1 label sl chipped. *(Finch)* £950 [≈ $1,823]
- The History of Tom Jones, a Foundling. London: for A. Millar, 1749. 3rd edn. 4 vols. 12mo. Intl ff of vol 3 wormed at lower edge. Sl browning, v occas staining. Contemp calf, gilt spines, mor labels, crack in 1 jnt, 1 label damaged. *(Finch)* £475 [≈ $911]
- The History of Tom Jones, a Foundling. London: for A. Millar, 1750. 4th edn, rvsd. 4 vols. 12mo. Contemp speckled calf, gilt spines, red & green labels.
(Jarndyce) £260 [≈ $499]
- The History of Tom Jones, a Foundling. London: W. Strahan ..., 1773. 4 vols. Lge 12mo. Contemp calf, hinges cracking, some spine extremities chipped.
(Bookpress) $425 [≈ £221]
- The History of Tom Jones, a Foundling. New Edition. London: Strahan ..., 1782. 4 vols. 4 frontis. Contemp tree calf, elab gilt dec spines, upper jnt vol 1 sl split.
(Gough) £325 [≈ $623]
- The History of Tom Jones ... New Edition. London: Strahan ..., 1782. 4 vols. xx,304;

viii,330; x,288; xii,347 pp. 4 frontis. Contemp tree calf, elab gilt dec spines (with foxes), upper jnt vol 1 split but sound.
(Gough) £250 [≈ $479]
- The History of Tom Jones, a Foundling ... New Edition. London: Longman ..., 1792. 3 vols. 12mo. xxiii,[i],284; [xii],368; xii,324 pp. Half-titles. 3 frontis, 1 other plate. Contemp calf, minor wear at extremities, sev labels sl defective. *(Clark)* £45 [≈ $86]

Fielding, Sir John
- The Universal Mentor; or, Entertaining Instructor. Consisting of Essays on the most Important Subjects in Life ... New Edition. London: for T. Evans, 1777. 12mo. [viii],vii, [v],254 pp. Contemp calf, mor label, spine & crnrs worn, sides rubbed, front jnt cracked.
(Finch) £25 [≈ $47]

Fielding, Sarah
- The Adventures of David Simple ... By A Lady. London: for A. Millar, 1744. 1st edn. 2 vols. 12mo. Few sl signs of age & use. Contemp calf gilt, reprd. Anon.
(Ash) £500 [≈ $959]
- The Governess; or, Little Female Academy. Being the History of Mrs Teachum, and her Nine Girls ... By the Author of David Simple. The Fourth Edition. Cork: for T. White & W. Flynn, [ca 1770?]. 12mo. xiv,213 pp. Some wear & sm reprs. Calf, renewed. Anon.
(Bickersteth) £110 [≈ $211]

Finch, Anne, Countess of Winchelsea
- Miscellany Poems, on Several Occasions. Written by a Lady. London: for J.B., & sold by Tooke, Taylor, Round, 1713. 1st edn. Issue without author's name on title. 8vo. 16 advt pp at end. Contemp calf, spine rubbed, jnts worn, front cvr almost loose. Cloth case. Anon. *(Ximenes)* $400 [≈ £208]

First ...
- First Elements of Astronomy and Natural Philosophy ... For the Use of Private Families, and Public Schools. London: for G. Sael, 1798. 4th edn, crrctd. Cr 8vo. Plate. Contemp mor backed mrbld bds.
(Stewart) £45 [≈ $86]
- The First of April ... see Combe, William.

Fisher, George
- The Instructor: or Young Man's Best Companion ... The Twenty-Seventh Edition, Corrected and Improved. London: W. Osborne & T. Griffin; Gainsborough: J.

Mozley, 1788. 12mo. 384 pp. Frontis, 3 plates. Orig calf, sl defective.
(*Bickersteth*) £45 [≈ $86]

Fisher, Samuel
- The Testimony of Truth Exalted ... London: 1679. 1st edn. Folio. [xii], "89" [ie 92], 97-692, 695-856,42, 45-98,[16] pp. 5 secondary titles. Occas foxing, 1st few ff stained. Contemp calf, rebacked, crnrs & edges sl worn. Wing F.1058.
(*Clark*) £125 [≈ $239]

Fitzherbert, Thomas
- A Treatise concerning Policy and Religion. London: for Abel Roper, 1652. 4to. Red & black title. Contemp sheep, spine worn & chipped, front inner hinge cracked. Wing F.1102.
(*Sanders*) £85 [≈ $163]

Fitzosborne, Sir Thomas (pseud.)
- See Melmoth, William.

Five Pieces of Runic Poetry ...
- See Percy, Thomas (ed.).

Flavel, John
- The Method of Grace in Bringing Home the Eternal Redemption ... Second Edition very much corrected. London: Th. Parkhurst, 1699. 4to. [40],538,[12 advt] pp. 19th c half calf, some wear, rebacked. Wing F.1170.
(*Humber*) £78 [≈ $149]
- A Token for Mourners, or, the Advice of Christ to a Distressed Mother, Bewailing the Death of her Dear and Only Son. London: Robert Boulter, 1680. Tall 12mo. [12],156 pp. Sl browning & wear. Old calf, rather worn, rebacked. Wing F.1198.
(*Humber*) £48 [≈ $92]

Fleetwood, William
- A Sermon Against Clipping ... London: Tho. Hodgkin, sold by John Whitlock ..., 1694. 1st edn. 4to. [iv],32 pp. Half-title brittle, sev gatherings browned, final leaf stained. Mod bds. Wing F.1248. (*Pickering*) $250 [≈ £130]
- A Sermon Preach'd before the Right Honourable the Lord Mayor and Court of Aldermen ... 11th of April, 1692 ... London: for Thomas newborough ..., 1692. Only edn. 4to. 30 pp. Disbound. Wing F.1253.
(*Young's*) £32 [≈ $61]
- The Thirteenth Chapter to the Romans, Vindicated from the Abusive Senses put upon it. London: for A. Baldwin, 1710. 8vo in 4s. Disbound. Anon. (*Sanders*) £15 [≈ $28]

Fleming, Robert, the younger
- Discourses on Several Subjects. The first containing a New Account of the Rise and Fall of the Papacy ... London: for Andr. Bell ..., 1701. 1st edn. 8vo. [8],clxxvii,248,[16] pp. Contemp panelled calf, mor label, upper hinge broken but secure on 3 cords.
(*Claude Cox*) £30 [≈ $57]

Fletcher, A.
- The Universal Measurer. In Two Parts ... Whitehaven: ptd by W. Masheder, 1752-53. 1st edn. 2 parts in one vol. 8vo. xiv,[2 advt], 282; vi,284 pp. Num text engvs. 2 sm reprs. Half-title creased. Old calf, sl worn.
(*Young's*) £300 [≈ $575]

Fletcher, Andrew, of Saltoun
- A Discourse of Government with Relation to Militias. London: reprinted for M. Cooper, 1755. 2nd edn. 8vo. 60 pp. Blank ft of title torn away. Stitched as issued, uncut.
(*Young's*) £40 [≈ $76]
- Two Discourses Concerning the Affairs of Scotland; written in the Year 1698. Edinburgh: 1698. 1st edn. 2 parts sep paged but continuously sgnd. Few crnrs sl dogeared. Orig mrbld wraps, uncut, edges v sl frayed. Wing F.1298. Anon. (*Sanders*) £200 [≈ $383]

Fletcher, John William
- An Appeal to Matter of Fact and Common Sense ... Phila: ptd by R. Aitken & Son, & sold by John Dickins, 1794. 2nd Amer edn. 12mo. Contemp sheep, upper jnt cracking.
(*Sanders*) £50 [≈ $95]
- Logica Genevensis: or, A Fourth Check to Antinomianism. London: ptd by J. Paramore, 1786. 12mo. Disbound. Anon.
(*Sanders*) £60 [≈ $115]

Fletcher, Phineas
- Piscatory Eclogues, with other Poetical Miscellanies. Illustrated with Notes ... Edinburgh: Kincaid & Creech, 1771. 2nd edn. 8vo. viii,151,[4] pp. Half-title. Title vignette. Contemp style calf.
(*Young's*) £90 [≈ $172]

Fleury, Claude
- The History, Choice, and Method of Studies. London: for S. Keble, 1695. 188,3 advt pp. Contemp speckled sheep, brown label.
(*C.R. Johnson*) £550 [≈ $1,055]

Florio: a Tale ...
- See More, Hannah.

Fonseca, Christoval de
- Devout Contemplations Expressed in two and Fortie Sermons ... Englished by J.M. [James Mabbe] ... London: Adam Islip, 1629. 1st English edn. Folio. [iv],648,[18] pp. Engvd title. Orig calf, rebacked. STC 11126.
(Vanbrugh) £225 [≈ $431]
- Devout Contemplations Expressed in two and Fortie Sermons ... Englished by J.M. ... London: Adam Islip, 1629. Folio. [6],648,[18] pp. Engvd title. Occas sl discold. New qtr vellum. STC 11126.
(Humber) £135 [≈ $259]

Fontenelle, Bernard Le Bovier, Sieur de
- Dialogues of the Dead. London: W. Sandby, 1760. 8vo. 320 pp. Contemp calf, gilt spine, hinges cracked, spine ends worn, lacks label. Anon. *(Chapel Hill)* $85 [≈ £44]
- The History of Oracles, and the Cheats of the Pagan Priests, in Two Parts. Made English. London: ptd in the year, 1688. 1st edn in English. 8vo. [xii],227,[v] pp. Paper browned. Minor staining & soiling. Old calf backed bds, vellum tips. Wing F.1413. Anon.
(Clark) £65 [≈ $124]
- A Plurality of Worlds. Written in French by the Author of the Dialogues of the Dead. Translated into English by Mr. Glanvill. London: Bentley & Magnes, 1688. 1st English edn. 8vo. [xii],152 pp. Sl marg stains. Contemp calf, front jnt cracked at hd. Wing F.1416. Anon. *(Finch)* £450 [≈ $863]

Foot, Jesse
- The Life of John Hunter. London: T. Becket, 1794. 287 pp. Contemp tree calf, red label, spine sl rubbed.
(C.R. Johnson) £475 [≈ $911]

Foote, Samuel
- The Tailors; A Tragedy for Warm Weather ... London: for T. Cadell, 1778. 1st edn. 8vo. Disbound. *(Dramatis Personae)* $40 [≈ £20]

Forbes, Duncan
- Reflexions on the Sources of Incredulity with regard to Religion. Edinburgh: Sands, Murray & Cochran ..., 1750. 1st edn. Sm 8vo in 4s. [iv],119,[i] pp. Sl browning of page edges. Contemp calf, gilt spine, sl rubbed. Anon. *(Clark)* £85 [≈ $163]
- Reflexions on the Sources of Incredulity with regard to Religion. Edinburgh: Sands, Murray & Cochran ..., 1750. 1st edn. 8vo. [iv], 119 pp. Contemp calf, gilt spine.

(Young's) £90 [≈ $172]
- Reflexions on the Sources of Incredulity with regard to Religion. Edinburgh: Sands, Murray & Cochrane, for Hamilton, Balfour, 1750. 2nd edn. 8vo. [iv],87 pp. Rec qtr calf. Anon. *(Burmester)* £110 [≈ $211]

Fordyce, David
- Dialogues concerning Education. The Second Edition. London: Printed in the Year 1745-48. 1st edn of vol 2. 2 vols. Title vignettes. Contemp calf, rubbed, gilt spines & dentelles, sm splits in hinges. Anon.
(Jarndyce) £280 [≈ $537]

Fordyce, G.
- Elements of the Practice of Physic, in Two Parts ... London: 1771. 3rd edn. viii,380 pp. 2 sm lib stamps. Contemp leather, rebacked. *(Whitehart)* £180 [≈ $345]

Fordyce, James
- A Collection of Hymns and Sacred Poems. Edinburgh: for the publisher, 1788. 263 pp. Qtr calf, mrbld bds.
(C.R. Johnson) £180 [≈ $345]
- Poems. London: Cadell, 1786. Half-title,265 pp. Orig calf, rebacked.
(C.R. Johnson) £145 [≈ $278]
- Sermons to Young Women, in Two Volumes. The Second Edition, Corrected. London: Millar & Cadell, 1766. 2 vols. 308; 313 pp. 19th c calf. *(C.R. Johnson)* £75 [≈ $143]

Foreign Essays ...
- Foreign Essays on Agriculture and the Arts. Consisting Chiefly of the Most Curious Discoveries ... Communicated ... for the Improvement of British Husbandry ... London: for R. Davis ..., 1766. 1st edn. 8vo. viii, 392 pp. Sl marg worm. Orig calf.
(Bickersteth) £120 [≈ $230]

Forrester, James
- The Polite Philosopher or, an Essay on that Art which makes a Man Happy in himself and agreeable to others. Edinburgh: Robert Freebairn, 1734. 1st edn. Sm marg loss to title. Disbound. Anon.
(Waterfield's) £45 [≈ $86]

Foster, John
- An Essay on the Different Nature of Accent and Quantity with their Use and Application in the English, Latin, and Greek Languages ... Second Edition, Corrected and much

enlarged ... Eton: J. Pote, 1763. 8vo. 3 advt pp. Contemp French calf, gilt spine.
(Georges) **£200 [≈ $383]**

Foster, Sir Michael
- A Report of Some Proceedings on the Commission of Oyer and Terminer and Goal [sic] Delivery for the Trial of the Rebels in the Year 1746 in the County of Surry ... Dublin: 1762. x,412,[18] pp. Some marg damp staining. Cloth, cvr damp stained. Anon.
(Wreden) **$150 [≈ £78]**

Foulkes, Robert
- An Alarme for Sinners ... London: Langley Curtis, 1679. Only edn. 4to. [iv],36 pp. Crnrs of last few ff torn with sl loss. Lib stamp on title verso. Disbound. Wing F.1644.
(Clark) **£45 [≈ $86]**

Fowke, Sir John
- Alderman Fowke's Speech at the Delivery of a Petition from the Lord Mayor, Aldermen and Commons in Common-Councill Assembled ... concerning the Militia ... London: 1659. Only edn. 4to. 8 pp. Caption title. Outer ff sl dusty. Disbound. Wing F.1690.
(Clark) **£100 [≈ $191]**

Fox, Charles (ed.)
- A Series of Poems, containing the Plaints, Consolations, and Delights of Achmed Ardebeili, a Persian Exile. With Notes ... Bristol: Bulgin & Rosser, for J. Cottle ..., 1797. 4 pp subscribers. Contemp calf, gilt spine sl rubbed.
(Jarndyce) **£150 [≈ $287]**

Fox, Charles James
- A Letter ... to the Worthy and Independent Electors of the City and Liberty of Westminster. The Tenth Edition. London: J. Debrett, 1793. 43,4 advt pp. Disbound.
(C.R. Johnson) **£25 [≈ $47]**

Fox, George
- A Collection of many Select and Christian Epistles, Letters and Testimonies ... The Second Volume [ie Journal vol 2]. London: T. Sowle, 1698. 1st edn. Folio. [6],557,[7],[3 advt] pp. 3Y4 a cancel. Repr to title. Contemp calf, reprd. Wing F.1764.
(Fenning) **£250 [≈ $479]**
- Gospel-Truth Demonstrated, in a Collection of Doctrinal Books ... London: T. Sowle, 1706. 1st edn. Folio. [14],1090,[6] pp. Clean tear without loss in 2 ff. Contemp calf, crnrs worn.
(Fenning) **£185 [≈ $355]**

- A Journal or Historical Account of the Life, Travels, Sufferings, Christian Experiences, and Labour of Love of George Fox ... Third Edition, Corrected. London: ... sold by Luke Hinde, 1765. Folio. [ii],lix, [i], 679, [xxix] pp. Contemp calf, backstrip relaid, reprd.
(Clark) **£75 [≈ $143]**

Fox, Henry
- A New Dictionary, in French and English ... London: Nourse, Hooper, 1769. 1st edn. 12mo. Contemp sheep, spine worn, lower jnt tender.
(Burmester) **£120 [≈ $230]**

Fragments of Ancient Poetry ...
- See Macpherson, James.

Frain du Tremblay, Jean
- A Treatise of Languages ... now Translated into English by M.H. London: for D. Leach, 1725. 1st edn in English. 8vo. [viii],171,[5] pp. Contemp panelled calf, rebacked.
(Burmester) **£275 [≈ $527]**

Francis de Sales, Saint
- An Introduction to a Deuoute Life ... Translated into Enlisg [sic] By I.Y. [J. Yakesley] the last edition. Paris: Mistrise Blangeart, 1637. 1st Paris edn. Sm 8vo. [xxxii], 728, [12] pp. Engvd title. Contemp mor gilt, sl worn. STC 11322(2).
(Vanbrugh) **£110 [≈ $211]**

Francis, Anne
- Miscellaneous Poems. London: for the author, & sold by T. Becket ..., 1790. 1st edn. 8vo. [iv],275 pp. Name cut from title marg. Contemp gilt panelled calf, 1 jnt strengthened.
(Gough) **£75 [≈ $143]**

Francis, Philip
- Constantine: A Tragedy. London: for A. Millar, 1754. 1st edn. 8vo. Title spotted & torn at inner marg. Disbound, backed with cloth tape. Anon.
(Dramatis Personae) **$40 [≈ £20]**

Francis, Richard
- Maxims of Equity, Collected from, and proved by Cases ... in the High Court of Chancery. London: Nutt, Gosling ..., 1727. 1st edn. Folio. Blank, title, 3 ff, 72 pp, 7 ff, 20 pp, blank. Contemp calf, sl rubbed, jnts cracking, sm piece of label missing. Anon.
(Meyer Boswell) **$850 [≈ £442]**

Francklin, Thomas
- The Epistles of Phalaris. Translated from the Greek. To which are added, Some Select Epistles of the most eminent Greek Writers ... London: for R. Francklin ..., 1749. 1st edn. 8vo. [xiv],xxiii,224 pp. Half-title, subscribers. Frontis. Calf, rebacked.
(Young's) **£38 [≈ $72]**
- The Epistles of Phalaris. Translated from the Greek. To which are added, Some Select Epistles from the most eminent Greek Writers. London: for R. Francklin, 1749. 8vo. [xvi], xxiv, 224 pp. Half-title. Frontis (sl torn at fold). Some foxing. Period calf, lacks label. *(Rankin)* **£50 [≈ $95]**
- The Epistles of Phalaris. Translated from the Greek. To which is added, Some Select Epistles ... London: for R. Francklin, 1749. 1st edn thus. 8vo. [xvi],xxiv,224 pp. Frontis. Contemp calf gilt, front jnt ends cracking, spine ends worn. *(Finch)* **£90 [≈ $172]**

Fransham, John
- The Criterion: or, Touchstone, by which to Judge of the Principles of High and Low-Church. In a Letter to a Friend. London: B. Bragge, 1710. 1st edn. 12mo. 16 pp. Middle-Hill wraps. Anon. *(Burmester)* **£65 [≈ $124]**

Fraser, Simon, Lord Lovat
- See Lovat, Simon Fraser, Lord.

Frauds ...
- The Frauds and Abuses of Coal-Dealers detected and exposed: in a Letter to an Alderman of London. The Third Edition. London: M. Cooper, 1747. 33 pp. Rec wraps. *(C.R. Johnson)* **£95 [≈ $182]**

Freame, John
- Scripture-Instruction digested into Several Sections, by Way of Question and Answer ... Third Edition. Bristol: S. Farley, (1769). 12mo. Sl marg worm. Contemp sheep, sl rubbed. *(Jarndyce)* **£25 [≈ $47]**

Freart, Roland, Sieur de Chambray.
- See Chambray, Roland Freart, Sieur de.

Frederick II, King of Prussia
- Memoirs of the House of Brandenburg ... By the Hand of a Master ... added ... Two Dissertations ... London: for J. Nourse, 1751. 1 blank crnr torn. Contemp calf, rubbed, lacks label. Anon. *(Waterfield's)* **£50 [≈ $95]**

The Free-Holder ...
- See Addison, Joseph.

Freind, John
- Nine Commentaries upon Fevers: and Two Epistles concerning the Small-Pox ... London: T. Cox, 1730. 1st edn in English. Sm 8vo. [xii], 137 pp. Name removed from title. Later mor. *(Bookpress)* **$300 [≈ £156]**

Freke, William
- Select Essays tending to the Universal Reformation of Learning; concluding with the Art of War ... London: Tho. Minors, 1693. Imprimatur leaf, 279 pp. Rebound in period calf. Wing F.2165.
(C.R. Johnson) **£350 [≈ $671]**

Frere, George
- A Short History of Barbados, from its First Discovery and Settlement, to the End of the Year 1767. London: Dodsley, 1768. 1st edn. 8vo. viii,121,[3] pp. Thick paper. 19th c half calf, rebacked. Anon.
(Burmester) **£175 [≈ $335]**

Friendly and Seasonable Advice ...
- Friendly and Seasonable Advice to the Roman Catholics of England ... see Comber, Thomas.

A Frivolous Paper ...
- A Frivolous Paper, In Form of a Petition: Framed and composed by a Disaffected Party in this City of London ... By a Well-willer to Peace and truth. London: W. Ley & F.I., 1642. 1st edn. 4to. 8 pp. Some browning. Disbound. Wing F.2231.
(Clark) **£65 [≈ $124]**

Fry, Edmund
- Pantographia; containing Accurate Copies of all the Known Alphabets of the World ... London: for John & Arthur Arch, 1799. 1st edn. Roy 8vo. xxxvi,320 pp. Endpapers & outer ff faintly discold. Contemp diced calf gilt, reprd. *(Ash)* **£500 [≈ $959]**
- Pantographia; containing Accurate Copies of all Known Alphabets of the World ... London: for John & Arthur Arch ..., 1799. 1st edn. [4],xxxvi,320 pp. Contemp diced calf gilt, hinges cracked but secure.
(Claude Cox) **£300 [≈ $575]**

Fry, John
- An Alphabetical Extract of all the Annual

Printed Epistles which have been sent to the several Quarterly-Meetings of the People called Quakers ... 1682 to 1762 ... London: for the author at Sutton Benger ..., n.d. 1st edn. 8vo. xiv,127 pp. Disbound.
(Young's) **£60 [≈ $115]**

- A Serious and Affectionate Address to the People called Quakers ... London: Luke Hinde ..., 1758. 1st edn. 8vo. iv,35 pp. Disbound.   *(Young's)* **£35 [≈ $67]**

Fugitive Pieces ...
- Fugitive Pieces, on Various Subjects. By Several Authors. The Third Edition. London: Dodsley, 1771. Contemp calf.
(C.R. Johnson) **£95 [≈ $182]**

Fuller, Samuel
- Practical Astronomy ... Collected from the Best Authors ... For the Use of Young Students. Dublin: by and for Samuel Fuller, 1732. 1st edn. 8vo. x,237,[1 advt] pp. 10 fldg plates. 1 plate reprd. Contemp calf, spine ends reprd, label chipped.
(Gaskell) **£400 [≈ $767]**

Fuller, Thomas, 1608-1661
- The Church-History of Britain ... London: John Williams, 1655. 1st edn. Folio. [viii], 1-171, [ix], 1-200, (153)-427,[ix], 1-235, [ix], 1-114,[vi], 117-238,[x], 1-172,22,[xx] pp. Fldg plan, 4 plates. Few sl marks. Contemp calf, rebacked & recrnrd. Wing F.2416.
(Clark) **£260 [≈ $499]**
- The Holy State. Cambridge: Roger Daniel for John Williams, 1642. 1st edn. Folio. Engvd title (edges browned). Tear at hd of 1 leaf with loss of 2 words in running title. Lib stamp. Contemp calf, spine ends & crnrs reprd. Wing F.2443.   *(Jarndyce)* **£140 [≈ $268]**
- A Pisgah-Sight of Palestine ... London: J.F. for John Williams, 1650. 1st edn. Lge folio. [viii],442,202,[17] pp. 20 maps, 8 plans, engvd arms in text. Contemp panelled calf, gilt spine, hinges strengthened.
(Vanbrugh) **£1,255 [≈ $2,409]**

Fuller, Thomas, 1654-1734
- Exanthematologia: or, An Attempt to Give a Rational Account of Fevers, especially Measles and Small Pox ... Appendix concerning Inoculation. London: 1730 [-29]. 1st edn. 2 parts & appendix in 1 vol with continuous pagination. 4to. xxvi,[17]-439 pp, advt leaf. Orig calf, rebacked.
(Bickersteth) **£440 [≈ $844]**

Fulton, Robert
- A Treatise on the Importance of Canal Navigation ... London: 1796. 1st edn. 4to. [2], vii-xvi,144 pp, advt leaf. 17 plates. Lacks half-title & dedic ff. Contemp calf.
(Fenning) **£200 [≈ $383]**

Fyfe, Andrew
- A System of Anatomy and Physiology, with the Comparative Anatomy of Animals. Compiled from the Latest and Best Authors ... Edinburgh: 1791. 3 vols. 506; 471; 467 pp. 20 plates. Leather, bds detached or missing, backstrips intact.   *(Fye)* **$100 [≈ £52]**

Gadbury, John
- [Greek title: Genethlialogia]. Or, the Doctrine of Nativities ... London: William Miller, 1661. 2nd edn. Folio. [xviii],276, [ii], "294" [ie 298],[x] pp. 2 secondary title-pages dated 1658. Sl marked. Contemp calf, rebacked & recrnrd, rubbed. Wing G.84A.
(Clark) **£325 [≈ $623]**

Gage, Thomas
- The English-American his Travail by Sea and Land: or, a New Survey of the West-Indias [sic] ... London: 1648. 1st edn. Folio in 6s. [x], 220,[12] pp. Lacks intl blank. Title sl soiled, sl wear & marks. Old sheep, sl worn & scuffed. Wing G.109.
(Clark) **£1,500 [≈ $2,879]**
- A New Survey of the West-Indies ... London: J. Nicholson & T. Newborough, 1699. 4th edn. 8vo. viii,477,[18] pp. Fldg map. Some worming to 1st few ff. Contemp calf, worn.
(Bookpress) **£650 [≈ £338]**
- A New Survey of the West-Indies: or, The English American His Travel by Sea and Land ... London: A. Clark ..., 1677. 3rd edn. 8vo. "577" [ie 477],[18] pp. Lacks map. Occas v sl foxing at end. Early 20th c red mor gilt, a.e.g.   *(Chapel Hill)* **$750 [≈ £390]**

Gairdner, Andrew
- An Historical Account of the Old Peoples Hospital, commonly called the Trinity Hospital, in Edinburgh ... Edinburgh: ptd in the year, 1734. 2nd (?) edn. 8vo. viii,56 pp. Disbound.   *(Bickersteth)* **£130 [≈ $249]**

Gale, John
- Cabinet of Knowledge, or Miscellaneous Recreations, including the most celebrated Card Deceptions ever Exhibited ... Magical Experiments ... Second Edition, considerably enlarged. London: James Wallis, 1797. 12mo.

6 plates. Contemp sheep, rebacked in calf, crnrs rubbed.
(Dramatis Personae) **$475 [≈ £247]**

Galen of Pergamon
- Galen's Method of Physick: or, his Great Master-Peece ... translator, Peter English. Edinburgh: 1656. Only edn. 12mo. [4],344 pp. Some quires loose. Contemp calf, front hinge & spine split. Wing G.161.
(Hemlock) **$750 [≈ £390]**

Galliae Notitia ...
- See Besongne, Nicholas.

Gambado, Geoffrey
- Annals of Horsemanship ... see Bunbury, Henry W.

Ganganelli, John Vincent Antonio
- Interesting Letters of Pope Clement XIV. (Ganganelli.) ... Translated from the French ... The Second Edition. London: Becket, 1777. 2 vols. 12mo. [iv],lxiv,285,[i]; [iv],273,[3] pp. Half-titles. Contemp calf backed bds, vellum tips, sl rubbed.
(Clark) **£48 [≈ $92]**

Garat, D.J.
- Memoirs of the Revolution; or, An Apology for my Conduct in the Public Employments which I have held ... Edinburgh: G. Mudie & Son, 1797. 1st edn. 8vo. iii,281 pp. Half calf, edges sl rubbed. *(Young's)* **£40 [≈ $76]**

Gardiner, Ralph
- Englands Grievance Discovered, in relation to the Coal Trade; with the Map of the River Tine, and Situation of the Town and Corporation of Newcastle ... Newcastle: 1796. 2nd edn. 8vo. viii,216 pp. Fldg map, 17 ports, 3 other plates. 19th c half calf, rubbed. *(Young's)* **£100 [≈ $191]**

Garencieres, Theophilus
- General Instructions, Divine, Moral, Historical, Figurative, &c. shewing the Progress of Religion ... York: J. White for the author, 1728. 8vo. 2 sections sl loose. Lacks f.e.p. Contemp sheep, worn but sound.
(Waterfield's) **£45 [≈ $86]**

Garnett, John
- A Sermon Preached at Christ-Church, Dublin. On the 28th of March, 1756. Before the Incorporated Society for Promoting Protestant Schools in Ireland ... Dublin: S.

Powell, 1756. 1st edn. 4to. Disbound. Anon.
(Young's) **£40 [≈ $76]**

Garrick, David
- Bon Ton; or High Life Above Stairs. A Comedy. London: for T. Becket, 1775. 1st edn. Variant with p 32 unnumbered. 8vo. Mod bds. Anon.
(Dramatis Personae) **$150 [≈ £78]**
- The Dramatic Works ... [with] A Life of the Author. London: for A. Millar, 1796. 3 vols. 12mo. Contemp calf, upper hinges cracked, lacks labels. *(Claude Cox)* **£35 [≈ $67]**
- The Dramatic Works, to which is prefixed A Life of the Author. London [Scotland?]: for A. Millar, 1798. Pirated edn. 3 vols. 12mo. Contemp calf, spines rubbed, lacks labels, upper hinges cracking.
(Jarndyce) **£60 [≈ $115]**
- The Poetical Works ... Now First Collected into Two Volumes. With Explanatory Notes ... London: Kearsley, 1785. 1st edn. 2 vols. 8vo. [iv],lvii,[i],224; [iv],[225]-540,[3 advt] pp. Contemp tree calf, elab gilt spines, spines chipped at hd, jnts just cracked but firm.
(Finch) **£185 [≈ $355]**
- The Sick Monkey, a Fable. London: for J. Fletcher, 1765. 1st edn. 4to. Half-title. Frontis. Disbound. Anon.
(Ximenes) **$1,250 [≈ £651]**

Garth, Samuel
- The Dispensary. A Poem ... With severall Descriptions and Episodes never before Printed ... London: for J.T. ..., 1726. 9th edn. 8vo. [xx],84 pp. 7 plates. Edges browned. New bds. Anon. *(Young's)* **£55 [≈ $105]**

Gataker, T.
- Essays on Medical Subjects, originally printed separately; to which is now prefixed an Introduction relating to the Use of Hemlock and Corrosive Sublimate ... London: 1764. lii,284 pp. Contemp leather, hinges sl weak. *(Whitehart)* **£180 [≈ $345]**

Gauden, John
- Considerations touching the Liturgy of the Church of England in reference to his Majesties late Gracious Declaration ... London: J.G. for John Playford, 1661. With A1 blank. Disbound. Wing G.348.
(Waterfield's) **£40 [≈ $76]**
- The Love of Truth and Peace. A Sermon ... Novemb. 29. 1640. London: T.C. for Andrew Crooke, 1641. 1st edn. 4to. [vi],46 pp. Some

damp stains, pen trials on title. Later wraps.
Wing G.362.   *(Clark)* **£25 [** ≈ **$47]**
- [Greek title: Megaleia Theou] Gods great
Demonstrations and Demands of Justice,
Mercy and Humility, Set forth in a Sermon ...
April 30. 1660. London: J. Best, for Andrew
Crook, 1660. Only edn. 4to. [x],67,[i] pp. Lib
stamp on title verso. Later wraps. Wing
G.364.   *(Clark)* **£30 [** ≈ **$57]**

Gavin, D. Antonio
- A Master-Key to Popery: in Five Parts ...
London printed. Newport, R.I.: reprinted,
1773. 1st recorded Amer edn. 300 pp. Foxed.
Later three qtr mor.   *(Reese)* **$200 [** ≈ **£104]**
- See also Emiliane, Gabriel d'.

Gay, John
- The Beggar's Opera ... Fourth Edition: To
which is added, the Ouverture in Score; and
the Musick ... London: for John Watts, 1735.
8vo. [viii],8 music,76 pp. Occas sl mark, 1 sm
marg repr. 19th c half calf, rubbed.
                  (Finch) **£75 [** ≈ **$143]**
- The Beggar's Opera and Polly: An Opera.
Being the Second Part of the Beggar's Opera.
Glasgow: Robert Urie, 1750. 1st Scottish edn.
12mo. Sm stain on 1 leaf not affecting text.
Contemp leather, worn, rebacked.
            (Dramatis Personae) **$80 [** ≈ **£41]**
- The Beggar's Opera. As it is acted at the
Theatre-Royal in Lincolns-Inn Fields.
London: for A. Scot, 1763. 8vo. 72 pp. Sl
dusty at ends. Disbound, largely uncut.
                  (Rankin) **£50 [** ≈ **$95]**
- Fables in Two Parts. Newcastle upon Tyne:
1765. Fcap 8vo. viii,176 pp. Occas soiling.
Contemp calf, backstrip relaid.
                 (Spelman) **£60 [** ≈ **$115]**
- Fables ... In One Volume Complete. London:
J. Buckland ..., 1778. 12mo. 240 pp. Frontis,
num plates. Sl soiling. Contemp calf.
               (Chapel Hill) **$150 [** ≈ **£78]**
- Fables. London: Longman ..., 1796. 2 parts
in 1 vol. Frontis, 67 half-page w'cuts.
Contemp calf, rebacked.
                 (Stewart) **£65 [** ≈ **$124]**
- Plays ... To which is prefixed an Account of
the Life and Writings of the Author. London:
for W. Strahan ..., 1772. 12mo. 359 pp. Port.
Contemp speckled calf, v sl worn.
                (Burmester) **£65 [** ≈ **$124]**
- Poems on Several Occasions. London:
Tonson & Lintot, 1731. 2nd coll edn. 2 vols.
12mo. Frontis vol 1, 2 plates. Occas v sl water
stains. Contemp calf, gilt spines rubbed, 1 jnt

tender.   *(Ximenes)* **$250 [** ≈ **£130]**
- Poems on Several Occasions. Glasgow:
Robert & Andrew Foulis, 1770. 2 vols. 12mo.
Contemp calf. *(Waterfield's)* **£100 [** ≈ **$191]**
- Polly: An Opera. being the Second Part of the
Beggar's Opera ... London: for T. Astley ...,
1742. 2nd edn. 4to. [viii],72 pp. Disbound.
                   (Young's) **£50 [** ≈ **$95]**
- The Shepherd's Week. In Six Pastorals ...
London: Ferd. Burleigh, 1714. 1st edn. 8vo.
[xvi],60,[4] pp. 7 engvd plates (inc frontis) inc
in pagination & collation. Sl browned, Rec
half calf.   *(Finch)* **£150 [** ≈ **$287]**

Gemelli Careri, John Francis
- A Voyage Round the World ... [London:
1732]. Extract from Churchill's Collection of
Voyages Vol 4. 572 pp. Map, 8 plates, text
engvs. Some wear & marking. Contemp calf,
backstrip relaid.   *(Reese)* **$550 [** ≈ **£286]**

Genard, Francois
- The School of Man. London: Lockyer Davis,
1753. 1st English edn. Lge 12mo. xvi,384,[8]
pp. Contemp calf, rubbed. Anon.
                (Bookpress) **$200 [** ≈ **£104]**

The General History of the Highways ...
- See Bergier, Nicolas.

Gent, Thomas
- The Antient and Modern History of the
Famous City of York ... York: for Thomas
Hammond, 1730. 1st edn. 1st imp, with
crown w'cut at p 84. Fcap 8vo. viii,256,[8] pp.
Fldg plan, fldg view, 6 w'cut ills & decs.
Without the inserted w'cut at p 171 as usual.
Contemp calf, rebacked.
                 (Spelman) **£180 [** ≈ **$345]**

Gentleman ...
- The Gentleman and Lady's Key to Polite
Literature: or a Compendious Dictionary of
Fabulous History ... London: for T. Carnan,
1788. 12mo. Unpaginated. Engvd frontis &
title. Contemp sheep, jnts cracked, spine sl
worn.   *(Burmester)* **£20 [** ≈ **$38]**
- The Gentleman Instructed ... see Darrell,
William; Hickes, George.

Gentleman, Francis
- Prolegomena to the Dramatic Writings of
Will. Shakespere. London: for John Bell,
1793. 2 vols. 12mo. 296; [ii],297-558 pp.
Contemp calf, vol 1 lacks labels, sl worn.
Anon.   *(Claude Cox)* **£30 [** ≈ **$57]**

- Royal Fables. London: Becket & de Hondt, 1766. 1st edn. Sm 8vo. Frontis. Contemp mottled calf gilt, rebacked.
 (Ximenes) **$400 [≈£208]**
- Royal Fables. London: Becket & De Hondt, 1766. 184 pp. Frontis. Contemp calf, rebacked. *(C.R. Johnson)* **£125 [≈$239]**

A Geographical Dictionary ...
- See Du Val, Claude.

Georgirenes, Joseph
- A Description of the Present State of Samos, Nicaria, Patmos, and Mount Athos ... London: W.G. & Moses Pitt, 1678. Contemp sheep, sl rubbed. Wing G.536.
 (C.R. Johnson) **£750 [≈$1,439]**

Gibbon, Edward
- The History of the Decline and Fall of the Roman Empire ... London: Strahan & Cadell, 1776 [-88]. 1st edn. 6 vols. 4to. Port frontis, 3 fldg maps. Lacks half-titles & final blank vol 6. Contemp half calf, gilt spines, sl rubbed, 4 jnts sl tender. *(Finch)* **£6,000 [≈$11,519]**
- The History of the Decline and Fall of the Roman Empire. London: Strahan & Cadell, 1791-92. 12 vols. 8vo. Frontis port, 2 fldg maps. Sl foxing. Contemp tree calf gilt, extremities rubbed, spines faded.
 (Heritage) **$400 [≈£208]**
- An Essay on the Study of Literature. Written Originally in French, Now first translated into English. London: Becket & De Hondt, 1764. Final 2 advt ff. Contemp sprinkled calf, label. *(Sanders)* **£1,500 [≈$2,879]**
- Miscellaneous Works ... with Memoirs of his Life and Writings, composed by himself ... London: Strahan, 1796. 1st edn. 2 vols. 4to. xxv,1 errata,703; viii,726,2 errata,advt pp. Silhouette port vol 1. Contemp calf, rebacked. A 3rd vol was published in 1815.
 (Young's) **£80 [≈$153]**
- Miscellaneous Works. With Memoirs of his Life and Writings ... Notes ... by John Lord Sheffield. Dublin: for P. Wogan ..., 1796. 1st Dublin edn. 3 vols. Half-titles vols 2 & 3. Frontis vol 1. Contemp calf, red & blue labels, spines sl rubbed.
 (Jarndyce) **£220 [≈$422]**
- Miscellaneous Works ... With Memoirs of his Life and Writings ... Notes by John Lord Sheffield. Dublin: P. Wogan ..., 1796. Silhouette frontis. Contemp qtr russia, mrbld bds. *(C.R. Johnson)* **£240 [≈$460]**

Gibbons, Thomas
- Memoirs of the Rev. Isaac Watts. London: James Buckland and Thomas Gibbons, 1780. 1st edn. 8vo. [xii],491,[ix] pp. 8 advt pp at end. Port frontis. Rec half calf, untrimmed.
 (Clark) **£110 [≈$211]**
- Memoirs of the Rev. Isaac Watts, D.D.. London: James Buckland & Thomas Gibbons, 1780. 1st edn. 8vo. ix,[iii],491,[[1],[8] pp. Port. Contemp sheep, spine sl worn but sound.
 (Burmester) **£50 [≈$95]**

Gibbs, James
- A Book of Architecture, containing Designs of Buildings and Ornaments. London: W. Innys ..., 1739. 2nd edn. Lge folio. [iv],xxv pp. 150 plates. 1 plate reprd. Contemp calf, rebacked. *(Bookpress)* **$1,850 [≈£963]**
- A Book of Architecture, containing Designs of Buildings and ornaments. The Second Edition. London: 1739. Folio. [iv],xxv,[i blank] pp. 148 (of 150, lacks nos 21 & 111) plates. Sev plates laid down or reprd. Some stains. Old calf gilt, sl worn.
 (Bow Windows) **£1,600 [≈$3,071]**

Gibson, John
- Atlas Minimus, or a new Set of Pocket Maps of the ... Known World ... Revis'd ... by Eman: Bowen ... London: 1758. 1st edn. 24mo. Frontis, 3 ff, 52 maps ptd on rectos only. Contemp colouring. Old calf gilt, rebacked. *(Reese)* **$1,500 [≈£781]**
- The Frequent Service of God in Publick, the Way to Long Life, Honour, and undoubted happiness: set forth in a Sermon ... Oxford: 1719. 1st edn. 4to. [viii],22 pp. Half-title. Disbound. *(Young's)* **£28 [≈$53]**

Gibson, Thomas
- The Anatomy of Human Bodies Epitomized. Wherein all the Parts of Man's Body, with their Actions and Uses, are succinctly described ... Sixth Edition. London: 1703. 8vo. [xvi],vii,632 pp. 20 plates. V sl hole in title. Sl marg water stain on a few ff. Orig calf. *(Bickersteth)* **£225 [≈$431]**

Gibson, William
- A New Treatise on the Diseases of Horses ... London: A. Millar, 1751. 1st edn. Large Paper. 4to. [12],464,[12] pp. Frontis, 31 plates. Contemp MS receipts on intl blanks. Contemp calf, rebacked.
 (Rootenberg) **$650 [≈£338]**

Gildon, Charles
- The Complete Art of Poetry. In Six Parts ... London: for Charles Rivington, 1718. 1st edn. 2 vols. 12mo. Contemp calf gilt, fine.
  (Ximenes) **$1,500 [≈ £781]**
- The Life of Mr. Thomas Betterton, the late Eminent Tragedian ... London: Robert Gosling, 1710. 1st edn. 8vo. Author's name ptd at end. Later port inserted. Occas foxing. Mod panelled calf antique. Anon.
  (Dramatis Personae) **$200 [≈ £104]**

Giles, Joseph
- Miscellaneous Poems: on Various Subjects, and Occasions. Revised and Corrected by the late Mr. Shenstone. London: for J. Godwin ..., 1771. 1st edn. 8vo. 19th c half calf, gilt spine (rubbed). Anon.
  (Ximenes) **$650 [≈ £338]**

Gilkie, James
- Every Man his own Procurator; or, The Country Gentleman's Vade-mecum. Edinburgh: for the author, 1778. Contemp qtr calf, sl rubbed.
  (Meyer Boswell) **$500 [≈ £260]**

Gill, John
- Levi's Urim and Thummin found with Christ. A Discourse on Deut. xxxiii.8 ... London: for Aaron Ward ..., 1725. 1st edn. 8vo. 42,2 advt pp. Title sl soiled. Disbound.
  (Young's) **£48 [≈ $92]**

Gillett, R.
- The Pleasures of Reason: or, The Hundred Thoughts of a Sensible Young Lady ... Third Edition ... London: for G. Sael, 1798. 12mo. 4,[18],168 pp. Frontis, map. Contemp calf, rubbed, outer hinges partly cracked but sound.
  (Karmiole) **$125 [≈ £65]**

Gillies, John
- Aristotle's Ethics and Politics ... Translated from the Greek. Illustrated by Introductiona and Notes ... Life ... London: Strahan ..., 1797. 1st edn. 2 vols. 4to. Contemp calf, gilt, red labels.
  (Young's) **£80 [≈ $153]**
- Memoirs of the Life of the Reverend George Whitefield, M.A. ... London: Dilly, 1772. 1st edn. 8vo. xvi,357,[1,2 advt] pp. Port. Rec calf.
  (Young's) **£65 [≈ $124]**

Gillingwater, Edmund
- An Historical Account of the Ancient Town of Lowestoft ... London: Robinson ... &

Stevenson, Norwich, [1790]. 4to. xv,485,[i errata],[4 index]. Half-title. Subscribers. Few sm marg reprs. Mod mor gilt, unopened.
  (Lamb) **£160 [≈ $307]**

Gillum, William
- Miscellaneous Poems ... London: for W. Lane, 1787. 1st edn. 8vo. Orig bds, some wear.
  (Ximenes) **$650 [≈ £338]**

Gilpin, William
- An Essay on Prints. Fourth Edition. London: for R. Blamire, 1792. 8vo. xvi,174, xii pp. V sl foxing. Period half calf, mrbld sides, rebacked.
  (Rankin) **£75 [≈ $143]**
- An Essay on Prints. Fourth Edition. London: R. Blamire, 1792. 8vo. xiii,[3],174, xi,[1 errata] pp. Orig bds, uncut, respined.
  (Spelman) **£130 [≈ $249]**
- An Essay on Prints. Fourth Edition. London: R. Blamire, 1792. 8vo. xiii,[3],174, xi,[1 errata] pp. Contemp tree calf, gilt ruled spine, red gilt label.
  (Spelman) **£200 [≈ $383]**
- The Lives of John Wicliff; and of the most Eminent of His Disciples ... Second Edition, corrected and improved. London: for J. Robson, 1766. 8vo. 5 ports. Contemp calf, gilt spine, red label, jnts weak.
  (Sanders) **£25 [≈ $47]**
- Observations, relative chiefly to Picturesque Beauty ... on several Parts of Great Britain; particularly the High-Lands of Scotland. London: Blamire, 1789. 1st edn. 2 vols. 8vo. vii,[i],xi,[i], 221,[i],[iv], 196, xx, [ii] pp. 40 plates. Minor marks. Rec half calf.
  (Clark) **£125 [≈ $239]**
- Observations relative chiefly to Picturesque Beauty ... on several Parts of England; particularly the Mountains, and Lakes of Cumberland, and Westmoreland. Second Edition. London: Cadell & Davies, 1788. 2 vols. 8vo. 30 aquatint plates. Contemp calf, jnts cracked.
  (Spelman) **£180 [≈ $345]**
- Observations on the River Wye, and several parts of South Wales, &c. relative chiefly to Picturesque Beauty ... Second Edition. London: Blamire, 1789. 8vo. xvi,152 pp. 17 oval aquatint plates. Contemp tree calf, rebacked.
  (Spelman) **£140 [≈ $268]**
- Observations on the Western Parts of England, relative chiefly to Picturesque Beauty ... added, a few Remarks on ... the Isle of Wight. London: Cadell & Davies, 1798. 1st edn. 8vo. xvi,359,[i] pp. 18 plates. Sl spotting. Contemp calf, rebacked.
  (Clark) **£120 [≈ $230]**

- Remarks on Forest Scenery, and other Woodland Views ... Illustrated by the Scenes of New-Forest in Hampshire. Second Edition. London: Blamire, 1794. 2 vols. 8vo. Dble-page map, 31 aquatint plates. Contemp tree calf gilt. *(Spelman)* **£160 [≈ $307]**

Gisborne, Thomas
- An Enquiry into the Duties of Men in the Higher and Middle Classes of Society in Great Britain ... Dublin: J. Exshaw, 1795. 1st Irish edn. 8vo. xv,[1],561 pp, advt leaf. Contemp calf, spine sl worn.
(Fenning) **£145 [≈ $278]**
- Poems, Sacred and Moral. London: Cadell & Davies, 1798. 1st edn. Sm 8vo. Half-title. Contemp calf, spine gilt, sl scuffed, hinges tender. *(Ximenes)* **$150 [≈ £78]**
- The Principles of Moral Philosophy Investigated, and briefly applied to the Constitution of Civil Society ... Third Edition, corrected ... added ... Appendix ... Abolition of the Slave Trade. London: White, 1795. Half-title, 367 pp. Orig bds, uncut, hinges cracked.
(C.R. Johnson) **£120 [≈ $230]**
- Walks in a Forest: or, Poems ... Second Edition, corrected and enlarged. London: Davis, for White, 1796. 8vo. [xii],123 pp. Some misbinding. Contemp polished tan calf, red mor label, smooth spine, gilt bands, front jnt sl tender. *(Finch)* **£90 [≈ $172]**

Glanvill, Joseph
- Essays on several Important Subjects in Philosophy and Religion ... London: J.D. for John Baker, & Henry Mortlock, 1676. 1st edn. Sm 4to. [xvi],66,[ii],56, [ii],43,[iii],28, [ii],61, [iii],58,[3 advt] pp. A few sl marks. Old style calf. Wing G.809.
(Finch) **£385 [≈ $739]**
- Lux Orientalis, or An Enquiry into the Opinion of the Eastern Sages, Concerning the Praeexistence of Souls ... London, Cambridge & Oxford: 1662. 1st edn. 8vo. [xl],192 pp. Sl marks. Contemp calf, gilt border, hd of spine sl defective, jnts cracked but firm. Wing G.814. Anon. *(Clark)* **£250 [≈ $479]**
- Sadducismus Triumphatus: or, a Full and Plain Evidence, concerning Witches and Apparitions ... London: Bettesworth ..., 1726. Folio. [xii],1-35,[36-50], 498,[4 advt] pp. Frontis, frontis to 2nd part, 1 other engvd illust. Contemp calf, sometime rebacked.
(Vanbrugh) **£375 [≈ $719]**
- Sadducismus Triumphatus: or, a Full and Plain Evidence concerning Witches and

Apparitions ... The Fourth Edition, with Additions ... London: 1726. 8vo. [12],35, [10], 161,[4], [12],223-498, [4 advt] pp. Frontis, 2 plates. Rec qtr calf.
(Fenning) **£225 [≈ $431]**
- Scepsis Scientifica: or Confest Ignorance, the Way to Science; in a Essay on the Vanity of Dogmatizing, and Confident Opinion ... London: E. Cotes for Henry Eversden, 1665. 8vo. Some sm lib stamps. Contemp sheep, recased. Wing G.827-8.
(Waterfield's) **£400 [≈ $767]**
- The Zealous, and Impartial Protestant, shewing Some great, but less heeded Dangers of Popery ... London: M.C. for Henry Brome, 1681. 1st edn. Sm 4to. [ii],60,[iv] pp. Disbound. Wing G.837. Anon.
(Finch) **£120 [≈ $230]**

Glass, Samuel
- An Essay on Magnesia Alba ... Oxford: for R. Davies, 1764. Only edn. 8vo. 6,38 pp. Stitched as issued, uncut.
(Young's) **£120 [≈ $230]**

Glasse, Hannah
- The Complete Confectioner ... London: for J. Cooke, [ca 1765]. 8vo. iv,304,xvi pp. Some spotting, lacks endpapers. Contemp sheep, spine worn but sound.
(Burmester) **£200 [≈ $383]**

Glenn, James
- A Description of South Carolina ... London: 1761. [8],110,[2] pp. Red polished calf. Anon.
(Reese) **$3,500 [≈ £1,822]**

Glover, Richard
- Boadicia. A Tragedy. London: Dodsley & Cooper, 1753. 1st edn. Issue with Cooper's name in imprint. 8vo. Title & last leaf dusty. Closed tear in B2. Disbound.
(Dramatis Personae) **$60 [≈ £31]**
- London: or, the Progress of Commerce. A Poem. London: T. Cooper, 1739. 4to. Title & last leaf sl dusty. Rebound in qtr calf.
(C.R. Johnson) **£245 [≈ $470]**
- Medea. A Tragedy. London: ptd by H. Woodfall, & sold by J. Morgan, 1761. 1st edn. 4to. Mod wraps. Anon.
(Waterfield's) **£65 [≈ $124]**
- Medea. A Tragedy. London: ptd by H. Woodfall, & sold by J. Morgan, 1761. 1st edn. 4to. State with price ptd below imprint. Title & final verso sl dusty. Disbound.
(Sanders) **£65 [≈ $124]**

Glynn, Robert
- The Day of Judgement: a Poetical Essay. The Third Edition. Cambridge: J. Bentham, 1758. 4to. Sm blot on title. Disbound.
                    (Waterfield's) £40 [≈ $76]

Godwin or Godwyn, Thomas
- Moses and Aaron, Civil and Ecclesiastical Rites Used by the Ancient Hebrews ... London: John Haviland & R. Royston, 1631. 4th edn. 4to. [8],300,[12] pp. Title stained at ft, sl marg wear. Contemp calf, rebacked. STC 11954.   *(Humber)* £58 [≈ $111]
- Moses & Aaron: Civil and Ecclesiastical Rites Used by the Ancient Hebrews ... Twelfth Edition ... London: Richard Hodgkinson ..., 1672. 4to in 8s. [viii],266,[12] pp. Title sl dust soiled. Rec calf backed bds. Wing G.982.
                    (Vanbrugh) £165 [≈ $316]
- Romanae Historiae ... An English Exposition of the Roman Antiquities ... For the Use of Abingdon School ... London: R.W. for Peter Parker, 1661. 4to. 270,[18] pp. Some edge browning. Rec contemp style calf.
                    (Young's) £40 [≈ $76]
- Romanae Historiae Anthologia recognita et aucta. An English Exposition of the Roman Antiquities ... Newly revised and enlarged by the Author. London: R.W. for Henry Cripps, 1661. Sm 4to. Title sl defective & reprd. Mod half mor. Wing G.990. *(Stewart)* £35 [≈ $67]
- Romanae Historiae ... An English Exposition of the Roman Antiquities ... London: for Peter Parker, 1668. iv,270,[18] pp. Qtr leather, recased.   *(Gage)* £25 [≈ $47]
- Romanae Historiae Anthologia recognita et aucta. An English Exposition of the Roman Antiquities ... London: J.C. for Peter Parker, 1671. Sm 4to. Wing G.993.
                    (Stewart) £45 [≈ $86]
- Romanae Historiae ... An English Exposition of the Roman Antiquities ... For the Use of Abingdon School ... London: R.W. for Peter Parker, 1674. 4to. [vi],270,[20] pp. Rec calf backed bds. Wing G.994.
                    (Vanbrugh) £165 [≈ $316]

Godwin, William
- The Enquirer. Reflections on Education, Manners and Literature in a Series of Essays. Dublin: for J. Moore, 1798. 8vo. Sm repr to title. Later half calf, rebacked.
                    (Waterfield's) £300 [≈ $575]
- An Enquiry concerning Political Justice, and its Influence on General Virtue and Happiness ... London: Robinson, 1793. 1st

edn. 2 vols. 4to. [iii]-xiii,[xxi], 378; [xxvi], [379]-895, [2 errata] pp. Lacks half-titles. Sgntr 3P misbound. Rec calf.
                    (Pickering) $6,000 [≈ £3,125]
- Enquiry Concerning Political Justice, and Its Influence on Morals and Happiness. Phila: Bioren & Madan, 1796. 1st Amer edn. xvi, [21]-362; viii,400 pp. Half-titles. Usual tanning, occas old water stains. Mod cloth & mrbld bds.   *(Reese)* $650 [≈ £338]
- Inquiry concerning Political Justice and its Influence on Morals and Happiness ... The Second Edition corrected. London: Robinson, 1796. 2nd edn, rvsd. 2 vols. 8vo. Sm lib stamp on titles. Minor marg paper reprs. Mod qtr calf, vellum tips.
                    (Waterfield's) £750 [≈ $1,439]
- Enquiry concerning Political Justice, and its Influence on Morals and Happiness. The Second Edition corrected. London: Robinson, 1796. 2 vols. Half-titles. Contemp tree calf, gilt spines (sl rubbed).
                    (Jarndyce) £600 [≈ $1,151]
- Memoirs of the Author of A Vindication of the Rights of Woman. The Second Edition Corrected. London: for J. Johnson, 1796. Half-title. Port frontis (marg sl stained). Orig bds, edges rubbed & bumped, rebacked, new endpapers.   *(Jarndyce)* £300 [≈ $575]
- Things as they are; or, the Adventures of Caleb Williams. London: for B. Crosby, 1794. 1st edn. 3 vols. Half-titles. Vol 1 lacks flyleaves. 12mo. Contemp paper backed bds, labelled in MS, sl rubbed. Cloth slipcase.
                    (Ximenes) $3,750 [≈ £1,953]
- Things As They Are; or, The Adventures of Caleb Williams. The Second Edition corrected. London: Robinson, 1796. 3 vols. Lacks half-titles. Sl later half calf, gilt spines, red & green labels, v sm reprs to hd of spines.
                    (Jarndyce) £320 [≈ $614]

Godwyn, Thomas
- See Godwin or Godwyn, Thomas.

Goethe, Johann Wolfgang von
- The Sorrows of Werter: a German Story. New Edition. London: for J. Dodsley, 1784. 2 vols in one. 12mo. viii,163; [ii],168 pp. Early 19th c half calf, gilt spines, sides sl rubbed. Anon.   *(Burmester)* £110 [≈ $211]
- The Sorrows of Werter: a German Story. A New Edition. London: for J. Dodsley, 1784. 2 vols. Calf, hinges sl weak, lacks 1 label. Anon.   *(Jarndyce)* £48 [≈ $92]

Goldsmith, Oliver
- The Citizen of the World ... London: for the author ..., 1762. 1st edn. 2 vols. 12mo. vii, [i],286; [ii],238,[xvi] pp. Page [vii] vol 1 misnumbered v. Lacks final blanks. Rec old style qtr calf, vellum tips. Anon.
(Finch) £275 [≈ $527]
- The Citizen of the World; or, Letters from a Chinese Philosopher residing in London to his Friends in the East. London: for J. Newbery, 1762. 1st coll edn. 2 vols. 8vo. Contemp sheep, rebacked.
(Waterfield's) £350 [≈ $671]
- The Citizen of the World ... London: for Vernor, Otridge ..., 1792. 2 vols. 12mo. Engvd titles only. Contemp calf, red labels, hinges sl rubbed. *(Jarndyce)* £65 [≈ $124]
- The Deserted Village. A Poem. London: for W. Griffith, 1770. 1st edn. 4to. Half-title. Engvd title-vignette. Crushed levant mor, inner dentelles gilt, a.e.g., by Riviere.
(Black Sun) $1,850 [≈ £963]
- Essays. London: for W. Griffin, 1765. 1st edn. 12mo. Engvd title vignette. Contemp calf, crnrs bumped, jnts sl worn but firm.
(Chapel Hill) £650 [≈ £338]
- Essays. London: for W. Griffin, 1765. The (probably pirated) edn with letterpress title. Contemp calf, paper label, hinges sl rubbed.
(Jarndyce) £90 [≈ $172]
- The Haunch of Venison, a Poetical Epistle to Lord Clare. London: for G. Kearsly, & J. Ridley, 1776. 1st edn. 4to. Frontis port. Sm repr to last leaf. Lacks half-title. Rebound in half calf. *(Jarndyce)* £140 [≈ $268]
- The Miscellaneous Works ... London: for W. Osborne, & T. Griffin, 1782. 12mo. 230 pp. Lacks half-title. Contemp sheep, spine sl worn. *(Burmester)* £50 [≈ $95]
- The Miscellaneous Works ... Now First Uniformly Collected. Perth: R. Morison junior ..., 1792. 7 vols. Frontis & engvd title vol 1. Some spotting. Contemp tree calf, gilt spines & borders, red & green labels, some wear to spine ends. *(Jarndyce)* £90 [≈ $172]
- The Poetical Works ... With the Life of the Author. Hereford: D. Walker, 1794. 1st edn thus. 24mo. 95 pp. 6 w'engvd ills by Thomas Bewick. Edges of 3 ff ragged. Calf, rebacked, new endpapers. *(Larkhill)* £190 [≈ $364]
- The Roman History ... London: for S. Baker & G. Leigh, T. Davies, & L. Davis, 1769. 1st edn. 2 vols. 8vo. Lacks final blank vol 1. 19th c half calf, gilt spines, jnts sl rubbed.
(Sanders) £75 [≈ $143]

- The Roman History ... Sixth Edition. London: 1789. 2 vols. 8vo. [2],x,487,[12]; [2],viii,501,[10] pp. Vol 2 half-title only. 1st title sl foxed & abraded. Later 19th c dark blue half calf, red & yellow labels.
(Fenning) £45 [≈ $86]
- The Traveller, a Poem. London: for Carnan & Newbery, 1770. 4to. [ii],iv,23,[1] pp. Engvd title. Lacks half-title. Mod wraps.
(Claude Cox) £45 [≈ $86]
- The Vicar of Wakefield: a Tale. The Fourth Edition. London: Carnan & Newbery, 1770. 2 vols. Fcap 8vo. [8],214; [6],223 pp. Contemp calf gilt, 1 backstrip relaid.
(Spelman) £100 [≈ $191]
- The Vicar of Wakefield; a Tale. London: for T. Carnan & F. Newbery, 1773. 5th edn. 2 vols. 12mo. Contemp calf, gilt spines, jnts cracked, 1 jnt reprd. Anon.
(Burmester) £75 [≈ $143]
- The Vicar of Wakefield: a Tale ... London: for J. Davies, T. Smith ..., 1783. 2 vols in one. 12mo. 135; 128 pp. Contemp mottled calf, gilt spine, jnts cracked, spine ends worn.
(Burmester) £55 [≈ $105]
- See also Kull, Owen.

Good-Nature ...
- Good-Nature. A Poem. [By a] Young Gentleman. London: for M. Cooper, [1744]. 1st edn. 4to. xii,23 pp. Piece scraped from surface of title. Stain in 3 margs. Lacks half-title. Disbound. *(Burmester)* £60 [≈ $115]

Goodman, John
- Winter Evening Conference between Neighbours. In Two Parts. The Second Edition, Corrected. London: J.M. for R. Royston, 1684. 8vo. [iv],232 pp. Contemp mor gilt, a.e.g. Wing G.1131. Anon.
(Claude Cox) £65 [≈ $124]

Goodricke, Henry
- A Speech on some Political Topics the Substance of which was intended to have been delivered in the House of Commons on Monday the 14th of December 1778 ... London: Cadell, 1779. Marg repr to title. Disbound. Anon. *(Waterfield's)* £65 [≈ $124]

Goodwin, John
- Apolutrosis Apolutroseos or Redemption Redeemed wherein the Most Glorious Work of the Redemption of the World ... Vindicated ... London: John Macock for Lodowick Lloyd & Henry Cripps, 1651. Sm folio.

[38],570,[17] pp. New half calf. Wing
G.1149.   *(Humber)* **£125 [≈ $239]**

Gookin, Daniel
- Historical Collections of the Indians in New
England. Of their Several Nations, Numbers,
Customs, Manners, Religion and
Government, before the English Planted
There ... [Boston]: 1792. [141]-232 pp. Mod
half cloth.   *(Reese)* **$250 [≈ £130]**

Goold, Thomas
- A Vindication of the Right Hon. Edmund
Burke's Reflections on the Revolution in
France ... Dublin: William Porter, for P.
Wogan ..., 1791. Rec cloth.
              (Jarndyce) **£120 [≈ $230]**

Gordon, George
- An Introduction to Geography, Astronomy,
and Dialling ... London: Senex, Strahan ... &
the author, 1726. 1st edn. 8vo. [xii],iv, 188,
40 pp. 11 engvs on 10 fldg plates. 19th c half
calf, rubbed, rebacked.
              (Burmester) **£120 [≈ $230]**

Gordon, Revd John
- Memoirs of the Life of John Gordon of
Glencat, in the County of Aberdeen in
Scotland, who was Thirteen Years in the
Scots College in Paris. London: Oswald,
1734. 8vo. 2 engvs. Calf, rebacked.
              (Emerald Isle) **£65 [≈ $124]**

Gosling, Mrs
- Moral Essays and Reflections. Sheffield: ptd
by W. Ward; & sold by G.G.J. & J. Robinson,
London, 1789. 1st edn. 8vo. [xvi], 127 pp.
Subscribers. Rec qtr calf, uncut.
              (Burmester) **£150 [≈ $287]**

Gother, John
- Pulpit-Sayings, or, The Characters of the
Pulpit-Papist Examined ... London: for
Henry Hills, 1688. 4to. [14],58,[1] pp. Title sl
dusty & creased. Lib stamp. Some browning.
Disbound. Wing G.1347. Anon.
              (Jarndyce) **£25 [≈ $47]**

Gouge, William
- A Learned and Very Useful Commentary on
the Whole Epistle to the Hebrews ... London:
A.M. & S.G. for Joshua Kirton, 1655. Thick
folio. [22],528, 534,384, 157,[32] pp. Port.
Occas sl browning, few minor blemishes.
New amateur goatskin. Wing G.1391.
              (Humber) **£195 [≈ $374]**

Gough, Strickland
- An Enquiry into the Causes of the Decay of
the Dissenting Interest in a Letter to a
Dissenting Minister ... Second Edition.
London: for J. Roberts, 1730. Disbound.
Anon.   *(Waterfield's)* **£40 [≈ $76]**

Gould, William
- An Account of English Ants ... London: for
A. Millar, 1747. 1st edn. Sm 8vo. Final advt
leaf. New sprinkled calf, label.
              (Georges) **£400 [≈ $767]**

The Governess ...
- See Fielding, Sarah.

The Graces ...
- The Graces: A Poetical Epistle from a
Gentleman to his Son. London: for the
author, 1774. 4to. 12 pp. Disbound.
              (C.R. Johnson) **£165 [≈ $316]**

Graeme, James
- Poems on Several Occasions. Edinburgh: A.
Donaldson, for W. Somerville, Lanark, 1773.
ix, [1],242 pp. Contemp calf, jnt broken.
              (C.R. Johnson) **£185 [≈ $355]**
- Poems on Several Occasions. Edinburgh: A
Donaldson, 1773. 1st edn. 12mo. 242 pp.
Orig half calf, some rubbing, wear hd of
spine.   *(Chapel Hill)* **$250 [≈ £130]**

Grafigny, Francoise P. Huguet de
- Letters Written by a Peruvian Princess. A
New Edition. Dublin: for William Colles, &
Rich. Moncrieffe, 1774. 2 vols in one. 12mo.
Continuous pagination & sgntrs. Contemp
calf, red label, 1 hinge reprd. Anon.
              (Jarndyce) **£120 [≈ $230]**

Graham, James
- The General State of Medical Chirurgical
Practice, Exhibited, shewing them to be
Inadequate, Ineffectual, Absurd and
Ridiculous ... Sixth Edition. London: 1779.
12mo. 248 pp. Rec leatherette.
              (Hemlock) **$300 [≈ £156]**

Graham, William
- The Art of Making Wines from Fruits,
Flowers, and Herbs, all the Native growth of
Great Britain ... New Edition. Revised,
Corrected, and greatly Enlarged. London: for
R. Baldwin, 1783. 8vo. [iv],68 pp. New bds.
              (Georges) **£250 [≈ $479]**
- The Scriptural Doctrine of Water Baptism.

Richmond: William Rind, 1799. 1st edn. 4to.
41 pp. Orig wraps, unopened.
(Bookpress) $250 [≈ £130]

Grainger, James
- The Sugar-Cane: a Poem. In Four Books.
With Notes. London: Dodsley, 1764. 1st edn.
4to. Half-title. Frontis. Disbound.
(Ximenes) $850 [≈ £442]

Granger, James
- A Biographical History of England ... adapted
to a methodical Catalogue of Engraved British
Heads. London: for D. Davies, 1769-1774. 3
vols in 5 inc 1774 Supplement. 4to. Port in
vol 1. Contemp calf, mor labels, jnts cracked,
Supplement not quite uniform.
(Waterfield's) £150 [≈ $287]

Grantham, Thomas
- A Marriage Sermon, called A Wife Mistaken,
or A Wife and No Wife ... London: H. Hills,
1710. 16 pp. Lib stamp. Disbound.
(Jarndyce) £25 [≈ $47]

Granville, George, Lord Lansdowne
- See Lansdowne, George Granville, Lord.

Graves, Richard
- Columella; or, the Distressed Anchoret. A
Colloquial tale. London: Dodsley, 1779. 1st
edn. 2 vols. 12mo. iv,240; [ii],248 pp. 2
frontis. Contemp tree calf, gilt spines, jnts
reprd, new labels. Anon.
(Burmester) £350 [≈ $671]
- Euphrosyne: or, Amusements on the Road of
Life by the Author of the Spiritual Quixote.
London: Dodsley, 1776. 1st edn. 8vo.
Frontis. Strip cut from hd of title. Contemp
calf, jnts cracked, lacks label, crnrs worn.
Anon.   *(Waterfield's)* £130 [≈ $230]

Gravesande, W.J.
- Mathematical Elements of Natural
Philosophy confirmed by Experiments, or an
Introduction to Sir Isaac Newton's
Philosophy ... London: 1720. 1st English
edn. xxii,259, [2] pp. 33 fldg plates (2 loose).
2 sm marg reprs. Contemp leather, new
endpapers, spine sl worn. A further vol was
published in 1721.
(Whitehart) £180 [≈ $345]

Gray, John
- A Treatise on Gunnery. London: for William
Innys, 1731. 2nd edn. 8vo. [iv],xliii,94 pp. 1
fldg plate, 2 engvd text figs, num w'cut text

figs. Orig calf.   *(Bickersteth)* £350 [≈ $671]

Gray, John
- A Plan for finally settling the Government of
Ireland upon Constitutional Principles; and
the Chief Cause of the unprosperous State of
that Country explained. London: John
Stockdale, 1785. 79 pp. Disbound. Anon.
(C.R. Johnson) £95 [≈ $182]

Gray, Thomas
- Designs by Mr. R. Bentley, for Six Poems by
Mr. T. Gray. London: for R. Dodsley, 1753.
1st edn. 1st issue, with half-title reading
"Drawings &c". 4to. [iv] pp, 36 ff ptd on 1
side only, [iv] pp. 6 plates. 2 sm marg reprs.
V occas dust flecks. Rec half mor.
(Rankin) £350 [≈ $671]
- An Elegy written in a Country Church Yard.
A New Edition. London: Dodsley, 1763. 4to.
11 pp. 20th c tree calf, dec gilt spine,
contrasting label. Anon.
(Sotheran's) £285 [≈ $547]
- Odes by Mr. Gray. [Twickenham:
Strawberry-Hill Press] R. & J. Dodsley, 1757.
1st edn, 1st issue. 4to. 21 pp. Sl soiling. Later
red mor.   *(Bookpress)* £550 [≈ £286]
- The Poems ... Memoirs of his Life and
Writings by W. Mason ... York & London:
1775. 1st coll edn. 4to. [iv],416,111,[iii] pp.
Errata leaf. Port. Kk2, h1 & h4 cancels. Occas
foxing. Contemp half calf, untrimmed,
extremities worn, sm splits in jnts.
(Clark) £75 [≈ $143]
- Poems. Dublin: William Sleater, 1775. 2
parts in 1 vol. 12mo. 185,[6],180-211,[1];
[189]-211, [1] pp. Engvd frontis, 2nd title-
page dated 1776, engvd & w'cut ills. Blank
crnr torn from 1 leaf. Contemp calf, spine sl
worn, upper jnt cracked.
(Burmester) £120 [≈ $230]
- The Poems of Mr. Gray. To which are added
Memoirs of his Life and Writings, by W.
Mason, M.A. York: A. Ward, 1778. 1st 8vo
edn. 4 vols. Port frontis. Lacks 1 endpaper.
Period qtr calf, mrbld sides, jnts weakening.
(Young's) £68 [≈ $130]
- The Poetical Works: with Some Account of
his Life and Writings ... Revised ... London:
for J. Scatcherd, 1799. 2 advt pp. Frontis &
plates. Contemp diced calf gilt, spine ends sl
rubbed.   *(Jarndyce)* £35 [≈ $67]

Greatheed, Bertie
- The Regent: A Tragedy ... Dublin: for
Messrs Burnet ..., 1788. 1st Dublin edn. 8vo.

[iv], 67, [5] pp. Disbound.
(Young's) £25 [≈ $47]

Green, Matthew •
- The Spleen ... To which is added, Some other Pieces by the Same Hand ... London: A. Dodd ..., 1738. 3rd edn crrctd. 8vo. iv,67 pp. Disbound. *(Young's)* £45 [≈ $86]

Green, Valentine
- The History and Antiquities of the City and Suburbs of Worcester. London: for the author by W. Bulmer & Co ..., 1796. 1st edn. 2 vols. 4to. xviii,300; iii,112,clv,[v] pp. Port, fldg plan (torn in fold), 24 plates (mostly browned or foxed). Later buckram.
(Hollett) £110 [≈ $211]

Greenwood, James
- The Virgin Muse. Being a Collection of Poems from our most celebrated English Poets ... Notes ... Index ... London: 1717. 1st edn. xii,220 pp. Frontis. Sl soiling. Rebound in half calf. *(C.R. Johnson)* £265 [≈ $508]

Greenwood, Jonathan
- The Sailing and Fighting Instructions or Signals as they are observed in the Royal Navy of Great Britain. (London: 1715). 1st edn. 12mo. 5 engvd ff of text, 67 plates, mostly hand cold. Contemp panelled sheep, spine worn. Anon.
(Ximenes) $2,000 [≈ £1,041]

Gregory, George
- The Economy of Nature explained and illustrated on the Principles of Modern Philosophy ... London: J. Johnson, 1796. 1st edn. 3 vols. xxiii,543; xv,592; xvi,569,[6] pp. Plates. New cloth. *(Wreden)* $275 [≈ £143]

Gregory, John
- A Comparative View of the State and Faculties of Man with those of the Animal World. London: Dodsley, 1765. 1st edn. Sm 8vo. Contemp calf gilt, spine worn. Anon.
(Hannas) £75 [≈ $143]
- A Comparative View of the State and Faculties of Man with those of the Animal World. A New Edition. London: Dodsley, 1785. 8vo. [4],xx,286,[9] pp. Half-title. Lacks a blank flyleaf. Contemp calf gilt.
(Hannas) £45 [≈ $86]
- A Father's Legacy to his Daughters. A New Edition ... London: for William Lane at the Minerva Press, 1795. viii,[9]-142,[2 advt] pp. Frontis. Contemp sheep, hinges sl worn.

Anon.   *(C.R. Johnson)* £150 [≈ $287]

Grew, Nehemiah
- The Anatomy of Plants ... London: 1682. Folio. [xxii],24,[x], 304,[20] pp. Usual mispagination at pp 213-220. 83 plates (plate 15 is numbered 6). Sl used, last 3 plates mtd. Mod calf, antique style.
(Wheldon & Wesley) £550 [≈ $1,055]
- The Anatomy of Vegetables Begun ... London: for Spencer Highman, 1672. 1st edn. 8vo. 16 ff, 198 pp, 11 ff. 2 (of 3) plates. Contemp calf, front hinge starting. Wing G.1946. *(Hemlock)* $875 [≈ £455]
- Musaeum Regalis Societatis ... whereunto is subjoyned the Comparative Anatomy of Stomachs and Guts. London: W. Rawlins, for the author, 1681. 1st edn. 2 parts in one vol. Folio. [12],386,[4], [2],43 pp. 31 plates. Port frontis. Orig calf, rebacked. Wing G.1952
(Rootenberg) $950 [≈ £494]

Grey, Richard
- Memoria Technica: or, A New Method of Artificial Memory ... London: for Charles King, 1730. 1st edn. xviii,[6],120 pp. Red & black title. Contemp panelled calf, hd of spine sl chipped. Anon. *(Karmiole)* $650 [≈ £338]
- Memoria Technica: or, a New Method of Artificial Memory ... New Edition, Corrected. Wolverhampton: J. Smart, for W. Lowndes, London, 1790. 12mo. [iv],xxvi,159,[i blank], [xxv], [i advt] pp. Contemp sheep, yellow edges, jnts just cracking. *(Finch)* £25 [≈ $47]

Grey, Thomas de
- The Compleat Horseman and Expert Farrier. In Two Books. London: Thomas Harper ..., 1639. 1st edn. Folio. Frontis, facing leaf of explanation. Sl soil at beginning, few minor stains. Contemp calf, some rubbing, spine sl worn. STC 12206.
(Ximenes) $1,200 [≈ £625]

Griffin, Geoffrey
- The Microcosm ... see Canning, George, et al.

Griffin, Philip
- Juvenile Poems on Several Occasions. By a Gentleman of Oxford. Oxford: for Daniel Prince ..., 1764. 1st edn. 12mo. [iv],128 pp. Half-title. Occas v sl spot. Contemp half calf, sides rubbed, crnrs bumped. Anon.
(Finch) £225 [≈ $431]

Griffith, John
- A Journal of the Life, Travel, and Labours in the Work of the Ministry ... London: James Phillips, 1779. 1st edn. 8vo. iv,427 pp. Contemp calf, sl rubbed, jnts partly cracked.
(Young's) **£40 [≈ $76]**
- A Journal of the Life, Travels, and Labours in the Work of the Ministry. London: James Phillips, 1779. 1st edn. 8vo. iv,427 pp. Orig calf, rebacked, new endpapers.
(Bickersteth) **£55 [≈ $105]**
- A Journal of the Life, Travels, and Labours in the Work of the Ministry, of John Griffith. Phila: Joseph Crukshank, 1780. 8vo. [2],iv, 426,[8], 112 pp. Contemp calf, hd of spine chipped, crnrs sl bumped.
(Karmiole) **$150 [≈ £78]**
- Some Brief Remarks on Sundry Subjects, Necessary to be Understood and Attended to by all professing the Christian Religion. Principally addressed to the People called Quakers. London: Richardson & Clark, 1765. 1st edn. 8vo. [viii],100 pp. Contemp wraps.
(Young's) **£22 [≈ $42]**

Griffith, Matthew
- A Pathetical Perswasion to Pray for Publick Peace: propounded in a Sermon ... London: for Richard Royston, 1642. 4to. [v], 27 pp. Sl browned, sl cut down at top edge. Mod half calf gilt by Bayntun. Wing G.2016.
(Hollett) **£50 [≈ $95]**

Griffith, Richard
- The Posthumous Works of the Celebrated Dr. Sterne, Deceased. London: ptd in the year 1775. 2nd edn. 2 vols in one. 12mo. viii, [iv], 216; 214, [2] pp. 19th c mrbld bds, new calf spine. Imitation of Sterne.
(Burmester) **£180 [≈ $345]**

Grose, Francis
- The Antiquities of Ireland. London: for Hooper & Wigstead, 1797. 2 vols. 4to. 260 engvd plates. Old milled calf, rebacked.
(Hollett) **£275 [≈ $527]**
- A Provincial Glossary, with a Collection of Local Proverbs, and Popular Superstitions. London: for S. Hooper, 1787. 1st edn. 2 parts in one vol. 8vo. 19th c half calf, sl rubbed. Port bound in.
(Jarndyce) **£120 [≈ $230]**
- A Provincial Glossary ... London: S. Hooper, 1790. 2nd edn. 8vo. viii,(324),57,[3] pp. Ptd on wove paper. Contemp mottled calf, lacks label. The Downes copy.
(Bookpress) **$375 [≈ £195]**

- A Provincial Glossary; with a Collection of Local Proverbs, and Popular Superstitions. London: for S. Hooper, 1790. 2nd edn, enlgd. 12mo. Contemp half mor, gilt spine, uncut, a bit rubbed.
(Ximenes) **$275 [≈ £143]**
- Rules for Drawing Caricaturas: with an Essay on Comic Painting ... Second Edition. London: for S. Hooper, 1791. 8vo. 40 pp. 21 plates. 1 leaf torn without loss. Some old water staining. Later bds, uncut, rather frayed & dusty along outer edges. Phillipps copy.
(Spelman) **£120 [≈ $230]**

Grosvenor, Benjamin
- Health, an Essay on its Nature, Value, Uncertainty, Preservation, and Best Improvement. The Second Edition. London: for H. Piers, R. Hett, 1748. 12mo. [viii],xi,242 pp, advt leaf. Orig calf, rebacked.
(Bickersteth) **£85 [≈ $163]**

Grou, Jean N.
- The Characters of Real Devotion ... from the French ... by Alexander Clinton. The Second Edition. Dublin: Mehain, Cross, 1795. Lge 12mo. 158,[2 advt] pp. Contemp sheep, sl worn.
(Fenning) **£75 [≈ $143]**

Grubb, Sarah
- Some Account of the Life and Religious Labours of Sarah Grubb with an Appendix containing an Account of Ackworth School ... Dublin: for R. Jackson, 1792. 1st Irish edn. 8vo. Contemp calf, jnts cracked, some wear at crnrs.
(Waterfield's) **£70 [≈ $134]**
- Some Account of the Life and Religious Labours of Sarah Grubb with an Appendix containing an Account of Ackworth School ... Edited by Lindley Murray. London: James Phillip, 1794. 2nd edn. 8vo. [6],438 pp. Few marks. 19th c half calf. *(Humber)* **£35 [≈ $67]**

The Guardian ...
- See Addison, Joseph, et al.

Guarini, Giovanni Battista
- Il Pastor Fido ... see Fanshawe, Sir Richard.

Guazzo, Stephen
- The Art of Conversation. In Three Parts ... Translated ... into English. London: for J. Brett, 1738. 1st English edn. 4to. Errata leaf. Frontis (amateur hand colouring). Title v sl soiled. Contemp vellum.
(Vanbrugh) **£175 [≈ $335]**

Guellette, Thomas Simon
- Chinese Tales ... Translated by Mr. Stackhouse ... London: for J. Hodges, 1745. 3rd edn. Cr 8vo. Lacks endpaper, title reprd, few sections loose. Contemp calf.
(Stewart) £100 [≈ $191]
- Tartarian Tales: or, a Thousand and One Quarters of Hours ... Now for the First Time Translated into English, by Thomas Flloyd. London: Tonson, 1759. 1st edn in English. 12mo. xii,369 pp. Frontis. Contemp calf, spine sl rubbed, lacks label.
(Burmester) £300 [≈ $575]

Guibert, Jacques Antoine Hippolyte, Comte de
- Observations on the Military Establishment and Discipline of His Majesty the King of Prussia; with an Account of the Private Life of that celebrated Monarch ... London: Fielding & Walker, 1780. 1st English edn. 8vo. [iv],101,[3 advt] pp. Disbound. Anon.
(Young's) £95 [≈ $182]

A Guide to the Lakes ...
- See West, Thomas.

Guidott, Thomas
- A Discourse of Bathe, and the Hot Waters there ... London: for Henry Brome, 1676. 1st edn. 8vo. [xxxii],200 pp. Engvd & ptd titles. 3 fldg plates. Ruled in red throughout. Edges browned. Contemp style calf. Wing G.2192.
(Young's) £220 [≈ $422]
- A Discourse of Bathe, and the Hot Waters there ... London: for Henry Brome, 1676. 1st edn. 8vo. [xxxii],200 pp. 2 sep titles dated 1676, 1677. Frontis explanation leaf. Frontis, 3 plates, fldg map. Orig calf, rebacked, crnrs v sl worn. Wing G.2192.
(Vanbrugh) £395 [≈ $758]
- A Discourse of Bathe, and the Hot Waters There ... London: for Henry Brome, 1676. 1st edn. [xxvi],200 pp. Engvd frontis & explanatory sheet, fldg plan, 3 plates, 1 text illust on a fldg page (foredge sl worn). Old sheep, spine rubbed. *(Hollett)* £160 [≈ $307]

Guillet de Saint-George, Georges
- The Gentleman's Dictionary. In Three Parts ... Riding ... Military Art ... Navigation ... London: Bonwicke, Goodwin ..., 1705. 1st English edn. Half-title. Proposal ff after parts 2 & 3. 3 fldg plates, ills. Sl marg worm to prelims. Contemp calf, hinges sl weak.
(Jarndyce) £380 [≈ $729]

Gumble, Thomas
- The Life of General Monck, Duke of Albemarle ... London: J.S. for Thomas Basset, 1671. 1st edn. 8vo. [xxii],486 pp. Port frontis. Some browning & minor spotting. Rec qtr calf. Wing G.2230.
(Clark) £90 [≈ $172]

Gunning, Mrs
- A Letter from ... Addressed to His Grace the Duke of Argyll. London: for the author, sold by Ridgway ..., 1791. 3rd edn. 8vo. [iv], 147, [1 errata] pp. Half-title. Orig wraps, uncut.
(Young's) £44 [≈ $84]

Gunning, Peter
- The Paschal or Lent Fast Apostolicall and Perpetuall ... With an Appendix ... London: R. Norton for Timothy Garthwait, 1662. 4to. [10], 242, 433-542,[7] pp. Title vignette. A few stains. 19th c panelled calf, rebacked. Wing G.2236.
(Humber) £125 [≈ $239]

Gunter, E.
- The Works. London: Francis Eglesfield, 1662. 4th edn. Cr 8vo. x,152,40, 111,166, 64, 150 pp. Rebound in leather.
(Gemmary) $1,250 [≈ £651]

Gurney, Thomas
- Brachygraphy: or an Easy and Compendious System of Short-Hand ... Tenth Edition. London: for J. & M. Gurney; sold by M. Gurney, 1785. 12mo. Frontis, engvd title only, plates. Contemp speckled calf.
(Jarndyce) £58 [≈ $111]

Gyllenborg, Karl
- Letters which passed between Count Gyllenborg, the Barons Gortz, Sparre and others ... Edinburgh: reprinted in the year, 1717. 1st Edinburgh edn. 8vo. 70,[2 blank] pp. Foxed. Disbound. *(Hannas)* £55 [≈ $105]

H., J.
- Astronomical Dialogues; Three Treatises ... see Harris, James.

H., P.
- Annotations on Milton's Paradise Lost ... see Hume, Patrick.

H., W.
- The Holy Sinner ... see Hodson, William.

Habington, William
- The Historie of Edward the Fovrth, King of England ... London: Tho. Cotes for William Cooke, 1640. 1st edn. Sm folio. [iv],232 pp. Port frontis (sm marg damp stain). Occas v sm marg worm. Orig sheep, spine sl worn. STC 12586.   *(Vanbrugh)* £220 [≈ $422]

Hackett, John
- Select and Remarkable Epitaphs on Illustrious and Other Persons, in Several Parts of Europe ... London: T. Osborne, J. Shipton, 1757. Only edn. 2 vols. 12mo. Frontis in vol 1. Indexes at end of vol 2. Orig calf, gilt spines.   *(Bickersteth)* £130 [≈ $249]

Hadley, George
- Introductory Grammatical Remarks on the Persian Language. With a Vocabulary, English and Persian ... Bath: R. Cruttwell, for the author, 1776. 4to. iv,9-215 pp. Blank section missing from inner marg of title. Sm marg tear in last leaf. Disbound.
            (C.R. Johnson) £525 [≈ $1,007]

Hailes, Sir David Dalrymple, Lord
- A Catalogue of the Lords of Session, From the Institution of The College of Justice, In the year 1532. With Historical Notes. Edinburgh: Sands, Murray, & Cochran, 1767. 1st edn. 4to. Corrigenda pasted to verso of leaf after title. Browning. New qtr calf. Anon.   *(Meyer Boswell)* $350 [≈ £182]

Hakewill, William
- The Liberty of the Subject: against the Pretended Power of Impositions ... London: R.H., 1641. 4to. [viii],142,[2] pp. Final imprimatur leaf. Title dusty with sm hole sl affecting imprint. Disbound, stitching broken. Wing H.210. *(Clark)* £100 [≈ $191]
- The Manner of holding Parliaments in England. Collected forth of our Ancient Records ... London: 1641. 1st edn. Sm 4to. [58] pp. Frontis. New period style calf by Middleton. Wing H.214. Anon.
            (Sotheran's) £285 [≈ $547]

Hale, Sir Matthew
- The Analysis of the Law ... In the Savoy: Nutt & Gosling for T. Waller, 1739. 3rd edn. Sl foxing & browning. New qtr calf.
            (Meyer Boswell) $250 [≈ £130]
- Contemplations Moral and Divine: In Two Parts. London: for William Shrowsbery, 1685. 8vo. [xii],360; [viii],308 pp. Frontis port. Lacks final blank. Some foxing & sl

fingering, marg tears in 3 ff. Period calf, rebacked.   *(Rankin)* £75 [≈ $143]
- The Primitive Origination of Mankind, Considered and examined according to the Light of Nature ... London: Godwin for Shrowsbery, 1677. 1st edn. Folio. [x],380 pp. Port frontis. Contemp sheep, rebacked. Wing H.258.   *(Vanbrugh)* £235 [≈ $451]

Hales, John
- Golden Remains ... London: for Tim Garthwait, 1659. 1st edn. 4to. [x],188,80,48 pp. Engvd frontis & title by Hollar. Orig bndg, rebacked. Wing H.269.
            (Vanbrugh) £255 [≈ $489]
- The Works ... now first collected together in Three Volumes. Glasgow: Robert & Andrew Foulis, 1765. Post 8vo issue. 3 vols. Contemp calf, gilt spine, lacks labels, some wear at extremities. Earl of Lisburne b'plate.
            (Waterfield's) £135 [≈ $259]

Hales, Stephen
- Some Considerations on the Causes of Earthquakes which were read before the Royal Society, April 5, 1750. The Second Edition, Corrected. London: for R. Manby & H.S. Cox, 1750. 23 pp. Disbound.
            (C.R. Johnson) £250 [≈ $479]
- Statical Essays ... Second Edition, with Amendments. Volume I [only]. London: for W. Innys ..., 1731. 8vo. 19 plates. Lib stamp on title, old marg stain to a few ff, 1 blank crnr torn away. Contemp calf, sl worn, jnts weak.   *(Stewart)* £200 [≈ $383]
- Statical Essays: containing Haemastaticks; or, an Account of some Hydraulic and Hydrostatical Experiments made on the Blood and Blood-Vessels of Animals. London: 1740. 2nd edn. 356, index pp. Leather, front bd detached, rear hinge strengthened.
            (Fye) $500 [≈ £260]
- Statical Essays: containing Haemastatics; or, an Account of some Hydraulic and Hydrostatical Experiments made on the Blood and Blood-Vessels of Animals. London: 1769. 3rd edn. 356 pp. Leather, front bd detached, spine & rear hinge cracked.
            (Fye) $375 [≈ £195]
- Vegetable Staticks ... Being an Essay towards a Natural History of Vegetation. London: 1727. 1st edn. [vii],vii, [ii],376 pp. 19 plates. Contemp calf, rebacked.
            (Wheldon & Wesley) £600 [≈ $1,151]

Halfpenny, Joseph
- Gothic Ornaments in the Cathedral Church

of York. York: Geo. Peacock, printer, 1795. 1st edn. Folio. 26 ff. Subscribers. 105 engvd plates (95 & 96 hand cold). Sl foxing. New qtr leather.   *(Bookpress)* **$575 [≈£299]**

Halfpenny, William
- A New and Complete System of Architecture Delineated ... London: John Brindley, 1749. 1st edn. Oblong 4to. [iv],25 pp. 47 plates. Contemp calf, worn.
        (Bookpress) **$2,250 [≈£1,171]**
- Practical Architecture, or a Sure Guide to the True Working according to the Rules of that Science ... London: Thomas Bowles, (1724). 1st edn. 12mo. [3],48 ff, engvd throughout. Contemporary calf, rebacked.
        (Bookpress) **$1,200 [≈£625]**
- Useful Architecture ... With Full and Clear Instructions, in every particular, for erecting Parsonage- Houses, Farm-Houses, and Inns ... London: Robert Sayer, 1755. 2nd edn. Sm 8vo. [iv],82 pp. 25 designs on 21 plates. Later half calf.   *(Bookpress)* **$1,450 [≈£755]**

Halfpenny, William & John
- Rural Architecture in the Gothick Taste. London: Robert Sayer, 1752. Only edn. Sm 8vo. 8 pp. 16 plates. Later bds.
        (Bookpress) **$1,500 [≈£781]**

Halhed, Nathaniel Brassey
- A Calculation on the Commencement of the Millenium ... London: B. Crosby, 1795. 52 pp. Frontis port. Orig wraps, uncut.
        (C.R. Johnson) **£55 [≈$105]**
- Testimony of the Authenticity of the Prophecies of Richard Brothers and of his Mission to recall the Jews. Second Edition. London: H.D. Symonds, 1795. 40 pp. Disbound.   *(C.R. Johnson)* **£55 [≈$105]**

Halifax, George Savile, Marquis of
- The Character of a Trimmer. His Opinion ... By the Honourable, Sir W. Coventry. The Second Edition, carefully corrected ... London: for Richard Baldwin, 1689. 4to. [4], 43 pp. Sl browned. Disbound. Wing H.247. Anon.   *(Jarndyce)* **£40 [≈$76]**

Hall, Captain John
- The History of the Civil War in America. Volume I [all published]. London: 1780. 2nd edn. 6 ff, 467 pp. Lge fldg map (tear reprd). Antique half calf & mrbld bds. Anon.
        (Reese) **$600 [≈£312]**

Hall, Joseph
- The Balm of Gilead or, Comforts for the Distressed; both Morall and Divine, most fit for these Woful Times. London: Thos. Newcomb, 1650. 12mo. xvii,396 pp. Front endpapers torn. Leather, rear bd detached.
        (Gage) **£45 [≈$86]**
- The Works. London: for Thomas Pavier, Miles Flesher & John Haviland, 1625. x,1395, index pp. Engvd title. Final pp of index v frayed. Leather, soiled & worn.
        (Gage) **£50 [≈$95]**

Hall-Stevenson, John
- Makarony Fables; Fables for Grown Gentlemen; Lyrick Epistles; and several other Poems; by the Author of Crazy Tales. Dublin: Thomas Ewing, 1772. 1st coll edn. Contemp calf, sl rubbed, split in hinge. Anon.
        (Jarndyce) **£150 [≈$287]**

Hallam, Isaac
- The Cocker: a Poem. In imitation of Virgil's Third Georgic. Humbly inscrib'd to the Honourable Society of Sportsmen at Grantham. Stamford: Francis Howgrave, 1742. 1st edn. 4to. 2 pp subscribers. Frontis. Old half sheep, lacks spine, 1 bd detached.
        (Ximenes) **$1,500 [≈£781]**

Haller, Albrecht von, Baron
- Usong. An Eastern Narrative. Written in German. London: for the translator ..., 1772. 1st English edn. 2 vols. Errata on p viii vol 1 & title verso vol 2. Contemp calf, gilt spines & borders, red & green labels, fine.
        (Jarndyce) **£680 [≈$1,305]**

Hallett, Joseph
- The Consistent Christian: Being a Confutation of the Errors advanced in Mr. Chubb's late Book ... London: for John Noon ..., 1738. 1st edn. 8vo. 44 pp. Disbound.
        (Young's) **£32 [≈$61]**

Hamilton, Alexander
- Outlines of the Theory and Practice of Midwifery. From the Last British Edition. The Third American Edition. Northampton: 1797. 8vo. 288 pp. Browned & foxed. Orig calf, worn.   *(Goodrich)* **$135 [≈£70]**

Hamilton, Count Anthony
- Memoirs of the Count Grammont ... A New Translation, with Notes and Illustrations ... London: for S. & E. Harding, (1793). 8vo. iii, 363, lxxxiv, 6 pp. 76 ports. 19th c calf, a.e.g.,

sometime rebacked. *(Young's)* **£80 [≈ $153]**

Hamilton, J.
- Stereography, or, a Compleat Body of Perspective, in all its Branches ... London: W. Bowyer for the author, 1738. 1st edn. 2 vols in one. Folio. [16],208, [2],[209-]400 pp. 130 plates. Some v sl foxing & sl marg worming. Contemp calf, backstrip relaid.
(Spelman) **£900 [≈ $1,727]**

Hamilton, William
- Letters concerning the Northern Coast of C. Antrim, containing a Natural History of its Basaltes, with an Account of Antiquities, Manners and Customs of that Country ... Dublin: Bonham, 1786. 8vo. Fldg map. Contemp calf, rebacked.
(Emerald Isle) **£135 [≈ $259]**
- Letters concerning the Northern Coast of the County of Antrim ... Dublin: Bonham, 1790. Fldg maps & plates. Contemp Irish tree calf, head band chipped.
(Emerald Isle) **£145 [≈ $278]**

Hamilton, Sir William
- Observations on Mount Vesuvius, Mount Etna, and other Volcanos ... Second Edition. London: Cadell, 1773. 8vo. iv,179,[i] pp. Fldg map (reprd), 5 plates. Orig sheep, rebacked. *(Frew Mackenzie)* **£300 [≈ $575]**
- Observations on Mount Vesuvius, Mount Etna, and other Volcanos ... Second Edition. London: Cadell, 1773. Sm 8vo. iv,180 pp. Fldg map, 5 plates. Crnr of title torn away. Contemp calf, rebacked. "From the Author" on title. *(Karmiole)* **£250 [≈ £130]**

Hamilton, William, of Bangour
- Poems on Several Occasions. Edinburgh: for W. Gordon, 1760. 8vo. Port frontis. Contemp calf. *(Buccleuch)* **£70 [≈ $134]**

Hamilton, William, of Gilbertsfield
- A New Edition of the Life and Heroick Actions of the Renoun'd Sir William Wallace ... Glasgow: William Duncan, 1722. 1st edn [sic]. 8vo. xxxvi,365 pp. Generally sl soiled, old doodling on title. Contemp calf, later endpapers. *(Burmester)* **£75 [≈ $143]**

Hammond, Henry
- A Brief Vindication of three passages in the Practical Catechisme, from the Censures affixt on them by the Ministers of London ... London: Richard Royston, 1648. 1st edn. 4to. [ii], 13, [i] pp. Disbound, stitching broken.

Wing H.518. *(Clark)* **£28 [≈ $53]**
- Of the Power of the Keyes: or, Binding and Loosing. London: Richard Royston, 1647. 1st edn. 4to. [xii],141,[i] pp. Blank leaf before title. Errata on final page. Occas sl browning. Disbound. Wing H.567. Anon.
(Clark) **£45 [≈ $86]**
- A Practical Catechism ... Fourteenth Edition ... Whereunto is added The Reasonableness of the Christian Religion. London: Tho. Newborough ..., 1700. 8vo. [12], 482, index pp. 19th c calf. *(Humber)* **£45 [≈ $86]**

Hammond, N.
- The Elements of Algebra in a New and Easy Method ... London: 1752. 2nd edn. xxiv,328 pp. New leather. *(Whitehart)* **£80 [≈ $153]**

Hanger, George
- Military Reflections on the Attack and Defence of London ... London: J. Debrett, 1795. Rebound in qtr calf.
(C.R. Johnson) **£75 [≈ $143]**

Hanway, Jonas
- Midnight the Signal. In Sixteen Letters to a Lady of Quality. London: Dodsley, 1779. 1st edn. 2 vols. Sm 8vo. Pp 193-4 omitted in pagination of vol 2. Engvd titles. Contemp calf, gilt spines, contrasting mor labels (sl rubbed). Anon. *(Ximenes)* **$2,000 [≈ £1,041]**
- Virtue in Humble Life ... The Second Edition, Amply Corrected, and Enlarged an Half Part. London: Dodsley, 1777. 2 vols in one. 4to. [4],xvii,viii,412; [2],viii,524 pp. 2 frontis. Rebound in cloth & bds.
(Karmiole) **$125 [≈ £65]**

Harbin, George
- The Hereditary Right of the Crown of England Asserted ... By a Gentleman. London: G. James, for Richard Smith, 1713. Folio. [vi], 274, lxiii, [5] pp. Sl browning. Old polished calf, rebacked, edges reprd. Anon.
(Hollett) **£150 [≈ $287]**

Harcourt, Robert
- The Relation of a Voyage to Guiana. Describing the Climate, Situation, Fertilitie, & Commodities of that Country ... Enlarged ... River of the Amazones ... London: 1626. 2nd edn, with addtns. Sm 4to. [16], 264 pp. Sl remarg a few ff. Crushed mor gilt. STC 12755. *(Reese)* **$3,000 [≈ £1,562]**

Hardinge, George
- A Series of Letters to the Right Hon.

Edmund Burke ... London: T. Cadell, 1791. 199 pp. Disbound.
(C.R. Johnson) **£65** [≈ $124]

Harington, Edward
- A Schizzo on the Genius of Man: in which, among Various Subjects, the Merit of Mr Thomas Barker, the celebrated young Painter of Bath, is particularly considered ... Bath: Cruttwell, 1793. 8vo. Half-title. Intl blank. 2 plates. Rec qtr leather.
(Spelman) **£280** [≈ $537]
- A Schizzo on the Genius of Man ... Bath: Cruttwell, Robinson, London ..., 1793. 1st edn. 8vo. xlviii,[ii],390,[i] pp. 2 plates. Contemp half calf, front sl tender at hd, bds rubbed. Anon. *(Finch)* **£375** [≈ $719]

Harley, George Davies
- Poems: by G.D. Harley, of the Theatre Royal, Covent Garden. London: for the author by J. Jarvis, 1796. 12mo. Half-title. 4 pp subscribers. Engvd port (1793) loosely insrtd Orig pink bds, uncut, later paper spine, paper label, sm split in hinge, some rubbing.
(Jarndyce) **£120** [≈ $230]

Harmer, Thomas
- The Outline of a New Commentary on Solomon's Song ... By the Author of Observations in Divers Passages of Scripture. London: for J. Buckland, 1768. 8vo. Inc addtnl index sheet Cc added in 1775. Title vignette. Sm lib stamp. 19th c calf. Anon.
(Waterfield's) **£50** [≈ $95]

Harper, Robert G.
- Observations on the Dispute between the United States and France, addressed ... to his Constituents, in May, 1797. Second Edition. Philadelphia Printed. London: reptd ..., 1798. 8vo. viii, (5)-109, [1 errata] pp, postscript leaf. Rec wraps.
(Fenning) **£38.50** [≈ $74]

Harrington, James
- The Oceana and Other Works ... With an Account of his Life by John Toland. London: Becket & Cadell, 1771. 4to. [iv],xl,598, [xvi], 2 advt pp. Port frontis, plate. V occas foxing. Contemp calf, hinges strengthened, sl scuffed. *(Rankin)* **£175** [≈ $335]

Harris, James
- Hermes or a Philosophical Inquiry concerning Universal Grammar ... London: for John Nourse ..., 1765. 2nd edn, rvsd &

crrctd. 8vo. xix,442,29 pp. Old calf, worn, rebacked. *(Young's)* **£70** [≈ $134]
- Hermes or a Philosophical Inquiry concerning Universal Grammar ... The Fifth Edition. London: for E. Wingrave ..., 1794. 8vo. Frontis. Contemp tree calf gilt, black label. *(Jarndyce)* **£90** [≈ $172]
- Philosophical Arrangements. London: John Nourse, 1775. 1st edn. 8vo. xiv,1-278, *277-485, [xxxiii] pp. F4 a cancel. Extra leaf *T3 after p 278. Frontis. Browned. Red qtr calf. *(Clark)* **£110** [≈ $211]
- Three Treatises: the First concerning Art, the Second Music, Painting and Poetry, the Third concerning Happiness. By J.H. London: H. Woodfall, jun., 1744. 1st edn. 8vo. K3 S4 cancelled. Later port inserted. Contemp calf, backstrip relaid.
(Waterfield's) **£135** [≈ $259]
- Three Treatises: the First Concerning Art; the Second concerning Music, Painting, and Poetry; the Third concerning Happiness ... Second Edition, revised and corrected. London: Nourse & Vaillant, 1765. 8vo. [ii], 377, [xviii] pp. Contemp calf, gilt spine, ft of spine sl chipped. *(Finch)* **£50** [≈ $95]

Harris, John, ?1666-1719
- Astronomical Dialogues between a Gentleman and a Lady ... The Second Edition. By J.H. F.R.S. London: for John Horsfield, 1725. 8vo. [2], vi,184 pp. 6 plates. Calf antique. *(Fenning)* **£125** [≈ $239]
- The Description and Use of the Celestial and Terrestrial Globes; and of Collins's Pocket Quadrant. London: 1703. 1st edn. 8vo. [vi],62,[4 advt] pp. Frontis. Contemp sheep, rubbed, crnrs worn, upper jnt split at hd.
(Gaskell) **£600** [≈ $1,151]
- The Description and Use of the Celestial and Terrestrial Globes ... The Sixth Edition. London: for D. Midwinter, 1725. Sm 8vo. [vi], 62, 4 advt pp. Frontis. Orig calf, front hinge cracked, sl damage to spine ends.
(Vanbrugh) **£75** [≈ $143]
- The Description and Use of the Globes, and the Orrery. To which is prefixed ... a Brief Account of the Solar System. London: 1734. 3rd edn. viii,190 pp. Frontis, 5 fldg plates. Water stain on top & outer marg of most pp. Contemp leather, rebacked.
(Whitehart) **£140** [≈ $268]

Harris, M.
- An Exposition of British Insects ... Bees, Flies and Libellulae. London: 1786. 2nd edn, 2nd

issue. 4to. viii,9-166,[4] pp. Engvd title, cold chart, plain plate, 50 hand cold plates. Minor browning. Contemp calf, rebacked, trifle worn. *(Wheldon & Wesley)* **£600 [≈ $1,151]**

Harris, W.
- A Discourse concerning Transubstantiation ... London: for R. Ford ..., 1735. 2nd edn. 8vo. 43,6 pp. Half-title. Disbound.
(Young's) **£18 [≈ $34]**

Harris, Walter & Smith, J.
- The Antient and Present State of the County of Down, containing a Chorographical Description ... with a Survey of the New Canal. Dublin: Reilly, 1744. 8vo. Map in facs. Contemp calf, rebacked. Anon.
(Emerald Isle) **£145 [≈ $278]**

Harris, William
- An Historical and Critical Account of the Life of Charles the Second ... London: A. Millar, 1766. 2 vols. [Bound with] An Historical and Critical Account of Hugh Peters. London: Noon & Millar, 1751. 1st edns. [viii],414,[ii]; [viii],400; 72 pp. Contemp calf, sl worn.
(Clark) **£70 [≈ $134]**

Harrison, Henry
- The Last Words of a Dying Penitent ... London: Randal Taylor, 1692. 1st edn. 4to. 31 pp. Last leaf cut close. Browned. Disbound. Wing H.892.
(Young's) **£45 [≈ $86]**

Hart, Joseph
- Hymns, &c. Composed on Various Subjects. The Tenth Edition ... Supplement ... Appendix. London: ptd by H. Trapp ..., 1784. 12mo. Rec qtr calf.
(Sanders) **£65 [≈ $124]**

Harte, Revd William
- An Essay on Reason [:a Poem]. London: J. Wright for Lawton Gulliver, 1735. 1st edn. Folio. [iv],40 pp,errata leaf. Title dusty & crnr reprd. Old ink page numbers. Mod wraps. Anon. *(Bickersteth)* **£65 [≈ $124]**

Hartley, David
- Observations on Man, his Frame, his Duty, and his Expectations. In Two Parts. London: S. Richardson, for James Leake & Wm. Frederick, Bath, 1749. Contemp calf, sl rubbed, lacks 1 label.
(C.R. Johnson) **£1,200 [≈ $2,303]**

Hartley, Thomas
- Sermons on Various Subjects; with a Prefatory Discourse ... Second Edition. London: for R. Manby, 1755. viii,308 pp. Leather, crnrs bumped. *(Gage)* **£25 [≈ $47]**

Hartson, Hall
- The Countess of Salisbury. A Tragedy ... London: for W. Griffin ..., 1767. 2nd edn. 8vo. [viii],72 pp. Disbound.
(Young's) **£22 [≈ $42]**

Harvey, James
- Praesagium Medicum, or the Prognostick Signs of Acute Diseases ... London: 1706. xxix, 216 pp. New qtr leather, garish endpapers. *(Whitehart)* **£160 [≈ $307]**
- Praesagium Medicum, or the Prognostick Signs of Acute Diseases; Established by Ancient Observations, and Explain'd by the Best Modern Discoveries. London: Strahan, 1706. 1st edn. 8vo. xxix,216 pp. Panelled calf. *(Goodrich)* **$395 [≈ £205]**

Harvey, William
- The Anatomical Exercises of Dr. William Harvey ... added the Discourse of James de Back ... London: Lowndes, 1673. 2nd edn in English. Sm 8vo. [xxiv],107, [xx],172 pp. Title mtd & reprd. Contemp calf, reprd.
(Bookpress) **$1,200 [≈ £625]**

Harwood, Edward
- A View of the Various Editions of the Greek and Roman Classics ... London: Becket, 1775. 1st edn. 8vo. xxiv,229,[3] pp. Some misbndg in preface. Contemp half calf, lacks label, jnts cracked but firm, sides darkened.
(Finch) **£120 [≈ $230]**

Hassell, John
- Tour of the Isle of Wight. London: John Jarvis, 1790. 1st edn. 2 vols. 8vo. xxiv,224; viii, 248, subscribers pp. 2 engvd titles, 30 oval tinted aquatint plates. Contemp tree calf, yellow edges, rebacked.
(Spelman) **£220 [≈ $422]**

Hasselquist, Frederick
- Voyages and Travels in the Levant in the Years 1749-52 ... London: 1766. 1st edn in English. 8vo. [viii],viii,1-268, 273-307, 380-456 pp, complete. Fldg map. Sl water stained at ends. Contemp calf, rebacked.
(Wheldon & Wesley) **£350 [≈ $671]**

Haudicquer de Blancourt, Jean
- The Art of Glass. Shewing how to make all Sorts of Glass, Crystal and Enamel ... With an Appendix ... London: 1699. 1st edn in English. [xvi],335,[13] pp. Half-title. 9 plates. Occas sl wear & tear. Rec calf. Wing H.1150.
(Clark) **£1,100 [≈ $2,111]**

Haversham, John
- Memoirs of the late Right Honourable John Lord Haversham from the year 1640 to 1710. London: 1711. 1st edn. 4to. xxiv,56 pp. Occas sl staining & fraying. Mod wraps.
(Robertshaw) **£18 [≈ $34]**

Hawkesworth, John
- An Account of the Voyages undertaken by the Order of His Present Majesty for Making Discoveries in the Southern Hemisphere ... London: 1773. 2nd edn. 3 vols. Lge 4to. [10], xxxvi, [12], 456; xiv, 410; 395 pp. Maps, plates. Occas sl marg foxing. Mod half calf.
(Reese) **$3,000 [≈ £1,562]**
- Almoran and Hamet: an Oriental Tale. Dublin: for W. Smith ..., 1761. 1st irish edn. 2 vols in one (as issued). 12mo. Half-title. Contemp calf, minor rubbing. Anon.
(Ximenes) **$150 [≈ £78]**

Hawkins, Sir John
- A General History of the Science and Practice of Music. London: for T. Payne & Son, 1776. 5 vols. 4to. Half-titles. Frontis vol 1, ills. Sl spotting. Later cloth backed green bds, uncut, crnrs sl rubbed. *(Jarndyce)* **£650 [≈ $1,247]**
- The Life of Samuel Johnson. London: for J. Buckland, 1787. 1st sep edn, "Vol.I" not present at ft of 1st leaf of each gathering. Lge 8vo. [2],602,[15] pp. Orig (?) bds, uncut, early cvrd with plain paper with painted gold lines, some wear. *(Spelman)* **£220 [≈ $422]**
- The Life of Samuel Johnson. The Second Edition, revised and Corrected. London: for J. Buckland ..., 1787. Contemp calf, hinges rubbed with sm splits at ends.
(Jarndyce) **£220 [≈ $422]**
- See also Probationary Odes for the Laureateship ... .

Hawney, William
- The Complete Measurer ... The Sixteenth Edition revised and corrected ... Appendix ... London: 1789. 12mo. x,[iii], 346 pp, advt leaf. Orig sheep. *(Bickersteth)* **£38 [≈ $72]**

Hay, William
- Religio Philosophici: or, the Principles of Morality and Christianity Illustrated from a View of the Universe, and of Man's Situation in it ... London: Dodsley, 1753. Disbound.
(Waterfield's) **£85 [≈ $163]**

Hayes, Richard
- Interest at One View calculated to a Farthing ... The Seventh Edition, with Additions. London: for W. Meadows, 1747. 16mo. Contemp calf, rebacked, crnrs reprd.
(Waterfield's) **£75 [≈ $143]**
- The Negociator's Magazine of Monies and Exchanges. In Three Parts. The Third Edition; the whole being intirely new wrote and much alter'd ... London: for W. Meadows, 1730. Intl advt leaf. Name cut from blank hd of title. Sl damage to f.e.p. Contemp calf, rebacked.
(Jarndyce) **£620 [≈ $1,190]**

Hayley, William
- Plays of Three Acts; written for a Private Theatre ... London: Cadell, 1784. 1st edn. 4to. [iii]-xv,[i],430 pp. Lacks half-title. Old style half calf. *(Finch)* **£95 [≈ $182]**
- A Poetical Epistle to an Eminent Painter [George Romney]. London: for T. Payne & Son, 1778. 4to. Disbound. Anon.
(Waterfield's) **£40 [≈ $76]**
- The Triumphs of Temper; a Poem ... London: Cadell & Davies, 1799. 10th edn. Cr 8vo. 7 engvs after Stothard. Crushed red mor, a.e.g., sl rubbed. *(Stewart)* **£25 [≈ $47]**

Hayward, Sir John
- A Reporte of a Discourse concerning Supreme Power in Affaires of Religion ... London: F.K. for John Hardie ..., 1606. 1st edn. 4to. [vi],52 pp. 1st & last blanks present. Imprint sl cropped. Unbound. STC 13001. Anon. *(Vanbrugh)* **£175 [≈ $335]**

Head, Richard
- Proteus Redivivus or the Art of Wheedling, of Insinuation ... collected and methodized by the Author of the First Part of the English Rogue. London: ptd by W.D., 1675. 8vo. Somewhat used. Contemp sheep, rebacked, crnrs reprd. Anon.
(Waterfield's) **£295 [≈ $566]**

Healde, Thomas
- The New Pharmacopoeia of the Royal College of Physicians of London. Translated

into English, with Notes ... Third Edition, corrected. London: J.W. Galabin, for T. Longman, 1788. 8vo. xvi,368 pp. Approbation leaf. Contemp calf, green edges.
(Finch) **£120 [≈ $230]**

Hearne, Samuel

- A Journey from Prince of Wale's [sic] Fort on Hudson's Bay to the Northern Ocean ... Dublin: P. Byrne, 1796. 1st Irish edn. 8vo. xlix, 458 pp. 5 fldg maps, 4 plates. Little foxing. Calf, rebacked, new endpapers.
(West Side) **$625 [≈ £325]**

Heathcote, Ralph

- Sylva; or the Wood: Being a Collection of Anecdotes ... By a Society of the Learned. The Second Edition, Corrected and Enlarged. London: for T. Payne & Son, 1788. 8vo. xvi, 368 pp. Some foxing. Period calf, backstrip relaid. Anon.
(Rankin) **£125 [≈ $239]**

Hedges, Sir Charles

- Reasons for Setling Admiralty-Jurisdiction, and Giving Encouragement to Merchants, Owners, Commanders, Masters of Ships ... [London]: 1690. 4to. [ii],21 pp. Sl dampstains. Cut a bit close. New qtr calf. Wing H.1350. Anon.
(Meyer Boswell) **$650 [≈ £338]**

Helsham, Richard

- A Course of Lectures in Natural Philosophy. Published by Bryan Robinson, M.D. The Second Edition. London: J. Nourse, 1743. 404 pp. Advt leaf. Fldg plates. Contemp calf, rebacked.
(C.R. Johnson) **£150 [≈ $287]**

- A Course of Lectures in Natural Philosophy ... Published by Bryan Robinson ... The Sixth Edition. Dublin: Sleater & M'Kenzie, 1793. 1st Irish edn. 11 fldg plates. Contemp half russia.
(Waterfield's) **£115 [≈ $220]**

- A Course of Lectures in Natural Philosophy ... Published by Bryan Robinson. The Sixth Edition. Dublin: Sleater & M'Kenzie, 1793. 8vo. 11 plates, some fldg. Contemp mottled sheep, sl wear to spine ends & hinges.
(Jarndyce) **£58 [≈ $111]**

Henckel, J.F.

- Pyritologia: or, a History of the Pyrites, the Principal Body in the Mineral Kingdom. London: 1757. 8vo. xviii,382 pp. Frontis. Blind stamp on title. New cloth.
(Wheldon & Wesley) **£150 [≈ $287]**

Henderson, William Augustus

- The Housekeeper's Instructor; or, Universal Family Cook ... London: W. & J. Stratford, [1790]. 1st edn. 8vo. 456,[xxiv] pp. Frontis, 10 plates (2 fldg). Occas v sl spotting. Rebound (1957) in crushed mor.
(Finch) **£240 [≈ $460]**

- The Housekeeper's Instructor. London: W. & J. Stratford, [1790?]. 1st edn in book form, bound from the magazine parts. Fcap 4to. 456, [xxiv] pp. 12 engvd plates. Some discoloration & sl flaws. Later panelled calf.
(Ash) **£350 [≈ $671]**

Henry, David

- The Complete English Farmer. London: for F. Newbery, 1771. 1st edn. Demy 8vo. [xxviii], 432, 2 pp. 2 plates. Sl foxing. Mod half calf gilt. Anon.
(Ash) **£200 [≈ $383]**

Henry, Mathew

- The Communicant's Companion ... London: for J. Buckland, 1772. 16th edn. 8vo. Red mor gilt, a.e.g., sl soiled.
(Young's) **£18 [≈ $34]**

Hentzner, Paulus

- A Journey into England ... In the Year M.D.XC.VIII. Strawberry-Hill: 1757. 8vo. With the 9 of p 39 present. Title vignette of Strawberry Hill. Red mor. Case. One of 220.
(Rostenberg & Stern) **$375 [≈ £195]**

- Travels in England, during the Reign of Queen Elizabeth ... To which is now added, Sir Robert Naunton's Regalia. London: Jeffrey, 1797. 8vo. Frontis, 11 plates partly in colour. Qtr calf.
(Rostenberg & Stern) **$325 [≈ £169]**

- Paul Hentzner's Travels in England ... Translated by Horace, late Earl of Orford, and first printed by him at Strawberry-Hill ... added, Sir Robert Naunton's Fragmenta Regalia ... London: Jeffery, 1797. Frontis, 10 plates. Sl wear. Later half mor.
(Jarndyce) **£55 [≈ $105]**

Herbert, Edward, Lord Cherbury

- The Life ... Written by Himself. London: Dodsley, 1770. 1st 'published' edn (Strawberry Hill precedes). Sm 4to. [xx],173 pp. Fldg port. Contemp calf, red edges, jnts split but sound, sl worn.
(Sotheran's) **£88 [≈ $168]**

- The Life Written by Himself. Dublin: for H. Saunders ..., 1771. 1st Dublin edn. 12mo. [xiv], 246 pp. Contemp calf, raised bands,

black label.   *(Young's)* **£130 [≈ $249]**
- The Life and Reign of King Henry the Eighth ... London: Mary Clark, for Ann Mearn ..., 1683. 7th edn. Folio. [vi],636,[13] pp. Port frontis. Some worming in lower blank marg throughout. 19th c half calf, spine with sl worm & v sl damage to headcap. Wing H.1507.   *(Vanbrugh)* **£175 [≈ $335]**

Herbert, George
- A Priest to the Temple ... The Third Impression. London: T.R. for Benj. Tooke, 1675. 12mo. Frontis port instead of imprimatur leaf. 8 pp ctlg misbound. 19th c calf, rubbed. Wing H.1514.
        (Jarndyce) **£110 [≈ $211]**

Herd, David (ed.)
- Antient and Modern Scotish [sic] Songs Heroic Ballads &c. Edinburgh: for Lawrie & Symington & Thomas Brown, 1791. 3rd edn. 2 vols. 12mo. Engvd titles with vignettes. Contemp sheep, scuffed, spines v worn. Anon.   *(Sanders)* **£50 [≈ $95]**

The Hereditary Right of the Crown of England Asserted ...
- See Harbin, George.

Herle, Charles
- Ahab's Fall by his Prophets Flatteries: Being the Substance of Three Sermons ... London: R.A. for J. Wright, 1644. 4to. [ii], 42 pp. Mod polished calf gilt. Hailstone b'plate.
        (Hollett) **£75 [≈ $143]**

The Hermit of Warkworth ...
- See Percy, Thomas.

Hernandez, James
- A Philosophical and Practical Essay on the Gold and Silver Mines of Mexico and Peru ... Translated from a Letter wrote in Spanish ... London: J. Scott, 1755. 86 pp. Rec wraps.
        (C.R. Johnson) **£750 [≈ $1,439]**

Hervey, Thomas
- A Letter from the Hon. Thomas Hervey, to Sir Thomas Hanmer, Bart. London: for the author, & sold by J.H., (1741). 1st edn. 8vo. [iv], 60 pp. Half-title. Disbound, uncut.
        (Young's) **£50 [≈ $95]**

Hesketh, Henry
- A Sermon Preached before the Right Honourable Lord Mayor and Aldermen of the

City of London ... January 30th 1677/78 ... London: Will. Leach ..., 1678. 1st edn. 4to. [vi], 50 pp. Disbound. Wing H.1615.
        (Young's) **£35 [≈ $67]**

Hetley, Sir Thomas
- Reports and Cases taken in the Third, Fourth, Fifth, Sixth, and Seventh Years of the late King Charles ... Now Englished ... London: 1657. Only edn. Folio. [xii],177,[i] pp. Title marg soiled, sm nick at hd. Contemp sheep, extremities sl worn. Wing H.1627.   *(Clark)* **£100 [≈ $191]**

Hewatt, Alexander
- An Historical Account of the Rise and Progress of the Colonies of South Carolina and Georgia ... London: 1779. 2 vols. xiv, 347; ix, 309 pp. Contemp calf. Anon.
        (Reese) **$3,000 [≈ £1,562]**

Hey, Richard
- A Dissertation on Duelling. Cambridge: Archdeacon, 1784. 97 pp. Disbound.
        (C.R. Johnson) **£85 [≈ $163]**
- A Dissertation on Suicide. Cambridge: Archdeacon, 1785. 90 pp. Disbound.
        (C.R. Johnson) **£85 [≈ $163]**

Heylyn, Peter
- A Brief Relation of the Death and Sufferings of the most Reverend and renowned Prelate the L. Archbishop of Canterbury ... "Oxford" [actually London]: 1644. 2nd edn. 4to. [ii],30 pp. Lib stamp title verso. Sl browning. Later wraps. Wing H.1685. Anon.
        (Clark) **£85 [≈ $163]**

Heynes, S.
- A Treatise of Trigonometry, Plane and Spherical, Theoretical and Practical ... Treatise of Stereographic and Orthographic Projection of the Sphere ... London: 1701. [2], 135, [52],[92],8 pp. Sep titles for 1st 3 sections. 16 plates. Sl marks. Old calf, sl worn.   *(Whitehart)* **£150 [≈ $287]**

Heywood, Thomas
- The Hierarchie of the Blessed Angels ... London: Adam Islip, 1635. 1st edn. Folio. [xii], 622,[8] pp. Licence leaf, errata page. Engvd title, 9 plates. Contemp sheep gilt, spine reprd. STC 13327.
        (Vanbrugh) **£855 [≈ $1,641]**

Hickes, George
- The Case of Infant Baptism in Five

Questions. London: Bassett, Tooke, & Gardiner, 1683. 4to. [4],106 pp. Cloth. Wing H.1842. Inscrbd "ex dono authoris".
(Humber) **£58 [≈ $111]**
- The Gentleman Instructed in the Conduct of a Virtuous and Happy Life. In Three Parts ... added, A Word to the Ladies ... London: W.B. for E. Smith ..., 1720. 7th edn. 8vo. [xxiv], 584 pp. Orig panelled calf, gilt dec spine, mor label. Anon.
(Vanbrugh) **£165 [≈ $316]**
- See also Darrell, William.

Higgons, Bevill
- A Short View of the English History: with Reflections ... Hague [ie London? Dublin?]: ptd by T. Johnston, 1727. Pirated edn. 8vo. [ii], 374,[2] pp. Inner upper marg of 1st few ff water stained. Contemp calf, traces of wear, label defective.   *(Burmester)* **£80 [≈ $153]**

The High German Doctor ...
- See Horneck, Phillip.

Hildersham, Arthur
- Lectures Upon the Fourth of John Preached at Ashby-de-la-Zouch in Leicestershire. London: G.M. for Edward Brewster, 1629. 1st edn. Sm folio. [2],457 pp. Engvd title. No endpapers, minor marks, sl wear to title. Contemp calf, sl worn. STC 13461.
(Humber) **£135 [≈ $259]**

Hildrop, John
- Reflections upon Reason by Phileleutherus Britannicus ... Second Edition. London: Innys, 1722. Disbound.
(Waterfield's) **£80 [≈ $153]**

Hill, Aaron
- Free Thoughts upon Faith: or, the Religion of Reason. A Poem. London: for J. Osborn, 1746. 1st edn. Folio. Disbound. Anon.
(Ximenes) **$675 [≈ £351]**

Hill, Abraham
- Familiar Letters which passed between Abraham Hill, Esq ... and Several eminent and ingenious Persons of the last Century ... London: W. Johnston, 1767. 1st edn. 8vo. [iv], xxxii, 241, [i] pp. Half-title. Rec qtr calf.
(Clark) **£90 [≈ $172]**
- Familiar Letters which passed between Abraham Hill, Esq ... and Several eminent and ingenious Persons of the last Century ... London: for W. Johnston, 1767. 1st edn. 8vo.

Half-title. 2 sm lib stamps. Half calf, gilt spine.   *(Ximenes)* **$300 [≈ £156]**

Hill, Brian
- Henry and Acasto. A Moral Tale in Verse. Embellished with Three Plates. London: Stockdale, 1798. 115,[1] pp. Contemp tree calf gilt, black label.
(C.R. Johnson) **£125 [≈ $239]**

Hill, "Sir" John
- The Actor: a Treatise on the Art of Playing ... London: R. Griffiths, 1750. 1st edn. 12mo. Lacks free endpapers. Calf, red label. Anon.
(Jarndyce) **£180 [≈ $345]**
- The Actor: or, A Treatise on the Art of Playing ... Adapted to the Present State of the Theatres ... London: for R. Griffiths, 1755. 1st edn. 12mo. Contemp calf, gilt dentelles, edges chafed. Anon.
(Dramatis Personae) **$250 [≈ £130]**
- Circumstances which preceded the Letters to the Earl of ------; and may tend to a Discovery of the Author. London: T. Evans, 1775. Half-title, 19 pp. Disbound. Anon.
(C.R. Johnson) **£145 [≈ $278]**
- Essays in Natural History and Philosophy. Containing a Series of Discoveries, by the Assistance of Microscopes. London: J. Whiston & B. White, 1752. 415 pp. Contemp calf, red label. *(C.R. Johnson)* **£260 [≈ $499]**
- A General Natural History or New and Accurate Description of the Animals, Vegetables and Minerals of the Different Parts of the World. London: 1748-52. 3 vols. Folio. Fldg table, 56 plates. Few sl blemishes. Rec half calf, antique style.
(Wheldon & Wesley) **£450 [≈ $863]**
- A General Natural History. Volume I. A History of Fossils. London: 1748. Folio. [xii], 1-228, 333-592, 457-654,[6] pp, complete. Fldg table, 12 hand cold plates. Some foxing & browning. Marg MS notes. Old half calf, worn, jnts cracked.
(Wheldon & Wesley) **£300 [≈ $575]**
- Lucina sine Concubitu. A Letter humbly address'd to the Royal Society ... that a Woman may conceive and be brought to Bed without any Commerce with Man. London: 1750. 2nd edn. 8vo. Title marg strengthened. Mod half calf. Anon.
(Robertshaw) **£125 [≈ $239]**
- A Method of producing Double Flowers from Single by a regular Course of Culture. London: 1758. 2nd edn. 8vo. 40 pp. 8 plates. Mod bds. Anon.

(Wheldon & Wesley) **£75 [≈ $143]**
- The Story of Elizabeth Canning considered by Dr. Hill. With Remarks ... London: M. Cooper, 1753. 53 pp. Rebound in mrbld wraps. *(C.R. Johnson)* **£95 [≈ $182]**
- See also La Solle, H.F. de.

The Hind and the Panther ...
- See Dryden, John.

Hippocrates
- Hippocrates Upon Air, Water, and Situation; upon Epidemical Diseases; and upon Prognosticks ... London: J. Watts, 1734. 1st edn. 8vo. [viii],xxiv, [xviii],389,[1] pp. Frontis. Contemp calf, hinges cracked.
(Bookpress) **$375 [≈ £195]**

Historical ...
- An Historical Account of ... South Carolina and Georgia ... see Hewatt, Alexander.
- An Historical Account of the Expedition against the Ohio Indians ... see Smith, William Provost.
- An Historical Account of the Origin, Progress, and Present State of the Bethlehem Hospital, founded by Henry the Eighth, for the Cure of Lunatics ... London: ptd in the year, 1783. 16 pp. Engvd frontis. Disbound.
(C.R. Johnson) **£1,250 [≈ $2,399]**
- An Historical, Genealogical and Poetical Dictionary ... Done from the Best Authors, and very Useful for Schools and all Young Gentlemen ... London: for Henry Rhodes ..., 1703. 1st edn. 12mo. (364) pp, final advt leaf. Occas soiling. Contemp calf.
(Burmester) **£48 [≈ $92]**

History ...
- The Historie of the Life and Death of Mary Stuart ... see Udall, William.
- The History and Adventures of an Atom ... see Smollett, Tobias.
- The History of England, from the Earliest Accounts of Time, to the Death of the late Queen Anne. London: 1722. 1st edn. 4 vols. 8vo. Frontis in vol 1, num engvd ports. Contemp calf. *(Robertshaw)* **£130 [≈ $249]**
- The History of Female Favourites ... see La Roche-Guilhem, Anne, de,
- The History of Lady Julia Mandeville ... see Brooke, Frances, nee Moore.
- The History of Nourjahad ... see Sheridan, Frances.
- The History of Oracles ... see Fontenelle,

Bernard de.
- The History of Pompey the Little ... see Coventry, Francis.
- The History of Prince Mirabel's Infancy, Rise and Disgrace, with the Sudden Promotion of Novicius ... Collected from the Memoirs of a Courtier lately Deceas'd. London: for J. Baker, 1712. 1st edn. 3 vols in one. 8vo. [x], 90; 80; 80 pp. Water stain. Later sheep, rebacked. *(Burmester)* **£500 [≈ $959]**
- The History of Sandford and Merton ... see Day, Thomas.
- The History of Sin and Heresie attempted ... see Leslie, Charles.
- The History of Sir Charles Grandison ... see Richardson, Samuel.
- The History of Sir William Harrington ... see Meades, Anna.
- The History of the Adventures of Joseph Andrews ... see Fielding, Henry.
- The History of the Bucaniers of America ... see Exquemeling, Alexandre Olivier.
- The History of the Civil War in America ... see Hall, Captain John.
- The History of the Devil ... see Defoe, Daniel.
- The History of the Famous Edict of Nantes ... see Benoist, Elie.
- The History of the Great Plague in London ... see Defoe, Daniel.
- The History of the Imperiall Estate of the Grand Seigneurs ... see Baudier, Michel.
- The History of the Theatres of London ... see Oulton, Walley Chamberlain.
- The History of the Voyages of Christopher Columbus, in order to discover America and the West-Indies. London: sold by D. Midwinter ..., 1777. 190 pp. Contemp sheep, rebacked, *(C.R. Johnson)* **£125 [≈ $239]**
- The History of Tom Jones the Foundling, in his Married State. London: for J. Robinson, 1750. 1st edn. 12mo. Contemp mottled calf, spine worn. *(Hannas)* **£550 [≈ $1,055]**
- The History of Tom Jones the Foundling, in his Married State. The Second Edition Corrected, with an Additional Chapter ... London: for J. Robinson, 1750. 12mo. [xiv], 336 pp. Half-title dusty. Crnr torn from 1 leaf. Sm marg wormhole in 5 ff. Calf antique.
(Burmester) **£175 [≈ $335]**
- The History of Vanillo Gonzales, surnamed the Merry Batchelor. From the French of Alain-Rene Le Sage. London: Robinson, 1797. 1st edn (?). 2 vols. 12mo. Half-titles.

Errata leaf vol 1. 19th c calf, spines sl scuffed.
(Burmester) **£280 [≈ $537]**

Hitt, Thomas
- A Treatise of Fruit Trees ... London: for the author, & sold by T. Osborne, 1755. 1st edn. 8vo. [xvi],392 pp. 7 fldg engvd plates (1 or 2 tears). Contemp sprinkled calf, upper jnt cracked but sound. *(Gaskell)* **£300 [≈ $575]**
- A Treatise of Fruit Trees. London: 1768. 3rd edn. 8vo. viii,394,[6] pp. 7 fldg plates. Tear in 1 plate reprd. Contemp calf, jnts weakening.
(Henly) **£95 [≈ $182]**
- A Treatise of Fruit-Trees. London: for Robinson & Roberts, 1768. 3rd edn. viii, 394, [iv] pp. 7 fldg plates. Contemp calf gilt, spine darkened, sm defect in bottom panel.
(Hollett) **£150 [≈ $287]**

Hoadley, Benjamin
- An Enquiry into the Reasons of the Conduct of Great Britain with relation to the Present State of Affairs in Europe. London: James Roberts, 1727. 1st edn. Disbound. Anon.
(Waterfield's) **£40 [≈ $76]**
- A Preservative against the Principles and Practices of the Nonjurors both in Church and State ... London: Knapton ..., 1716. 3rd edn. 8vo. [iv],102,2 advt pp. Disbound. Anon. *(Young's)* **£40 [≈ $76]**

Hobbes, Thomas
- Hobb's Tripos. In Three Discourses ... The Third Edition ... London: for Gilliflower, Rogers, Fox ..., 1684. 1st coll edn. 8vo. [xiv], 317,[3 advt] pp. Lacks intl blank. 19th c half calf, sl rubbed, backstrip relaid. Wing H.2266. *(Pickering)* **$1,200 [≈ £625]**
- A Letter about Liberty & Necessity. Written to the Duke of Newcastle ... With Observations ... by Benjamin Laney ... London: 1677. 2nd edn. 12mo. [ii],104, [12 advt] pp. Contemp sheep, reprd. Wing H.2245B. *(Burmester)* **£300 [≈ $575]**
- A Letter about Liberty and Necessity. Written to the Duke of Newcastle ... With Observations ... by Benjamin Laney ... London: J.C. for W. Crook, 1677. 2nd edn. 12mo. Blank marg of title sl chipped. Sheep antique. Wing H.2245B.
(Ximenes) **$900 [≈ £468]**
- Leviathan. London: for Andrew Crooke, 1651. 1st edn. 1st issue, with the "head" ornament on ptd title. Demy 4to. [vi],396 pp. Addtnl engvd title. Fldg table. A few sl marks & blemishes. Rec mor. *(Ash)* **£2,000 [≈ $3,839]**

- Leviathan. London: for Andrew Crooke, 1651. 2nd edn. Folio. [viii], "394" [ie 396] pp. Engvd title, fldg table, 'bear' ornament on title. V sl browned. Contemp calf, rehinged. Wing H.2247. *(Pickering)* **$2,250 [≈ £1,171]**
- Tracts of Mr. Thomas Hobbs of Malmesbury ... London: for W. Crooke, 1682. 5 advt pp after Behemoth, 2 advt pp at end. Frontis port, fldg plate. Contemp calf, rubbed & scarred, hinges weakening but sound. Wing H.2265 (& 2215, 2211, 2259).
(Jarndyce) **£550 [≈ $1,055]**

Hockin, Thomas
- A Discourse on the Nature of God's Decrees: Being an Answer to a Letter from a Person of Quality concerning them. London: for Edward Vize, 1684. 1st edn. 8vo. [xxii], 390 pp. Edge browned. New calf.
(Young's) **£65 [≈ $124]**

Hodges, William
- Travels in India, during the Years 1780 ... 1783. The Second Edition, corrected. London: for the author, & sold by J. Edwards, 1794. 4to. [viii],154 pp. Fldg map, 14 plates. Some foxing, mainly of early ff. Contemp calf, rebacked. *(Clark)* **£160 [≈ $307]**

Hodson, William
- The Holy Sinner. A Tractate meditated on some Passages of the Storie of the Penitent Woman ... By W.H. ... [Cambridge: for] Andrew Crooke, 1639. 1st edn. 12mo. [ii],98,[xii] pp. Engvd title (defective at hd) & frontis. Some staining. Rec sheep. STC 13555. *(Clark)* **£120 [≈ $230]**

Hog, James
- Otia Christiana: or, Christian Recreations. Being a Conference betwixt Nicon and Philotheus ... Edinburgh: James Watson, 1708. 1st edn. 12mo. vii,[i],220 pp. Some browning. Contemp sheep, rubbed. By J.H.
(Clark) **£180 [≈ $345]**

Holberg, Ludvig, Baron
- An Introduction to Universal History. Translated from the Latin of Baron Holberg; With Notes ... by Gregory Sharpe ... London: for L. Davis ..., 1787. 3rd edn. 8vo. xxv, [ii], 354 pp. Old calf, sl worn.
(Young's) **£40 [≈ $76]**
- A Journey to the World Under-Ground. By Nicholas Klimius. Translated from the Original. London: for T. Astley; & B. Collins, 1742. 1st English edn. 12mo. 12 advt ff at

end. Mod old style panelled calf. Anon.
(Hannas) **£380 [≈ $729]**

Holcroft, Thomas

- Caroline of Lichtfield: A Novel. Translated from the French [of Baroness Montolieu]. Second Edition. London: Robinson, 1797. 2 vols. 8vo. Occas sl foxing. Period calf, gilt spines & labels.   *(Rankin)* **£65 [≈ $124]**
- Duplicity: A Comedy. London: for G. Robinson, 1781. 1st edn. Disbound.
(Dramatis Personae) **$85 [≈ £44]**

Hole, Richard

- Remarks on the Arabian Nights' Entertainments; in which the Origin of Sindbad's Voyages, and other Oriental Fictions, is particularly considered. London: Cadell & Davies, 1797. 1st edn. 8vo. iv,258, [2 errata] pp. Sm lib blind stamp. Sm reprs. Rec qtr calf.   *(Burmester)* **£75 [≈ $143]**

Holland, P.

- Select Views of the Lakes in Cumberland, Westmorland & Lancashire; from Drawings made by P. Holland. Engraved by C. Rosenberg. Liverpool: 1792. Only edn. Sm oblong 4to. Engvd title / dedic, 20 uncold aquatint plates. Some marks. Mid 19th c limp cloth, edges rubbed. *(Hollett)* **£380 [≈ $729]**

Holles, Denzil Holles, Baron

- Memoirs of Denzil Lord Holles, Baron of Ifield in Sussex, from the year 1641 to 1648. London: for Tim. Goodwin, 1699. Frontis. MS index on endpaper. Contemp calf, sometime rebacked, rubbed, crnrs worn.
(Waterfield's) **£65 [≈ $124]**

Holt, John

- Characters of the Kings and Queens of England, selected from the Different Histories ... particularly intended for the Instruction of Youth ... London: Robinson, 1786-87-88. 207; 212; 346 pp. Half-titles in vols 1 & 2. Contemp calf, spine ends v sl worn.   *(C.R. Johnson)* **£245 [≈ $470]**
- General View of the Agriculture of the County of Lancaster ... London: J. Nichols, 1794. Large Paper. Sq 4to. 114 pp. Fldg map, 1 plate. Half mor gilt by Fazakerley.
(Hollett) **£95 [≈ $182]**

Holwell, John Zephaniah

- Interesting Historical Events, relative to the Provinces of Bengal, and the Empire of Indostan ... London: Becket & De Hondt,

1766-71. Part 1 "Second Edition corrected, with a supplement". 3 parts in one. 8vo. Fldg maps. Minor foxing. Mod buckram.
(McBlain) **$275 [≈ £143]**

Home, Everard

- A Dissertation on the Properties of Pus ... London: John Richardson, 1788. 1st edn. Sm 4to. 63 pp. Lacks half-title. Last 4 pp sl marked. Old half calf, rubbed, sl wear to jnts.
(Bickersteth) **£65 [≈ $124]**

Home, Henry, Lord Kames

- See Kames, Henry Home, Lord.

Homer

- The Iliad ... Translated by Alexander Pope. London: Lintot, 1750. 6 vols. 12mo. Intl licence ff. Frontises, plates. Contemp speckled calf gilt, some rubbing & sl wear to hd of spines, 2 hinges sl splitting.
·   *(Jarndyce)* **£60 [≈ $115]**
- The Iliad ... Translated by Alexander Pope. Glasgow: Robert & Andrew Foulis, 1771. 4 vols. 12mo. Fldg map in vol 1. Contemp calf, lacks labels.   *(Waterfield's)* **£125 [≈ $239]**

The Honours of the Table ...

- See Trusler, J.

Hooke, Andrew

- An Essay on the National Debt, and National Capital ... London: W. Owen, 1750. Half-title, 59 pp. Authenticating sgntr of the author. Disbound, uncut.
(C.R. Johnson) **£240 [≈ $460]**

Hooke, Nathaniel

- An Account of the Conduct of the Dowager Dutchess of Marlborough ... to ... 1710. Dublin: for George Faulkner, 1742. 1st Irish edn. 12mo. 171,[1 advt] pp. Signs of use. Calf backed bds, uncut. Anon.
(Fenning) **£28.50 [≈ $55]**

Hooker, Richard

- A Faithful Abridgment of the Works of ... Richard Hooker. In Eight Books of Ecclesiastical Polity ... With an Account of his Life. By a Divine of the Church of England. London: Benjamin Bragg, 1705. [6], 350 pp. Old panelled calf, rebacked.
(Karmiole) **£85 [≈ £44]**
- Of the Laws of Ecclesiastical Politie. London: William Stansbye, 1622. 6th edn of books 1-4. Folio. [lviii],583,[xv] pp. 19th c tree calf, jnts

cracked but bds firm.
(Bookpress) **$500** [≈ £260]
- Of the Laws of Ecclesiastical Politie. Eight
Bookes. London: William Stansbye for
George Latham, 1632-31. 6th edn. Folio.
[lvi], 583,[18] pp. Engvd genl title (sl
browned) & 4 sep ptd titles. Orig sheep, spine
reprd. STC 13718.
(Vanbrugh) **£225** [≈ $431]
- Of the Lawes of Ecclesiastical Politie.
London: Andrew Crooke, 1666. Folio.
[xii],36, [xxvi], 579,[i] pp. Engvd frontis &
title (both mtd & reprd in margs). Minor marg
worm, occas staining. Contemp calf,
rebacked, recrnrd. Wing H.2637.
(Clark) **£65** [≈ $124]
- The Works ... With an Account of his Life
and Death. London: Thomas Newcomb for
Andrew Crook, 1666. Folio. Engvd title,
frontis port. A few minor stains. Contemp
calf, sl worn, reprs to jnts. Wing H.2631.
(Ximenes) **$350** [≈ £182]
- The Works: of the Laws of Ecclesiastical
Politie. London: 1676. Folio. Engvd port &
title. Margs cut close just touching a few
running titles. Amateur half leatherette. Wing
H.2632. *(Lamb)* **£35** [≈ $67]
- The Works ... London: for John Walthoe ...,
1723. New edn, with addtns. Folio. lxxxviii,
518,[8] pp. Port, addtnl engvd title. Orig calf,
rebacked. *(Vanbrugh)* **£175** [≈ $335]

Hooper, Jacob
- An Impartial History of the Rebellion and
Civil Wars in England, during the Reign of
King Charles the First ... London: 1738. 1st
edn. Folio. 628 pp. Frontis, 24 plates. Orig
panelled calf, spine reprd.
(Vanbrugh) **£175** [≈ $335]

Hooper, John
- A Commentarie or Cleare Confession of the
Christian Faith ... London: Christopher
Barker, (1583). Sm 8vo. W'cut title border.
Lacks Mii. New calf. STC 1220.
(Stewart) **£450** [≈ $863]

Hooper, William
- Rational Recreations, In which the Principles
of Numbers and Natural Philosophy are
clearly and copiously elucidated ... Third
Edition, Corrected. London: for J. Davies ...,
1787. 4 vols. 8vo. 65 fldg plates. Contemp
tree calf, gilt spines & dentelles.
(Dramatis Personae) **$900** [≈ £468]

Hope, Sir William
- A New, Short, and Easy Method of Fencing
... Edinburgh: by James Watson, 1707. 1st
edn. Sm 4to. xv,[iii],288 pp. Fldg table, fldg
plate. Contemp sprinkled calf, mor label. The
Colquhoun copy. *(Finch)* **£950** [≈ $1,823]

Hopkins, Charles
- Friendship Improv'd; or, the Female
Warriour. A Tragedy ... London: Tonson,
1700. 1st edn. 4to. [viii],56 pp. Paper
browned, inner marg damp stained. Rec
wraps. Wing H.2723. *(Clark)* **£60** [≈ $115]

Hopkins, Ezekiel
- The Doctrine of the Two Sacraments. The
Way of Salvation ... In the Savoy: John Nutt
for Richard Smith, 1712. 8vo. [26],448 pp.
Port. Contemp calf, jnts cracked, split up
spine. *(Humber)* **£35** [≈ $67]

Hoppus, Edward
- The Gentleman's and Builder's Repository;
or, Architecture Display'd ... London: for
James Hodges, & Benjamin Cole, 1737. 1st
edn. 4to. [ii],101,[i] pp. 86 (on 85) plates, num
text engvs. Contemp calf gilt, v sl rubbed.
(Finch) **£750** [≈ $1,439]

Horne, Andrew
- The Mirrour of Justices: Written Originally
in the old French ... and many things added.
London: for J. Worrall ..., 1768. 8vo.
[32],288, 287-325,[8] pp. Some browning &
foxing. Few sm marg reprs. Mod qtr calf.
(Meyer Boswell) **$450** [≈ £234]

Horne, George
- A Fair, Candid and Impartial State of the
Case between Sir Isaac Newton and Mr
Hutchinson ... Oxford: at the Theatre for S.
Parker ..., 1753. 1st edn. [iv],76 pp. Half-
titles. Wrappers, uncut.
(C.R. Johnson) **£275** [≈ $527]

Horne, Henry
- Essays concerning Iron and Steel ... London:
T. Cadell, 1773. 1st edn. 12mo. iii, 223 pp.
Later polished calf, backstrip relaid. The
Boulton copy. *(Bookpress)* **$2,500** [≈ £1,302]

Horne, Melvill
- Letters on Missions. Schenectady: C.P.
Wyckoff, 1797. 1st edn. 12mo. xiv,124,[2
advt] pp. Disbound. *(Bookpress)* **$150** [≈ £78]

Horneck, Phillip
- The High German Doctor with many Additions and Alterations ... Index. London: the booksellers, 1720. 1st coll edn. 2 vols. 8vo. Foredges of the earlier ff in each vol pulpy with damp. Contemp calf. Anon.
(Waterfield's) **£225 [≈$431]**

Horsley, Samuel
- A Charge delivered to the Clergy of the Archdeaconry of St. Albans at a Visitation holden May 22d, 1783 ... London: for J. Robson, 1783. Disbound.
(Waterfield's) **£75 [≈$143]**
- Tracts in Controversy with Dr. Priestley upon the Principal Question of the Belief of the First Ages in Our Lord's Divinity ... Now revised and augmented ... Glocester: R. Raikes, 1789. 8vo. Orig bds, front cvr detached. *(Waterfield's)* **£125 [≈$239]**

Howard, John
- An Account of the Principal Lazarettos in Europe ... Warrington: William Eyres, 1789. 4to. viii,259,[xiii] pp. 22 fldg plates, fldg table. Qtr mor. *(Lamb)* **£350 [≈$671]**
- The State of the Prisons in England and Wales ... London: J. Johnson, 1792. 4th edn. 4to. [viii],540,[1] pp. 22 plates. Contemp calf, jnts reprd. *(Bookpress)* **$650 [≈£338]**

Howard, Sir Robert
- The Life and Reign of King Richard the Second. By a Person of Quality. London: for M.L. & L.C. ..., 1681. 1st edn. 8vo. [viii], 240 pp. Contemp sheep. Wing H.3001. Anon.
(Vanbrugh) **£225 [≈$431]**

Howe, John
- A Funeral Sermon on the Death of that Pious Gentlewoman Mrs. Judith Hammond. London: Tho. Parkhurst, 1696. Only edn. 4to. [iv], 31,[i] pp. Lib stamp on title verso. remains of old lower wrapper. Wing H.3029.
(Clark) **£48 [≈$92]**

Howell, James
- Dodonas Grove, Or the Vocall Forrest. The Third Edition ... with the Addition of two other Tracts. Cambridge: 1645. 12mo. [xxiv], 191, 23 pp. Frontis, 2 fldg plates (1 reprd). Early 19th c calf, front bd detached. Wing H.3060, 3070, 3106.
(Vanbrugh) **£225 [≈$431]**
- Epistolae Ho-Elianae. Familiar Letters Domestic and Forren ... Third Edition. With

a Fourth Volume of New Letters ... London: Moseley, 1655. 1st coll edn. 8vo. Red & black title. Fldg frontis. Calf. Wing H.3073.
(Sotheran's) **£398 [≈$764]**
- Lustra Ludovici, or the Life of the late victorious King of France, Lewis XIII ... London: for Humphrey Moseley, 1646. 1st edn. Sm folio. [12],188,[8] pp. Engvd decs. Contemp calf, rebacked. Wing H.3092.
(Karmiole) **$375 [≈£195]**
- Lustra Ludovici, or the Life of the late Victorious King of France, Lewis the XIII ... London: for Humphrey Moseley, 1646. 1st edn. Folio. [xii],188,[8] pp. Port in text. Sm piece torn from title marg. Contemp style mod calf. Wing H.3092.
(Vanbrugh) **£225 [≈$431]**

Hoyland, Francis
- Poems and Translations. London: W. Bristow ... & C. Etherington, in York, 1763. 4to. 54 pp. Disbound.
(C.R. Johnson) **£120 [≈$230]**

Hoyle, Edmond
- Mr. Hoyle's Games of Whist, Quadrille, Piquet, Chess, and Back-Gammon ... The Thirteenth Edition ... London: for Thomas Osborne, Henry Woodfall, Richard Baldwin, (1763). 12mo. Edges sl browned. Rebound in half calf. Sgnd by Hoyle & Thomas Osborne.
(Jarndyce) **£70 [≈$134]**

Huarte Navarro, Juan de Dios
- Examen de Ingenios: or, the Tryal of Wits ... made English from the most Correct Edition by Mr Bellamy. London: Richard Sare, 1698. 8vo. [4],502 pp, advt leaf. Foxed. Contemp calf, rebacked, sl wear to hd of spine. Wing H.3205. *(Spelman)* **£120 [≈$230]**

Huber, Marie
- The World Unmask'd; or, the Philosopher the greatest Cheat; in Twenty-Four Dialogues. A New Edition. Translated from the French. London: J. Phillips, 1786. 12mo. x, 356, [4 advt] pp. Sl marg damp stain on a few ff. Contemp sheep, rebacked, edges worn. Anon. *(Burmester)* **£50 [≈$95]**

Huddesford, George
- A Proper reply to a Pamphlet entitled A Defence of the Rector and Fellows of Exeter College, &c. Oxford: at the Theatre, 1755. 4to. Disbound. *(Waterfield's)* **£25 [≈$47]**
- Topsy Turvy: with Anecdotes and Observations illustrative of Leading

Characters in the Present Government of France. London: for the author ..., 1793. 3rd edn, enlgd. 8vo. [iv],66,[2] pp. Half-title. Disbound. Anon. *(Burmester)* **£30 [≈$57]**

Hudson, Thomas
- Poems on Several Occasions. Newcastle upon Tyne: I. Thompson & Co, 1752. xxiv,[4],228 pp. Contemp calf, red label.
(C.R. Johnson) **£280 [≈$537]**

Hues, Robert
- A Learned Treatise of Globes ... now ... made English ... by John [but Edmund] Chilmead. London: J.S. for Andrew Kemb, 1659. 2nd English edn. 8vo. [xxxvii],209, 220-241, 142-186, [1] pp. C4 & U8 blank. Occas sl water stain. Contemp calf, ft of spine chipped. Wing H.3298.
(Gaskell) **£1,200 [≈$2,303]**

Hull, Thomas
- Moral Tales in Verse, founded on Real Events. London: for George Cawthorn, 1797. 1st edn. 2 vols. 8vo. Half-titles, subscribers. Port. Contemp tree calf, gilt spines.
(Ximenes) **$350 [≈£182]**
- Richard Plantagenet a Legendary Tale, now First Published. London: for J. Bell, & C. Etherington, York, (1774). 4to. Half-title with date. The title is engvd. Old blue wraps.
(Jarndyce) **£40 [≈$76]**
- Richard Plantagenet a Legendary Tale. Now First Published ... London: for J. Bell, [1774]. 1st edn. 4to. [iv],iv,30 pp. Half-title detached. Disbound. *(Finch)* **£75 [≈$143]**

Hume, David
- Dialogues concerning Natural Religion ... Second Edition. London: 1779. 8vo. Contemp tree calf, rebacked, new endpapers.
(Waterfield's) **£350 [≈$671]**
- An Enquiry concerning the Principles of Morals. London: A. Millar, 1751. 1st edn. Earlier state, with L3 uncancelled. 12mo. Advt ff at end. Lib blind stamp. Contemp style roan.
(Frew Mackenzie) **£1,100 [≈$2,111]**
- Essays and Treatises on Several Subjects ... New Edition. Dublin: J. Williams, 1779. Contemp tree calf, rebacked.
(C.R. Johnson) **£350 [≈$671]**
- Essays and Treatises on Several Subjects. A New Edition. London: for T. Cadell ..., 1786. 2 vols. 8vo. Contemp calf, gilt borders, hinges sl rubbed. *(Jarndyce)* **£220 [≈$422]**

- Essays and Treatises on Several Subjects. In Two Volumes. Containing Essays, Moral, Political, and Literary. A New Edition. London: for T. Cadell, 1788. 2 vols. Contemp calf, black labels.
(C.R. Johnson) **£265 [≈$508]**
- Essays, Moral and Political. The Third Edition, corrected, with additions. London: for A. Millar, & A. Kincaid in Edinburgh, 1748. 12mo. Orig calf, sl rubbed, early reback retaining backstrip. *(Jarndyce)* **£280 [≈$537]**
- The History of England under the House of Tudor ... London: for A. Millar, 1759. 1st edn. 2 vols. 4to. Contemp calf, rebacked, new free endpapers in vol 2.
(Waterfield's) **£265 [≈$508]**
- The History of England ... New Edition, with the Author's Last Corrections and Improvements ... Short Account of his Life ... London: Cadell, 1786. 8 vols. Contemp calf, sl fraying & cracking, lacks labels.
(Bell) **£120 [≈$230]**
- Philosophical Essays concerning Human Understanding. By the Author of the Essays Moral and Political. London: for A. Millar ..., 1748. 1st edn. 12mo. iv,256,[4 advt] pp. Sl browning. Contemp calf, rec label. Anon.
(Pickering) **$3,750 [≈£1,953]**
- A True Account of the Behaviour and Conduct of Archibald Stewart, Esq; late Lord Provost of Edinburgh. In a Letter to a Friend. London: for M. Cooper, 1748. 1st edn. Todd's state "d". 8vo. 51,[1] pp. Outer ff sl dusty. Old wraps. Anon.
(Burmester) **£1,450 [≈$2,783]**

Hume, Patrick
- Annotations on Milton's Paradise Lost ... By P.H. ... London: Tonson, 1695. 1st edn. Folio in 2s. [ii],321 pp. Port frontis. Some faint browning, 1st 2 ff sl soiled in lower marg. Old mrbld bds, vellum crnrs, rec calf spine. Wing H.3663. *(Finch)* **£600 [≈$1,151]**

Humfrey, John
- An Answer to Dr. Stillingfleet's Book of the Unreasonableness of Separation ... London: for Thomas Packhurst, [1682]. Sole edn. Sm 4to. 39 pp. Title sl soiled. Disbound. Wing H.3667. Anon. *(Finch)* **£70 [≈$134]**
- A Case of Conscience, Whether a Nonconformist, who hath not taken the Oxford Oath, may come to live at London, or at any Corporate-Town ... and yet be a good Christian? ... London: in the year 1669. Sole edn. Sm 4to. 31 pp. Disbound. Wing H.3673A. Anon. *(Finch)* **£85 [≈$163]**

Humphries, John

- Vindiciae Veritatis. A Narrative Vindicating the Truth, against the Invective, Malicious, and Slanderous Back-biting Aspersions of certain Nonconformists ... London: in the Year 1660. Sole edn. Sm 4to. [ii], 10 pp. Disbound. Wing H.3723.
(Finch) **£75 [≈ $143]**

Hunter, Alexander

- Georgical Essays ... York: by A. Ward, for J. Dodsley ..., 1777. All published in this edn. 8vo. [iv],560,[vii] pp. 3 fldg plates. Contemp calf backed bds, mor label, jnts cracked, spine ends worn, crnrs knocked, sides rubbed.
(Finch) **£45 [≈ $86]**

- Outlines of Agriculture, addressed to Sir John Sinclair, Bart. President of the Board of Agriculture. The Second Edition. York: Wilson, Spence & Mawman, 1797. 47 pp. 2 fldg plates. Orig mrbld wraps.
(C.R. Johnson) **£165 [≈ $316]**

Hunter, John, Admiral

- An Historical Journal of the Transactions at Port Jackson, and Norfolk Island ... London: for John Stockdale, 1793. 8vo. xxi, [3], (17)-525, [3 advt] pp. Port, vignette title (v sl shaved), fldg map (sm repr), fldg plate by William Blake. Rec qtr calf.
(Fenning) **£850 [≈ $1,631]**

Hunter, John, F.R.S.

- Observations on Certain Parts of the Animal Oeconomy. London: sold at No. 13, Castle-Street, Leicester-Square, 1786. 1st edn. 4to. 18 plates. Orig bds, minor rubbing. Cloth case.   *(Ximenes)* **$3,500 [≈ £1,822]**

Hunter, William

- Two Introductory Lectures, delivered by Dr. William Hunter, to his Last Course of Anatomical Lectures ... added, Some Papers relating to ... Plan for ... a Museum ... London: J. Johnson, 1784. 4to. 130 pp. Half-title. Fldg plate. Orig qtr calf, uncut.
(Goodrich) **$1,950 [≈ £1,015]**

Hurd, Richard

- Dialogues on the Uses of Foreign Travel; considered as a Part of an English Gentleman's Education: between Lord Shaftesbury and Mr. Locke. London: W.B. for A. Millar, 1764. 1st edn. 8vo. [iv],201 pp. Later half mor. Anon.
(Bookpress) **$375 [≈ £195]**

Hurdis, James

- Tears of Affection, a Poem, occasioned by the Death of a Sister tenderly beloved. London: for J. Johnson, 1794. 1st edn. 8vo. Half-title. Advt leaf at end. Disbound.
(Ximenes) **$100 [≈ £52]**

Husbands, John (ed.)

- A Miscellany of Poems by Several Hands. Oxford: Leon. Lichfield, 1731. 1st edn. 8vo. 19 pp subscribers. Contemp calf, gilt spine, some rubbing but sound.
(Ximenes) **$7,500 [≈ £3,906]**

Hutcheson, Francis

- An Essay on the Nature and Conduct of the Passions and Affections with Illustrations on the Moral Sense. London: Knapton ..., 1730. 1st edn, 2nd issue (ie reissue of 1728 edn with a cancel title-page). 8vo. Contemp Cambridge style panelled calf, rebacked.
(Waterfield's) **£675 [≈ $1,295]**

- An Essay on the Nature and Conduct of the Passions and Affections. With Illustrations of the Moral Sense. London: For Knapton ..., 1730. 2nd London edn. 8vo. xxii,[ii],333 pp, advt leaf. Orig calf, rebacked.
(Bickersteth) **£440 [≈ $844]**

- An Inquiry into the Original of Our Ideas of Beauty and Virtue; In Two Treatises ... Second Edition, Corrected and Enlarg'd. London: for J. Darby ..., 1726. 8vo. Contemp panelled calf, rebacked. Anon.
(Waterfield's) **£350 [≈ $671]**

- An Inquiry into the Original of our Ideas of Beauty and Virtue; In Two Treatises ... Second Edition, Corrected and Enlarg'd. London: for J. Darby ..., 1726. 8vo. xxvi, [ii], 304 pp. Contemp calf, mor label, red sprinkled edges, rubbed, jnts cracked but firm, sl worn. Anon   *(Finch)* **£300 [≈ $575]**

- An Inquiry into the Original of our Ideas of Beauty and Virtue ... Fourth Edition, Corrected. London: for D. Midwinter ..., 1738. 8vo. xxi,[iii],304,[viii] pp. Contemp calf, relabelled, sides rubbed, hd of spine reprd. Anon.   *(Finch)* **£340 [≈ $652]**

- Letters concerning the True Foundation of Virtue or Moral Goodness, wrote in a Correspondence between Mr Gilbert Burnet and Mr Francis Hutcheson ... Glasgow: Foulis, 1772. Sm 8vo. viii,(9)-158 pp. Orig calf, jnts cracked, hd of spine sl worn.
(Bickersteth) **£650 [≈ $1,247]**

Hutchinson, Francis
- An Historical Essay Concerning Witchcraft. London: Knaplock, 1718. 8vo. Calf, rebacked. *(Emerald Isle)* **£200 [≃ $383]**
- An Historical Essay concerning Witchcraft ... Second Edition, with considerable Additions. London: R. Knaplock ..., 1720. 8vo. [32],336 pp. Minor marg worm. Contemp calf, spine rubbed & worn.
(Frew Mackenzie) **£250 [≃ $479]**

Hutchinson, John
- An Abstract from the Works of John Hutchinson Esq., being a Summary of his Discoveries in Philosophy and Divinity. The Second Edition, corrected. London: for E. Withers, 1755. 8vo. Title-leaf a cancel. Contemp calf. *(Waterfield's)* **£225 [≃ $431]**

Hutchinson, W.
- The History of the County of Cumberland ... Carlisle: F. Jollie, 1794. 1st edn. 2 vols. 4to. 600; 686 pp. 2 engvd titles, lge fldg map, 3 fldg plans, 51 plates, num text ills. Occas sl spotting. Half calf gilt, rebacked, edges sl rubbed. *(Hollett)* **£275 [≃ $527]**

Hutchinson, William
- The Spirit of Masonry in Moral and Elucidatory Lectures. London: for J. Wilkie & W. Goldsmith, 1775. 8vo. Engvd title with vignette, 1 plate, 1 vignette in text. Contemp qtr calf, vellum tips, some wear, jnts cracking. Letter from Locke in appendix is spurious.
(Sanders) **£85 [≃ $163]**

Hutton, Charles
- A Mathematical and Philosophical Dictionary ... London: J. Davis, 1796-95. 1st edn. 2 vols. 4to. [iii]-viii,650; [ii],756 pp. 37 plates, text ills. Lacks half-titles. Occas sl marks. Contemp calf, rebacked, crnrs sl worn. *(Clark)* **£225 [≃ $431]**
- Miscellanea Mathematica: consisting of a Large Collection of Curious Mathematical Problems ... London: Baldwin, 1775. 1st edn. All published. 12mo. iv, 342, [2 errata & advt] pp. Text diags. Contemp calf backed mrbld bds, bds rubbed. *(Gaskell)* **£265 [≃ $508]**

Hutton, William
- The Battle of Bosworth Field ... Birmingham: Pearson & Rollason, 1788. 1st edn. 8vo. Title, (v)-lxxiv, 180 pp. Lacks b2 (dedic?). Port, plan. Occas browning. Contemp calf, rebacked. *(Bow Windows)* **£105 [≃ $201]**

- A Journey from Birmingham to London. Birmingham: Pearson & Rollason; sold by Baldwin & Lowndes, London, 1785. 8vo. Frontis. Some spotting. Contemp calf, gilt borders, Signet Library stamp, rebacked.
(Jarndyce) **£110 [≃ $211]**

Huygens, Christian
- The Celestial Worlds Discover'd ... The Second Edition, Corrected and Enlarged. London: 1722. Sm 8vo. vi,162 pp. 5 fldg plates (sev foxed or dust marked, 1 reprd on reverse). Old calf, rebacked, crnr tips worn.
(Bow Windows) **£175 [≃ $335]**

Icelandic Poetry ...
- Icelandic Poetry, or The Edda of Saemund translated into English Verse, by A.S. Cottle. Bristol: N. Biggs for Joseph Cottle ..., 1797. 1st English edn. 8vo.. Final errata leaf. Contemp half roan, rubbed.
(Hannas) **£200 [≃ $383]**

Ideas for Rustic Furniture ...
- See Taylor, I. & J.

The Idler ...
- See Johnson, Samuel.

Ignoramus: or, the English Lawyer ...
- See Ruggle, George.

Il Putanismo di Roma ...
- See Leti, Gregorio.

Imison, John
- The School of Arts. The Second Edition, with very considerable additions. London: for the author ... by John Murray, [ca 1790]. 8vo. xv,[i],[errata leaf], 319,[i],2, [advt leaf], [4 contents],176 pp. 24 plates. Rec qtr calf gilt.
(Spelman) **£180 [≃ $345]**
- A Treatise of the Mechanical Powers. I. Of the Lever, II. The Wheel ... VI. The Inclined Plane. To which are added Several Useful Improvements ... London: for the author ..., [1787]. 8vo. [iv],39 pp. 2 fldg plates (1 sm tear, no loss) inc frontis. Mod qtr calf.
(Finch) **£225 [≃ $431]**

Imitations ...
- Imitations of the Characters of Theophrastus. London: for S. Leacroft, 1774. 1st edn. 8vo. [vi],xxx,[ii],112 pp. Half-title. Contemp mor backed bds. *(Burmester)* **£150 [≃ $287]**

Imlay, Gilbert
- A Topographical Description of the Western Territory of North America ... By George [sic] Imlay. London: Debrett, 1793. 2nd edn. 8vo. "171" [ie 433],[19],[1],[2 advt] pp. 2 fldg maps, fldg plan, fldg table. Contemp calf, jnts weak but holding, sl rubbed.
 (Chapel Hill) **$1,250** [≈ £651]

Improved Method ...
- An Improved Method of Opening the Temporal Artery ... see Butter, William.

Inett, John
- Origines Anglicanae: Or, A History of the English Church ... London: T.H. for M. Wotton ..., 1704. 1st edn. Folio. [vi],x,[xiv], 390, [10] pp. Contemp panelled calf, rebacked. *(Young's)* **£85** [≈ $163]

Ingelo, Nathaniel
- Bentivolio and Urania in Six Books ... Third Edition, with some Amendments. London: T.R. for Richard Marriott, 1673. Folio. Mod half calf. Wing I.177.
 (Waterfield's) **£120** [≈ $230]

Inglis, Mrs Richmond
- Anna and Edgar: or, Love and Ambition. A Tale. Edinburgh: Murray & Cochrane for the author ..., 1781. 4to. New bds.
 (C.R. Johnson) **£165** [≈ $316]

Inquiry ...
- An Inquiry into the Original of our Ideas of Beauty and Virtue ... see Hutcheson, Francis.

Institution ...
- The Institution of a Christian Man, conteynynge the Exposytion of the Crede ... (London: Berthelet, 1537). Sm 8vo. Lacks a1-4 (title & prelims). Few marg tears. Colophon reprd. 19th c mor. STC 5167.
 (Stewart) **£450** [≈ $863]

Instructions ...
- Instructions for the Education of a Daughter ... see Fenelon, Salignac de la Mothe.

Interest ...
- The Interest of Great Britain Considered, with regard to Her Colonies ... see Jackson, Richard.
- The Interest of the Three Kingdom's, With respect to the Business of the Black Box, And all the other Pretentions of His Grace the

Duke of Monmouth ... London: in the year, 1680. Sm 4to. [ii],32 pp. Disbound. Wing I270A. *(Finch)* **£60** [≈ $115]

Ireland, J.
- Vindiciae Regiae; or, a defence of the Kingly Office. In Two Letters to the Earl of Stanhope. The Second Edition. London: for J. Wright, 1797. 8vo. 79 pp. Half-title, 4 advt pp. Sm piece torn from final advt leaf. New bds. *(Claude Cox)* **£15** [≈ $28]

Isham, Zachary
- A Sermon preached at the Funeral of the Reverend John Scott D.D. ... March 15, 1694-5. London: for Walter Kettilby, 1695. Half-title. Disbound. Wing I.1068.
 (Waterfield's) **£20** [≈ $38]

Isocrates
- The Orations and Epistles of Isocrates. Translated from the Greek by Mr. Joshua Dinsdale. And revised by the Rev. Mr. Young. London: for T. Waller, 1752. 1st edn. 8vo. Advt leaf at end. Contemp calf, gilt dec spine. *(Ximenes)* **$250** [≈ £130]

Ives, John
- Select Papers chiefly relating to English Antiquities ... London: Hingeston, 1773 [-75]. 4to. [viii],170 pp. Port frontis inserted. 3 plates (1 fldg). Contemp calf, rebacked.
 (Lamb) **£150** [≈ $287]

Izacke, Richard
- Remarkable Antiquities of the City of Exeter. Giving an Account of the Laws and Customs of the Place ... London: Rowland Reynolds, 1681. 2nd edn. [vi],191,[lxiii] pp. Frontis, fldg map. Sm reprs. Old sheep, rebacked, crnrs sl worn. Wing I.1111.
 (Clark) **£110** [≈ $211]

Jackson, John
- The History of the Scottish Stage ... Edinburgh: Peter Hill, 1793. 424,41 pp. Early 19th c calf & bds.
 (C.R. Johnson) **£325** [≈ $623]

Jackson, John Baptist
- An Essay on the Invention of Engraving and Printing in Chiaro Oscuro ... London: for A. Millar, S. Baker ..., 1754. 4to. 19 pp. 8 engvd & cold plates (rather spotted & offset). Mod calf. *(Hollett)* **£4,850** [≈ $9,311]

Jackson, Richard
- The Interest of Great Britain Considered, with regard to Her Colonies, and the Acquisitions of Canada and Guadeloupe ... London: 1760. 1st edn. 58 pp. Antique qtr calf. Anon.   *(Reese)* **$650 [≈£338]**

Jackson, Robert
- A Treatise on the Fevers of Jamaica ... Phila: Robert Campbell, 1795. 1st Amer edn. 12mo. 276,19,[5] pp. 4 advt pp. Contemp sheep.   *(Bookpress)* **$250 [≈£130]**
- A Treatise on the Fevers of Jamaica ... Phila: 1795. 8vo. xi,296,19 pp. 5 pp ctlg of Robert Campbell. Sl browning. Contemp tree calf, front hinge cracked. *(Hemlock)* **$275 [≈£143]**

Jackson, Thomas
- The Works of the Reverend and Learned Divine ... London: Andrew Clark, 1673. 3 vols. Folio. Sl marg worm in vol 3. New bds. Wing J.90.   *(Stewart)* **£100 [≈$191]**

Jacob, Giles
- The Compleat Court-Keeper: or, Land-Steward's Assistant ... Second Edition: with Additions and Amendments. London: John Nutt ... for Lintot, Ward, 1715. 8vo. viii, 480, [21],[3 advt] pp. Contemp calf, new label.   *(Fenning)* **£85 [≈$163]**
- The Compleat Parish-Officer ... Sixth Edition with additions ... added, the Office of Constables, written by Sir Francis Bacon ... London: Nutt, Gosling ..., 1731. 12mo. Sl staining. New rear f.e.p. Contemp sheep, rubbed, sm repr. Anon.   *(Jarndyce)* **£150 [≈$287]**
- The Complete Court-Keeper: or, Land-Steward's Assistant ... London: 1764. 6th edn. 8vo. viii,534,25 pp. Minor worming. Old calf.   *(Young's)* **£75 [≈$143]**
- The Modern Justice: Containing the Business of A Justice of Peace ... [with] A New Appendix to the Modern Justice ... London: Nutt & Gosling ..., 1720-22. 8vo. [8], 502,[42], [ii],48, 33-48, 49-60,[22] pp. Some browning & foxing. Contemp calf, rebacked.   *(Meyer Boswell)* **$275 [≈£143]**
- A New Law-Dictionary ... Fourth Edition. In the Savoy: Nutt & Gosling, 1739. Folio. Few ff dusty. Later three qtr mor & buckram bds, rubbed.   *(Meyer Boswell)* **$300 [≈£156]**
- A New Law-Dictionary ... The Fifth Edition, with great Additions and Improvements ... In the Savoy: Lintot ..., 1744. Folio. Contemp calf, rubbed, wear at spine ends, splits in

hinges.   *(Jarndyce)* **£200 [≈$383]**
- The Poetical Register: or, the Lives and Characters of all the English Poets ... London: Bettesworth, Taylor ..., 1723. 2 vols. 8vo. xxvi,[vi],328, [xxviii]; vii,[i blank],[xi],[i blank],444 pp. 14 ports inc frontises. Contemp calf, sl worn. Anon.   *(Finch)* **£300 [≈$575]**

Jago, Richard
- Edge-Hill, or, the Rural Retreat delineated and moralised. A Poem in Four Books. London: Dodsley, 1767. 4to. 4 vignettes. Mod bds.   *(Waterfield's)* **£125 [≈$239]**

James I, King of Scotland
- Poetical Remains. Edinburgh: for J. & E. Balfour, 1783. 8vo. Mod qtr calf.   *(Waterfield's)* **£85 [≈$163]**

James, Charles
- Poems by the Author of Hints to Lord Rawdon on some Military Abuses ... London: J. Davis ..., 1792. Frontis port. Orig mrbld bds, paper spine, uncut, defective in places.   *(C.R. Johnson)* **£185 [≈$355]**

James, Thomas
- The Jesuits Downfall, Threatened Against Them by the Secvlar Priests for their wicked Lives ... Together with the Life of Father Parsons ... Oxford: Joseph Barnes ..., 1612. 1st edn. 4to. [xii],72 pp. Unbound & stitched as issued. STC 14459.   *(Vanbrugh)* **£295 [≈$566]**

Jameson, E.
- An Outline of the Mineralogy of the Shetland Islands and of the Island of Arran, with an Appendix ... Edinburgh: 1798. 8vo. xiv, 202 pp. 2 maps, plate. Blind stamp on title. Some browning. Orig bds, rebacked.   *(Wheldon & Wesley)* **£150 [≈$287]**

Jefferys, Thomas
- An Exact Chart of the River St. Laurence, from Fort Frontenac to the Island of Anticosti shewing the Soundings, Rocks, Shoals, &c. with Views of the Lands. London: 1768. Lge fldg linen backed cold map, 37 x 24 inches. 2 sl stains at folds. Orig mrbld paper slipcase.   *(Reese)* **$1,250 [≈£651]**

Jenkins, Joseph
- A Sermon Occasioned by a Dreadful Explosion of Gun-Powder, in Chester ... November 5th, 1772. Wrexham: Richard

Martin, [1772]. 36 pp. Mod half calf gilt. *(Hollett)* £175 [≈ $335]

Jenks, Benjamin
- The Glorious Victory of Chastity; in Joseph's Hard Conflict, and His Happy Escape. London: J. Buckland, 1761. 106,[2 advt] pp. Contemp calf, extremities worn, front bd detached. *(Wreden)* $30 [≈ £15]

Jenner, Charles
- Poems. Cambridge: J. Bentham ..., 1766. 1st edn. 4to. 82 pp. Lacks half-title. Title sl soiled. Lib blind stamp & ink stamp. Old bds, lacks backstrip. *(Burmester)* £50 [≈ $95]

Jennings, D.
- An Introduction to the Globes and the Orrery: as also the Application of Astronomy to Chronology ... London: 1752. [xii],178 pp. 13 figs on 5 fldg plates. Old leather gilt, crudely rebacked, inner hinge sl cracked. *(Whitehart)* £50 [≈ $95]

Jenyns, Soame
- A Scheme for the Coalition of Parties humbly submitted to the Publick. London: Wilkie, 1772. 34 pp. Half-title. Disbound. Anon. *(C.R. Johnson)* £65 [≈ $124]
- A View of the Internal Evidence of the Christian Religion. London: Dodsley, 1776. 2nd edn. 8vo. 191 pp. Half-title. Near contemp half calf, backstrip relaid. Anon. *(Young's)* £50 [≈ $95]
- The Works ... To which are prefixed ... History of the Author's Family, and also of his Life; by Charles Nelson Cole. London: Cadell, 1790. 1st coll edn. 4 vols. 8vo. Port. Contemp calf, spines darkened & sl rubbed, lacks labels. *(Burmester)* £50 [≈ $95]

Jephson, Robert
- Braganza. A Tragedy ... New Edition corrected by the Author. London: Evans, Davies, [1775]. 8vo. [iv],76,[i] pp. Engvd title with vignette. Disbound. *(Bickersteth)* £25 [≈ $47]

Jerningham, Edward
- Poems on Various Subjects ... London: for J. Robson, 1767. 1st coll edn. 8vo. [iv],119 pp. Occas marg stains. Contemp calf, gilt spine sl chipped at ends. *(Rankin)* £65 [≈ $124]

Jessop, Edmund
- A Discovery of the Errors of the English Anabaptists ... London: W. Iones for Robert

Bird ..., 1623. 1st edn. 4to. [12],103 pp. Wraps. STC 14520. *(Fenning)* £110 [≈ $211]

Jessop, Thomas
- The Jesuites Ghostly Wayes to Draw other persons over to their Damnable Principle ... London: for Will. Bowtel, 1679. 4to. 25 pp. Lacks A1 (probably blank). Mod half calf. Wing J.716. *(Hollett)* £75 [≈ $143]

The Jesuit's Memorial ...
- See Parsons, Robert.

Johnson, John
- The Clergy-Man's Vade Mecum, or an Account of the Antient and Present State of the Church of England. The Rights and Duties of the Clergy. London: Nicholson, 1707. 8vo. Ca 350 pp. Contemp calf. Anon. *(Emerald Isle)* £45 [≈ $86]
- The Clergyman's Vade-Mecum: or, an Account of the Ancient and Present Church of England ... Third Edition, with large additions. London: for John Nicholson ..., 1709. Lge 12mo. [24],351,[32] pp. Contemp calf. Anon. *(Fenning)* £45 [≈ $86]

Johnson, Mary
- Madam Johnson's Present: or, Every Young Woman's Companion, in Useful and Universal Knowledge ... London: for W. Nicoll, 1769. 5th edn. iv,5-197, [17],2 advt] pp. Few sl marks. Contemp calf backed mrbld bds, rubbed & worn. *(Hollett)* £225 [≈ $431]

Johnson, Richard
- Blossoms of Morality. Intended for the Amusement of Young Ladies & Gentlemen. By the Editor of the Looking-Glass for the Mind. London: E. Newbery, 1789. 1st edn. Sm 8vo. [vii], 212 pp. Engvd frontis & title. Contemp calf, sl rubbed, ft of spine chipped. Anon. *(Bromer)* $450 [≈ £234]
- The Juvenile Biographer ... The First Worcester Edition. Worcester: Isaiah Thomas, 1787. 12mo. 119,[4 advt] pp. Frontis, w'cuts in text. Half mor, mrbld bds, t.e.g., others uncut. *(Bromer)* $1,750 [≈ £911]

Johnson, Revd Samuel
- The Absolute Impossibility of Transubstantiation Demonstrated. London: for William Rogers, 1688. 1st edn. 4to. xv,54,[2 advt] pp. Half-title. Ex-lib. Sm tear in half-title, wormhole in blank marg. Bds. Wing J.819. Anon. *(Wreden)* $60 [≈ £31]

Johnson, Samuel
- An Account of the Life of Mr. Richard Savage, son of the Earl Rivers. London: for J. Roberts, 1744. 1st edn. Issue without a single erratum at end. 8vo. Lacks half-title & final blank. Edges sl browned. Blank marg of last leaf sl trimmed. Half mor gilt. Anon.
(Ximenes) **$475 [≈ £247]**
- A Dictionary of the English Language ... London: Strahan, Knapton ..., 1755. 1st edn. 2 vols. Folio. Few sm tears reprd without loss. V sl even browning. Antique style panelled calf, red & green mor labels.
(Finch) **£4,750 [≈ $9,119]**
- A Dictionary of the English Language ... The Third Edition, Corrected. London: for A. Millar; W. Strahan ..., 1766. 2 vols. Occas sl staining. Rebound in half calf.
(Jarndyce) **£200 [≈ $383]**
- A Dictionary of the English Language ... The Third Edition, Corrected. London: A. Millar, 1766. 2 vols. Contemp calf, red labels, sl worn. *(C.R. Johnson)* **£285 [≈ $547]**
- A Dictionary of the English Language ... The Fourth Edition, Corrected. London: for Strahan, Rivington ..., 1770. 2 vols. Contemp calf, gilt spines, red labels, sl scuffed, split in hinge. *(Jarndyce)* **£200 [≈ $383]**
- A Dictionary of the English Language. London: W. Strahan, 1773. 5th edn. 2 vols. 8vo. Contemp calf, sl worn, spines sl darkened. *(Bookpress)* **$500 [≈ £260]**
- A Dictionary of the English Language ... Abstracted from the Folio Edition, by the Author ... Fifth Edition, Corrected ... London: for W. Strahan ..., 1773. 2 vols. 8vo. Titles sl creased. Contemp calf, sl insect damage along jnts. *(Burmester)* **£160 [≈ $307]**
- A Dictionary of the English Language ... The Fourth Edition, revised by the Author. Dublin: for Thomas Ewing, 1775. 2 vols. 4to. Contemp speckled calf, rebacked, orig red & green labels retained.
(Jarndyce) **£480 [≈ $921]**
- A Dictionary of the English Language ... The Sixth Edition, Corrected by the Author. London: for Strahan, Rivington ..., 1778. 2 vols. Rebound in half calf.
(Jarndyce) **£220 [≈ $422]**
- A Dictionary of the English Language ... The Seventh Edition. London: Rivington ..., 1785. 1st 1-vol folio edn. Folio. Sl spotting. Contemp style speckled calf, vellum tips.
(Frew Mackenzie) **£650 [≈ $1,247]**
- A Dictionary of the English Language ... The Sixth Edition. London: 1785. 2nd 4to edn. 2

vols. 4to. Port in vol 1. Contemp calf, rebacked, rubbed, hd of spines a little worn, ends of upper jnts starting to crack but firm.
(Bickersteth) **£280 [≈ $537]**
- A Dictionary of the English Language ... The Sixth Edition. London: 1785. 2 vols. 4to. Frontis port. Contemp russia, hinges weakening. *(C.R. Johnson)* **£485 [≈ $931]**
- A Dictionary of the English Language ... Sixth Edition. London: Rivington, 1785. 2 vols. Thick 4to. Half-title in vol 1. Frontis port. Old calf gilt, rebacked, v rubbed & scratched, edges defective in places, 1 hinge cracked.. *(Hollett)* **£220 [≈ $422]**
- A Dictionary of the English Language ... London: for Harrison & Co, 1786. Folio. Red & black title. frontis. Prelims sl dusty, creases in final ff. Contemp reversed calf, sl rubbed & marked. *(Jarndyce)* **£620 [≈ $1,190]**
- A Dictionary of the English Language ... The Eighth Edition. London: for A. Millar; Edinburgh: Brown & Doig; Gainsborough: Mozley; Stirling: Anderson, 1792. 2 vols in one. Blank crnr torn from title. Contemp tree sheep, worn, rebacked & reprd, new endpapers. *(Jarndyce)* **£200 [≈ $383]**
- Dr. Johnson's Table-Talk ... Selected and Arranged from Mr. Boswell's Life of Johnson. London: for C. Dilly, 1798. 1st edn. Sl spotting. Later half calf, t,e,g, backstrip relaid, sl rubbed, label chipped.
(Jarndyce) **£120 [≈ $230]**
- Extracts from the Publications of Mr. Knox, Dr. Anderson, Mr. Pennant, and Dr. Johnson; relative to the Northern and North-Western Coasts of Great Britain. London: C. Macrae, 1787. 1st edn. 8vo. 31 pp. Lower part sl damp stained. Rec wraps.
(Burmester) **£45 [≈ $86]**
- The False Alarm. The Second Edition. London: Cadell, 1770. Half-title, 53 pp. V sl traces of damp on a few ff. Rebound in qtr calf. *(C.R. Johnson)* **£280 [≈ $537]**
- The Idler. By the Author of the Rambler. With Additional Essays. The Fourth Edition. London: Rivington, Carnan ..., 1783. 2 vols. 12mo. Contemp speckled calf, sl rubbed, split in hinge, lacks 1 label. Anon.
(Jarndyce) **£58 [≈ $111]**
- Irene: a Tragedy ... London: for R. Dodsley, & sold by M. Cooper, 1749. 1st edn. 8vo. [vi],86 pp. Lacks advt leaf & half-title. MS index on intl blank. Some browning & staining. Contemp vellum gilt. Bound with 6 other plays. *(Finch)* **£500 [≈ $959]**
- A Journey to the Western Islands of Scotland.

Dublin: for A. Leathley, J. Exshaw, H. Saunders ..., 1775. Probable 1st Dublin edn. 2 vols in one. 12mo. Rebound in half calf.
(Jarndyce) **£180 [≈ $345]**

- Letters to and from the late Samuel Johnson ... Published ... by Hester Lynch Piozzi. London: Strahan & Cadell, 1788. 1st edn. 2 vols. 8vo. [ii],xv,397; xi,424 pp. Lacks intl blank & errata slip (as usual). Sl foxing. Victorian half calf, dec spines gilt.
(Sotheran's) **£350 [≈ $671]**

- Letters to and from the late Samuel Johnson ... London: Strahan & Cadell, 1788. 1st edn. 2 vols. demy 8vo. Few sl marks. Lacks errata leaf. Contemp calf, gilt spine, sl rubbed, jnts tender & split but bds firm on cords.
(Ash) **£350 [≈ $671]**

- The Life of Mr. Richard Savage son of the Earl Rivers. The Fourth Edition. To which are added, the Lives of Sir Francis Drake, and Admiral Blake ... by the Author of the Rambler. London: F. Newbery, 1777. 298 pp. Qtr calf, rebacked. Anon.
(C.R. Johnson) **£125 [≈ $239]**

- The Lives of the most Eminent English Poets. London: C. Bathurst ..., 1783. New edn. 4 vols. 8vo. Contemp calf, outer hinges cracked, spine leather brittle.
(Bookpress) **$250 [≈ £130]**

- The Lives of the most Eminent English Poets ... New Edition, corrected. London: 1790-91. 4 vols. 8vo. iii,452; iii,464; [3],436; [3],492 pp. Port. Contemp tree calf gilt, red & green labels, some wear to spines & headbands.
(Fenning) **£95 [≈ $182]**

- The Lives of the most Eminent English Poets, with Critical Observations ... A New Edition, corrected. London: Rivington ..., 1790. 4 vols. 8vo. Port in vol 1. Contemp calf, mor labels, spines rubbed & sl worn at ends.
(Finch) **£140 [≈ $268]**

- Johnson's Lives of the English Poets, abridged ... Designed for the Improvement of Youth ... Some Account of the Life of Dr. Johnson. London: for E. Newbery, 1797. 1st edn thus. 12mo. Frontis. Contemp sheep, gilt spine, v sm crack in hinge.
(Ximenes) **$450 [≈ £234]**

- The Poetical Works. Cook's Edition. London: C. Cook, [ca 1779]. The cheap issue without the extra engvd plates. 12mo. 83,[5 advt] pp. Frontis, 1 engvd & 2 ptd titles. Contemp tree calf, gilt spine.
(Spelman) **£35 [≈ $67]**

- The Poetical Works. A New Edition. London: W. Osborne & T. Griffin ..., 1785.

Contemp calf, black label.
(C.R. Johnson) **£125 [≈ $239]**

- The Poetical Works. Complete in One Volume. A New Edition. London: for W. Osborne & T. Griffin; & J. Mozley, Gainsborough, 1785. Sm 8vo in 4s. 2 half-titles before title. Contemp sheep, spine ends & 2 patches on upper bd defective.
(Sanders) **£55 [≈ $105]**

- The Poetical Works ... Complete in One Volume. A New Edition. London: W. Osborne & T. Griffin, & J. Mozley, Gainsborough, 1785. Half-title. Contemp calf, lacks label.
(C.R. Johnson) **£100 [≈ $191]**

- The Poetical Works ... Complete in One Volume. A New Edition. London: for W. Osborne & T. Griffin; & J. Mozley, Gainsborough, 1785. 2nd edn. Sm 8vo. viii,152 pp. Contemp calf, mor label, mark to upper cvr.
(Finch) **£125 [≈ $239]**

- The Poetical Works. A New Edition considerably enlarged. London: George Kearsley, 1789. Half-title,212,12 advt pp. Rebound in qtr calf.
(C.R. Johnson) **£85 [≈ $163]**

- Prayers and Meditations ... Published from his Manuscripts ... by George Strahan. Dublin: White, Byrne & Cash, 1785. 1st Irish edn. 269 pp. Rebound in qtr calf.
(C.R. Johnson) **£225 [≈ $431]**

- Prayers and Meditations ... Published from his Manuscripts, by George Strahan. The Second Edition. London: for T. Cadell, 1785. Rebound in half calf.
(Jarndyce) **£120 [≈ $230]**

- The Prince of Abissinia. A Tale ... The Fourth Edition. London: for W. Strahan ..., 1766. 2 vols. 12mo. Contemp calf, rebacked. Anon.
(Waterfield's) **£165 [≈ $316]**

- The Prince of Abissinia. A Tale. The Seventh Edition. London: Rivington ..., 1786. 12mo. Contemp tree calf, rubbed, hinges splitting.
(Jarndyce) **£40 [≈ $76]**

- The Prince of Abissinia. A Tale. The Ninth Edition. London: Rivington ..., 1793. Tall 12mo. 304 pp. Orig mottled calf, rec rebacked, later endpapers. Anon.
(Limestone Hills) **$75 [≈ £39]**

- The Prince of Abissinia. A Tale. The Ninth Edition. London: Rivington ..., 1793. 12mo. Contemp tree calf, gilt spine sl rubbed, label sl chipped.   *(Jarndyce)* **£40 [≈ $76]**

- The Prince of Abissinia. A Tale. The Tenth Edition. London: Rivington ..., 1798. 12mo. Contemp tree calf, gilt spine, label.

(Jarndyce) **£65** [≈ $124]
- The Rambler ... Thirteenth Edition. London: for T. Longman ..., 1794. 3 vols. 8vo. 3 frontis. Contemp tree calf, rebacked.
(Waterfield's) **£70** [≈ $134]
- Rasselas, Prince of Abissinia ... London: for E. & S. Harding ..., 1796. New edn. 8vo. 236, 2 advt pp. Half-title. 4 plates. Contemp mor, a.e.g., rubbed. *(Young's)* **£45** [≈ $86]
- Taxation No Tyranny; an Answer to the Resolutions and Address of the American Congress. The Fourth Edition. London: Cadell, 1775. 91 pp. Coffee stains on 4 pp. Disbound. Anon.
(C.R. Johnson) **£60** [≈ $115]
- See also Husbands, John (ed.).
- See also The Matrimonial Preceptor.

Johnstone, Charles
- Crysal: or, the Adventures of a Guinea ... By an Adept. London: for J. Watson ..., 1785. 4 vols. 8vo. Period calf, contrasting labels (2 missing). Anon. *(Rankin)* **£85** [≈ $163]
- The Reverie: or, A Flight to the Paradise of Fools. Published by the Editor of The Adventures of a Guinea. London: Becket & De Hondt, 1763. 1st edn. 2 vols. 12mo. Errata leaf vol 2. Repr to vol 2 title verso. Speckled calf, red labels.
(Jarndyce) **£120** [≈ $230]

Jones, A.
- The Art of Playing at Skittles ... London: for the author & sold by T. Wilkie, 1773. 56, 4 advt pp. Rec calf, uncut.
(C.R. Johnson) **£850** [≈ $1,631]

Jones, David
- A Compleat History of Europe ... Third Edition, Corrected, and very much Enlarged. London: Nicholson, Harris, Bell, 1701. 8vo. Contemp calf, lacks label, spine ends chipped, crnrs sl worn. Anon. *(Sanders)* **£32** [≈ $61]
- The Secret History of White-Hall, from the Restoration of Charles II ... London: R. Baldwin, 1697. 1st edn. [xii],80, 80,80, 64, 80, 110 pp. Old calf gilt, worn, hinges cracked. Wing J.9347.
(Hollett) **£140** [≈ $268]

Jones, Henry, Bishop of Clogher
- A Sermon Preach't at Christs-Church Dublin ... May 24. 1660. London: J.C. for J. Crook, 1660. 1st edn. 4to. [iv],28 pp. Outer ff dusty, lib stamp on title verso. Later wraps. Wing J.952. *(Clark)* **£65** [≈ $124]

Jones, Henry
- Kew Garden. A Poem. In Two Cantos. London: J. Browne, 1767. 4to. 45 pp. Qtr calf, mrbld bds.
(C.R. Johnson) **£285** [≈ $547]

Jones, Inigo
- The Designs ... see Kent, William.

Jones, Jenkin
- Hobby Horses, a Poetic Allegory, in Five Parts. London: for M. Allen, [1797]. 1st edn. Sm 8vo. Frontis. 1 section spotted. Contemp green calf, gilt spine (rubbed, label chipped).
(Ximenes) **$275** [≈ £143]

Jones, John
- The New Returna Brevium or the Law Returned from Westminster ... London: William Du-gard, 1650. 1st edn. 12mo. [xii],83 pp. Sl stained. Rec half calf. Wing J.972. *(Vanbrugh)* **£155** [≈ $297]
- The Peace of Justice, or the Authoritie of a Justice of Peace ... London: Bentley for Shears, 1650. 1st edn. 12mo. [viii],23,[3] pp. 1st leaf blank save for w'cut device on recto. Sm 8vo. Sm hole in title. Sl stained. Rec half calf. Wing J.973. *(Vanbrugh)* **£155** [≈ $297]

Jones, Sir William
- A Grammar of the Persian Language. London: W. & J. Richardson, 1771. 1st edn. 4to. [2], xxiv, 153,[1] pp, errata leaf. Plate. Presumably lacks half-title. Rec bds.
(Fenning) **£165** [≈ $316]

Jones, Revd William
- An Essay on the First Principles of Natural Philosophy ... Oxford: S. Parker ..., 1762. 1st edn. 4to. [vi],281 pp. 3 plates (2 fldg). Contemp calf, rebacked.
(Bookpress) **$600** [≈ £312]

Jones, William
- The Gentlemens or Builders Companion ... London: for the author, 1739. 2nd edn, enlgd. Sm 4to. 7 engvd ff. 56 plates (the last 4 are dble & are numbered 53-60). Contemp calf, red edges, rebacked, worn.
(Bookpress) **$1,950** [≈ £1,015]

Jonson, Ben
- The Works ... With Additions never before Published. London: Thomas Hodgkin ..., 1692. 1st complete coll edn. Lge folio. [x],1-744, [4] pp, with minor mispagination.

Port frontis. Contemp calf, Victorian reback,
sl worn. Wing J.1006.
                    (Vanbrugh) **£455 [≈ $873]**
- The Works ... Collated with all the Former
  Editions ... by Peter Whalley. London: for D.
  Midwinter ..., 1756. 7 vols. Port in vol 1.
  Contemp calf, labels lacking or defective.
                    (Waterfield's) **£135 [≈ $259]**

Jortin, John
- Discourses concerning the Truth of the
  Christian Religion. The Second Edition.
  London: for John Whiston, 1747. 8vo. 1 sm
  repr. Contemp calf, jnts cracked but sound,
  lacks label. Anon. *(Waterfield's)* **£45 [≈ $86]**
- The Life of Erasmus ... London: for J.
  Whiston & B. White, 1758. 1st edn. Lge 4to.
  [viii],630,[2] pp. Mezzotint port frontis (sm
  worm hole on lower part), 1 other plate.
  Contemp tree calf, sl worn.
                    (Vanbrugh) **£155 [≈ $297]**
- The Life of Erasmus. London: J. Whiston &
  B. White, 1758. Lge 4to. [8],631 pp.
  Contemp tree calf, jnts weak.
                    (Humber) **£48 [≈ $92]**

Judgement ...
- The Judgement of Foreign Divines
  concerning the Liturgy and Ceremonies of
  the Church of England. London: Richard
  Baldwin, 1690. 8vo. Disbound. Wing J.1177.
                    (Waterfield's) **£45 [≈ $86]**

Julia de Roubigne, a Tale ...
- See Mackenzie, Henry.

Junius
- The Letters of Junius. London: for J.
  Wheble, in Paternoster Row, 1770. 1st
  Wheble edn. 8vo. [iv],232 pp. Wheble
  imprint below "cap of liberty" vignette on
  title. Old calf, rebacked.
                    (Young's) **£55 [≈ $105]**
- Junius [Letters]. London: for Henry Sampson
  Woodfall, 1772. 1st authorised edn. 2 vols.
  Engvd titles only. Early orange bds, brown
  paper spines, uncut, crnrs sl rubbed, sl wear
  to 1 hinge.   *(Jarndyce)* **£100 [≈ $191]**
- [Letters]. Stat Nominis Umbra. London: T.
  Bensley for Vernor & Hood, 1796. 2 vols.
  8vo. [6],xl,325; [2],366 pp. Addtnl engvd
  titles, 16 ports (spotted). Late 19th c half calf,
  mor labels, sl rubbed & worn.
                    (Claude Cox) **£25 [≈ $47]**
- The Letters. London: for J. Mundell & Co,
  1798. 8vo. viii,316 pp. Buckram.

                    (Young's) **£18 [≈ $34]**
- The Letters of Junius. London: J. Mundell,
  1798. Tall 8vo. [8],316 pp. Some stains.
  Contemp calf, worn. *(Humber)* **£28 [≈ $53]**

Justice, J.
- The British Gardener's New Director.
  Dublin: 1765. 4th edn. 8vo. [xvi],xxvi, 443,
  [12] pp. 4 plates. Upper crnr of title cut away,
  sl water stain at end. Tear in 1 plate reprd.
  New cloth. *(Wheldon & Wesley)* **£60 [≈ $115]**

Juvenal
- The Satires ... Translated into English Verse
  by Mr. Dryden and several other eminent
  Hands. Together with the Satires of Aulus
  Persius Flaccus ... London: Tonson, 1693.
  1st edn. Folio. Rec reversed sheep & mrbld
  bds. Wing J.1288.   *(Stewart)* **£120 [≈ $230]**

Juvenile Poems on Several Occasions ...
- See Griffin, Philip.

Kalm, Peter
- Travels into North America ... Warrington &
  London: 1770-71. 1st English edn. 3 vols.
  xvi, 400; 352; viii,310,[8 index],[8
  subscribers] pp. Lge fldg map, 6 plates. Neat
  reprs to some map folds. 2 ff damp stained.
  Contemp calf, rebacked.
                    (Reese) **$4,250 [≈ £2,213]**

Kames, Henry Home, Lord
- Elements of Criticism. Edinburgh: for A.
  Millar, London; & A. Kincaid & J. Bell,
  Edinburgh, 1762. 1st edn. 3 vols. 8vo. Some
  faint marg damp stain. Contemp calf, gilt dec
  spines, contrasting mor labels, pale green
  edges, sides rubbed. Anon.
                    (Finch) **£700 [≈ $1,343]**
- Elements of Criticism. The Fifth Edition.
  With Additions and Improvements. Dublin:
  Charles Ingham, 1772. 329; 342,index pp.
  Contemp calf, red & green labels.
                    (C.R. Johnson) **£165 [≈ $316]**
- Loose Hints upon Education chiefly
  concerning the Culture of the Heart. Second
  Edition, enlarged. Edinburgh: for John Bell,
  1782. 419 pp. Contemp calf, rebacked. Anon.
                    (C.R. Johnson) **£350 [≈ $671]**

Keate, George
- An Epistle from Lady Jane Gray to Lord
  Guilford Dudley supposed to have been
  written in the Tower a few days before they
  suffered. London: Dodsley, 1762. 4to. Mod

wraps. Anon. *(Waterfield's)* £135 [≈$259]
- A Short Account of the Ancient History, Present Government, and Laws of the Republic of Geneva. London: George Keate, 1761. 1st edn. 8vo. xv,[i],218,[4] pp. Fldg map. Some offsetting. Rec half calf.
(Clark) £200 [≈$383]

Keepe, Henry
- Monumenta Westmonasteriensia: or an Historical Account of ... St. Peter's, or the Abby [sic] Church of Westminster. With all the Epitaphs, Inscriptions ... Monuments ... described ... By H.K. ... London: 1682. 1st edn. 8vo. [xvi],368 pp. Orig sheep, rebacked. Wing K.126. *(Vanbrugh)* £195 [≈$374]

Keill, James
- An Account of Animal Secretion ... London: Strahan, 1708. 1st edn. 8vo. xxviii,187,[1] pp. Text ills. Minor staining & soiling. Contemp calf, headcap chipped, spine & crnrs rubbed, lacks label. *(Gaskell)* £525 [≈$1,007]

Kelham, Robert
- A Dictionary of the Norman or Old French Language ... London: for Edward Brooke ..., 1779. 1st edn. 8vo. viii,259,[i], xii,88 pp. Orig bds, uncut, 19th c paper reback, upper jnt cracked but holding, spine extremities chipped. Middle Hill copy.
(Finch) £350 [≈$671]

Kelly, Hugh
- The School for Wives, a Comedy. London: for T. Becket, 1774. 1st edn. Title coming detached, sl damaged in gutter. Mod wraps. Anon. *(Waterfield's)* £20 [≈$38]

Kelly, James
- A Complete Collection of Scotish Proverbs explained and made intelligible to the English Reader. London: for William & John Innys, 1721. 8vo. Sl staining. Mod qtr calf.
(Waterfield's) £115 [≈$220]

Ken, Thomas
- A Manual of Prayers for the Use of the Scholars of Winchester College, and all other Devout Christians ... Twenty-third Edition ... Account of his Lordship's Life. London: for J. Hazard, 1728. 12mo. 4 pp advts at end. Port. Contemp sheep, somewhat worn but sound. *(Sanders)* £30 [≈$57]

Kennedy, John
- A Treatise upon Planting, Gardening, and

the Management of the Hot-House. Dublin: for W. Wilson, 1784. 1st Dublin edn. 8vo. xiii, [iii], 462,[ii advt] pp. Sl browned, occas spot. Contemp tree calf, mor label, spine worn, sides rubbed, crnrs bumped.
(Finch) £75 [≈$143]

Kennett, Basil
- A Brief Exposition of the Apostles Creed, According to Bishop Pearson, In a New Method, by way of Paraphrase and Annotation. London: for A. & J. Churchill ..., 1705. 1st edn. 8vo. xxiv,191 pp. Sm rust hole in 1 leaf. Contemp panelled calf.
(Young's) £55 [≈$105]
- Roma Antiqua Notitia: or, the Antiquities of Rome ... London: for T. Child ..., 1717. 6th edn. 8vo. xxx,375,26,2 advt pp. Frontis, 13 plates (some fldg). Contemp calf, rebacked.
(Young's) £46 [≈$88]
- Roma Antiqua Notitia: or the Antiquities of Rome ... The Tenth Edition. London: Knapton ..., 1737. Frontis, 8 plates (some fldg). Contemp sheep, rebacked.
(Waterfield's) £65 [≈$124]

Kennett, White
- The Case of Impropriations, and of the Augmentation of Vicarages ... Stated by History and Law ... London: Churchill, 1704. 8vo. A few pencil notes. Orig panelled calf (hinges cracked). Anon.
(Stewart) £55 [≈$105]
- The Duties of rejoycing in a Day of Prosperity. Recommended in a Sermon ... June 23, 1706 ... London: H. Hills, for the benefit of the poor, (1708). 1st edn. 8vo. 16 pp. Disbound. *(Young's)* £20 [≈$38]

Kenrick, William
- Falstaff's Wedding: A Comedy. Being A Sequel to the Second Part of the Play of King Henry the Fourth. Writen in Imitation of Shakespeare ... London: for J. Wilkie ..., 1760 [1766]. 1st edn. Mod wraps.
(Dramatis Personae) $85 [≈£44]
- The Lady of the Manor, a Comic Opera ... The Songs set to Music by Mr. Hook. London: Dilly ..., 1778. 1st edn. 8vo. [vi],65 pp. Lacks half-title. Final p sl soiled. Disbound. *(Bickersteth)* £25 [≈$47]
- Letter to David Garrick, Esq. Occasioned by his having moved the Court of King's Bench against the Publisher of Love in the Suds ... London: for J. Wheble, 1772. 1st edn. 4to. Disbound.
(Dramatis Personae) $225 [≈£117]

Kent, James
- Dissertations; being the Preliminary Part of a Course of Law Lectures. New York: George Forman, for the author, 1795. 1st edn. 8vo. Sl browning. Disbound.
(Ximenes) $750 [≈ £390]

Kent, Nathaniel
- General View of the Agriculture of the County of Norfolk ... for the Consideration of the Board of Agriculture ... Norwich: at the Norfolk Press ..., 1796. 2nd edn. 8vo. xvi, 236,[i errata] pp. Fldg map, 3 plates. Orig bds, uncut, paper label, spine worn.
(Finch) £100 [≈ $191]
- Hints to Gentlemen of Landed Property. London: Dodsley, 1775. 1st edn. 8vo. vii,[i], 268 pp. 10 fldg plates. Tables in text. Contemp calf, mor label, dec gilt spine, spine chipped at hd, crnrs worn, jnts cracked.
(Finch) £165 [≈ $316]
- Hints to Gentlemen of Landed Property ... London: Dodsley, 1776. 2nd edn. 8vo. vii,282 pp. 9 fldg plates. Single persistent worm hole. Rec half calf.
(Young's) £120 [≈ $230]

Kent, William
- The Designs of Inigo Jones ... [London]: 1727. 1st edn. Folio. 2 vols in one. [14]; [8] pp. 73 + 63 plates. Lacks frontis. Contemp reversed calf, rebacked, sl soiled.
(Bookpress) $2,750 [≈ £1,432]

Ker, John
- The Memoirs ... London: the author, 1726. 1st edns. 2 vols. 8vo. xi,[i],iv,180, [4]; [ii], viii,184, [6],16 pp. [Vol 1] orig bds, uncut, worn, [vol 2] contemp calf, hinges cracked.
(Bookpress) $450 [≈ £234]

Keys, J.
- The Antient Bee-Master's Farewell; or, Full and Plain Directions for the Management of Bees. London: 1796. 1st edn. 8vo. xvi,273 pp. 2 plates. Trifle foxed. Calf, reprd.
(Wheldon & Wesley) £175 [≈ $335]

Keysler, John George
- Travels through Germany, Bohemia, Hungary, Switzerland, Italy, and Lorrain ... Second Edition. London: Linde, Field, 1756-57. 4 vols. 4to. 8 plates. Orig calf, rubbed, jnts cracked but firm, spine ends worn, new labels. (Bickersteth) £285 [≈ $547]

Kidder, Richard
- A Demonstration of the Messias in which the Truth of the Christian Religion is Proved, against all Enemies thereof; but especially against the Jews ... Second Edition revised. London: Osborn ..., 1726. Folio. Contemp calf, upper cvr detached. (Lamb) £35 [≈ $67]

Kilburn, Richard
- Choice Presidents upon all Acts of Parliament, relating to the Office and Duty of a Justice of Peace ... Seventh Edition, very much enlarged ... By G.F. of Grays-Inn, Esq. London: for Jacob Tonson, 1703. 497 pp. Table. Contemp calf, jnts cracking.
(C.R. Johnson) £200 [≈ $383]

Kimber, E. & Johnson, R.
- The Baronetage of England ... and a Dictionary of Heraldry ... London: for G. Woodfall, 1771. 1st edn. 3 vols. 8vo. xii, 530; vii,540; vii,485,32 pp. 36 pp of engvd coats of arms. Contemp tree calf, jnts weakening, spines sl worn. (Young's) £95 [≈ $182]

Kindersley, Mrs Nathaniel Edward
- Letters from the Island of Teneriffe, Brazil, the Cape of Good Hope and the East Indies. London: 1777. [4],302 pp. Engvd frontis. Contemp calf. (McBlain) $475 [≈ £247]

King, Edward
- Morsels of Criticism tending to illustrate some Few Passages in the Holy Scriptures upon Philosophical Principles and an enlarged View of Things. London: J. Nichols, 1788. 4to. Contemp half calf, leather renewed. (Waterfield's) £85 [≈ $163]

King, William
- Doctor King's Apology: or, Vindication of himself from the Several Matters charged on him by the Society of Informers. Oxford: at the Theatre, 1755. Sm marg loss on last leaf. Disbound. (Waterfield's) £25 [≈ $47]
- An Essay on the Origin of Evil ... translated from the Latin with large notes ... the Fourth Edition corrected by Edmund Law. Cambridge: Thirlbourn & Woodyer, 1758. 8vo. Contemp calf, front jnt cracked but sound, sl worn. (Waterfield's) £80 [≈ $153]
- Miscellanies in Prose and Verse. London: Lintott & Clements, [1709]. 1st edn. Large & Fine Paper. 8vo. [xxxii],536,[ii] pp. Occas sl damp stains. Contemp calf, gilt spine, worn but sound. (Sotheran's) £200 [≈ $383]

- Miscellanies in Prose and Verse. London: Lintott & Clements, [1709]. 1st coll edn. Fine Paper issue with no watermark. 8vo. [xxxii], 536 pp. Sep titles to the various works. Lacks Nn1 Table. Contemp calf, sl worn & chipped.
  (Clark) £140 [≈ $268]

Kippis, Andrew
- The Life of Captain James Cook. Dublin: for H. Chamberlaine, W. Colles ..., 1788. Half-title, 527 pp. Contemp calf, red label.
  (C.R. Johnson) £750 [≈ $1,439]
- A Sermon Preached at the Old Jewry, on the Fourth of November, 1788 ... London: Robinson ..., 1788. 1st edn. 8vo. [iv],47,[1 advt] pp. Disbound. *(Young's)* £28 [≈ $53]

Kirby, Joshua
- Dr. Brook Taylor's Method of Perspective made Easy ... Second Edition. London: ptd by W. Craighton, for the author, Ipswich, 1755. 2 vols in one. 4to. [4],iv subscribers, xvi, 78; [2],84,[15] pp, directions leaf. Frontis, 51 plates. Contemp half calf, rebacked. *(Claude Cox)* £320 [≈ $614]

Kirkby, John
- The Capacity and Extent of the Human Understanding; exemplified in the Extraordinary Case of Automathes ... Fourth Edition. Dublin: Faulkner, 1747. 12mo. 228 pp. Title sl soiled & with 2 sm marg tears. Rec half calf. *(Burmester)* £150 [≈ $287]

Kirkman, James Thomas
- Memoirs of the Life of Charles Macklin, Esq. Principally Compiled from His Own Papers and Memorandums ... Forming a ... History of the Stage ... London: Lackington, Allen, 1799. 1st edn. 2 vols. 8vo. Frontis ports. Titles sl offset. Orig bds, rebacked, sl rubbed. *(Dramatis Personae)* $325 [≈ £169]

Kirwan, Richard
- An Essay on the Analysis of Mineral Waters. London: J.W. Myers for D. Bremner, 1799. 1st edn. 8vo. vii,279 pp. Errata slip mtd on last contents page. 7 fldg tables. Sl marg water stain. Orig bds, uncut, lacks most of paper spine. *(Bickersteth)* £170 [≈ $326]
- An Estimate of the Temperature of Different Latitudes. London: J. Davis, for P. Elmsley, 1787. 1st edn. 8vo. viii,114 pp. Title & last page a little dusty. Disbound.
  (Bickersteth) £120 [≈ $230]
- Geological Essays. London: 1799. 1st edn. 8vo. xvi,502 pp. Some marks. Lib stamp on

title verso & last leaf, label on endpaper. Old mrbld bds, rec calf spine.
  (Bow Windows) £305 [≈ $585]
- The Manures most advantageously applicable to the Various Sorts of Soils, and the Causes of their Beneficial Effect ... London: for Vernor & Hood, 1796. 4th edn. 8vo. Title sl soiled. New wraps. *(Stewart)* £85 [≈ $163]

Klimius, Nicholas (pseud.)
- A Journey to the World Under-Ground ... see Holberg, Ludvig.

Knight, Cornelia
- Dinarbas; a Tale: being a Continuation of Rasselas, Prince of Abyssinia. London: for C. Dilly, 1790. 1st edn. 12mo. xxii,336 pp. Contemp sheep, rebacked. Anon.
  (Bickersteth) £200 [≈ $383]

Knowles, Charles
- An Account of the Expedition to Carthagena, with Explanatory Notes and Observations. London: 1743. 58 pp. Half-title. Disbound. Anon. *(Reese)* $350 [≈ £182]

Knox, John
- A Tour through the Highlands of Scotland, and the Hebride Isles, in 1786. London: for J. Walter ..., 1787. Sole edn. 8vo. clxxvi, 276, 103, [1] pp. Sl marked. Orig calf, rebacked.
  (Bickersteth) £140 [≈ $268]

Knox, Robert
- An Historical Relation of the Island of Ceylon ... London: Chiswell, 1681. 1st edn. Folio. [23],189,[2 advt] pp. Fldg map, 15 plates. Occas sl browning, few v sm reprs. Contemp calf, gilt spine, extremities & inner hinges sometime reprd. Wing K.742.
  (Frew Mackenzie) £925 [≈ $1,775]

Knox, Vicesimus
- Essays Moral and Literary. London: for Charles Dilly, 1782. 3rd edn. 2 vols. 12mo. Engvd frontis & vignette to each vol. Contemp calf, spines worn, 1 jnt weak.
  (Young's) £29 [≈ $55]
- Essays, Moral and Literary. The Fourteenth Edition. London: for Charles Dilly, 1795. 2 vols. 12mo. Contemp tree calf.
  (Hannas) £20 [≈ $38]
- Liberal Education: or, A Practical Treatise on the Methods of acquiring Useful and Polite Learning. The Third Edition. London: Charles Dilly, 1781. 8vo. Half-title. Sl intl

staining. Rebound in half calf.
(Jarndyce) **£85 [≈ $163]**
- Liberal Education ... The Eleventh Edition, corrected and enlarged. London: Charles Dilly, 1795. 2 vols in one. 12mo. Sl foxing. Later half calf.   *(Jarndyce)* **£48 [≈ $92]**
- Personal Nobility: or, Letters to a Young Nobleman, on the Conduct of his Studies, and the Dignity of the Peerage. London: Dilly, 1793. 1st edn. 12mo. xxxvi,363 pp. Title vignette. Lacks half-title. Contemp tree calf, gilt spine. Anon.
(Claude Cox) **£45 [≈ $86]**

Knox, William
- Observations upon the Liturgy. With a Proposal for its Reform ... By a Layman of the Church of England ... added, the Journals of the American Convention ... London: for J. Debrett, 1789. 1st edn. 212, [1 errata] pp. V sl foxing. 19th c cloth. Anon.
(Wreden) **$200 [≈ £104]**

Koehoorn, Minno, Baron of
- The New Method of Fortification. Translated from the Original Dutch of the late famous Engineer ... By Thomas Savery Gent. London: for Daniel Midwinter, 1705. 1st edn in English. Folio. xx,182 pp. 16 plates. 1 sm marg hole. Lib stamp on title verso. Rec mor.   *(Young's)* **£150 [≈ $287]**

The Koran
- The Alcoran of Mahomet, translated out of Arabique into French ... and newly Englished, for the satisfaction of all that desire to look into the Turkish Vanities. London: Printed, 1649. 1st edn in English. 8vo. Contemp sheep, rebacked. Wing K.747A.   *(Waterfield's)* **$300 [≈ $575]**
- The Alcoran of Mahomet, translated out of Arabique into French ... and newly Englished, for the satisfaction of all that desire to look into the Turkish Vanities. London: Printed, 1649. 1st English edn, 8vo version. Rebound in calf. Wing K.747A.
(Jarndyce) **£320 [≈ $614]**

Kull, Owen (pseudonym)
- Sandfordiana Hibernica. Volume II. Chapter V. Containing the Writings, Sayings, and Actions of Lady Ann Sandford, during the Month of April, MDCCXLIX. Kinnard: Hughy Macquaid, 1749. 1st edn. 8vo. Disbound.   Unrecorded.   By Oliver Goldsmith?   *(Ximenes)* **$1,750 [≈ £911]**

Labelye, Charles
- A Description of Westminster Bridge. To which are added, an Account of the Methods made use of in laying the Foundation of its Piers ... London: W. Strahan, for the author, 1731. 1st edn. 8vo. 2 plates called for in title but never issued. Disbound.
(Ximenes) **$250 [≈ £130]**
- The Present State of Westminster Bridge ... in a Letter to a Friend. London: J. Millan, 1743. 1st edn. 8vo. 30,[2] pp. V sl waterstain. Later bds. Anon. *(Bookpress)* **$350 [≈ £182]**

La Bruyere, Jean de
- The Works ... In Two Volumes ... Sixth Edition ... London: Curll & Pemberton, 1713. 2 vols. 8vo. [vi],119, [iii],xxiv,58, [ii], xviii, 18, [ii],8,[iv]; [iv],400, [xii] pp. Frontis. Sectional titles in vol 1. Contemp calf, later labels, sl worn.   *(Clark)* **£30 [≈ $57]**
- The Works in Two Volumes. To which is added the Characters of Theophrastus ... By N. Rowe ... London: for J. Bell, 1776. 2 vols. 8vo. ix,[i],311; [iv],247 pp. Sm piece cut from title. Contemp calf, spine hds worn.
(Young's) **£30 [≈ $57]**

La Calprenede, Gaultier de Coste, Sieur de
- Cassandra: the fam'd Romance ... rendred into English by Sir Charles Cotterell ... London: for Humphry Moseley, 1661. Folio. Addtnl engvd title (reprd). Sl dusty at end. Contemp calf, rubbed & grazed, worm at ft of spine, split at hd. Wing L.107.
(Jarndyce) **£140 [≈ $268]**

La Chambre, Marin Cureau de
- The Art how to Know Men. London: T.R. for Thomas Dring, 1665. 1st edn in English. 8vo. Frontis. 19th c red half mor gilt, gilt spine, sl rubbed. Wing L.128.
(Ximenes) **$475 [≈ £247]**

Laclos,   Pierre   Ambroise   Francois, Choderlos de
- Dangerous Connections ... By M. C**** de L***. London: for T. Hookham, 1784. 1st English edn. 4 vols. 12mo. Contemp calf, gilt spines, red & blue labels (1 chipped), vol 1 rebacked to style.
(Jarndyce) **£1,200 [≈ $2,303]**

Laconics ...
- Laconics: or, New Maxims of State and Conversation. Relating to the Affairs and Manners of the Present Times. In Three Parts. London: Thomas Hodgson, 1701. 1st

edn. 8vo. [viii], 120 pp. Rec bds.
(*Burmester*) **£140 [≈ $268]**

The Ladies Calling ...
- See Allestree, Richard.

The Ladies' Library ...
- See Wray, Mary.

La Fare, Charles Augustus de
- Memoirs and Reflections upon the Principal Passages of the Reign of Louis the XIVth ... By Monsieur L.M.D.F. translated from the French. London: for Mary Kettilby ..., 1719. 8vo. Contemp calf, rubbed, sm chip hd of spine. Anon. (*Waterfield's*) **£75 [≈ $143]**

La Fontaine, Jean de
- The Loves of Cupid and Psyche. In Verse and prose ... With a New Life of La Fontaine ... London: for H. Chapelle, 1744. 1st edn in English. 8vo. Lacks half-title. 19th c calf gilt, gilt spine, a.e.g., by Riviere, rebacked, traces of rubbing. (*Ximenes*) **$275 [≈ £143]**

Lairesse, Gerard de
- The Art of Painting, in all its Branches, methodically demonstrated ... Translated by J.J. Fritsch. London: for S. Vandenbergh ..., 1778. 4to. 71 plates. A few spots. Contemp calf, sl rubbed. (*Stewart*) **£300 [≈ $575]**

La Martiniere, Pierre Martin de
- A New Voyage into the Northern Countries, describing the ... Norwegians, Laponians, Kilops, Borandians, Siberians ... London: for John Starkey, 1674. 1st English edn. 12mo. Cancel title. As always lacks A1, presumed blank. Mod calf. Wing L.204.
(*Hannas*) **£1,500 [≈ $2,879]**

Lamb, Charles
- A Tale of Rosamund Gray and Old Blind Margaret. London: for Lee & Hurst, 1798. 1st edn. Probable 2nd issue, with London (not Birmingham) imprint. Sm 8vo. Half calf antique. Cloth case.
(*Ximenes*) **$1,250 [≈ £651]**

Lambarde, William
- Archeion, or, a Discourse upon the High Courts of Justice in England ... Newly corrected, and enlarged ... London: E.P. for Henry Seile, 1635. Some ff browned, stained or dusty at edges. Contemp sheep, sl rubbed, later label. STC 15144.
(*Jarndyce*) **£160 [≈ $307]**

- A Perambulation of Kent ... London: Bollifant, 1596. 2nd edn. 4to. [x],588,[5] pp. Fldg map, full-page map in text. Contemp sheep, backstrip relaid. STC 15176.
(*Vanbrugh*) **£975 [≈ $1,871]**

Lambe, Robert
- An Exact and Circumstantial History of the Battle of Floddon. In Verse. Written about the Time of Queen Elizabeth ... Berwick upon Tweed: R. Taylor, 1774. 1st edn. 8vo. 126,i erratum, 156 pp. Frontis. 1 sm repr. Contemp style half calf, uncut.
(*Young's*) **£110 [≈ $211]**

Lamy, Bernard
- Apparatus Biblicus: or an Introduction to the Holy Scriptures in Three Books ... Done into English from the French ... London: S. Palmer, 1723. 4to. xxviii,540 pp. 30 plates (some fldg). Leather, jnts taped, crnrs bumped. (*Gage*) **£35 [≈ $67]**
- The Art of Speaking: written in French by Messieurs du Port Royal ... Rendred into English. London: for M. Pitt, 1676. 1st edn in English. 8vo. [xvi],1-148, 105-212, 1-164, [xx] pp. Blank leaf before title, 6 advt pp at end. Damp stains. Rec half calf. Wing 307A. Anon. (*Clark*) **£135 [≈ $259]**

Lancaster, Nathaniel
- The Pretty Gentleman: or, Softness of Manners vindicated from the False Ridicule exhibited under the Character of William Fribble, Esq. London: for M. Cooper, 1747. 1st edn. 8vo. Disbound. Anon.
(*Ximenes*) **$375 [≈ £195]**

Landen, John
- A Discourse concerning the Residual Analysis: a New Branch of the Algebraic Art ... London: Nourse, 1758. 1st edn. Sm 4to. Stitched as issued, largely unopened, trifle soiled. (*Ximenes*) **$850 [≈ £442]**
- Mathematical Memoirs respecting a Variety of Subjects ... London: for the author, & sold by J. Nourse, 1780. [With] Vol. II. London: sold by F. Wingrave, 1789. 1st edn. 2 vols in one. 4to. 11 fldg plates. 1st title sl browned, sl foxing. 19th c bds, later calf spine.
(*Ximenes*) **$1,000 [≈ £520]**

Langhorne, John
- Letters between Theodosius and Constantia ... A New Edition. London: Becket & De Hondt, 1770. 2 vols. Sm 8vo. 2 frontis. Orig calf, lacks labels. Anon.

(Bickersteth) **£45 [≈ $86]**

- Owen of Carron: a Poem. London: for Edward & Charles Dilly, 1778. Title vignette. Minor marg reprs to last ff. Disbound.
(Waterfield's) **£125 [≈ $239]**
- The Poetical Works ... London: Becket & De Hondt, 1766. 1st edn. 2 vols. 12mo. [iv],164; [viii], 181, [2] pp. Frontis. Contemp calf, hinges cracked.   *(Bookpress)* **$185 [≈ £96]**
- The Poetical Works ... London: Becket & De Hondt, 1766. 1st coll edn. 2 vols. Sm 8vo. Final advt leaf. Frontis. Contemp roan, rebacked.   *(Hannas)* **£250 [≈ $479]**
- The Viceroy: a Poem. Addressed to the Earl of Halifax. London: for H. Payne & W. Cropley, 1762. 1st edn. 4to. Half-title. Blank lower half of last leaf renewed (no loss of text). Disbound, stitching loose. Anon.
(Ximenes) **$100 [≈ £52]**

Langley, Batty
- The City and Country Builder's and Workman's Treasury of Designs ... London: S. Harding, 1750. 3rd edn. 4to. [ii],22 pp. 186 + 14 (appendix) plates. Contemp calf, rebacked, minor wear to tips.
(Bookpress) **$950 [≈ £494]**

Langley, Batty & Langley, Thomas
- The Builder's Jewel; or, The Youth's Instructor, and Workman's remembrancer ... London: Longman ..., 1797. Sm 4to. iv,5-46 pp. Engvd frontis, 99 numbered engvd plates. F4 blank. Contemp calf, gilt spine (sl worn).
(Vanbrugh) **£195 [≈ $374]**
- Gothic Architecture, Improved by Rules and Proportions. In Many Grand Designs ... London: John Millam, 1747. 4to. Engvd title, 64 engvd plates (numbered A-B,1-62). Sl foxing throughout, some plates sl water stained, 2 sm reprs. Half mor.
(Sotheran's) **£975 [≈ $1,871]**
- Gothic Architecture, Improved by Rules and Proportions In Many Grand Designs ... London: I. & J. Taylor, [ca 1787]. 3rd edn. Lge 4to. 7, [1] pp. Engvd title (sm tear in gutter marg), 64 plates. Old sheep, recased.
(Bookpress) **$1,350 [≈ £703]**

Lansdowne, George Granville, Lord
- Poems upon Several Occasions. The Second Edition. London: Tonson, 1716. 12mo. Disbound.   *(Waterfield's)* **£30 [≈ $57]**

La Roche-Guilhem, Anne de
- The History of Female Favourites. London:

Parker, 1722. 8vo. calf, front cvr detached. Anon.   *(Rostenberg & Stern)* **$200 [≈ £104]**

La Solle, Henri Francois de
- Memoirs of a Man of Pleasure, or the Adventures of Versorand. London: for T. Osborne, 1751. 1st edn. 2 vols. 12mo. 19th c mor, t.e.g., trifle rubbed. Purported translation by "Sir" John Hill.
(Ximenes) **$1,750 [≈ £911]**

Latimer, Hugh
- Sermons on Various Subjects ... To which is prefixed his Life. London: T. Pilcher, 1788. 2 vols in one. 8vo. [8],282,297,index pp. Old tree calf, cloth spine, crnrs worn & bumped.
(Humber) **£35 [≈ $67]**

Latin and English Poems ...
- See Loveling, Benjamin.

Latrobe, B.H.
- Characteristic Anecdotes, and Miscellaneous Authentic Papers, tending to illustrate the Character of Frederic II, late King of prussia. Dublin: for L. White ..., 1788. Cr 8vo. Name cut from title, marg of E9 torn touching text. Half mor, rubbed.   *(Stewart)* **£35 [≈ $67]**

Lauderdale, James Maitland, 8th Earl of
- Letters to the Peers of Scotland. London: for G.G. & J. Robinson, 1794. 1st edn. 8vo. Half-title. Final errata leaf. New bds.
(Georges) **£150 [≈ $287]**

The Laughing Philosopher ...
- The Laughing Philosopher. Dublin: for James Williams, 1777. 244 pp. Rebound in calf.   *(C.R. Johnson)* **£85 [≈ $163]**

Laurence, Edward
- A Dissertation on Estates upon Lives and Years whether in Lay or Church-Hands. With an Exact Calculation of their Real Worth, by proper Tables ... London: Knapton, 1730. 64 pp. Rebound in bds.
(C.R. Johnson) **£285 [≈ $547]**
- The Duty of a Steward to his Lord ... London: for John Shuckburgh, 1727. 1st edn. 4to. [iv],[xvi],212 pp. Dble-page map, dble-page plate. Contemp calf, rebacked.
(Vanbrugh) **£295 [≈ $566]**

Laurence, John
- The Fruit-Garden Kalendar; or, a Summary of the Art of Managing the Fruit-Garden ...

Appendix of the usefulness of the Barometer. London: for Bernard Lintot, 1718. 1st edn. 8vo. Half-title. 3 ctlg pp. Fldg frontis, 1 text ill. Mod bds. *(Stewart)* £100 [≈ $191]

Lavater, Johann Caspar

- Aphorisms on Man. Translated [by J.H. Fuseli] from the Original Manuscript ... Third Edition. London: for J. Johnson, 1794. 224 pp. Engvd frontis by William Blake after Fuseli. Contemp tree calf, red label.
(C.R. Johnson) £220 [≈ $422]

- Essays on Physiognomy ... Abridged from Mr. Holcroft's Translation. Boston: William Spotswood & David West, (1794). 1st Amer edn. 12mo. [6],272 pp. Engvd title, 7 plates. Minor foxing. Contemp calf.
(Karmiole) $300 [≈ £156]

Lavoisier, A.

- Elements of Chemistry. Translated from the French by Robert Kerr. Edinburgh: William Creech, 1796. 2nd edn. 8vo. 592 pp. 2 fldg tables, 13 fldg plates. Contemp calf, gilt spine. *(Gemmary)* $650 [≈ £338]

- Elements of Chemistry. Translated from the French by Robert Kerr. Edinburgh: William Creech, 1799. 4th edn. 8vo. 592 pp. 2 fldg tables, 13 fldg plates (foxed). Contemp calf, sl shaken & worn. *(Gemmary)* $450 [≈ £234]

Law Quibbles ...

- Law Quibbles: or, a Treatise of the Evasions, Tricks, Turns and Quibbles, commonly used in the Profession of the Law ... London: Nutt, Gosling ..., 1736. 4th edn, enlgd. [Blank], [8],132,135, [12],72, [blank] pp. Sl dusty & browned. New qtr calf.
(Meyer Boswell) $750 [≈ £390]

Law, William

- An Appeal to all that doubt, or disbelieve the Truths of the Gospel ... Second Edition. London: Innys & Richardson, 1756. Contemp calf, rebacked, crnrs reprd.
(Waterfield's) £85 [≈ $163]

- A Practical Treatise upon Christian Perfection. London: William & John Innys, 1726. 1st edn. 8vo. [viii],546,[ii] pp. Blank before title, final advt leaf. Contemp calf, extremities sl worn. *(Clark)* £100 [≈ $191]

- A Practical Treatise upon Christian Perfection ... The Second Edition. London: Innys, 1728. 8vo. Contemp calf, rebacked.
(Waterfield's) £90 [≈ $172]

- A Serious Call to a Devout and Holy Life ...

The Eighth Edition. London: J. Richardson, 1761. 8vo. [6],354 pp. Wormed in lower inner marg towards end. Polished calf, jnts cracked.
(Humber) £35 [≈ $67]

The Law-French Dictionary ...

- The Law-French Dictionary alphabetically digested ... added, The Law-Latin Dictionary ... The Second Edition, corrected and enlarg'd. In the Savoy: Nutt, Gosling ..., 1718. 8vo. Contemp calf, rubbed, splits hd of spine, lacks label. *(Jarndyce)* £120 [≈ $230]

Lawrence, Herbert

- The Life and Adventures of Common Sense: an Historical Allegory. London: for Montagu Lawrence, 1769. 1st edn. 2 vols. 8vo. Contemp calf, gilt spine, mor labels, minor rubbing. Anon. *(Ximenes)* $1,500 [≈ £781]

Lawrence, Thomas Dawson

- The Miscellaneous Works. Published for the Benefit of the Sunday School at Lawrence Town, County Down. Dublin: R. Marchbank, 1789. 99 pp. Contemp calf, red label, rebacked, some signs of use.
(C.R. Johnson) £240 [≈ $460]

Lawrence, William

- Two Great Questions Determined by the Principles of Reason & Divinity ... London: for Richard Janeway, 1681. Folio. [4],35 pp. Disbound. Wing L.692A. Anon.
(Jarndyce) £85 [≈ $163]

Lawson, John

- The History of Carolina; containing the Exact Description and Natural History of that Country ... London: Taylor & Baker, 1714. 1st edn, 2nd issue. Sm 4to. [3] ff,258,[1] pp. Fldg map (sl foxed), plate. Contemp panelled calf, rebacked, crnrs rubbed.
(Chapel Hill) $8,500 [≈ £4,427]

Lawson, William

- A New Orchard and Garden, or the Best Way of Planting ... With The Country Housewifes Garden for Hearbes ... London: Edward Griffin, 1638. 3rd edn, enlgd. Sm 8vo. [viii], 123 pp. Ills. Old reprs to last 12 ff. Disbound.
(Bookpress) $450 [≈ £234]

The Layman's Vindication of the Church of England

- See Defoe, Daniel.

Layng, Henry
- The Rod, a Poem. Oxford: W. Jackson, 1754. 4to. 46 pp. Frontis. Occas sl dusty or spotted. Lib stamp on title verso. 19th c buckram.
  (Hollett) **£180 [≈ $345]**

Leake, John
- The Scholar's Manual. Being a Collection of Meditations... design'd for Establishing and Promoting Christian Principles and Practice ... By a Gentleman of Oxford. London: Rivington, 1733. 1st edn. 8vo. x, [xxiv], 312 pp, 2 advt ff. Orig calf, sm crack to jnt, lacks label.   *(Bickersteth)* **£165 [≈ $316]**

Learmont, John
- Poems Pastoral, Satirical, Tragic, and Comic. Carefully corrected by the Author. Edinburgh: for the author, 1791. 414 pp. Subscribers. Som ff in 1st gathering affected by coffee stains. Contemp qtr calf, rebacked.
  (C.R. Johnson) **£120 [≈ $230]**

Lechevalier, Jean Baptiste
- Description of the Plain of Troy: with a Map of that Region ... Edinburgh: T. Cadell, 1791. 1st edn. 4to. [iii]-xv [ie xix], 154, [10] pp. 4 maps (3 fldg). Contemp calf, front hinge cracking.   *(Bookpress)* **$425 [≈ £221]**

Le Clerc, Jean
- A Compendium of Universal History ... Done into English. London: 1699. 1st edn in English. 8vo. [viii],195,[29] pp. Frontis. Browned. Contemp sheep, backstrip relaid, crnrs sl worn. Wing L.814.
  (Clark) **£125 [≈ $239]**

Le Clerc, Sebastian
- Practical Geometry: or, a New and Easy Method of Treating that Art. London: T. & J. Bowles, 1742. 4th edn. 12mo. [ii],185,[7] pp. Contemp calf, rebacked, later endpapers.
  (Bookpress) **$425 [≈ £221]**

Le Courayer, Pierre Francois
- A Defence of the Dissertation on the Validity of the English ordination ... London: Innys, 1728. 1st edn. 2 vols. 8vo. xx, 520,4 advt; [vi], 2 advt,584 pp. Contemp panelled calf, spine hds nicked. Anon.   *(Young's)* **£100 [≈ $191]**

Lee, James
- An Introduction to Botany. Containing an Explanation of the Theory of that Science; extracted from the Works of Dr. Linnaeus ... Third Edition, corrected, with large

Additions. London: 1776. 8vo. xxiv,432 pp. 12 plates. Contemp calf, hinges cracking but sound.   *(Claude Cox)* **£55 [≈ $105]**

Lee, Nathaniel
- Caesar Borgia; Son of Pope Alexander the Sixth: A Tragedy. London: Bentley & Magnes, 1680. 1st edn. Sm 4to. [viii],70,[2] pp. Disbound.   *(Bookpress)* **$185 [≈ £96]**
- Lucius Junius Brutus; Father of his Country. A Tragedy ... London: Tonson, 1681. 1st' edn. 4to. [viii],72,[2] pp. Browned. Rec bds. Wing L.852.   *(Clark)* **£65 [≈ $124]**
- Lucius Junius Brutus; Father of his Country. A Tragedy. London: Tonson, 1681. 1st edn. Sm 4to. [viii],72,[2] pp. Disbound.
  (Bookpress) **$185 [≈ £96]**
- Theodosius: or, The Force of Love. A Tragedy ... London: Th. Chapman, 1692. 4to. [iv], 60,[ii] pp. Browned. Disbound. Wing L.879.   *(Clark)* **£32 [≈ $61]**

Lee, Sophia
- The Recess; or, a Tale of the Time. London: Cadell, 1792. 4th edn, crrctd. 3 vols. 12mo. Half-titles. Contemp tree calf, gilt spines, sl rubbed, sl worn at extremities.
  (Burmester) **£150 [≈ $287]**

Leeds, Francis Osborne, 5th Duke of Leeds
- An Address to the Independent Members of both Houses of Parliament ... London: for R. Faulder ..., 1782. 1st edn. 8vo. [iv],26 pp. Wraps. Anon.   *(Young's)* **£30 [≈ $57]**

Leeds, Sir Thomas Osborne, Duke of
- The Thoughts of a Private Person; About the Justice of the Gentlemens undertaking at York. Nov. 1688 ... London: Printed in the Year, 1689. Only edn. 4to. [iv],26 pp. Lib stamp on title verso, some marks & cropping. Later wraps. Wing L.923A. Anon.
  (Clark) **£60 [≈ $115]**

L'Enclos, Ninon de
- The Memoirs ... with her Letters to Monsr. de St. Evremond and to the Marquis de Sevigne ... translated from the French by a Lady [Elizabeth Griffith] ... London: Dodsley & Johnstone, 1776. 2 vols. 8vo. Contemp tree calf, gilt spines, dble mor labels.
  (Waterfield's) **£200 [≈ $383]**

L'Estrange, Hamon
- The Reign of King Charles: an History ... London: E.C. for Edward Dod ..., 1655. 1st

edn. 4to. [viii],266,[vi] pp. Engvd frontis. 1 sm marg repr. Contemp panelled calf, red speckled edges, jnts split at ends. Wing L.1189. Anon. *(Sotheran's)* £285 [≈ $547]

L'Estrange, Sir Roger
- Considerations upon a Printed Sheet entituled the Speech of the late Lord Russel to the Sheriffs ... London: T.B. for Joanna Brome, 1683. 1st edn. 4to. 52 pp. Outer ff dusty, lib stamp on title verso. Disbound. Wing L.1230. Anon. *(Clark)* £50 [≈ $95]
- A Discourse of the Fishery ... London: for Henry Brome, 1674. 1st edn. 4to. [ii],10 pp. Title sl dust soiled, 2 sm marg stains. New bds. Wing L.1236.
(Pickering) $1,000 [≈ £520]
- The Dissenter's Sayings, In Requital for L'Estrange's Sayings. Published in Their Own Words, for the Information of the People. London: for Henry Brome, 1681. 1st edn. Sm 4to. [iv],46 pp. Disbound. Wing L.1240. *(Finch)* £60 [≈ $115]
- The Observator, in Dialogue. London: J. Bennet for William Abington, 1684-87. 1st coll edn. 3 vols in 2. Folio. 2 port frontis. Contemp calf, extremities sl worn, minor loss at spine ends. *(Clark)* £550 [≈ $1,055]
- A Reply to the Reasons of the Oxford-Clergy against Addressing. London: for Henry Hills, 1687. 4to. 20 pp. Disbound. Wing L.1297. Anon. *(Jarndyce)* £30 [≈ $57]
- See also under Aesop; Seneca.

Leigh, Charles
- The Natural History of Lancashire, Cheshire and the Peak in Derbyshire ... Oxford: 1700. Folio. Engvd port, title, imprimatur, dble page map, 24 plates. Occas offsetting. Half calf, rebacked, crnrs reprd.
(Henly) £315 [≈ $604]
- The Natural History of Lancashire, Cheshire, and the Peak, in Derbyshire ... Oxford: for the author, 1700. Folio. [xx],4 subscribers, [2 advt],112,[36 index] pp. Port, map, 24 plates. Contemp polished calf gilt, edges & hinges worn, jnts cracked. *(Hollett)* £280 [≈ $537]

Leland, John
- A View of the Principal Deistical Writers [Part 1] ... in Several Letters to a Friend. London: 1754. 8vo. Occas sl marg spotting. Owner's name cut from title. Contemp calf, hd of spine chipped. *(Buccleuch)* £60 [≈ $115]

Le Lievre, -
- Observations on the Baume de Vie, first Discovered by Mr Le Lievre, the King's Apothecary at Paris ... London: ptd by W. Griffin ..., 1765. 8vo. Title,49,[iii] pp. 2 sm tears reprd. Mod wraps.
(Bickersteth) £145 [≈ $278]

Lemery, Nicholas
- A Course of Chymistry. Containing an easie Method of preparing those Chymical Medicins which are used in Physick ... Translated by Walter Harris, M.D. London: 1686. 2nd edn in English. 8vo. [28], 548,[14], 2 advt pp. Imprimatur leaf. 3 plates. Prelims browned. Half calf.
(Rootenberg) $650 [≈ £338]

Lemery, Nicolas (attributed author)
- Modern Curiosities of Art & Nature ... London: for Matthew Gilliflower, & James Partridge, 1685. 1st edn in English. 12mo. Engvd title with facing leaf of explanation. Contemp calf, rebacked, edges rubbed, inner hinges strengthened. Wing L.1041.
(Ximenes) $1,750 [≈ £911]

Lemnius, Levinus
- An Herbal for the Bible ... Drawen into English by Thomas Newton. London: Edmund Bollifant, 1587. 8vo. [6],287,[9] pp, last page blank. With 1st & last blank ff. Q8 in photostat facs. Contemp limp vellum, browned. STC 15454.
(Hemlock) $750 [≈ £390]

Lempriere, John
- Bibliotheca Classica; or, A Classical Dictionary, containing a Full Account of all the Proper Names mentioned in Antient Authors ... Third Edition, greatly enlarged. London: Cadell & Davies, 1797. 8vo. Contemp calf, red label, sl rubbed.
(Jarndyce) £75 [≈ $143]

Lendrum, J.
- A Concise and Impartial History of the American Revolution, to which is prefixed, a General History of North and South America ... Account of the Discovery and Settlement of North America. Boston: 1795. 2 vols. [8], 13-339; [8],13,411 pp. Leather backed cloth bds. *(Reese)* $150 [≈ £78]

Leonardo da Vinci
- A Treatise of Painting, translated from the Original Italian ... prefixed the Author's Life.

London: Senex & Taylor, 1721. 1st English edn. 8 ff, 189 pp, 9 ff. Port, 35 engvd plates. Contemp calf, rebacked, sl worn.
(Ars Artis) **£450 [≈ $863]**
- A Treatise on Painting ... to which is added a Life of the Author. London: I. & J. Taylor, 1796. 2nd English edn. xii,189 pp,10 ff. 29 plates. Sl stain blank marg 1st ff. Cloth, sl worn.   *(Ars Artis)* **£95 [≈ $182]**

Le Poivre, M.
- Travels of a Philosopher: or Observations on the Manners and Arts of Various Nations in Africa and Asia ... Dublin: for P. & W. Wilson ..., 1770. 1st Dublin edn. 12mo. vi, [ii], 183 pp. Contemp calf.
(Young's) **£230 [≈ $441]**

Le Sage, Alain Rene
- See The History of Vanillo Gonzales ... .

Leslie, Charles
- The Good Old Cause, Further Discuss'd. In a Letter to the Author of the Jacobite's Hopes Reviv'd ... London: printed ..., 1710. 1st edn. 8vo. 32,4 pp. 1st & last ff soiled. Disbound. Anon   *(Young's)* **£40 [≈ $76]**
- The History of Sin and Heresie attempted ... in some Meditations upon the Feast of St. Michael and all Angels. London: H. Hindmarsh, 1698. 1st edn. 4to. [viii],60 pp. Some spotting & browning. Disbound. Wing L.1135.   *(Clark)* **£36 [≈ $69]**
- Satan Disrobed from his Disguise of Light: or, The Quakers Last Shift to Cover their Monstrous Heresies ... Second Edition, with some Improvements ... London: C. Brome ..., 1698. 4to. [xii],100 pp. Minor stain, 1 sm repr. Disbound. Wing L.1151.
(Clark) **£24 [≈ $46]**

Leti, Gregorio
- Il Putanismo di Roma, or the History of the Whores and Whoredom of the Popes, Cardinals and Clergy of Rome ... Now made English by I.D. London: ptd 1670. 8vo. [vi], 136 pp. Frontis. Sm hole in 1 leaf. Polished calf antique, t.e.g., by Hatchards. Wing L.1340A. Anon   *(Bickersteth)* **£360 [≈ $691]**

Letter(s) ...
- A Letter Concerning Libels, Warrants, the Seizure of Papers, and Sureties for the Peace of Behaviours ... Fourth Edition, enlarged and improved. London: for J. Almon, 1765. Disbound.   *(Waterfield's)* **£40 [≈ $76]**

- A Letter from a Gentleman in Scotland to his Friend at London ... see Defoe, Daniel.
- A Letter from a Gentleman in Town to a Friend in the Country, concerning the Present State of the Fishing-Copartnery in North-Britain. Edinburgh: ptd in the year, 1723. 4to. 16 pp. Disbound.
(C.R. Johnson) **£280 [≈ $537]**
- A Letter from a Gentleman in Town to his Friend in the Country, recommending the Necessity of Frugality. London: for W. Webb ..., 1751. 3rd edn. 8vo. 24 pp. Marg of last leaf sl defective.   *(Young's)* **£20 [≈ $38]**
- A Letter to a Member of Parliament. Concerning the Present State of Affairs at Home and Abroad. By a True Lover of the People. London: for T. Cooper ..., 1740. 1st edn. 8vo. [iv],60 pp. Half-title. End ff trifle dusty. Disbound.   *(Young's)* **£45 [≈ $86]**
- A Letter to Monsieur Boileau Depreaux ... see Prior, Matthew.
- A Letter to the Oxford Tories. By An Englishman. London: for M. Cooper, 1750. 8vo. Mod sheep. Cordeaux & Merry attribute to Henry Brooke. *(Waterfield's)* **£40 [≈ $76]**
- A Letter to the Reverend Dr. Lowth ... see Bridle, John.
- A Letter to the Right Honourable William Pulteney Esq occasion'd by a Bill depending in the House of Commons for raising One Hundred Thousand Pounds upon the Roman-Catholicks. By a Member of the House of Commons. London: 1723. Folio. Sl wear. Sewn as issued.
(Waterfield's) **£225 [≈ $431]**
- A Letter to the Right Honourable The Lord B----y. Being an Inquiry into the Merit of his Defence of Minorca. London: for R. May ..., 1757. 1st edn. 8vo. [iv],47 pp. Stitched as issued.   *(Young's)* **£70 [≈ $134]**
- A Letter to the Town, concerning the Man and the Bottle ... London: W. Reeve ..., 1749. Only edn. 8vo. 20 pp. Disbound.
(Young's) **£85 [≈ $163]**
- A Letter to the Whigs. London: for J. Almon, 1779. 1st edn. 8vo. Disbound.
(Ximenes) **£350 [≈ £182]**
- Letters and Tracts on the Choice of Company ... see Bolton, Robert.
- Letters between Theodosius and Constantia ... see Langhorne, John.
- Letters concerning the Present State of England. Particularly respecting the Politics, Arts, Manners, and Literature of the Times. London: for J. Almon, 1772. 1st edn. 8vo.

Usual gap in pagination between pp ii & 9. Contemp calf, gilt spine (a bit rubbed).
(Ximenes) **$600 [≈ £312]**
- Letters from a Farmer in Pennsylvania ... see Dickinson, John.
- Letters from Edinburgh ... see Topham, Edward.
- Letters from Paris, during the Summer of 1791 ... London: for J. Debrett ..., 1792. 1st edn. 8vo. xx,347 pp. Frontis. Title & frontis sl spotted. Old calf, sl rubbed, back jnt partly split. (Young's) **£58 [≈ $111]**
- Letters from the Manuscript in the Library at Woburn Abbey ... see Russell, Rachel, Lady.
- The Letters of Atticus ... see Cooke, Thomas.

- Letters of Religion and Virtue, to several Gentlemen and Ladies. With some short Reflections on Divers Subjects. London: for Henry Bonwicke, 1695. Only edn. Imprimatur leaf, 216 pp. Contemp calf, rebacked. Ducal b'plates. Wing L.1786.
(C.R. Johnson) **£165 [≈ $316]**
- Letters supposed to have been written by Yorick and Eliza ... see Combe, William.
- Letters written by a Peruvian Princess ... see Grafigny, Francoise P. Huguet de.

Lettice, John
- Letters on a Tour through Various Parts of Scotland, in the Year 1792. London: for T. Cadell, 1794. 1st edn. 8vo. Sl foxing. Contemp half calf. (Ximenes) **$325 [≈ £169]**

Lettsom, J.C.
- The Naturalist's and Traveller's Companion, containing Instructions for Collecting and Preserving Objects of Natural History. London: 1774. 2nd edn. 8vo. xvi, 89, [8] pp. Cold frontis, cold title vignette. Half calf.
(Wheldon & Wesley) **£85 [≈ $163]**

Levaillant, Auguste-Nicolas
- New Travels into the Interior Part of Africa. By Way of the Cape of Good Hope in the Years 1783, 84 & 85 ... London: Robinson, 1798. 1st edn. 3 vols. 8vo. xlix,288; 383; 488 pp. Fldg map, 22 plates (5 fldg). Map torn but complete, some browning. Calf, 4 bds loose.
(Terramedia) **$300 [≈ £156]**
- Travels into the Interior Parts of Africa ... Translated from the French ... Perth: ptd by R. Morison Junior ..., 1791. 2 vols. 8vo. [iv], 207; 204 pp. 2 frontis, 4 plates. Faint damp stain on 2 plates. Orig tree calf, gilt spines.

(Vanbrugh) **£175 [≈ $335]**

Levesque de Pouilly, Louis Jean
- The Theory of Agreeable Sensations: in which the Laws observed by Nature in the Distribution of Pleasure are Investigated ... New Edition. London: W. Owen, 1774. 216,6 advt pp. Contemp tree calf, red label. Anon.
(C.R. Johnson) **£185 [≈ $355]**

Lewis, Matthew Gregory
- The Castle Spectre: A Drama ... London: for J. Bell ..., 1798. 1st edn. 8vo. viii,102 pp. Outer ff soiled. Disbound.
(Young's) **£30 [≈ $57]**

Lewis, Thomas
- Origines Hebraeae: The Antiquities of the Hebrew Republick. London: Illidge & Hooke, 1724-25. 1st edn. 4 vols. Post 8vo. Fldg engvd plate, engvd decs. Sl browning. Contemp Cambridge calf, contrasting labels, sl rubbed. (Ash) **£250 [≈ $479]**
- The Scourge in Vindication of the Church of England. London: Printed in the Year, 1717. 1st coll edn. 12mo. [ii],368 pp. Some staining at ends. Rec half calf. Anon.
(Clark) **£65 [≈ $124]**

Lewis, William
- The New Dispensatory: containing I. The Elements of Pharmacy. II. The Materia Medica. III. The Preparations and Compositions of the new London and Edinburgh Pharmacopoeias ... London: Nourse, 1785. 5th edn. 8vo. x,[v],688 pp. Sl marg water stain. Orig calf, sl rubbed.
(Bickersteth) **£65 [≈ $124]**

Leybourn, William
- The Complete Surveyor: Containing the whole Art of Surveying of Land ... London: 1653. 1st edn. Sm folio. [xii],279 pp. Port frontis, num w'cut ills. Sm burn hole in A4. Orig vellum, top edge front cvr sl damaged. Wing L.1907. (Vanbrugh) **£525 [≈ $1,007]**
- Compleat Surveyor: or, the Whole Art of Surveying of Land. London: Samuel Ballard, 1722. 5th edn. Folio. Frontis, 14 fldg plates. Lib stamp & b'plate. Contemp calf, rebacked.
(Bookpress) **$575 [≈ £299]**
- An Introduction to Astronomy and Geography ... London: 1675. 8vo. Fldg plate. Occas headline shaved. Contemp calf, rebacked. Wing L. 1915.
(Waterfield's) **£125 [≈ $239]**

Life ...
- The Life and Adventures of Common Sense
... see Lawrence, Herbert.
- The Life and Astonishing Adventures of John
Daniel ... see Morris, Ralph (supposed
author).
- The Life and Reign of King Richard the
Second ... see Howard, Sir Robert.
- The Life of Mr. Richard Savage ... see
Johnson, Samuel.
- The Life of Mr. Thomas Betterton ... see
Gildon, Charles.

Lightfoot, John
- The Temple Service as it stood in the Dayes
of Our Saviour. London: R. Cotes for Andrew
Crook, (1649). 4to. [12],200 pp. Sl worn.
Contemp calf, rebacked. Wing L.2072.
(Humber) £85 [≈ $163]

Lilly, W. & Colet, J.
- A Short Introduction of Grammar. Generally
to be used; compiled and set forth for the ...
Knowledge of the Latin Tongue. Oxford:
1714. 8vo. [14],62, blank leaf, title leaf, 206
pp. Contemp calf, hd of spine worn.
(Spelman) £70 [≈ $134]
- A Short Introduction to Grammar. Generally
to be used, compiled and set forth for the ...
Knowledge of the Latin Tongue. London:
Buckley & Longman, 1760. Part 1 only. Sm
8vo. [10], 62 pp. W'cut title. Sm hole without
loss to title & A2. Orig drab bd cvrs.
(Spelman) £60 [≈ $115]

Lilly, William
- Mr. William Lilly's True History of King
James the First, and King Charles the First ...
London: J. Roberts, 1715. 12mo. [ii],vii, [i],
108 pp. Lacks intl blank. Browned. 19th c
half calf, gilt spine, sl rubbed.
(Clark) £75 [≈ $143]

Lind, J.
- An Essay on Diseases incidental to Europeans
in Hot Climates with the Methods of
preventing their Fatal Consequences.
London: 1792. 5th edn. xvi,366 pp. Leather,
new label, spine sl rubbed.
(Whitehart) £190 [≈ $364]

Lindsay, David
- The Works of the Famous and Worthy
Knight, Sir David Lindsay ... Newly
Corrected ... Augmented ... Edinburgh: 1720.
2nd edn. 12mo. 264 pp. Orig calf, spine sl

worn, hinges cracked but firm.
(Vanbrugh) £95 [≈ $182]

Ling, Nicholas
- Politeuphia, Wits Common-Wealth. Newly
Corrected and Amended. London: W.S. for I.
Smethwicke, [1620?]. "10th edn". 12mo. [8],
513,[7] pp. Title soiled & backed. Old calf,
rubbed, hinges partly cracked but sound.
STC 15688. Anon. *(Karmiole)* $250 [≈ £130]

Linnaeus, C.
- Miscellaneous Tracts relating to Natural
History, Husbandry, and Physick, to which is
added the Calendar of Flora, by B.
Stillingfleet. London: 1762. 2nd edn. 8vo.
[xxxii], 391 pp. 11 plates. Contemp calf.
(Wheldon & Wesley) £75 [≈ $143]
- Miscellaneous Tracts ... see also Stillingfleet,
B.
- A System of Vegetables ... Translated ... By a
Botanical Society of Lichfield. Lichfield:
1783. 2 vols. 8vo. Half-titles (sl soiled). 11
plates. Sm ink spot on vol 2 title. Mod qtr
calf.   *(Wheldon & Wesley)* £250 [≈ $479]

Lipscomb, William
- Verses on the Beneficial Effects of
Inoculation, which obtained One of the
Chancellor's Prizes at the University of
Oxford in the Year 1772. Now republished ...
London: J. Davis, 1793. 4to. 8 pp. Disbound.
(C.R. Johnson) £275 [≈ $527]

Little, Janet
- The Poetical Works of Janet Little, the
Scotch Milkmaid. Air: John & Peter Wilson,
1792. 1st edn. 8vo. Subscribers. Contemp
half calf, worn.   *(Hannas)* £280 [≈ $537]

Littleton, Sir Thomas
- Littletons Tenvres in English, lately perused
and amended. London: Companie of
Stationers, 1616. Sm 8vo. 142,[2] ff. Black
Letter. Contemp style calf. STC 15781.
(Vanbrugh) £225 [≈ $431]

The Lively Oracles Given to Us ...
- See Allestree, Richard.

LL., M.
- Men-Miracles. With other Poemes. By
M.LL. ... see Llewellyn, Martin.

Llewellyn, Martin
- Men-Miracles. With other Poemes. By

M.LL. St. of Ch. Ch. in Oxon. London: for
Will. Shears Junior, 1656. Sm 8vo. [xvi],112
pp. Lacks intl blank. Occas sl staining.
Prelims erratically sgnd. Contemp sheep,
rebacked, crnrs sl worn. Wing L.2626.
(Clark) **£220 [≈ $422]**

Lloyd, Charles
- The Anatomy of a Late Negociation.
Earnestly Addressed to the Serious
Consideration of the People of Great-Britain
... London: for J. Wilkie ..., 1763. 1st edn.
4to. 28 pp. No half-title. New qtr calf. Anon.
(Young's) **£35 [≈ $67]**
- The Anatomy of a Late Negociation earnestly
Addressed to the Serious Consideration of the
People of Great-Britain. London: by J.
Wilkie, 1763. 4to. Half-title. Disbound.
Anon. *(Waterfield's)* **£65 [≈ $124]**

Lloyd, David
- Fair Warnings to a Careless World ...
London: for Samuel Speed, 1665. 1st edn. Sm
4to. Advt leaf at end. Margs trimmed sl close.
Buckram. Wing L.2640A. Anon.
(Ximenes) **$250 [≈ £130]**
- Memoirs of the Lives, Actions, Suffering and
Death of the Noble Personages that suffered
Death ... for the Protestant Religion ...
1637-1660 ... London: 1668. Sm folio.
[16],708,[1] pp. Port. Inner edge 1st 4 ff
strengthened. 19th c cloth. Wing L.2642.
(Humber) **£98 [≈ $188]**

Lloyd, John
- Thesaurus Ecclesiasticus: An improved
edition of The Liber Valorum ... With an
Appendix ... London: Longman ..., 1796. 1st
edn. 8vo. xi,504 pp. Orig bds, uncut &
unopened. *(Young's)* **£65 [≈ $124]**

Lloyd, Robert
- Poems ... London: for the author, by Dryden
Leach; & sold by T. Davies, 1762. 1st edn.
4to. xix,[i],277 pp. Half-title. Subscribers.
Minor paper reprs. Some tiny worming at hd.
Contemp calf, lacks label, rubbed, extremities
worn, jnts cracking at ft but firm.
(Finch) **£95 [≈ $182]**
- The Poetical Works ... prefixed an Account of
the Life and Writings of the Author. By W.
Kenrick ... London: T. Evans, 1774. 2 vols.
8vo. [iv],xliii,[i],195; [iv],iv,242,[2 advt] pp.
Half-titles. Title vignettes. Contemp calf,
rebacked. *(Burmester)* **£110 [≈ $211]**

Lobb, T.
- A Practical Treatise of Painful Distempers,
with some Effectual Methods of curing them,
exemplified in a great Variety of suitable
Histories. London: 1739. xxx,[2], 320, [14]
pp. Contemp calf, rebacked, edges & crnrs
worn. *(Whitehart)* **£120 [≈ $230]**

Lobo, Jerome
- A Voyage to Abyssinia ... From the French
[translated by Samuel Johnson]. London
[actually Birmingham: for Thomas Warren]:
for A. Bettesworth & C. Hitch, 1735. 1st edn
in English. 8vo. xii,396,[viii] pp. Unusually
clean copy. Contemp calf, rubbed, sl surface
damage *(Finch)* **£600 [≈ $1,151]**

Lochee, Lewis
- An Essay on Military Education. London: for
the author ..., 1776. 2nd edn. 8vo. 106 pp.
Text ends on p 106 in mid-sentence & with a
catchword, but the verso is blank. Disbound.
(Young's) **£50 [≈ $95]**

Locke, John
- The Conduct of the Understanding. To
which is added, An Abstract of Mr. Locke's
Essay on Human Understanding. Cambridge:
J. Archdeacon, for J. Nicholson ..., 1781. 4
advt pp. Rebound in half calf, a.e.g.
(Jarndyce) **£140 [≈ $268]**
- An Essay concerning Humane Understanding
... The Third Edition. London: Churchill,
Manship, 1695. Folio. [xl],407,[13] pp. Port
frontis. 2 sm tears, occas sl marg damp stain,
occas sl soiling. Mod calf. Wing L.2741.
(Clark) **£320 [≈ $614]**
- An Essay concerning Humane Understanding
... The Third Edition. London: Churchill,
Manship, 1695. Folio. Frontis. Contemp calf,
front jnt cracked, minor loss at hd of jnts.
Wing L.2741. *(Waterfield's)* **£635 [≈ $1,219]**
- An Essay concerning Human Understanding
... Eleventh Edition. London: for Edmund
Parker, 1735. 2 vols. 8vo. [xxxiii],372; [xvi],
340,[28] pp. Contemp calf, rubbed & worn,
hinges cracked, labels defective.
(Claude Cox) **£50 [≈ $95]**
- An Essay concerning Human Understanding
... Twentieth Edition. London: for Longman,
by Law & Son ..., 1796. 2 vols. 8vo. xxx,510;
xiv,459,[xxvi] pp. Fldg table. Contemp tree
calf, rebacked. *(Gough)* **£95 [≈ $182]**
- Some Thoughts Concerning Education ... the
Fourth Edition enlarged. London: for A. & J.
Churchill, 1699. 4th edn. 8vo. [viii],380,[2]

pp. Contemp calf, lacks label, hd of spine chipped, spine & jnts rubbed. Wing L.2764. Anon.   *(Pickering)* **$1,250 [≃ £651]**
- Some Thoughts Concerning Education. The Fourteenth Edition. London: Whiston, Strahan ..., 1772. 12mo. [viii],325,[3] pp. Contemp sheep, rebacked.
                (Burmester) **£90 [≃ $172]**
- The Works ... Third Edition. London: for Bettesworth, Parker ..., 1727. Vol 3 bears no edn note. 3 vols. Folio. Frontis port & funeral plate vol 1. Contemp calf, gilt backstrips relaid, some rubbing at crnrs.
                (Jarndyce) **£380 [≃ $729]**
- The Works ... Fifth Edition. To which is now first added, The Life of the Author ... London: S. Birt ..., 1751. 3 vols. Folio. Port. Occas sl spotting & browning. Contemp calf, rebacked. *(Frew Mackenzie)* **£620 [≃ $1,190]**
- The Works. Seventh Edition. London: H. Woodfall ..., 1768. 4 vols. 4to. Marg worm at end of vol 1. Contemp polished calf, gilt spines, red & black labels, jnts cracked but firm, minor chips to spine ends.
                (Frew Mackenzie) **£400 [≃ $767]**

Lockhart, George
- Memoirs Concerning the Affairs of Scotland ... London: sold by J. Baker, 1714. 1st edn. 8vo. xxx,[23 Key (2nd edn, dated 1714)],420 pp. Occas stains. Contemp calf, crnrs bumped, sm defect hd of spine. Anon.
                (Young's) **£50 [≃ $95]**

Loder, Robert
- The History of Framlingham, in the County of Suffolk ... Woodbridge: for R. Loder, 1798. 1st edn. [One of 250]. 4to. xii,453,[1 blank], [2] pp. Subscribers. 10 plates. Few sl marks. Contemp bds, uncut, later cloth spine sl worn at ends.
                (Bow Windows) **£180 [≃ $345]**

Logan, John
- Poems, by the Rev. Mr. Logan, one of the Ministers of Leith. London: Cadell, 1781. 1st edn. 8vo. Half-title. Lacks final blank leaf. Occas sl finger marks. Price erased from title. Early half mor, rubbed.
                (Hannas) **£40 [≃ $76]**
- Poems. [Londonderry?:] Printed in the year, 1782. Disbound. *(Waterfield's)* **£150 [≃ $287]**

Logic; or, The Art of Thinking ...
- See Arnaud, Antoine & Nicole, Pierre.

The Loiterer: a Periodical Work ...
- See Austen, James (? & Jane).

Lomazzo, G.P.
- A Tracte containing the Arts of curious Paintinge, Carvinge & Buildinge ... Englished by R.H. [Richard Haydock]. Oxford: 1598. 1st edn in English. 11 ff,119,218 pp. 13 engvd ills. Engvd title in facs. Lacks last leaf with printer's mark. Sl marks. Calf, rebacked.
                (Ars Artis) **£1,000 [≃ $1,919]**

Longinus
- Dionysius Longinus On the Sublime. Translated from the Greek, with Notes ... By William Smith. Third Edition, corrected and Improved. London: for B. Dod, 1752. 8vo. [xvi], xxxiv, 180 pp, advt leaf. Frontis. Engvd arms to dedic. Period calf, sl worn.
                (Rankin) **£35 [≃ $67]**

The Looking Glass for the Mind ...
- See Berquin, Arnaud.

Loose Hints upon Education ...
- See Kames, Henry Home, Lord.

Lorgna, A.M.
- A Dissertation on the Summation of Infinite Converging Series with Algebraic Divisors ... (Translated by H. Clarke). London: for the author, 1779. 4to. xx,222 pp. 2 fldg plates. Contemp roan backed bds, v sl rubbed, sl worn.   *(Whitehart)* **£60 [≃ $115]**

Lothian, William
- The History of the United Provinces of the Netherlands, from the Death of Philip II, King of Spain ... Dublin: Whitestone ..., 1780. 8vo. xiii,463 pp. Period calf, sl worn.
                (Rankin) **£50 [≃ $95]**

The Lottery ...
- The Lottery, or Midsummer Recess; intended for the Information and Amusement of Young Persons of both Sexes. Uttoxeter: ptd & sold by R. Richards, 1797. 2nd edn. Cr 8vo. Lower crnr of all ff gnawed away (no loss of text). Contemp calf.
                (Stewart) **£65 [≃ $124]**

Louthian, John
- The Form of Process before the Court of Justiciary in Scotland ... Edinburgh: Robert Fleming & Co for William Hamilton, 1732. 8vo. vi,301 pp, errata leaf. Some browning.

Period calf. *(Rankin)* £50 [≈ $95]
- The Form of Process before the Court of Justiciary in Scotland ... Second Edition, with Additions and Amendments. Edinburgh: Hamilton, Balfour & Neill, 1752. 8vo. viii, 288 pp. Period calf, spine ends sl chipped.
(Rankin) £50 [≈ $95]

Lovat, Simon Fraser, Lord
- Genuine Memoirs of the Life of Simon Lord Fraser of Lovat. London: for M. Cooper, 1746. 1st edn. 12mo. 40 pp. 19th c mor gilt, front hinge cracked.
(Chapel Hill) $150 [≈ £78]
- Memoirs of the Life of Simon Lord Lovat; written by himself, in the French Language; and now first translated [by William Godwin], from the Original Manuscript. London: Nicol ..., 1797. 1st edn of this translation. 8vo. [iv], [ii blank], 468 pp. Contemp calf, backstrip relaid.
(Pickering) $500 [≈ £260]

Love ...
- Love and Folly ... see Selden, Ambrose.
- Love of Fame ... see Young, Edward.

Love, John
- The New Waymouth [sic] Guide ... Waymouth: ptd for & sold by J. Love ..., (1788). Sm 8vo. 67,[i advt] pp. Orig mrbld wraps, ptd paper label on front wrapper, lacks most of backstrip. *(Georges)* £180 [≈ $345]

Loveling, Benjamin
- Latin and English Poems. By a Gentleman of Trinity College, Oxford. London: C. Bathurst, 1741. 2nd edn. 12mo. Sm blank crnr torn from title. Contemp calf gilt.
(Ximenes) $150 [≈ £78]

The Lover's Secretary ...
- The Lover's Secretary; or, the Adventures of Lindamira, a Lady of Quality ... Revis'd and Corrected by Mr. Tho. Brown. London: for W. Feales ..., 1734. 3rd edn. 12mo. [iv],228, [4 advt] pp. Sl used & marked. 18th c sheep backed bds, sl worn.
(Burmester) £360 [≈ $691]

Lowth, Robert
- The Life of William of Wykeham, Bishop of Winchester ... London: for A. Millar, 1759. 2nd edn. 8vo. xxxiv,357,liv pp. Frontis, fldg table. 1st & last ff discold. Contemp calf, rubbed, jnts cracked. *(Young's)* £50 [≈ $95]

- A Short Introduction to English Grammar: with Critical Notes. The Second Edition, Corrected. London: for Millar ... Dodsley, 1763. 12mo. Half-title. Contemp calf, gilt spine, label. Anon. *(Georges)* £75 [≈ $143]
- A Short Introduction to English Grammar: with Critical Notes. A New Edition, corrected. London: Dodsley, 1772. 221 pp,advt leaf. Contemp calf, hinges weakening, spine dried. Anon. *(C.R. Johnson)* £145 [≈ $278]
- A Short Introduction to English Grammar: with Critical Notes. London: for J. Dodsley, 1783. xv,221,[1] pp. 19th c qtr calf. Anon.
(C.R. Johnson) £110 [≈ $211]
- A Short Introduction to English Grammar: with Critical Notes. A New Edition Corrected. London: Dodsley & Cadell, 1789. 184 pp. Contemp calf, red label. Anon.
(C.R. Johnson) £95 [≈ $182]

Lowth, William
- Directions for the Profitable Reading of the Holy Scriptures ... Third Edition ... London: J. Bettenham ..., 1726. 12mo. [xii], 153, [iii advt] pp. Contemp calf, crnrs sl worn, sm split 1 jnt. *(Clark)* £32 [≈ $61]

Lucas, Richard
- An Inquiry after Happiness. In Three Parts ... Edinburgh: William Gray ..., 1754. 8th edn. 2 vols. 8vo. xi,371; iv,345 pp. Contemp calf, twin labels. *(Young's)* £120 [≈ $230]

Lucian
- The Select Dialogues ... To which is added a new Literal Translation ... by Edward Murphy. Dublin: reprinted by John Exshaw, 1771. 8vo. Contemp sheep, sl scuffed.
(Waterfield's) £45 [≈ $86]

Lucina sine Concubitu ...
- See Hill, "Sir" John.

Luckombe, Philip
- The History and Art of Printing ... London: Adlard & Browne, for J. Johnson, 1771. 1st edn. 8vo. With 2 titles (of 1st & 2nd issues, 1st issue reads "The Concise History of the Origin and Progress of Printing'). W'cut frontis, num text ills. Half calf antique.
(Ximenes) $850 [≈ £442]
- The History and Art of Printing. London: J. Johnson, 1771. 2nd edn. Post 4to. [xiv], 502, [4] pp. Type specimens, ornaments, &c. Some staining & thumbing. Mod qtr calf gilt.
(Ash) £300 [≈ $575]

Lucretius Carus, Titus
- Titus Lucretius Carus, His Six Books of Epicurean Philosophy. London: Thomas Sawbridge, 1683. 3rd edn of this translation. [xlii], 223,60,[6] pp. Frontis. Contemp calf, rebacked & recrnrd.
(Bookpress) **$450 [≈ £234]**

Ludlow, Edmund
- Memoirs ... [London]: "Switzerland, Printed at Vivay in the Canton of Bern", 1698-99. 1st edn. 3 vols. [ii],viii,430,[ii]; [ii], 435-878; [x],402,[lvi] pp. Port in vol 1. Blank leaf at end of vol 1. Occas browning. Rec bds. Wing L.3460, L.3462. *(Clark)* **£150 [≈ $287]**
- Memoirs ... With a Collection of Original Papers, and the Case of King Charles the First. London: for Becket & De Hondt, & Cadell, & Evans, 1771, New edn. Lge 4to. xii, 558, 19,[28],2 ctlg pp. Orig calf gilt, elab gilt spine, mor label. *(Vanbrugh)* **£175 [≈ $335]**
- Memoirs ... With a Collection of Original Papers, and the Case of King Charles the First. London: for Becket & De Hondt, & Cadell, & Evans, 1771, 4to. xii,558,19,[31] pp. Port. Contemp speckled calf, some wear, lower jnt partly cracked, spine ends sl worn. *(Burmester)* **£90 [≈ $172]**

Lumisden, Andrew
- Remarks on the Antiquities of Rome and its Environs ... Illustrated with Engravings. London: ptd by Bulmer & Co, sold by G. Nicol, 1797. 1st edn. 4to. iv,478,[12] pp. Port, 12 plates & maps. Contemp calf, rebacked. *(Claude Cox)* **£120 [≈ $230]**

Lupton, Donald
- The Glory of their Times, or the Lives of the Primitive Fathers ... London: I. Oken, 1640. 1st edn. 4to. [viii],538 pp. Engvd title, num engvd ports in text. Orig sheep, ft of spine v sl damaged. STC 16943.
(Vanbrugh) **£225 [≈ $431]**

Lupton, Thomas
- A Thousand Memorable Things. Containing Modern Curiosities ... London: for G. Conyers, [?early 1700s]. 12mo. [ii],264,[x] pp. Some wear & tear, marg worm in 3 prelims. New qtr calf. Anon. *(Rankin)* **£85 [≈ $163]**

Lupton, William
- A Discourse of Murther, Preach'd in the Chapel at Lincoln's-Inn ... London: for S. Keble ..., 1725. Only edn. 8vo in 4s. 32 pp. Sl foxing & browning, title dusty. new qtr

calf. *(Meyer Boswell)* **$175 [≈ £91]**

Luther, Martin
- Several Choice Prophecyes ... As Also, The Remarkable Prophecy of the Learned and Reverend Dr Musculus. Collected by R.C. M.A. London: 1666. 1st edn. Sm 4to. [ii],'37" [ie 47] pp. Sl spotting. 18th c qtr mor. Wing L.3515, C115. *(Vanbrugh)* **£1,555 [≈ $2,985]**

Lux Orientalis ...
- See Glanvill, Joseph.

Luxborough, Henrietta Knight, Lady
- Letters ... to William Shenstone, Esq. London: Dodsley, 1775. Orig calf, sl wear to spine ends. *(C.R. Johnson)* **£125 [≈ $239]**

Lynch, Bernard
- A Guide to Health through the Various Stages of Life. London: for the author, & sold by Mrs. Cooper ..., 1744. 8vo. 5 pp subscribers. Contemp calf, gilt borders, spine rubbed & chipped at hd.
(Jarndyce) **£140 [≈ $268]**

Lynde, Humphrey
- Via Devia: The By-Way: Mis-Leading the Weake and Unstable into Dangerous Paths of Error ... London: Aug. M. for Rob. Milbourne, 1630. Thick tall 12mo. [70],684 pp. Minor wear. 18th c calf. STC 17095.
(Humber) **£88 [≈ $168]**

Lysons, Daniel
- The Environs of London ... London: Strahan for Cadell & Davies, 1792-96. 1st edn. 4 vols. 4to. 3 maps, 4 engvd titles, 60 plates (3 hand cold), 2 pedigrees. Occas sl spotting or browning. Half mor gilt, rubbed & scraped.
(Hollett) **£275 [≈ $527]**

Lyttelton, George, 1st Baron Lyttelton
- Dialogues of the Dead. London: W. Sandby, 1760. 1st edn. 8vo. xii,320 pp. Title dusty, few pencil notes. Rec qtr calf. Anon.
(Clark) **£35 [≈ $67]**
- Dialogues of the Dead. London: [Samuel Richardson for] W. Sandby, 1760. 1st edn. The state with Sale's ornament 34 on p 3. 8vo. Occas sl foxing. Contemp calf, rebacked.
(Sanders) **£125 [≈ $239]**
- Dialogues of the Dead. London: W. Sandby, 1760. 2nd edn. 8vo. xii,320 pp. Contemp qtr calf, hinges cracked. Anon.
(Bookpress) **$225 [≈ £117]**

- The History of the Life of Henry the Second ... Third Edition. London: Dodsley, 1769-71. 6 vols. 8vo. Later (French?) roan, sl scuffed.
  (Waterfield's) £120 [≈ $230]
- Observations on the Conversion and Apostleship of St. Paul. In a Letter to Gilbert West, Esq. London: Dodsley, 1747. 1st edn. 110 pp. Disbound. Anon.
  (Wreden) $75 [≈ £39]
- Observations on the Conversion and Apostleship of St. Paul. In a Letter to Gilbert West, Esq; The Third Edition. London: for R. Dodsley, sold by M. Cooper, 1747. 8vo. Half-title & final blank. Disbound. Anon.
  (Sanders) £15 [≈ $28]

Lyttelton, Thomas, 2nd Baron Lyttelton
- Letters of the late Lord Lyttelton. Third Edition. London: J. Bew, 1780. 8vo. [ii],vii, [i], 222 pp. Title soiled & inner marg reinforced. Last 2 ff torn without loss. Contemp qtr calf, vellum tips, rubbed, hd of spine chipped.
  (Clark) £24 [≈ $46]

M., G.
- Country Contentments; The English House-Wife ... see Markham, Gervase.
- Miscellanea ... see Miege, Guy.
- The Praise of Yorkshire Ale ... see Meriton, George.

Mably, Gabriel Bonnot, Abbe
- Phocion's Conversations ... Originally translated by Abbe Mably, from a Greek Manuscript of Nicocles; with Notes by William Macbean, A.M. London: for the author, & sold by Dodsley, 1769. 1st edn in English. 8vo. vi, civ, [ii], 303,[1] pp. Subscribers. Contemp calf, sl worn.
  (Burmester) £85 [≈ $163]

Macarius of Egypt
- Primitive Morality, or the Spiritual Homilies of St. Macarius the Egyptian ... Done out of Greek ... by a Presbyter of the Church of England [Thomas Haywood]. London: W. Taylor ..., 1721. xii,482 pp. Contemp calf, sl worn.
  (Gage) £30 [≈ $57]

Macaulay, Alexander
- An Inquiry into the Legality of Pensions on the Irish Establishment. London Printed by J. Wilkie. Dublin: reprinted & sold by the booksellers, 1763. 16 pp. Disbound.
  (C.R. Johnson) £30 [≈ $57]

Macaulay, Aulay
- Polygraphy, or Short-Hand made easy ... London: the author, 1742. 1st edn. 12mo. [2], viii, 119 pp, engvd throughout. Frontis. Authenticating sgntr. Mor, hinges cracked.
  (Bookpress) $285 [≈ £148]

M'Cormick, Charles
- Memoirs of the Right Honourable Edmund Burke ... London: for the author, 1797. 1st edn. 4to. 383 pp. 19th c qtr calf.
  (C.R. Johnson) £225 [≈ $431]
- Memoirs of the Right Honourable Edmund Burke ... The Second Edition. London: for Lee & Hurst, 1798. 4to. Port frontis (borders sl stained). New half calf.
  (Georges) £100 [≈ $191]

M'Donald, Alexander
- A Galick and English Vocabulary ... Edinburgh: Robert Fleming, 1741. 194 pp. 2 title pages (Gaelic, English). Contemp qtr calf, mrbld bds, respined.
  (C.R. Johnson) £475 [≈ $911]

McFarlan, John
- Inquiries concerning the Poor. Edinburgh: for T. Longman, London; & J. Dickson, Edinburgh, 1780. 1st edn. 8vo. Few spots in prelims. Contemp speckled calf, edges sl rubbed, rec reback.
  (Jarndyce) £720 [≈ $1,382]

MacGilvray, John
- Poems. By John MacGilvray; A.M. Master of the Grammar School of Lestwithiel. London: J. Bew, 1787. 4to. 109 pp. Sl marg damp stains. Orig bds, uncut, backstrip worn.
  (C.R. Johnson) £325 [≈ $623]

Macgreggor, Malcolm (pseud.)
- See Mason, William.

Mackenzie, Sir George
- Reason. An Essay. London: Joseph Hindmarsh & Richard Sare, 1695. 2nd edn. 12mo. [x], 3-158 pp. Title marg reprd, minor browning & soiling. Contemp calf, old reback, rubbed, crnrs worn. Wing M.194.
  (Clark) £85 [≈ $163]
- A Vindication of the Government in Scotland during the Reign of King Charles II ... London: for J. Hindmarsh, 1691. 1st edn. Sm 4to. 66 pp. Mod wraps.
  (Chapel Hill) $150 [≈ £78]

Mackenzie, George, Earl of Cromarty
- An Historical Account of the Conspiracies by the Earls of Gowry and Robert Logan of Restalrig, against King James V ... Edinburgh: James Watson, 1713. 8vo. xvi, 127,80 pp. Half-title. Prelims sl foxed. New bds.   *(Rankin)* £75 [≈ $143]

Mackenzie, Henry
- Julia de Roubigne, a Tale ... Third Edition. London: Strahan ..., 1782. 2 vols. 12mo. xii,195,[i]; vii,[i],202,[ii advt] pp. Half-titles. Contemp sheep, extremities sl worn, sm defect in leather on 1 bd. Anon.
            (Clark) £65 [≈ $124]
- The Man of Feeling. The Second Edition, Corrected. London: for T. Cadell, 1771. 8vo. viii, 286 pp. Period calf, surface of spine sl cracked. Anon.   *(Rankin)* £125 [≈ $239]
- The Man of Feeling. London: for W. Strahan ..., 1783. New edn. 8vo. viii,278 pp. Frontis. Old calf, worn. Anon. *(Young's)* £40 [≈ $76]
- The Man of the World. London: Strahan & Cadell, 1773. 1st edn. 2 vols. 12mo. Half-titles. 1 sm marg repr. Contemp calf gilt, red labels, sl rubbed. Anon.
            (Jarndyce) £140 [≈ $268]
- The Man of the World ... Fifth Edition. London: Strahan & Cadell, 1795. 2 vols. 12mo. [iv],300; [iv],228 pp. Half-titles. Occas sl staining. Contemp tree calf, gilt spines, dble labels, minor wear at extremities. Anon.
            (Clark) £65 [≈ $124]
- The Pursuit of Happiness. Inscribed to a Friend. London: T. Cadell, 1781. 4to. Half-title. Orig mrbld wraps. Anon.
            (C.R. Johnson) £175 [≈ $335]

Mackenzie, Henry, et al.
- The Mirror. A Periodical Paper published at Edinburgh in the Years 1779 and 1780. Ninth Edition. London: 1792. 2 vols. 8vo. Contemp tree calf gilt, gilt spines, contrasting labels. Anon.   *(Buccleuch)* £130 [≈ $249]

Mackenzie, J.
- The History of Health and the Art of Preserving It ... Edinburgh: 1759. 2nd edn. xii, 436 pp. Leather, hd of spine sl chipped.
            (Whitehart) £180 [≈ $345]

Mackenzie, James
- A Treatise concerning the Origin and Progress of Fees ... Being a Supplement to Spotiswood's Introduction ... Edinburgh: Ruddimans, 1734. 1st edn. 8vo in 4s. xii,276

pp. Few pp browned. Contemp calf, gilt spine. Anon.   *(Clark)* £50 [≈ $95]

Mackintosh, Sir James
- A Discourse on the Study of the Law of Nature and Nations; Introductory to a Course of Lectures on that Science ... Second Edition. London: Cadell & Davies, 1799. 8vo. [iv],68 pp. Some dusting, sm hole in 1 leaf. New qtr mor. *(Meyer Boswell)* £350 [≈ £182]
- Vindiciae Gallicae. Defence of the French Revolution and its English Admirers against the Accusations of Edmund Burke ... London: Robinson, 1791. 1st edn. 8vo. A few pencil marks. Contemp half calf, sometime rebacked, inner hinges reinforced with cloth tape.   *(Jarndyce)* £45 [≈ $86]
- Vindiciae Gallicae. Defence of the French Revolution and its English Admirers against the Accusations of the Right Hon. Edmund Burke ... London: ·Robinson, 1791. 1st edn. 8vo. 351 pp. Rec half calf.
            (Young's) £130 [≈ $249]
- Vindiciae Gallicae. Defence of the French revolution and its English Admirers against the Accusations of the Right Hon. Edmund Burke ... Dublin: W. Corbet, 1791. 167 pp. Disbound.   *(C.R. Johnson)* £45 [≈ $86]

Macklin, Charles
- The Man of the World. A Comedy ... Dublin: 1785. 1st edn. 12mo. Disbound, uncut.
            (Dramatis Personae) $40 [≈ £20]

Mackworth, Humphrey
- Peace at Home: or, a Vindication of the Proceedings of the Honourable House of Commons ... London: Freeman Collins, J. Nutt, 1703. 2nd edn. Folio. [viii],12 pp. Outer marg of 1 leaf trimmed. Disbound.
            (Burmester) £25 [≈ $47]
- Peace at Home: or, a Vindication of the proceedings of the Honourable House of Commons ... London: Freeman Collins, 1703. 3rd edn. 8vo. [viii],16 pp. Contemp wraps.   *(Burmester)* £30 [≈ $57]
- A Vindication of the Rights of Commons of England. By a Member of the Honourable the House of Commons. London: J. Nutt, 1701. 1st edn. Folio. [xii],40 pp. Outer ff sl dusty. Disbound.   *(Burmester)* £35 [≈ $67]

Maclaurin, Colin
- An Account of Sir Isaac Newton's Philosophical Discoveries ... Publish'd from the Author's Manuscript Papers, by Patrick

Murdoch. London: for the author's children, 1748. 1st edn 4to. xx, [xx subscribers],392 pp. Half-title. 5 plates. Sl marked at end. Mod half calf gilt. *(Hollett)* **£250 [≈ $479]**

- An Account of Sir Isaac Newton's Philosophical Discoveries, in Four Books. London: A. Millar, 1750. 2nd edn. 8vo. xxvi, 412 pp. 6 fldg plates. Sl foxed. New leather. *(Gemmary)* **$400 [≈ £208]**

- A Treatise of Algebra, in Three Parts ... added an Appendix ... London: Millar & Nourse, 1748. 1st edn. 8vo. xiv,366,[2], 65, [1] pp. 12 fldg plates. Contemp sprinkled calf, mor label, hd of spine worn & chipped, jnts cracked but sound. *(Gaskell)* **£400 [≈ $767]**

Macnab, D.

- An Exact Description of the Island and Kingdom of Sicily ... added, a Short Narrative of the Island and Kingdom of Sardinia. Falkirk: Patrick Mair, for the translator, 1784. 1st edn. 8vo. Contemp mrbld bds, uncut, later paper spine. *(Ximenes)* **$325 [≈ £169]**

M'Nicol, Donald

- Remarks on Dr Samuel Johnson's Journey to the Hebrides ... London: T. Cadell, 1779. Half-title. Contemp calf, backstrip sometime relaid. *(C.R. Johnson)* **£225 [≈ $431]**

Macpherson, James

- Fingal, An Ancient Epic Poem ... Together with Several other Poems, composed by Ossian the Son of Fingal. Translated from the Galic Language by James Macpherson. London: Becket & De Hondt, 1762. 1st edn. 4to. Contemp calf gilt, a.e.g., v sl worn. *(Buccleuch)* **£150 [≈ $287]**

- Fingal, An Ancient Epic Poem ... Together with Several other Poems, composed by Ossian the Son of Fingal. Translated from the Galic Language ... Dublin: for Richard Fitzsimons, 1762. 1st Dublin edn. 12mo. [xvi],xx,304 pp. Sm stain on 1 leaf. Contemp calf *(Young's)* **£130 [≈ $249]**

- Fragments of Ancient Poetry ... Translated from the Galic or Erse Language. The Second Edition. Edinburgh: for Hamilton & Balfour, 1760. Advt leaf at end. Orig blue bds, uncut, sl spotted, cream paper spine sl defective. Anon. *(Jarndyce)* **£220 [≈ $422]**

- The Poems of Ossian. Translated by James Macpherson. A New Edition, carefully corrected and greatly improved. London: Strahan, Becket, 1773. 2nd coll edn. 2 vols. 8vo. xiii,[iii],404; [vi],435 pp. Half-titles.

Contemp calf, hd of spines sl worn. *(Burmester)* **£80 [≈ $153]**

- The Works of Ossian the Son of Fingal. Translated from the Galic Language by James McPherson. Paris: ptd by J.Fr. Valade & sold by Theophilus Barrois, 1783. 3 vols. Cr 8vo. Orig wraps, unopened. *(Stewart)* **£75 [≈ $143]**

Madan, Spencer

- A Letter to Doctor Priestley in consequence of his 'Familiar Letters addressed to the Inhabitants of the Town of Birmingham, &c.'. Birmingham: E. Piercy, [1790]. Disbound. *(Waterfield's)* **£110 [≈ $211]**

- The Principal Claims of the Dissenters, considered, in a Sermon preached ... 14th of February, 1790. Birmingham: E. Piercy, [1790]. Sm blank piece missing from hd of title. Disbound. Anon. *(Waterfield's)* **£60 [≈ $115]**

Madden, Samuel

- Themistocles, The Lover of His Country. A Tragedy. London: for R. King, 1729. 1st edn. 2nd imp, with crrctns & unsigned dedic. 8vo. Ends sl dusty. Disbound. Anon. *(Dramatis Personae)* **$80 [≈ £41]**

Madox, Thomas

- Baronia Anglica. An History of Land-Honors and Baronies and of Tenure in Capite verified by Records. London: for Francis Gosling, 1741. Folio. Publisher's (?) bds, uncut. *(Waterfield's)* **£135 [≈ $259]**

Maffei, Scipio

- A Compleat History of the Ancient Amphitheatres ... London: W. Sare, (1735). 2nd edn. 8vo. xvi,412 pp. 15 plates (some hand cold). Contemp sheep, worn. *(Bookpress)* **$175 [≈ £91]**

Magna Charta ...

- Magna Charta, Made in the Ninth Year of K. Henry the Third ... With some Short, but Necessary Observations ... Translated ... By Edw. Cooke ... London: 1680. 1st edn thus. Sm 4to. [viii],68,[ii] pp. Disbound. Wing M.253. *(Finch)* **£275 [≈ $527]**

Mahomet, Lewis Maximilian

- Some Memoirs of the Life of Lewis Maximilian Mahomet, Gent. Late Servant to His Majesty ... Written by Himself. London: for H. Curll, 1727. 20 pp. Sl browned. Disbound. *(Jarndyce)* **£30 [≈ $57]**

Maillet, Benoit de

- Telliamed; or, the World Explain'd: containing Discourses between an Indian Philosopher and a Missionary ... A Very Curious Work. Baltimore: W. Pechelin for D. Porter, 1797. 1st Amer edn. 8vo. 268 pp. Sl browned. Contemp calf. Anon.
(Rootenberg) **$600 [≃ £312]**

Maintenon, Francoise d'Aubigne, Marchioness

- The Letters of Madame de Maintenon; and other Eminent Persons ... Translated from the French. Dublin: George Faulkner, 1753. 1st Irish edn. 12mo. viii,254,[2 advt] pp. Contemp calf.   *(Burmester)* **£35 [≃ $67]**

Mainwaring, J.

- Memoirs of the Life of the late George Frederic Handel ... London: Dodsley, 1760. 1st edn. 8vo. [4],208 pp. Half-title. Port. Sl browning. Contemp calf, rebacked. Anon.
(Claude Cox) **£220 [≃ $422]**

Mainwaring, Sir Thomas

- A Reply to an Answer to the Defence of Amicia ... London: for S. Lowndes, 1673. 1st edn. Sm 8vo. [ii],105 pp. Red & black title. Rec calf. Wing M.303.
(Burmester) **£140 [≃ $268]**

Maitland, William

- The History of Edinburgh ... Edinburgh: Hamilton, Balfour & Neill, 1753. Folio. viii, 518 pp. Fldg plan frontis, fldg hand cold map, fldg plan, 2 fldg engvs, fldg ground plan, 18 ills. Few sm reprs. Qtr calf, rebacked, crnrs sl dented.
(Rankin) **£275 [≃ $527]**

Makarony Fables ...

- See Hall-Stevenson, John.

Malcolm, William, James, & Jacob

- General View of the Agriculture of the County of Buckingham ... Drawn up for the consideration of the Board of Agriculture and Internal Improvement. London: Colin Macrae, 1794. 1st edn. 4to. 63 pp. Disbound, sewing defective.   *(Bickersteth)* **£45 [≃ $86]**

Malcolme, David

- Letters, Essays and Other Tracts Illustrating the Antiquities of Great Britain and Ireland, together with ... the Affinity betwixt the Languages of the Americans and the Ancient Britons ... London: Millan, 1744. 8vo. Mod

bds.   *(Emerald Isle)* **£150 [≃ $287]**

Mallet, David

- The Life of Francis Bacon, Lord Chancellor of England. London: for A. Millar, 1740. 8vo. viii, 197,3 advt pp. Period calf, lacks label, 1 jnt reprd, spine ends sl chipped.
(Rankin) **£45 [≃ $86]**
- Mustapha. A Tragedy. London: for A. Millar, 1739. 1st edn. 8vo. Last p sl soiled. Disbound. Anon.
(Dramatis Personae) **$50 [≃ £26]**

Mallet, Paul Henry

- Northern Antiquities: or, a Description of the Manners, Customs, Religions, and Laws of the Ancient Danes, and other Northern Nations ... London: 1770. 1st edn in English. 2 vols. 8vo. [10],lvi,415; [8],356 pp. Half-title vol 2. Some prelim spotting. Half cloth.
(Young's) **£120 [≃ $230]**
- Northern Antiquities: or, a Description of the Manners, Customs, Religions, and Laws of the Ancient Danes, and other Northern Nations ... London: Carnan, 1770. 1st English edn. 2 vols. 8vo. Half-titles, 2 inserted dedic ff. Contemp calf, rebacked.
(Hannas) **£160 [≃ $307]**

Malton, James

- An Essay on British Cottage Architecture. London: Hookham & Carpenter, 1798. 4to. [4], 27, [1] pp. 21 aquatint plates printed in bistre. Some sl foxing on plates. Half calf & mrbld bds.   *(Sotheran's)* **£875 [≃ $1,679]**

Malton, Thomas

- A Compleat Treatise on Perspective ... see Taylor, Brook.

Malvezzi, Virgilio

- Discourses upon Cornelius Tacitus ... translated into English by Sir Richard Baker. London: E.G. for Whitaker ..., 1642. 1st English edn. Folio. W'cut title-border. Mod half sheep. Wing M.359.
(Waterfield's) **£125 [≃ $239]**

Man ...

- The Man of Feeling; The Man of the World ... see Mackenzie, Henry.

Manchester, Henry Montagu, Earl of

- Contemplatio Mortis, & Immortalitatis. The fifth Impression much enlarged. London: Francis Constable, 1642. 12mo. Port, addtnl engvd title (both rather soiled). Some soiling & staining. Later half mor gilt, jnts rubbed. Wing M.404. *(Frew Mackenzie)* **£45 [≈ $86]**

Mandeville, Bernard de

- An Enquiry into the Origin of Honour, and the Usefulness of Christianity in War. By the Author of the Fable of the Bees. London: for John Brotherton, 1732. 1st edn. Later half calf, spine rubbed. *(Jarndyce)* **£380 [≈ $729]**

- The Fable of the Bees: or, Private Vices, Publick Benefits ... Sixth Edition ... London: Tonson, 1729. 12mo. Contemp calf, reprd, hinges rubbed, new label.
  (Jarndyce) **£220 [≈ $422]**

Manheim, Frederic

- Affecting History of the Dreadful Distresses of Frederic Manheim's Family. Phila: Matthew Carey, 1794. 2nd edn. 8vo. 48 pp. Lacks frontis. Lacks blank half of A2. Some discolouration at ends. Disbound.
  (Bookpress) **$275 [≈ £143]**

Manley, Mary Delariviere

- Memoirs of Europe, towards the Close of the Eighth Century. Written by Eginardus ... and done into English by the Translator of the New Atlantis. The Second Edition, Corrected. London: for John Morphew, 1711. 8vo. [16, 4 key], 334 pp. Sl marks. Contemp calf, rebacked. Anon
  (Claude Cox) **£45 [≈ $86]**

- The Power of Love: in Seven Novels ... London: for C. Davis, 1741. Later issue of 1st edn of 1720, with cancel title. Lacks half-title. Sl browned. Contemp calf, rebacked, hinges rubbed. *(Jarndyce)* **£250 [≈ $479]**

Manning, Francis

- Of Levity and Steadiness. A Poem. In an Epistle to a Friend, who was in doubt what course to take in Difficult Times. London: J. Roberts, 1735. Foxon's variant without price after imprint. 4to. Rebound in half calf.
  (C.R. Johnson) **£185 [≈ $355]**

Manning, Henry

- Modern Improvements in the Practice of Physic. London: Robinson, Murray, 1780. 1st edn. 8vo. [viii],'240" [ie 440] pp. Sl dust soiled. Contemp half calf, worn, label defective. *(Gaskell)* **£180 [≈ $345]**

Manning, Owen

- Considerations on the State of Subscription to the Articles and Liturgy of the Church of

England, towards the Close of the Year 1773 ... By a Consistent Protestant. London: for J. Wilkie, 1774. Disbound. Anon.
  (Waterfield's) **£45 [≈ $86]**

Manstein, Baron de

- Memoirs of Russia. From the Year 1727 to the Year 1744. Translated from the Original Manuscript ... Second Edition ... Improved. London: Becket ..., 1773. 4to. xxvi,418,index pp. 10 fldg maps & plans. Rec qtr mor.
  (Terramedia) **$750 [≈ £390]**

Manton, Thomas

- A Practical Exposition on the Whole Fifty Third Chapter of Isaiah ... London: Parkhurst, Robinson, 1703. Only edn. 8vo. vi, 595, [1] pp. Port. Rec bds.
  (Fenning) **£35 [≈ $67]**

Manwood, John

- A Treatise of the Lawes of the Forest ... London: Societie of Stationers, 1615. 4to. Some sl wear & tear. Contemp calf, rebacked. STC 17292. *(Meyer Boswell)* **$500 [≈ £260]**

- A Treatise of the Lawes of the Forest ... London: Societie of Stationers, 1615. 2nd edn. Sm 4to. [xv], 258 ff. Contemp calf, rebacked. STC 17292.
  (Bookpress) **$500 [≈ £260]**

Marchant, Mr.

- Observations on Mr. Fielding's Plan for a Preservatory and Reformatory. London: for W. Reeve, 1758. Only edn. Title,22 pp. Some foxing & browning. Last leaf reprd without loss. Mod linen backed mrbld bds.
  (Meyer Boswell) **$250 [≈ £130]**

The Margate New Guide ...

- See Sharpe, Richard Scrafton.

Markham, Francis

- The Booke of Honovr. or, Five Decads of Epistles of Honovr. London: Augustine Matthewes, 1625. 1st edn. Sm folio. Usual mispagination. Some browning & spots. Later polished calf gilt, a.e.g. STC 17331.
  (Bow Windows) **£325 [≈ $623]**

Markham, Gervase

- Country Contentments ... By G.M. ... Newly Corrected ... London: Harper for Harison sic, 1633. 5th edn. 4to. [viii],118 pp. Rec half calf. STC 17345. *(Vanbrugh)* **£155 [≈ $297]**

- The English House-Wife. Containing the

inward and outward Vertues which ought to be in a compleat Woman ... By G.M. Now the fourth time much augmented ... London: Nicholas Oak for Iohn Harison, 1631. Sm 4to. [x], 252 pp. Lacks A1 blank. Old calf, backstrip relaid. *(Bickersteth)* £420 [≈$806]

- The Inrichment of the Weald of Kent ... Revised, Enlarged and Corrected ... London: for Hannah Sawbridge, 1683. Sm sq 4to. [ii], 126, [4] pp. Few text w'cuts. 2 sm blind stamps, a few spots. Rec calf gilt.
(Hollett) £120 [≈$230]

- Markham's Farewell to Husbandry: or, the Enriching of all Sorts of Barren and Sterile Grounds in our Nation. London: 1653. Sm 4to. [vi], 126,[4] pp. W'cuts in text. New calf.
(Wheldon & Wesley) £120 [≈$230]

Marmet, Melchior de

- Entertainments of the Cours: or, Academical Conversations. Held upon the Cours at Paris ... London: 1658. 1st edn in English. 8vo. [lii],207,[1],[2 errata] pp. Addtnl engvd title (outer edge sl shaved). Contemp sheep. The Earl of Hadington's copy. Wing M.701.
(Burmester) £300 [≈$575]

Marr, John

- Marriage Promoted. In a Discourse of its Ancient and Modern Practice ... By a Person of Quality. London: Baldwin, 1690. 1st edn under this title. 4to. [viii],63,[i] pp. Half-title. Lib stamp on title verso. Outer ff dusty. Disbound, loose. Wing M.710. Anon.
(Clark) £65 [≈$124]

Marriage Asserted ...

- Marriage Asserted: In Answer to a Book Entituled Conjugium Conjurgium ... by William Seymar, Esq. Written by a Country Gentleman. London: Henry Herringman, 1674. Only edn. 8vo. [xxviii],98 pp. Lacks A1 (presumed blank). Polished calf antique, t.e.g., by Hatchards.
(Bickersteth) £360 [≈$691]

Marriott, Thomas

- Female Conduct: being an Essay on the Art of Pleasing. To be practised by the Fair Sex, before, and after Marriage. A Poem ... London: for W. Owen, 1759. 1st edn. Contemp calf, rebacked.
(Jarndyce) £250 [≈$479]

Marshall, Stephen

- A Sacred Record to be made of Gods Mercies to Zion ... London: Rich. Cotes for Stephen

Bowtell ..., [n.d.]. Only edn. 4to. [iv],36 pp. Disbound. Wing M.773.
(Young's) £45 [≈$86]

Marshall, William

- Planting and Ornamental Gardening: a Practical Treatise. London: Dodsley, 1785. 1st edn. 8vo. xi,[5],638 pp. Half-title. Some browning. Full leather, orig label preserved.
(Spelman) £120 [≈$230]

- Planting and Ornamental Gardening: a Practical Treatise. London: 1785. 1st edn. 8vo. xv,638 pp. Mod bds. Anon.
(Wheldon & Wesley) £75 [≈$143]

- Planting and Rural Ornament ... London: G. Nicol, 1796. 2nd edn. 2 vols. 8vo. xxxii, 408, [8]; xx,454,[6] pp. Sl marg water stain few ff. Contemp sheep, some wear.
(Bookpress) £450 [≈£234]

- Planting and Rural Ornament. Being a Second Edition, with Large Additions, of Planting and Ornamental Gardening. London: 1796. 2 vols. 8vo. xxxii,408,[8]; xx,454,[6] pp. Contemp tree calf, 1 label defective. *(Henly)* £152 [≈$291]

Martial

- Select Epigrams of Martial. Translated and Imitated by William Hay, Esq; with an Appendix of some by Cowley ... London: Dodsley, 1755. 1st edn. 8vo. [xii],239,23,4 advt pp. Parallel Latin & English text. Old calf, rebacked. *(Young's)* £36 [≈$69]

- Select Epigrams of Martial. Translated and Imitated by William Hay, Esq; with an Appendix ... London: Dodsley, 1755. Fcap 8vo. [12], 239,[21] pp, advt leaf. Latin & English text. Contemp calf, backstrip relaid.
(Spelman) £45 [≈$86]

Martin, Benjamin

- Biographica Philosophica. Being an Account of the Lives, Writings, and Inventions of the most eminent Philosophers and Mathematicians ... to the Present Time. London: W. Owen & the author, 1764. 1st edn. 8vo. [iv],565,[3] pp. Port. Some margs cut close. Rec qtr calf.
(Burmester) £180 [≈$345]

- The Description and Use of a Case of Mathematical Instruments ... London: the author ..., 1771. 8vo. [ii],18 pp. New bds.
(Georges) £150 [≈$287]

- Lingua Britannica Reformata: or, a New English Dictionary ... London: for J. Hodges ..., 1749. 8vo. Sep title to the Institutes of

Language dated 1748. 6 plates. Some wear & tear. Contemp calf, worn, jnts cracked, some loss on backstrip.   *(Clark)* **£150 [≈ $287]**
- Logarithmologia or the Whole Doctrine of Logarithms, Common and Logistical, in Theory and Practice. London: J. Hodges, 1740. 8vo. xii, 248,64 pp. Calf.
(Gemmary) **$650 [≈ £338]**

Martin, John
- The History and Antiquities of Naseby, in the County of Northampton. Cambridge: Francis Hodson, 1792. 8vo. 206 pp. Subscribers. Old polished calf, worn, hinges cracked.   *(Hollett)* **£45 [≈ $86]**

Martin, T. or J.
- Mary Magdalen's Tears Wip't Off; or, The Voice of Peace to an Unquiet Conscience ... London: for Robert Pawlett, 1676. 3rd edn. [iv], 155,[4 advt] pp. Engvd frontis vignette, red & black title. Old calf, rebacked, edges worn. Wing M.851. Anon.
(Hollett) **£95 [≈ $182]**

Martyn, Benjamin
- Timoleon. A Tragedy ... London: for J. Watts ..., 1730. 2nd edn. 8vo. [xvi],66,[6] pp. Half-title. 2 sm reprs. New bds. Anon.
(Young's) **£35 [≈ $67]**

Martyn, John
- The Bucolicks of Virgil with an English Translation and Notes by J. Martyn. London: 1749. 2nd edn. xcix,[i],390, 7,[11] pp. Port, 2 maps, 2 plates. Calf, jnts cracked.
(Wheldon & Wesley) **£50 [≈ $95]**

Martyn, Thomas, entomologist
- The English Entomologist exhibiting all the Coleopterous Insects found in England. London: 1792. Text in English & French. Roy 4to. [v],33,[vi], 41,[4] pp. 2 engvd titles, 2 plates of medals, 42 hand cold plates. Contemp half russia, rebacked, crnrs reprd.
(Wheldon & Wesley) **£750 [≈ $1,439]**

Martyn, Thomas, F.R.S.
- Flora Rustica: exhibiting Accurate Figures of such Plants as are either Useful or Injurious in Husbandry, drawn and engraved by Frederick P. Nodder ... London: 1792-94. 4 vols. 8vo. 144 hand cold plates. Occas sl browning. Qtr calf, uncut, rebacked.
(Henly) **£580 [≈ $1,113]**
- Thirty-Eight Plates ... to illustrate Linnaeus's System of Vegetables. London: 1799. 8vo. 38

plain plates. Half mor.
(Wheldon & Wesley) **£20 [≈ $38]**
- Thirty-Eight Plates ... to illustrate Linnaeus's System of Vegetables ... London: 1799. 8vo. vi,72 pp. 38 hand cold plates. Calf, worn & broken.   *(Wheldon & Wesley)* **£80 [≈ $153]**

Martyn, Thomas
- A Chronological Series of Engravers from the Invention of the Art to the Beginning of the Present Century. Cambridge: UP, 1770. 1st edn. 12mo. [iv],xii, 128,[16] pp. 3 fldg plates. Few contemp MS notes. Contemp qtr calf, yellow edges. Anon.
(Bookpress) **$325 [≈ £169]**

Marvell, Andrew
- The Rehearsal Transprosed or Animadversions Upon a Late Book ... 2nd Impression with Additions and Amendments. London: 1672. 8vo. [1],326 pp. Sm hole last leaf. Calf, worn. Wing M.878.
(Humber) **£75 [≈ $143]**
- A Short Historical Essay touching General Councils, Creeds, and Impositions in Matters of Religion ... London: ptd in the year 1680. 1st sep edn. 4to. Title sl stained. Early doodles on title & verso of final blank. New wraps. Wing M.888. *(Stewart)* **£140 [≈ $268]**

Mary Magdalen's Tears ...
- See Martin, T. or J.

Maseres, Francis
- A Review of the Government and Grievances of the Province of Quebec, since the Conquest of it by British Arms. To which is added, An Appendix ... London: Logographic Press, 1788. Half-title, 111 pp. Disbound. Anon.
(C.R. Johnson) **£350 [≈ $671]**

Mason, George
- An Essay on Design in Gardening. London: for B. White, 1768. 1st edn. Sm 8vo. [4],54 pp. Half-title. Lacks final blank. Contemp calf, rebacked. Anon.
(Fenning) **£350 [≈ $671]**

Mason, John
- An Essay on Elocution, or, Pronunciation ... Third Edition. London: for R. Hett ..., 1751. 8vo. 43 pp. Disbound.
(Jarndyce) **£110 [≈ $211]**
- An Essay on Elocution, or, Pronunciation ... London: for J. Buckland, 1757. 4th edn. 8vo. 52,[1 advt] pp. Disbound.
(Young's) **£65 [≈ $124]**

Mason, William
- Caractacus, a Dramatic Poem ... By the Author of Elfrida. London: Knapton & Dodsley, 1759. 4to. Press figs on M2v, M3v; N2 sgnd N3. Lacks half-title. Disbound, sewing perished. Anon.
  (Waterfield's) £40 [≈ $76]
- Elfrida, a Dramatic Poem ... Second Edition. London: Knapton, 1752. 8vo. [iv],xx, 80 pp. Mod wraps.   *(Claude Cox)* £15 [≈ $28]
- The English Garden: a Poem. Book the First ... Second Edition. London: sold by R. Horsefield ..., 1772. 4to. Half-title. Disbound. Anon. *(Waterfield's)* £40 [≈ $76]
- The English Garden: a Poem ... A New Edition, corrected. To which are added a Commentary and Notes, by W. Burgh ... York: A. Ward ..., 1783. 1st complete edn. 8vo. ix, [i], 243 pp. Early 19th c half sheep, spine sl worn. *(Burmester)* £75 [≈ $143]
- An Epistle to Dr Shebbeare to which is added an Ode to Sir Fletcher Norton ... By Malcolm Macgreggor of Knightsbridge [pseud.] ... Third Edition. London: for J. Almon, 1777. 4to. Disbound. Anon.
  (Waterfield's) £40 [≈ $76]

The Massacre of Glenco ...
- The Massacre of Glenco. being a True Narrative of the Barbarous Murder of the Glenco-Men, in the Highlands of Scotland ... 13th of Feb. 1692 ... London: B. Bragg, 1703. 1st edn. 4to. 32 pp. Rebound in qtr calf. Anon. Attributed to George Ridpath or Charles Leslie. *(Burmester)* £280 [≈ $537]

Masters, Mary
- Familiar Letters and Poems on Several Occasions. London: for the author, by D. Henry & R. Cave, 1755. 336 pp. Subscribers. Contemp calf. *(C.R. Johnson)* £850 [≈ $1,631]

Masters, Samuel
- The Case of Allegiance in Our Present Circumstances Consider'd in a Letter from a Minister in the City to a Minister in the Country. London: for Ric. Chiswell, 1689. Mod wraps. Wing M.1067. Anon.
  (Waterfield's) £30 [≈ $57]

Mather, Increase
- A Discourse concerning Faith and Fervency in Prayer ... Boston: B. Green, for Samuel Gerrish, 1710. 1st edn. 12mo. Some soiling & use. Disbound, stitching loose.
  (Ximenes) $750 [≈ £390]

- A Disquisition concerning Ecclesiastical Councils ... Boston: for N. Boone, 1716. 1st edn. 12mo. Contemp sheep, a bit worn, old paper label on spine.
  (Ximenes) $1,500 [≈ £781]

Mather, Samuel
- The Life of the Very Reverend and Learned Cotton Mather ... Boston: Samuel Gerrish, 1729. 1st edn. 8vo. [ii],vi,6, 10,186 pp. Subscribers. Some foxing & water staining. Later half mor, t.e.g.
  (Bookpress) $650 [≈ £338]
- Memoirs of the Life of the late Reverend Increase Mather, D.D. who died August 23, 1723. London: 1725. Sm 4to. [6],88 pp. Mezzotint port. Decs. Some foxing. Hole in 1 leaf not affecting text. Contemp mrbld wraps. The Brinley copy. Anon.
  (Reese) $2,000 [≈ £1,041]

Mathias, Thomas James
- The Pursuits of Literature. A Satirical Poem, in Four Dialogues. With Notes. Dublin: for J. Milliken, 1798. 8th edn. xxxi,380 pp. Mor. Anon. *(Young's)* £50 [≈ $95]

The Matrimonial Preceptor ...
- The Matrimonial Preceptor. A Collection of Examples and Precepts relating to the Married State from the most celebrated Writers Ancient and Modern. London: for T. Lownds ..., [1765]. 3rd edn. 12mo. Contemp calf gilt. Pieces by Dr. Johnson & others.
  (Ximenes) $900 [≈ £468]

Maude, Thomas
- Verbeia; or Wharfdale, a Poem Descriptive and Didactic with Historical Remarks. York: E. Blanchard, 1782. 4to. Half-title,44,45 pp. Disbound. Anon.
  (C.R. Johnson) £225 [≈ $431]
- Viator a Poem: or, a Journey from London to Scarborough, by way of York. With Notes Historical and Topographical. London: B. White ..., 1782. Half-title, 40,xix pp. Disbound. Anon.
  (C.R. Johnson) £225 [≈ $431]
- Wensley-Dale; or Rural Contemplations: a Poem. Third Edition. London: James Dixwell, 1780. 4to. Frontis, plates. Rebound in qtr calf. Anon.
  (C.R. Johnson) £145 [≈ $278]

Maupertius, Pierre Louis Moreau de
- The Figure of the Earth, determined from Observations ... at the Polar Circle ...

London: Cox, Davis ..., 1738. 1st edn in English. 8vo. vii,[i],232 pp. Fldg map, 9 fldg plates. Title backed. Contemp calf, sl later mor label. *(Burmester)* **£200 [≈ $383]**

Maurice, Henry
- A Defence of Diocesan Episcopacy ... London: Hannah Clark for James Adamson, 1691. 1st edn. 8vo. [viii],456 pp. Contemp calf, hd of spine worn. Wing M.1360.
(Lloyd-Roberts) **£35 [≈ $67]**
- The Lawfulness of taking the New Oaths Asserted. London: J. Mills, sold by Randal Taylor, 1689. 1st edn. 4to. [ii],13,[i] pp. Dusty, some staining, lib stamp on title verso. Later wraps, untrimmed. Wing M.1364. Anon. *(Clark)* **£20 [≈ $38]**

Maurice, Thomas
- The School-Boy. A Poem. In Imitation of Mr. Phillips's Splendid Shilling. Oxford: for the author, & sold by J. & J. Fletcher, [1775]. 4to. 12 pp. Disbound. Anon.
(C.R. Johnson) **£165 [≈ $316]**

Maury, Jean Siffrein
- The Principles of Eloquence; adapted to the Pulpit and the Bar. Translated from the French, with Additional Notes, by John Neal Lake. London: Cadell, Dilly, 1793. 1st edn in English. 8vo. xvi,242,[2 errata], 16 advt pp. Orig bds, respined. *(Burmester)* **£90 [≈ $172]**

Mavor, William Fordyce
- The Juvenile Olio; or Mental Medley: containing Original Essays ... Tales ... Written by a Father chiefly for the Use of his Children. London: for E. Newborn, 1796. 266, 2 advt pp. Frontis. Contemp calf, red label. *(C.R. Johnson)* **£70 [≈ $134]**
- Youth's Miscellany; or, a Father's Gift to his Children ... London: E. Newbery, 1798. Sm 8vo. xi,286,[2 advt] pp. Frontis. Sl damp stain bottom edge. Mod calf, gilt spine, orig endpapers. *(Bromer)* **$400 [≈ £208]**

Mawe, Thomas & Abercrombie, John
- Every Man his Own Gardener ... Dublin: for P. Byrne, 1798. 14th edn. 8vo. [iv],626,[19] pp. Old sheep, rubbed. *(Young's)* **£42 [≈ $80]**
- Every Man His Own Gardener ... The Twelfth Edition ... London: 1788. 12mo. [iv],616, [xix] pp. Frontis. Orig calf, rubbed, hd of spine sl worn, upper jnt cracked but firm. *(Bickersteth)* **£56 [≈ $107]**

Maxims of Equity ...
- See Francis, Richard.

Maxwell, Henry
- An Essay towards an Union of Ireland with England ... London: Timothy Goodwin, 1703. 4to. 56 pp. Disbound. Anon.
(C.R. Johnson) **£250 [≈ $479]**

Maxwell, R.
- The Practical Husbandman: being a Collection of Miscellaneous Papers on Husbandry. Edinburgh: 1757. 8vo. xii,432,4 pp. Verso of title sgnd by the author. Half calf, backstrip relaid.a *(Henly)* **£60 [≈ $115]**

Maxwell, Robert
- The Practical Husbandman ... Edinburgh: the author, 1758. 1st edn. 8vo. xii,432,[6] pp. 1 plate. Contemp calf.
(Bookpress) **$475 [≈ £247]**

May, Thomas
- A Discourse concerning the Successe of Former Parliaments. London: 1642. 1st edn. 4to. [2],12 pp. Lacks blank at end. Rec wraps. Wing M.1406. Anon. *(Fenning)* **£65 [≈ $124]**

Mead, Richard
- A Discourse on the Plague. The Ninth Edition corrected and enlarged. London: 1744. 8vo. [viii],164 pp. Strip cut from top of title. Old lib stamp on p. 1. Old half calf, upper jnt cracked. *(Bickersteth)* **£45 [≈ $86]**
- A Mechanical Account of Poisons in Several Essays. The Second Edition, revised, with Additions. London: J.M. for Ralph Smith, 1708. 8vo. [16],189,[2] pp. Half-title. Fldg engvd plate. Sl worming in inner blank marg. Rec qtr calf. *(Fenning)* **£85 [≈ $163]**
- A Mechanical Account of Poisons, in Several Essays ... London: J. Brindley, 1745. 3rd edn. 8vo. xlviii,319,[1] pp. 4 plates (1 fldg). Contemp calf, rear hinge cracked.
(Bookpress) **$300 [≈ £156]**
- Medica Sacra; or, a Commentary on the most Remarkable Diseases, mentioned in the Holy Scriptures. London: 1755. 120 pp. Contemp panelled calf, rebacked.
(Whitehart) **£295 [≈ $566]**
- Medical Precepts and Cautions ... London: J. Brindley, 1755. 2nd edn. 8vo. xvi,311,[1] pp. Contemp calf, hinges cracked.
(Bookpress) **$185 [≈ £96]**
- Monita et Precepta Medica. London: Brindley, 1751. 1st edn. 8vo. [xii],272 pp.

Later half calf. *(Bookpress)* $225 [≈ £117]
- A Treatise concerning the Influence of the Sun and Moon upon Human Bodies and the Diseases thereby produced. Translated from the Latin by Thomas Stack. London: Brindley, 1748. 2 vols in one. 8vo. 130, 204 pp. Title dusty & chipped at foredge. New antique style bds. *(Goodrich)* $145 [≈ £75]
- A Treatise on the Small Pox and Measles ... London: for the translator, & sold by R. Griffiths, 1747. 1st edn in English. 8vo. Errata leaf. Old wraps.
(Ximenes) $250 [≈ £130]

Meades, Anna
- The History of Sir William Harrington ... Revised and Corrected by the late Mr. Richardson. London: for John Bell, & C. Etherington, York, 1771. 1st edn. 4 vols. 12mo. Half-titles & final advts in vols 1-3, crrctly. Sl used. Contemp calf, sl worn. Anon.
(Ximenes) $850 [≈ £442]

Meadows, Sir Philip
- A Narrative of the Principal Actions occurring in the Wars between Sueden and Denmark. Before and after the Roschild Treaty. London: A.C. for H. brome, 1677. 1st edn. 12mo. Minor stains. Contemp calf, worn. Wing M.1566.
(Hannas) £150 [≈ $287]

Meadows, Samuel
- A Warning to the Sluggard; or, A Picture of a Slothful Man Void of Understanding ... London: for the author ..., 1768. 1st edn. 8vo. 39 pp. Disbound. *(Young's)* £35 [≈ $67]

Mede, Joseph
- The Reverence of Gods House A Sermon preached ... on St. Matthies day, Anno 1635/6 ... London: M.F. for John Clark ..., 1638. 1st edn. 4to. 71 pp. Title & next leaf reprd. Stained. Disbound. STC 17769.
(Young's) £35 [≈ $67]

Medea, a Tragedy ...
- See Glover, Richard.

Meeks, Carroll L.V.
- Italian Architecture, 1750-1914. New Haven & London: Yale UP, 1966. Lge stout 4to. xxviii, 546 pp. 266 ills. Cloth. Dw.
(Ars Libri) $150 [≈ £78]

Meier, George Frederick
- The Merry Philosopher; or, Thoughts on Jesting ... Now first Translated into English from the German original. London: Newbery, Nicoll, 1764. 1st edn in English. Sm 8vo. [iv], 213,[3 blank & advt] pp. Name erased from title. Rec cloth.
(Burmester) £150 [≈ $287]

Melmoth, William
- Letters of Sir Thomas Fitzosborne, on Several Subjects. London: Dodsley, 1769. 7th edn. 8vo. xii,452 pp. Contemp calf, front jnt weakening. Anon. *(Young's)* £25 [≈ $47]

Melville, Sir James
- The Memoirs ... Published from the Original Manuscript by George Scott ... Third Edition, corrected. Glasgow, Robert Urie, 1751. 8vo. Contemp sheep, backstrip worn, jnts cracked but sound.
(Waterfield's) £55 [≈ $105]

Memoirs ...
- Memoirs of a Cavalier ... see Defoe, Daniel.
- Memoirs of a Man of Pleasure ... see La Solle, H.F. de.
- Memoirs of George Anne Bellamy, including all her Intrigues ... By a Gentleman of Covent-Garden Theatre. London: J. Walker, 1785. Issue with pp 199/200 condensed. 204 pp. Contemp qtr calf, hinges worn.
(C.R. Johnson) £180 [≈ $345]
- Memoirs of the Cardinal de Retz ... London: for J. Brotherton ..., 1723. 8vo. viii, [iv],332 pp. Contemp half calf, sl rubbed.
(Young's) £30 [≈ $57]
- Memoirs of the House of Brandenburg ... see Frederick II, King of Prussia.
- Memoirs of the Life and Administration of the late Andrew- Hercules Fleury, Cardinal of the Roman Church ... By an Impartial Hand. The Second Edition. London: J. Roberts, 1743. 8vo. 101 pp. Title sl dusty. New bds.
(Claude Cox) £15 [≈ $28]
- Memoirs of the Life and Gallant Exploits of the Old Highlander, Sergeant Donald Macleod, who having returned, wounded, with the Corpse of General Wolfe, from Quebec, was admitted an out-pensioner of Chelsea Hospital ... London: 1791. 90 pp. Qtr calf. *(C.R. Johnson)* £180 [≈ $345]
- Memoirs of the Life of Simon Fraser, Lord Lovat. London: for M. Cooper, 1746. 1st edn. 8vo. [iv],123 pp. Half-title. Title marg & final leaf reprd. *(Young's)* £45 [≈ $86]

- Memoirs of the Life of the late Reverend Increase Mather ... see Mather, Samuel.
- Memoirs of the Life of the late George Frederic Handel ... see Mainwaring, J.
- The Memoirs of the Marquess de Langallerie ... see Courtilz de Sandras, Gatien de (supposed author).
- Memoirs of the Year Two Thousand Five Hundred ... see Mercier, L.S.
- Memoirs relating to the Restoration of King James I. of Scotland ... London: for W. Jones ..., 1716. 1st edn. 8vo. 32 pp. Browned. Disbound. *(Young's)* **£25 [≈ $47]**

Memoria Technica ...
- See Grey, Richard.

Memorial ...
- The Memorial of the Church of England humbly offer'd to the Considerations of all true Lovers of our Church and Constitution. London: printed in the year, 1705. Setting with catchword '-ing' on p 16. Sometimes attributed to W. Pittis, J. Drake & H. Pooley. *(Waterfield's)* **£35 [≈ $67]**

Memorials ...
- Memorials and Letters relating to the History of Britain in the Reign of Charles I. Published from Originals. Glasgow: Robert & Andrew Foulis, 1766. 1st edn. 8vo. xxxii,191 pp. Contemp mottled calf. *(Gough)* **£55 [≈ $105]**

Mendoza, Daniel
- The Art of Boxing: with a Statement of the Transactions that have passed between Mr. Humphreys and myself since our Battle at Oldham. (London): for Daniel Mendoza ..., (1789). 1st edn. 12mo. Half-title. Frontis. A bit used. Rec amateur calf. *(Ximenes)* **$1,250 [≈ £651]**

Mengs, A.R.
- The Works of Anthony Raphael Mengs ... published by Chev. Don Joseph Nicholas D'Azara. London: Faulder, 1796. 1st English edn. 3 vols in 2. Errata leaf at end. Half leather. *(Ars Artis)* **£210 [≈ $403]**

Menzies, John
- Papismus Lucifugus, A faithfull Copie of the Papers exchanged ... Aberdene: John Forbes younger, 1668. 1st edn. 4to. [xxxvi], 272 pp. No front free endpaper. Contemp sheep, rebacked, crnrs reprd. Wing M.1725. *(Clark)* **£150 [≈ $287]**

Mercier, Louis Sebastien
- Memoirs of the Year Two Thousand Five Hundred. London: for G. Robinson, 1772. 1st edn in English. 12mo. Contemp calf, gilt spines, sl rubbed, 1 jnt cracked. Anon. *(Ximenes)* **$950 [≈ £494]**

Meriton, George
- The Praise of Yorkshire Ale ... The Third Edition ... by G.M. Gent. York: J. White for Francis Hildyard, 1697. 8vo. Title laid down & browned, few sm holes in title. 19th c calf, rebacked. *(Waterfield's)* **£135 [≈ $259]**

Merry, Robert
- The Pains of Memory. A Poem. London: Robinson, 1796. 4to. 36 pp. Rec mrbld wraps. *(C.R. Johnson)* **£250 [≈ $479]**

Mesnager, Mons.
- Minutes of the Negotiations ... see Defoe, Daniel.

Methodical ...
- A Methodical Treatise of Replevins, Distresses, Avowries, &c. Containing the Method of Proceedings therein in the Courts at Westminster ... In the Savoy: Nutt & Gosling ..., 1739. 2nd edn, crrctd. Damp staining at ends. Contemp calf, sl worn. *(Meyer Boswell)* **$175 [≈ £91]**

Michaelis, Sebastian
- The Admirable Historie of the Possession and Conversion of a Penitent Woman ... Translated into English by W.B. London: for William Apsley, 1613. 1st English edn, 2nd issue. Sm 4to. [xlviii],418,[x], 154,[34] pp. V sl marg worm. 18th c qtr calf, rebacked. STC 17854A. *(Vanbrugh)* **£1,555 [≈ $2,985]**

Michell, John
- A Treatise of Artificial Magnets ... Second Edition, Corrected and Improved. Cambridge: Joseph Bentham, 1751. 78 pp. Fldg plate. Cased in cloth bds. *(C.R. Johnson)* **£180 [≈ $345]**

Mickle, William Julius
- Poems and a Tragedy. London: A. Paris, for J. Egerton ..., 1794. 1st coll edn. 4to. Half-title. 7 pp subscribers. Frontis port. Lib stamps. Rec lib cloth. *(Jarndyce)* **£35 [≈ $67]**
- Pollio: an Elegiac Ode ... Oxford: at the Clarendon Press ..., 1766. 1st edn. 4to. Disbound. Anon. *(Ximenes)* **$275 [≈ £143]**

The Microcosm ...
- See Canning, George, et al.

Middleton, Charles
- Picturesque and Architectural Views for Cottages, Farm Houses and Country Villas. London: for Edward Jeffrey, 1793. 1st edn. Folio. [2],16 pp. 21 aquatint plates (11 dble page, 10 cold). Qtr calf & mrbld bds.
(Sotheran's) **£1,850 [≈ $3,551]**

Middleton, Conyers
- A Dissertation concerning the Origin of Printing in England ... Cambridge: for W. Thurlbourn ..., 1735. 1st edn. 4to. [iv],29, [1], [2 advt] pp. Half-title. Vignette on title. Rec bds. *(Burmester)* **£250 [≈ $479]**
- A Free Inquiry into the Miraculous Powers which are supposed to have subsisted in the Christian Church, from the Earliest Ages ... London: for Manby & Cox, 1749. 4to. Some browning of title & half-title. Contemp calf, worn, front jnt breaking.
(Waterfield's) **£45 [≈ $86]**
- The History of the Life of Marcus Tullius Cicero. Dublin: for John Smith & Abraham Bradley, 1741. 2 vols. 8vo. Contemp speckled calf, green labels, some wear to spine ends & crnrs, jnts cracking.
(Waterfield's) **£50 [≈ $95]**
- A Letter from Rome, Showing an Exact Conformity between Popery and Paganism ... The Third Edition, with Additions. London: for William Innys & Richard Manby, 1733. 4to. Disbound. *(Sanders)* **£35 [≈ $67]**
- The Miscellaneous Works ... London: Richard Manby, 1752. 1st edn. 4 vols. 4to. xcvi, 400; x,500; iv,502,[2]; [iv],x,437, [51] pp. Frontis vol 1, 24 plates. Red half mor.
(Bookpress) **$350 [≈ £182]**

Midnight the Signal ...
- See Hanway, Jonas.

Miege, Guy
- Miscellanea: or, a Choice Collection of Wise and Ingenious Sayings ... by G.M. ... London: for William Lindsey, 1694. 1st edn. Sm 8vo. Title sl soiled. 19th c half calf, gilt spine (sl rubbed). Wing M.2014.
(Ximenes) **$600 [≈ £312]**
- The Present State of Denmark. London: for Tho. Basset, 1683. 1st edn. Sm 8vo. [8],159 pp. Contemp sheep, rebacked. Wing M.2024.
(Fenning) **£350 [≈ $671]**
- The Present State of Great Britain, and

Ireland, in Three Parts ... London: for J. Brotherton ..., 1738. 8th edn, enlgd. 8vo. 308; 251,[4 advt] pp. Port frontis. V sl foxing. Orig calf, hinges cracked, spine ends & crnrs rubbed. Anon. *(Chapel Hill)* **$85 [≈ £44]**
- A Relation of Three Embassies from His Sacred Majestie Charles II to the Great Duke of Muscovie, the King of Sweden, and King of Denmark ... London: 1669. 1st edn. 8vo. 3 advt pp. 2 ports (frontis laid down). Contemp calf, rebacked. Wing M.2025.
(Hannas) **£240 [≈ $460]**

Mihles, Samuel
- The Elements of Surgery ... Adapted to the Use of the Camp and Navy, as well as of the Domestic Surgeon. London: Knapton, 1746. 1st edn. 8vo. [vi],324,[12] pp & inserted leaf after p 271. 25 plates (I-III, A-Y). Contemp polished calf, mor label, fine.
(Gaskell) **£850 [≈ $1,631]**

Mildmay, Sir William
- An Account of the Southern Maritime Provinces of France ... London: Thomas Garrison, 1764. 4to. 133,2 pp. 2 fldg plans. Disbound. Anon.
(C.R. Johnson) **£450 [≈ $863]**
- The Police of France: or, an Account of the Laws and Regulations established in that Kingdom, for the Preservation of Peace and the Preventing of Robberies ... London: E. Owen & T. Harrison, 1763. 4to. 138 pp. Disbound. Anon.
(C.R. Johnson) **£450 [≈ $863]**

Miles, William
- A Letter to Henry Duncombe, Esq. Member for the County of York, on the Subject of a very extraordinary Pamphlet lately addressed by Mr. Burke, to a Noble Lord. The Second Edition. London: Debrett, 1796. 100 pp. Rebound in bds. *(C.R. Johnson)* **£45 [≈ $86]**

Millar, G.H.
- A New ... Body or System of Natural History. London: [1785]. Folio. [iv], 5-618, [2] pp. Frontis, 85 plates. Frontis mtd, title creased. Mod bds. *(Wheldon & Wesley)* **£225 [≈ $431]**

Miller, Philip
- The Gardener's Dictionary ... London: for the author, & sold by C. Rivington, 1731. 1st edn. Folio. xvi,[iv], B1-8D2, a1-zz2 in 2s pp. Frontis, 4 fldg plates. Occas minor staining, sl marg worm. Sm hole affecting a few lines. Contemp calf, rebacked, crnrs reprd.

(Clark) **£280 [≈ $537]**
- The Gardeners Dictionary ... abridged from the last folio edition. London: 1754. 4th edn. 3 vols. 8vo. Frontis, 3 plates. Contemp calf, rebacked with mor.
(Wheldon & Wesley) **£160 [≈ $307]**
- The Gardener's Dictionary ... London: the author, (1756)-1759. 7th edn. Folio. Unpaginated. Contemp calf.
(Bookpress) **$1,500 [≈ £781]**
- The Gardener's Kalendar ... The Eighth Edition ... added a List of the Medicinal Plants ... London: Rivington, 1748. 8vo. [2], xvi,343,10,1 advt pp. Frontis. No intl blank. Tear in dedic. Final blank defective. Contemp calf gilt, short crack in upper jnt.
(Beech) **£70 [≈ $134]**
- The Gardener's Kalendar ... London: Rivington, 1751. 9th edn. 8vo. Frontis. Contemp calf, gilt spine (trifle rubbed).
(Ximenes) **$150 [≈ £78]**
- The Gardeners Kalendar; directing what works are necessary to be performed every Month in the Kitchen, Fruit, and Pleasure-Gardens. London: 1760. 12th edn. 8vo. xiv,429,1 advt pp. Frontis, 5 fldg plates. Addtnl MS index inserted. Calf, sl worn.
(Henly) **£65 [≈ $124]**
- The Gardeners Kalendar. London: 1769. 15th edn. 8vo. lxvi,382,[21] pp. Frontis, 5 plates. Contemp calf, jnts cracking.
(Wheldon & Wesley) **£45 [≈ $86]**

Millot, Claude F.X.
- Elements of General History. Translated from the French ... Dublin: for Price, Potts ..., 1779. 1st Irish edn. 5 vols. 8vo. xxiii, 564; xii,571; xvi,[9],435; [15],518,[2 blank]; [12],500 pp. Few flyleaves lacking. Contemp calf, red & green labels, 2 vols sl rubbed.
(Fenning) **£45 [≈ $86]**

Mills, John
- Essays Moral, Philosophical, and Political. London: for S. Hooper, 1772. viii, [2], 340,xxi,[1] pp. Rebound in qtr calf.
(C.R. Johnson) **£285 [≈ $547]**

Milns, William
- The Penman's Repository ... London: the author, 1787. 1st edn. Oblong 4to. 32 ff, engvd throughout. V sl soiling at some crnrs. New qtr calf, slipcase.
(Bookpress) **$1,250 [≈ £651]**

Milton, John
- Accedence Commenc't Grammar, Supply'd with sufficient Rules, For the use of such (Younger or Elder) as are desirous ... to attain the Latin Tongue ... London: for S.S. & sold by John Starkey, 1669. 12mo. [4],65, [1] pp. 18th c qtr calf. Wing M.2088.
(C.R. Johnson) **£8,500 [≈ $16,319]**
- Paradise Lost ... Twelfth Edition ... Account of his Life. London: Tonson, 1725. Lge 12mo. xxviii,[8],350,[46] pp. Port, 12 plates. Sl foxing throughout. Rec bds.
(Fenning) **£85 [≈ $163]**
- Paradise Lost ... Fourteenth Edition, to which is prefix'd An Account of his Life. London: Tonson, 1741. 8vo. Frontis, 12 plates. Contemp calf, rebacked.
(Stewart) **£75 [≈ $143]**
- Paradise Lost. London: for Tonson ..., 1751. Cr 8vo. Frontis, 12 plates. Some old staining. New bds.
(Stewart) **£45 [≈ $86]**
- Paradise Lost ... Birmingham: John Baskerville for J. & R. Tonson, London, 1758. 1st Baskerville edn. 8vo. [30],[xix],416 pp. 18 pp subscribers. Rebound in mod panelled calf, gilt spine.
(Claude Cox) **£110 [≈ $211]**
- Paradise Lost. London: for London: Hawes ..., 1764. Cr 8vo. Port, 12 engvd plates by Hayman. Contemp calf, crudely rebacked, crnrs worn.
(Stewart) **£30 [≈ $57]**
- Paradise Lost: a Poem. Glasgow: Robert & Andrew Foulis, 1770. Folio. Some reprs to gutter of title. Occas sl spotting. B1 apparently cancelled as usual. Mod qtr mor.
(Waterfield's) **£150 [≈ $287]**
- Paradise Lost ... With a Biographical and Critical Account of the Author and his Writings. London: A. Law, W. Miller, & R. Cater, 1795. New edn. 12mo. 299 pp. Port, 12 plates. Good reading copy only. Contemp sheep, upper jnt split but sound.
(Gough) **£20 [≈ $38]**
- Paradise Lost. London: Longman, Law ..., 1795. 8vo. Title vignette. Contemp calf, upper jnt broken. *(Stewart)* **£25 [≈ $47]**
- Paradise Regain'd ... added Samson Agonistes ... London: for John Starkey, 1680. 2nd edn. Sm 8vo. 2 ctlg ff at end. Lacks licence leaf. Blank foredge of title reprd. Sl soiling. 1 tear reprd. Mor gilt, a.e.g. Wing M.2153.
(Georges) **£200 [≈ $383]**
- Paradise Regain'd ... To which is added Samson Agonistes. And Poems upon several Occasions. With a Tractate of Education. The Fifth Edition ... London: Tonson, 1713.

12mo. Frontis, 10 plates. Occas browning. 1 page rubbed with v sl loss. Old calf, rebacked.
(Sanders) £85 [≈ $163]

- Paradise Regain'd ... added Samson Agonistes; and Poems upon several Occasions. With a Tractate of Education. London: for J. & R. Tonson, 1742. 8th edn, crrctd. 8vo. New bds. *(Stewart)* £45 [≈ $86]

- Paradise Regain'd ... Samson Agonistes; and Poems upon Several Occasions, with a Tractate of Education. The Eighth Edition. London: Tonson ..., 1743. Lge 12mo. [8],352 pp. Frontis. Contemp calf gilt, jnts cracked but firm.   *(Fenning)* £65 [≈ $124]

- Paradise Regain'd ... Samson Agonistes ... Poems on Several Occasions ... Birmingham: John Baskerville for J. & R. Tonson, 1758. 1st Baskerville edn. 8vo. 390 pp. Bound without the Life. Contemp calf, elab gilt spine, upper hinge cracked, extremities rubbed.
(Claude Cox) £85 [≈ $163]

- A Treatise of Civil Power in Ecclesiastical Causes shewing that it is not lawful for any Power on Earth to compel in Matters of Religion. London: reptd for J. Johnson, 1790. 8vo. Title frayed & laid down. Mod qtr calf.
(Waterfield's) £115 [≈ $220]

Minsheu, John
- Ductor in Linguas, The Guide into Tongues ... London: 1617. 1st edn. Lge folio. [xvi], 543 pp. Some marg worm at end. Mid 18th c calf, hinges cracked. Duke of Bedford b'plate. STC 17944.   *(Vanbrugh)* £475 [≈ $911]

- The Gvide into Tongves [Latin title] ... London: Iohn Haviland, 1627. 2nd edn. Folio.. [iv] pp, 760 columns. Occas sm marg tears, sl spotting & browning. Contemp calf, upper jnt & spine ends reprd. STC 17947.
(Burmester) £350 [≈ $671]

The Mirror ...
- See Mackenzie, Henry, et al.

Miscellaneous Poems ...
- Miscellaneous Poems: on Various Subjects, and Occasions ... see Giles, Joseph.

Miscellany Poems ...
- Miscellany Poems, on Several Occasions ... see Finch, Anne, Countess of Winchelsea.

Mitchell, John
- The Present State of Great Britain and North America, with regard to Agriculture, Population, Trade, and Manufactures,

Impartially Considered. London: 1767. Only edn. xvi,363 pp, errata. Half-title. Foxed. Mod polished calf. Anon.
(Reese) $1,250 [≈ £651]

Mitchell, Joseph
- The Highland Fair; or The Union of the Clans. An Opera ... London: for J. Watts, 1731. 1st edn. 8vo. Frontis. Prelims inc 4 advt pp. Ends sl dusty. Disbound.
(Dramatis Personae) $300 [≈ £156]

- The Highland Fair; or, Union of the Clans. An Opera ... London: J. Watts, 1731. 1st edn. 8vo. [xiv],78 pp. Frontis by Hogarth. W'cut music. Some foxing of text. Mod half calf.
(Bookpress) $275 [≈ £143]

Mitford, William
- An Essay upon the Harmony of Language, intended principally to illustrate that of the English Language. London: Scott, 1774. iv, 288 pp. Contemp calf, red label. Anon.
(C.R. Johnson) £350 [≈ $671]

Modern ...
- The Modern Family Physician, or the Art of Healing Made Easy ... Adapted to the Use of private Families. London: F. Newbery, 1775. 279 pp. Contemp sheep, jnt broken.
(C.R. Johnson) £185 [≈ $355]

- The Modern Practice of the London Hospitals ... A New Edition. With an useful Index of Diseases, and their Remedies. London: for G. Lister, [1785]. 121 pp. Engvd frontis. Rec bds.
(C.R. Johnson) £225 [≈ $431]

Moellenbrock, Andreas Valentin
- Cochlearie Curiosa: or the Curiosities of Scurvygrass ... London: S. & B. Griffin for William Cademan, 1676. 1st edn in English. Trans by Thomas Sherley. 8vo. [16],195,[29] pp. 4 fldg plates. Sl browning. Calf, rebacked. Wing M.2381.   *(Rootenberg)* $950 [≈ £494]

Molesworth, Robert
- An Account of Denmark, as it was in the Year 1692. London: Printed in the Year 1694. 1st edn. 8vo. [lii],271,[i] pp. Minor marg spotting. Contemp calf, some wear at extremities, sm splits in jnts, sl loose. Wing M.2382A. Anon.   *(Clark)* £125 [≈ $239]

Molyneux, William
- The Case of Ireland's being bound by Acts of Parliament in England, stated ... Dublin: ptd by & for J.R., & sold by Clavel, Churchill ...

London, 1698. 1st edn, London issue. 8vo. [xvi],174 pp. Contemp calf, rebacked. Wing M.2403.   *(Pickering)* **$850 [≈ £442]**

Monier, Pierre
- The History of Painting, Architecture, Sculpture, Graving ... In Three Books ... London: for T. Bennet ..., 1699. 1st edn. 8vo. [xxx],192,[14],[4 advt] pp. Frontis. Errata on A8v. Orig panelled calf, sl worn, hinges cracked but firm. Wing M.2419.
(Vanbrugh) **£285 [≈ $547]**

Monk, John (ed.)
- An Agricultural Dictionary, consisting of Extracts from the most Celebrated Authors and Papers. London: G. Woodfall, 1794. 3 vols. 384; 372; 374 pp. Contemp qtr calf, mrbld bds. Matthew Boulton's copy.
(C.R. Johnson) **£225 [≈ $431]**
- An Agricultural Dictionary, consisting of Extracts from the most celebrated Authors and Papers. London: Woodfall for the author ..., 1794. 1st edn. 3 vols. 8vo. 384; 372; 374 pp. Contemp qtr calf, sl rubbed.
(Burmester) **£225 [≈ $431]**

Monro, A.
- The Structure and Physiology of Fishes explained ... Edinburgh: 1785. Large Paper. Folio (455 x 285 mm). 128 pp. 50 engvd plates on 44 ff (numbered 1-44, 3*, 9*,10*,14*, 15*, 40*). Occas minor foxing. 2 marg tears reprd. Contemp bds, rebacked in calf.   *(Wheldon & Wesley)* **£400 [≈ $767]**

Monro, Alexander
- Presbyterian Inquisition; as it was lately practised against the Professors of the College of Edinburgh August and September 1690 ... London: for J. Hindmarsh, 1691. Mod wraps. Wing M.2443. Anon.
(Waterfield's) **£30 [≈ $57]**

Monro, Thomas, et al.
- The Olla Podrida, a Periodical Work, Complete in Forty-Four Numbers ... London: J. Nichols ..., 1788. 1st edn thus. 8vo. 443 pp. Half calf. Anon.   *(Young's)* **£80 [≈ $153]**

Monroe, James
- A View of the Conduct of the Executive, in the Foreign Affairs of the United States, connected with the Mission to the French Republic ... 1794-1796. Phila: Benjamin Franklin Bache, 1797. 1st edn. 8vo. [iv],lx, 407 pp. Occas foxing. Contemp bds, rebacked

in cloth.   *(Bookpress)* **$250 [≈ £130]**

Monroe, Thomas
- Essays on Various Subjects. London: J. Nichols, 1790. Half-title, 228 pp. Lib stamp on title. Orig bds, uncut.
(C.R. Johnson) **£180 [≈ $345]**

Montagu, Richard
- Appello Caesarem. A Iust Appeale from Two Uniust Informers. London: H.L. for Mathew Lownes, 1625. Sm 4to. Old damp stain in 1st half. New calf. STC 18031.
(Georges) **£135 [≈ $259]**

Montague, Lady Mary Wortley
- Letters ... written, during her Travels ... London: 1763. 3rd edn. 3 vols. 12mo. xii, 165; 167; 134 pp. Mod qtr calf.
(Lewis) **£95 [≈ $182]**
- Letters ... written, during her Travels in Europe, Asia and Africa ... London: Becket & De Hondt, 1769. New edn. 3 vols. Contemp half calf, sl worn. *(Bookpress)* **$350 [≈ £182]**

Montaigne, Michel de
- The Essayes ... The Third Edition whereunto is now newly added an Index ... London: M. Flesher for Rich. Royston, 1632. Folio. Engvd title & verse "To the Beholder". Sm repr to crnr of 1 leaf. Panelled calf, rebacked, crnrs reprd. STC 18043.
(Jarndyce) **£350 [≈ $671]**

Montesquieu, Charles de Secondat, Baron de
- Miscellaneous Pieces ... Translated from the New Edition of his Works printed at Paris. London: for D. Wilson, 1759. 8vo. Blank segment of half-title lacking. 2 ff sl sprung. Contemp calf, jnts cracked but sound, clumsy repr to top jnt. *(Waterfield's)* **£425 [≈ $815]**
- Reflections on the Causes of the Rise and Fall of the Roman Empire: translated from the French ... The Fourth Edition ... Glasgow: Robert Urie, 1758. 8vo. Contemp speckled calf, red label.   *(Jarndyce)* **£85 [≈ $163]**
- The Spirit of Laws ... With Corrections and Additions communicated by the Author. London: Nourse & Vaillant, 1750. 1st English edn. 2 vols. 8vo. viii,[xx],452,[ii]; [ii], xvi, 483,[xlvi],[ii] pp. Occas browning & spotting. Contemp calf, rebacked.
(Sotheran's) **£985 [≈ $1,891]**
- The Spirit of the Laws. Translated from the French ... by Mr. Nugent ... The Second

Edition corrected ... London: Nourse & Vaillant, 1752. 2 vols. 8vo. xl,[xx],452; [ii], [ii advt], xvi,484, [xxxvi],[2 advt] pp. Contemp calf, ft of spine vol 2 'sl damaged.
(Finch) **£575 [≈ $1,103]**
- The Spirit of Laws translated from the French ... by Mr. Nugent ... The Second Edition, corrected ... London: Nourse & Vaillant, 1752. 2nd English edn. 2 vols. 8vo. Contemp calf, new labels.
(Waterfield's) **£400 [≈ $767]**

Montfaucon, Bernard de
- The Antiquities of Italy. being the Travels ... made English ... Second Edition, revis'd ... the Editor John Henley ... London: 1725. Folio. [ii],xxxviii,331,[i] pp. Vignette ills. Title trimmed & mtd without loss. Contemp calf, rebacked, crnrs reprd. *(Clark)* **£185 [≈ $355]**

Moore, Edward
- The Gamester. A Tragedy. London: for R. Francklin, 1753. 1st edn. Pott 4to. Sl browning. Later wraps, worn & split, upper wrapper detached. Anon.
(Ash) **£200 [≈ $383]**

Moore, Isabella
- The Useful and Entertaining Family Miscellany ... The Complete English Housekeeper's Companion ... near Five Hundred Receipts ... London: for Thomas Palmer, 1766. 1st edn. Post 8vo. vii,[i],112 pp. A few sl marks & creases. Mod half mor.
(Ash) **£500 [≈ $959]**

Moore, John
- A View of Society and Manners in France, Switzerland, and Germany. London: Strahan & Cadell, 1783. 5th edn. 2 vols. Demy 8vo. [iv], xvi,(452); [xvi],440 pp. Contemp mrbld calf, gilt dec spines in Adam style, contrasting oval numbers, sl worn. *(Ash)* **£100 [≈ $191]**
- A View of Society and Manners in France, Switzerland, and Germany ... London: Strahan & Cadell, 1786. 6th edn. 2 vols. 8vo. xvi, 420; xii,420 pp. Sm piece torn from last f.e.p. Contemp tree calf, elab gilt dec spines, 2-cold labels, fine. *(Gough)* **£225 [≈ $431]**
- A View of Society and Manners in France, Switzerland, and Germany ... London: Strahan, 1786. 6th edn, crrctd. 2 vols. 8vo. xvi,420; xii, 420 pp. Old calf, rebacked.
(Young's) **£55 [≈ $105]**
- A View of the Causes and Progress of the French Revolution. London: Robinson, 1795. 1st edn. 2 vols. 8vo. Contemp half calf, spines

sl cracked with sm hole in following hinge vol 1, new labels.   *(Jarndyce)* **£120 [≈ $230]**

Moore, John
- The Objections against the Duty of Prayer, Answer'd. In a Sermon ... February 17, 1705/6. L; for W. Rogers, 1706. 1st edn. 4to. [4], 49, [2 advt] pp. Rec wraps.
(Fenning) **£24.50 [≈ $47]**

Moral ...
- Moral Amusement; or, a Selection of Tales, Histories, and Interesting Anecdotes; intended to amuse and instruct Young Minds. London: for Vernor & Hood, 1799. Sm 8vo. Frontis. Morocco backed mrbld bds. Possibly by Charlotte Smith. *(Stewart)* **£65 [≈ $124]**
- Moral and Historical Memoirs ... see Temple, Revd William Johnston.

More, Hannah
- An Estimate of the Religion of the Fashionable World. By One of the Laity. Second Edition. London: Cadell, 1791. Fcap 8vo. [6],261,[i] pp,advt leaf. Orig wraps, uncut, some creasing & chipping to edges.
(Spelman) **£40 [≈ $76]**
- Florio: a Tale, for Fine Gentlemen and Fine Ladies: and The Bas Bleu or Conversation: Two Poems. London: Cadell, 1786. 1st edn. 4to. Half-title. Disbound. Anon.
(Waterfield's) **£165 [≈ $316]**
- Sacred Dramas; Chiefly intended for Young Persons ... added, Sensibility, a Poem. Second Edition. London: Cadell, 1782. 8vo. Orig calf, red label, leading hinge weak.
(Jarndyce) **£20 [≈ $38]**
- Slavery, a Poem. London: Cadell, 1788. 4to. 20 pp. Lacks half-title. Mod wraps.
(C.R. Johnson) **£285 [≈ $547]**
- Thoughts on the Importance of the Manners of the Great to general Society. London: Cadell & Davies, 1799. 9th edn. 8vo. Half-title. Contemp tree calf, hinge splitting. Anon.   *(Jarndyce)* **£45 [≈ $86]**

More, Henry
- An Explanation of the Grand Mystery of Godliness ... London: J. Flesher for W. Norden, Cambridge, 1660. Folio. Contemp calf rebacked. Wing M.2658.
(Waterfield's) **£250 [≈ $479]**
- Philosophicall Poems. Cambridge: Roger Daniel, 1647. 8vo. C3 & C6 sl damaged without loss, laminated & rather discold. Mod calf, 20th c notebook bound in at end. Wing

M.2670. *(Waterfield's)* **£150 [≈ $287]**

More, Sir Thomas
- Sir Thomas Moore's Vtopia ... Translated into English by Raphe Robinson ... newly Corrected ... London: Bernard Alsop, 1624. 4th English edn. 4to. [viii],138,[5] pp. Damage to blank margs last 3 ff affecting 2 catchwords. 19th c bds, rebacked. STC 18097. *(Vanbrugh)* **£225 [≈ $431]**

Morell, Sir Charles
- Pseudonym used by James Ridley, q.v.

Morgan, Sylvanus
- The Sphere of Gentry. London: William Leybourn, for the author, 1661. 1st edn. Folio. [xvi],120,118, 119,116,[xx] pp. Num engvd plates & ills, ports, arms, text w'cuts. Traces of old colour to a few plates. Lacks the Howard tree. Old calf, rebacked, sl bruised.
(Ash) **£500 [≈ $959]**

Morgan, William
- Facts addressed to the Serious Attention of the People of Great Britain respecting the Expense of the War and the State of the National Debt ... Third Edition revised ... [With his] Additional Facts. London: for J. Debrett, 1796. 2 items. Disbound.
(Waterfield's) **£120 [≈ $230]**

Morgann, Maurice
- An Essay on the Dramatic Character of Sir John Falstaff. London: for T. Davies, 1777. 1st edn. 8vo. With blank N6 & errata leaf. Lacks half-title. 19th c qtr calf. Anon.
(Dramatis Personae) **$150 [≈ £78]**

Morland, Samuel
- The History of the Evangelical Churches of the Valleys of Piemont ... London: Henry Hills, for Adoniram Byfield, 1658. Sm folio. [70], [1],709 pp. Port, fldg map, 26 plates. Minor marg wear. Rebound in divinity calf. Wing M.2779. *(Humber)* **£250 [≈ $479]**

Morris, Edward
- A Short Inquiry into the Nature of Monopoly and Forestalling ... London: Cadell & Davies, 1795. 1st edn. 8vo (in 4s). [iv],27 pp. Half-title. Orig wraps, uncut, sl dusty.
(Meyer Boswell) **$350 [≈ £182]**

Morris, Matthias
- Social Religion Exemplified, in an Account of the First Settlement of Christianity in the City

of Caerludd in Several Dialogues. Revised and Abridged by Edward Williams. Shrewsbury: J. Eddowes, 1786. 12mo. xxiii, 422, index pp. Half leather, worn. *(Gage)* **£25 [≈ $47]**

Morris, Ralph (supposed author)
- The Life and Astonishing Adventures of John Daniel, a Smith at Royston in Hertfordshire ... Travels ... Shipwreck ... Eagle ... on which he flew to the Moon ... London: T. Parker, 1770. 2nd edn. 12mo. [ii], 319 pp. Contemp bds, new calf spine. Anon.
(Burmester) **£450 [≈ $863]**

Morse, Jedidiah
- The American Geography ... With a particular Description of Kentucky ... Second Edition. London: Stockdale, 1792. 8vo. xvi, 536 pp. 2 fldg maps, fldg table. 2 sm tears in maps (no loss). Rec half calf.
(Clark) **£220 [≈ $422]**
- A New and Correct Edition of the American Geography ... Edinburgh: for R. Morison & Son ... & Vernor & Hood, 1795. 5th edn. 8vo. 531 pp. 7 fldg maps (linen backed). Contemp half calf, front jnt cracked but holding.
(Chapel Hill) **$650 [≈ £338]**

Morton, Thomas
- A Cure for Heart-Ache; A Comedy ... London: for Longman ..., 1797. 1st edn. 8vo. 87 pp. Closed tear in last leaf. Disbound.
(Young's) **£21 [≈ $40]**
- An Exact Discoverie of Romish Doctrine in the Case of Conspiracie and Rebellion ... London: Felix Kyngston ..., 1605. 1st edn. 4to. [iv],54 pp. Catchwords & imprint shaved. Stitched as issued. STC 18184. Anon.
(Vanbrugh) **£155 [≈ $297]**

Morvan de Bellegarde, Jean Baptiste
- Reflexions upon Ridicule ... Wherein are represented the Different Manners and Characters of Persons of the Present Age ... London: 1739. 5th edn. 2 vols. 12mo. [xvi], 298, [22]; [xii],243,[32] pp. 18th c tree calf, elab gilt spines, 1 spine hd worn. Anon.
(Young's) **£150 [≈ $287]**

Moryson, Fynes
- An Itinerary ... London: John Beale, 1617. 1st edn. Folio. [xiv],(296), (302),(292) pp. W'cut plans. Italic variant of dble-leaf title. Faint marg stains, sl marg worming. Lacks 1st & last blanks. Victorian calf, gilt spine, rebacked. STC 18205.
(Ash) **£1,000 [≈ $1,919]**

Moseley, Walter Michael
- An Essay on Archery: describing the Practice of that Art, in all Ages and Nations. Worcester & London: 1792. 1st edn. 8vo. [i],x,348 pp. Addtnl engvd title & frontis, 4 plates. Later polished half calf, gilt spine, v sl rubbed. Inscrbd 'from the author'.
  (Finch) £225 [≈ $431]

Moser, Joseph
- The Adventures of Timothy Twig, Esq. in a Series of Poetical Epistles. London: for E. & T. Williams, 1794. 1st edn. 2 vols in one. 8vo. Contemp half calf, v worn.
  (Hannas) £240 [≈ $460]
- The Adventures of Timothy Twig, Esq. in a Series of Poetical Epistles. London: for E. & T. Williams, 1794. 1st edn. 2 vols. 8vo. Port in vol 1. Contemp calf, rebacked.
  (Bickersteth) £200 [≈ $383]

Mosheim, John Lawrence
- An Ecclesiastical History, Antient and Modern ... Translated ... by Archibald Maclaine. London: for A. Millar, 1765. 1st edn. 2 vols. 4to. xxix,807; 681 pp. Contemp speckled calf, raised bands, contrasting labels.
  (Young's) £80 [≈ $153]

Moss, Thomas
- Poems on Several Occasions. Wolverhampton: ptd & sold by G. Smart, 1769. 4to. 61 pp. Qtr calf, mrbld bds. Anon.
  (C.R. Johnson) £385 [≈ $739]

Motherby, George
- A New Medical Dictionary; or General Repository of Physic ... Second Edition, considerably enlarged and improved ... London: for J. Johnson ..., 1785. Folio. Ms notes. 26 plates. Contemp calf, rebacked, orig label preserved.
  (Frew Mackenzie) £265 [≈ $508]

Motte, Andrew
- A Treatise of the Mechanical Powers, wherein the Laws of Motion, and the Properties of those Powers are Explained and Demonstrated ... London: Motte, 1727. 1st edn. 8vo. [8],222,[2] pp, inc errata & advt leaf. 3 plates, text w'cuts (1 full page). Contemp calf, rebacked. *(Rootenberg)* £950 [≈ £494]

Mowbray, Geoffrey
- Remarks on the Conduct of Opposition during the Present Parliament ... London: for J. Wright ..., 1798. 1st edn. 8vo. 117 pp. Stiff

wraps. *(Young's)* £25 [≈ $47]

Mozeen, Thomas
- Young Scarron. London: T. Trye, W. Reeve, 1752. 1st edn. 12mo. [iv],viii,[iv],17-182 pp. Half-title. Some brown staining. Contemp calf, sl worn, upper jnt cracked but firm. Anon. *(Burmester)* £275 [≈ $527]

Mumbo Chumbo ...
- Mumbo Chumbo: a Tale written in Antient Manner recommended to Modern Devotees. London: for Becket & De Hondt, 1765. 4to. Title vignette. Browned. Disbound.
  (Waterfield's) £125 [≈ $239]

Munro, Hugh
- A Compendious System of the Theory and Practice of Modern Surgery ... in the Form of a Dialogue. London: Hodson, 1792. 8vo. 352, [10] pp. Fldg table (reprd). Blank hd of title reprd. New qtr calf, mrbld bds, uncut.
  (Goodrich) $250 [≈ £130]

Munro, Thomas
- Philocletes in Lemnos. A Drama ... To which is prefixed, A Green Room Scene ... London: William Bingley, 1795. 1st edn. Sm crnr ink stain. Disbound. Anon.
  (Dramatis Personae) $100 [≈ £52]

Muralto, Onuphrio
- The Castle of Otranto ... see Walpole, Horace.

Murdoch, Patrick
- Mercator's Sailing applied to the Time Figure of the Earth with an Introduction concerning the Discovery and Determination of that Figure. London: for A. Millar, 1741. 4to. xxvii,38,[2 advt] pp. 3 fldg plans & diags. Bds. *(Lamb)* £125 [≈ $239]

Murphy, Arthur
- The School for Guardians. A Comedy ... London: for P. Vaillant, 1767. 1st edn. Disbound, sewing loose.
  (Dramatis Personae) $40 [≈ £20]
- Zenobia: A Tragedy ... London: for W. Griffin ..., 1768. 1st edn. 8vo. [vi],82,[2] pp. Disbound. *(Young's)* £25 [≈ $47]

Murphy, James
- Plans, Elevations, Sections and Views of the Church at Batalha, in the Province of Estremadura in Portugal ... London: I. & J.

Taylor, 1795. 1st edn. Folio. Engvd title, engvd dedic, 25 engvd plates (2 dble page). Half calf. *(Sotheran's)* **£500 [≈ $959]**

Murray, Lord George
- A Particular Account of the Battle of Culloden, April 16, 1746. In a Letter from an Officer of the Highland Army ... London: for T. Warner ..., 1749. 1st edn. 8vo. 25 pp. Half-title. Disbound. Anon.
(Young's) **£70 [≈ $134]**

Murray, James
- Sermons to Asses. London: for J. Johnson, T. Cadell, & W. Charnley (Newcastle), 1768. 1st edn. 8vo. Title vignette. Contemp calf gilt, sl worn, crnrs bumped. Anon.
(Buccleuch) **£75 [≈ $143]**

Murray, Lindley
- English Exercises, adapted to the Grammar lately published, Digested for the Benefit of Private Learners ... Fourth Edition, corrected. London: Longman ..., 1799. 182 pp. Contemp sheep, spine sl cracked.
(C.R. Johnson) **£45 [≈ $86]**

Murray, Mungo
- A Treatise on Ship-Building and Navigation. In Three Parts ... London: Henry & Cave, for the author ..., 1754. 1st edn. 4to. 18 fldg plates & lge volvelle (1 fold strengthened on verso). Contemp mottled calf gilt, gilt spine, mor label. *(Ximenes)* **$3,500 [≈ £1,822]**

Musculus, Wolfgang
- Commonplaces of Christian Religion for the use of such as desire the Knowledge of Godly Truth. London: 1563. 1st edn. Thick 4to. 1340, 42 pp. Title & preface in facs. Lacks final leaf of table at end. New vellum. STC 18308. *(Humber)* **£195 [≈ $374]**

Museum Rusticum ...
- Museum Rusticum et Commerciale: or, Select Papers on Agriculture, Commerce, Arts, and Manufactures ... London: 1766-64-66. 3rd edn vol 1, 1st edn vols 2-6. 6 vols. 8vo. 11 plates, plans & tables. Orig calf, sl wear hd of spines.
(Bickersteth) **£280 [≈ $537]**

Nabbes, Thomas
- The Bride, A Comedie. Acted in the yeere 1638, at the Private-House in Drury-lane ... London: for Laurence Blaikelocke, 1640. 1st edn. Sm 4to. Imprimatur leaf at end.

Browned, shaved close. Closed tear to D2. Disbound.
(Dramatis Personae) **$500 [≈ £260]**

Naismith, John
- Thoughts on Various Objects of Industry pursued in Scotland ... Edinburgh: for the author, sold by Bell & Bradfute, 1790. 1st edn. 8vo. Sep paged appendix. Later half calf, spine rubbed. *(Jarndyce)* **£350 [≈ $671]**

Nalson, John
- Foxes and Fire-brands: or a Specimen of the Danger and Harmony of Popery and Separation ... The Second Edition. London: Tooke, 1681. 4to. [iv],33,[i] pp. Some staining at ends, lib stamp on title verso. Later wraps. Wing N.103. Anon.
(Clark) **£24 [≈ $46]**

Natter, Johann Lorenz
- A Treatise on the Ancient Method of Engraving on Precious Stones, compared with the Modern ... By Laurentius Natter. London: for the author, 1754. 1st edn in English. Sm folio. xxxvi [ie xxxvii],[i], 54,[ii] pp. Engvd dedic, 37 plates. Contemp half calf, rebacked & recrnrd.
(Finch) **£650 [≈ $1,247]**

The Natural History of Bees ...
- See Bazin, G.A.

The Naturalist's Journal ...
- See Barrington, Daines.

Naunton, Robert
- Fragmenta Regalia, or Observations on the late Queen Elizabeth, her Times and Favorites. [London]: 1641. 1st edn. Sm 4to. 43 pp. Sl cropped at hd without loss. New mor. Wing N.249. *(Bookpress)* **$285 [≈ £148]**

Neal, Daniel
- A Funeral Sermon occasioned by the Death of the late reverend Mr Matthew Clarke. London: for John Clark, Richard Hett, Samuel Chandler, 1726. Disbound.
(Waterfield's) **£20 [≈ $38]**

Neale, George
- Some Observations on the Use of the Agaric ... London: for Jacob Robinson, 1757. 1st edn. 8vo. Mod bds. *(Ximenes)* **$275 [≈ £143]**

Neale, T.H.
- A Proposal for Amending the Silver Coins of England, and the Possibility of it, without any Great Charge to the Nation ... London: for the author, 1696. 60 pp. Mod half calf gilt. Wing N.349. Anon. *(Hollett)* £350 [≈ $671]

Necker, Jacques
- Of the Importance of Religious Opinions. Boston: Hall, 1796. 2nd Amer edn. 8vo. Foxed. Orig calf, rebacked, reprd. Translated by Mary Wollstonecraft.
(Rostenberg & Stern) $285 [≈ £148]

Nelson, James
- An Essay on the Government of Children, under Three General Heads: viz. Health, Manners and Education. London: Dodsley, 1753. 1st edn. 8vo. vii,[xxi],420 pp. Marg reprs to worm in crnr of 1st 11 ff. Contemp calf, jnts reprd, new label.
(Burmester) £300 [≈ $575]

Nelson, Robert
- An Address to Persons of Quality and Estate. To which is added, an Appendix of some Original and Valuable Papers. London: G. James, for R.S., & sold by Rivington, 1715. 1st edn. 1st issue, with frontis & 9 lines of text on last page. Foredges damped. Contemp calf, sl worn. *(Jarndyce)* £180 [≈ $345]
- An Address to Persons of Quality and Estate ... London: G. James, for R.S., & sold by Rivington, 1715. 1st edn. 2nd issue, without port, & with 10-line addtn to last page of advts. 3 advt pp. Sl marg worm at end. Contemp calf, sl worn.
(Jarndyce) £160 [≈ $307]

Nelson, W.
- The Office and Chief Authority of a Justice of Peace ... Tenth Edition, Corrected, Amended, and Continued ... London: E. & R. Nutt ..., 1729. 8vo. [2],iv,756 pp. Contemp calf, spine ends chipped, extremities sl worn.
(Claude Cox) £75 [≈ $143]

Neve, Richard
- The City and Country Purchaser, and Builder's Dictionary: or, the Compleat Builders Guide ... London: D. Brown, 1726. 2nd edn, enlgd. 8vo. [xii],xx,(288) pp. Contemp calf, gilt spine, hinges sl worn.
(Bookpress) $1,100 [≈ £572]

Neville, Henry
- Plato Redivivus: or a Dialogue concerning

Government ... London: for S.I., 1681. 8vo. Contemp calf, rebacked. Wing N.513.
(Waterfield's) £250 [≈ $479]

New ...
- A New Adventure of Telemachus ... see Stubbes, George.
- A New and General Biographical Dictionary ... see Owen, William & Johnston, William.
- The New Bath Guide ... see Anstey, Christopher.
- A New Collection of Enigmas, Charades, Transpositions, etc. London: Hookham, Carpenter, 1791. 1st edn. 2 vols in 1. 12mo. xv, [1],96; [iv],116 pp. Subscribers. Answers pencilled in. Contemp calf, rebacked.
(Burmester) £250 [≈ $479]
- A New Description of Merryland ... see Stretser, Thomas.
- The New Dunciad ... see Pope, Alexander.
- The New Handmaid to Arts, Sciences, Agriculture, &c. London: Clements & Sadler, 1790. 1st edn. Sm 8vo. [ii],118 pp. Contemp qtr calf, rubbed. *(Bookpress)* $850 [≈ £442]
- New Remarks of London: or, A Survey of the Cities of London and Westminster, of Southwark and part of Middlesex and Surrey ... Collected by the Company of Parish-Clerks ..., London: 1732. 1st edn. 8vo. viii,408 pp. W'cut ill. Lacks corrigenda leaf. Contemp calf, sl worn. *(Frew Mackenzie)* £80 [≈ $153]
- New Travels in the United States of America ... see Brissot de Warville, Jacques Pierre.
- A New Treatise on the Laws concerning Tithes ... Second Edition, corrected and enlarged ... London: W. Griffin, 1766. 298, [8] pp. Half-title. Portion of upper marg of title torn away. Contemp calf.
(Wreden) $75 [≈ £39]
- A New Treatise on the Laws Concerning Tithes ... see also Cunningham, Timothy.

Newarke, Viscount
- See Dorchester, Henry Pierpoint, Marquess of.

Newcome, Peter
- A Sermon [on Matt.XXIV.12] ... to the Societies for Reformation of Manners ... December the 26th 1709 ... London: J.L. for John Wyat, 1710. 1st edn. 4to. [4],24 pp. Half-title. Rec wraps.
(Fenning) £28.50 [≈ $55]

Newcome, William
- An Attempt towards an Improved Version, a

Metrical Arrangement, and an Explanation of the Twelve Minor Prophets. London: 1785. 1st edn. 4to. [lvi],246 pp. Contemp bds, uncut, edges & crnrs sl worn.
(Bow Windows) £80 [≈ $153]

Newman, Samuel
- A Large and Complete Concordance to the Bible in English ... Third Impression corrected and amended. London: for Thomas Downes & Andrew Crook, 1658. Lge thick folio. Unpaginated. Contemp calf, sl worn. Wing N.931. *(Lloyd-Roberts)* £150 [≈ $287]

News from Purgatory ...
- News from Purgatory. or, the Jesuit's Legacy to all Countries. [London: 1679?]. Folio. 4 pp. Disbound. Wing N.993.
(C.R. Johnson) £65 [≈ $124]

Newton, Sir Isaac
- Mathematical Principles of Natural Philosophy ... Translated into English, and illustrated with a Commentary, by Robert Thorp, M.A. Volume I [all published] London: 1777. 1st edn. 4to. xlviii,[1],360 pp. 22 fldg plates. Lacks half-title. Occas sl foxing. Contemp half roan, sl worn.
(Whitehart) £1,500 [≈ $2,879]
- Opticks ... London: Smith & Walford, 1704. 1st edn, 1st issue. 4to. 2 ff, 144,211 pp. Red & black title. 19 fldg plates. Contemp calf, backstrip relaid, new endpapers.
(Offenbacher) $7,500 [≈ £3,906]
- Opticks: or, a Treatise of the Reflections, Refractions, Inflections and Colours of Light. London: Innys, 1718. 2nd edn, 2nd issue. 8vo. [6],382,[2 ctlg] pp. 12 fldg plates. Minor foxing. Mod leather.
(Gemmary) $1,000 [≈ £520]
- Opticks ... The Fourth Edition, Corrected. London: for William Innys, 1730. 8vo. viii, 382, [2 advt] pp. 12 fldg plates (numbered 1-5, 1-2, 1-4, 1). Contemp sprinkled polished calf, gilt ruled sides & spine, crnrs worn.
(Gaskell) £800 [≈ $1,535]
- The System of the World demonstrated in an Easy and Popular Manner ... Second Edition, Corrected and Improved. London: for J. Robinson, 1740. Reissue of 1st edn of 1731. 8vo. 2 plates. Title-page is a cancel. Contemp calf, jnt cracked, lacks label.
(Waterfield's) £400 [≈ $767]

Newton, J.
- A Complete Herbal ... London: 1798. 8vo. 176 plates inc port. Sm but rather heavy stain

on text & 1st 12 plates. Mod calf antique style. *(Wheldon & Wesley)* £180 [≈ $345]

Newton, Richard
- University Education: or, an Explication and Emendment of the Statute ... Second Edition. London: for G. Strahan, 1726, reprinted 1733. 8vo. 271,[i errata] pp. Contemp calf gilt, mor label, jnts worn, hd of lower jnt cracking. *(Finch)* £240 [≈ $460]

Nicholas, George
- A Letter from George Nicholas of Kentucky to his Friend in Virginia ... Phila: James Carey, 1799. 2nd edn. 8vo. 39 pp. Later qtr mor. *(Bookpress)* $450 [≈ £234]

Nicholls, William
- The Sunday and Holiday Service of the Book of Common Prayer ... with the Psalms of David, Paraphrased. London: J. Barber, for J. Holland & W. Taylor, 1707. 1st edn. 8vo. [xvi], 255, [i],[vi], Aa-Ss8, Tt1-4. Half-title. Later calf, sl rubbed. *(Clark)* £48 [≈ $92]

Nichols, John
- Biographical and Literary Anecdotes of William Bowyer, Printer, F.S.A., and of many of his Learned Friends ... London: the author, 1782. 1st edn. 4to. viii,666 pp. Frontis. Contemp calf, hinges weak.
(Bookpress) £400 [≈ £208]
- Biographical Anecdotes of William Hogarth with a Catalogue of his Works ... and Occasional Remarks. London: John Nichols, 1785. 3rd edn, enlgd. 8vo. xx,529 pp. Addtnl engvd title. 19th c calf, gilt spine. Anon. *(Lloyd-Roberts)* £60 [≈ $115]

Nichols, Thomas
- Observations on the Propagation and Management of Oak Trees in general; but more immediately applying to His Majesty's New-Forest, in Hampshire ... Southampton: T. Baker, [1791]. Mrbld wraps.
(C.R. Johnson) £120 [≈ $230]

Nicholson, J. & Burn, R.
- The History and Antiquities of the Counties of Westmorland and Cumberland. London: for Strahan & Cadell, 1777. 1st edn. 4to. cxxxiv,630; 615,[8 index] pp. 2 lge fldg maps. Qtr calf gilt, rubbed, bds worn, hinges cracked. *(Hollett)* £350 [≈ $671]

Nicholson, Peter
- The Principles of Architecture ... London: J.

Barfield, [1795-98]. 1st edns. 3 vols. 8vo. Over 200 plates. Contemp reversed calf, 2 hinges reinforced. •
(Bookpress) **$1,250 [≈£651]**

Nicholson, William
- The Irish Historical Library, pointing at Most of the Authors and Records in print, and MSS which may be serviceable to the Compilers of a General History of Ireland. Dublin: Aaron Rhames, 1724. 8vo. [xl],246,[x] pp. Contemp calf, rebacked.
(Emerald Isle) **£200 [≈$383]**

Nicholson, William (ed.)
- A Journal of Natural Philosophy, Chemistry, and the Arts: illustrated with Engravings. London: Robinson, 1797-1801. 1st edn, 1st series. 4 vols. 4to. xxviii,600; xxiii, [1],285-564; xix,[1],552; xvi,562 pp. 85 plates. Few ff damp stained. Contemp calf & half calf, 1 vol rebacked.
(Rootenberg) **$1,250 [≈£651]**

Nicol, W.
- The Scotch Forcing and Kitchen Gardener; being a Second Edition with Extensive Additions of The Scotch Forcing Gardener. Edinburgh: for the author, 1798. [ii], 9, [vii]-xii, [ii], 248 pp. 5 fldg plates (foxed). Half calf, rubbed.
(Wheldon & Wesley) **£40 [≈$76]**

Nicolson, William
- The English Historical Library ... London: Timothy Childe, 1714. 2nd edn. Folio. xviii, 169, 176-272 pp. Lower marg of last few ff water stained. Contemp calf, rebacked.
(Bookpress) **$450 [≈£234]**
- The English, Scotch and Irish Historical Libraries ... Third Edition, Corrected and Augmented ... London: 1736. 1st coll edn. Folio. xviii,272,18, xviii,[ii],148, xvi,118 pp. Sl marg stains. Orig calf, old reback, sl worn.
(Vanbrugh) **£225 [≈$431]**

Nimmo, William
- A General History of Stirlingshire ... Edinburgh: William Creech, 1777. 1st edn. vii, 527 pp. Fldg map. Contemp half calf, lower jnt sl split.   *(Gough)* **£225 [≈$431]**

Nisbet, Alexander
- An Essay on the Ancient and Modern Use of Armories ... Edinburgh: William Adams Junior for James MackEven, 1718. 4to. viii,[vi], 224, [xvi] pp. 6 pp subscribers. 7

plates. Some wear & tear. Old ink notes. Period calf, sl worn. *(Rankin)* **£150 [≈$287]**

Nisbet, Charles
- An Address to the Students of Dickinson College, Carlisle. On his re-election to the Office of Principal of said College. Edinburgh: W. Martin, 1786. 12 pp. Rec wraps.   *(C.R. Johnson)* **£125 [≈$239]**

Noble, Mark
- Memoirs of the Protectoral-House of Cromwell ... Third Edition, with Improvements. London: Robinson, 1787. 2 vols. 8vo. 10 pp subscribers. Plates, ports, tables. Lib labels. Contemp diced calf gilt, rebacked, crnrs chipped
(Jarndyce) **£75 [≈$143]**

The Nonpareil ...
- See Smart, Christopher.

Norden, Frederick Lewis
- Travels in Egypt and Nubia ... Translated ... and Enlarged ... by Dr. Peter Templeman. London: Davis & Reymers, 1757. 1st English edn. 2 vols in one. 8vo. 154; 232, [6 advt] pp. Orig calf, lacks label, sl rubbed.
(Chapel Hill) **$300 [≈£156]**

Norris, John
- A Collection of Miscellanies: consisting of Poems, Essays, Discourses & Letters ... Second Edition corrected. London: for J. Crisley & Samuel Manship, 1692. 8vo. Contemp calf, rebacked. Wing N.1249.
(Waterfield's) **£135 [≈$259]**

North, Roger
- A Discourse of Fish and Fish-Ponds ... Dome by a Person of Honour. London: for E. Curll, 1713. 1st edn. 8vo. viii,79,[1] pp. Some worming in lower blank margs. Contemp sheep.   *(Gaskell)* **£250 [≈$479]**

Northleigh, John
- The Parallel: Or, The New Specious Association an Old Rebellious Covenant ... London: for B. Tooke, 1682. Only edn. Folio. 34 pp. Dusty. Rec bds. Wing N.1301. Anon.
(Young's) **£35 [≈$67]**

Nostradamus, Michel
- The True Prophecies or Prognostications of Michael Nostradamus ... Translated and Commented by Theophilus de Garencieres ... London: Ratcliffe & Thompson ..., 1672. 1st

edn in English. Folio. [xxxii],522 pp. Engvd frontis, title, dedic. Rec calf.
(Frew Mackenzie) **£1,100 [≈ $2,111]**

Nott, John, cook
- The Cooks and Confectioners Dictionary: Or, The Accomplish'd Housewifes Companion ... The Third Edition with Additions. London: Rivington, 1726. Engvd frontis. Contemp panelled calf, hinges cracking, spine ends sl worn. *(C.R. Johnson)* **£475 [≈ $911]**

Nott, John, of Bristol
- Alonzo; or, the Youthful Solitaire. A Tale. London: J. Robson, 1772. 4to. 24 pp. Disbound. *(C.R. Johnson)* **£165 [≈ $316]**

Nottingham, Daniel Finch, Earl of
- The Answer of the Earl of Nottingham to Mr Whiston's Letter to him concerning the Eternity of the Son of God ... Seventh Edition ... London: for Edward Valentine, 1721. 8vo. Mod bds. *(Waterfield's)* **£40 [≈ $76]**

The Novelist's Magazine ...
- The Novelist's Magazine Vol.1 containing Almoran and Hamet [by John Hawkesworth], Joseph Andrews [by Henry Fielding], and Amelia [by Henry Fielding]. London: for Harrison & Co, 1781. 8vo. 2 + 4 + 6 (of 7) plates. Mod qtr calf.
(Waterfield's) **£60 [≈ $115]**

Noy, William
- The Grounds and Maxims of the English Law. To which is annexed, A Treatise of Estates, by Sir John Doderidge ... Fifth Edition with additions. In the Savoy: Henry Lintot, for J. Worrall, 1757. 12mo. 4 advt pp. Contemp calf, red label.
(Jarndyce) **£95 [≈ $182]**

Nugent, Robert Craggs
- Considerations upon a Reduction of the Land-Tax. London: R. Griffiths, at the Dunciad, 1749. Half-title, 67 pp. Fldg table (sm tear, no loss). Disbound, uncut.
(C.R. Johnson) **£200 [≈ $383]**

Nugent, Thomas
- The Grand Tour. Containing an Exact Description of most of the Cities, Towns, and remarkable Places of Europe ... London: S. Birt ..., 1749. 1st edn. 4 vols. 12mo. Contemp calf, spines trifle worn, minor chipping to hds. *(Frew Mackenzie)* **£295 [≈ $566]**
- The Grand Tour, or, a Journey through the

Netherlands, Germany, Italy, and France ... London: for D. Browne, 1756. 2nd edn, crrctd. 4 vols. 8vo. Contemp sprinkled calf, gilt, later labels. *(Young's)* **£120 [≈ $230]**

O'Begley, Conor
- The English Irish Dictionary. Paris: Seamus Guerin, 1732. 1st edn. 4to. [viii],717 pp. Some worming at ft at end touching 1 letter. Contemp sheep, mor label, gilt dec spine (worn at ends), sides scratched & rubbed. Anon. Clanricarde - Phillipps copy.
(Finch) **£575 [≈ $1,103]**

O'Conor, Daniel Patrick
- The Works ... consisting of Moral, Sentimental, Pathetick, and Descriptive Pieces, in Prose and Verse ... Cork: J. Connor, [1798?]. 1st edn. 2 vols. 8vo. 1st few ff vol 2 sl affected by damp. Contemp half calf, gilt spines (rubbed), hd of 1 spine worn. *(Ximenes)* **$225 [≈ £117]**

Observations ...
- Observations made during a Tour through Parts of England ... see Sullivan, Richard Joseph.
- Observations on Modern Gardening ... see Whately, Thomas.
- Observations on the Conversion and Apostleship of St. Paul ... see Lyttelton, George, 1st Lord Lyttelton.
- Observations on the Correspondence between Poetry and Music ... see Webb, Daniel.
- Observations on the Importance and Use of Theatres; their Present Regulation, and Possible Improvements. London: for M. Cooper, & J. Jackson, 1759. 1st edn. 8vo. Half-title. Mod wraps.
(Ximenes) **$850 [≈ £442]**
- Observations on the Inslaving ... of Negroes ... see Benezet, Anthony.
- Observations on the Military Establishment and Discipline of His Majesty the King of Prussia ... see Guibert, J.A.H., Comte de.
- Observations on the Swedish History. Very Proper to be read by the Subjects of a Free Government. London: for T. Cooper, 1743. 1st edn. 8vo. [4],45 pp inc half-title. Disbound. *(Hannas)* **£160 [≈ $307]**
- Observations upon a Late Pamphlet [by John, Baron Hervey], entitled, Miscellaneous Thoughts &c. In a Letter to the Noble Author. London: for T. Cooper, [1742]. Mod wraps. *(Waterfield's)* **£40 [≈ $76]**

The Observer ...
- See Cumberland, Richard.

Oculus Britanniae ...
- See Amhurst, Nicholas.

Ode ...
- Ode for Thanksgiving Day ... see Walsh, William.
- An Ode upon the Present Period of Time; with a Letter to the Right Honourable George Grenville. London: J. Almon, 1769. 4to. 12 pp. Disbound. *(C.R. Johnson)* £165 [≈ $316]

The Oeconomy of Human Life ...
- See Dodsley, Robert.

The Officer's Manual ...
- The Officer's Manual in the Field; or, a Series of Military Plans, representing the Principal Operations of a Campaign. Translated from the German. London: Bensley for Egerton ..., 1798. Sq 8vo. [viii],70 pp. 60 plates (sl offsetting). Rebound in qtr calf. *(Rankin)* £85 [≈ $163]

The Old English Baron ...
- See Reeve, Clara.

Oldfield, T.H.B.
- An Entire and Complete History, Political and Personal, of the Boroughs of Great Britain ... London: for G. Riley ..., 1792. 1st edn. 3 vols. 8vo. Half-titles. Orig bds, rebacked. Anon.   *(Young's)* £165 [≈ $316]
- History of the Original Constitution of Parliaments from the Time of the Britons to the Present Day. London: 1797. 8vo. Mod cloth backed bds. *(Waterfield's)* £40 [≈ $76]

Oldham, John
- The Works ... Seventh Edition, Corrected. London: for Dan. browne ..., 1710. 8vo. [iv], 328, [xvi],86 pp. Frontis port. Sep titles to 'Satyrs', 'Poems and Translations', and 'Remains'. Some browning. Period calf, rebacked.   *(Rankin)* £125 [≈ $239]

Oldys, William
- The British Librarian ... London: for T. Osborne, 1738. 8vo. Orig title to Part 5 retained together with 1 advt leaf. Some tears reprd without loss. Contemp calf, crnrs worn. Anon.   *(Waterfield's)* £100 [≈ $191]
- Collection of Epigrams to which is Prefix'd, A

Critical Dissertation on this Species of Poetry. London: for J. Walthoe ..., 1727. 1st edn. 8vo. xxiii,(264) pp. Sm piece cut from top of half-title. Sl stains at end. Contemp calf, rebacked. Anon. *(Young's)* £65 [≈ $124]

Olivier, J.
- Fencing Familiarized: or, a New Treatise on the Art of Sword Play ... London: for John Bell, & C. Etherington, York, [1771-72]. 1st edn. 8vo. xlix,196,5 advt pp. Fldg frontis, 8 plates. English & french text & titles. Sl offset on plates. Contemp calf, rebacked.
(Vanbrugh) £295 [≈ $566]

The Opera Rumpus ...
- The Opera Rumpus; or, The Ladies in the Wrong Box! A Serio- Comic- Operatic Burlesque Poem! ... London: Baldwin, 1783. 1st edn. 4to. viii,20 pp. Old mrbld bds, rebacked in calf gilt. *(Hollett)* £180 [≈ $345]

Orem, William
- A Description of the Chanonry in Old Aberdeen in the years 1724 and 1725. (Bibliotheca Topographica Britannica No. III). London: J. Nichols, 1782. 4to. Fldg map. Mod half calf.
(Waterfield's) £95 [≈ $182]

The Origin of Printing ...
- See Bowyer, William & Nichols, John (eds.).

Original Poems ...
- Original Poems, On Various Occasions. By a Lady ... see Cowper, M.F.C.

Ornithologia Nova ...
- Ornithologia Nova; or a New General History of Birds, Extracted from the Best Authorities ... Birmingham: T. Warren, 1743-45. 1st edn. 2 vols. 12mo. 340; viii, 314,6 pp. 2-cold titles. 347 w'engvd plates. Contemp tree sheep, jnts reprd.   *(Gough)* £395 [≈ $758]

Orrery, John Boyle, Earl of
- See Boyle, John, Earl of Cork and Orrery.

Osborne, Francis
- Advice to a Son ... Oxford: H. Hall, 1656. Contemp calf, hinge sl rubbed. Wing O.509. Anon.   *(Jarndyce)* £140 [≈ $268]
- A Miscellany of Sundry Essays, Paradoxes, and Problematicall Discourses, Letters and Characters ... London: J. Grismond, for R. Royston, 1659. 1st edn. 12mo. xxxvi,260 pp.

Occas sm lib stamp. Contemp sheep, spine ends sl worn, old lib label on spine. Wing O516A. *(Burmester)* £280 [≈$537]

Ossian
- See under Macpherson, James.

Otway, Thomas
- Alcibiades. A Tragedy ... London: for R. Bentley & S. Magnes, 1687. 3rd edn. Sm 4to. Mod qtr calf. Wing O.540.
(Dramatis Personae) $65 [≈£33]

Oulton, Walley Chamberlain
- The History of the Theatres of London ... London: Martin & Bain, 1796. 2 vols in one. Half-titles. Contemp qtr calf, red labels. Anon. *(C.R. Johnson)* £340 [≈$652]

Over, Charles
- Ornamental Architecture in the Gothic, Chinese and Modern Taste ... London: Robert Sayer, [175-?]. Sm 8vo. 8 pp. 54 plates. Later bds.
(Bookpress) $1,500 [≈£781]

Overall, John
- Bishop Queall's Convocation Book, MDCVI, concerning the Government of God's Catholick Church ... London: Walter Kettilby, 1690. 4to. iv,338 pp. Title torn. Lacks 2 ports. Contemp calf, spine damaged, crnrs bumped. *(Gage)* £50 [≈$95]

Ovid
- Ovid's Metamorphoses Epitomized in an English Poetical Style. For the Use and Entertainment of the Ladies of Great Britain. London: for Robert Horsfield, 1760. 8vo. xv, 236, 3 advt pp, inc intl blank. Sl foxing. Period calf gilt, sl cracks to upper jnt.
(Rankin) £75 [≈$143]
- See also Sandys, George.

Owen, Charles
- An Essay towards a Natural History of Serpents: In two Parts. London: for the author, 1742. 1st edn. 4to. xxiii,240,[12] pp. 7 full page ills. Errata, directions to binder, 15 pp subscribers. Rec half calf.
(Rootenberg) $550 [≈£286]
- An Essay towards a Natural History of Serpents ... London: the author, 1742. 1st edn. 4to. xxiii,240,[12] pp. Subscribers. 7 plates. Sev reprs, name clipped from title. Half calf. *(Bookpress)* $600 [≈£312]

Owen, Revd Henry
- Sixteen Sermons on Various Subjects. London: for J. Nichols, 1797. 1st edn. 8vo. viii, 351, xlvi subscribers pp. Spotted. Cloth, stained. *(Young's)* £20 [≈$38]

Owen, J.
- Travels into Different Parts of Europe in the Years 1791 and 1792 ... London: 1796. 1st edn. 2 vols. 8vo. Errata leaf in vol 2. Tree calf. *(Henly)* £60 [≈$115]

Owen, John
- Meditations and Discourses on the Glory of Christ ... London: B.A., 1691. Sm 8vo. [22], 200 pp. Sl marg wear & browning. Calf, rebacked. Wing O.769A.
(Humber) £85 [≈$163]
- Meditations and Discourses on the Glory of Christ ... Sheffield: W. Ward, 1792. New edn. 8vo. [xvi],284 pp. Contemp calf.
(Young's) £25 [≈$47]
- [Greek title: Phronema tou Pneumatos, then] or The Grace and Duty of being Spiritually-Minded. London: J.G. for Nathaniel Ponder, 1681. 4to. Contemp Cambridge calf, jnts cracked, spine & crnrs worn. Wing O.792.
(Sanders) £45 [≈$86]

Owen, William
- Geriadur Cynmraeg a Saesoneg ... see Pughe, William Owen.
- Owen's New Book of Fairs ... New Edition. London: B. Law ..., 1792. 12mo. Intl licence leaf. 4 advt pp (ink scrawls). Disbound.
(Jarndyce) £45 [≈$86]

Owen, William & Johnston, William
- A New and General Biographical Dictionary ... London: T. Osborne ..., 1761-67. 1st edn. 12 vols. 8vo. B'plates removed. Contemp calf, few hinges started. Anon.
(Bookpress) $585 [≈£304]

Pagan, Blaise Francois, Comte de
- An Historical & Geographical Description of the Great Country and River of the Amazones in America ... Now Translated into English by William Hamilton ... London: Starkey, 1661. 8vo. 15 ff,153 pp. Fldg map. Later limp vellum. *(Frew Mackenzie)* £1,800 [≈$3,455]

Pagasse, Mr.
- The French Preceptor; or, Principles of the French Language ... Dublin: R.M. Butler, 1795. 1st edn. 8vo. Contemp tree calf gilt,

lacks label.   *(Ximenes)* **$275 [≃£143]**

Page, John
- Receipts for Preparing and Compounding the Principal Medicines made Use of by the late Mr. Ward ... London: Henry Whitridge ..., 1763. 1st edn. 8vo. [2],33 pp. Disbound.
(Young's) **£200 [≃$383]**

Paget, Thomas Catesby, Lord
- Some Reflections upon the Administration of Government ... London: Dodsley, 1740. 1st edn. 8vo. [iv],104 pp. Half-title. Red & black title. Marg hole. Disbound. Anon.
(Young's) **£55 [≃$105]**

Pagett, Thomas Catesby, Baron
- An Essay on Human Life. London: for Fletcher Gyles, 1737. 3rd edn, enlgd. 8vo. Title sl dusty. Disbound.
(Ximenes) **$100 [≃£52]**

Pagitt, Ephraim
- Heresiography, Or a Description and History of the Hereticks and Sectaries Sprang up in these latter Times ... London: for William Lee ..., 1662. 6th edn. 8vo. [xxx], 309, [6] pp. Frontis (partly torn away). text w'cuts. Rather shabby. New bds. Wing P.182.
(Young's) **£38 [≃$72]**

Pain, William
- The Practical House Carpenter; or, Youth's Instructor ... List of Prices ... Fourth Edition, with large Additions. London: 1792. 4to. [8],[30],22 pp. 148 engvd plates (6 fldg). Crnr of 1 plate sl defective. Lacks pp 3-4 of price list. Sl used. Rec qtr calf.
(Fenning) **£225 [≃$431]**
- The Practical House Carpenter; or, Youth's Instructor ... Phila: Thomas Dobson, 1797. 2nd Amer edn. 4to. v,15 pp. 148 plates, inc the 2 plates facing pp 3 & 65. Title marg reprd, few marg tears. Occas foxing. Contemp calf, rebacked.   *(Bookpress)* **$1,850 [≃£963]**

Pain, William & James
- Pain's British Palladio: or, The Builder's General Assistant ... London: the authors, 1786. 1st edn. Folio. [ii],14 pp. 42 plates (1 dble). Sm repr to 1 plate. Later half calf.
(Bookpress) **$1,750 [≃£911]**

Paine, Thomas
- Address and Declaration of the Friends of Universal Peace and Liberty ... August 20th, 1791. Together with some Verses ... [London:

1793?]. 8vo. 8 pp. Disbound.
(Bow Windows) **£150 [≃$287]**
- The Age of Reason ... Paris: ptd by Barrois, 1794. 8vo. [ii],[ii],55,[1 blank] pp. Disbound.
(Bow Windows) **£120 [≃$230]**
- The Age of Reason. Part the Second ... London: 1795. 1st edn. 8vo. xii,107,[1 blank] pp. Few sm marks. Disbound.
(Bow Windows) **£135 [≃$259]**
- Common Sense ... London: 1792. 8vo. 71,[1 blank] pp. Disbound.
(Bow Windows) **£120 [≃$230]**
- Dissertation   of   First-Principles   of Government. London: 1795. 1st edn. 8vo. 47,[1 blank] pp. Laid paper, watermark dated 1796. Disbound.
(Bow Windows) **£165 [≃$316]**
- A Letter Addressed to the Abbe Raynal on the Affairs of North America ... London: 1791. 8vo. [ii],vi,66 pp. Lacks a leaf at end (?). Disbound.   *(Bow Windows)* **£85 [≃$163]**
- A Letter addressed to the Abbe Raynal, on the affairs of North-America ... London: J. Ridgway, 1792. 46 pp,advt leaf. Disbound.
(C.R. Johnson) **£75 [≃$143]**
- Letter addressed to the Addressers, on the late Proclamation. London: ptd by H.D. Symonds, & Thomas Clio Rickman, 1792. Probably the 1st edn, with 78 pp of text & final advt leaf. Minor crease in title. Stitched as issued. Fldg case. *(Ximenes)* **$400 [≃£208]**
- Letter from Thomas Paine to George Washington ... London: 1797. 8vo. [ii],77,[1 blank] pp. Some dust marks. Disbound.
(Bow Windows) **£85 [≃$163]**
- A Letter to the Earl of Shelburne ... on his Speech July 10, 1782 ... New Edition. London: for J. Ridgway, 1791. 8vo. (3)-58 pp. Lacks port & half-title. Disbound.
(Bow Windows) **£55 [≃$105]**
- Letters addressed to the Addressers, of the late Proclamation ... Second Edition. London: for H.D. Symonds, 1792. Cr 8vo. Sl browning. New bds. *(Stewart)* **£75 [≃$143]**
- Prospects on the War and Paper Currency of Great Britain. The Third Edition. London: 1793. 8vo. viii,68 pp. Some foxing of outer ff. Disbound.   *(Bow Windows)* **£70 [≃$134]**
- Rights of Man. Part the Second ... Seventh Edition. London: 1792. 8vo. (iii)-xv,[i Contents], 178 pp. Lacks half-title. Title dusty. Disbound.
(Bow Windows) **£60 [≃$115]**
- The Rights of Man. For the Use and Benefit of all Mankind. London: Citizen Daniel Isaac

Eaton ..., 1795. 8vo. vii,[i blank],151,1 blank] pp. Lacks advt pp. Title foxed. Disbound.
(Bow Windows) £60 [≈ $115]

Painting Illustrated in Three Diallogues ...
- See Aglionby, William.

Paley, William
- The Principles of Moral and Political Philosophy. The Second Edition, Corrected. London: J. Davies, 1786. 4to. Half-title, 657 pp. Contemp tree calf.
(C.R. Johnson) £175 [≈ $335]
- The Principles of Moral and Political Philosophy ... Eleventh Edition, corrected. London: R. Faulder, 1796. 2 vols. 8vo. xxxiii, [v],378; [viii],433 pp. Orig bds, uncut, vol 1 early rebacked, sl soiled, crnrs bumped, 2 sm tears in paper of sides. *(Finch)* £45 [≈ $86]

Palladio, Andrea
- The Architecture ... in Four Books ... With Notes and Remarks of Inigo Jones ... London: A. Ward ..., 1742. 3rd edn. 2 vols in one. Lge folio. viii,104; 100 pp. Frontis, port, 230 plates. Occas sl foxing. Contemp reversed sheep, rebacked, some wear.
(Bookpress) $2,850 [≈ £1,484]
- The First Book of Architecture ... Translated out of the Italian with an Appendix ... London: 1708. 7th edn. 2 ff, "239" [ie 237, 173/4 not issued] pp. Frontis, 7 fldg & 63 other plates (2 sl defective). Few stains. Sm marg worm to a few pp. Contemp leather, rebacked. *(Ars Artis)* £250 [≈ $479]
- The Four Books of Architecture ... London: Isaac Ware, 1738. 6 ff,110 pp. 4 engvd titles (general & 1,2,3), 212 engvd plates (7 in text), 6 text ills. Contemp leather, worn, jnts cracked, spine lettering v faint.
(Ars Artis) £750 [≈ $1,439]

Palmer, John
- A New Scheme of Short-Hand ... London: J. Johnson, 1774. 1st edn. 8vo. 2,xv,[i],175 pp. 9 plates. Contemp half calf, lacks free endpapers, bds worn.
(Bookpress) $475 [≈ £247]
- A New Scheme of Short-Hand; being an Improvement upon Mr. Byrom's Short-Hand. London: for J. Johnson, 1774. 1st edn. 8vo. 9 plates. Rec bds. *(Ximenes)* $125 [≈ £65]
- Papers relative to the Agreement made by Government with Mr. Palmer, for the Reform and Improvement of the Posts. London: Cadell & Davies, 1797. 1st edn. 4to.

Mod wraps. *(Ximenes)* $225 [≈ £117]

Palmer, Samuel
- A General History of Printing ... London: A. Bettesworth ..., 1733. 2nd edn. 4to. vii, [v], 400 pp. Contemp calf, rubbed, backstrip relaid. *(Bookpress)* $725 [≈ £377]
- A General History of Printing from the First Invention of it in the City of Mentz ... London: for A. Bettesworth ..., 1733. 2nd edn. 4to. xii,400 pp, some irregular pagination. Some sl marks. Contemp calf, rebacked. *(Claude Cox)* £275 [≈ $527]

The Paphian Dove ...
- The Paphian Dove. Being a Selection of Admired Pieces on the Kiss ... Dublin: for John Rice ..., 1798. 1st edn. 8vo. 110 pp. Occas sl spotting. Disbound.
(Young's) £80 [≈ $153]

Park, Mungo
- Travels in the Interior Districts of Africa. London: W. Bulmer & Co for the author, 1799. 1st edn. 4to. 3 fldg maps & charts, 6 plates. Some tears with sl loss on 1 map. Later half calf gilt.
(Central Africana) £275 [≈ $527]

Park, Thomas
- Sonnets, and Other Small Poems. London: for G. Sael, 1797. 1st edn. Large Paper (?). 8vo. Engvd title & 5 plates. Early 19th c half calf gilt, by Quinton of Norwich, spine sl rubbed. *(Ximenes)* $250 [≈ £130]
- Sonnets, and Other Small Poems. London: for G. Sael, 1797. 1st edn. Large Paper (?). 8vo. 4 pp subscribers. Engvd title, 5 plates. Early 19th c half calf gilt, trifle rubbed.
(Ximenes) $250 [≈ £130]

Parker, Benjamin
- Philosophical Meditations with Divine Inferences. London: for the author, 1734. Disbound. *(Waterfield's)* £90 [≈ $172]

Parker, George
- Life's Painter of Variegated Characters in Public and Private Life. London: for James Ridgway, 1789. 1st edn. 8vo. 45 pp subscribers. 19th c half rose calf gilt, gilt spine, front bd loose, ft of spine chipped.
(Ximenes) $650 [≈ £338]

Parker, Samuel
- A Discourse of Ecclesiastical Politie ...

London: for John Martin ..., 1670. 1st edn.
8vo. (i)-xxiii, xxxii-lvi (without loss), 326, [1
errata,1 blank] pp. Occas marg worm. Some
use. Old sheep, rebacked with calf. Wing
P.459. Anon.   *(Bow Windows)* **£55 [≈ $105]**

Parkinson, John
- Theatrum Botanicum, The Theater of Plants,
or An Universall and Compleate Herball.
London: 1640. Folio. xviii,1755 pp,errata
leaf. Addtnl engvd title, over 2700 w'cut ills.
A few edges strengthened. Some marginalia.
18th c calf, rebacked, new endpapers.
                    (Henly) **£1,250 [≈ $2,399]**
- Theatrum Botanicum. London: Thomas
Cotes, 1640. 1st edn. Folio. [xx],1746,[2] pp.
Water stain to last few ff. Contemp calf bds,
rebacked.   *(Bookpress)* **$2,750 [≈ £1,432]**

Parnell, Thomas
- An Essay on the Different Stiles of Poetry.
London: for Benj. Tooke, 1713. 1st edn. 8vo.
Half-title. Disbound, trimmed a trifle close.
Anon.   *(Ximenes)* **$1,000 [≈ £520]**
- Poems on Several Occasions ... Published by
Mr. Pope. London: Lintot, 1722. 1st edn.
8vo. [viii],221,[iii] pp. Minor browning.
Contemp calf, gilt spine, minor wear to spine
ends, jnts cracked but secure.
                        (Clark) **£75 [≈ $143]**
- Poems on Several Occasions ... Published by
Mr. Pope. London: Lintot, 1726. 2nd edn.
8vo. [viii],221,[35 advt] pp. Red & black title.
Marg worm at end. Contemp calf, spine ends
worn.   *(Burmester)* **£30 [≈ $57]**
- Poems on Several Occasions ... Published by
Mr. Pope. Sixth Edition. Dublin: R. Reilly,
1735. 12mo. [vi],186 pp. Red & black title.
Contemp calf, sl wear to upper jnt.
                        (Young's) **£80 [≈ $153]**
- The Poetical Works of Dr. Thomas Parnell,
late Archdeacon of Clogher. Glasgow:
Andrew Foulis, 1786. Folio. Contemp calf,
spine gilt extra, rebacked.
                    (Emerald Isle) **£200 [≈ $383]**

Parr, Samuel
- A Free Translation of the Preface to
Bellendenus; containing Animated Strictures
on the Great Political Characters of the
Present Time. London: Stafford & Davenport
..., 1788. 1st edn. 8vo. xii,159 pp. New bds.
Anon.   *(Young's)* **£40 [≈ $76]**
- A Sequel to the Printed Paper lately
circulated in Warwickshire by the Rev.
Charles Curtis ... London: for Charles Dilly,

1792. 1st edn. 8vo. Disbound. Anon.
                    (Ximenes) **$150 [≈ £78]**

Parry, Edward, Bishop of Killaloe
- David Restored. Or an Antidote against the
Prosperity of the Wicked and the Afflictions
of the Just ... Oxford: Joseph Godwin, 1660.
Only edn. 8vo. [xlviii],311, [iii],20,[ii] pp.
Transverse title, final advt leaf. Some marks.
Later qtr mor, rubbed. Wing P.556.
                        (Clark) **£85 [≈ $163]**

Parry, Richard
- The Genealogies of Jesus Christ in Matthew
and Luke explained; and the Jewish
Objections removed. London: 1771. Only
edn. 8vo. 61 pp. Fldg table. Old calf.
                    (Bickersteth) **£22 [≈ $42]**

Parsons, Robert
- The Jesuit's Memorial, for the Intended
Reformation of England ... With an
Introduction ... by Edward Gee. London:
Richard Chiswel, 1690. 8vo. [iv],lvi,[xvi], 262
pp. Half-title. Stained. Disbound. Wing
P.569. Anon.   *(Clark)* **£32 [≈ $61]**
- A Sermon Preached At the Funeral of the Rt
Honorable John [Wilmot] Earl of Rochester.
Oxford: at the Theater ..., 1680. 1st edn. 4to.
Crnrs v sl dogeared. Disbound. Wing P.570.
                    (Sanders) **£60 [≈ $115]**

Parsons, Colonel William
- Chronological Tables of Europe ... Ninth
Impression, with alterations and amendments
... London: for B. Barker & C. King, 1726.
Oblong 16mo. Engvd throughout by Sturt on
47 plates. Contemp calf gilt, spine sl worn.
                    (Ximenes) **$250 [≈ £130]**

Partridge, John
- Annus Mirabilis or Strange and Wonderful
Predictions and Observations Gathered out of
Mr. J. Partridges Almanack 1688 ... London:
Randal Taylor, 1689. 4to. [iv],32 pp. Lib
stamp on title verso. Sl dusty. Disbound.
Wing A.2018.   *(Clark)* **£85 [≈ $163]**
- Mene Mene, Tekel Upharsim. The Second
Part of Mene Tekel: Treating of the Year
MCCLXXXIX [sic] ... London: Baldwin,
1689. 1st edn. 4to. [viii],32 pp. Outer ff
dusty. Crnr of last leaf torn. Disbound. Wing
P.619.   *(Clark)* **£60 [≈ $115]**

Pascal, Blaise
- The Life of Mr. Paschal, with his Letters
relating to the Jesuits ... Translated into

English by W.A. [William Andrews]. London: James Bettenham for the author, 1744. 2 vols. 8vo. 2 frontis. Contemp calf, sl worn. *(Waterfield's)* **£200 [≈$383]**

Pasquin, Anthony
- See Williams, John (Anthony Pasquin).

Paterson, Daniel
- A New and Accurate Description of all the Direct and Principal Cross Roads in England and Wales ... Seventh Edition, corrected, and greatly improved ... London: for T. Carnan, 1786. viii,xxiv pp, 284 columns, 285-293, [1 advt] pp. Fldg map. Sl used. Orig sheep. *(Fenning)* **£45 [≈$86]**

The Path to Riches ...
- See Sullivan, James.

Patrick, Symon
- Angliae Speculum: A Glass that Flatters Not; Presented to a Country Congregation at the Solemn Fast, April 24, 1678 ... London: for Richard Royston ..., 1678. 1st edn. 4to. 38 pp. Some staining. Disbound. Wing P.744. Anon. *(Young's)* **£75 [≈$143]**
- An Answer to a Book spread abroad by Romish Priests, intitled The Touchstone of the Reformed Gospel ... London: 1692. Sm 8vo. Contemp leather, rear bd held by 1 cord. *(Gage)* **£25 [≈$47]**
- The Christian Sacrifice. A Treatise shewing the Necessity, End and Manner of receiving the Holy Communion ... London: R.N. for Rich. Royston, 1685. 8th edn, crrctd. Cr 8vo. Frontis. Final ff stained. Contemp calf, rebacked. Wing P.767. *(Stewart)* **£40 [≈$76]**
- The Christian Sacrifice ... In Four Parts ... London: J.H. for L. Meredith, 1693. 10th edn. 12mo. [24],528 pp. 1 plate. 18th c calf, jnt cracked. Wing P.769A. *(Humber)* **£55 [≈$105]**
- A Commentary upon the Two Books of Samuel ... London: Chiswell, 1703. 4to. Orig calf, worn. *(Stewart)* **£25 [≈$47]**
- The Devout Christian Instructed How to Pray and Give Thanks to God or a Book of Devotions for Families. London: J. Walthoe ..., 1730. 16th edn. 8vo. 22,476,4 pp. Frontis. Sl wear. Contemp calf, spine worn, jnts cracked. *(Humber)* **£28 [≈$53]**
- An Exhortation Sent to the Clergy of the Diocese of Ely. London: for Ri. Chiswell, 1704. 12mo. 5 old lib stamps. 19th c cloth backed bds. *(Sanders)* **£32 [≈$61]**

- The Parable of the Pilgrim: written to a Friend. London: Robert White for Francis Tyson, 1678. 4to. xii,527 pp. Contemp leather, sl worn & soiled, hinges weak. *(Gage)* **£30 [≈$57]**
- A Sermon preached upon St. Peter's Day ... By a Divine of the Church of England. London: for Ric. Chiswell, 1687. Imprimatur leaf. Mod buckram. Wing P.845. Anon. *(Waterfield's)* **£40 [≈$76]**
- The Witnesses to Christianity ... London: for R. Royston, 1675. 1st edn of this 1st part. 8vo. [xviii],662 pp. Contemp black mor gilt, a.e.g., sl rubbed, headband lacking. Wing P.864. *(Sotheran's)* **£88 [≈$168]**

Patten, Thomas
- King David Vindicated from a Late Misrepresentation of his Character. In a Letter to His Grace the Archbishop of Canterbury ... Oxford: Clarendon Press, 1762. 1st edn. 8vo. [iv],131 pp. Disbound. *(Young's)* **£30 [≈$57]**

Paul, John
- Every Landlord or Tenant his own Lawyer ... London: Strahan & Woodfall, 1775. 144 pp. Sl dusty at ends. Disbound. *(C.R. Johnson)* **£75 [≈$143]**

Pax in Bello ...
- Pax in Bello; or, A Few Reflections on the Prospect of Peace, arising out of the Present Circumstances of the War ... London: for J. Owen ..., 1796. Only edn. 8vo. [iv],88 pp. Disbound. *(Young's)* **£55 [≈$105]**

Peake, John
- Brown Beer: a Poem. London: for the author, & sold by J. Williams, "MDLLLXII" [ie 1762]. 1st edn. 4to. 2 old lib marks. Rec calf. *(Ximenes)* **$900 [≈£468]**

Peake, John, victualler
- Brown Beer: A Poem. London: for the author, 1762. 4to. iv,5-20 pp. Late 19th c buckram, hinge split. *(Hollett)* **£175 [≈$335]**

Pearson, Anthony
- The Great Case of Tithes truly stated, clearly open'd, and fully resolved ... with an Appendix. London: assigns of J. Sowle, 1732. 8 advt pp at end. Orig wraps. *(Waterfield's)* **£50 [≈$95]**

Pearson, John
- An Exposition of the Creed. London: Roger Daniel for John Williams, 1659. 1st edn. 4to. [16], 785 pp. New mor. Wing P.995.
(Humber) **£95 [≈ $182]**
- An Exposition of the Creed. The Fourth Edition revised and now more Enlarged. London: J.M. for John Williams, 1676. Folio. Port. Red ruled title. Contemp calf, jnts cracked. Wing P.998. *(Lamb)* **£45 [≈ $86]**

Pechey, J.
- The Complete Herbal of Physical Plants ... London: 1707. 2nd edn. Sm 8vo. [viii],1-248, 193-336, 331-349, [29] pp, complete. Some mostly marg worm of 1st 20 ff, loss of a few letters. Few sl stains, few blank crnrs sl defective. Mod calf.
(Wheldon & Wesley) **£180 [≈ $345]**

Peele, J.
- The Art of Drawing, and Painting in Water Colours ... With Instructions ... chiefly from a manuscript of the great Mr Boyle ... Second Edition, with large additions. London: for J. Peele, 1732. 8vo. 70 pp, index leaf. 1 text w'cut. Some browning. Rec half sheep. Anon.
(Spelman) **£380 [≈ $729]**

Pegge, Samuel
- An Essay on the Coins of Cunobelin. London: Bowyer, 1766. 1st edn. Post 4to. iv, (136) pp. Plates. Mod qtr mor. 200 copies ptd. *(Ash)* **£100 [≈ $191]**

Peirce, James
- A Vindication of the Disenters ... Second Edition, Corrected. London: for John Clark, 1718. 575 pp. Leather gilt, rebacked, crnrs bumped. *(Gage)* **£45 [≈ $86]**

Pelling, Edward
- A Practical Discourse Concerning the Redeeming of Time ... London: for John Everingham ..., 1695. 1st edn. 8vo. 104,[5], [3 advt] pp. Old sheep, rebacked. Wing P.1085.
(Young's) **£165 [≈ $316]**
- A Sermon Preached at Westminster-Abbey On the 26th of July, 1685 ... London: Keble & Davis, 1685. 4to. [ii],36 pp. Red-ruled throughout. Outer ff dusty, some marg tears. Lib stamp title verso. Disbound. Wing P.1098. *(Clark)* **£20 [≈ $38]**

Pemberton, Henry
- The Dispensatory of the Royal College of Physicians, London ... London: 1748. 2nd edn. x, 414 pp. Contemp calf, gilt borders, mor label, edges of crnrs worn.
(Whitehart) **£135 [≈ $259]**
- A View of Sir Isaac Newton's Philosophy. London: S. Palmer, 1728. 1st edn. 4to. [48], 407 pp. 12 fldg plates. Qtr leather, rebacked.
(Gemmary) **£750 [≈ £390]**
- A View of Sir Isaac Newton's Philosophy. London: S. Palmer, 1728. 4to. Subscribers. 12 plates, num text decs by Pine. Few sm marg worm holes. Contemp calf, rebacked. Anon. *(Waterfield's)* **£450 [≈ $863]**
- A View of Sir Isaac Newton's Philosophy. Dublin: re-printed by & for John Hyde, 1728. 44, 333 pp. 12 fldg plates. Contemp calf, red label. *(C.R. Johnson)* **£425 [≈ $815]**

Pemble, William
- Salomons Recantation and Repentance: or, the Book of Ecclesiastes briefly and fully explained. London: J.H. for John Bartlet, 1628. Sm 4to. New qtr calf. STC 19584.
(Stewart) **£85 [≈ $163]**
- Vindiciae Fidei, or a Treatise of Justification by Faith ... Second Edition. Oxford: John Lichfield for Edward Forrest, 1629. 4to. [viii],248 pp. Sl damp staining throughout. Contemp limp vellum, soiled. STC 19590.
(Frew Mackenzie) **£110 [≈ $211]**

Pendlebury, Henry
- A Plain Representation of Transubstantiation. As it is received in the Church of Rome ... London: for J. Johnson, 1687. 4to. vi,68 pp. Title & last leaf v dusty, 1 leaf creased. Later wraps. Wing P.1141. Anon. *(Hollett)* **£50 [≈ $95]**

Pendragon ...
- Pendragon; or, the Carpet Knight his Kalendar. London: for John Newton, 1698. 1st edn. 8vo. [viii],186 pp. Sl browned. 18th c sheep, rebacked. Wing P.1142.
(Burmester) **£350 [≈ $671]**

Penn, James
- Sermons and Tracts. London: Printed in the Year 1777. 1st edn. 8vo. xvi,191,[i] pp. 10 pp subscribers. Title sl soiled. Rec half calf.
(Clark) **£65 [≈ $124]**
- Various Tracts. London: Charles Say for the author, (1762). 8vo. Subscribers. Contemp calf backed bds, uncut. *(Lamb)* **£25 [≈ $47]**

Penn, William
- A Brief Account of the Rise and Progress of the People called Quakers ... Ninth Edition. London: James Phillips, 1786. 12mo. Final advt leaf. Contemp sheep, scarred, hinges splitting. *(Jarndyce)* £30 [≈ $57]

Pennant, Thomas
- Arctic Zoology. London: 1792. 2nd edn. 3 vols. 4to. Frontis, 2 title vignettes, 23 plates. Lacks the 2 fldg maps. Without the 2 unnumbered plates sometimes found. Some offsetting from plates. 2 sm tears reprd. Contemp calf, worn, rebacked, jnts sl weak. *(Wheldon & Wesley)* £400 [≈ $767]
- British Zoology. Warrington & London: 1776-77. 4th edn. 4 vols. 8vo. Engvd titles (vol 2 title comprises plate 60 of Birds), fldg music plate, 280 plates. Contemp calf, jnts beginning to crack. *(Wheldon & Wesley)* £180 [≈ $345]
- Genera of Birds. London: for B. White, 1781. 2nd (1st 4to) edn. Post 4to. [iv], [xxvi], (70) pp. Engvd title & 15 plates, all hand cold in a later hand. Washed & reprd, new tissue guards. Rec 18th c style mor. *(Ash)* £300 [≈ $575]
- The History of the Parishes of Whiteford and Holywell. London: for B. & J. White ..., 1796. 1st edn. 4to. [viii],328 pp. 2 titles with engvd vignettes, 22 plates. A few spots, sl offsetting from plates. Old polished half calf, uncut, sl rubbed, edges sl worn. *(Hollett)* £185 [≈ $355]
- The Journey from Chester to London. Dublin: for Luke White, 1783. 1st Irish edn. 8vo. [2],ii,468,[6] pp. Sgntr F misbound but complete. 19th c half calf. *(Fenning)* £65 [≈ $124]
- The Literary Life of the late Thomas Pennant Esq. By Himself. London: B. & J. White, R. Faulder, 1793. 4to. Frontis port. Sl stained. faint lib stamps. Rec half calf, uncut. *(Jarndyce)* £90 [≈ $172]
- The Literary Life of the late Thomas Pennant Esq. By Himself. London: B. & J. White, Robt. Faulder, 1793. 1st edn. 4to. vi, 144 pp. 2 plates. Contemp calf, rebacked. *(Lloyd-Roberts)* £120 [≈ $230]
- Some Account of London. Third Edition. Dublin: for John Archer, 1791. 1st Irish edn. Roy 8vo. iv,[8 subscribers],[2],479,[8] pp. Engvd title, fldg map, 15 plates. Sl used. Contemp calf gilt. *(Fenning)* £75 [≈ $143]
- Some Account of London. London: for Robt. Faulder, 1793. 3rd edn. 4to. viii,502 pp. 15

plates (inc fldg plan). Plan split at folds, frontis reprd & tissue lined. Rebound in half calf. *(Lloyd-Roberts)* £110 [≈ $211]
- A Tour in Scotland MDCCLXIX. Chester: John Monk, 1771. 1st edn. 8vo. 316 pp. 18 plates, 1 text ill. Contemp calf. *(Chapel Hill)* $250 [≈ £130]
- A Tour in Scotland. MDCCLXIX. Chester: John Monk, 1771. [With] Supplement to the Tour in Scotland. Chester: John Monk, 1772. 18 plates, ills. Contemp calf, spine ends sl worn, hinge splitting. Anon. *(Jarndyce)* £120 [≈ $230]
- A Tour in Wales. Volume 1. London: for Benjamin White, 1784. Sm 4to. [8],488,[viii] pp. Engvd title, 26 plates, 2 extra plates. Occas spotting. 2 sm blind stamps. Old calf gilt, reprd, rebacked. *(Hollett)* £180 [≈ $345]
- The View of Hindoostan. London: Henry Hughes, 1798. 2 vols. 4to. xv,273; x,387 pp. Fldg map, 20 plates, 2 head-pieces. Some plates water stained, 1 torn without loss, 1 marked twice in ink. Contemp leather gilt, spines & extremities worn. Anon. *(Bates & Hindmarch)* £225 [≈ $431]

Pennington, Isaac
- Letters ... added Letters of Stephen Crisp, William Penn ... London: James Phillips, 1796. 8vo. Half mor. *(Stewart)* £20 [≈ $38]
- The Works of the Long Mournful and Sore-Distressed Isaac Pennington whom the Lord visited and relieved by that Despised People called Quakers. London: James Philips, 1784. 4 vols. Tall 8vo. Contemp tree calf, sl worn. *(Humber)* £55 [≈ $105]

Penrose, Thomas, Sr.
- Address to the Genius of Great Britain. London: S. Crowder, & J. Willis (Newbury), [1775]. 1st edn. 4to. Half-title (sl soiled). Disbound. *(Ximenes)* £650 [≈ £338]
- Poems. London: J. Walker, 1781. Contemp calf, jnts broken. *(C.R. Johnson)* £120 [≈ $230]

Penrose, Thomas, Jr.
- A Sketch of the Lives and Writings of Dante and Petrarch. With some Account of Italian and Latin Literature in the Fourteenth Century. London: Stockdale, 1790. 1st edn. 12mo. [ii],114 pp. Lacks half-title. 19th c half calf, rubbed, hd of spine worn. Anon. *(Burmester)* £65 [≈ $124]

Penton, Stephen
- The Guardian's Instruction, or, The Gentleman's Romance. Written for the Diversion and Service of the Gentry ... London: for the authour ..., 1688. Only edn. 12mo. [xvi],92 pp. Some sm reprs. Rec contemp style calf. Wing P.1429. Anon.
(Young's) **£245 [≈ $470]**

Pentweazle, Ebenezer (pseud.)
- The Horatian Canons of Friendship ... see Smart, Christopher.

Percy, Thomas
- Five Pieces of Runic Poetry, translated from the Icelandic Language [by Thomas Percy]. London: Dodsley, 1763. 1st edn. 8vo. Contemp calf gilt. *(Hannas)* **£120 [≈ $230]**
- Five Pieces of Runic Poetry. London: Dodsley, 1763. 1st edn. Post 8vo. Contemp green vellum later label, sl worn, sl discold. Anon. *(Ash)* **£200 [≈ $383]**
- The Hermit of Warkworth. A Northumberland Ballad ... London: for T. Davies, & S. Leacroft, 1771. 1st edn. 4to. viii,52 pp. Title vignette. Occas mark. Later card wraps. Anon. *(Finch)* **£45 [≈ $86]**

Perkins, William
- A Commentary or Exposition upon the Five First Chapters to the Galatians ... With a Supplement ... by Ralph Cudworth. London: John Legatt for the Univ of Cambridge, 1617. 4to. [10],584,[21] pp. Sl wear & tear. Calf. STC 19681. *(Humber)* **£125 [≈ $239]**

Perrault, C.
- The Natural History of Animals ... Done into English by a fellow of the Royal Society [A. Pitfield] ... London: 1702. 3rd English edn of the 'Parisian Memoirs'. Folio. [x], 3-267, [13],40 pp. Frontis, 35 plates. Some wear & tear. Calf, rebacked. *(Wheldon & Wesley)* **£180 [≈ $345]**

Perry, John
- The State of Russia under the Present Czar. London: for Benjamin Tooke, 1716. 1st edn. Post 8vo. [viii],280 pp. Fldg map by Moll. Few minor flaws. Contemp calf, sl marked & rubbed. *(Ash)* **£400 [≈ $767]**

Persian ...
- Persian Eclogues ... see Collins, William.
- Persian Tales ... see The Arabian Nights.

Personal Nobility ...
- See Knox, Vicesimus.

Petrarch, Francesco
- Sonnets and Odes translated from the Italian ... with the Original text and Some Account of his Life. London: for T. Davies, 1777. 8vo. Contemp qtr sheep, hd of spine defective. *(Waterfield's)* **£50 [≈ $95]**

Petty, William
- Political Survey of Ireland ... Second Edition, carefully corrected, with additions. London: D. Browne, 1719. 2nd edn. 8vo. [xvi], 223, [1 blank],[2 advt] pp. Title & some ff browned. 19th c half sheep. *(Pickering)* **$1,250 [≈ £651]**

Phalaris
- The Epistles of Phalaris ... see Francklin, Thomas.

Phelpes, Charles
- A Caveat against Drunkenness, especially in Evil Times. London: Tho. Parkhurst, 1676. 1st edn. [xiv],167 pp. 1st few ff sl stained & fragile. Some cropping of top edge. Old calf, worn, rebacked. Wing P.1975. *(Hollett)* **£95 [≈ $182]**

Philippos, N.B. (pseud.)
- The Farrier's and Horseman's Dictionary ... By N.B. [name in Greek]. London: for J. Darby ..., 1726. 1st edn. 8vo. viii,454 pp. Contemp calf, jnts reprd, new label. *(Burmester)* **£250 [≈ $479]**

Philips, Ambrose
- The Briton. A Tragedy. London: for B. Lintott, 1722. 1st edn. 8vo. Sl stain to half-title & last leaf. Disbound. *(Dramatis Personae)* **$50 [≈ £26]**

Philips, John
- Blenheim, a Poem ... The Second Edition. London: for Tho. Bennet, 1705. Folio. Occas sl staining & browning. Mod qtr calf, uncut. *(Waterfield's)* **£135 [≈ $259]**
- Cyder. A Poem. In Two Books. London: Tonson, 1708. 1st edn. 8vo. [vi],89 pp. Fly-title (soiled & stained) bound before frontis. Mod calf gilt. Anon. *(Claude Cox)* **£95 [≈ $182]**
- Cyder, a Poem in Two Books. London: Tonson, 1708. 1st edn, ordinary paper issue. 8vo. Frontis. Contemp panelled calf.

(Waterfield's) **£200 [≈ $383]**
- Cider, a Poem in Two Books. With Notes ... by Charles Dunster. London: George Stafford, for T. Cadell, 1791. 1st edn thus. 8vo. [iv], 183 pp. Sl marg worm. Contemp tree calf, spine sl rubbed.
(Burmester) **£150 [≈ $287]**
- Poems on Several Occasions. The Fourth Edition. London: Thomas Astley, 1728. 12mo. 46,23,72 pp. Sep pagination & sgntr for each section. The Splendid Shilling & Blenheim have Curll's imprint & date 1726, Cyder 3rd edn, Tonson, 1727. Orig calf, rebacked, rubbed. *(Bickersteth)* **£45 [≈ $86]**
- The Splendid Shilling. An Imitation of Milton. The Third Correct Edition. London: G.J. for Hen. Clements, 1719. Sm 8vo. 28 pp. Occas soiling. Later bds.
(Spelman) **£25 [≈ $47]**

Philips, Katherine
- Poems by the most deservedly admired Mrs Katherine Philips, The Matchless Orinda ...L: T.N. for Henry Herringman, 1678. 2nd edn. Folio. [xxxiv],198,[viii],124 pp. Port frontis. Wormhole in blank marg throughout. Orig calf, rebacked. Wing P.2035.
(Vanbrugh) **£255 [≈ $489]**
- Poems. London: Tonson, 1710. New edn. [46], 562 pp. Plate, port. Contemp bds, mod spine. *(Bell)* **£65 [≈ $124]**

Philosophical ...
- The Philosophical Dictionary, For the Pocket ... see Voltaire, F.M.A. de.

Phipps, Constantine John
- A Voyage towards the North Pole ... London: Bowyer & Nichols, 1774. 4to. vii,253 pp. 15 plates & maps, fldg tables. Half-title. Contemp speckled calf, rebacked to style.
(High Latitude) **$995 [≈ £518]**

Pic, Jean
- The Dream of Alcibiades. Translated from the Greek. London: H. Kent ..., 1749. 1st edn. 8vo. viii,48 pp. Disbound. Anon.
(Young's) **£90 [≈ $172]**

Pickering, Amelia
- The Sorrows of Werter: A Poem. London: Cadell, 1788. Half-title, xxii, 69 pp. Disbound. *(C.R. Johnson)* **£250 [≈ $479]**

Pigott, Charles
- The Female Jockey Club, or a Sketch of the

Manners of the Age. By the Author of the Former Jockey Club. London: for the author, 1794. 199 pp. Wraps. Anon.
(Wreden) **$40 [≈ £20]**
- The Female Jockey Club, or a Sketch of the Manners of the Age. By the Author of 'The Former Jockey Club'. London: for D.I. Easton, 1794. 3rd edn. 8vo. Title foxed, marg paper flaw in 1 leaf. 19th c mor bds, new mor spine. Anon. *(Stewart)* **£60 [≈ $115]**
- A Political Dictionary: explaining the True Meaning of Words ... London: for D.I. Eaton, 1795. 8vo. [ii],126 pp. Title dusty, prelims & last few ff damp stained in lower outer crnrs. Early bds, later cloth spine & crnrs, uncut, some wear to bds. *(Rankin)* **£60 [≈ $115]**

Piles, Roger de
- The Art of Painting, and the Lives of the Painters ... London: Nutt, 1706. 1st English edn. 8vo. [14],466 pp. Frontis. Contemp panelled calf, lower spine chipped.
(Bernett) **$325 [≈ £169]**
- The Principles of Painting ... Now First Translated into English. By a Painter. London: for J. Osborn, 1743. 1st English translation. 8vo. xii,300, [viii] pp. 2 plates. Sl spots, 1 sm repr. Contemp sprinkled calf, mor label, red sprinkled edges, spine just worn at hd. *(Finch)* **£120 [≈ $230]**

Pilkington, Mary
- Biography for Girls; or, Moral and Instructive Examples, for Young Ladies. London: for Vernor & Hood, 1799. Sm 8vo. Frontis. Mor backed mrbld bds.
(Stewart) **£55 [≈ $105]**

Pinchard, Elizabeth
- The Blind Child, or Anecdotes of the Wyndham Family. Written for the Use of Young People. By a Lady. London: for E. Newbery, 1791. 1st edn. 8vo. 178,[ii] pp. Final advt leaf. Frontis. Contemp tree calf, dec spine relaid. Anon. *(Finch)* **£110 [≈ $211]**
- The Blind Child, or Anecdotes of the Wyndham Family. Written for the Use of Young People. By a Lady. The Third Edition. London: for E. Newbery, 1795. 12mo. Frontis. Contemp sheep, rather worn, upper jnt broken. Anon.
(Sanders) **£35 [≈ $67]**
- Dramatic Dialogues, for the Use of Young Persons. By the Author of 'The Blind Child'. London: for E. Newbery, 1792. 2nd edn. 2 vols. Cr 8vo. 2 frontis, 4 plates. Contemp calf, gilt ruled spines. Anon.

(Stewart) **£100 [≈ $191]**
- The Two Cousins, a Moral Story, for the Use of Young Persons ... London: for E. Newbery, 1794. 2nd edn. Cr 8vo. Frontis (sl spotted). Contemp calf (upper jnt cracked). Anon.   *(Stewart)* **£75 [≈ $143]**

Pindar, Peter (John Wolcot)
- An Apologetic Postscript to Ode upon Ode or a Peep at St. James's. London: for G. Kearsley, 1787. 1st edn. 4to. [iv],23 pp. Half-title. Disbound.   *(Bickersteth)* **£25 [≈ $47]**

Pindar, Peter (pseudonym)
- The Kirwanade: or Poetical Epistle humbly addressed to the Modern Apostle in consequence of his very spirited behaviour in the Chapter held lately at St. Patrick's. Dublin: for the author, 1791. Disbound, sewing broken.   *(Waterfield's)* **£50 [≈ $95]**

Pineda, Pedro
- A Short and Compendious Method for Learning to Speak, Read, and Write, the English and Spanish Languages ... Third Impression, Corrected and Amended. London: for J. Nourse, 1762. 8vo. xii,361,[3 advt] pp. Early 19th c half calf, gilt spine.   *(Burmester)* **£70 [≈ $134]**

Piozzi, Hester Lynch
- Anecdotes of the late Samuel Johnson, LL.D. during the last Twenty Years of his Life. London: Cadell, 1786. 1st edn. 8vo. viii,306,[ii] pp. Half-title. Postscript leaf (without errata slip). Occas sl foxing. Contemp calf, sometime rebacked.
        (Sotheran's) **£300 [≈ $575]**
- Anecdotes of the late Samuel Johnson ... London: 1786. 2nd edn. 8vo. viii,306,[1] pp. Occas sl spotting. Lacks half-title & errata slip. Cloth.   *(Young's)* **£65 [≈ $124]**

Pitman, Henry
- A Relation of the Great Sufferings and Strange Adventures of Henry Pitman, Chyrurgion of the late Duke of Monmouth ... London: ptd by Andrew Sowle ..., 1689. Only edn. 4to. 38,[2 advt] pp. Sl browned. Lib stamp title verso. Disbound. Wing P.2298.   *(Clark)* **£250 [≈ $479]**

Pitt, Christopher
- Vida's Art of Poetry, translated into English Verse. London: Palmer for Bettesworth, 1725. 1st edn in English. 12mo. [iv], 118 pp, advt leaf. Orig calf, jnts cracked.

(Bickersteth) **£75 [≈ $143]**

Pittis, William
- Dr Ratcliffe's Life and Letters. The Fourth Edition. London: for A. Bettesworth ..., 1736. 8vo. [vi],102 pp. Sm piece chipped from title. 19th c half calf. Anon.
        (Claude Cox) **£45 [≈ $86]**

Planting and Rural Ornament ...
- See Marshall, William.

Plat, Hugh
- The Garden of Eden: or, an Accurate Description of all Flowers and Fruits now growing in England ... London: Leake, 1675. 6th edn. 2 parts in one vol. Sm 8vo. [xxvi], 148, [xvi],159 pp. Contemp sheep, rebacked & recrnrd.   *(Bookpress)* **$650 [≈ £338]**
- The Jewel House of Art and Nature ... London: Bernard Alsop, 1653. 2nd edn. Text w'cuts. Inkstains to prelims to A4. Mod qtr calf. Wing P.3290.
        (Dramatis Personae) **$850 [≈ £442]**

Platina, Bartolomeo
- The Lives of the Popes From the Time of Our Saviour Jesus Christ to the reign of Sixtus IV ... Translated ... by Sir Paul Rycaut. The Second Edition, Corrected. London: 1688. Folio. [xxxii],416,394,[18] pp. Port. A few marg stains & chips. Rec half calf. Wing P.2404. *(Bow Windows)* **£125 [≈ $239]**
- The Lives of the Popes, from the Time of Our Saviour Jesus Christ, to the Reign of Sixtus IV ... Translated ... by Sir Paul Rycaut. The Second Edition, Corrected. London: 1688. Folio. [xxxii],394,[16] pp. Port. Few sm lib stamps. Contemp calf, rebacked. Wing P.2404.
        (Young's) **£60 [≈ $115]**

Platus, Hueronymus
- The Happiness of a Religious State ... Translated into English. (Rouen: J. Cousturier), 1632. 4to. Early crnrs sl frayed, 3Mi torn. Vellum, reprd. STC 20001.
        (Stewart) **£100 [≈ $191]**

Plautus
- Plautus's Comedies, Amphitryon, Epidicius, and Rudens, Made English: With Critical Remarks upon each Play. By Laurence Echard ... Second Edition Corrected. London: 1716. 12mo. Frontis. Contemp sprinkled calf, sl rubbed.
        (Dramatis Personae) **$95 [≈ £49]**

Plaw, John
- Rural Architecture; or Designs from the Simple Cottage to the Decorated Villa ... London: the author, 1790. 2nd edn. 4to. 8,viii pp. Frontis, 60 aquatint plates. Contemp calf, rebacked, minor wear to tips.
(Bookpress) **$1,450 [≈ £755]**

Plowden, Francis
- A Short History of the British Empire during the last Twenty Months; viz. from May 1792 to the Close of the Year 1793. London: Robinson, 1794. 8vo. Half-title. Contemp calf gilt, spine sl rubbed. *(Jarndyce)* **£70 [≈ $134]**
- A Short History of the British Empire during the Last Twenty Months; viz. from May 1792 to the close of the year 1793. London: 1794. 1st edn. Contemp half calf, spine rubbed.
(Robertshaw) **£26 [≈ $49]**
- A Supplement to the Investigation of the Native Rights of British Subjects. London: for the author ..., 1785. 1st edn. 8vo. xi, 151 pp. Half-title. Contemp half calf, sl rubbed.
(Young's) **£45 [≈ $86]**

Pluche, Noel Antoine
- The History of the Heavens, considered according to the Notions of the Poets and Philosophers, compared with the Doctrines of Moses. Translated ... by J.B. De Freval. London: 1740. 1st edn in English. 2 vols. 8vo. 25 plates. Orig calf, rubbed, jnt cracked.
(Bickersteth) **£110 [≈ $211]**
- Spectacle de la Nature: or, Nature Display'd ... Translated from the Original French, By Mr. Humphreys. The Fourth Edition. London: L. Francklin, Davis ..., 1740. 7 vols. 8vo. 7 frontis, num plates. Contemp calf, sl worn. Anon. *(Finch)* **£325 [≈ $623]**

A Plurality of Worlds ...
- See Fontenelle, B. le B., Sieur de.

Plutarch
- The Philosophy, Commonly Called, The Morals ... Translated ... By Philemon Holland ... Newly revised and Corrected. London: S.G. for J. Kirton, 1657. 2nd edn. Folio. [viii], 1108, [56] pp. Sm stain at ends. Orig calf gilt, spine sl faded & worn. Wing P.2655. *(Vanbrugh)* **£295 [≈ $566]**

A Pocket Companion for Oxford ...
- A Pocket Companion for Oxford. Containing, An Accurate Description of the Public Edifices ... Oxford: R. Clements; & R.

Baldwin, (1744). 1st edn. 8vo. 4 plates. Title sl browned. Rebound in half calf.
(Jarndyce) **£85 [≈ $163]**

Pococke, Edward
- A Commentary on the Prophecy of Hosea ... Oxford: at the Theatre, 1685. Folio. [8],816, 40 pp. Early calf, rebacked. Wing P.2660.
(Humber) **£125 [≈ $239]**

Pococke, Richard
- A Description of the East ... London: for the author by W. Bowyer, 1743-45. 1st edn. 2 vols. Folio. vi,[viii],310; xii,268, viii,308 pp. Engvd title vignettes, dedic, 178 maps & plates. No plate 33 vol 1 as always. Few sm nicks. Later half calf, reprd.
(Frew Mackenzie) **£1,200 [≈ $2,303]**

Poems ...
- Poems on Several Occasions. London: Lintot, 1717 ... see Fenton, Elijah.
- Poems on Several Occasions ... London: 1727 ... see Thomas, Elizabeth.
- Poems on Several Occasions ... Edinburgh: 1754 ... see Blacklock, Thomas.
- Poems on Several Occasions. Wolverhampton, 1769 ... see Moss, Thomas.
- Poems on Several Subjects ... see Cooper, John Gilbert.
- Poems to Thespia ... see Downman, Hugh.
- Poems upon Various Subjects, Latin and English ... see Browne, Isaac Hawkins.

Poetical ...
- Poetical Excursions in the Isle of Wight. London: N. Conant, 1777. 4to. 42 pp. Title vignette. Contemp qtr calf, mrbld bds, mor label, some wear.
(C.R. Johnson) **£350 [≈ $671]**
- The Poetical Register ... see Jacob, Giles.

Poetry of the Anti-Jacobin ...
- See Canning, George, et al.

Pointer, John
- A Rational Account of the Weather, shewing signs of its several Changes and Alterations, together with the Philosophical Reasons of them. Oxford: L.L. for S. Wilmot ..., 1723. 76 pp. Rebound in panelled calf.
(C.R. Johnson) **£240 [≈ $460]**
- A Rational Account of the Weather ... Second Edition corrected and much enlarg'd ... added, Three Essays ... London: for Aaron

Ward, 1738. 8vo. Half-title. Contemp calf, rebacked, crnrs reprd.
(Georges) £200 [≈ $383]

Polano, Pietro Soave
- See Sarpi, Paolo.

Pole, Thomas
- The Anatomical Instructor ... Preparing and Preserving the different Parts of the Human Body, and of Quadrupeds ... London: the author, Darton & Co, 1790. 1st edn. 8vo. lxxx, [xii],304, [xv] pp, errata leaf. 10 plates (spotted). 19th c half mor, rubbed.
(Bickersteth) £110 [≈ $211]
- The Anatomical Instructor. London: the author & W. Darton, 1790. 1st edn. 8vo. lxxx, [xii], 304,[15] pp. 10 plates. 1 index leaf defective. Contemp tree calf, hinges starting to crack.
(Bookpress) $450 [≈ £234]
- The Anatomical Instructor; or, an Illustration of the Modern and Most Approved Methods of Preparing and Preserving the Different Parts of the Human Body and of Quadrupeds ... London: 1790. 8vo. lxxx, [6], 304,[7] pp. 10 plates. Calf, jnts split.
(Goodrich) $125 [≈ £65]

Polite ...
- The Polite Gamester: or, The Humours of Whist. A Dramatic Satire ... London: M. Cooper, W. Reive, C. Sympson, 1753. 1st edn thus. 8vo. Frontis. Disbound.
(Dramatis Personae) $100 [≈ £52]
- The Polite Philosopher ... see Forrester, James.

Politeuphia, Wits Common-Wealth ...
- See Ling, Nicholas.

Political ...
- Political Catechism ... see Robinson, Robert.
- A Political Essay upon the English and French Colonies in Northern and Southern America, considered in a New Light. By A Patriot. London: G. Woodfall, 1760. Half-title, 15 pp. Disbound.
(C.R. Johnson) £240 [≈ $460]

Pomfret, John
- Poems upon several Occasions ... Fourth Edition, Corrected. London: for E. Curll, & W. Taylor, 1716. 12mo. [vi],148 pp. Frontis. Contemp calf, sometime rebacked, extremities rubbed.
(Finch) £35 [≈ $67]
- Poems upon several Occasions. Eighth Edition, corrected. With some Account of his Life and Writings ... added, his Remains. London: [Samuel Richardson] for J. Walthoe, 1731. 8vo. frontis. Lacks 1st blank. New cloth.
(Stewart) £85 [≈ $163]
- Poems upon Several Occasions ... To which are added, His Remains. London: for D. Brown ..., [ca 1760]. 11th edn. 8vo. xii,132, vi,17 pp. Frontis. Some spotting. Old sheep, rebacked.
(Young's) £12 [≈ $23]

Pontoppidan, Erich
- The Natural History of Norway ... together with the Customs and Manner of Living of the Inhabitants ... London: for A. Linde, 1755. 1st English translation. Folio. xxiii,[i], 206, vii,[i], 291,[xii] pp. Fldg map, 26 plates. V sl marg worm at end. Contemp polished calf, gilt spine.
(Finch) £575 [≈ $1,103]

Poole, Joshua
- The English Parnassus: or, a Helpe to English Poesie ... London: Tho. Johnson, 1657. 1st edn. 8vo. [xxxii],1-288, 239-572 pp. Blank leaf before title. Some damp staining. Pen-trials on title. Rec half calf. Wing P.2814. Lowndes calls for a frontis in error.
(Clark) £150 [≈ $287]

Pope, Alexander
- The Dunciad with Notes Variorum, and the Prolegomena of Scriblerus. The Second Edition, with some Additional Notes. London: Gilliver, 1729. 232, errata pp. Frontis. red & black title. Contemp calf, brown label. Anon.
(C.R. Johnson) £135 [≈ $259]
- The Dunciad. With Notes Variorum, and the Prolegomena of Scriblerus. London: Gilliver, 1729. 8vo. 221,[xiii] pp. Frontis of the Ass, plate of the Owl. Contemp panelled calf, red edges, no free endpapers, jnts split at ends. Anon.
(Sotheran's) £225 [≈ $431]
- An Essay on Criticism. The Sixth Edition corrected. London: Lintot, 1719. Frontis. New bds.
(C.R. Johnson) £90 [≈ $172]
- The New Dunciad: as it was found in the year MDCCXLI. With the Illustrations of Scriblerus, and Notes Variorum. London: for F. Cooper, 1742. 1st edn of Book IV. 4to. [vi], 44 pp. Lacks half-title. Spotted. Disbound. Anon.
(Burmester) £110 [≈ $211]
- The New Dunciad: as it was found in the Year 1741. With the Illustrations of Scriblerus, and Notes Variorum. London: for T. Cooper, 1742. 2nd edn of Book IV of the Dunciad. 4to. Half-title. Mod half calf gilt.

(Ximenes) **$250 [≈ £130]**
- The Rape of the Lock ... Second Edition. London: Lintot, 1714. 48 pp. Frontis, 5 plates. Disbound.
(C.R. Johnson) **£245 [≈ $470]**
- The Temple of Fame: a Vision. The Second Edition. London: Lintot, 1715. 4 advt pp. Frontis. New bds. Anon.
(C.R. Johnson) **£125 [≈ $239]**
- The Works ... London: 1717-35-37-41. 1st edns. Vols 1 & 3 1st issues. 4 vols. 4to. Half-titles. Fldg port frontis vol 1. Contemp calf gilt, rebacked, bds worn.
(Young's) **£500 [≈ $959]**
- The Works ... with his last Corrections, Additions and Improvements; together with the Commentary and Notes of his Editor [W. Warburton]. London: for C. Bathurst ..., 1770. 9 vols. 8vo. Contemp calf, rubbed, crnrs worn, jnts cracked, lacks labels.
(Waterfield's) **£60 [≈ $115]**

Porny, Marc Antoine (Antoine Pyron du Martre)
- The Elements of Heraldry ... Fifth Edition with considerable Alterations and Additions. London: Robinson ..., 1795. 8vo. 24 plates. Later half calf, rubbed.
(Jarndyce) **£58 [≈ $111]**
- The Elements of Heraldry ... Fifth Edition. London: Robinson ..., 1795. 8vo. 24 plates. Mod qtr calf. *(Waterfield's)* **£45 [≈ $86]**

Portal, Abraham
- Poems. London: for the author, 1781. 1st edn. 8vo. [iv],7,[i],295 pp. Subscribers. Occas sl spotting & soiling. Contemp calf, rebacked, crnrs sl worn. *(Burmester)* **£180 [≈ $345]**

Portlock, Nathaniel
- A Voyage round the World; but more particularly to the North-West Coast of America ... London: 1789. 1st edn. Thick paper issue. 4to. Port, fldg chart, 18 plates & maps (5 cold). Contemp half russia & blue mrbld bds gilt, uncut, spine & hinges sl rubbed. *(Ximenes)* **$4,500 [≈ £2,343]**

Postlethwayt, Malachy
- Great-Britain's True System ... London: for A. Millar ..., 1757. 1st edn. 8vo. [viii], cl, 363 pp. Some childish marginalia on a few pp. Mod half calf. *(Pickering)* **$1,250 [≈ £651]**
- The Merchant's Advocate: Or, An Enquiry, whether the Merchants are not intitled to a Discount of 5 per Cent ... London: M.

Cooper, 1749. Half-title, 20 pp. Anon.
(C.R. Johnson) **£360 [≈ $691]**

Pote, Joseph
- The History and Antiquities of Windsor Castle, and the Royal College ... Account of the Town and Corporation of Windsor ... Eton: Joseph Pote, 1749. 1st edn. Sm 4to. [xx],431 pp. Licence. Port, plan, 12 plates. Early 20th c levant mor gilt, a.e.g.
(Hollett) **£175 [≈ $335]**

Pott, Joseph Holden
- An Essay on the Landscape Painting. With Remarks General and Critical, on the Different Schools and Masters, Ancient or Modern. London: for J. Johnson, 1782. 104 pp. Contemp calf, rebacked. Anon.
(C.R. Johnson) **£245 [≈ $470]**

Pott, Percival
- An Account of the Method of obtaining a Perfect or Radical Cure of the Hydrocele, or Watry Rupture, by means of a Seton. The Second Edition. London: Hawes, Clarke, Collins, 1772. 8vo. [iv],43 pp. 1 plate. Old half calf, rebacked. *(Bickersteth)* **£85 [≈ $163]**
- Chirurgical Observations relative to the Cataract, the Polypus of the Nose, the Cancer of the Scrotum ... London: Carnegy, 1775. 8vo. [iv],xi,[i],208 pp. Later half calf. Bound with Thomas Percival's Essays Medical and Experimental Vol II, London, 1773.
(Goodrich) **$3,750 [≈ £1,953]**
- A Treatise on the Hydrocele, or Watry Rupture, and other Diseases of the Testicle ... Third Edition, improved with very considerable Additions. London: Hawes, Clarke, Collins, 1773. 8vo. vii,[iii],372 pp. 2 plates. Title sl marked. Orig calf, rebacked.
(Bickersteth) **£180 [≈ $345]**

Potter, Francis
- An Interpretation of the Number 666 ... Oxford: Leonard Lichfield, 1642. 1st edn. Sm 4to. [9] ff,214 pp. Title reprd. New qtr calf. Wing P.3028. *(Chapel Hill)* **$900 [≈ £468]**

Potter, John, 1674?-1747
- Archaeologia Graeca: or, the Antiquities of Greece. The Second Edition. London: for S. & J. Sprint ..., 1706. 2 vols. 8vo. 9 + 18 plates. Contemp panelled calf, mor labels, crnrs reprd. James Gibb's b'plates.
(Waterfield's) **£155 [≈ $297]**

Potter, John
- The Curate of Coventry: A Tale. In Two Volumes. London: F. Newbery, 1771. 2 vols. 219; 263 pp. Half-title. Blank crnrs clipped from half-title & title of vol 2. Contemp calf, spines sl rubbed.
                (C.R. Johnson) **£850 [≈ $1,631]**

Potter, John, musician (ed.)
- Festivious Notes on the History and Adventures of the Renowned Don Quixote ... Second Edition. London: for F. Newbery ..., 1771. 12mo. xii,255,[21] pp. Half-title. Errata leaf. Contemp calf gilt, spine darkened, upper jnt tender, label chipped.
                (Burmester) **£120 [≈ $230]**

Potter, Robert
- An Inquiry into some Passages in Dr. Johnson's Lives of the Poets ... London: Dodsley, 1783. 1st edn. 4to. [iv],50 pp. Sep title to 'The Ninth Pythian Ode'. Port frontis. Half-title sl dusty. Disbound.
                (Finch) **£475 [≈ $911]**
- Observations on the Poor Laws, on the Present State of the Poor, and on Houses of Industry. London: for J. Wilkie, 1775. 1st edn. [ii],72 pp. Mod half calf gilt.
                (Hollett) **£195 [≈ $374]**

Potter, Thomas
- The Expedition against Rochfort fully stated and considered in a Letter ... By A Country Gentleman. The Second Edition, Corrected. London: J. Towers, 1758. 68 pp. Disbound. Anon.   *(C.R. Johnson)* **£25 [≈ $47]**

Pownall, Thomas
- The Right, Interest and Duty of the State as concerned in the Affairs of the East Indies. London: S. Bladon, 1773. Half-title, 48 pp. Disbound.   *(C.R. Johnson)* **£75 [≈ $143]**

Pozzo, Andrea
- Rules and Examples of Perspective Proper for Painters and Architects. London: Benjamin Motte, 1707. 1st edn in English. Demy folio. [vi],[102],[viii] pp. Engvd titles, 101 plates, engvs. Pict title mtd. Occas lib stamps, sl marks & chips. Rec half mor.
                (Ash) **£500 [≈ $959]**
- Rules and Examples of Perspective Proper for Painters and Architects ... London: Benjamin Motte, 1707. 1st edn in English. Folio. [xx],130 pp. 103 plates (inc 2 engvd titles). Contemp calf, spine darkened, hinges cracking. Earl of Coningsby (subscriber)'s

copy.   *(Bookpress)* **$3,500 [≈ £1,822]**

The Practice of Perspective ...
- See Dubreuil, Jean.

The Preceptor ...
- See Dodsley, Robert.

Present ...
- The Present Necessity of distinguishing Publick Spirit from party. London Printed. Edinburgh: reptd, 1736. 8vo. Mod wraps.
                (Waterfield's) **£45 [≈ $86]**
- The Present State of England, Set Forth in a Dialogue between Jehu and Jeroboam. London: for Richard Janeway, 1681. Sole edn. Sm 4to. 20 pp. Disbound. Wing P.3263.
                (Finch) **£90 [≈ $172]**
- The Present State of Great Britain and North America ... see Mitchell, John.
- The Present State of Great Britain ... see Miege, Guy.
- The Present State of Westminster Bridge ... see Labelye, Charles.

Price, Francis
- The British Carpenter, or a Treatise on Carpentry ... London: the author, 1735. 2nd edn. Sm 4to. [xii],52, (supplement) [iv],16 pp. 60 engvs. Mod qtr calf.
                (Bookpress) **$500 [≈ £260]**

Price, Howell ap David
- A Genuine Account of the Life and Transactions of Howell ap David Price, Gentleman of Wales ... Written by Himself ... London: for T. Osborne ..., 1752. Only edn. 12mo. viii,302 pp. Crnr torn from title affecting 3 letters. Lacks rear wrapper. Boxed.
                (Young's) **£200 [≈ $383]**

Price, Richard
- Additional Observations on the Nature and Value of Civil Liberty, and the War with America ... Second Edition. London: Cadell, 1776. 176 pp. Qtr mor, contemp mrbld bds, respined.   *(C.R. Johnson)* **£145 [≈ $278]**
- An Appeal to the Public, on the Subject of the National Debt. A New Edition. With an Appendix ... London: Cadell, 1774. 3rd edn, enlgd. [3],iv-vi, [3],x-xvi, [1],2-97,[1] pp. Rec wraps.   *(C.R. Johnson)* **£165 [≈ $316]**
- An Essay on the Population of England, from the Revolution to the Present Time. With an Appendix ... The Second Edition, with

Corrections and Additions. London: for T. Cadell, 1780. 88 pp. Contemp calf, rebacked.
(C.R. Johnson) £450 [≈ $863]
- Four Dissertations ... The Fourth Edition, with Additions. London: Cadell, 1777. 8vo. Some browning. Contemp calf, jnts cracked but sound. *(Waterfield's)* £125 [≈ $239]
- Four Dissertations ... The Fourth Edition, with Additions. London: Cadell, 1777. 464 pp. Contemp calf, rebacked.
(C.R. Johnson) £75 [≈ $143]
- Observations on the Nature of Civil Liberty, the Principles of Government, and the Justice and Policy of the War with America ... Third Edition. London: Cadell, 1776. 1st edn, 3rd imp. 8vo. Lacks half-title. Mod qtr calf.
(Waterfield's) £155 [≈ $297]
- Observations on the Nature of Civil Liberty, the Principles of Government, and the Justice and Policy of the War with America. Boston: reptd & sold by T. & J. Fleet, 1776. 1st Amer edn. Some loss on top crnr of title affecting 5 letters. Mod qtr calf.
(Waterfield's) £250 [≈ $479]
- A Review of the Principal Questions and Difficulties in Morals ... London: for A. Millar, 1758. 1st edn. 486,2 advt pp. Sm old lib stamp. Rebound in qtr calf, elab gilt spine.
(C.R. Johnson) £2,750 [≈ $5,279]

Price, Uvedale
- An Essay on the Picturesque, as compared with the Sublime; and, on the Use of Studying Pictures, for the Purpose of Improving Real Landscape. London: J. Robson, 1794. 1st edn. 8vo. xv,[i],288 pp. 19th c half calf. *(Spelman)* £280 [≈ $537]

Prideaux, Humphrey
- Directions to Church-Wardens for the faithful Discharge of their Office. For the Use of the Arch-Deaconry of Suffolk. The Second Edition, with Additions. Norwich: ptd by F. Burges, 1704. 4to. 41 pp. Disbound.
(C.R. Johnson) £125 [≈ $239]
- The Old and New Testaments connected in the History of the Jews and Neighbouring Nations ... London: Knaplock & Tonson, 1729. 10th edn. 4 vols. 8vo. 6 fldg maps, 10 plates (3 fldg). Contemp calf, spines rubbed.
(Lloyd-Roberts) £55 [≈ $105]

Priestley, Joseph
- An Appeal to the Public, on the Subject of the Riots in Birmingham ... added, Strictures of a Pamphlet, intitled "Thoughts on the late

Riot..." Birmingham: 1792. 2nd edn. 2 vols. Sm 8vo. xxxix,184; xxviii,210 pp. Crnr of vol 2 title clipped. New qtr leather.
(Whitehart) £255 [≈ $489]
- A Comparison of the Institutions of Moses with those of the Hindoos and other Ancient Nations ... Northumberland: for the author by A. Kennedy, 1799. 8vo. Contemp tree calf, hd of spine & crnrs worn.
(Waterfield's) £300 [≈ $575]
- A Description of a Chart of Biography ... Second Edition. Warrington: for the author ..., 1765. 12mo. 120, [1 errata, with errata slip mtd on blank verso] pp. 2 fldg plates. Last 2 ff stained. Rec wraps.
(Fenning) £58.50 [≈ $113]
- Disquisitions relating to Matter and Spirit ... London: for J. Johnson, 1777. 1st edn. 8vo. Q2,7 cancelled as usual. Frontis (sl foxed). Contemp tree calf, front jnt cracked but sound. Lacks label.
(Waterfield's) £325 [≈ $623]
- An Essay on the First Principles of Government; and on the Nature of Political, Civil, and Religious Liberty. London: for J. Dodsley ..., 1768. 1st edn. 8vo. Title sl soiled & marg reprd. Half calf antique, gilt spine.
(Ximenes) $900 [≈ £468]
- Experiments and Observations on Different Kinds of Air. London: 1775-76. 2nd edn. 2 vols (only, of 3). xxiii,[2],324; xliv,399, [8] pp. 4 plates. Contemp leather, rebacked.
(Whitehart) £180 [≈ $345]
- Hartley's Theory of the Human Mind, on the Principle of the Association of Ideas ... London: for J. Johnson, 1775. 372,3 advt pp,errata. Rebound.
(C.R. Johnson) £550 [≈ $1,055]
- The History and Present State of Discoveries relating to Vision, Light, and Colours. London: J. Johnson, 1772. 1st edn. 2 vols. 4to. v,[1],xvi,422; [2],423-812,[20] pp. Subscribers. Errata leaf. Frontis, 24 plates. Some browning & offsetting of plates. Contemp calf, rehinged.
(Rootenberg) $1,600 [≈ £833]
- The History and Present State of Electricity ... Third Edition, corrected and enlarged. London: for C. Bathurst ..., 1775. 2 vols. 8vo. Usual mispaginations. Ctlg inserted in vol 2. 8 fldg plates. Contemp calf, sl worn at ft of spine, new label. *(Waterfield's)* £220 [≈ $422]
- Lectures on History and General Policy to which is prefixed, an Essay upon a Course of Liberal Education for Civil and Active Life ... Third Edition. Dublin: White & Byrne, 1791.

8vo. Contemp tree calf, rebacked.
(Waterfield's) **£90 [≈ $172]**
- Lectures on History, and General Policy: to which is prefixed, an Essay on a Course of Liberal Education for Civil and Active Life. London: 1793. 2 vols. xvi,408; vii,488 pp. 2 fldg frontis. Mottled paper bndg, uncut.
(Whitehart) **£350 [≈ $671]**
- A Letter to the Right Honourable William Pitt ... on the Subjects of Toleration and Church Establishment occasioned by his Speech ... 28th of March 1787. London: for J. Johnson, 1787. Disbound.
(Waterfield's) **£85 [≈ $163]**
- Letters to a Philosophical Unbeliever Part I ... [Part II] ... Birmingham: Pearson & Rollason for J. Johnson, 1787. 2nd edn Part 1, 1st edn Part 2. 2 vols in one. 8vo. Mod qtr calf.
(Waterfield's) **£685 [≈ $1,315]**
- Letters to the Right Honourable Edmund Burke, occasioned by his Reflections on the French Revolution. Birmingham: Thomas Pearson, 1791. 1st edn. 8vo. Mod qtr calf.
(Waterfield's) **£225 [≈ $431]**
- Letters to the Right Honourable Edmund Burke occasioned by his Reflections of the Revolution in France, &c. The Third Edition, corrected. Birmingham: Thomas Pearson, sold By J. Johnson, London, 1791. 7 advt pp. Pp (5-6) misbound but complete. Rec cloth.
(Jarndyce) **£65 [≈ $124]**
- Letters to the Right Honourable Edmund Burke occasioned by his Reflections on the Revolution in France. Birmingham: Thomas Pearson, 1791. Disbound.
(Waterfield's) **£125 [≈ $239]**
- Observations on the Increase of Infidelity. The Third Edition, to which are added, Animadversions ... Phila: for Thomas Dobson, 1797. Orig blue wraps, uncut, sl bumped & dusty, backstrip worn.
(Jarndyce) **£90 [≈ $172]**
- Two Discourses. I. On Habitual Devotion. II. On the Duty of not living to Ourselves ... Birmingham: Piercy & Jones for J. Johnson, 1783. 8vo. Mod qtr calf.
(Waterfield's) **£175 [≈ $335]**
- The Use of Christianity, especially in Difficult Times ... The Author's Farewell Discourse to his Congregation. London: for J. Johnson, 1794. 1st edn. 8 ctlg pp. Lacks half-title. Rebound in half calf.
(Jarndyce) **£65 [≈ $124]**
- The Use of Christianity, especially in difficult Times: a Sermon ... March 30, 1794 ... being the Author's Farewell Discourse to

his Congregation. Dublin: William Folds, 1794. 1st Irish edn. 8vo. Half-title. Disbound.
(Waterfield's) **£110 [≈ $211]**

The Prince of Abyssinia ...
- See Johnson, Samuel.

Prince, Thomas
- The Vade Mecum for America: or a Companion for Traders and Travellers ... Boston: S. Kneeland, 1732. 2nd edn. Narrow 4to. [8],220 pp. Contemp calf, rebacked, some wear, crnrs bumped. Anon.
(Reese) **$2,750 [≈ £1,432]**

Pringle, John
- Observations on the Diseases of the Army ... Fourth Edition enlarged. London: Millar, Wilson ..., 1764. xxvii,355, cxxviii,[30] pp. Engvd title. Ex-lib. Lacks half-title. Calf gilt, scuffed, front jnt cracked but holding.
(Wreden) **$50 [≈ £26]**

Prior, Matthew
- The History of His Own Time ... Copied fair for the Press by Mr. Adrian Drift, His Executor. London: for the editor, 1740. 8vo. viii, 472,[8] pp. Port frontis. Lib stamp title verso, few marg blind stamps. Mod calf gilt.
(Hollett) **£95 [≈ $182]**
- A Letter to Monsieur Boileau Depreaux; Occasion'd by the Victory at Blenheim. London: Tonson, 1704. 1st edn. Folio. [ii],10 pp. Sl spotting, edges browned, inner title marg stained. Foredge of 1 leaf trimmed around 1 word (no loss). Later wraps. Anon.
(Finch) **£30 [≈ $57]**
- An Ode humbly inscrib'd to the Queen on the late glorious Success of Her Majesty's Arms. Written in Imitation of Spencer's Style. London: Tonson, 1706. Folio. Lacks half-title. Mod wraps.
(Waterfield's) **£100 [≈ $191]**
- Poems on Several Occasions ... Glasgow: Foulis, 1751. 2 vols in one. 8vo. 219; 214, [6,4 advt] pp. Contemp calf, gilt spine, red label, sl rubbed.
(Young's) **£40 [≈ $76]**

Prior, Thomas
- An Authentic Narrative of the Success of Tar-Water, In curing a great Number and Variety of Distempers ... New Edition, Complete. London: Dublin ptd, London reptd, for W. Innys ..., 1746. 8vo. 88 pp. Orig wraps, uncut, wraps detached, edges sl frayed.
(Finch) **£180 [≈ $345]**

Privileges ...

- The Privileges and Practice of Parliaments in England: Collected out of the Common Laws of this Land ... London: for Robert Harford, 1680. 4to. title,contents leaf,34 pp. Marg blind stamp on title. Later half roan, edges worn. Wing P.3535. *(Hollett)* £75 [≈ $143]

Probationary Odes for the Laureateship ...

- Probationary Odes for the Laureateship: with a Preliminary Discourse by Sir John Hawkins, Knt [pseud.]. London: for James Ridgway, 1785. 8vo. Half-title. Period qtr sheep, sl worn. By Tickell, Fitzpatrick, et al. *(Rankin)* £75 [≈ $143]

The Project. A Poem ...

- See Tickell, Richard.

Prolegomena ...

- Prolegomena to the Dramatic Writings of Will. Shakespere ... see Gentleman, Francis.

The Protical Son ...

- The Protical Son: A Welch Preachment, by the Parson of Llangtyddre. On the Return of his Protical Son ... London: for H. Carpenter ..., 1750. 1st edn. 8vo. 23 pp. Half-title. Disbound. *(Young's)* £150 [≈ $287]

Pryce, William

- Archaeologia [sic] Cornu-Britannica; or, An Essay to preserve the Ancient Cornish Language ... Sherborne: W. Crutwell, 1790. 65, 176 pp. Disbound.
(C.R. Johnson) £320 [≈ $614]
- Bibliotheca [sic] Cornu-Britannica; or, An Essay to preserve the Ancient Cornish Language ... Sherborne: W. Cruttwell ..., 1790. 1st edn. 4to. [xxiv],65,[176] pp. Rec qtr calf. *(Burmester)* £320 [≈ $614]
- Mineralogia Cornubiensis; a Treatise on Minerals, Mines, and Mining ... London: for the author, by James Phillips, 1778. 1st edn. Folio. [36],xiv,[2],331,[1] pp. Frontis port, 7 plates (3 fldg), 2 fldg tables. Few sl marks. Orig bds, backed in cloth, worn.
(Rootenberg) $1,200 [≈ £625]

Prynne, William

- A Counter-plea to the Cowards Apologie ... [London: 1647]. The edn without imprint or date. 4to. 4 pp. Drophead title. Torn at edges, sl dusty. Disbound. Wing P.3932. Anon.
(Jarndyce) £40 [≈ $76]
- Histrio-Mastix. The Player's Scourge, or,

Actor's Tragedie ... London: Michael Sparke, 1633 [1632]. 1st edn. 4to. 2 closed tears. Dust soiling to edges. Contemp calf, rebacked. STC 20464A.
(Dramatis Personae) $1,200 [≈ £625]
- An Humble Remonstrance to His Maiesty, against the Tax of Ship-Money ... [London]: Printed Anno 1641. 1st edn. Sm 4to. [ii],68 pp. Last 3 ff mispaginated 39-44. New wraps. Wing P.3983. Anon.
(Pickering) $750 [≈ £390]
- The Perpetuitie of a Regenerate Mans Estate ... Second Edition Perused and Enlarged. London: William Jones, 1627. 4to. 46,548 pp. Tiny marg worm hole. Minor marks. Contemp calf with 4 ties. STC 20472.
(Humber) £130 [≈ $249]
- A Plea for the Lords ... London: for Michael Spark, 1648. 4to. [iv],69 pp. A few spots. Blind stamp on title & final leaf. Old calf gilt, rebacked, edges rubbed. Wing P.4034.
(Hollett) £75 [≈ $143]
- A Vindication of the Imprisoned and Secluded Members of the House of Commons, from the Aspersions ... in a Paper lately printed and published ... London: for Michael Spark ..., 1649. 1st edn. 4to. 28 pp. Disbound. Wing P.4128. Anon.
(Young's) £70 [≈ $134]

Psalmanazar, George

- Memoirs of ****, commonly known by the name of George Psalmanazar; a Reputed Native of Formosa. Written by himself ... London: for R. Davis ..., 1765. 2nd edn. 307 pp. Port frontis. Few lib blind stamps. Old calf, rebacked. *(Hollett)* £160 [≈ $307]

Puddicomb, John Newell

- The British Hero in Captivity. A Poem ... London: J. Robson ..., 1782. 1st edn. 4to. 23 pp. Disbound. Anon.
(Bookpress) $1,500 [≈ £781]

Pugh, John

- Remarkable Occurrences in the Life of Jonas Hanway, Esq. London: for the author by J. Davies, 1787. x,262 pp. Fldg map frontis. Sev neat lib stamps. Contemp calf, spine worn.
(C.R. Johnson) £225 [≈ $360]

Pughe, William Owen

- Geriadur Cynmraeg a Seasoneg. A Welsh and English Dictionary ... prefixed, A Welsh Grammar. By William Owen [Pughe]. London: for E. & T. Williams, 1793. 1st edn. 2 vols. 8vo. Unpaginated. Contemp tree calf,

rebacked. Thoresby Park b'plates.
(Finch) **£300 [≈ $575]**

Pulteney, Richard
- A General View of the Writings of Linnaeus. London: 1781. 1st edn. 8vo. iv,425, [1] pp. Contemp calf.
(Wheldon & Wesley) **£175 [≈ $335]**

Pulteney, William
- The Budget Opened. Or an Answer to a Pamphlet Intituled, A Letter from a member of Parliament to his Friends in the Country, concerning the Duties of Wine and Tobacco. London: H. Haines, 1733. 1st edn. 8vo. 34,[1] pp. Wraps. Anon.   *(Young's)* **£65 [≈ $124]**
- Considerations on the Present State of Public Affairs and the Means of Raising the Necessary Supplies. London: 1779. 1st edn. 52 pp. Disbound. *(Robertshaw)* **£25 [≈ $47]**
- An Enquiry into the Conduct of our Domestic Affairs, from the Year 1721, to the Present Time ... Being a Sequel to Politicks on both sides. London: H. Haines, 1734. 68 pp. Mod half calf gilt. Anon.
(Hollett) **£150 [≈ $287]**
- A Letter from a Member of Parliament to a Friend in the Country, concerning the Sum of 115,000l. ... London: for Jeffrey Walker, (1729). 1st edn. 8vo. 24 pp. Some page numerals shaved. Stitched. Anon.
(Young's) **£45 [≈ $86]**
- Thoughts on the Present State of Affairs with America ... London: Dodsley, 1778. 4th edn. 8vo. [ii],102 pp. Later wraps.
(Bookpress) **$175 [≈ £91]**

Pulton, Ferdinando
- De Pace Regis et Regni, viz. A Treatise declaring which be the great and generall Offences of the Realme ... London: Companie of Stationers, 1615. 3rd edn. Folio in 6s. Few sm marg reprs & wormings. Contemp calf, rebacked, rear cvr sl stained. STC 20497.
(Meyer Boswell) **$500 [≈ £260]**

Purcell, John
- A Treatise of the Cholick; containing Analytical Proof of its Many Causes ... London: J. Morphew, 1715. 2nd edn. Sm 8vo. [xvi], 188, [12] pp. Contemp calf, rebacked.   *(Bookpress)* **$300 [≈ £156]**

Purchas, Samuel
- Purchas His Pilgrimage ... London: William Stansby for Henrie Featherstone ..., 1613. 1st

edn. 4to. [xxvi],752,[xx] pp. Usual misnumberings. Some wear & tear. Later half mor. STC 20505.
(Sotheran's) **£990 [≈ $1,900]**

Purney, Thomas
- Pastorals. After the Simple Manner of Theocritus. Second Edition Corrected. London: ptd by H. Parker, for J. Brown, & R. Burleigh, 1717. 1st edn. 8vo. Mod bds.   *(Ximenes)* **$475 [≈ £247]**

The Pursuit of Happiness ...
- See Mackenzie, Henry.

The Pursuits of Literature ...
- See Mathias, Thomas James.

Pye, Henry James
- Beauty, a Poetical Essay. In Three Parts. London: Becket & De Hondt, 1766. 1st edn. 4to. [2],26 pp. Disbound. Anon.
(Hannas) **£100 [≈ $191]**
- Shooting, a Poem. London: J. Davis ..., 1784. 49 pp. Half-title. New wraps. Anon.
(C.R. Johnson) **£325 [≈ $623]**

Quarles, Francis
- Emblems, Divine and Moral: together with Hieroglyphicks of the Life of Man. London: Elizabeth Nutt for T. Horn ..., 1718. iv,375 pp. Num engvs in text. Cloth, spine faded.
(Gage) **£40 [≈ $76]**
- A Feast for Wormes. Set forth in a Poeme of the History of Ionah. London: Felix Kyngston, for Richard Moore, 1626. 2nd edn. 2 parts in one, with continuous register. Sm 4to. W'cut on title. All side-notes intact. Lacks intl blank leaf. Calf antique. STC 20545.   *(Georges)* **£350 [≈ $671]**
- Institutions, Essays and Maxims, Political Moral and Divine divided into Four Centuries. London: for Sam. Briscoe, 1695. 12mo. Index, 286 pp. Last leaf N1 sl torn without loss. Leather, spine damaged.
(Gage) **£40 [≈ $76]**

Quillet, Claude
- Callipaedia: or, the Art of Getting Pretty Children ... Translated from the Original Latin of Claudius Quilletus. By Several Hands. London: Lintott, 1710. 1st edn of this translation. Sm 8vo. [xvi],72,[viii] pp. Contemp calf, jnt ends split.
(Sotheran's) **£185 [≈ $355]**

Quincy, John
- The Dispensatory of the Royal College of Physicians in London. London: R. Knaplock ..., 1721. 1st edn. 8vo. xvi,362,[15] pp. Frontis. Contemp calf, rebacked.
  (Bookpress) **$475 [≈ £247]**
- Lexicon Physico-Medicum; or, a New Physical Dictionary ... London: Andrew Bell, 1719. 1st edn. 8vo. xvi,462,[2 advt] pp. Contemp sheep, rebacked.
  (Gough) **£100 [≈ $191]**
- See also under Sanctorius.

Quintilian
- The Declamations of ... Translated ... by a learned and ingenious hand [J. Warr]. London: J.R. for John Taylor, 1686. 1st edn in English. 8vo. [16],272, 259 (bis)-474 pp. Sl worming. Contemp calf, rebacked. Wing Q.224.
  (Fenning) **£85 [≈ $163]**

Radcliffe, Ann
- The Italian, or the Confessional of the Black Penitents ... London: Cadell & Davies, 1797. 1st edn. 3 vols. 12mo. xii,336; [2], 360; [2],444 pp. Occas soiling & sl browning. 3 margs tears reprd, 1 crnr torn. Contemp calf backed bds, rebacked, vellum tips.
  (Claude Cox) **£95 [≈ $182]**
- A Journey made in the Summer of 1794, through Holland and the Western Frontier of Germany ... added Observations during a Tour to the Lakes of Lancashire, Westmorland and Cumberland. London: 1795. 4to. x,500 pp. Lacks half-title. Contemp half russia, sl worn.
  (Rankin) **£175 [≈ $335]**
- The Mysteries of Udolpho ... London: Robinson, 1794. 1st edn. 4 vols. 12mo. Few sm tears. Lacks half-titles. Contemp calf, gilt spines reprd. *(Burmester)* **£400 [≈ $767]**

Radcliffe, John
- Dr. Radcliffe's Life and Letters, with A True Copy of his Last Will and Testament ... London: for E. Curll ..., 1716. 3rd edn. 8vo. [iv],100 pp. Edge browned. Title partly defaced. New calf. *(Young's)* **£85 [≈ $163]**
- Pharmacopoeia Radcliffeana: or, Dr. Radcliff's Prescriptions, faithfully gathered from his Original Recipe's ... by Edward Strother. London: Rivington, 1716. 1st edn. 12mo. xii,166,2 advt pp. Possibly lacks a port. Marg browning. Half calf.
  (Rootenberg) **$400 [≈ £208]**

Raffald, Elizabeth
- The Experienced English Housekeeper, for the use of Ladies, Housekeepers, Cooks ... New Edition ... London: Millar, Law & Cater [ie York: Wilson, Spence & Mawman], 1791. W'cut frontis, 3 fldg plates. Mod buckram.
  (Waterfield's) **£150 [≈ $287]**

Raleigh, Sir Walter
- The History of the World ... London: for Walter Burre ... , 1614 (colophon 1634). Folio. [lxii],555,[i], 669,[55] pp. Title vignette port, 'Minde of the Front' leaf, 8 maps & engvs. Occas v sl marks & marg tears. Contemp sheep, rebacked. STC 20641.
  (Vanbrugh) **£475 [≈ $911]**
- The History of the World ... London: for Robert White ..., 1677. Folio. Addtnl engvd title, port, 8 maps. Table. Occas worm in inner margs. Contemp calf, rubbed & reprd, rebacked. Wing R.167.
  (Jarndyce) **£650 [≈ $1,247]**
- Three Discourses ... Published by Philip Ralegh, Esq; his only grandson. London: for Benjamin Barker, 1702. 1st edn thus. 8vo. Sep title (dated 1701) to 2nd essay. Advt leaf at end. Port. Contemp sheep, sl rubbed, jnts sl worn. *(Ximenes)* **$350 [≈ £182]**

Ralph, James
- The Case of Authors by Profession or Trade Stated. With regard to Booksellers, the Stage, and the Public. No Matter by Whom. London: for R. Griffiths, 1758. 1st edn. [iv], 72, 65-68 pp. Title & last leaf sl soiled. 19th c half mor, jnts rubbed.
  (C.R. Johnson) **£350 [≈ $671]**
- The Taste of the Town: or, A Guide to All Publick Diversions ... London: the booksellers, 1731. 12mo. Contemp calf, rebacked. Anon.
  (Dramatis Personae) **$500 [≈ £260]**

Ramsay, Allan
- The Gentle Shepherd ... Glossary ... Newcastle: printed in the year 1763. 8vo. 64, [xii] pp. Title & last leaf dusty. Tear (no loss). Disbound. *(Rankin)* **£50 [≈ $95]**
- The Gentle Shepherd ... Glasgow: ptd by A. Foulis, sold by D. Allan, Edinburgh ..., 1788. 4to. Half-title. Port frontis, 12 aquatint plates, 18 pp engvd music. Orig tissue guards. Old stain on 1 opening. Contemp diced calf gilt, rebacked. *(Sanders)* **£225 [≈ $431]**
- The Gentle Shepherd, a Scotch Pastoral. London: for the author, by T. Bensley ...,

1790. 1st edn of this version. 8vo. 11 pp
subscribers. Errata leaf. Contemp half calf,
minor wear to spine. *(Ximenes)* **$150 [≈£78]**

- The Gentle Shepherd ... Attempted in
English by Margaret Turner. London: for the
author, by T. Bensley, 1790. 8vo. viii,206,6
pp, errata leaf. 11 pp subscribers. 3 lib
stamps. Rec qtr calf. *(Rankin)* **£65 [≈$124]**

- The Gentle Shepherd: A Scot's [sic] Pastoral
Comedy. Embellished with Five Engravings
... Edinburgh: Geo. Reid & Co, 1798. 8vo.
Half-title. Disbound, partly unopened.
(Dramatis Personae) **$60 [≈£31]**

- Poems. Edinburgh: Thomas Ruddiman, for
the author, 1721. 1st coll edn. 4to. xxviii,400
pp. Occas sl marg fingering.
Period speckled calf, gilt spine, upper jnts sl
cracked.   *(Rankin)* **£250 [≈$479]**

- Poems. Glasgow: for Peter Tait, 1770. 8vo.
Early 19th c diced calf.
(Waterfield's) **£125 [≈$239]**

Ramsay, David

- The History of the American Revolution.
Phila: Aitken & Son, 1789. 1st edn. 2 vols in
one. [6],359; [6],360 pp. Mod calf backed
mrbld bds.   *(Reese)* **$600 [≈£312]**

- The History of the American Revolution.
London: 1791. 1st British edn. 2 vols in one.
viii,vi,360; vi,360 pp. Errata. Contemp calf &
bds, backstrips relaid. *(Reese)* **$400 [≈£208]**

- The History of the American Revolution.
Dublin: William Jones, 1795. 2 vols in one.
Continuous pagination. Contemp tree calf,
black label, ft of spine sl chipped, hinges
weakening.   *(C.R. Johnson)* **£180 [≈$345]**

- The History of the Revolution of South-
Carolina, from a British Province to an
Independent State. Trenton: Isaac Collins,
1785. 1st edn. 2 vols. 8vo. 453; 574 pp. 5
maps. Orig tree calf, fine.
(Chapel Hill) **$3,000 [≈£1,562]**

Ramsay, James

- An Essay on the Treatment and Conversion
of African Slaves in the British Sugar
Colonies. London: James Phillips, 1784. 8vo.
Half calf, mrbld bds, rebacked.
(Jarndyce) **£450 [≈$863]**

- Examination of Rev. Mr. Harris's Scriptural
Researches on the Licitness of the Slave-
Trade. London: James Phillips, 1788. 1st
edn. 8vo. Advt leaf at end. Qtr mor.
(Ximenes) **$125 [≈£65]**

- Objections to the Abolition of the Slave
Trade, with Answers ... London: James

Phillips, 1788. Half-title, 60 pp. Disbound.
(C.R. Johnson) **£250 [≈$479]**

Ramsey, William

- Conjugium Conjurgium: or, some Serious
Considerations on Marriage ... By William
Seymar [pseud.] Esquire. The Seventh
Edition Corrected. London: [1675]. 8vo.
[xix],92,[4 advt] pp. Frontis. Date on title
erased. Calf antique, t.e.g., by Hatchards.
Wing R.229.   *(Bickersteth)* **£360 [≈$691]**

Rapin, Rene

- Rapin of Gardens. A Latin Poem ... English'd
by Mr. Gardiner. London: Bowyer for
Lintott, (1706). 1st edn of this translation.
8vo. 5 advt pp. Frontis, 4 plates. Contemp
black mor gilt, a.e.g., spine faded & sl rubbed.
(Ximenes) **$600 [≈£312]**

- Rapin of Gardens. A Latin Poem in Four
Books. English'd by Mr. [James] Gardiner.
London: Bowyer for Lintot, 1718. Rvsd edn.
8vo. Port frontis, 4 plates. Contemp panelled
calf, rebacked, new endpapers but retaining
orig pastedowns. *(Waterfield's)* **£115 [≈$220]**

- Reflections on Aristotle's Treatise of Poesie
... London: for T.N. for H. Herringman,
1674. 1st edn in English. 8vo. Contemp calf,
sl worn. Wing R.270.
(Ximenes) **$650 [≈£338]**

- Reflections upon the Eloquence of these
Times; particularly of the Barr and Pulpit.
London; for Richard Preston, 1672. 1st edn
of this translation. 8vo. Licence leaf. Errata
leaf. Contemp calf, jnts sl worn. Wing R.274.
Anon.   *(Ximenes)* **$350 [≈£182]**

Raspe, Rudolph Eric

- An Account of some German Volcanos, and
their Productions ... London: Lockyer Davis,
1776. 1st edn. 8vo. xix,[1],140 pp, inc 4 advt
pp. Half-title. 2 fldg plates. Contemp calf,
rebacked.   *(Rootenberg)* **$500 [≈£260]**

Ravenscroft, Edward

- The Italian Husband. A Tragedy. London:
for Isaac Cleave, 1698. 1st edn. 4to. Foxed.
Mod cloth. Wing R.330.
(Ximenes) **$325 [≈£169]**

Rawlinson, Richard

- The English Topographer. London: T.
Jauncy, 1720. 1st edn. 8vo. [viii], xliv, 275,
[13] pp. Contemp calf, spine extremities sl
chipped, hinges starting. Anon.
(Bookpress) **$600 [≈£312]**

Ray, John

- A Collection of Curious Travels & Voyages. In Two Tomes ... London: for S. Smith & B. Walford ..., 1693. 1st edn, mixed issue. [xxviii], 396, 186,45,[i] pp. Imprimatur leaf. Lacks final advt leaf. Old calf, surface of lower bd sl abraded. Wing R.386; Keynes 92/93. *(Hollett)* **£350 [≃ $671]**

- A Collection of English Words Not Generally used ... with ... an Account of the preparing and refining such Metals and Minerals as are gotten in England. London: 1674. 1st edn. 8vo. [xiv],178 pp. Lacks A1 (blank). Contemp sheep, sometime reprd, worn. Wing R.388. *(Gaskell)* **£525 [≃ $1,007]**

- A Collection of English Words not generally used ... Second Edition, augmented ... London: Christopher Wilkinson, 1691. 211, 5 advt pp. Calf, rebacked. Wing R.389. *(C.R. Johnson)* **£280 [≃ $537]**

- A Compleat Collection of English Proverbs ... The Fourth Edition. London: for W. Otridge ..., 1768. 8vo. Contemp calf, rebacked. *(Waterfield's)* **£180 [≃ $345]**

- Philosophical Letters between the late learned Mr. Ray and several of his Ingenious Correspondents ... Published by W. Derham. London: 1718. 1st edn. 8vo. [viii],376, [10], [2] pp. Contemp calf, rebacked. *(Wheldon & Wesley)* **£150 [≃ $287]**

- Three Physico-Theological Discourses ... Second Edition Corrected, very much enlarged ... London: Sam. Smith, 1693. 8vo. [xxiv], 1-160, [viii], 161-406, [ii] pp. Final advt leaf. 4 plates. Some browning, occas marg staining. Rec half calf. Wing R.409. *(Clark)* **£285 [≃ $547]**

- The Wisdom of God, manifested in the Works of the Creation. London: 1717. 7th edn. 8vo. [xxvi],17-405, [3] pp. Port. Endpapers & last 2 ff v sl foxed. Contemp calf, rebacked. *(Wheldon & Wesley)* **£175 [≃ $335]**

- The Wisdom of God Manifested in the Works of Creation In Two Parts ... Tenth Edition. London: William Innys & Richard Manly, 1735. Tall 8vo. [24],405,[3] pp. 18th c calf, rebacked, crnrs bumped. *(Humber)* **£38 [≃ $72]**

Raynal, Guillaume Thomas

- A Philosophical and Political History of the Settlements and Trades of the Europeans in the East and West Indies. London: Cadell, 1776. 1st edn in English. 4 vols. 8vo. x,503; viii,530; vi,559; vi,552 pp. Rebacked, orig backstrips relaid. *(Gough)* **£120 [≃ $230]**

- A Philosophical and Political History of the British Settlements and Trade in North America ... With an Introductory Preface ... Present War in America ... Edinburgh: 1779. 12mo. xii, "410" [ie 412] pp. Half title. Contemp sheep, worn, jnts broken. *(Bow Windows)* **£50 [≃ $95]**

- A Philosophical and Political History of the British Settlements and Trade in North America. From the French ... With an Introductory Preface, not in the First Edition. Edinburgh: 1779. Half-title, 410 pp. Contemp sheep. *(C.R. Johnson)* **£85 [≃ $163]**

Rayner, William

- Miscellanies in Prose and Verse, Original and Translated. Ipswich: for the author, by M. Craighton & W. Jackson, 1767. 4to. 151, subscribers pp. Some browning & spotting. Contemp tree calf, red label. Stradbroke copy. *(C.R. Johnson)* **£385 [≃ $739]**

Rede, Leman Thomas

- Bibliotheca Americana; or a Chronological Catalogue of the most Curious and Interesting Books, Pamphlets, State Papers, &c. upon the Subject of North and South America ... London: 1789. 4to. iv,271 pp. Occas foxing. Old half vellum, mrbld bds. *(Reese)* **$1,000 [≃ £520]**

Redhead, William, et al.

- Observations on the Different Breeds of Sheep, and the State of Sheep Farming in some of the Principal Counties of England ... Edinburgh: ptd by W. Smellie ..., 1792. 1st edn. 8vo. 7,[i],xviii,99 pp. Half-title stained. 1 sm repr. Old wraps. *(Burmester)* **£250 [≃ $479]**

Reeve, Clara

- The Old English Baron. A Gothic Story. A New Edition. London: for Charles Dilly, 1784. 8vo. Sl foxing. Period calf, new label. *(Rankin)* **£50 [≃ $95]**

- The Old English Baron: a Gothic Story. A New Edition. London: for Charles Dilly, 1787. 12mo. Frontis (dated 1777), plate. Contemp sheep, sl worn, rebacked. Anon. *(Jarndyce)* **£58 [≃ $111]**

Reflections ...

- Reflections upon Learning ... see Baker, Thomas.

- Reflections upon Polygamy ... see Delany, Patrick.

- Reflections upon Reason ... see Hildrop, John.
- Reflections upon the Eloquence of these Times ... see Rapin, Rene.

Reflexions ...
- Reflexions on Dr. Gilbert Burnet's Travels ... see Varillas, Antoine.
- Reflexions on the Sources of Incredulity ... see Forbes, Duncan.
- Reflexions upon Ridicule ... see Morvan de Bellegarde, J.B.

Reform or Run ...
- See Bowdler, John.

Regimen Sanitatis Salerni ...
- Regimen Sanitatis Salerni: or, The Schoole of Salernes Regiment of Health ... London: B. Alsop, 1649. 1st edn of this translation. Sm 4to. [iv],220,[3] pp. Lib stamps on title & 2nd leaf. New qtr mor. *(Bookpress)* **$785 [≈£408]**

Regiomontanus, Johannes ...
- See Angelus, Johannes.

Regnault, Noel
- Philosophical Conversations: or, a New System of Physics, by Way of Dialogue. Translated into English and Illustrated with Notes by Thomas Dale, M.D. London: 1731. 1st edn in English. 3 vols. 8vo. 89 plates. Contemp calf, spines sl rubbed with some wear at ends. *(Burmester)* **£600 [≈$1,151]**

Reign ...
- The Reign of King Charles ... see L'Estrange, Hamon.

Relation ...
- A Relation of Several Hundreds of Children & Others that Prophesie and Preach in their Sleep, &c. ... London: Richard Baldwin, 1689. Only edn. 4to. [ii],35,[i] pp. No imprimatur leaf. Outer ff dusty. 1 headline cropped. Disbound. Wing R.808. *(Clark)* **£140 [≈$268]**
- A Relation of the Barbarous and Bloody Massacre of about an Hundred Thousand Protestants, begun at Paris ... London: Richard Chiswel, 1678. Only edn. 4to. 47,[i] pp. Outer ff dusty, backstrip reinforced, few sm tears, lib stamp title verso. Disbound. Wing R.814. *(Clark)* **£30 [≈$57]**

Relph, Josiah (Joseph)
- A Miscellany of Poems, consisting of Original Poems, Translations, Pastorals in the Cumberland Dialect ... Glasgow: Robert Foulis for Mr. Thomlinson (Wigton), 1747. 1st edn. 8vo. 33 pp subscribers. Sl foxing. Contemp calf, rebacked. *(Ximenes)* **$450 [≈£234]**
- Poems, with the Life of the Author. Embellished with Picturesque Engravings on Wood by Mr. T. Bewick, of Newcastle. Carlisle: J. Mitchell, 1798. Early half calf, mrbld bds, vellum crnrs. *(C.R. Johnson)* **£285 [≈$547]**

Rennell, James
- Observations on a Current that often prevails to the Westward of Scilly; endangering the Safety of Ships that approach the British Channel. London: 1793. 1st edn. 8vo. Half-title (torn, no loss). Fldg chart. Disbound. *(Ximenes)* **$150 [≈£78]**

Report ...
- A Report of Some Proceedings on the Commission of Oyer and Terminer ... see Foster, Sir Michael.

Reresby, Sir John
- The Memoirs of the Honourable Sir John Reresby, Bart and last Governor of York ... London: for Samuel Harding, 1735. 8vo. red & black title. Contemp speckled calf, mor label. *(Waterfield's)* **£65 [≈$124]**

Reresby, Tamworth
- A Miscellany of Ingenious Thoughts and Reflections, in Verse and Prose ... London: H. Mears, 1721. 4to. Some sl marg spotting. Contemp qtr calf. *(Waterfield's)* **£225 [≈$431]**
- A Miscellany of Ingenius Thoughts and Reflections, In Verse and Prose ... London: H. Meere for the author, 1721. 1st edn. 4to. [viii], 422,[ii] pp. Occas spotting & staining. Rebacked in sheep, sides in calf gilt, sides worn, crnrs bumped. *(Finch)* **£95 [≈$182]**

Resta, Sebastiano
- An Historical and Chronological Series of the most Eminent Painters ... London: Joseph Duke, 1739. 18 pp. New wraps. *(Ars Artis)* **£35 [≈$67]**
- The True Effigies of the Most Eminent Painters, and Other Famous Artists that have Flourished in Europe ... London: for D.

Browne, 1694. Folio. [2],18 pp. 126 plates. Lacks addtnl engvd title. Contemp calf, rebacked. Wing R.1174. Anon.
(Karmiole) **$650 [≈ £338]**

The Resurrection of Jesus Considered ...
- See Annet, Peter.

The Reverie ...
- See Johnstone, Charles.

Revesi Bruti, Ottavio
- A New and Accurate Method of Delineating all the Parts of the Different Orders in Architecture ... London: Fletcher Gyles, 1787. 1st English edn. Folio. [viii],52 pp. 51 plates. Contemp calf, backstrip relaid.
(Bookpress) **$1,850 [≈ £963]**

Review ...
- A Review of the Characters of the Principal Nations in Europe ... see Andrews, John.

Reynardson, Francis
- The Stage: a Poem. Inscrib'd to Joseph Addison, Esq; by Mr. Webster [pseud.] of Christ-Church, Oxon. London: for E. Curll, 1713. 1st edn. 8vo. 1st word of title sl shaved. Disbound. Anon. *(Ximenes)* **$900 [≈ £468]**

Reynolds, Edward
- The Works ... Corrected and Amended. London: T. Newcomb for George Thomason, 1658. Large Paper. Folio. [16],1010,[3] pp. Port (mtd). 18th c dark blue Cambridge bndg, elab gilt, a.e.g., edges sl rubbed, ends of top jnt cracked. Wing R.1234.
(Humber) **£250 [≈ $479]**

Reynolds, John
- The Triumph of Gods Revenge against the crying and execrable Sinne of (wilful and premeditated) Murther ... Fourth Edition ... London: Sarah Griffin for William Lee, 1663. Folio. Engvd frontis & ills. A few marks. Contemp calf, rebacked. Wing R.1311.
(Jarndyce) **£240 [≈ $460]**

Reynolds, Sir Joshua
- A Discourse delivered to the Students of the Royal Academy ... London: Thomas Davies, 1769. 1st edn. 4to. [ii],23 pp. Frontis port (apparently added to this copy). Lacks A1 (blank or half-title?). Later wraps.
(Bookpress) **$175 [≈ £91]**
- Seven Discourses delivered in the Royal

Academy by the President. London: for T. Cadell, 1778. 1st coll edn. 8vo. Half-title, advt leaf at end. Contemp calf, rebacked.
(Ximenes) **$475 [≈ £247]**
- Seven Discourses Delivered in the Royal Academy by the President. London: 1778. 1st coll edn. 8vo. [viii],326,[2] pp. Some wear & tear. Old roan backed bds, spine ends worn, jnts cracking. Anon.
(Bow Windows) **£35 [≈ $67]**
- Seven Discourses Delivered in the Royal Academy by the President. London: Cadell, 1778. 8vo. [viii],326 pp, advt leaf. Half-title. Period speckled calf, v sl cracks in jnts, spine ends sl chipped. Anon.
(Rankin) **£100 [≈ $191]**

Rhyme and Reason ...
- See Bentham, Jeremy.

Riccoboni, Marie Jeanne
- Letters from Elizabeth Sophia de Valiere to her Friend Louisa Hortensia de Canteleu ... Translated from the French by Mr. Maceuen. London: Becket & De Hondt, 1772. 1st edn in English. 2 vols. 12mo. Half-titles. Errata leaf & 2 advt ff vol 2. Contemp calf gilt, sl rubbed.
(Ximenes) **$650 [≈ £338]**

Rice, Woodford
- The Rutland Volunteer Influenza'd: or, a Receipt to a Patriot, a Soldier, or a Poet. London: for G. Kearsley, 1783. 1st edn. 4to. Half-title. Errata slip pasted to title verso. Frontis. Disbound.
(Ximenes) **$1,250 [≈ £651]**

Rich, Robert
- A Letter ... to the Right Honourable Lord Viscount Barrington, His Majesty's Secretary at War ... London: for P. Mitchell ..., 1775. 1st edn. 4to. [ii],63, xxv,[1 errata] pp. Appendix & table. Disbound.
(Young's) **£70 [≈ $134]**

Richardson, Jonathan, Sr.
- The Works containing I. Theory of Painting. II. Essay on the Art of Criticism ... III. The Science of a Connoisseur ... "Strawberry Hill" [ie London]: sold by B. White & Son ..., 1792. 1st edn. 4to. vii,287 pp. 12 plates. Contemp calf, hinges cracked but firm.
(Claude Cox) **£165 [≈ $316]**

Richardson, Jonathan, Sr. & Jonathan, Jnr.
- Account of Some of the Statues, Bas-Reliefs, Drawings and Pictures in Italy, etc. with

Remarks. London: Knapton, 1722. 1st edn. 25 ff, 362 pp. Frontis. Contemp leather, somewhat worn.   *(Ars Artis)* **£250 [≈ $479]**

Richardson, Robert

- A State of the Evidence in the cause between his Grace the Duke of Hamilton and others, pursuers of Archibald Douglas, of Douglas ... London: C. Bathurst, 1769. 8vo. Later half calf, dble labels. *(Waterfield's)* **£65 [≈ $124]**

Richardson, Samuel

- A Collection of the Moral and Instructive Sentiments, Maxims, Cautions, and Reflections, contained in the Histories of Pamela, Clarissa, and Sir Charles Grandison. London: for S. Richardson ..., 1755. 1st edn. 12mo. Contemp calf, gilt spine, minor repr.   *(Ximenes)* **$450 [≈ £234]**
- Pamela: or, Virtue Rewarded ... London: Rivington, Osborn ..., 1741. 2nd edn vols 1 & 2, 1st edn vols 3 & 4. 4 vols. 12mo. Sl marg staining vol 4, 1 crnr reprd. Later half mor.   *(Jarndyce)* **£520 [≈ $998]**
- The History of Sir Charles Grandison ... London: for S. Richardson, 1754. 1st edn. 7 vols. 12mo. The 8 cancelled ff all present. Vol 6 p 279 catchword not crrctd, indicating early issue. Rec contemp style calf. Anon.   *(Young's)* **£340 [≈ $652]**
- The History of Sir Charles Grandison ... Third Edition. London: for S. Richardson, & sold by Hitch, Hawes ..., 1754. 7 vols. 12mo. Contemp sheep, gilt borders, rubbed, splits in some hinges.   *(Jarndyce)* **£120 [≈ $230]**
- See also Meades, Anna.

Richardson, William

- Cursory Remarks on Tragedy, on Shakespear, and on certain French and Italian Poets, principally Tragedians. London: for W. Owen, 1774. 1st edn. 8vo. Half-title, final advt leaf. Contemp tree calf, gilt spine, minor rubbing. Anon.   *(Ximenes)* **$450 [≈ £234]**
- Cursory Remarks on Tragedy, on Shakespeare and on certain French and Italian Poets, principally Tragedians. London: for W. Owen, 1774. 2nd edn. 8vo. Disbound. Anon. Often attributed to Edward Taylor.   *(Dramatis Personae)* **$100 [≈ £52]**
- Essays on Shakespeare's Dramatic Characters of Richard the Third, King Lear, and Timon of Athens ... added, an Essay on the Faults of Shakespeare; and Additional Observations on ... Hamlet. London: Murray, 1784. 1st edn. Half-title, 270,4 advt pp. Contemp calf,

hinges sl cracked.
    (C.R. Johnson) **£160 [≈ $307]**
- Essays on Shakespeare's Dramatic Characters of Richard the Third, King Lear, and Timon of Athens ... added, an Essay on the Faults of Shakespeare; and Additional Observations on ... Hamlet. London: Murray, 1784. 1st edn. Sm 8vo. Mod bds.
    (Dramatis Personae) **$200 [≈ £104]**
- Essays on Shakespeare's Dramatic Characters of Richard the Third, King Lear, and Timon of Athens ... London: for J. Murray, 1784. 1st edn. 8vo. Paste-on errata slip at end. Contemp calf, trifle rubbed. *(Ximenes)* **$275 [≈ £143]**
- A Philosophical Analysis and Illustration of some of Shakespeare's Remarkable Characters. The Second Edition, corrected. London: for John Murray, 1774. Sm 8vo. [iv], 204 inc advt pp. Period calf, lacks label, upper jnt cracked but firm, sl chip hd of spine.   *(Rankin)* **£60 [≈ $115]**
- Poems Chiefly Rural. The Third Edition, corrected. Glasgow: Robert & Andrew Foulis, 1776. 144 pp. Contemp calf, gilt spine, hinges sl weak. *(C.R. Johnson)* **£100 [≈ $191]**

Richer, Adrien

- Great Events from Little Causes ... Translated from the French. London: for F. Newbery, 1767. 1st edn in English. 12mo. 4 advt ff at end. Sgntr clipped from title marg. Contemp sheep, gilt spine, jnts cracked.
    (Ximenes) **$150 [≈ £78]**

Richers, Thomas

- The History of the Royal Genealogy of Spain ... Made English from the French Copy ... With several useful Notes ... London: James Round, 1724. 1st edn. 8vo. [viii], xxii, [2], 437,[11] pp. Port. 14 pp subscribers. Contemp calf, red label.
    (Young's) **£120 [≈ $230]**

Ridley, James

- The Tales of the Genii ... Faithfully translated from the Persian Manuscript ... By Sir Charles Morell [pseud.] ... London: Wilkie, 1786. 2 vols. 8vo. 2 frontis, 12 plates. Possibly lacks half-title in vol 2, not called for in vol 1. 19th c half calf, sl rubbed.
    (Bickersteth) **£160 [≈ $307]**
- The Tales of the Genii ... Faithfully translated from the Persian Manuscript ... By Sir Charles Morell [pseud.] ... The Fifth Edition. London: Wilkie, 1786. 2 vols. 12mo. Contemp tree calf, gilt spines, green & red labels.   *(Jarndyce)* **£220 [≈ $422]**

Ripley, James
- Select Original Letters on various Subjects by James Ripley, now, and for Thirty Years Past, Oastler at the Red-Lion, Barnet. London: for the author ..., 1781. 123 pp. Frontis port. Rebound in blue mor.
(C.R. Johnson) **£225 [≈ $431]**

Ripperda, Jan Wilhelm
- Memoirs of the Duke of Ripperda ... London: Stagg, Browne, 1740. 1st edn in English. 8vo. xv,[i],344,[viii] pp. Orig calf, jnts cracked. BLC attributes to John Campbell.
(Bickersteth) **£60 [≈ $115]**

Ritson, Joseph (ed.)
- Robin Hood: a Collection of all the Ancient Poems, Songs, and Ballads, now extant ... London: Egerton, 1795. 1st edn. 2 vols. [2], cxviii, [2],167; [6],229,[4] pp. 63 w'engvs by T. & J. Bewick. Some foxing & minor soiling. 19th c mrbld bds, rebacked.
(Spelman) **£280 [≈ $537]**

Roberte the Deuyil ...
- Roberte the Deuyil. A Metrical Romance, from an Ancient Illuminated Manuscript. London: I. Herbert, 1798. 1st edn. 8vo. viii, 49 pp. 14 plates. Contemp calf, some wear.
(Bookpress) **$285 [≈ £148]**

Roberts, Alexander
- An Exposition upon the Hundred and Thirtie Psalme gathered out of some of the Ancient Fathers and later Writers. London: Iohn Winder for Robert Runckworth, 1610. Few side-notes in last gathering sl shaved. Later wraps. STC 21073.
(Waterfield's) **£40 [≈ $76]**

Roberts, Francis
- Clavis Bibliorum, The Key of the Bible Unlocking the Richest Treasury of Holy Scripture ... Second Edition Enlarged. London: T.R. & E.M. for G. Calvert, 1649. O.T. vol only. 8vo. [6],66,624 pp. 18th c calf, minor wear. Wing R.1584 (Part 1).
(Humber) **£48 [≈ $92]**

Roberts, Miss R.
- Albert, Edward and Laura and the Hermit of Priestland. Three Legendary Tales ... London: Cadell, 1783. 4to. Without the engvd title sometimes found. Disbound.
(Waterfield's) **£40 [≈ $76]**

Roberts, William Hayward
- Poems. London: for J. Wilkie, T. Payne, W. Frederic at Bath ..., 1774. 1st coll edn. Contemp calf, rubbed, hinges weakening.
(Jarndyce) **£110 [≈ $211]**
- A Poetical Essay on the Existence of God ... London: J. & J. Hughs, 1771. 1st edn. 4to. 24,28,32 pp. New qtr calf.
(Young's) **£70 [≈ $134]**

Robertson, Alexander
- Poems on Various Subjects and Occasions ... mostly taken from his own Original Manuscripts. Edinburgh: for C. Alexander ..., [1751?]. Contemp sheep.
(C.R. Johnson) **£145 [≈ $278]**

Robertson, Archibald
- A Topographical Survey of the Great Road from London to Bath and Bristol ... London: for the author ... & William Faden, 1792. 1st edn. 2 vols. 8vo. [2],xvi,154; viii,190 pp, errata leaf. 11 maps, 63 (of 65) aquatint plates. Later 19th c cloth, sl rubbed & chipped.
(Claude Cox) **£300 [≈ $575]**

Robertson, David
- Poems. Edinburgh: Creech, 1784. Half-title. Rebound in calf & mrbld bds.
(C.R. Johnson) **£285 [≈ $547]**

Robertson, John
- Tables of Difference of Latitude and Departure. Phila: Joseph Cruikshank, 1790. 1st edn. 8vo. [i],90 pp. Later wraps.
(Bookpress) **$225 [≈ £117]**

Robertson, Joseph
- An Essay on Punctuation. London: for J. Walter, 1785. 1st edn. Half-title, 177 pp, advt leaf. Contemp calf. Anon.
(C.R. Johnson) **£280 [≈ $537]**

Robertson, Robert
- An Essay on Fevers ... London: !790. 1st edn. 286 pp. Ex-lib. Leather, lacks backstrip, spine scorched.
(Fye) **$150 [≈ £78]**

Robertson, William, lexicographer
- Phraseologia Generalis ... A full, large, and general Phrase Book ... Cambridge: ptd by John Hayes, & sold by Daniel Browne ... London, 1693. Intl advt leaf. Final leaf "Cambridge Phrases". Sl staining. Sl later calf, rubbed, lacks label. Wing R.1617A.
(Jarndyce) **£220 [≈ $422]**

Robertson, William
- An Historical Disquisition concerning the Knowledge which the Ancients had of India ... With an Appendix ... London: Strahan, 1791. 1st edn. 4to. xii,364,[10] pp. 2 fldg maps. Contemp qtr calf, rebacked.
　　　　　　　(*Young's*) **£85 [≈ $163]**
- An Historical Disquisition concerning the Knowledge which the Ancients had of India. Dublin: 1791. 8vo. 349,14 index pp. Calf, hinges tender.　(*Terramedia*) **$60 [≈ £31]**
- The History of America ... London: W. Strahan, 1777. 1st edn. 4to. xvii,[vii],488; [ii], 535,[19],[1 errata] pp. 4 maps, 1 fldg plate. Some offsetting, occas sl foxing. Contemp tree calf, gilt spine, extremities rubbed, jnts reprd.　(*Pickering*) **$950 [≈ £494]**
- The History of America. London: for Strahan, Cadell, Balfour, 1777. 1st edn. 2 vols. 4to. xvii,[7],488; [2],535,[20] pp. Fldg plate. Lacks the maps. Sl spotting. 19th c calf, gilt spines, sides sl rubbed & marked.
　　　　　　(*Claude Cox*) **£65 [≈ $124]**
- The History of Ancient Greece ... Second Edition. Edinburgh: for Charles Elliot, 1778. 8vo. xx,558,[xxii] pp. Sl foxing. Period sheep, sl worn.　(*Rankin*) **£65 [≈ $124]**

Robinson, Nicholas
- A Compleat Treatise of the Gravel and Stone, with all their Causes, Symptoms, and Cures ... Second Edition, with large Additions. London: B. Cowse, 1723. 8vo. [24], 284, [10],[8 advt] pp. Some damp staining mainly at the end. Contemp calf.
　　　　　　(*Spelman*) **£140 [≈ $268]**
- The Heroick Christian: or, the Man of Honour ... London: for Mary Smith, 1721. Only edn. 8vo. [xvi],149,3 advt pp. Light edge staining.　(*Young's*) **£160 [≈ $307]**

Robinson, Robert
- The General Doctrine of Toleration applied to the particular Case of Free Communion. Cambridge: Francis Hodson, 1781. Disbound.　(*Waterfield's*) **£45 [≈ $86]**
- A Political Catechism. London: for J. Buckland ..., 1782. 1st edn. 8vo. [iv],140 pp. Disbound. Anon.　(*Burmester*) **£85 [≈ $163]**
- Political Catechism. London: for J. Buckland ..., 1782. 1st edn. 8vo. Mod qtr calf. Anon.
　　　　　　(*Waterfield's*) **£75 [≈ $143]**

Robinson, Thomas
- An Essay towards a Natural History of Westmorland and Cumberland ... London:

J.L. for W. Freeman, 1709. 1st edn. [xiv],118,[2 advt] pp. Old calf, rebacked, new endpapers. Earl of Derby's b'plates (dated 1702).　(*Hollett*) **£225 [≈ $431]**

Rochon, Alexis
- A Voyage to Madagascar, and the East Indies. Translated from the French ... added a Memoir on the Chinese Trade. London: 1792. 1st English edn. 475 pp. Fldg map of Madagascar. Sm blind stamp on title. Contemp half leather, worn, front hinge cracking.　(*Trophy Room*) **$400 [≈ £208]**
- A Voyage to Madagascar, and the East Indies. London: for G.G.J. & J. Robinson, 1792. 1st edn in English. 8vo. Fldg map. Contemp calf, rebacked.　(*Ximenes*) **$500 [≈ £260]**

Roderick, John & Williams, John
- English and Welch Dictionary ... Shrewsbury: Thomas Durston, 1737. 2nd edn. 12mo. Orig calf backed bds.
　　　　　　(*Chapel Hill*) **$150 [≈ £78]**

Rodriguez, Alonso
- The Practice of Christian Perfection ... Translated into English out of the French Copy ... "London" [actually St. Omer]: ptd by Thomas Hales, 1697-99. 1st complete edn in English. 3 vols. Sm 4to. Contemp calf, used but sound.　(*Sotheran's*) **£168 [≈ $322]**

Rogers, Richard
- A Commentary Upon the Whole Booke of Judges ... London: Felix Kyngston for Thomas Man, 1615. Sm thick folio. [16],970,[1] pp. Few sm stains. Contemp polished calf. STC 21204.
　　　　　　(*Humber*) **£250 [≈ $479]**

Rogers, Robert
- A Concise Account of North America ... London: 1765. 264 pp. Old lib stamp on title. Occas sl foxing. Antique calf, leather label.　(*Reese*) **$1,500 [≈ £781]**

Rogers, Timothy
- Early Religion: or a Discourse of the Duty and Interest of Youth ... Second Edition much enlarged. London: for John Dunton, 1691. 118 pp, advt leaf. Contemp calf, some wear. Wing R.1849A.
　　　　　　(*C.R. Johnson*) **£150 [≈ $287]**

Rogers, Woodes
- A Cruising Voyage Round the World ... London: for Bell & Lintot, 1712. 1st edn.

8vo. 5 fldg maps (2 sl torn, no loss). Contemp panelled calf, spine ends sl chipped, some splitting at hinges.
(Jarndyce) **£1,200 [≈ $2,303]**

The Rolliad ...

- The Rolliad, in Two Parts: Probationary Odes for the Laureateship; and Political Miscellanies: with Criticisms and Illustrations. Revised, Corrected and Enlarged by the Original Authors. London: Ridgway, 1795. 2 vols. Frontis. 19th c three qtr calf. *(Limestone Hills)* **$130 [≈ £67]**

Rolt, Richard

- The Lives of the Principal Reformers, both Englishmen and Foreigners ... London: Bakewell ..., 1759. 1st edn. Folio. xii,[ii], 202 pp. 21 mezzotint ports. Contemp calf backed green bds, gilt spine.
(Frew Mackenzie) **£475 [≈ $911]**

Romaine, William

- The Knowledge of Salvation Precious in the Hour of Death, proved in a Sermon ... upon the Death of the Rev. Mr. James Hervey ... The Third Edition. London: for J. Worrall, & M. Withers, 1759. 8vo in 4s. Final advt leaf. Title soiled. Disbound. *(Sanders)* **£45 [≈ $86]**

Ronayne, Philip

- A Treatise of Algebra in Two Books ... Second Edition with Additions. London: Innys, 1727. 8vo. [viii],v,[iii], 160,177-461,[3 advt] pp. Text diags. Contemp sprinkled calf, worn, upper jnt cracked.
(Gaskell) **£375 [≈ $719]**

Roome, Edward

- The Jovial Crew. A Comic-Opera. As it is Acted at the Theatre-Royal ... London: for J. Watts ..., 1731. 1st edn. 8vo. [viii],68 pp. Engvd music before each song. Wraps. Anon.
(Young's) **£75 [≈ $143]**

Rose, George

- The Proposed System of Trade with Ireland Explained. London: Nichols, 1785. 8vo. 58 pp. Mrbld bds. Anon.
(Emerald Isle) **£65 [≈ $124]**
- The Proposed System of Trade with Ireland explained. London: John Nichols, 1785. Half-title, 58 pp. Disbound. Anon.
(C.R. Johnson) **£125 [≈ $239]**

Rose, John Augustus

- An Impartial History of the late Disturbances

in Bristol ... Bristol: the editor, 1793. 16 pp. Disbound. *(C.R. Johnson)* **£125 [≈ $239]**

Ross, Robert

- The American Lati[n] Grammar; or, a Compleat Introduction to the Latin Tongue ... Providence: 1780. 5th edn. 12mo. 112 pp. Sm chip to title, foredge marg shaved. Orig calf backed paper over birch bds, paper label defective, ft of spine chipped. Anon.
(Reese) **$150 [≈ £78]**

Rous, Francis

- Archaeologiae Atticae Libri Septem ... The Description of the Citties ... within the Athenian Territories ... Oxford: Lichfield & Hall, 1658. 5th edn, crrctd & enlgd. Sm 4to. Final index leaf defective. Mod half mor. Wing R.2036. *(Stewart)* **£75 [≈ $143]**
- Archaeologiae Atticae Libri Septem ... The Description of the Citties ... within the Athenian Territories ... Oxford: Hall for Adams & Forrest, 1671. 7th edn, crrctd & enlgd. 4to. [vi],375,[9] pp. Contemp calf, rebacked. Wing R.2039.
(Vanbrugh) **£165 [≈ $316]**

Rousseau, Jean Jacques

- Emilius; or, an Essay on Education. Translated from the French by Mr. Nugent. London: Nourse & Vaillant, 1763. 1st edn of this translation. 4 parts in 2 vols. 8vo. [ii], xvi,[ii], 406,[2 advt]; [ii],406,[18] pp. Frontis, 5 plates. Contemp calf, jnts reprd.
(Burmester) **£1,250 [≈ $2,399]**
- Emilius and Sophia; or a New System of Education. Translated ... by the Translator of Eloisa. London: H. Baldwin, 1783. 4 vols. 12mo. Port, frontises. Orig tree calf, gilt spines. *(Chapel Hill)* **$165 [≈ £85]**
- An Inquiry into the Nature of the Social Contract; or Principles of Political Right. Translated from the French. London: Robinson, 1791. 1st edn of the 2nd English translation. A few marg pencil lines. Rebound in half calf. *(Jarndyce)* **£480 [≈ $921]**
- Letters on the Elements of Botany. Addressed to a Lady. Translated into English with Notes and Twenty-Four Additional Letters ... by Thomas Martyn. London: White, 1785. 1st edn in English. 8vo. xxiv,503,[28] pp. Fldg table. Contemp calf, v faint mark back bd.
(Gough) **£125 [≈ $239]**
- Letters on the Elements of Botany. Addressed to a Lady. With Notes, and Twenty-Four Additional Letters, fully explaining the System of Linnaeus. London: 1787.

Translated by T. Martyn. xxv,500,[28] pp. Fldg table. Contemp calf, rebacked.
(Whitehart) **£85 [≈ $163]**

- Original Letters, to M. de Malesherbes, M. D'Alembert, Madame la M. de Luxembourg ... Translated from the French. London: C. Whittingham, for H.D. Symonds, 1799. 1st edn. 8vo. Half-title. Port frontis, fldg plate, engvd music. Rec rebacked half calf.
(Jarndyce) **£85 [≈ $163]**

Rowe, Elizabeth

- Poems on Several Occasions. To which is prefixed, An Account of her Life and Writings. A New Edition. London: 1778. 12mo. 206 pp. Orig sheep, rubbed, spine ends sl worn, lacks label. *(Bickersteth)* **£45 [≈ $86]**

Rowe, Henry

- Poems. London: for the author, & sold by Cadell & Davies, 1796. 1st edn. 2 vols. 8vo. 14, [iv],135, [i]; [vi],128 pp. Subscribers. Half-titles. Some damp staining outer margs. Orig bds, uncut, rebacked in mod calf.
(Lamb) **£65 [≈ $124]**

Rowlands, alias Verstegen, Richard

- A Restitution of Decayed Intelligence in Antiquities. Concerning the most noble and renvvmed [sic] English Nation. By the Studie and Travaile of R.V. ... Antwerp: 1605. 1st edn. 4to. [xxiv],338,[13] pp. Num text ills. Sl browning. 19th c calf, rebacked. STC 21361.
(Vanbrugh) **£275 [≈ $527]**

- A Restitution of Decayed Intelligence ... By the Study, and travell [sic] of R.V. London: Iohn Norton for Ioyce Norton, 1634. Sm 4to. [xxiv],338,[12] pp. 11 text engvs inc 1 on title. Sm stain on title. Old calf, rebacked. STC 21363.
(Bow Windows) **£110 [≈ $211]**

Rowlands, Henry

- Mona Antiqua Restaurata; An Archaeological Discourse on the Antiquities ... of the Isle of Anglesea ... Second Edition, corrected and improved. London: J. Knox, 1766. 4to. xvi, 357, [ii] pp. Map, 12 plates. Contemp calf gilt, backstrip relaid. *(Gough)* **£75 [≈ $143]**

The Royal Interview ...

- See Combe, William.

Ruffhead, Owen

- The Life of Alexander Pope ... London: for C. Bathurst, 1769. 1st edn. 8vo. [vi],578 pp. Frontis. Old calf, raised bands, sl worn.
(Young's) **£70 [≈ $134]**

Ruggle, George

- Ignoramus. Comoedia corum Regia Majestate Jacobi Regis Angliae ... London: impensis J. S[pencer], 1630. 1st edn. 12mo. [ii],187 pp. Frontis. Orig vellum. STC 21445.
(Vanbrugh) **£165 [≈ $316]**

- Ignoramus ... London: impensis G.S., (1707). Stated 5th but 6th edn. Sm 8vo. Lacks endpaper. Contemp sheep, worn, upper jnt reprd. *(Stewart)* **£60 [≈ $115]**

- Ignoramus: or, The English Lawyer. A Comedy ... London: for W. Feales, 1736. 8vo. 72 pp. Frontis. Disbound. Anon.
(Young's) **£25 [≈ $47]**

Rules and Regulations ...

- Rules and Regulations for the Sword Exercise of the Cavalry ... see Fawcett, William.

- Rules and Regulations of the Royal Edinburgh Light Dragoons ... see Scott, Sir Walter.

Rural Oeconomy ...

- See Young, Arthur.

Russell, John

- A Complete and Useful Book of Cyphers. London: Sayer & Bennett, [17--?]. 1st edn. 4to. Engvd throughout. 25 plates. Later calf.
(Bookpress) **$425 [≈ £221]**

Russell, Rachel, Lady

- Letters, from the Manuscript in the Library at Woburn Abbey ... London: Dilly, 1773. 1st edn. 4to. lxxxi,216 pp. Orig bds, uncut.
(Bickersteth) **£70 [≈ $134]**

- Letters of Lady Rachel Russell; from the Manuscript in the Library at Woburn Abbey ... London: Dilly, 1773. 2nd edn. 4to. lxxii,216 pp. Contemp calf, spine ends reprd, some scuffing to bds. *(Spelman)* **£50 [≈ $95]**

- Letters from the Manuscript in the Library at Woburn Abbey ... London: Dilly, 1774. 3rd edn. 8vo. cxii,332 pp. Calf gilt, jnts splitting but holding firm. Anon.
(Young's) **£20 [≈ $38]**

Russell, Richard

- Dissertation concerning the Use of Sea Water in Diseases of the Glands ... Oxford: At the Theatre, 1753. 1st edn containing both parts. xvi,398,[2] pp. Licence leaf, errata at end. 7 plates. Contemp calf, spine extremities sl rubbed. *(Karmiole)* **$400 [≈ £208]**

- A Dissertation of the Use of Sea-Water in the Diseases of the Glands ... Third Edition, revised and corrected ... London: for W. Owen, 1755. 8vo. Frontis, plate. 1 marg tear. Sl spotting. Contemp calf, gilt, sl rubbed, wear at spine ends, splits in hinge.
(Jarndyce) **£140 [≈ $268]**
- The Oeconomy of Nature in Acute and Chronical Diseases of the Glands ... London: 1755. 1st edn. 8vo. [iv],253,[1 blank,1 advt, 1 blank] pp. 1 plate. Old jotting on title verso. Old calf, rebacked, crnrs worn.
(Bow Windows) **£175 [≈ $335]**

Rutherford, Samuel
- Joshua Redivivus, or Mr. Rutherfoord's Letters ... The Second Edition.. [Edinburgh?]: Printed in the Yeer 1671. 8vo. Title & final verso sl soiled. Cut rather close. 19th c calf, a.e.g. Wing R.2382.
(Sanders) **£85 [≈ $163]**

Rutherforth, Thomas
- A System of Natural Philosophy ... Cambridge: J. Bentham, 1748. 1st edn. 2 vols. 4to. [24],496; [4],497-1105,[7] pp. Subscribers. Fldg map, 31 plates. Minimal browning. Contemp tree calf, elab gilt spine (sl worn).
(Rootenberg) **$500 [≈ £260]**

Rycaut, Sir Paul
- The Present State of the Ottoman Empire ... London: for John Starkey & Henry Brome, 1668. 2nd edn. Folio. [xii],218 pp. Frontis. 2 plates, text ills. Orig sheep, sl damage to hd of spine & lower front hinge. Wing R.2413.
(Vanbrugh) **£425 [≈ $815]**

Ryland, John
- An Address to the Ingenious Youth of Great-Britain ... To which is subjoined a Plan of Education ... London: H.D. Symonds, 1792. 1st edn. 12mo. [iv],ii-111.143,[3 advt] pp. Port. Orig bds, rebacked.
(Burmester) **£120 [≈ $230]**

Rymer, Thomas
- Edgar, or the English Monarch; An Heroick Tragedy. London: for Richard Tonson, 1677. 1st edn. 4to. A few headlines trimmed. Later qtr calf, jnts & spine rubbed. Wing R.2423.
(Dramatis Personae) **$225 [≈ £117]**
- A Short View of Tragedy; it's Original, Excellency, and Corruption. With some Reflections of Shakespear ... London: Richard Baldwin, 1693. 1st edn. 8vo. [xvi],182,[2] pp. Intl blank, final advt leaf.

Contemp calf, rebacked. Wing R.2429.
(Burmester) **£300 [≈ $575]**

S., H.
- Memorials of the Method and Manner of Proceedings in Parliament ... see Scobell, Henry.

S., J. (ed.)
- Poetical Beauties of Modern Writers. London: for I. Wallis ..., 1798. 192 pp. Vignette title. Contemp tree calf. Poems by Coleridge, Crabbe, Southey, &c.
(C.R. Johnson) **£275 [≈ $527]**

S., T.
- Arts Improvement ... see Snow, T. (pseud.).

Sacheverell, Henry
- False Notions of Liberty in Religion and Government Destructive of Both. A Sermon ... May 29, 1713. London: Henry Clements, 1713. 1st edn. 23 pp. Half-title. browned. Disbound.
(Wreden) **$40 [≈ £20]**

Sacheverell, William
- An Account of the Isle of Man ... London: for J. Hartley ..., 1702. 1st edn. 12mo. [xv], 175 pp. Contemp calf, sl worn, upper jnt tender.
(Burmester) **£120 [≈ $230]**

Sackville, Charles
- A Treatise concerning the Militia, in Four Sections ... London: J. Millan, 1752. Half-title, 68 pp. Disbound. Anon.
(C.R. Johnson) **£55 [≈ $105]**

Sadler, John
- Rights of the Kingdom; or Customs of our Ancestours ... London: Richard Bishop, 1649. 1st edn. 4to. [8],93,30-48, 75,48-184,[4],[4 blank] pp, complete. Some browning, sl wear. Contemp calf, elab gilt spine, sl worn. Wing S.278A. Anon.
(Meyer Boswell) **$350 [≈ £182]**

Sage, John
- An Account of the Late Establishment of Presbyterian Government by the Parliament of Scotland in Anno 1690 ... London: for Jos. Hindmarsh, 1693. 1st edn. Sm 4to. 100 pp. V sl foxing. Mod wraps. Anon.
(Chapel Hill) **$110 [≈ £57]**

The Sailing and Fighting Instructions ...
- See Greenwood, Jonathan.

Saint Evremond, Charles de M. de St. denis

- The Works. Made English from the French Originals ... Second Edition, corrected and enlarged. London: 1728. 3 vols. 8vo. 2 ports. Contemp calf, rubbed but sound, vols 2 & 3 wrongly numbered on spines.
(Bickersteth) **£55 [≈ $105]**

St. George, Arthur

- The Blessings of Christian Philosophy; being a Treatise on the Beatitudes ... Dublin: S. Powell for George Risk, 1737. 1st edn. 8vo. xliii,[i],331,[i] pp. Faint damp staining. Contemp calf, rubbed. *(Clark)* **£35 [≈ $67]**

St. Germain, Christopher

- Two Dialogues in English, between a Doctor of Divinity, and a Student in the Laws of England ... London: 1673. New edn. 8vo. 366, [8] pp. Rec half calf. Wing S.317A. Anon. *(Young's)* **£90 [≈ $172]**

St. John, Henry, 1st Viscount Bolingbroke

- See Bolingbroke, Henry St. John, 1st Viscount.

Salmon, Thomas

- The Modern Gazeteer [sic]; or, A Short View of the Several Nations of the World ... London: for S. & E. Ballard ..., 1756. 3rd edn, with addtns. 8vo. Lacks free endpapers. Orig calf, sl rubbed & spotted, paper label defective. *(Chapel Hill)* **$200 [≈ £104]**

Sancho, Ignatius

- Letters ... prefixed, Memoirs of his Life. London: ptd by John Nichols ... , 1782. 1st edn. 2 vols. 8vo. Half-title. 2 frontis. Contemp tree calf, spines worn, jnts cracked.
(Ximenes) **$375 [≈ £195]**

Sancroft, William

- Lex Ignea: or The School of Righteousness. A Sermon ... Octob. 10. 1666 ... London: for R. Pawlett, (1666). 4to. 36 pp. Lib stamp. Disbound. Wing S.553.
(Jarndyce) **£50 [≈ $95]**

Sanctorius, Sanctorius

- Medicina Statica: being the Aphorisms ... Translated into English with large Explanations ... By John Quincy. London: for William Newton, 1712. 1st edn. 8vo. lvi, "112" [ie 312] pp. Frontis, fldg plate. Faintly browned. Contemp calf, sl worn.
(Finch) **£150 [≈ $287]**

- Medicina Statica: being the Aphorisms ... Translated into English with large Explanations ... added, Dr. Keil's Medicina Statica ... Essays ... by John Quincy ... London: 1723. 3rd edn. 8vo. viii,344,xxiv,116 pp. Frontis, fldg plate. Orig calf, rebacked. *(Bickersteth)* **£85 [≈ $163]**

- Medicina Statica: being the Aphorisms ... Translated into English with large Explanations ... By John Quincy ... added, Dr. Keil's Medicina Statica ... London: 1737. 5th edn. 463 pp. Fldg plate. Leather, rebacked, new endpapers.
(Fye) **$400 [≈ £208]**

Sanders, Jonathan

- A New Narrative of a Fiery Apparition seen on several Days about Tower-Hill ... [London: 1681]. Folio. 4 pp. Uncut. Wing S.746C. *(C.R. Johnson)* **£85 [≈ $163]**

Sanders, Mark

- Poems on Occasional Subjects ... Written between the Fourteenth and Twentieth Years, of the Author's Age. Dublin: Robert Jackson, 1778. 1st edn. 12mo. 2 pp subscribers. Some water stains. Contemp calf, gilt spine, rubbed. *(Ximenes)* **$400 [≈ £208]**

- Poems on Occasional Subjects. Dublin: Jackson, 1788. 8vo. 143 pp. Calf, rubbed.
(Emerald Isle) **£75 [≈ $143]**

Sandys, George

- Ovids Metamorphosis Englished ... London: 1626. 1st edn. Folio. [xx],326,[5] pp. Engvd frontis & title. Contemp calf, worn, piece missing from spine. Slipcase.
(Bookpress) **$1,250 [≈ £651]**

- A Paraphrase upon the Divine Poems. [London]: 1648. 3rd edn. 8vo. [xxii],224, 17,[1], 11,[1], 27 pp. Later calf. 1 marg reprd, stain on hd of 1st ff. Wing S.673.
(Bookpress) **$225 [≈ £117]**

- A Relation of a Journey begun An Dom 1610 ... London: for Ro. Allot, 1632. 3rd edn. Folio. [4],309 pp. Engvd title, 49 engvs (2 fldg). Tears to fldg plates, 1 engv defaced. Contemp calf, worn, cvrs detached, lacks backstrip. *(Worldwide)* **$350 [≈ £182]**

- A Relation of a Journey begun An: Dom: 1610. Foure Bookes. Containing a Description of the Turkish Empire, of Egypt, of the Holy Land ... London: Allot, 1632. 3rd edn. 4to. 309 pp. Engvd title, maps, ills. 18th c calf, rebacked. *(Chapel Hill)* **$850 [≈ £442]**

- Sandys Travails ... Turkish Empire ... Greece

... Aegypt ... Holy-Land ... Italy ... The Fift [sic] Edition. London: 1652. Sm folio. Title,[ii],240 pp. Map (worm holes), fldg view (defective), 47 text engvs. Occas spotting, sm tear (no loss). Later half calf. Wing S.677. *(Frew Mackenzie)* **£300 [≈ $575]**

Sargent, John
- The Mine: a Dramatic Poem. London: T. Cadell, 1775. 4to. Disbound.
    (C.R. Johnson) **£145 [≈ $278]**
- The Mine: A Dramatic Poem. To which are added Two Historic Odes. The Third Edition. London: Cadell & Davies, 1796. Sm 8vo. Frontis, 4 plates. Contemp dark blue straight grained mor gilt, a.e.g., jnts v sl rubbed. Princess Sophia's b'plate.
    (Sanders) **£30 [≈ $57]**

Sandeman, Robert
- The Honor of Marriage opposed to all Impurities: an Essay. London: for T. Vernor, 1777. 1st edn. Wrappers, apparently as issued. *(Waterfield's)* **£125 [≈ $239]**

Sarpi, Paolo
- The History of the Council of Trent ... London: 1676. 1st edn. Folio. [xvi],civ, 889, [47] pp. Red & black title. Old calf, rebacked. Wing S.696. *(Young's)* **£85 [≈ $163]**
- The History of the Council of Trent ... Written in Italian by Pietro Soave Polano [pseud.], and faithfully translated by Nathanael Brent ... London: 1676. 4to. [xi], cvi, 889,[47] pp. Contemp calf, worn. Wing S.696. *(Wreden)* **$85 [≈ £44]**

Saunders, Charles
- Tamerlane the Great. A Tragedy ... London: for Richard Bentley & M. Magnus, 1681. 1st edn. Sm 4to. Mod wraps.
    (Dramatis Personae) **$400 [≈ £208]**

Saunders, William
- A Treatise on the Structure, Economy, and Diseases of the Liver ... London: 1793. 1st edn. 232 pp. Wormhole affecting marg of 25 ff. Rec qtr leather. *(Fye)* **$250 [≈ £130]**
- A Treatise on the Structure, Economy, and Diseases of the Liver; together with an Inquiry into the Properties and Component Parts of the Bile and Biliary Concretions. London: 1795. 2nd edn. xxvi,261 pp. Few sm ink stains. Half leather, rebacked, sl worn.
    (Whitehart) **£90 [≈ $172]**

Savary, Claude Etienne
- Letters on Egypt ... Dublin: for Luke White & P. Byrne, 1787. 2 vols. 2 fldg maps, 1 fldg plate. Contemp calf, red & green labels, vol 1 rubbed at ft of spine, vol 2 with 1 worm hole at ft of hinge. *(Jarndyce)* **£140 [≈ $268]**

Saxe, Maurice de
- Reveries or Memoirs upon the Art of War. London: Nourse, 1758. 1st English edn. 4to. Publisher's list at end. 40 fldg plates. Calf, rebacked, sl scuffed.
    (Rostenberg & Stern) **$385 [≈ £200]**

Saywell, William
- A Serious Inquiry into the Means of an Happy Union ... prevent Popery ... London: A.G. & J.P., sold by Rand. Taylor, 1681. Sole edn. Sm 4to. [ii],48 pp. Disbound. Wing S.805. *(Finch)* **£50 [≈ $95]**

Scale, Bernard
- An Hibernian Atlas, or General Description of the Kingdom of Ireland. London: for Robert Sayer, 1776. 1st edn. Sm 4to. Cold maps. Previous owner's stamp on verso of some maps. Contemp calf, rebacked.
    (Emerald Isle) **£650 [≈ $1,247]**

Scamozzi, V.
- The Mirror of Architecture ... Fifth Edition whereunto is added, A Compendium of the Art of Building ... by William Leyburn. London: John Sprint, 1708. 3 ff, 112 pp. Frontis, 40 plates, 4 fldg diags, 1 engvd plate in text. Sm marg worm hole. Contemp leather, reprd. *(Ars Artis)* **£450 [≈ $863]**
- The Mirror of Architecture ... whereunto is added, A Compendium of the Art of Building ... by William Leyburn. London: J. & B. Sprint, 1721. 6th edn. 3 ff, 112 pp. Addtnl engvd title with port, 53 plates (7 fldg). Some browning. Contemp sheep, worn.
    (Ars Artis) **£250 [≈ $479]**

Scarron, Paul
- The Comic Romance of Monsieur Scarron translated by Oliver Goldsmith ... London: for W. Griffin, 1775. 2 vols. 8vo. Usual typographic peculiarities. Contemp calf, front jnts cracked, sometime roughly reprd.
    (Waterfield's) **£300 [≈ $575]**

Scawen, John
- New Spain, Or, Love in Mexico: An Opera, in Three Acts ... London: Robinson, 1790. 1st edn. 8vo. [iv],61 pp. Disbound. Anon.

(Young's) **£30 [≃ $57]**

Scheffer, John
- The History of Lapland ... Oxford: at the Theatre, 1674. 1st edn in English. 4to. Engvd title, [2],147, [1] pp. Fldg map (sl loss top edge). Occas foxing & dust soiling, minor creasing. Three qtr red mor, spine gilt extra, t.e.g., by Ganford. Wing S.851.
(Reese) **$750 [≃ £390]**

Scheuchzer, John Gaspar
- An Account of the Success of Inoculating the Small-Pox in Great Britain, for the Years 1727 and 1728 ... London: for J. Peele ..., 1729. 1st edn. 8vo. 63 pp. Page numerals & 1 catchword partly cropped. Wraps.
(Young's) **£290 [≃ $556]**

Schiller, Friedrich
- The Robbers. A Tragedy. Translated from the German [by A.F. Tytler, later Lord Woodhouselee]. London: Robinson, 1792. 1st edn in English. 8vo. xviii,[i],220 pp. Lacks half title. Last leaf torn without loss. Last p sl soiled. Early cloth, spine ends worn.
(Bickersteth) **£95 [≃ $182]**

A Schizzo on the Genius of Man ...
- See Harington, Edward.

The Scholar's Manual ...
- See Leake, John.

Schomberg, Alexander Crowcher
- Bagley; a Descriptive Poem. With the Annotations of Scriblerus Secundus ... prefixed ... Prologomena on the Poetry of the Present Age. Oxford: for J. & J. Fletcher, 1777. 1st edn. 4to. Mod wraps. Anon. Sometimes ascribed to Thomas Burgess.
(Ximenes) **$400 [≃ £208]**

School ...
- The School for Wives ... see Kelly, Hugh.
- School Occurrences ... see Fenn, Eleanor.
- The School of Man ... see Genard, Francois.

Sclater, Edward
- Consensus Veterum: or, the Reasons of Edward Sclater Minister of Putney, for his Conversion to the Catholic Faith and Communion. London: 1686. 4to. 100 pp. Title sl soiled. Disbound. Wing S.910.
(Robertshaw) **£20 [≃ $38]**

Scobell, Henry
- Memorials of the Method and Manner of Proceedings in Parliament Passing Bills ... Gathered ... By H.S., E.C.P. London: printed in the year 1670. Sl browning.. Contemp sheep, rubbed, rebacked. Wing S.924.
(Meyer Boswell) **$225 [≃ £117]**

Scot, Alexander
- Rudiments and Practical Exercises, for learning the French Language, by an Easy Method ... Fourth Edition, with several new Chapters ... Edinburgh: for William Creech ..., 1794. 8vo. Sl staining. Contemp sheep, rubbed, rebacked. *(Jarndyce)* **£70 [≃ $134]**

Scot, Sir John
- The Staggering State of the Scots Statesmen ... Now published, from an Original Manuscript. Edinburgh: Ruddiman for Nimmo, 1754. 1st edn. 12mo. [ii],xxxiv,190 pp. Some staining, endpapers frayed. Contemp sheep, lacks label.
(Clark) **£60 [≃ $115]**

Scott, James
- Odes on Several Subjects. Cambridge: J. Bentham, 1761. 4to. Mod mrbld bds.
(Waterfield's) **£135 [≃ $259]**

Scott, John
- Amwell. A Descriptive Poem. Dublin: for S. Price ..., 1776. 1st Dublin edn. 12mo. 32 pp inc half-title. Rec wraps.
(Fenning) **£110 [≃ $211]**

Scott, Jonathan (translator)
- Bahar-Danush; or, Garden of Knowledge. An Oriental Romance. Translated from the Persian of Einaiut Oollah. Shrewsbury: J. & W. Eddowes, for Cadell & Davies, 1799. 1st edn of this translation. 3 vols. 8vo. Contemp calf gilt, sl rubbed. The Currer set.
(Ximenes) **$650 [≃ £338]**

Scott, Sir Walter
- Rules and Regulations of the Royal Edinburgh Light Dragoons. [Edinburgh]: 1798. Vignette title, 26,[34 blank],[4],[8 blank] pp. Contemp red mor, a,.e.g. Anon.
(C.R. Johnson) **£1,800 [≃ $3,455]**

Scourge ...
- The Scourge in Vindication of the Church of England ... see Lewis, Thomas.

Scrafton, Luke

- Reflections on the Government of Indostan. With a Short Sketch of the History of Bengal ... London, Printed 1763. London: reptd by Strahan, for Kearsley & Cadell, 1770. 2nd London edn. 8vo. Contemp calf, sl rubbed.
(Ximenes) **$250 [≈£130]**

Scudery, George de

- Curia Politiae: or, The Apologies of Severall Princes. London: Moseley, 1654. 1st English edn. Sm folio. Engvd title, 11 ports. Calf. Wing S.2140.
(Rostenberg & Stern) **$300 [≈£156]**

Seagrave, Robert

- Observations upon the Conduct of the Clergy, in Relation to the Thirty Nine Articles ... London: for R. Hett ..., 1738. 1st edn. 8vo. 67 pp. Disbound.
(Young's) **£45 [≈$86]**

Seale, John Barlow

- An Analysis of the Greek Metres, for the Use of Students at the Universities. Third Edition. Cambridge: John Burgess, 1798. 63 pp. Disbound. Anon.
(C.R. Johnson) **£30 [≈$57]**

Secker, Thomas

- Sermons on Several Subjects. London: Rivington, 1771. 7 vols. Leather, some vols sl damaged, some bds detached, spines worn.
(Gage) **£40 [≈$76]**

Sedgwick, Obadiah

- England's Preservation or, A Sermon discovering the onely way to prevent destroying Judgements ... London: R.B. for Samuel Gellibrand, 1642. Only edn. 4to. [vi], 52 pp. Disbound. Wing S.2372.
(Young's) **£45 [≈$86]**
- Haman's Vanity, or, A Sermon Displaying the Birthless Issues of Church-destroying Adversaries ... London: R. Bishop ..., 1643. Only edn. 4to. [vi],32 pp. Disbound. Wing S.2374.
(Young's) **£45 [≈$86]**
- The Shepherd of Israel or Gods Pastoral Care Over His People Delivered in Divers Sermons ... London: D. Maxwell for S. Gellibrand, 1658. 4to. [8],432 pp. Title mtd with loss of 2 letters. Minor blemishes. 19th c half calf, hd of top jnt cracked. Wing S.2380.
(Humber) **£135 [≈$259]**

Selden, Ambrose

- Love and Folly. A Poem. In Four Canto's. London: for W. Johnston, 1749. 1st edn. Presumed early issue without errata slip pasted to p.xviii. 8vo. [ii],xvii, [i],296 pp. Half-title. Contemp style half calf. Anon.
(Burmester) **£150 [≈$287]**

Selden, John

- The Historie of Tithes. [London]: 1618. 1st edn. Sm 4to. [vi],xxii,[12], 491,[5] pp. Contemp calf, gilt spine, outer hinges cracking. STC 22172.
(Bookpress) **$325 [≈£169]**
- Of the Judicature in Parliaments, A Posthumous Treatise ... London: for Joseph Lawson ..., [1689]. 2nd edn. 8vo. [8],188 pp. Sl foxing & browning. Contemp calf, worn, rebacked. Wing S.2433.
(Meyer Boswell) **$450 [≈£234]**
- Table-Talk. London: Tonson, 1696. 2nd edn. 8vo. [viii],192 pp. Contemp calf, rebacked, lacks pastedowns. STC 2438.
(Bookpress) **$185 [≈£96]**

Select Essays ...

- Select Essays on Husbandry. Extracted from the Museum Rusticum, and Foreign Essays on Agriculture ... Experiments ... in Scotland. Edinburgh: Balfour, 1767. 1st edn. 8vo. viii, 408 pp. Advt leaf after title. 2 plates, fldg table. Some (mostly marg) staining. Contemp calf, rubbed.
(Finch) **£135 [≈$259]**

Seller, Abednego

- Remarques relating to the State of the Church of the First Centuries ... London: Richard Chiswell, 1680. xxxviii,476 pp. Some damp stains. Marg ink notes. Leather, rebacked, crnrs bumped.
(Gage) **£40 [≈$76]**

Semple, George

- A Treatise on Building in Water ... Dublin: for the author, by J.A. Husband, 1776. 4to. [vi],157 pp. 63 plates. Mod half calf gilt.
(Hollett) **£1,500 [≈$2,879]**

The Senators ...

- See Delamayne, Thomas Hallie.

Seneca

- Morals by Way of Abstract ... London: Tonson, 1705. L'Estrange's translation. 9th edn. 8vo. [xxx],524,[12] pp. Frontis. Lacks front free endpaper. Contemp calf, outer hinges cracked.
(Bookpress) **$225 [≈£117]**

- Seneca's Morals by way of Abstract ...
Adorned with Cuts. By Sir Roger L'Estrange.
London: Tonson ..., 1764. Lge 12mo.
[24],383 pp. 7 plates. Contemp calf gilt, worn
but sound.   *(Fenning)* **£28.50 [≈ $55]**

Sermons to Asses ...
- See Murray, James.

Settle, Elkanah
- Absalom Senior: or, Achitophel Transpros'd.
A Poem. London: for S.E. & sold by Langley
Curtis, 1682. 1st edn. Folio. 38, [2] pp. A few
spots. Lacks L2 (blank). Rec polished calf gilt.
Wing S.2652. Anon. *(Hollett)* **£120 [≈ $230]**

Several Discourses and Characters ...
- See Shannon, Francis Boyle, Viscount.

Several Years Travel through Portugal ...
- See Bromley, William.

Seward, William
- Anecdotes of Some Distinguished Persons ...
London: Cadell & Davies, 1795-96. 2nd edn
vols 1 & 2, 1st edns vols 3 & 4. 4 vols. 8vo.
15 plates, 14 engvd pp of music. Contemp
calf gilt, 1 hinge just holding, sl rubbed.
Anon.   *(Lloyd-Roberts)* **£100 [≈ $191]**

Seymar, William (pseud.)
- See Ramsey, William.

Seymour, Richard
- The Compleat Gamester: in Three Parts ...
Written for the Use of the Young Princesses.
The Seventh Edition. London: for J. Hodges,
1750. 12mo. Frontis (sm marg crnr torn).
Contemp calf, red label.
          (Jarndyce) **£280 [≈ $537]**

Shadwell, Thomas
- Bury-Fair. A Comedy ... London: for James
Knapton, 1689. 1st edn. Sm 4to. Title & final
leaf sl dusty. Sm blank piece torn from marg
of advt leaf. Disbound.
          (Dramatis Personae) **$450 [≈ £234]**
- The History of Timon of Athens ... Made
into a Play ... "Shakespeare's Play Gently
Alter'd" ... London: for Henry Herringman,
1688. 3rd edn. 4to. Lacks part of title inc
imprint. Later half calf.
          (Dramatis Personae) **$50 [≈ £26]**

**Shaftesbury, Anthony Ashley Cooper, 3rd
Earl of**
- Characteristicks of Men, Manners, Opinions,
Times. The Third Edition. London: 1723. 3
vols. 8vo. Port, frontis, 8 vignettes. Occas
browning. Contemp calf gilt, new labels,
rubbed, jnts starting.
          (Frew Mackenzie) **£165 [≈ $316]**
- Characteristicks of Men, Manners, Opinions,
Times in Three Volumes. Birmingham: John
Baskerville, 1773. 3 vols. Contemp calf,
rebacked, elab gilt spines.
          (Lamb) **£180 [≈ $345]**
- Characteristics of Men, Manners, Opinions,
Times, with a Collection of Letters. Basil: for
J. Tourneisen & J.L. Legrand, 1790. 3 vols.
8vo. Near contemp blue bds, leather labels,
spines sl chipped, edges rubbed.
          (Buccleuch) **£125 [≈ $239]**

Shakespeare, William
- Poems. London: Reprinted for Thomas
Evans, (1775). Horizontal chain lines. Port on
title. Contemp speckled calf gilt, rebacked.
          (Jarndyce) **£150 [≈ $287]**
- The Winter's Tale, a Play. Alter'd from
Shakespear, by Charles Marsh. The Second
Edition. With a Preface ... London: for
Charles Marsh, 1756. 8vo. vi,78 pp. 19th c
half mor, a.e.g.   *(Burmester)* **£100 [≈ $191]**
- The Plays, From the Text of Dr. Johnson.
With the Prefaces, Notes, &c. of Rowe, Pope
... Dublin: Thomas Ewing, 1771. 7 vols in 13.
8vo. 1 frontis, engvd title to each half-vol of
the plays. 1 leaf held by a pin. Contemp mor,
lacks labels, some spines sl worn.
          (Sanders) **£250 [≈ $479]**
- The Dramatic Works. With Notes by Joseph
Rann. Oxford: Clarendon Press, 1786. Only
Rann edn. 6 vols. 8vo. Lacks vol 3 epilogue
leaf. Early 19th c half calf, sl worn.
          (Young's) **£150 [≈ $287]**
- Dramatic Works; with Explanatory Notes. A
New Edition. To which is now added, a
Copious Index ... by the Rev. Samuel
Ayscough. London: Stockdale, 1790. 1st
Ayscough edn. 3 vols. Lge 8vo. Subscribers.
4 advt ff vol 3. Port. Contemp calf, sl worn.
          (Burmester) **£175 [≈ $335]**
- The Plays ... From the Text of Mr. Steevens's
Last Edition. London: H. Baldwin & Son ...,
1798. 9 vols. 12mo. Half-titles. Contemp tree
calf, gilt dec spines, dble mor labels.
          (Vanbrugh) **£255 [≈ $489]**
- The Plays ... accurately printed from the Text
of Mr. Steevens's last Edition. London:

Baldwin & Sons for Dilly, Johnson ..., 1798. 9 vols. 12mo. Half-titles. Sl spotting. Contemp tree sheep, sl rubbed, some wear at spine ends. *(Jarndyce)* £85 [≈ $163]

Shannon, Francis Boyle, Viscount
- Several Discourses and Characters address'd to the Ladies of the Age. Wherein the Vanities of the Modish Women are discovered ... By a Person of Honour. London: 1689. 1st edn. 8vo. [xvi],199 pp. Marg worm hole in 17 ff. Contemp sheep, hd of spine sl worn. Wing S.2965A. Anon. *(Burmester)* £450 [≈ $863]

Sharp, Granville
- A General Plan for laying out Towns and Townships on the New Acquired Lands in the East-Indies, America, or Elsewhere ... [London]: 1794. 1st edn. 8vo. 24 pp. Lge fldg plate (few tears along fold). Later qtr leather. *(Bookpress)* $2,750 [≈ £1,432]

Sharp, Samuel
- A Critical Enquiry into the Present State of Surgery. Second Edition. London: Tonson, 1750. 8vo. [8],294 pp. Contemp unlettered calf, lacks f.e.p. *(Spelman)* £160 [≈ $307]
- Letters from Italy ... The Years 1765, and 1766. London: R. Cave for W. Nicol, 1766. 1st edn. Post 8vo. [vi],312 pp. E8 & M4 are cancels. Few minor marks & flaws. Contemp calf, gilt spine, reprd. *(Ash)* £200 [≈ $383]
- Letters from Italy, describing the Customs and Manners of that Country ... Dublin: P. Wilson ..., [ca 1767]. 3rd edn. 12mo. vi,380 pp. Contemp calf, spine ends chipped, extremities sl rubbed. *(Frew Mackenzie)* £60 [≈ $115]
- A Treatise on the Operations of Surgery, with a Description and Representation of the Instruments used in performing them ... London: 1761. 8th edn. 234 pp. Plates. Rec qtr leather. *(Fye)* $400 [≈ £208]
- A Treatise on the Operations of Surgery, with a Description and Representation of the Instruments used ... Eighth Edition. London: Tonson, 1761. 8vo. [viii],liv,234 pp. 14 plates. Contemp calf, spine sl rubbed & chipped at hd. *(Frew Mackenzie)* £285 [≈ $547]

Sharp, Thomas
- The Necessary Knowledge of the Lord's Supper ... In a Sermon preach'd at the Cathedral of York, March 29th, 1727 ... Third Edition. York: for John Hildyard, by

Thomas Gent, 1737. 8vo. [2],ii,44 pp. 19th c half mor. *(Spelman)* £90 [≈ $172]

Sharpe, Richard Scrafton
- The Margate New Guide; or Memoirs of Five Families out of Six; who ... make Margate the Place of their Summer Migration ... London: R. Dutton, 1799. 123 pp. Contemp calf, rebacked. Anon. *(C.R. Johnson)* £160 [≈ $307]

Shaw, Cuthbert
- Monody to the Memory of a Young Lady who died in Child-Bed ... added, an Evening Address to a Nightingale. London: for J. Dodsley ..., 1770. 3rd edn, enlgd. 4to. iv,23 pp. Disbound. *(Burmester)* £50 [≈ $95]

Shaw, Joseph
- Parish Law: or, a Guide to Justices of the Peace, Ministers, Church-Wardens, Overseers of the Poor ... In the Savoy: Henry Lintot ..., 1743. 5th edn. 8vo. [vi],374,[12] pp. Final gathering loosening. Old calf, upper jnt cracking. *(Young's)* £75 [≈ $143]

Shaw, Peter
- The Dispensatory of the Royal College of Physicians in Edinburgh. London: 1727. xii, 281 pp. Sl foxing. New leather. *(Whitehart)* £150 [≈ $287]
- The Juice of the Grape: or, Wine Preferable to Water. A Treatise, wherein Wine is shewn to be the Grand Preserver of Health ... London: for W. Lewis ..., 1724. 1st edn. xii, 56 pp. Mod half calf gilt. Hailstone b'plate. Anon. *(Hollett)* £350 [≈ $671]
- A New Practice of Physic ... London: Longman, 1753. 7th edn. 2 vols. 8vo. [xvi], 415; [ii], 413-712, [22] pp. Contemp calf, spines sl darkened, some hinges starting. *(Bookpress)* $325 [≈ £169]
- The Tablet, or Pictures of Real Life ... London: Longman, 1762. 371 pp. Contemp calf. Anon. *(C.R. Johnson)* £220 [≈ $422]

Shaw, Stebbing
- A Tour to the West of England, in 1788. London: Robson & Clarke, 1789. 602 pp. Contemp calf, green label, 1 hinge worn in places. *(C.R. Johnson)* £135 [≈ $259]

Shaw, Thomas
- Travels, or Observations relating to several parts of Barbary and the Levant. Oxford: 1738. 1st edn. Folio. [8],xviii, 444, 68 pp.

Engvd title, 35 maps & plates (7 fldg), num text ills. Few sl tears. Contemp calf, v worn, cvrs detached.   *(Worldwide)* **£325** [≈ £169]

Sheffield, John, Duke of Buckingham
- See Buckingham, John Sheffield, Duke of.

Shenstone, William
- The Works ... In Two Volumes with Decorations. London: Dodsley, 1764. 2 vols. 8vo. 2 frontis, fldg plate vol 2. Sev lib blind stamps, occas sl spot. Mod qtr calf.
(Waterfield's) **£185** [≈ $355]
- The Works in Verse and Prose ... London: Dodsley, 1764-69. 1st coll edn. 3 vols. 8vo. 2 "Contents" ff vol 2. Frontis & title vignettes in vols 1 & 2, fldg plan vol 2. Sm marg tear 3 ff. Contemp calf, v sl worn.
(Burmester) **£110** [≈ $211]
- The Works in Prose and Verse. London: J. Hughs for J. Dodsley, 1765-9. 2nd edn. 3 vols. 8vo. Frontis & vignette titles in vols 1 & 2. Lacks plan from vol 2. Old calf, sometime rebacked.   *(Young's)* **£30** [≈ $57]
- See also Giles, Joseph.

Sheppard or Shepheard, William
- Of Corporations, Fraternities, and Guilds ... London: Twyford, Dring ..., 1659. Only edn. 8vo. 3 blanks, title, 2 ff, 187 pp, 2 blanks. Sl foxed & browned. Contemp sheep, backstrip relaid. Wing S.3195.
(Meyer Boswell) **$1,250** [≈ £651]
- The Practical Counsellor in the Law. Touching Fines, Common Recoveries, Judgements and the Execution thereof ... London: for A. Crooke ..., 1671. Folio. [iv],500,[6],[2 blank] pp. Some stains. Old calf, rebacked & reprd. Wing S.3208.
(Bow Windows) **£260** [≈ $499]
- The Touch-Stone of Common Assurances ... London: M.F. for W. Lee ..., 1648. 1st edn. 4to in 8s. [xii],529,[14] pp. 4 blank ff at end. Few crnrs frayed, sl marg browning. Contemp sheep, rebacked, crnrs reprd. Wing S.3214.   *(Clark)* **£160** [≈ $307]
- The Touch-Stone of Common Assurances ... London: for W. Lee ..., 1651. 3rd edn. 4to. [xii], 529,[5] pp. Contemp sheep, elab gilt spine, fine. Wing S.3215A.
(Vanbrugh) **£325** [≈ $623]

Sheraton, T.
- The Cabinetmaker and Upholsterer's Drawing Book, with Appendix, Accompaniment, and List of Subscribers.

London: Bensley, 1793-95. 115 engvd plates, many fldg. frontis cut down & mtd. 10 plates reprd in fold. 19th c half mor.
(Phillips) **£875** [≈ $1,679]

Sheridan, Charles Francis
- A History of the Late Revolution in Sweden ... London: Dilly, 1778. 1st edn. 8vo. Errata leaf. Sl foxing. Contemp calf, jnts cracking.
(Hannas) **£50** [≈ $95]
- A History of the Late Revolution in Sweden ... Dublin: M. Mills, 1778. 1st Dublin & 1st authorized edn. 8vo. Marg water stains at end. Contemp calf, sl worn.
(Hannas) **£55** [≈ $105]

Sheridan, Frances
- The Discovery. A Comedy ... Written by the Editor of Miss Sidney Biddulph. London: for T. Davies ..., 1763. 1st edn. 8vo. Title browned & sl frayed at hd. Disbound. Anon.
(Dramatis Personae) **$60** [≈ £31]
- The History of Nourjahad. London: Dodsley, 1767. 1st edn. 12mo. [iv],240 pp. Half-title. Contemp calf, upper jnt reprd. Anon.
(Burmester) **£150** [≈ $287]

Sheridan, Richard Brinsley
- The Duenna: a Comic Opera. London: T.N. Longman, 1794. 1st edn. 8vo. [iv],(9)-78 pp. No half-title. Disbound. *(Clark)* **£60** [≈ $115]
- Pizarro; a Tragedy ... taken from the German Drama of Kotzebue ... London: James Ridgway, 1799. 1st edn, ordinary paper issue. 8vo. [viii],76,[4] pp. Minor foxing, few ff sl creased. Rec wraps.   *(Clark)* **£40** [≈ $76]
- Pizarro; a Tragedy ... taken from the German Drama of Kotzebue ... London: James Ridgeway, 1799. 1st edn. 8vo. [viii],79 pp. Rec mor.   *(Young's)* **£95** [≈ $182]
- A Trip to Scarborough. A Comedy ... Altered from Vanbrugh's Relapse ... London: G. Wilkie, 1781. 1st edn. 8vo. [vi],104 pp. No half-title. Disbound. *(Clark)* **£75** [≈ $143]
- A Trip to Scarborough. A Comedy ... Altered from Vanbrugh's Relapse ... Dublin: R. Marchbank, 1781. 1st Dublin edn. 8vo. [vi], 72 pp. No half-title. Some marg worm. Later wraps.   *(Clark)* **£35** [≈ $67]
- Verses to the Memory of Garrick. Spoken as A Monody, at the Theatre Royal in Drury-Lane. London: T. Evans ..., 1779. 1st edn. 4to. 15 pp. Frontis. Later qtr calf, crnrs knocked. Anon.   *(Clark)* **£120** [≈ $230]

Sheridan, Thomas

- A Complete Dictionary of the English Language ... The Third Edition, revised, corrected and enlarged ... London: Charles Dilly, 1790. 2 vols. 8vo. calf, rebacked, rubbed. *(Jarndyce)* **£160 [≈ $307]**
- A Course of Lectures on Elocution together with Two Dissertations on Language and some Other Tracts ... London: Strahan, for Millar sic, Dodsley ..., 1762. 1st edn. 4to. Early half calf, rubbed. *(Buccleuch)* **£180 [≈ $345]**
- A Course of Lectures on Elocution ... London: Strahan, 1762. 1st edn. 4to. 262 pp. Rebound in qtr calf. *(C.R. Johnson)* **£225 [≈ $431]**
- A Course of Lectures on Elocution: together with Two Dissertations on Language ... New Edition. London: Dodsley, 1781. 8vo. 19th c half calf, uncut. *(Jarndyce)* **£110 [≈ $211]**
- A Course of Lectures on Elocution: together with Two Dissertations on Language ... New Edition. London: for C. Dilly ..., 1798. 8vo. Contemp calf, black label, spine sl rubbed. *(Jarndyce)* **£45 [≈ $86]**
- Lectures on the Art of Reading. London: Dodsley ..., 1775. 2 vols. 8vo. Contemp calf, rebacked, crnrs worn. *(Waterfield's)* **£225 [≈ $431]**
- Lectures on the Art of Reading. London: Dilly, 1794. 4th edn. 8vo. Contemp calf, rebacked. *(Emerald Isle)* **£50 [≈ $95]**
- Sheridan's and Henderson's Practical Method of Reading and Reciting English Poetry, elucidated by a Variety of Examples ... London: E. Newbery, 1796. 264 pp. Contemp sheep. *(C.R. Johnson)* **£120 [≈ $230]**

Sherlock, Thomas

- Bishop Sherlock's Arguments against a Repeal of the Corporation and Test Acts ... Oxford: Clarendon Press ..., 1790. 8vo. [iv], 74 pp. Title sl soiled. Disbound. *(Burmester)* **£25 [≈ $47]**

Sherlock, William

- An Answer to a Discourse Intituled, Papists Protesting against Protestant-Popery ... London: for John Amery, 1686. 1st edn. 4to. [iv], 130 pp. Imprimatur leaf reprd. Some staining. New bds. Wing S.3259. Anon. *(Young's)* **£55 [≈ $105]**
- A Discourse Concerning the Divine Providence ... London: William Rogers, 1705. 4th edn. 8vo. [12], 480 pp. Few sl damp

marks. 18th c polished calf, rebacked, crnrs bumped. *(Humber)* **£45 [≈ $86]**
- A Discourse Concerning the Nature, Unity, and Communion of the Catholick Church ... London: for William Rogers, 1688. 1st edn. 4to. [iv], 60, 4 advt pp. Imprimatur leaf. Disbound. Wing S.3291. *(Young's)* **£35 [≈ $67]**

Shirley, William

- The Parricide; or, Innocence in Distress. A Tragedy. London: for J. Watts, 1739. 1st edn. Post 8vo. Lacks half-title. Cropped sl close at hd. Some browning. Later half calf, sl rubbed & split. *(Ash)* **£100 [≈ $191]**

Shirrefs, Andrew

- Poems, chiefly in the Scottish Dialect. Edinburgh: for the author, 1790. Half-title. Frontis port. Rec bds, uncut. *(C.R. Johnson)* **£125 [≈ $239]**
- Poems, chiefly in the Scottish Dialect. Edinburgh: for the author, 1790. 8vo. Half-title. Frontis. Mod half calf, uncut. *(Waterfield's)* **£115 [≈ $220]**

Short ...

- A Short Account of the late Application to Parliament made by the Merchants of London upon the Neglect of their Trade ... London: T. Cooper, 1742. 2nd edn. 8vo. 61 pp. Disbound. *(Burmester)* **£48 [≈ $92]**
- A Short Critical Review of the Political Life of Oliver Cromwell ... see Banks, John.
- A Short History of Barbados ... see Frere, George.
- A Short History of Insects ... see Lever, Lady.
- A Short History of Standing Armies in England ... See Trenchard, John.
- A Short History of the Rise, Reign, and Ruin of the Antinomians ... see Welde, Thomas.
- A Short Introduction to English Grammar ... see Lowth, Robert.

Short, Thomas

- A Comparative History of the Increase and Decrease of Mankind in England and several Countries abroad ... General States of Health, Air, Seasons and Food ... London: 1767. 1st edn. 4to. [xii], 213 pp. Title laid down. Some soiling. Mod half leather, uncut. *(Whitehart)* **£200 [≈ $383]**
- The Natural, Experimental, and Medicinal History of the Mineral Waters of Derbyshire,

Lincolnshire, and Yorkshire, particularly those of Scarborough ... London: 1734. [xx], xxii,362 pp. 4 plates. Last few ff sl wormed. Reversed calf, v sl worn.
(Whitehart) **£250 [≈ $479]**

- The Natural, Experimental, and Medicinal History of the Mineral Waters. London: for the author, 1734. 1st edn. Cr 4to. [xx],xxii, 362 pp. 5 plates. 1 leaf sl flawed. Lacks addtnl disclaimer leaf Uu2 found in BL copy. Mod half calf.   *(Ash)* **£125 [≈ $239]**

Shorter Examples ...

- Shorter Examples or, Second Book of English Examples, to be rendered into Latin adapted to the Use of Youth of the Lower Class. Eton: T. Pote, 1791. 12mo. Contemp sheep, paper label on spine, jnts cracked.
(Waterfield's) **£35 [≈ $67]**

Sibbes, Richard

- The Bruised Reede and Smoaking Flax. Some Sermons ... Sixt Edition. London: M.F. for R. Dawlman & L. Fawne, 1638. 12mo. [50],336 pp. Num marg ink marks, marg burn mark at end. New qtr calf. STC 22484.
(Humber) **£55 [≈ $105]**

Sibly, Ebenezer

- The Medical Mirror. Or Treatise on the Impregnation of the Human Female. Shewing the Origin of Diseases ... Second Edition. London: for the author ..., [plates dated 1794]. 8vo. 184,8 pp. Port frontis, 4 plates. Orig bds, uncut, sl soiled, spine defective at ft.   *(Finch)* **£140 [≈ $268]**

- A New and Complete Illustration of the Celestial Science of Astrology ... In Four Parts ... London: for the proprietor ..., 1784-84-87-88. 1st edn. 4to. 1126,[4] pp. 29 plates (1 fldg). Some marks, chiefly marginal, few sm reprs. Antique half calf.
(Finch) **£200 [≈ $383]**

- A New and Complete Illustration of the Celestial Science of Astrology ... In Four Books ... London: for the proprietor & sold by W. Nicoll, 1784-88. 1st edn of the 4 parts. 4to. 1126,[4] pp. Frontis, 29 plates. Some wear & tear. Contemp style half calf.
(Gough) **£295 [≈ $566]**

Sidney, Algernon

- Discourses concerning Government ... London: the booksellers, 1698. Folio. Contemp calf, rubbed, crnrs reprd. Wing S.3761.   *(Waterfield's)* **£300 [≈ $575]**

- Discourses Concerning Government ...

London: J. Darby, 1704. 2nd edn. Folio. [viii], 424,[58] pp. Orig panelled calf, spine renewed, edges reprd.
(Vanbrugh) **£175 [≈ $335]**

- Letters ... to the Honourable Henry Savile ... Now First printed ... London: Dodsley, 1742. 1st edn. 8vo. 176 pp. Half-title soiled. 1st few ff sl stained. Reversed calf.
(Young's) **£38 [≈ $72]**

Sidney, Sir Philip

- The Countesse of Pembrokes Arcadia ... Now the ninth time published, with a Two Fold Supplement ... also added a sixth Booke, by R.B. ... London: Waterson & Young, 1638. 9th edn. Folio. [vi],624,[19] pp. Dec title border. Occas sl wear. Contemp calf. STC 22550.   *(Vanbrugh)* **£355 [≈ $681]**

- The Countesse of Pembrokes Arcadia ... Thirteenth Edition. With his Life and Death ... London: for George Calvert, 1674. 13th edn. Folio. [xxxii],624,[26] pp. Port frontis. Contemp sheep, backstrip relaid. Wing S.3770.   *(Vanbrugh)* **£175 [≈ $335]**

Sillar, David

- Poems. Kilmarnock: John Wilson, 1789. 1st edn. 8vo. Half calf, t.e.g., by Bayntun.
(Georges) **£160 [≈ $307]**

Simes, Thomas

- A Military Course for the Government and Conduct of a Battalion ... London: for the author ..., 1777. 14 pp subscribers. Cold frontis & plates. Sl staining. Contemp calf, rec reback.   *(Jarndyce)* **£120 [≈ $230]**

Simmons, Samuel

- Elements of Anatomy and the Animal Economy. From the French of M. Person. Corrected ... Augmented with Notes. London: Wilie, 1775. 1st edn. 8vo. xii,396 pp, errata leaf. 3 plates. Light pencilling. Old qtr calf, worn.   *(Goodrich)* **$75 [≈ £39]**

Simmons, Samuel Foart

- An Account of the Tenia, and Method of Treating It. London: J. Wilkie, 1778. 2nd edn. 8vo. (iii)-xxi,77 pp. 2 fldg plates. Lacks half-title. Later bds. Anon.
(Bookpress) **$275 [≈ £143]**

Simon, James

- An Essay towards an Historical Account of Irish Coins ... Dublin: S. Powell for the author ..., 1749. 1st edn. 4to. xv,[1 blank], 184 pp. 8 plates. Sm worm hole not affecting text. Contemp calf, spine rubbed, hinge ends starting to split.   *(Pickering)* **$500 [≈ £260]**

Simpson, Thomas, 1710-61
- The Doctrine and Application of Fluxions ... Second Edition, revised and carefully corrected. London: for John Nourse, 1776. 2 vols. 8vo. xii, 274,[2 advt]; [ii], 275-576 pp. Name torn from hd of vol 2 title. Contemp sheep, rebacked, sides scuffed.
    (Burmester) **£175 [≈ $335]**
- Essays on Several Curious and Useful Subjects, in Speculative and Mix't Mathematicks ... London: H. Woodfall, for J. Nourse, 1740. 1st edn. 4to. viii,142,[1 errata], [1 advt] pp. W'cut text diags. Contemp panelled calf, label chipped, spine & crnrs sl worn.   *(Gaskell)* **£400 [≈ $767]**
- Essays on Several Curious and Useful Subjects, in Speculative and Mix'd Mathematicks. London: H. Woodfall, for J. Nourse, 1740. 1st edn. 4to. viii,142,[2] pp. Errata. Ctlg. W'cut diags. Rec half calf gilt.   *(Rootenberg)* **$750 [≈ £390]**
- Select Exercises for Young Proficients in the Mathematics ... A New Edition ... Account of the Life and Writings of the Author, by Charles Hutton. London: for F. Wingrave, 1792. 8vo. [4],iv, xxiii,[i], 252 pp. Ink splashes on 4 pp. Contemp calf.
    (Fenning) **£45 [≈ $86]**

Simson, Patrick
- The History of the Church since the Days of Our Saviour ... London: for John Bellamy, 1624. 1st edn. Sm 4to. "770" [ie 700] pp. Early 19th c half calf, some rubbing, crnrs sl bumped.   *(Chapel Hill)* **$250 [≈ £130]**

Simson, Robert
- Elements of the Conic Sections ... The First Three Books, translated from the Latin Original ... Edinburgh: for Charles Elliot ..., 1775. 1st edn in English. 8vo. [vi],255 pp. 14 fldg plates. Contemp calf backed bds, vellum crnrs, jnts rubbed.   *(Gaskell)* **£125 [≈ $239]**

Simson, Thomas, 1696-1764
- An Inquiry how far the Vital and Animal Actions of the more Perfect Animals can be accounted for Independent of the Brain. Edinburgh: 1752. 1st edn. 4to. [4],16, 270, [2] pp. Errata after title. 2 fldg plates. V sl browning. Contemp calf, rebacked.
    (Rootenberg) **$650 [≈ £338]**

Sinclair, George
- Satan's Invisible World Discovered ... Edinburgh: A. Jardine, [ca 1780]. 16mo. 170 pp. Contemp half calf.
    (Chapel Hill) **$150 [≈ £78]**

Sinclair, John
- Observations on the Scottish Dialect. London: for Strahan & Cadell, & W. Creech, Edinburgh, 1782. 8vo. Marg stain in 1st 2 gatherings. Some spotting. Contemp half calf, rubbed, spine worn, hinges weak, lacks label.
    (Jarndyce) **£120 [≈ $230]**

Sketch(es) ...
- A Sketch of the Lives and Writings of Dante and Petrarch ... see Penrose, Thomas, Jr.
- Sketches chiefly relating to the History ... of the Hindoos ... see Craufurd, Quintin.

Sloane, Hans
- A Voyage to the Islands Madera, Barbados, Nieves, S. Christophers and Jamaica ... London: 1707-25. 4 vols. Folio. Fldg map, 284 dble-page plates. 4 plates defective & reprd with facs, another plate 2 blank crnrs reprd. Contemp calf, trifle rubbed.
    (Wheldon & Wesley) **£2,400 [≈ $4,607]**

Smart, Christopher
- The Horatian Canons of Friendship ... By Ebenezer Pentweazle ... London: for the author, & J. Newbery, 1750. 1st edn. 4to. viii, 19, [1 advt] pp. Occas spotting, final leaf sl soiled. Mod calf gilt.
    (Hollett) **£1,500 [≈ $2,879]**
- The Nonpareil; or, The Quintessence of Wit and Humour ... London: for T. Carnan, 1757. 1st edn. 8vo. xii,230, ii,68 pp. Lacks frontis & rear free endpaper. Page 1 sl soiled. Old calf gilt, sl worn, spine creased & defective at ends. Anon.
    (Hollett) **£220 [≈ $422]**
- The Poems ... Prefixed, an Account of his Life and Writings ... Reading: ptd by Smart & Cowslade, & sold by F. Power & Co, London, 1791. 1st coll edn. 2 vols. 4 advt pp vol 2. Frontis vol 1. Contemp tree calf, gilt spines, red & green labels.
    (Jarndyce) **£320 [≈ $614]**
- A Poetical Translation of the Fables of Phaedrus ... London: Dodsley, 1765. 1st edn. xvii, 221, index pp. Frontis. Contemp sheep, rebacked.   *(C.R. Johnson)* **£165 [≈ $316]**

Smart, John

- Tables of Interest, Discount, Annuities &c. London: J. Darby & T. Browne, 1726. [iv], 123 pp. Half-title. Mod half calf gilt.
(Hollett) **£120 [≈ $230]**

Smeaton, John

- Experimental Enquiry concerning the Natural Powers of Wind and Water to turn Mills and other Machines depending on a Circular Motion ... London: Taylor, 1794. 110 pp. 5 fldg plates. Qtr calf, mrbld bds.
(C.R. Johnson) **£350 [≈ $671]**

- Experimental Enquiry concerning the Natural Powers of Wind and Water to Turn Mills and Other Machines ... Second Edition. London: I. & J. Taylor, 1795. Tall 8vo. 5 fldg plates, 2 fldg tables. Advt leaf at end. 3 ff soiled. Rec calf, v sl bowed.
(Georges) **£350 [≈ $671]**

Smellie, William

- The Philosophy of Natural History. Dublin: William Porter ..., 1790. 2nd edn. 2 vols. 8vo. Sl wear & tear. Contemp half calf, jnts reprd.
(Stewart) **£300 [≈ $575]**

Smethurst, G.

- Tables of Time: whereby the Day of the Month ... Manchester: 1749. Sm 8vo. viii,132, 48 pp. Sev lib blind stamps. Later lib cloth, spine dull.   *(Whitehart)* **£40 [≈ $76]**

Smith, Adam

- Essays on Philosophical Subjects ... prefixed, An Account of the Life and Writings of the Author; by Dugald Stewart. Dublin: 1795. 1st Dublin edn. 8vo. cxxiii, [1 blank], 332 pp. 1 sm repr, sl marg damp stain, blank piece cut from title. Contemp sheep, rebacked.
(Pickering) **$2,500 [≈ £1,302]**

- An Inquiry into the Nature and Causes of the Wealth of Nations. London: Strahan & Cadell, 1776. 1st edn. 2 vols. 4to (11 3/4 x 9 3/8 inches). Half-titles, final blank vol 1, advts end of vol 2. 4 cancels (1: M3, 2Z3, 3A4; 2: 3Z4). Orig bds, untrimmed. Qtr mor slipcase.
(Book Block) **$55,000 [≈ £28,645]**

- An Inquiry into the Nature and Causes of the Wealth of Nations ... The Eighth Edition. London: Strahan & Cadell, 1796. 3 vols. Half-titles. Contemp tree calf, red labels, hinges weakening.   *(C.R. Johnson)* **£180 [≈ $345]**

- The Theory of Moral Sentiments ... Eighth Edition. London: Strahan & Cadell, 1797. 2 vols. Half-titles. Contemp tree calf, red labels.

(C.R. Johnson) **£850 [≈ $1,631]**

Smith, Charles

- The Ancient and Present State of the County and City of Cork, containing a Natural, Civil, Ecclesiastical, Historical and Topographical Description thereof. Dublin: Wilson, 1774. 2nd edn. 2 vols. 8vo. 14 maps & plates. A few reprs. Half calf. *(Emerald Isle)* **£250 [≈ $479]**

- The Antient and Present State of the County of Down ... with the Natural and Civil History of Same ... With a Survey of the New Canal ... Dublin: Reilly, 1744. 8vo. 271 pp. Fldg map. Antique style half calf. Anon.
(Emerald Isle) **£150 [≈ $287]**

- The Antient and Present State of the County and City of Waterford, being a Natural, Civil, Ecclesiastical, Historical and Topographical Description thereof ... Dublin: Reilly, 1746. 8vo. 380 pp. Maps, plates. Contemp Irish calf, sm repr at ft of spine.
(Emerald Isle) **£250 [≈ $479]**

- The Ancient and Present State of the County and City of Waterford ... Dublin: for W. Wilson, 1774. 8vo. xx,376,[6],[2 advt] pp. Port, fldg map, fldg plan, 3 fldg views, 2 other plates (1 fldg). Rec qtr calf.
(Fenning) **£185 [≈ $355]**

Smith, Charlotte

- Desmond. A Novel. London: for G.G.J. & J. Robinson, 1792. 1st edn. 3 vols. 12mo. Half-titles. 4 advt pp vol 3. B'plates removed. Contemp half calf, spines sl rubbed, vol 3 lacks label.   *(Jarndyce)* **£320 [≈ $614]**

- Elegiac Sonnets ... Fifth Edition, with Additional Sonnets and Other Poems. London: Cadell, 1789. 12mo. [iv], xxvi, 83 pp. Half-title. Subscribers. 5 plates. Some pencilled scribbling. Rec bds.
(Burmester) **£30 [≈ $57]**

- The Emigrants, A Poem, in Two Books. London: Cadell, 1793. 1st edn. 4to. ix,68 pp. Half-title. Marg blind stamp on prelims. Orig bds, sl rubbed & marked, rebacked. Half mor box.   *(Hollett)* **£350 [≈ $671]**

- Minor Morals, interspersed with Sketches of Natural History, Historical Anecdotes, and Original Stories. London: Sampson Low, 1799. 2nd edn. 2 vols. 12mo. Frontis. Contemp mor backed mrbld bds (crnrs worn).
(Stewart) **£45 [≈ $86]**

- Rural Walks: in Dialogues. Intended for the Use of Young Persons. The Second Edition. London: Cadell & Davies, 1795. 2 vols. 174; 184 pp. Contemp mrbld bds, rebacked in cloth. *(C.R. Johnson)* £125 [≈$239]

Smith, Edmund
- The Works ... to which is prefix'd, A Character of Mr. Smith by Mr. Oldisworth. London: Lintot, 1719. 3rd edn. 8vo. [xxxvi], 101 pp. Sl spotting & staining. New bds.
(Young's) £45 [≈$86]

Smith, Eliza
- The Compleat Housewife: or Accomplish'd Gentlewoman's Companion: being a Collection of Upwards of Six Hundred of the most Approved Receipts in Cookery ... Eighth Edition ... London: 1737. 8vo. [xviii], 354, xv, [3 advt] pp. Frontis, 6 fldg plates. Rec qtr calf. *(Burmester)* £275 [≈$527]
- The Compleat Housewife: or, Accomplish'd Gentlewoman's Companion ... London: for J. & J. Pemberton, 1737. 8th edn. [xvi],354,xv,[4 advt] pp. Frontis, 6 fldg plates. Sm worm track edge of frontis. Contemp calf, rather worn, jnts cracked.
(Hollett) £240 [≈$460]

Smith, Captain George
- An Universal Military Dictionary ... London: for J. Millan, 1779. 4to. ii,xi-xvii, i-viii, [ii], B1-Rr4 pp, seemingly complete. Engvd title, fldg table, 16 plates. Occas sl damp stain. Contemp calf gilt, edges darkened, edges of lower bd scraped. *(Hollett)* £285 [≈$547]

Smith, George, of Kendal
- A Compleat Body of Distilling, explaining the Mysteries of that Science ... Second Edition. London: for Henry Linton, 1731. 8vo. Intl advt leaf. Frontis. Contemp sheep, hinges sl cracked. *(Jarndyce)* £360 [≈$691]

Smith, Godfrey
- The Laboratory; or, School of Arts ... Fourth Edition, with Additions ... London: for James Hodges, 1755. 8vo. Frontis, plates (some fldg). Contemp speckled calf gilt, spine sl rubbed. *(Jarndyce)* £250 [≈$479]

Smith, Henry
- Two Sermons, of Jonah's Punishment ... London: T.C. for Cuthbert Burby, 1605. 2nd (?) edn. 8vo. [i],44 pp. 1 leaf torn affecting 6 letters. Disbound. STC 22753.
(Young's) £45 [≈$86]

Smith, Hugh
- Letters to Married Women. The Third Edition, Revised, and considerably Enlarged.

London: for the author, 1774. 256 pp. Contemp calf, hinges cracking.
(C.R. Johnson) £250 [≈$479]

Smith, Captain John
- England's Improvement Reviv'd: Digested into Six Books. London: In the Savoy, by Tho. Newcomb for the author, 1670. 1st edn. 4to. 270 pp. Contemp calf, gilt spine, red label. Wing S.4092.
(C.R. Johnson) £620 [≈$1,190]
- The True Travels, Adventures, and Observations of Captaine John Smith. London: Thomas Slater, 1630. 1st edn. 4 issue points noted. Sm folio. [xii],60 pp. Fldg plate in facs. Later mor, a.e.g., by Pratt.
(Bookpress) $3,250 [≈£1,692]

Smith, Dr John
- The Life of St. Columba ... Joint Patron of the Irish; commonly called Colum-Kille, The Apostle of the Highlands. Edinburgh: Mundell, 1798. 8vo. 168,10 advt pp. Contemp half calf. *(Emerald Isle)* £50 [≈$95]

Smith, John, of Colchester
- A Designed End to Socinian Controversy ... London: Printed in the Year 1695. Only edn. 63, [i] pp. Disbound. Sl dusty, blank crnrs of title torn, cropped at hd. Wing S.4109A.
(Clark) £120 [≈$230]

Smith, Joseph
- The Difference between the Nonjurors and the Present Publick Assemblies, not a Real, but Accidental Schism. London: J. Morphew, 1716. 1st edn. 8vo. 42 pp. Sm paper flaw in title. Disbound. Anon. *(Young's)* £50 [≈$95]

Smith, Matthew
- Memoirs of Secret Service. London: for A. Baldwin, 1699. 1st edn. 8vo. Final blank leaf. Trivial marg damp stain last few ff. Contemp calf, jnt ends cracking, water stain on lower cvr. Wing S.4131. *(Georges)* £200 [≈$383]

Smith, Robert, Rat-Catcher to the Princess Amelia
- The Complete Rat-Catcher ... London: for the daughters of the late R. Smith ..., [ca 1790]. 8vo. [ii],48 pp. 3 fldg plates (1 sl stained). Plate IV numbering altered by hand to I. Rec wraps. *(Burmester)* £60 [≈$115]
- The Universal Directory for Taking Alive and Destroying Rats, and all other Kinds of Four-Footed and Winged Vermin ... London: for the author, 1768. 1st edn. 8vo. vii,218 pp.

Author's note pasted to title verso. Sl wear & marks. 6 plates. Orig calf, rebacked.
(Bickersteth) **£130 [≈ $249]**

Smith, Thomas

- An Account of the Greek Church ... London: Miles Flesher for Richard Davis in Oxford, 1680. 1st edn in English. 8vo. [xxiv], 303, [13] pp. Blank leaf before title. 9 pp advts at end Contemp calf gilt, jnts cracked but firm, extremities sl worn, lacks label. Wing S.4232.
(Clark) **£150 [≈ $287]**

- A Sermon on the Credulity of the Mysteries of the Christian Religion preached before a learned Audience. London: Tho. Roycroft, 1675. Edges frayed, sl water staining in early ff. Sewn as issued. Wing S.4250.
(Waterfield's) **£40 [≈ $76]**

Smith, Sir Thomas

- De Republica Anglorum. The Manner of Gouernement or Policie of the Realme of England ... London: 1583. 1st edn. Sm 4to. [iv], 119,[1 blank] pp. Few reprs inc 2 in facs. 19th c mor gilt, a.e.g. The Stirling Maxwell copy. STC 22857.
(Pickering) **$2,500 [≈ £1,302]**

Smith, William

- The History of the Province of New-York ... London: 1757. 1st edn. 4to. xii,255 pp. Dble-page plate (loose). Sl foxing. Title darkened. Tear to 1 crnr without loss. Contemp sheep backed mrbld bds, worn, hinges cracked, lacks label.
(Reese) **$900 [≈ £468]**

- The History of the Province of New-York ... London: 1776. 2nd edn. viii,334 pp (misnumbered but complete). Sm hole to 2 ff sl affecting sidenote & page number. Contemp mottled calf, gilt spine, hinges worn, front weak but cords sound. Slipcase.
(Reese) **$600 [≈ £312]**

- The History of the Province of New York. London: 1776. 2nd edn. 8vo. Some browning. Contemp calf, outer hinges sl cracked.
(Black Sun) **$150 [≈ £78]**

- The History of the Province of New-York ... Phila: Mathew Carey, April 9, 1792. 1st Amer edn. 8vo. Tear in rear flyleaf. Contemp sprinkled sheep, gilt spine, v sl rubbing.
(Ximenes) **$450 [≈ £234]**

Smith, William

- The Poetic Works ... With Some Account of the Life and Writings of the Author by Thomas Crane. Chester: T. Crane ..., 1782. 52 pp. Disbound.

(C.R. Johnson) **£145 [≈ $278]**

Smith, William Provost

- An Historical Account of the Expedition against the Ohio Indians, in the Year MDCCLXIV, under the Command of Henry Bouquet, Esq. London: T. Jefferies, 1766. 1st English edn. 4to. [xvii], 71 pp. Map, 2 plans, 2 plates. Sl foxing. Half calf, sl worn. Anon.
(Bookpress) **$3,500 [≈ £1,822]**

Smollett, Tobias

- The Adventures of Ferdinand Count Fathom. By the Author of Roderick Random. London: 1753. 1st edn. Correct 1st edn, with 'W. Johnston' not 'T. Johnson' in imprint. 2 vols in one. 12mo. [ii], viii,262; [ii],315 pp. Lacks final blank vol 1. Contemp calf, rebacked, sm repr.
(Finch) **£300 [≈ $575]**

- The History and Adventures of an Atom. London: Robinson & Roberts, 1769. 1st edn. 2nd issue, with date crrctd from 1749 to 1769. 2 vols. 12mo. viii,227; [iv],190 pp. Contemp calf, rebacked, minor tip & edge wear. Anon.
(Bookpress) **$600 [≈ £312]**

- The Expedition of Humphry Clinker. By the Author of Roderick Random. Dublin: J. Exshaw, 1781. 3rd Dublin edn. 2 vols. 8vo. Contemp sheep, crnrs & hd of spines worn. Anon.
(Buccleuch) **£75 [≈ $143]**

- The Expedition of Humphry Clinker. London: for J. Wren, & W. Hodges, 1795. 2 vols. 12mo. Contemp sheep, red labels, spine ends worn, splits in hinges.
(Jarndyce) **£40 [≈ $76]**

- The Adventures of Peregrine Pickle ... London: for the author, & sold by D. Wilson, 1751. 1st edn. 4 vols. 12mo. Leaf L12 in vol 3 a cancel as usual. Contemp calf, backstrips relaid, vol 4 not quite uniform. Anon.
(Bickersteth) **£325 [≈ $623]**

- The Adventures of Peregrine Pickle. In which are included, Memoirs of a Lady of Quality. The Seventh Edition. London: Strahan, Rivington ..., 1784. 4 vols. 12mo. Frontises. 4 pp torn without loss. Contemp sheep, spine ends worn.
(Jarndyce) **£50 [≈ $95]**

- Plays and Poems ... With Memoirs of the Life and Writings of the Author. London: for T. Evans, & R. Baldwin, 1777. 1st edn. 8vo. [iv], xlvii, [ii], 4-272 pp. Half-title. Vignette port on title. Some foxing. Contemp calf, rubbed, spine ends worn, label defective.
(Burmester) **£110 [≈ $211]**

- Plays and Poems ... With Memoirs of the Life

and Writings of the Author. London: Evans &
Baldwin, 1777. 1st coll edn. Sm 8vo. Title
vignette. Half-title. Later half calf, crnrs
worn.   *(Buccleuch)* **£120 [≈ $230]**
- The Regicide: or, James the First, of
Scotland. A Tragedy. By the Author of
Roderick Random. London: for Osborn &
Millar, 1749. 1st edn. 19th c calf gilt by
Riviere. a.e.g., rebacked to style.
                       (Jarndyce) **£250 [≈ $479]**
- The Adventures of Roderick Random ...
Eighth Edition. London: Strahan ..., 1780. 2
vols. 12mo. xvi,280; xii,316 pp. Some
browning of page edges. Contemp calf,
rubbed, old tape marks at hd of spines. Anon.
                            (Clark) **£50 [≈ $95]**
- The Adventures of Roderick Random. Phila:
Mathew Carey, 1794. 1st Amer edn. 2 vols.
12mo. [iii],viii, 227,[7]; [ii],255 pp. Contemp
calf, v sl rubbed. *(Bookpress)* **£325 [≈ £169]**
- Travels through France and Italy ... London:
Baldwin, 1766. 1st edn. 2 vols. 8vo. 372; 296
pp. Lacks half-titles. Orig calf, rebacked to
style.   *(Frew Mackenzie)* **£260 [≈ $499]**
- Travels through France and Italy. London:
for R. Baldwin, 1766. 1st edn. 2 vols. Demy
8vo. Half-titles. Sl browning, few faint signs
of age. Mod calf gilt, mor labels.
                            (Ash) **£250 [≈ $479]**

Smyth, James Carmichael
- The Effects of the Nitrous Vapour in
Preventing and Destroying Contagion ...
made chiefly by the Surgeons of His Majesty's
Navy ... with an Introduction ... on Jail or
Hospital Fever ... Phila: Dobson, 1799. 8vo.
174 pp. Fldg table. Foxed. Early sheep,
rebacked.   *(Goodrich)* **$165 [≈ £85]**

Smyth, John Ferdinand Dalziel
- A Tour in the United States of America ...
London: G. Robinson ..., 1784. 1st edn. 2
vols. 8vo. x, [xiv],400; [xii], 455,[1] pp.
Contemp speckled calf, some spine wear,
lacks 1 label.   *(Bookpress)* **$1,600 [≈ £833]**

Snow, T. (pseud.)
- Arts Improvement: or Choice Experiments
and Observations in Building, Husbandry,
Gardening, Mechaniks, Chimistry, Painting,
Japanning ... By T.S. London: for D. Brown,
1703. 8vo. Contemp sheep, lacks label, hinges
reinforced.
                  (Dramatis Personae) **$1,200 [≈ £625]**

Soane, Sir John
- Plans, Elevations and Sections of Buildings ...
London: Taylor, 1788. 1st edn. Lge folio.
[vi],11,[2] pp, 16 ff. 47 plates. Sl foxing. Later
half calf.   *(Bookpress)* **$3,850 [≈ £2,005]**

Soave, Pietro, Polano (pseudonym)
- See Sarpi, Paolo.

Solis y Rivadeneyra, Antonio de
- The History of the Conquest of Mexico by
the Spaniards. Done into English ... by
Thomas Townsend. London: Woodward ...,
1724. 1st edn in English. Folio. [xviii],163,
252, 152 pp. Port, 8 maps & plates. Contemp
calf, extremities sl rubbed, jnts starting.
                  (Frew Mackenzie) **£850 [≈ $1,631]**
- The History of the Conquest of Mexico by
the Spaniards. Translated by Thomas
Townsend. London: 1753. 3rd English edn. 2
vols. 8vo. xvi, 383; x,386 pp. 2 fldg maps, 6
fldg plates (of 7?, see Sabin). Repr to frontis
reverse. Some browning, mostly marginal.
Rec bds.   *(Zwisohn)* **$400 [≈ £208]**

Some ...
- Some Observations on the Militia; with the
Sketch of a Plan for the Reform of it. London:
T. & J. Egerton, 1785. Half-title, 41 pp.
                     (C.R. Johnson) **£35 [≈ $67]**
- Some of the Quakers Principles and
Doctrines ... see Bugg, Francis.
- Some Thoughts Concerning Education ... see
Locke, John.
- Some Thoughts on the Present State of our
Trade to India. By a Merchant of London.
London: for M. Cooper, 1754. 1st edn. 4to.
Some foxing. Sm hole in last few ff.
Disbound. Cloth case.
                        (Ximenes) **$400 [≈ £208]**

Somers, John, Lord
- A Letter, ballancing the Necessity of Keeping
a Land-Force in Times of Peace: with the
Dangers that may follow on it. N.p.: Printed
in the Year 1697. 16 pp. Lacks intl blank.
Disbound. Wing S.4642.
                        (Jarndyce) **£55 [≈ $105]**
- The Security of Englishmen's Lives: or, the
Trust, Power and Duty of Grand Juries of
England Explained ... First printed in the
Year 1681 ... London: for J. Almon, 1766.
2nd edn. 8vo. 112 pp. Stitched as issued.
                        (Young's) **£45 [≈ $86]**

Somervile, William
- The Chace. A Poem. London: for G. Hawkins, 1735. 1st 8vo edn. 8vo. [xx],131 pp. Contemp calf, elab gilt border, gilt panelled spine, mrbld endpapers, sl worn.
(Young's) £85 [≈ $163]
- The Chase, a Poem: to which is added Hobbinol, or the Rural Games ... Birmingham: Robert Martin, 1767. Lge 8vo. 199 pp. Title sl browned. Contemp calf, mor label, extremities rubbed, short split in upper hinge. *(Claude Cox)* £55 [≈ $105]

Somerville, Thomas
- The History of Political Transactions, and of Parties, from the Restoration of Charles the Second to the Death of King William. London: for A. Strahan, 1792. 1st edn. 4to. xxiii, 599, [13],1 errata pp. Half-title. Occas spotting. Old qtr cloth, uncut, rebacked.
(Young's) £70 [≈ $134]

Somner, William
- A Treatise of Gavelkind, both name and Thing ... added, The Life of the Author, newly revis'd ... London: for F. Gyles ..., 1726. 2nd edn. Sm 4to. [xii],216,[8] pp. Frontis. *(Hollett)* £150 [≈ $287]

Sondes, Sir George
- Authentic Memorials of Remarkable Occurrences and Affecting Calamities in the Family of Sir George Sondes, Bart. In Two Parts ... Evesham: J. Agg ..., [ca 1790]. 12mo. 201 pp, advt leaf. Orig calf, rebacked, most of backstrip relaid. *(Bickersteth)* £68 [≈ $130]

The Sorrows of Werter ...
- See Goethe, Johann Wolfgang von.

Souligne, - de
- The Desolation of France Demonstrated ... By a Person of Quality, a Native of France. London: for John Salisbury, 1697. 1st edn. 8vo. [xiv], 280 pp. Sl browned. Contemp calf, rebacked & recrnrd, worn. Wing S.4718. Anon. *(Pickering)* $700 [≈ £364]

Southerne, Thomas
- The Works. London: J. Tonson ..., 1721. 1st coll edn. 2 vols. 12mo. Later cloth.
(Bookpress) $125 [≈ £65]

Southey, Robert
- Letters written during a Short Residence in Spain and Portugal. Second Edition. Bristol:

Biggs & Cottle, 1799. Contemp calf, red label. *(C.R. Johnson)* £150 [≈ $287]
- Letters written during a Short residence in Spain and Portugal. Second Edition. Bristol: Biggs & Cottle, 1799. 8vo. xiv, [ii], 483 pp, inc advt leaf. Lacks half-title. Sm crnr torn from Ff2. New half calf. Inscrbd "from the author" in Southey's hand.
(Rankin) £150 [≈ $287]
- Poems. Bristol: 1797-99. 1st edn of both vols. 2 vols. Sm 8vo. [viii],220, advt leaf; [vi], 232 pp. Mottled calf gilt, a.e.g., gilt spines, mor labels, by Bedford.
(Bickersteth) £520 [≈ $998]

Sowerby, J.
- Coloured Figures of English Fungi or Mushrooms. London: 1797-1803. 3 vols in one. Folio. 400 hand cold plates. Contemp calf gilt, rather worn. Without the unfinished supplement published in 1809-15 with 40 plates.
(Wheldon & Wesley) £2,750 [≈ $5,279]

Spallanzani, Lazzaro
- Dissertations relative to the Natural History of Animals and Vegetables. Translated from the Italian. A New Edition, Corrected and Enlarged. London: Murray, 1789. 2nd English edn. 2 vols. 8vo. 3 fldg plates. 1st vol sl spotted. Rec calf antique.
(Bickersteth) £225 [≈ $431]
- Travels in the Two Sicilies and Some Parts of the Apennines ... London: 1798. 4 vols. 8vo. 11 plates. Binder's cloth.
(Wheldon & Wesley) £300 [≈ $575]

Sparrman, Anders
- A Voyage to the Cape of Good Hope ... Second Edition, Corrected. London: Robinson, 1786. 2 vols. 4to. Advt leaf. Frontis (sm marg repr), map, 9 plates (erased lib stamp on verso of 1 plate). Occas sl stains. Contemp calf, rebacked & recrnrd.
(Hannas) £300 [≈ $575]
- A Voyage to the Cape of Good Hope ... Second Edition, Corrected. London: 1786. 2 vols. 4to. Frontis, map, 9 plates. Some foxing, mainly at ends, few marg tears. Orig bds, uncut, rebacked, trifle worn.
(Wheldon & Wesley) £325 [≈ $623]

Sparrow, John
- A Mechanical Dissertation upon the Lues Venerea. Proving not only the possibility, but certainty of curing that Disease ... By J.S. Surgeon. London: Richard King ..., 1731. 1st

edn. 43,[1] pp. Wraps (sl worn).
(Wreden) **$249.50 [≈ £130]**

Spectacle de la Nature ...
- See Pluche, Noel Antoine.

The Spectator ...
- See Addison, Joseph & Steele, Richard.

Speechly, William
- A Treatise on the Culture of the Pine Apple and the Management of the Hot-House ... York: 1779. 1st edn. Roy 8vo. xvii,[v],186 pp. Subscribers 5 pp. 2 plates. Sl soiling, lib b'plate. Cloth.
(Wheldon & Wesley) **£180 [≈ $345]**
- A Treatise on the Culture of the Vine ... New Hints on the Formation of Vineyards in England ... Dublin: 1791. 1st Dublin edn. 8vo. xxi,[i blank],307,[iv misbound after p 306] pp. 5 plates (1 fldg with sm marg tear). Contemp calf, gilt spine, mor label.
(Finch) **£180 [≈ $345]**

Speed, John
- The History of Great Britaine ... London: George Humble, 1623. 2nd edn, rvsd & enlgd. 4to. [6],[iv], 155-(924), [xliv] pp. Engvd title, plates, figs & ornaments. Some marks & minor reprs. Later Cambridge calf, rebacked.
(Ash) **£400 [≈ $767]**

Spelman, Sir Henry
- De non temerandis Ecclesiis, Churches not to be Violated. A Tract of the Rights and respects due unto Churches ... Oxford: H. Hall, for Amos Curteyn, 1668. 4th edn. 8vo. [xiv], 128 pp. Lacks endpapers. Old sheep. Wing S.4922.
(Young's) **£90 [≈ $172]**
- The History and Fate of Sacrilege, Discover'd by Examples ... London: John Hartley, 1698. 1st edn. 8vo. [viii],292,40 pp. Contemp calf, worn. Wing S.4927.
(Clark) **£40 [≈ $76]**
- The Larger Treatise concerning Tithes ... together with some other Tracts of the same Author ... Published by Jer: Stephens ... London: for Philemon Stephens, 1647. 1st edn. 4to. [xl],189, [i],27, [xxxviii] pp. Outer marg cropped. Disbound. Wing S.4928 & 4917.
(Clark) **£45 [≈ $86]**
- Villare Anglicum: or A View of the Townes of England. Collected by the appointment of Sir Henry Spelman. London: R. Hodgkinsonne, 1656. 1st edn. Sm 4to. Contemp calf, rubbed, jnts cracked. Wing S.4932.
(Frew Mackenzie) **£120 [≈ $230]**

Spence, Joseph
- A Parallel in the manner of Plutarch ... Strawberry Hill: ptd by William Robinson, 1758. One of 700. 8vo. Blank inner gutter of title reprd. Early 19th c half calf.
(Waterfield's) **£200 [≈ $383]**
- A Parallel; in the manner of Plutarch ... Strawberry Hill: ptd by William Robinson ..., 1758. 1st edn. One of 700. 8vo. 104 pp. Vignette on title. Occas sl foxing. Early 19th c calf, backstrip sometime relaid.
(Sotheran's) **£200 [≈ $383]**
- Polymetis: or, an Enquiry Concerning the Agreement between the Works of the Roman Poets, and the Remains of the Antient Artists ... London: Dodsley, 1747. 1st edn. Folio. xii, 362 pp. 41 plates, text engvs. Ex-lib. Some age browning, 1 marg tear. Contemp calf, rebacked, sl worn.
(Bernett) **$575 [≈ £299]**
- Polymetis or, an Enquiry Concerning the Agreement between the Works of the Roman Poets and the Remains of the Antient Artists ... London: Dodsley, 1747. Folio. Frontis port, 41 plates. Contemp calf, jnts cracked, some wear at crnrs.
(Waterfield's) **£250 [≈ $479]**
- Polymetis: or, An Enquiry concerning the Agreement between the Works of the Roman Poets, and the Remains of the Antient Artists ... London: 1755. 2nd edn. Folio. vi,361,[1] pp. Port, 41 plates, 16 text engvs. 3 sm reprs, few sm marks. Contemp calf, rebacked, reprd.
(Bow Windows) **£340 [≈ $652]**

Spencer, Benjamin
- Chrysomeson, a Golden Meane: or, a Middle Way for Christians to walk by ... London: for the author & sold by William Hope, 1659. Folio. [viii],289,[ii] pp. Frontis (rather cropped), plate explanation leaf (laid down). Old calf, reprd & rebacked. Wing S.4944.
(Hollett) **£150 [≈ $287]**

Spencer, John
- A Discourse concerning Prodigies: wherein the Vanity of Presages by them is reprehended ... Second Edition ... added a Short Treatise concerning Vulgar Prophecies. London: 1665. 8vo. [xxxii],408, [viii], 136,[6] pp. 18th c calf, rebacked. Wing S.4948.
(Finch) **£130 [≈ $249]**
- A Discourse concerning Prodigies ... The Second Edition Corrected and Enlarged ... London: J. Field for Will. Graves, 1665. 2 parts in one vol. Sm 8vo. [32],408], 136,[16] pp. Contemp calf, sl rubbed. Wing S.4948.
(Karmiole) **£200 [≈ $104]**

Spencer, John
- Hermes or the Acarian Shepherds: a Poem in Sixteen Books. Newcastle upon Tyne: T. Saint, 1782. 2 vols in one. Some staining & fraying on last 2 ff. Contemp calf, worn, rebacked.   *(Waterfield's)* **£185 [≈ $355]**

Spencer, Joshua
- Thoughts on an Union. Dublin: for William Jones, 1798. 3rd edn. 8vo. 35 pp. Wraps.
(Young's) **£38 [≈ $72]**

Spenser, Edmund
- The Faerie Queen. A New Edition, with Notes ... by Ralph Church. London: for the author by William Faden, 1758. 4 vols. 8vo. Errata leaf in each vol. Subscribers vol 4. Occas sl browning. Contemp calf, hinges of vol 2 cracked but secure, lacks labels.
(Claude Cox) **£55 [≈ $105]**

Spinckes, Nathaniel
- No Reason for Restoring the Prayers and Directions of Edward VI's Liturgy. By a Non-Juror. London: for John Morphew, [1717]. Undated title-page. Disbound. Anon.
(Waterfield's) **£45 [≈ $86]**
- No Sufficient Reason for Restoring the Prayers and Directions of King Edward the Sixth's First Liturgy. Part 1. By a Non-Juror. London: for John Morphew, 1718. Disbound. Anon.   *(Waterfield's)* **£45 [≈ $86]**

Spirit ...
- The Spirit of the Public Journals for 1797 ... Volume I. The Second Edition. London: for James Ridgway, 1799. Rec v nasty half calf.
(Jarndyce) **£25 [≈ $47]**

The Sportsman's Dictionary ...
- The Sportsman's Dictionary. Compiled by Experienced Gentlemen ..,. for Town and Country. London: for Fielding & Walker, 1778. 1st edn. Demy 4to. viii,[472] pp. Frontis, 15 plates. A few marks & creases. Old calf, rebacked.   *(Ash)* **£250 [≈ $479]**
- The Sportsman's Dictionary; or, the Gentleman's Companion for Town and Country ... Fourth Edition. London: Robinson, 1792. 4to. Frontis, 16 plates. Sm damp stain in lower margs. Contemp half calf & mrbld bds, rebacked.
(Sotheran's) **£198 [≈ $380]**

Spotswood, John
- The History of the Church of Scotland ...

London: J. Flesher for R. Royston, 1655. 1st edn. Folio. [xxii],546, [2],[10],[2 advt] pp. 2 ports. New linen backed bds. Wing S.5022.
(Young's) **£120 [≈ $230]**

Spottiswood, John
- An Introduction to the Knowledge of the Stile of Writs, Simple and Compound, made use of in Scotland ... Fifth Edition. Edinburgh: Kincaid & Bell ..., 1765. 12mo. [iv],587,[21] pp. Minor staining at ends. Contemp calf.   *(Clark)* **£35 [≈ $67]**

Sprat, Thomas
- The History of the Royal Society of London ... Third Edition Corrected. London: Knapton ..., 1722. Sm 4to. [xvi],438 pp. Frontis with imprimatur on recto, 2 fldg plates. Title & prelims sl fingered. Period panelled calf, sl worn.
(Rankin) **£125 [≈ $239]**
- A True Account and Declaration of the Horrid Conspiracy against the late King ... In the Savoy: Thomas Newcomb ..., 1685. 1st edn. 2 parts in one. Folio. [vi],167, [iii], 141 pp. Orig sheep, gilt spine reprd. Wing S.5065. Anon.   *(Vanbrugh)* **£275 [≈ $527]**
- A True Account and Declaration of the Horrid Conspiracy against the late King ... In the Savoy: Thomas Newcomb, 1685. 2nd edn. Folio. [vi],141 pp. Fldg plate of Rye House. Old calf, rebacked. Wing S.5065. Anon.   *(Young's)* **£80 [≈ $153]**

Squire, Francis
- A Pastoral Epistle on Occasion of the Present Unnatural Rebellion ... London: for John Whiston, 1746. Half-title. Sl later half calf, spine chipped at hd, split in hinge.
(Jarndyce) **£45 [≈ $86]**

Stafford, Richard
- A Clear Apology and Just Defence of Richard Stafford for Himself ... London: Printed in the Year 1690. 1st edn. 4to. [iv], 36 pp. Outer ff sl dusty, lib stamp title verso. Disbound. Wing S.5110.   *(Clark)* **£170 [≈ $326]**

Stanhope, Eugenia
- The Deportment of a Married Life ... London: Mason, 1798. 2nd edn. 8vo. [iii]-xi, 281 pp. Lacks 1st & last blanks. Contemp half calf, uncut, rubbed, some staining. Anon.
(Bookpress) **$325 [≈ £169]**

State ...
- The State of the Trade and Manufactory of

iron in Great-Britain Considered. [London]: 1750. 1st edn. 8vo. 15 pp. Disbound.
(Bookpress) **$650 [≈ £338]**

Staunton, Sir George

- An Authentic Account of an Embassy from the King of Great Britain to the Emperor of China ... taken from the Papers of the Earl of Macartney. Dublin: 1798. 2 vols. 8vo. xv, 449; xviii, 430 pp. 26 plates. Name cut from title. Contemp calf.   *(Lewis)* **£320 [≈ $614]**

Stearns, Charles

- The Ladies Philosophy of Love, a Poem in Four Cantos written in 1774 and now First Published according to Act of Congress. Leominster, Mass.: John Prentiss & Co. for the author, 1797. 4to. Sl browned. 1 leaf torn (no loss). Disbound.
(Waterfield's) **£200 [≈ $383]**

Stedman, Charles

- The History of the Origin, Progress, and Termination of the American War ... London: for the author ..., 1794. 2 vols. Lge 4to. xv, [1],399; xv,[1], 449,[13], 502 pp. 15 maps & plans (11 fldg). V occas sl foxing. Orig bds, untrimmed, later paper labels.
(Reese) **$4,500 [≈ £2,343]**

Steele, Elizabeth

- The Memoirs of Mrs. Sophia Baddeley, Late of Drury Lane Theatre. London: for the author, 1787. 1st edn. 6 vols. Sm 8vo. Orig bds, rebacked.
(Dramatis Personae) **$525 [≈ £273]**

Steele, Sir Richard

- The Christian Hero: an Argument proving that no Principles but those of Religion are sufficient to make a Great Man. The Fifth Edition. London: for J.T., 1711. 12mo. [xiv], 68 pp. Lacks half-title. Contemp calf, rubbed.
(Lamb) **£25 [≈ $47]**
- The Conscious Lovers. A Comedy ... London: Tonson, 1723. 1st edn. Lge 8vo. Later half calf, jnts worn, spine chipped.
(Dramatis Personae) **$125 [≈ £65]**
- The Importance of Dunkirk Consider'd ... London: for A. Baldwin, 1713. 2nd edn. 8vo. 40 pp. New bds.   *(Young's)* **£38 [≈ $72]**
- The Plebeians. By a Member of the House of Commons. The Sixth Edition. London: for S. Popping, 1719. 1st coll edn. 8vo. 67,[5] pp. Old wraps. Anon.   *(Burmester)* **£75 [≈ $143]**
- The Romish Ecclesiastical History of Late

Years. London: for J. Roberts, 1714. 1st edn. 8vo. [xiv],xii,vi, 167,1 errata pp. Frontis. F8, intended for cancellation, here present. 18th c calf, sometime rebacked.
(Young's) **£60 [≈ $115]**
- The Romish Ecclesiastical History of late Years. London: for J. Roberts, 1714. 8vo. F8, intended for cancellation, here present. Frontis. Contemp calf, front jnt cracking.
(Waterfield's) **£90 [≈ $172]**
- See also under Wray, Mary.

Stemmata Chicheleana ...

- See Buckler, Benjamin.

Stennett, Joseph

- God's Awful Summons to a Sinful Nation considered; In a Sermon ... in Commemoration of the Dreadful Storm of Wind ... London: for Aaron ward, 1738. 1st edn. 8vo. vii,48 pp. Disbound.
(Young's) **£46 [≈ $88]**

Stennett, Samuel

- Discourses on Personal Religion ... Second Edition. London: R. Hett, 1772. 2 vols. viii, 310; iv, 340 pp. Some ff stained from pressed flowers. Contemp calf, sl worn & scuffed.
(Wreden) **$50 [≈ £26]**

Sterling, John

- A System of Rhetorick, in a Method entirely new ... added, the Art of Rhetorick made easy ... by John Holmes. Dublin: John Exshaw, 1786. 12mo. viii,84 pp. Contemp sheep, sl worm damage.   *(Burmester)* **£75 [≈ $143]**

Sterne, Laurence

- The Beauties of Sterne ... New Edition. London: T. Davies ..., 1782. Half-title, 232 pp, advt leaf. Contemp calf.
(C.R. Johnson) **£40 [≈ $76]**
- The Beauties of Sterne ... Thirteenth Edition. London: Kearsley ..., 1799. 8vo. xxiv, 324 pp. Port frontis, 6 plates (dated 1793). 19th c half calf, spine rubbed.   *(Clark)* **£35 [≈ $67]**
- Letters of the late Rev. Mr. Laurence Sterne ... Memoirs of his Life and Family ... London: for T. Becket ..., 1775. 1st edn. 3 vols in one. Sm 8vo. Frontis port in vol 1. Contemp half calf, flat spine, mor label, edges of bds sl rubbed.   *(Finch)* **£350 [≈ $671]**
- Letters from Yorick to Eliza. A New Edition. London: for G. Kearsley, 1775. 2nd English edn. Sm 8vo. 104 pp, inc half-title. Occas v sl marg browning. Contemp tree calf, new label.

Anon. *(Rankin)* £50 [≈ $95]
- Letters from Yorick to Eliza, and Sterne's Letters to his Friends on Various Occasions. To which is added, His Watchcoat. Dublin: R. Steuart ..., 1776. 12mo. Half-title ('in two volumes'). Few ff spotted. 1 leaf torn (no loss). Contemp sheep, rebacked.
(Ximenes) $250 [≈ £130]
- Letters supposed to have been written by Yorick and Eliza ... see Combe, William.
- Original Letters of the late Reverend Mr. Laurence Sterne; never before Published. London: ptd at the Logographic Press ..., 1788. 1st edn. 12mo. Contemp speckled calf, gilt spine, red & green labels, jnts rubbed. Spurious fabrication by William Combe.
(Jarndyce) £90 [≈ $172]
- The Posthumous Works ... see Griffith, Richard.
- A Sentimental Journey through France and Italy. By Mr. Yorick. London: Becket & De Hondt, 1768. 1st edn. 2 vols. 12mo. xx,203; [4], 208 pp. Half-titles. 18th c calf gilt, hinges rubbed. Anon.
(Karmiole) $1,250 [≈ £651]
- A Sentimental Journey through France and Italy. By Mr. Yorick. The Second Edition. London: Beckett & De Hondt, 1768. 2 vols. Half-titles. Contemp calf, sl rubbed, hinges weakening. *(Jarndyce)* £120 [≈ $230]
- A Sentimental Journey through France and Italy. A New Edition. London: Strahan, Cadell ..., 1780. 12mo. [ii],340 pp. Lacks half-title. Contemp tree calf, lower jnt sl cracked. Anon. *(Burmester)* £50 [≈ $95]
- A Sentimental Journey through France and Italy. By Mr. Yorick. London: for J. Davies, T. Smith, N. Taylor, & W. Thompson, 1784. 4 parts, each with half-title, continuously paginated. 19th c half calf, hinges rubbed.
(Jarndyce) £80 [≈ $153]
- A Sentimental Journey through France and Italy. By Mr. Yorick. New Edition. London: Strahan for J. Johnson ..., 1790. 12mo. 251 pp. Half-title. 2 plates. Contemp calf style calf, orig backstrip laid down. Anon.
(Gough) £55 [≈ $105]
- A Sentimental Journey through France and Italy ... London: Cadell, 1794. 4 vols in one (inc Hall-Stevenson's continuation). 12mo. [ii], 311 pp. Contemp continental blue half calf, gilt spine, sm hole in spine, v sl rubbed. Anon. *(Burmester)* £90 [≈ $172]
- The Sermons of Mr. Yorick. The Tenth Edition. N.p.: ptd in the year, 1770. A pirated edn. 4 vols in 2. 8vo. Contemp calf, gilt

spines, labels (sl chipped), minimally worn.
(Sanders) £75 [≈ $143]
- The Sermons of Mr. Yorick. A New Edition. London: Dodsley, 1784. 6 vols. 8vo. Final advt leaf vol 6. Port frontis. Contemp calf, gilt rubbed, lacks numbering pieces, 2 jnts cracked. *(Clark)* £65 [≈ $124]
- The Works ... Dublin: Thomas Armitage, 1774. 2nd Irish coll edn. 7 vols. 12mo. Engvd titles, port in vol 1, frontises in 1 & 2. Final blank in vol 1. Occas sl marks. Contemp calf, some spines sl worn.
(Burmester) £180 [≈ $345]
- The Works ... London: Dodsley, 1793. 10 vols. 8vo. Contemp tree calf, gilt spines, labels, reprs to sev spine ends, gilt a little dull.
(Spelman) £360 [≈ $691]

Stevens, George Alexander
- A Lecture on Heads ... With Twenty-Four Heads by Nesbit, from Designs by Thurston. London: Bensley, 1799. 1st illust edn. Sm 8vo. Frontis. Foredges sl stained. Later bds.
(Dramatis Personae) $100 [≈ £52]
- Songs, Comic, and Satyrical.. Oxford: for the author ..., 1772. 1st edn. 12mo. 16,[ii], 247, [i] pp. Fldg frontis, 1 plate & w'engv in text. Occas sl foxing & pale marg damp staining at end. Late Victorian polished calf gilt, by Jenkins, jnts rubbed.
(Sotheran's) £285 [≈ $547]

Stevens, Sacheverell
- Miscellaneous Remarks made upon the Spot, in a late Tour through France, Italy, Germany and Holland ... London: S. Hooper, 1756. 8vo. [iv], 403,[i] pp. 7 plates (6 fldg). Occas sl spotting. Rec half calf.
(Frew Mackenzie) £80 [≈ $153]

Stewart, James
- Plocacosmos: or The Whole Art of Hair Dressing ... London: the author, 1782. 1st edn. Lge 8vo. [vi],435 pp. Frontis, 10 plates. Orig bds, uncut, spine chipped & cracked.
(Bookpress) $3,800 [≈ £1,979]

Stewart, Sir James
- The Index or Abridgement of the Acts of Parliament and Convention, from ... 1424 to ... 1707 ... Edinburgh: George Mossman, 1707. 12mo. [xii],297,[iii] pp. Final blank leaf. Minor marg browning. Contemp calf, rubbed, 1 hinge reprd. *(Clark)* £50 [≈ $95]

Stillingfleet, Benjamin

- An Essay on Conversation. London: for J. Gilliver & J. Clarke, 1737. Folio. Title sl foxed. Cut close at top affecting a few page numbers. Disbound.
(Waterfield's) **£105 [≈ $201]**

- Miscellaneous Tracts relating to Natural History, Husbandry, and Physick. Translated from the Latin ... with Notes. London: 1759. 1st edn. 8vo. xxx,[1],230 pp. Sl water stain at ends. Half calf, trifle used.
(Wheldon & Wesley) **£200 [≈ $383]**

- Miscellaneous Tracts relating to Natural History, Husbandry, and Physick ... The Second Edition ... London: 1762. 8vo. xxxi, 391 pp. Lib stamp on title. 11 plates. Contemp calf, rebacked. Author's pres copy.
(Goodrich) **$145 [≈ £75]**

- See also Linnaeus, C.

Stillingfleet, Edward

- The Grand Question, concerning the Bishops Right to Vote in Parliament in Cases Capital ... London: for M.P., & sold by Richard Rumball ..., 1680. 1st edn. 8vo. [iv],188 pp. New calf. Wing S.5594. Anon.
(Young's) **£95 [≈ $182]**

- Origines Britannicae, or, the Antiquities of the British Churches ... London: M. Flesher for Henry Mortlock, 1685. 1st edn. Folio. xxiii, [vi],[2 advt], 364 pp. Orig calf, front jnt cracked. Wing S.5615.
(Young's) **£75 [≈ $143]**

- Origines Britannicae, or the Antiquities of the British Churches ... London: M. Flesher for Henry Mortlock, 1685. 1st edn. Folio. [2],lxxiii, [8],364 pp. Contemp calf, worn but sound. Wing S.5615.
(Fenning) **£58.50 [≈ $113]**

- Sermons on Several Occasions. To which is added a Discourse concerning the True Reason of the Sufferings of Christ ... London: R. White for Henry Mortlock, 1673. Sm folio. [8], [16],384 pp. Title worn & mtd. Few sm marg holes & stains. 18th c half calf, worn. Wing S.5666.
(Humber) **£55 [≈ $105]**

- The Unreasonableness of Separation ... London: T.N. for Henry Mortlock, 1681. 1st edn. 4to. [1],[94], [8],450 pp. Minor blemishes. 18th c polished calf, sl rubbed. Wing S.5675.
(Humber) **£65 [≈ $124]**

Stirling, John

- A System of Rhetorick ... added, The Art of Rhetorick made Easy ... By John Holmes. Dublin: John Exshaw, 1786. Sl spotted & browned. Contemp sheep, spine chipped, jnts splitting.
(Jarndyce) **£140 [≈ $268]**

Stirling, Sir William Alexander, Earl of.

- See Alexander, Sir William, Earl of Stirling.

Stoddart, John

- A Brief Journal of the Life, Travels, and Labours of Love in the Work of the Ministry ... Thomas Wilson, who departed this Life ... 20th third Month, 1725. Dublin: Sam Fuller, 1728. 8vo. 98,2 advt pp. Contemp calf, cottage tooled. Anon.
(Emerald Isle) **£85 [≈ $163]**

Stoerck, Anthony

- An Essay on the Use and Effects of the Root of the Colchicum Autumnale, or Meadow Saffron ... with an Appendix concerning the Cicuta, or Hemlock ... London: Becket & De Hondt, 1764. 1st edn in English. 8vo. 47 pp. Fldg frontis. Later mor backed bds.
(Burmester) **£170 [≈ $326]**

Stone, Thomas

- An Essay on Agriculture, with a View to Inform Gentlemen of Landed Property, whether their Estates are managed to the Greatest Advantage. Lynn: W. Whittingham, 1785. 261 pp. Contemp qtr calf, mrbld bds. Matthew Boulton's copy.
(C.R. Johnson) **£160 [≈ $307]**

Stork, William

- A Description of East Florida, with a Journal, kept by John Bartram of Philadelphia ... London: 1769. 3rd edn, enlgd with sl altered title. 4to. [2],viii, 40,[2], xii,35 pp. Errata. Fldg frontis map (sm tears at folds), 2 fldg plans. Used. Later three qtr mor, worn. Anon.
(Reese) **$3,000 [≈ £1,562]**

Stout, Benjamin

- Narrative of the Loss of the Ship Hercules, commanded by Captain Benjamin Stout, on the Coast of Caffraria, the 16th of June, 1796 ... Travels through the Southern Deserts of Africa ... Cape of Good Hope. London: Johnson, 1798. 1st edn. 8vo. Some marks. Disbound.
(Ximenes) **$400 [≈ £208]**

Stow, John

- The Annales, or Generall Chronicle of England ... Continued ... by Edmond Howes. London: impensis Thomae Adams, 1615. Folio. [xx], 988, [30] pp. W'cut title. Early 19th c calf bds, rebacked, fine. STC 23338.
(Vanbrugh) **£575 [≈ $1,103]**

- Annales, or, A Generall Chronicle of England ... Continued ... by Edmund Howes. London: impensis Richard Meighen, 1631 (colophon: 1632). Folio. Engvd title (marg sl torn). 18th c speckled calf, gilt spine, hinges weakening. STC 23340.   *(Jarndyce)* **£650 [≃ $1,247]**
- A Summarie of the Chronicles of England ... London: Iohn Harison, 1604. 16mo. [xxx], 459, [30] pp. W'cut title border & intls. Errata leaf. 1 closed tear. Old calf, rubbed, upper jnt split but steady on cords. STC 23329.
          (Sotheran's) **£248 [≃ $476]**
- A Survay of London ... London: John Windet, 1603. 2nd edn. Sm 4to. Errata leaf & blank leaf at end. Sl marg staining. Contemp limp vellum, soiled, sl surface damage, lacks ties. STC 23343.   *(Georges)* **£350 [≃ $671]**
- A Survey of London. London: John Windet, 1603. 2nd edn. 4to. [viii],579,[2] pp. Occas foxing. Later calf. *(Bookpress)* **$475 [≃ £247]**

Stretser, Thomas
- A New Description of Merryland ... Tenth Edition. London: for E. Curll, 1742. 8vo. Few sm marg reprs. Green half mor gilt, a.e.g., by Bedford. Anon.
          (Ximenes) **$1,500 [≃ £781]**

Strother, Edward
- Criticon Febrium: or, a Critical Essay on Fevers ... London: Rivington, 1716. 1st edn. 8vo. [xii],211,[1] pp. Contemp calf, hinges cracked.   *(Bookpress)* **$375 [≃ £195]**
- An Essay on Sickness and Health. London: 1725. 1st edn. 8vo. lxviii,463,[1] pp. Contemp calf, split in lower hinge. The Plesch copy.   *(Hemlock)* **$375 [≃ £195]**
- Pharmacopoeia Radcliffeana ... see Radcliffe, John.

Strutton, Richard
- A True Relation of the Cruelties and Barbarities of the French, upon the English Prisoners of War ... London: Baldwin, 1690. Only edn. 4to. [iv],57,[i] pp. Lacks final advt leaf. Some wear & tear. Lib stamp title verso. Disbound. Wing S.6018.
          (Clark) **£200 [≃ $383]**

Strype, John
- Annals of the Reformation and Establishment of Religion and other various occurrences in the Church and State of England ... Third Edition, with large additions. London: Symon, 1735-38. Vols 3 & 4 2nd edn. 4 vols. Folio. Contemp calf, worn, 4 jnts cracked.

(Waterfield's) **£140 [≃ $268]**

Stuart, Andrew
- Letters to the Right Honourable Lord Mansfield ... London: printed in the Month of January 1773. 1st edn. 4to. [iv],39,63, 47,47 pp. Contemp qtr calf, rubbed.
          (Young's) **£70 [≃ $134]**
- Letters to the Rt. Hon. Lord Mansfield. London: printed in the Month of January 1773. 1st edn. 4to. [iv],39,[1], 63,[1], 47,[1], 47, [1] pp. Contemp calf, some wear hd of spine & crnrs.   *(Claude Cox)* **£80 [≃ $153]**
- Letters to the Rt. Hon. Lord Mansfield. London: printed in the Month of January 1773. 1st 8vo edn. 8vo. [ii],39,[1], 63,[1], 47, [1], 47,[1] pp. Engvd title. Later half cloth.
          (Claude Cox) **£30 [≃ $57]**

Stuart, James
- Critical Observations on the Buildings and Improvements of London. London: Dodsley, 1771. 2nd edn. 12mo. [ii],69 pp. Later qtr mor. Anon.   *(Bookpress)* **$500 [≃ £260]**

Stubbe, Henry
- The Miraculous Conformist: or An Account of several Marvailous Cures performed by the Stroaking of the Hands of Mr. Valentine Greatarick ... In a Letter to ... Robert Boyle ... Oxford: Hall, 1666. Sm 4to. 44 pp. Some blank crnrs chewed. New half calf. Wing S.6062.   *(Goodrich)* **$1,495 [≃ £778]**
- The Miraculous Conformist: or an Account of several Marvellous Cures performed by the stroking of the Hands of Mr Valentine Greatarick ... Oxford: H. Hall, 1666. 1st edn. Sm 4to. [vi],44, [2 blank] pp. Sl browned. 19th c mor gilt, a.e.g. Wing S.6062.
          (Finch) **£750 [≃ $1,439]**

Stubbes, George
- A New Adventure of Telemachus. By the Author of the Dialogue of Beauty ... London: W. Wilkins, 1731. 1st edn. 8vo. viii,56 pp. Title sl soiled & with 2 sm tears, a few other marg tears. Lib stamp. Early 19th c half calf, rebacked. Anon. *(Burmester)* **£300 [≃ $575]**

The Student's Companion ...
- The Student's Companion: being a Collection of Historical Quotations from the Best Ancient and Modern Authors ... London: for A. Millar, 1748. 12mo. Contemp calf, rubbed, hinges weakening.
          (Jarndyce) **£48 [≃ $92]**

Stukeley, William

- An Account of a large Silver Plate, of Antique Basso Relievo, Roman Workmanship, found in Derbyshire 1729 ... London: for G. Vandergucht, 1736. 4to. 11 pp. Lge fldg plate. Disbound. *(Waterfield's)* £85 [≈ $163]

Sturch, John

- A View of the Isle of Wight, in Four Letters to a Friend ... Newport, Isle of Wight: for the author, 1794. 5th edn. 12mo. 84 pp. Fldg map (somewhat soiled). Title & last few ff soiled. Orig mrbld paper wraps, cvrs worn, backstrip defective.
  (Frew Mackenzie) £30 [≈ $57]

Suckling, Sir John

- Fragmenta Aurea: a Collection of all the incomparable peeces written by Sir John Suckling ... London: for Humphrey Moseley, 1646. 1st edn. 8vo. Port. Contemp calf gilt, ft of front jnt cracked. Wing S.6126B. States of title & port noted.
  (Waterfield's) £450 [≈ $863]

Sullivan, James

- The Path to Riches. An Inquiry into the Origin and Use of Money; and into the Principles of Stocks and Banks. By a Citizen of Massachusetts. Boston: ptd by P. Edes, for I. Thomas & E.T. Andrews, 1792. 1st edn. 8vo. Few sl marg stains. Mod cloth. Anon.
  (Ximenes) $850 [≈ £442]

Sullivan, Richard Joseph

- Observations made during a Tour through Parts of England, Scotland, and Wales. In a Series of Letters. London: T. Becket, 1780. 4to. Half-title, 247,[1] pp. Early 19th c qtr calf, rebacked. Anon.
  (C.R. Johnson) £185 [≈ $355]
- A View of Nature, in Letters to a Traveller among the Alps ... London: for T. Becket ..., 1794. 1st edn. 6 vols. 8vo. Errata leaf in each vol. Occas foxing. Lacks vol 1 half-title (?). Contemp tree calf gilt, dble mor labels, some wear to spines, few labels chipped.
  (Sotheran's) £225 [≈ $431]

Suttor, William

- Dialogue between a Nobleman and a Farmer, upon the Reduction of the National Debt ... also the Distressed Condition of the Farmers in Scotland ... Edinburgh: the author, 1788. 12mo. Contemp qtr calf, red mor label.
  (Waterfield's) £350 [≈ $671]

Swan, Abraham

- A Collection of Designs in Architecture ... London: the author, [ca 1770]. 2nd edn. 2 vols in one. Folio. vi,8; iv,12 pp. 60 + 65 plates. Contemp reversed calf, worn.
  (Bookpress) $1,500 [≈ £781]

Swediaur, Francois

- Practical Observations on Venereal Complaints. New York: Samuel Campbell, 1788. 1st Amer edn. 8vo. [iv],128 pp. Browned. Contemp sheep, sl worn.
  (Bookpress) $650 [≈ £338]

Swift, Jonathan

- Directions to Servants in general ... Perth: R. Morison, 1778. 1st Scottish edn. 12mo. 19th c half calf, minor wear.
  (Ximenes) $650 [≈ £338]
- The Intelligencer. By the Author of a Tale of a Tub. The Second Edition. London: for Francis Cogan, 1730. 12mo. [viii],268 pp. Sl browned & used. Contemp calf, rebacked. Anon.
  (Sotheran's) £168 [≈ $322]
- The Life and Genuine Character of Doctor Swift. Written by himself. London: for J. Roberts, 1703. 1st edn. Folio. Half-title. Disbound. *(Ximenes)* $600 [≈ £312]
- A Tale of a Tub ... The Second Edition corrected. London: for John Nutt, 1704. Intl advt leaf. Later half calf, spine gilt extra, jnts sl rubbed. Anon. *(Jarndyce)* £220 [≈ $422]
- A Tale of a Tub ... Battle between the Ancient and Modern Books ... London: for John Nutt, 1704. 3rd edn, crrctd. 8vo. 19th c half mor (sl rubbed). mrbld bds. Anon.
  (Stewart) £125 [≈ $239]
- A Tale of a Tub ... London: for John Nutt, 1704. 3rd edn, crrctd. 8vo. [xii],322 pp. Blank top of title cut away. Contemp calf. Anon.
  (Young's) £100 [≈ $191]
- A Tale of a Tub ... to which is added, an Account of a Battle between the Ancient and Modern Books ... London: for Charles Bathurst, 1747. 11th edn. Sm 8vo. [ii], xvi, [vi], 220 pp. Frontis, 7 plates. Orig calf gilt, spine worn & ends chipped. Anon.
  (Vanbrugh) £145 [≈ $278]
- A Tale of a Tub ... added, An Account of a Battle between the Antient and Modern Books ... London: for Charles Bathurst, 1760. 8vo. Frontis, 7 plates. Contemp calf, gilt spine. Anon. *(Ximenes)* $175 [≈ £91]
- Travels into Several Remote Nations of the World by Lemuel Gulliver. London: Benjamin Motte, 1727. 3rd edn. 2 vols.

12mo. vi,[iv], xii,264; [vi],269 pp. 4 maps, 2 plans, 4 ills. Port frontis (not called for) inserted from another edn. Sl foxed. Half calf, rebacked. Anon.   *(Bookpress)* **$750 [≈ £390]**

Swift, Jonathan (attrib.)
- The Right of Precedence between Physicians and Civilians enquir'd into. Dublin, printed. London: reprinted for J. Roberts [ie Edmund Curll], 1720. 8vo. Half-title dusty. Disbound. Anon.   *(Ximenes)* **$350 [≈ £182]**

Switzer, Stephen
- An Introduction to a General System of Hydrostaticks and Hydraulicks ... London: T. Astley, 1729. 1st edn. 2 vols. 4to. [vi], xxxii, [4], 133,[15], 129-274,10; [viii], 275-352, 4, 353-413, [14] pp. 9 + 52 (numbered 10-60) plates. Contemp calf, rebacked.   *(Bookpress)* **$2,850 [≈ £1,484]**
- The Practical Fruit-Gardener. London: Thomas Woodward, 1724. 1st edn. 8vo. [xxvii], 333, [17] pp. 3 fldg plates. Occas v sl foxing. Contemp calf, minor chipping & cracking to spine. *(Bookpress)* **$450 [≈ £234]**

Sydenham, Thomas
- The Whole Works. London: for Wellington & Castle, 1696. 1st edn in English. Translated by John Pechy. Post 8vo. [xxiv], 1-248, 353-592 pp, complete. 1st 2 ff sl chipped. Some browning. Mod half calf.   *(Ash)* **£250 [≈ $479]**
- The Whole Works ... Translated from the Original Latin, by John Pechy ... London: Richard Wellington, 1696. 1st edn in English. 8vo. [xxiv], 248, 353-592 pp. Title dusty & creased, marg tears to 1st 2 ff. Sl marks. Rec half calf. Wing S.6305.   *(Clark)* **£380 [≈ $729]**
- The Entire Works ... Newly made English ... Notes ... By John Swan. London: Edward Cave, 1742. 1st edn of this translation. 8vo. [ii],xi, [i],xxiii, [vii],623,[xv] pp. Few pp sl dusty. Old calf, extremities sl worn, lacks label.   *(Clark)* **£200 [≈ $383]**

Sydney, Algernon
- See Sidney, Algernon.

Sykes, Arthur Ashley
- An Answer to the Nonjurors Charge of Schism upon the Church of England ... London: Knapton, 1716. 1st edn. 8vo. 47 pp. Bottom marg hole occas straying to a letter. Disbound. Anon.   *(Young's)* **£50 [≈ $95]**

- An Essay on the Nature, Design, and Origin, of Sacrifices. London: Knapton, 1748. Only edn. 8vo. viii,354,2 advt pp. Contemp calf. Anon.   *(Young's)* **£120 [≈ $230]**

The Sylph; a Novel ...
- See Devonshire, Georgiana Cavendish, Duchess of.

Sylva; or the Wood ...
- See Heathcote, Ralph.

Symson, Patrick
- See Simson, Patrick.

T., D.
- Hieraginisticon: or, Corah's Doom, being an Answer to Two Letters of Enquiry into the Grounds and Occasions of the Contempt of the Clergy and Religion ... London: Tho. Milbourn, 1672. Only edn. 8vo. [ii],198,[1 errata] pp. Rec contemp style calf. Wing T.4.   *(Young's)* **£120 [≈ $230]**

The Tablet ...
- The Tablet, or Pictures of Real Life ... see Shaw, Peter.

Tacitus
- The Works of Tacitus. With Political Discourses upon the Author. By Thomas Gordon. The Fourth Edition Corrected. London: Rivington ..., 1770. 5 vols. 8vo. Period speckled calf, red & green labels.   *(Rankin)* **£85 [≈ $163]**

Talbot, B.
- The New Art of Land Measuring; or, a Turnpike Road to Practical Surveying ... Wolverhampton: for the author ..., 1779. 1st edn. 8vo. xxiv,412 pp. 13 plates, fldg table. Contemp qtr calf, sl rubbed.   *(Burmester)* **£360 [≈ $691]**

A Tale of a Tub ...
- See Swift, Jonathan.

Tandon, J.E.
- A New French Grammar, teaching a Person of Common Capacity to Read, Speak, and Write that Tongue ... London: John Millan, 1760. 5th edn. 8vo. [iv],128 pp. Fldg table. Free endpapers defective. Contemp calf, chip to front bd.   *(Bookpress)* **$285 [≈ £148]**

Tanner, Thomas
- Notitia Monastica; or, an Account of all the Abbies, Priories, and Houses of Friers, heretofore in England and Wales ... London: John Tanner, 1744. 1st edn. Folio. Port, 3 plates. Some wear & tear. Old calf, worn, jnts broken. *(Bow Windows)* **£95 [≈$182]**
- Notitia Monastica; or, an Account of all the Abbies, Priories, and Houses of Friers, formerly in England and Wales ... Now reprinted with many additions, by James Nasmith. Cambridge: UP, 1787. Folio. Port. Reversed sheep, new spine.
(Stewart) **£150 [≈$287]**

Tansillo, Luigi
- The Nurse, a Poem translated from the Italian ... By William Roscoe. Liverpool: J. M'Creery, for Cadell & Davies, 1798. 1st English edn. 4to. [2],14, 67,[1], 12 pp, inc half-title. Contemp half calf, ft of spine v worn. *(Hannas)* **£45 [≈$86]**

Taplin, William
- The Gentleman's Stable Directory; or, Modern System of Farriery ... London: for G. Kearsley, 1788-91. 6th edn vol 1, 1st edn vol 2. 2 vols. 8vo. xxiii,448; viii,424 pp. Half-titles. Early 19th c calf, sometime rebacked. *(Young's)* **£110 [≈$211]**

Tasso, Torquato
- Godfrey of Bulloigne: or the Recovery of Jerusalem. Done into English Heroical Verse, by Edward Halifax ... London: J.M. for Henry Herringman, 1687. 1st 8vo edn. [xxxii],655 pp. Old calf, rehinged. Wing T.174. *(Young's)* **£60 [≈$115]**

The Taste of the Town ...
- See Ralph, James.

Tate, Nahum
- A Poem upon Tea; With a Discourse on its Sov'rain Virtues; and Directions in the Use of it for Health ... London: for J. Nutt, 1702. 2nd edn. 8vo. [xvi],47 pp. Stain at top of last 3 ff. Title dusty. Disbound. Mor backed box. *(Young's)* **£210 [≈$403]**

Taxation No Tyranny ...
- See Johnson, Samuel.

Taylor, Adam
- A Treatise on the Ananas or Pine-Apple, containing Plain and Easy Directions for raising this most excellent Fruit without Fire ... Devizes: 1769. 8vo. [2],vi,62 pp. 2 fldg hand cold plates. Rec half calf, gilt spine.
(Spelman) **£240 [≈$460]**

Taylor, Brook
- A Compleat Treatise on Perspective, In Theory and Practice ... [edited by] Thomas Malton. The Second Edition, Corrected and Improved. London: the author, 1778. Lge folio. [xii],296, 8,iv pp. Frontis, 48 plates. Occas sl foxing. Later half calf gilt.
(Vanbrugh) **£455 [≈$873]**

Taylor, George & Skinner, Andrew
- Maps of the Roads of Ireland Surveyed 1777. London: published for the authors as the Act Directs 14th Nov. 1778, sold by G. Nicol ..., (1778). 1st edn. 8vo. xvi,16 subscribers pp. 288 engvd road-maps ptd on both sides. General map (defective). Old calf, worn.
(Young's) **£90 [≈$172]**

Taylor, Henry
- The Apology of Benjamin Ben Mordecai to his Friends, for Embracing Christianity ... With Notes and Illustrations ... London: for J. Wilkie, 1771. 1st edn. 4to. viii, [1 errata], 128, v,205, v,187 pp. Calf backed bds, uncut. Anon. *(Young's)* **£75 [≈$143]**

Taylor, I. & J.
- Ideas for Rustic Furniture proper for Garden Seats, Summer Houses, Hermitages, Cottages, etc. London: Architectural Library, Holborn, [ca 1790]. 25 plates. Mod half mor.
(Phillips) **£875 [≈$1,679]**

Taylor, Jeremy
- Antiquitates Christianae: or the History of the Life and Death of the Holy Jesus, as also the Lives ... of His Apostles [by William Cave] ... In Two Parts ... London: 1684. 7th edn. Folio. Engvd & ptd titles, plates, text ills. Contemp calf. Wing T.288.
(Lloyd-Roberts) **£150 [≈$287]**
- A Course of Sermons for All the Sundays of the Year ... Third Edition Enlarged ... London: 1668. Folio. [xvi],250, [xiv],270, [iv],48, [viii],219, [iii], 21,[i] pp. Port (mtd). 10 secondary title-pp. Contemp calf, extremities worn, sm splits jnt ends. Wing T.331. *(Clark)* **£180 [≈$345]**
- Eniagmos. A Course of Sermons for all the Sundays of the Year ... With a Supplement of Eleven Sermons ... London: for Awnsham Churchill, 1673. 4th edn enlgd. Sm folio.

[20], 250,[12], 270,[8], 243,[1],79 pp. Port. Sl marg wear, sl damp stains. 19th c calf, sl worn. Wing T.332.   *(Humber)* **£85 [≈$163]**
- The Golden Grove. London: F. Walthoe ..., (1735). 27th edn. 12mo. [x],154,[6] pp. frontis. Contemp calf, a.e.g., minor wear.
     (Bookpress) **$75 [≈£39]**
- The Great Exemplar of Sanctity and Holy Life according to the Christian Institution ... London: R.N. for Francis Ash, 1649. 1st edn. Variant imprint with no address for Francis Ash. Sm 4to. Some worming in inner margs. Sl water stain at end. 19th c calf gilt, sl rubbed.   *(Ximenes)* **$350 [≈£182]**
- The Great Exemplar of Sanctity and Holy Life ... London: R.N. for Francis Ash, 1649. 1st edn. 4to. [xlii],166, [vi],168, [iv], 182,[18] pp. General title in red & black with vignette, 3 sep titles to the parts. Contemp calf, rebacked, sl worn. Wing T.342.
     (Clark) **£150 [≈$287]**
- The Great Exemplar of Sanctity and Holy Life according to the Christian Institution ... London: R. Norton for R. Royston, 1657. 3rd edn. Folio. [lii],600,[x] pp. Frontis, addtnl engvd title, 11 (of 12) plates. Stitching weak, well used. Contemp calf, spine chipped. Wing T.344.   *(Lloyd-Roberts)* **£60 [≈$115]**
- The Worthy Communicant ... With the Cases of Conscience ... As also Devotions. London: R.H. for Awnsham Churchill, 1683. 8vo. [16], 436 pp. Frontis. Few sl stains. Tear in title. Early calf. Wing T.421.
     (Humber) **£48 [≈$92]**

Taylor, Nathaniel
- A Preservative Against Deism Showing the Great Advantage of Revelation Above Reason ... London: John Laurance & Tho. Cockerill, 1698. 8vo. [38],266,[6] pp. Jnts cracked. Wing T.548.   *(Humber)* **£58 [≈$111]**

Taylor, Samuel
- An Essay intended to Establish a Standard for an Universal System of Stenography, or Short Hand Writing ... London: the author, 1786. 1st edn. 8vo. [xviii],98 pp. 11 plates. Contemp calf, backstrip relaid.
     (Bookpress) **$275 [≈£143]**

Taylor, William
- The Ready Reckoner, or, Trader's Correct Guide ... Birmingham: ptd by J. Belcher ..., 1792. 1st edn. 12mo. x,[ii],202,[2] pp. Occas sl marks. Contemp sheep, worn, lower jnt tender.   *(Burmester)* **£25 [≈$47]**

The Tell-Tale ...
- The Tell-Tale: or, Anecdotes expressive of Characters of Persons eminent for Rank, Learning, Wit, or Humour ... London: for R. Baldwin, 1756. 1st edn. 2 vols. 12mo. Contemp calf gilt, spines sl worn.
     (Ximenes) **$600 [≈£312]**

Telliamed; or, the World Explain'd ...
- See Maillet, Benoit de.

The Temperate Man ...
- See Cornaro, Luigi, et al.

Temple, R.
- Practice of Physic ... London: 1798. xiv, 344 pp. Interleaved with blanks. Occas sl foxing, ink notes on some blanks. New qtr leather.
     (Whitehart) **£240 [≈$460]**

Temple, Sir William
- An Introduction to the History of England. London: ptd by W.S. ..., 1708. 3rd edn. 8vo. [viii], 310 pp. Contemp speckled calf, sl rubbed.   *(Young's)* **£34 [≈$65]**
- Observations upon the United Provinces of the Netherlands. The Fourth Edition. London: for Edward gellibrand, 1680. 12mo. xvi,320 pp. Some margs sl damp stained. Period sheep, sm cracks in spine, crnrs sl worn, inner jnts sl loose.
     (Rankin) **£60 [≈$115]**
- Observations upon the United Provinces of the Netherlands. The Eighth Edition. Edinburgh: Hamilton & Balfour, 1747. 12mo. Contemp calf, red label.
     (Jarndyce) **£48 [≈$92]**
- The Works; to which is prefix'd Some Account of the Life and Writings of the Author. London: for A. Churchill ..., 1720. 1st coll edn. 2 vols. Folio. Frontis vol 1. Contemp panelled calf, rebacked.
     (Jarndyce) **£250 [≈$479]**
- The Works ... to which is prefixed, The Life and Character of Sir William Temple [by Lady Giffard] ... London: for J. Round ..., 1740. 2 vols. Folio. Port frontis. Contemp speckled calf, mor label, jnts cracking.
     (Waterfield's) **£150 [≈$287]**

Temple, Revd. William Johnston
- Moral and Historical Memoirs. London: 1779. 1st edn. 424 pp. Sl marg staining at ends. Contemp calf, jnts weak. Anon.
     (Robertshaw) **£38 [≈$72]**

Tenants Law ...
- Tenants Law: or, the Laws concerning Landlords, Tenants and Farmers ... Fifteenth Edition, with all the Modern Cases .... London: ptd by S. Richardson & C. Lintot ..., 1760. 12mo. 334,[38] pp. Contemp calf.
(Burmester) £120 [≃ $230]

Tenison, Thomas
- A Discourse concerning a Guide in Matters of Faith ... London: Ben. Tooke, 1683. 4to. vi, 43 pp. Mod bds.   *(Gage)* £18 [≃ $34]

Tennent, John
- Physical Enquiries. London: Andrew Millar, 1742. 1st edn. Sm 8vo. [x],69,[1] pp. Later half calf.   *(Bookpress)* $750 [≃ £390]

Terence
- The Comedies of Terence, Translated into Blank Verse, by George Colman. Dublin: Boulter Grierson, 1766. 8vo. lx,436 pp. Frontis, 1 plate. Damp stains on title & 1st leaf. Period sheep gilt, surface worm lower cvr.   *(Rankin)* £65 [≃ $124]

Terrae-Filius ...
- See Amhurst, Nicholas.

Theobald, Lewis
- The Cave of Poverty, a Poem. Written in Imitation of Shakespeare. London: for Jonas Browne, sold by J. Roberts, [1715]. 1st edn. 8vo. Half-title sl dusty. Disbound, stitching loose.   *(Ximenes)* $750 [≃ £390]

Theocritus
- The Idylliums ... with Rapin's Discourse upon Pastorals, made English by Mr. Creech ... Second Edition ... Life of Theocritus by Basil Kennet. London: for E. Curll, 1713. 8vo. Port. Contemp calf, bds not quite matching.   *(Waterfield's)* £45 [≃ $86]

The Theory of Agreeable Sensations ...
- See Levesque de Pouilly, Louis Jean.

Thevenot, Jean de
- The Travels of Monsieur de Thevenot into the Levant. In Three Parts ... Newly Done Out of French. London: H. Clarke, 1687. 1st edn in English. Folio. [xl],291,1; [ii],200; [ii], 114,4 pp. Port frontis, 3 plates. Rec half mor.   *(Terramedia)* $1,500 [≃ £781]

Things Divine and Supernatural ...
- See Browne, Peter.

Thomas, Elizabeth
- Poems on Several Occasions. To John Dryden Esq; Hen. Cromwel Esq; ... Written by a Lady. The Second Edition. London: for Tho. Astley, 1727. 8vo. [vi],295,[9] pp & 8 pp ctlg at end. Contemp calf, spine rubbed, lacks label, sl worn. Anon.
(Burmester) £350 [≃ $671]

Thomas, Joshua
- A History of the Baptist Association in Wales from the Year 1650, to the Year 1790 ... London: Dilly, Button & Thomas ..., 1795. 1st edn. 8vo. viii,88 pp. Disbound.
(Burmester) £75 [≃ $143]

Thomas, Robert
- Medical Advice to the Inhabitants of Warm Climates, on the Domestic Treatment of all the Diseases incidental thereon ... Nassau, New-Providence: John Wells, 1794. 12mo. [4], 192 pp. Sm ownership stamps. Contemp calf. Bound with sev other unimportant pieces.   *(Reese)* $12,500 [≃ £6,510]

Thompson, Charles
- Rules for Bad Horsemen, or those who depend upon Practice without Principles ... Fifth Edition, carefully corrected and revised. London: for R. Blamire, 1787. Lge 12mo. xii,88 pp. Half-title. Later half calf, spine defective but cords strong.
(Fenning) £65 [≃ $124]

Thompson, Edward
- The Court of Cupid. London: for C. Moran, 1770. 1st edn. 2 vols in one. Sm 8vo. Advt leaf end of vol 2. Contemp calf, gilt spine (sl worn). Anon.   *(Ximenes)* $450 [≃ £234]

Thompson, Isaac
- A Collection of Poems, Occasionally Writ on Several Subjects. Newcastle upon Tyne: John White for the author ..., 1731. Only edn. 8vo. xiv,176,[2 blank] pp. Orig calf, spine ends worn, vertical crack beginning in middle of spine.   *(Bickersteth)* £280 [≃ $537]

Thomson, Alexander
- Pictures of Poetry; Historical, Biographical and Critical. Edinburgh: Mundell & Son, 1799. Contemp red mor, spine rubbed.
(C.R. Johnson) £165 [≃ $316]

- Whist: a Poem, in Twelve Cantos. London: J. & B. Bell, 1791. 194,1 pp. Contemp calf, rebacked. Anon. *(C.R. Johnson)* **£85 [≈$163]**

Thomson, George
- The Spirit of General History in a Series of Lectures ... Carlisle: ptd by F. Jollie, & sold by B. Law, London, 1791. 1st edn. 8vo. Contemp calf, top hinge cracked but holding, crnrs bumped.   *(Buccleuch)* **£60 [≈$115]**

Thomson, James
- The Seasons, A Poem. London: for J. Millan sic, 1730. 1st 8vo edn. [iv],312, 16,20 pp. Some edge soiling. New period style calf.
    (Young's) **£70 [≈$134]**
- The Seasons. With his Life, an Index, and Glossary ... London: for A. Hamilton, 1793. 8vo. xxiv,227,[xix] pp. Title vignette, 5 plates, 6 text engvs. Sm tear in port, title sl spotted. Orig calf, gilt spine, sm crack ft of upper jnt.   *(Bickersteth)* **£48 [≈$92]**
- The Tragedy of Sophonisba. London: A. Millar, 1730. A2 uncancelled. Disbound.
    (C.R. Johnson) **£35 [≈$67]**

Thorold, John
- A View of Popery or Observations on the Twelve Articles of the Council of Trent ... London: for John Rivington, 1766. 183 pp. Contemp leather, sl scored, crnrs sl worn.
    (Gage) **£18 [≈$34]**

Thoughts ...
- The Thoughts of a Private Person ... see Leeds, Thomas Osborne, Duke of.
- Thoughts on Hunting ... see Beckford, Peter.
- Thoughts on the Importance of the Manners of the Great ... see More, Hannah.
- Thoughts on the Present Proceedings of the House of Commons. The Second Edition. London: for J. Debrett, 1788. 8vo. [iv],19 pp. Sl dusty at ends. Uncut, sewed as issued.
    (Bickersteth) **£25 [≈$47]**

A Thousand Memorable Things ...
- See Lupton, Thomas.

Thrale, Hester Lynch
- See Piozzi, Hester Lynch.

Three Letters ...
- Three Letters Concerning the Present State of Italy ... see Burnet, Gilbert.

Thucydides
- The History of the Peloponnesian War. London: John Watts, 1753. Translated by William Smith. 1st edn thus. 2 vols. 4to. [xxvi], lxxxiii, 308; 484,[12] pp. 2 fldg maps. Contemp calf, sl rubbed.
    (Bookpress) **$250 [≈£130]**

Thunberg, C.P.
- Travels in Europe, Africa, and Asia, made between the Years 1770 and 1779. London: 1795-96. 3rd edn. 4 vols. 8vo. 11 plates. Contemp qtr calf, trifle used.
    (Wheldon & Wesley) **£250 [≈$479]**

Thurston, Joseph
- The Toilette. London: for Benj. Motte, 1730. 2nd edn. 4to. 48 pp. Frontis. Rebound in tree calf.   *(Limestone Hills)* **$120 [≈£62]**

Tickell, Richard
- The Project. A Poem dedicated to Dean Tucker ... Second Edition. London: for T. Becket, 1788. 4to. Top right marg sl shaved. Disbound. Anon.   *(Waterfield's)* **£50 [≈$95]**

Tillotson, John
- A Discourse against Transubstantiation. London: M. Flesher for Brabazon Aylmer & William Rogers, 1684. Disbound. Wing T.1190. Anon.   *(Waterfield's)* **£30 [≈$57]**
- The Works ... London: for R. Ware ..., 1743. 12 vols. 8vo. Port frontis. Contemp speckled calf, gilt border on sides, some jnts cracked but sound, spines rubbed.
    (Sotheran's) **£235 [≈$451]**

Tilly, William
- The Nature and Necessity of Religious Resolution, in the Defence and Support of a Good Cause ... A Sermon ... July 19th. 1705. The Second Edition. Oxford: L. Lichfield ..., 1705. 4to. [4], "46" [ie 68] pp. Half-title. Rec wraps.   *(Fenning)* **£24.50 [≈$47]**

Tindal, Nicholas
- A Guide to Classical Learning: or, Polymetis Abridged ... Third Edition. London: for R. Horsfield, & J. Dodsley, 1768. 12mo. Frontis, plates. Contemp calf, rubbed.
    (Jarndyce) **£40 [≈$76]**

Tissot, Samuel A.D.
- Advice to the People in General, with Regard to their Health ... Translated from the French ... by J. Kirkpatrick. London: Becket & De

Hondt, 1765. 1st edn. 8vo. xxxii, 608, [4] pp. Rec contemp style calf.
(Young's) **£140 [≈ $268]**

- Advice to the People in General, with regard to their Health ... Translated by J. Kirkpatrick ... London: 1766. 2nd edn. xxxvi, 620 pp. Contemp leather, rubbed, sl marked.
(Whitehart) **£180 [≈ $345]**

- Advice to the People in General with Regard to their Health ... Translated from the French ... by J. Kirkpatrick. Third Edition. London: 1768. 8vo. 620 pp. Calf, jnts weak.
(Goodrich) **$60 [≈ £31]**

- Advice to People in General, with Respect [sic] to their Health. Edinburgh: A Donaldson, 1768. 2 vols. 12mo. xxi,261, vi, 364 pp. Contemp calf.
(Bookpress) **$285 [≈ £148]**

Tocquot, J.F.
- The Royal Pocket Dictionary, French and English, and English and French ... London: Robinson, Gardner ..., 1795. Only edn. 16mo. Contemp blue mor, a.e.g., spine rubbed.
(Jarndyce) **£48 [≈ $92]**

Tomkins, John & Kendall, John
- Piety Promoted, in Brief Memorials ... of some of the People called Quakers ... London: James Phillips, 1789. 1st edn thus. 3 vols. 8vo. vii,312; 308; 285,15 pp. Contemp calf, spines sl worn.
(Young's) **£50 [≈ $95]**

Tong, William
- An Account of the Life and Death of the late Reverend Mr Matthew Henry. London: for M. Lawrence ..., 1718. Port frontis. Contemp panelled calf, rebacked, crnrs reprd.
(Waterfield's) **£70 [≈ $134]**

Topham, Edward
- Letters from Edinburgh: written in the Years 1774 and 1775 ... London: Dodsley, 1776. 8vo. xv,383 pp. V occas foxing. Period calf, upper jnt cracked, lower jnt sl cracked, spine ends sl chipped. Anon.
(Rankin) **£150 [≈ $287]**

- Letters from Edinburgh: written in the Years 1774 and 1775 ... London: Dodsley, 1776. [xviii],383 pp. Sl spotting to title, occas v sl marg water stains. Rec qtr calf.
(Buccleuch) **£115 [≈ $220]**

- Letters from Edinburgh; written in the years 1774 and 1775 ... Dublin: for W. Watson, [1776?]. 2 vols. Sm chip in 1 endpaper. Contemp calf, rebacked. Anon.

(Wreden) **$250 [≈ £130]**

Topsy Turvy ...
- See Huddesford, George.

Torr, James
- The Antiquities of York City and the Civil Government thereof ... York: G. White for F. Hildyard ..., 1719. 1st edn. Sm 8vo. [viii], 148, [4] pp. Contemp calf, rebacked, crnrs reprd.
(Bow Windows) **£145 [≈ $278]**

Tosi, Pietro Francesco
- Observations on the Florid Song; or, Sentiments on the Ancient and Modern Singers. London: for J. Wilcox, 1742. 1st edn in English. 12mo. 6 fldg plates of music. Early bds, later paper spine, rubbed.
(Ximenes) **$850 [≈ £442]**

Tott, Francois de, Baron
- Memoirs ... containing the State of the Turkish Empire and the Crimea, during the late War with Russia ... Second Edition ... Translated from the French. London: Robinson, 1786. 2nd edn, enlgd. 2 vols. 8vo. Occas sl marks. Contemp qtr calf, rubbed, sl bumped.
(Finch) **£100 [≈ $191]**

Toulmin, Joshua
- Memoirs of the Life, Character, Sentiments, and Writings, of Faustus Socinus. Southwark: for the author, by J. Brown, Horsly-down ..., 1777. 1st edn. 8vo. 11 pp subscribers. No port ever bound in (called for?). Contemp calf, gilt spine.
(Georges) **£85 [≈ $163]**

Tour ...
- A Tour in Scotland ... see Pennant, Thomas.
- A Tour Thro' the Whole Island of Great Britain ... see Defoe, Daniel.

Tournay, Thomas
- The Cave of Death. An Elegy. Inscribed to the Memory of Deceased Relations of the Author. Canterbury: for the author, 1776. 4to. Half-title, 24 pp. Disbound. Anon.
(C.R. Johnson) **£265 [≈ $508]**

Towgood, Micajah
- A Calm and Plain Answer to the Enquiry Why are you a Dissenter from the Church of England? London: for Buckland, Dilly, Davies, & Cregg at Exeter, 1772. Disbound. Anon. *(Waterfield's)* **£30 [≈ $57]**
- A Dissent from the Church of England fully

justified ... the Fifth Edition. London: R.
Hurst, 1779. 8vo. Sm lib marks. Contemp
calf, rebacked.   *(Waterfield's)* £50 [≈ $95]
- High-Flown Episcopal and Priestly Claims
freely examin'd ... London: for J. Noon, 1737.
40 pp. Sl marg stain at end. Disbound. Anon.
(Jarndyce) £20 [≈ $38]

Townshend, Charles
- Remarks on the Letter addressed to two Great
Men. In a Letter to the Author of that Piece.
London: Printed in the Year 1760. 8vo. 38
pp. Disbound.   *(Rankin)* £50 [≈ $95]

The Tragedy of Nero ...
- The Tragedy of Nero. Newly Written.
London: Aug. Mathewes, for Thomas Jones,
1633. 2nd edn. 4to. [lxx] pp. With blank A1.
Outer ff dusty, crnrs sl frayed, sl marg worm,
hole in last 2 ff. Disbound. STC 18431.
(Clark) £85 [≈ $163]

Trapp, Joseph
- The Doctrine of the Most Holy, and Ever
Blessed Trinity briefly stated and proved ...
London: for J. Brotherton ..., [1730?]. 8vo.
Contemp calf, jnts cracked but sound.
(Waterfield's) £45 [≈ $86]

Trapp, Joseph (ed.)
- Proceedings   of   the   French   National
Convention on the Trial of Louix XVI.
London: for the author ..., 1793. 1st edn. 8vo.
Sl foxing. Contemp qtr calf, backstrip relaid.
(Meyer Boswell) $450 [≈ £234]

Travels through Flanders ...
- Travels   through   Flanders,   Holland,
Germany, Sweden, and Denmark ... with
necessary Instructions for Travellers ...
London: for Randal Taylor, 1693. 1st edn.
8vo. Text ends with catchword. 5 fldg plates
& plans. Contemp calf, edges rubbed,
rebacked. Wing T.2056A
(Ximenes) $750 [≈ £390]

Treatise ...
- A Treatise concerning Oaths and Perjury.
London: for J. Roberts, 1750. 1st edn. 8vo.
Half-title. Advt leaf. Disbound.
(Ximenes) $250 [≈ £130]
- A Treatise concerning the Militia ... see
Sackville, Charles.
- A Treatise concerning the Origin and
Progress of Fees ... see Mackenzie, James.

Trelawny, Sir John
- A Sermon ... before the Queen ... Nov. 12.
1702 ... London: T. Bennet, 1702. 1st edn.
4to. [4],43,[1 advt] pp. Licence leaf. Rec
wraps.   *(Fenning)* £24.50 [≈ $47]

Trenchard, John
- A   Short   History   of   Standing   Armies   in
England. [London]: 1698. 1st edn. 4to. viii,
46, [2] pp. Errata leaf. Brown stain on 2 ff.
Untrimmed. Contemp style half calf. Anon.
(Vanbrugh) £135 [≈ $259]
- A   Short   History   of   Standing   Armies   in
England. [London]: 1698. 1st edn, 3rd issue.
4to. viii,46 pp. Errata leaf. Browned. Mod
half calf gilt. Wing T.2116. Anon.
(Hollett) £130 [≈ $249]
- Standing Armies Standing Evils, and Prov'd
to be Foreign to the ... English Constitution
... London: ptd by T. Free for Old Lady
England ..., 1749. 2nd edn. 8vo. 63 pp.
Disbound.   *(Young's)* £48 [≈ $92]

Trenck, Friedrich von der, Baron
- The Life ... Translated from the German, by
Thomas Holcroft. Dublin: for Messrs.
Chamberlaine ..., 1788. 1st Irish edn of this
translation. 2 vols in 1. 8vo. [2],vi,220; 240
pp. Frontis. Contemp calf.
(Fenning) £45 [≈ $86]

Trial ...
- The Trial, Conviction and Condemnation of
Andrew Brommich and William Atkins, for
being Romish Priests ... at Summer Assizes
last at Stafford ... London: for Robert
Pawlett, 1679. Folio. 20 pp. Lib stamp on
title verso. Mod half calf gilt. Wing T.2176.
(Hollett) £120 [≈ $230]

Triall ...
- The Triall of a Black-Pudding. Or, The
unlawfulness of Eating Blood proved by
Scriptures, Before the Law, Under the Law,
and After the Law. By A well-wisher to
Ancient Truth. London: ptd by F.N., sold by
John Hancock, 1652. 4to. 22 pp. Mod half
calf gilt. Wing B.846. *(Hollett)* £140 [≈ $268]
- A Triall of the English Lyturgie. Wherein All
the material Objections raised in Defence
hereof are fully cleared and Answered.
London: for Ben. Allen, 1643. 1st edn. 4to.
22 pp. Late 19th c buckram, label defective.
Wing T.2226.   *(Hollett)* £60 [≈ $115]

Trimmer, Sarah

- An Easy Introduction to the Knowledge of Nature and Reading the Holy Scriptures adapted to the Capacities of Children. The Fourth Edition with Additions ... London: Longman, Robinson, Johnson, 1786. 12mo. xvi, 193, [5 advt] pp. Later half calf.
(Lamb) £35 [≈ $67]
- An Easy Introduction to the Knowledge of Nature, and Reading the Holy Scriptures. Adapted to the Capacities of Children. The Eighth Edition, with additions ... London: Longman ..., 1793. 12mo. Sl marg staining. Contemp sheep, sl rubbed, rebacked.
(Jarndyce) £75 [≈ $143]
- Fabulous Histories. Designed for the Instruction of Children, respecting their Treatment of Animals. London: for T. Longman ..., 1791. 4th edn. 8vo. Contemp calf, gilt ruled spine. *(Stewart)* £100 [≈ $191]
- Fabulous Histories. Designed for the Instruction of Children, respecting their Treatment of Animals. London: for T. Longman ..., 1793. 5th edn. 8vo. Lacks front endpaper. Contemp calf, gilt ruled spine.
(Stewart) £75 [≈ $143]
- Fabulous Histories. Designed for the Instruction of Children, respecting their Treatment of Animals. London: for T. Longman ..., 1793. 5th edn. 8vo. Contemp calf, gilt ruled spine. *(Stewart)* £100 [≈ $191]
- Fabulous Histories Designed for the Instruction of Children respecting their Treatment of Animals. London: for T. Longman ..., 1798. 6th edn. 172 pp. Early mrbld bds, new gilt calf spine.
(James) £75 [≈ $143]

Trot, John (pseud.)

- See Bolingbroke, Henry St. John, Viscount.

Trowell, Samuel

- A New Treatise of Husbandry, Gardening, and other Matters relating to Rural Affairs ... London: Olive Payne, 1739. 164 pp. Contemp calf, sl worn.
(C.R. Johnson) £285 [≈ $547]

Trusler, John

- Chronology; or, The Historian's Vade-Mecum ... Twelfth Edition. London: Logographic Press, for the author ..., (1786). 2 vols. 12mo. Contemp calf, sl rubbed.
(Jarndyce) £48 [≈ $92]
- The Difference between Words, esteemed Synonymous, in the English Language ...

Dublin: for R. Moncrieffe, 1776. 1st Irish edn. 2 vols in one. 8vo. Contemp speckled calf, hinge splitting at hd. Anon.
(Jarndyce) £185 [≈ $355]
- The Honours of the Table ... With the Whole Art of Carving ... Second Edition. London: Literary Press, 1791. 12mo. 120 pp. 28 w'cut ills. Contemp calf, spine roughly reprd. Anon. *(Karmiole)* $125 [≈ £65]
- A Summary of the Constitutional Laws of England, being an Abridgement of Blackstone's Commentaries. London: for the author, at the Literary- Press, (1796). Cr 8vo. Crnr torn from index leaf. Contemp calf backed mrbld bds. *(Stewart)* £55 [≈ $105]
- The Tablet of Memory, or Historian's Guide ... Dublin: Peter Hoey, 1782. Lge 12mo. "vi" [ie iv], 269,[3 advt] pp. Sl used, sm piece missing from 1 leaf with sl loss. Contemp calf, spine worn but strong.
(Fenning) £55 [≈ $105]

Tryon, Thomas

- The Way to Health, Long Life and Happiness ... added, a Treatise of most Sorts of English Herbs ... London: Andrew Sowle, 1683. 1st edn. 8vo. [xvi],669,[3 advt] pp. Sm rust hole in 1 leaf. Contemp calf, sm chips spine ends, crnrs worn. Wing T.3200.
(Gaskell) £1,200 [≈ $2,303]
- The Way to Health, Long Life and Happiness ... [Bound & continuously signed with] A Dialogue between an East-Indian Brackmanny ... and a French Gentleman ... London: D. Newman, 1691. 2nd edns. 8vo. [xiv],500; [2], 19 pp. Some worming. New sheep. Wing T.3201.
(Bookpress) $425 [≈ £221]

Tucker, John

- The Validity of Presbyterian Ordination Argued ... A Discourse delivered in the Chapel of Harvard- College in Cambridge, New England ... Boston, New England: Thomas & John Fleet, 1778. Disbound.
(Waterfield's) £35 [≈ $67]

Tucker, Josiah

- A Series of Answers to certain Popular Objections, against separating from the Rebellious Colonies ... Being the Concluding Tract of the Dean of Glocester, on the Subject of Indian Affairs. Glocester: 1776. 108, [11] pp. Sm marg repr to title. Mod half mor.
(Reese) $150 [≈ £78]

Tull, Jethro
- Horse-Hoeing Husbandry. London: A. Millar, 1751. 3rd edn. 8vo. xvi,432 pp. 7 plates. Contemp calf.
  (Bookpress) **$900 [≃ £468]**

Turnbull, George
- A Curious Collection of Ancient Paintings, accurately engraved from excellent Drawings ... London: S. Birt & B. Dod, 1744. Folio. [4], 42 pp. 55 plates (the last unnumbered & added from the 1st edn of 1740). Occas sl foxing. Contemp calf, rebacked.
  (Spelman) **£280 [≃ $537]**
- Observations upon Liberal Education, in all its Branches ... London: for A. Millar, 1742. Only edn. 8vo. Marg ink stain last 4 ff. Contemp speckled calf gilt, hd of spine rubbed.   *(Jarndyce)* **£140 [≃ $268]**

Turner, Daniel, M.D.
- De Morbis Cutaneis. A Treatise of Diseases Incident to the Skin. London: for R. Wilkin ..., 1736. 5th edn. xiv,x,524 pp. Port frontis (creased, sl soiled). Worm track in marg of prelims, 3 marg blind stamps. Contemp calf, sometime rebacked, extremities rubbed.
  (Hollett) **£140 [≃ $268]**
- A Discourse concerning Fevers. In Two Letters to a Young Physician. London: John Clarke, 1739. 3rd edn. 8vo. xii,364 pp. Frontis. Contemp calf, hinges cracked, wear to spine & tips. *(Bookpress)* **£285 [≃ $148]**
- Syphilis. A Practical Dissertation on the Venereal Disease ... Second Edition, revised ... London: 1724. 8vo. 16 ff, 376 pp, 4 ff. Contemp calf.   *(Hemlock)* **$275 [≃ £143]**
- Siphylis. A Practical Dissertation on the Venereal Disease. London: J. Walthoe ..., 1732. 4th edn. 8vo. [xxvi],476 pp. Frontis.
  (Bookpress) **$350 [≃ £182]**
- Syphilis. A Practical Dissertation on the Venereal Disease, in Two Parts. The Fourth Edition, still farther improved ... London: 1732. 8vo. [xxvi],476 pp. Port. Contemp panelled calf, rubbed, head of spine worn.
  (Bickersteth) **£120 [≃ $230]**

Turner, Daniel, of Abingdon
- Letters Religious and Moral; designed particularly for the Entertainment of Young Persons. London: for the author, & sold by Johnson, Davenport, Robinson, 1766. 1st edn. Sm 8vo. Advt leaf at end. Contemp calf gilt.   *(Ximenes)* **$225 [≃ £117]**

Turner, Richard, 1753-1788
- An Easy Introduction to the Arts and Sciences ... Second Edition. London: for S. Crowder, 1787. 12mo. [iv],154, [directions to binder], [5 advt] pp. 8 plates. Orig sheep, rubbed, edges sl worn, sm dent in spine, upper jnt cracked. *(Bickersteth)* **£50 [≃ $95]**
- The Heavens Survey'd, and the True System of the Universe delineated, so as to form a curious Astronomical Instrument. London: for S. Crowder, 1783. 1st edn. Folio. [ii],ii,53 pp. 3 plates, 2 text engvs. Sl used. Contemp wraps, worn, spine defective.
  (Gaskell) **£225 [≃ $431]**

Turner, William
- Sound Anatomiz'd, in a Philosophical Essay on Musick ... London: William Pearson, for the author ..., 1724. 1st edn. Sm 4to. Errata leaf. Fldg engvd plate of music. Sl foxing. 19th c cloth backed mrbld bds, a bit worn.
  (Ximenes) **$1,500 [≃ £781]**

Tusser, Thomas
- Five Hundred Points of Good Husbandry ... Corrected, better ordered, and newly augmented to a fourth part more ... London: T.R. & M.D. for the Company of Stationers, 1672. Sm 4to. 146,[ii] pp. Num early MS notes. 18th c calf, jnt cracked. Wing T.3369.
  (Bickersteth) **£145 [≃ $278]**

Twisse, William
- Of the Morality of the Fourthe Commandement, as still in Force to Binde Christians ... London: 1641. Only edn. Sm 4to. Title, [10] ff, 246,[19] pp. Title reprd at ft, sl affecting imprint. Contemp calf, backstrip relaid.   *(Reese)* **£150 [≃ £78]**

The Two Cousins ...
- See Pinchard, Elizabeth.

Two Letters ...
- Two Letters to the Right Honourable Viscount Townshend ... see Watts, Robert.

Tytler,   Alexander   Fraser,   Lord Woodhouselee
- Essay on the Life and Character of Petrarch. To which are added, Seven of his Sonnets, translated from the Italian. London: Cadell, 1784. 54 pp. Disbound. Anon.
  (C.R. Johnson) **£150 [≃ $287]**
- Plans and Outlines of a Course of Lectures on Universal History, Ancient and Modern ...

Edinburgh & London: 1782. 1st edn. 8vo. [4], 216, [3], 218-250 pp. Advt leaf Ee before table. 6 hand cold maps. Contemp mor, gilt spine (rubbed). *(Pickering)* **$350 [≈ £182]**

Udall, William
- The Historie of the Life and Death of Mary Stuart Queene of Scotland. London: Iohn Haviland ..., 1636. 12mo. [xx],493,[1 blank] pp. Usual mispagination. Port, engvd & ptd titles. Few v sl marks & tears. Crushed mor gilt, a.e.g., v sl rubbed. STC 24510. Anon.
  (Bow Windows) **£375 [≈ $719]**

Underwood, Thomas
- Poems. Bath: for the author by W. Archer, 1768. Subscribers. B2v sgnd by the author. Orig bds, uncut, rebacked.
  (C.R. Johnson) **£225 [≈ $431]**
- The Snarlers. A Poem. Second Edition. London: for the author, sold by Henry Webley, 1768. 4to. 27 pp. Lacks 1st leaf (half-title?). Title tipped onto a guard & sl defective in upper marg. Late 19th c buckram. Anon.
  (Hollett) **£150 [≈ $287]**

Uring, Nathaniel
- A History of the Voyages and Travels of Capt. Nathaniel Uring, with a New Draught of the Bay of Honduras, very useful for Masters of Ships that use the Leeward Island Trade, or Jamaica. London: 1749. 4th edn. [14],384 pp. Fldg map. Minor damp stains. Contemp calf, rebacked. *(Reese)* **$650 [≈ £338]**

Usefulness ...
- The Usefulness of the Stage to Religion and to Government ... see Dennis, John.

Ussher, James
- A Body of Divinity, or the Summe and Substance of the Christian Religion ... The sixth Edition, Corrected and much enlarged by the Author ... London: 1670. Folio. [xii], 3-451, [iii], 24,[xiv] pp. Marg fraying & worming. 19th c half calf, worn. Wing U.157.
  (Clark) **£45 [≈ $86]**

Uzziah and Jotham ...
- Uzziah and Jotham. A Poem ... London: for B. Motte & Randall Taylor, 1690. Folio. [ii], 32 pp. Some early MS crrctns. Later bds. Wing U.232. *(Hollett)* **£150 [≈ $287]**

V., R.
- A Restitution of Decayed Intelligence ... see Rowlands, Richard.

The Vade Mecum for America ...
- See Prince, Thomas.

Valerius Maximus
- Romae Antiquae Descriptio. A View of the Religion, Laws, Customs, Manneres and Dispositions of the Ancient Romans ... London: J.C. for Samuel Speed, 1678. 1st English translation. 8vo. [x],478 pp. Frontis. Sl stain last ff. Contemp calf, gilt spine. Wing V.34. *(Finch)* **£300 [≈ $575]**

Vallancey, Charles
- The Art of Tanning and Currying Leather: With an Account of all the Different Processes Made Use of in Europe and Asia, for Dying Leather Red and Yellow ... London: reptd for J. Nourse, 1780. 12mo. [ii], xx, 259, [i] pp. Antique style qtr calf. Anon.
  (Finch) **£400 [≈ $767]**
- An Essay on the Antiquity of the Irish Language ... Dublin: S. Powell, 1772. 1st edn. 8vo. x,[iii],63 pp. Some faint spotting towards end. Mod bds. Anon.
  (Finch) **£400 [≈ $767]**

Vallemont, Pierre le Lorrain de
- Curiosities of Nature and Art in Husbandry and Gardening. London: D. Brown ..., 1707. 1st edn in English. 8vo. [xvi],352 pp. 12 plates. Contemp calf, rebacked, some wear.
  (Bookpress) **$550 [≈ £286]**

Valuable Secrets ...
- Valuable Secrets concerning Arts and Trades, or, Approved Directions from the Best Artists ... London: William Hay, 1775. 1st edn. 16mo. [viii], xxxiv, 312 pp. Contemp calf.
  (Bookpress) **$1,350 [≈ £703]**
- Valuable Secrets concerning Arts and Trades ... Dublin: James Williams, 1778. 8vo. [viii], xxvii,[i], 312 pp. Contemp calf, spine ends reprd, new endpapers, jnts v sl cracked.
  (Spelman) **£350 [≈ $671]**

Van Kampen, Nicholas, & Son
- The Dutch Florist: or, True Method of Managing All Sorts of Flowers with Bulbous Roots. The Second Edition, to which is added the particular method of treating the Guernsey Lily. London: Baldwin, 1764. 8vo. [8], 104 pp. Half calf, extremities v sl rubbed.
  (Beech) **£60 [≈ $115]**

Vanbrugh, Sir John
- The Mistake. A Comedy ... by the author of

The Provok'd Wife, &c. London: Tonson,
1706. 1st edn. 8vo. Half-title, advt leaf. Some
browning. Mod qtr mor. Anon.
(Waterfield's) **£200 [≈ $383]**
- Plays ... London: Rivington, Longman ...,
1776. 2 vols. 12mo. 12,372; 340, [4],iv pp.
Contemp tree calf, old rebacking.
(Burmester) **£50 [≈ $95]**

The Vanity of Human Life ...
- The Vanity of Human Life, a Monody.
Sacred to the Memory of the most Hon.
Francis Russel, Marquis of Tavistock.
London: for J. Dodsley ..., 1767. 1st edn. 4to.
14 pp. Last leaf spotted. Disbound.
(Burmester) **£125 [≈ $239]**

Vansleb, F.
- The Present State of Egypt. or, a New
Relation of a Late Voyage into that Kingdom.
performed in the Years 1672 and 1673.
Englished by M.D. London: for John
Starkey, 1678. 1st edn. 12mo. [vii],253,index
pp. Top marg trimmed close. Contemp calf &
bds, jnts weak. *(Terramedia)* **$700 [≈ £364]**

Varillas, Antoine
- Reflexions on Dr. Gilbert Burnet's Travels
into Switzerland, Italy, and Certain Parts of
Germany and France ... London: Randal
Taylor, 1688. 1st edn. 8vo. [xlviii], 164 pp.
Fldg w'cut plate. New contemp style calf.
Wing V.114. Anon. *(Young's)* **£145 [≈ $278]**

Vassa, Gustavus
- The Interesting Narrative of the Life of
Olaudah Equiano, or Gustavus Vassa, the
African. Written by Himself. Fourth Edition,
Enlarged. Dublin: for the author, 1791. 8vo.
xxiv, 360 pp. Port frontis (spotted), 1 fldg
plate. Sl foxed. Later half calf, sl worn.
(Rankin) **£125 [≈ $239]**
- The Interesting Narrative of the Life of
Olaudah Equiano, or Gustavus Vassa, the
African. Sixth Edition, Enlarged. London: for
the author, 1793. 12mo. xxxiv,[ii], 360 pp.
Port frontis (spotted), 1 fldg plate. "Contents"
leaf cropped. Contemp style qtr calf.
(Frew Mackenzie) **£120 [≈ $230]**

Venegas, Miguel
- A Natural and Civil History of California ...
London: for James Rivington & James
Fletcher, 1759. 1st edn in English. 2 vols.
8vo. Fldg map, 4 plates. Contemp calf,
rebacked. *(Ximenes)* **$2,250 [≈ £1,171]**

Veneroni, Giovanni
- The Complete Italian Master; containing
The best and easiest Rules for Attaining that
Language   ...   New   Edition,   With
Considerable Improvements ... London: for J.
Nourse, 1778. 12mo. [iv],464,[208] pp.
Contemp calf, elab gilt spine, extremities
worn, jnts cracked but firm.
(Finch) **£40 [≈ $76]**
- The Italian Master ... Revised, corrected and
enlarged ... Second Edition ... added ... A
Dictionary   ...   translated   ...   by   Edward
Martin. London: for J. Walthoe ..., 1729.
Samuel Birt's 24 pp ctlg (ca 1736) bound in.
Contemp calf, spine rubbed, jnts sl worn.
(Jarndyce) **£160 [≈ $307]**

Venn, Henry
- The Duty of a Parish-Priest ... A Sermon ...
July 2, 1760. Leeds: ptd by G. Wright ...,
1760. 1st edn. 8vo in 4s. Sl browned.
Disbound. *(Sanders)* **£60 [≈ $115]**

Venner, Thomas
- Via Recta ad Vitam Longam. Or a Treatise
wherein the Right Way and Best Manner of
Living for attaining a Long and Healthfull
Life, is clearly Demonstrated ... London:
1650. Sm 4to. 12,417 pp. Minor marg
worming. Later contemp style calf. Wing
V.195. *(Frew Mackenzie)* **£300 [≈ $575]**

Verelst, Harry
- A View of the Rise, Progress and Present
State of the English Government in Bengal ...
London: for J. Nourse, 1772. 1st edn. 4to.
[xii], 148,4, 253 pp.. Title sl spotted.
Contemp half calf, sl rubbed.
(Young's) **£150 [≈ $287]**
- A View of the Rise, Progress, and Present
State of the English Government in Bengal ...
London: for J. Nourse ..., 1772. 1st edn. 4to.
[xii],148, [iv],253,[1 errata] pp. Title v sl dust
soiled. Orig bds, uncut, rebacked.
(Pickering) **$800 [≈ £416]**

The Vermin Killer ...
- The Vermin Killer. Being a Compleat and
Necessary Family-Book. London: W. Owen,
[17--?]. 12mo. 84 pp. Disbound.
(Bookpress) **$425 [≈ £221]**

Verstegen, Richard
- See Rowlands, alias Verstegen, Richard.

Vertot d'Aubeuf, Rene Aubert de
- The History of the Knights of Malta ... London: Strahan ..., 1728. 2 vols. Folio. 5 fldg maps. Lacks 6 plates. Some wear & tear. Contemp calf, rubbed, vol 1 spine defective & jnts cracked but sound.
(Waterfield's) **£125 [≈ $239]**
- The History of the Revolutions of Portugal. The Fifth Edition. Revised and considerably enlarged, by the Author ... London: 1754. 8vo. [xvi],138, [10],14, [2] pp. Frontis, 1 plate. Some marks. Rec bds.
(Bow Windows) **£48 [≈ $92]**

Veslingus, John
- The Anatomy of the Body of Man ... Englished by Nich. Culpeper ... London: peter Cole, 1653. 1st English edn. Sm folio. [xii], 192, [2] pp. 24 plates. Lacks frontis. Rec calf gilt. Wing V.286. *(Hollett)* **£350 [≈ $671]**

The Vicar of Wakefield ...
- See Goldsmith, Oliver.

Vicars, John
- Babylons-Beautie: or the Romish-Catholicks Sweet-Heart ... London: G.M. for Ralph Rounthwait, 1644. 1st edn. Thin 4to. [vi],130 pp. Dec title border (v sl ink stain on title). 19th c half calf. Wing V.293.
(Vanbrugh) **£125 [≈ $239]**

Victor, Benjamin
- The Widow of the Wood. London: for T. Corbett, 1755. 1st edn. 12mo. vii,208 pp. Contemp calf, crnrs & spine ends worn. Anon. *(Bickersteth)* **£85 [≈ $163]**
- The Widow of the Wood. London: for C. Corbett ..., 1755. 1st edn. 8vo. [ii],iv, 208, [1 advt] pp. 1 gathering loose. 20th c qtr calf. Anon. *(Young's)* **£180 [≈ $345]**
- The Widow of the Wood. London: C. sic Corbett, 1755. 1st edn. 12mo. vii,[i],208 pp. Half-title. Lib label on pastedown. Contemp half calf, spine ends worn, jnts cracked. Anon.
(Clark) **£220 [≈ $422]**

Vida, Marcus Hieronymus
- The Christiad, a Poem in Six Books; translated ... by J. Cranwell ... Cambridge: J. Archdeacon ..., 1768. 1st edn. 8vo. [xvi], 397 pp. Trivial worming upper inner crnr. Lacks f.e.p. Contemp qtr calf, spine ends worn, sides rubbed. *(Finch)* **£48 [≈ $92]**
- The Silkworm: A Poem. Dublin: the author, 1740. Translated by Samuel Pullein. 1st edn

thus. Sm 4to. [iv],141,[2] pp. Frontis. Contemp calf, rebacked.
(Bookpress) **$425 [≈ £221]**

View ...
- The View of Hindoostan ... see Pennant, Thomas.
- A View of Sir Isaac Newton's Philosophy ... see Pemberton, Henry.
- A View of the Internal Evidence of the Christian Religion ... see Jenyns, Soame.

Vieyra, Antonio
- A Dictionary of the Portuguese and English Languages ... London: for F. Wingrave ..., 1794. 2nd edn. 2 vols in one. 4to. Title to part 2 bound at beginning, appendix & errata at end. 1 closed tear. Contemp tree calf, rebacked, sides worn.
(Burmester) **£150 [≈ $287]**

Vignola Revived ...
- Vignola Revived; wherein is shewn the True and most Elegant Proportions of the Five Orders. London: Robert Sayer, 1761. Folio. [4] pp. 56 engvd plates. Tear in title reprd. Contemp calf, rebacked.
(Sotheran's) **£650 [≈ $1,247]**

Vigo, John
- The Whole Worke of that Famous Chirurgion Maister John Vigo; newly Corrected by men skilfull in that Arte ... Compiled and Published by Thomas Gale ... London: Thomas East, 1586. Sm thick 4to. [10],455 ff. Engvd title border. Black Letter. Early calf, rebacked.
(Goodrich) **$6,500 [≈ £3,385]**

Vincent, Nathaniel
- A Heaven or Hell Upon Earth, or a Discourse Concerning Conscience. London: T. Parkhurst, 1676. Sm 8vo. [16],317,[3] pp. Inner edge of title worn. Sl browned. 19th c calf, hinges weak. Wing V.409.
(Humber) **£58 [≈ $111]**

Vincent, William
- The Origination of the Greek Verb. An Hypothesis. London: Ginger, 1794. 1st edn. 8vo. 32 pp. 5 fldg tables. Title faintly spotted, lib stamp. Mod wraps. Anon.
(Finch) **£35 [≈ $67]**

Vincent, William
- The Voyage of Nearchus from the Indus to the Euphrates ... an Account of the First

Navigation attempted by Europeans in the Indian Ocean. London: 1797. Lge 4to. v,530, errata pp. 6 engvd charts. Frontis in facs. Contemp calf, reprd. *(Lewis)* £145 [≈ $278]

Vindication ...
- A Vindication of Her Late Majesty Queen Anne, of Glorious Memory; or His Grace the Duke of Ormonde; and of the Late Ministry ... London: for R. Burleigh ..., 1715. 1st edn. 8vo. 35 pp. Title sl spotted. Wraps.
(Young's) £55 [≈ $105]
- A Vindication of the Imprisoned and Secluded Members of the House of Commons ... see Prynne, William.
- A Vindication of the Presbyteriall-Government, and Ministry: Together, With an Exhortation ... London: for C. Meredith, 1650. 1st edn. 4to. [iv],175 pp. Later 19th c buckram, upper hinge cracked. Wing V.523.
(Hollett) £75 [≈ $143]

Vines, Richard
- A Treatise of the Institution, Right Administration and receiving of the Sacrament of the Lords Supper ... London: A.M. for Thomas Underhill, 1657. 4to. [19],375,[4] pp. Addtnl cancel title. Old calf, edges rubbed, rebacked. Wing V.572.
(Humber) £88 [≈ $168]

Virgil
- The Georgicks ... With an English Translation and Notes by John Martyn. London: R. Reilly for T. Osborne, 1746. 2nd edn. 8vo. 10 plates. 2 preface ff just cropped. Contemp calf (sl worn).
(Stewart) £85 [≈ $163]
- Georgicorum Libri Quatuor. The Georgicks of Virgil, with an English Translation and Notes by John Martyn ... London: for the editor by Richard Reily, 1741. 4to. [xxii], 403, [i],3,index pp. 10 cold plates (5 hand cold). Mod calf. *(Buccleuch)* £200 [≈ $383]
- Virgil's Husbandry, or an Essay on the Georgics: being the Second Book translated into English Verse [by William Benson] ... With Notes ... London: Innys, 1724. 1st edn of this translation. 8vo. [ii],xxviii, 50, [20] pp. Frontis, 1 plate. Lacks half-title. Disbound.
(Burmester) £50 [≈ $95]

The Virgin Muse ...
- The Virgin Muse. Being a Collection of Poems from our most celebrated English Poets. Designed for the Use of Young Gentlemen and Ladies at Schools ... Notes ...

Index ... by James Greenwood. London: 1717. 1st edn. 12mo. xii, 220 pp. Frontis. Sl used. New half calf.
(Burmester) £275 [≈ $527]

Virtue the Source of Pleasure ...
- See Barnard, E.

Visions in Verse ...
- See Cotton, Nathaniel.

Voiture, Vincent de
- The Works ... Compleat ... Made English by John Dryden ... Thomas Cheek ... Mr. Dennis ... [With] The Second Volume of the Works ... The Second Edition, with Additions]. London: for Sam. Briscoe ..., 1705. 1st edn thus. 2 vols in one. 8vo. Port. Contemp calf, sl worn
(Burmester) £120 [≈ $230]

Volney, M.C.
- Travels through Syria & Egypt in the Years 1783, 1784 & 1785 ... London: Robinson, 1787. 1st edn. 2 vols. 8vo. xii,418; iv,500,index pp. 2 fldg plates. Minor foxing & browning. Later half mor gilt.
(Terramedia) $350 [≈ £182]

Voltaire, Francois Marie Arouet de
- The History of Charles XII. King of Sweden. Translated from the French. London: for Alexander Lyon, 1732. 1st edn in English. 8vo. [2],194, 185,[3] pp. Errata leaf. Some marg worm at ends. Contemp calf, sl worn.
(Claude Cox) £45 [≈ $86]
- The History of the War of Seventeen Hundred and Forty One. London: for J. Nourse, 1756. 2nd edn. [ii],260 pp. Lib stamp on endpaper, faint stamp on title verso. Mod polished calf gilt. *(Hollett)* £70 [≈ $134]
- Letters ... to Several of his Friends. Translated from the French by the Rev. Dr. Franklin. London: for T. Davies, & J. Wheble, 1770. 1st edn. 12mo. [ii],234 pp. Lacks half-title. Contemp mrbld bds, rebacked in calf, sides rubbed.
(Burmester) £140 [≈ $268]
- Letters Concerning the English Nation. London: Davis & Lyon, 1733. 1st edn (precedes the French edn). Post 8vo. A few pencil notes. Rec qtr calf.
(Ash) £500 [≈ $959]
- Letters Concerning the English Nation. London: Davis & Lyon, 1733. 1st edn (precedes the French edn). 8vo. [16],253,

[1],[18] pp, inc errata, index & ctlg. Contemp panelled calf. *(Rootenberg)* **$1,250 [≈ £651]**
- Letters Concerning the English Nation. London: for Davis & Lyon, 1733. 1st edn (precedes the French text). Some staining, title sl dusty. Rec imitation calf.
(Jarndyce) **£220 [≈ $422]**
- Memoirs of the Life of Voltaire. Written by Himself. Translated from the French. London: for G. Robinson, 1784. 1st English edn. Half-title. 2 ff dusty with sm marg tears. Contemp calf, gilt spine, green label, upper jnt sl weak. *(Jarndyce)* **£55 [≈ $105]**
- Memoirs of the Life of Voltaire. Written by Himself. London: Robinson, 1784. 1st English translation. 8vo. Calf.
(Rostenberg & Stern) **$185 [≈ £96]**
- The Philosophical Dictionary, For the Pocket. Catskill: Creswell; New York: Duyckinck, 1796. 12mo. Title port. Browned. Lib stamp. Perf intls at ft of title. Panelled calf. Anon.
(Rostenberg & Stern) **$125 [≈ £65]**
- Le Taureau Blanc: or, The White Bull, from the French. Translated from the Syriac. London: Murray, 1774. 2nd edn. 8vo. 75 pp. Frontis (spotted). Title sl browned, stamp on verso. Cloth backed bds, soiled.
(Hollett) **£50 [≈ $95]**
- A Treatise on Toleration; The Ignorant Philosopher; and A Commentary on the Marquis of Becaria's Treatise on Crimes and Punishments. Translated ... by David Williams. London: for Fielding & Walker, 1779. 3 parts in one vol. Rebound in half calf.
(Jarndyce) **£120 [≈ $230]**

Vream, William
- A Description of the Air-Pump, according to the ... Best and Last Improvements ... London: J.H. for the author ..., 1717. 1st edn. 8vo. 3 fldg plates (versos strengthened). Lib stamp on title verso. Mod bds.
(Ximenes) **$1,250 [≈ £651]**

W., A.
- The Enormous Abomination of the Hoop-Petticoat, as the Fashion now is ... Humbly offer'd to the Consideration of Both Sexes; especially the Female. By A.W. Esq; London: for William Russel, 1745. 27,[1] pp. Rebound in qtr calf. *(C.R. Johnson)* **£550 [≈ $1,055]**

W., I.
- Philosophical Essays ... see Watts, Isaac.

W., P.
- A Prospect of the State of Ireland ... see Walsh, Peter.

Wagstaffe, William
- A Comment upon the History of Tom Thumb. London: for J. Morphew, 1711. 1st edn. 8vo. Title dusty. 2 old blind stamps. Disbound. Anon. *(Ximenes)* **$400 [≈ £208]**

Wake, William
- The Bishop of Lincoln's Charge to the Clergy ... in his Primary Visitation ... May the 20th, 1706. London: for Richard Sare, 1707. 1st edn. 4to. [4],55,[1 advt] pp. Rec wraps.
(Fenning) **£28.50 [≈ $55]**
- A Discourse of the Holy Eucharist ... London: R. Chiswell, 1687. 4to. [4],38, [6], 127 pp. Sm marg worm holes. New cloth. Wing W.240. *(Humber)* **£45 [≈ $86]**
- The Genuine Epistles of the Apostolical Fathers, Barnabas, Ignatius, Clement, Polycarp ... With a Preliminary Discourse by William Wake. London: W.B. for R. Sare, 1710. 2nd edn. 8vo. [8],357,[11] pp. Few marks, sl shaken. Contemp calf.
(Humber) **£48 [≈ $92]**
- Of Our Obligation to put Our Trust in God rather than Men ... a Sermon ... Fourth Edition. London: for R. Sare, 1695. Disbound. Wing W.250.
(Waterfield's) **£30 [≈ $57]**
- The Principles of the Christian Religion explained: in a Brief Commentary upon the Church Catechism ... Second Edition, corrected. London: for Richard Sare, 1700. 8vo. Lacks free endpapers. Contemp sheep, rubbed, hd of spine reprd. Wing W.259.
(Waterfield's) **£45 [≈ $86]**
- The Principles of the Christian Religion explained: in a Brief Commentary upon the Church-Catechism. London: for Richard Sare, 1708. 3rd edn, crrctd. Cr 8vo. Contemp calf. *(Stewart)* **£25 [≈ $47]**
- The Principles of the Christian Religion explained in a Brief Commentary upon the Church Catechism ... Fifth Edition, corrected. London: W. Bowyer for Richard Williamson, 1731. 8vo. Contemp Cambridge style calf, mor label, minor scuffing.
(Waterfield's) **£45 [≈ $86]**

Wakefield, Gilbert
- A Reply to the Letter of Edmund Burke, Esq. to a Noble Lord ... London: for the author, & sold by G. Kearsley ..., 1796. New edn. 8vo.

52 pp. Errata slip. Wraps.
(Young's) £40 [≈ $76]
- The Spirit of Christianity, Compared with
the Spirit of the Times in Great Britain ...
London: sold by Kearsley ..., 1796. New edn.
8vo. 41,2 advt pp. Half-title. Sgntr cut from
top marg of title. Disbound.
(Young's) £45 [≈ $86]

Wakely, Andrew
- The Mariner's Compass Rectified ...
Enlarged ... by J. Atkinson ... revised ... by
John Adams ... London: for Mount & Page,
1784. Lge 12mo. 272 pp. W'cut volvelle,
w'cut ill. Title dusty. Contemp calf.
(Vanbrugh) £175 [≈ $335]

Walker, Clement
- Relations and Observations, Historical and
Politick, upon the Parliament begun ... 1640
... With an Appendix ... [London]: Printed in
the Year, 1648. Later calf, gilt borders, hinge
splitting. Wing W.334A. Anon.
(Jarndyce) £120 [≈ $230]
- Relations and Observations, Historical and
Politick, upon the Parliament begun ... 1640
... With an Appendix ... [London]: Printed in
the Yeare, 1648. 1st edn. 4to. [vi],256,18 pp.
Fldg plate (edge reprd). Occas doodles. Old
sheep. Wing W.334B,317. Anon.
(Young's) £120 [≈ $230]

Walker, Sir Edward
- Historical   Discourses   upon   Several
Occasions: Together with Perfect Copies of
... the Treaty held at Newport, in the Isle of
Wight ... London: for Sam. Keble ..., 1705.
1st edn. Folio. [xvi],369,98 pp. Plate. Titles
to both parts. Lacks frontis. Old calf, sl worn.
(Young's) £70 [≈ $134]

Walker, James
- An Inquiry into Sterility in Both Sexes ...
Phila: E. Oswald, 1797. 1st edn. Sm 4to. 22
pp. Later qtr calf, front hinge & spine sl worn.
(Bookpress) $250 [≈ £130]

Walker, John
- An Attempt towards recovering an Account
of the Numbers and Sufferings of the Clergy
of the Church of England ... London: W.S.
for J. Nicholson ..., 1714. 1st edn. Folio. [iv],
li, [xvii], 204,436 pp. Errata leaf, subscribers.
2 ff creased. Rec half calf.
(Clark) £90 [≈ $172]

Walker, John
- A Critical Pronouncing Dictionary and
Expositor of the English Language ... Dublin:
for P. Wogan, 1794. 1st Irish edn. Contemp
calf, red label. *(C.R. Johnson)* £240 [≈ $460]
- A Critical Pronouncing Dictionary and
Expositor of the English Language ... The
Second   Edition;   with   considerable
improvements and large additions. London:
Robinson,   Cadell,   Davies,   1797.   4to.
Contemp calf, rubbed, rebacked.
(Jarndyce) £180 [≈ $345]

Walker, Obadiah
- Propositions concerning Optic-Glasses ...
Oxford: at the theater, 1679. 1st edn. 4to. [iv],
46 pp. Text diags. Faint water stains in inner
crnrs. Mod qtr mor. Wing W.409. Anon.
(Gaskell) £550 [≈ $1,055]

Walker, William
- Baptismon   Didache.   The   Doctrine   of
Baptisms, or a Discourse of Dipping and
Sprinkling ... London: Robert Pawlet, 1678.
8vo. 16,304 pp. Stitching weak in centre.
19th c qtr calf, worn, split up spine. Wing
W.417.   *(Humber)* £45 [≈ $86]

Wallace, James, M.D.
- An Account of the Islands of Orkney ...
London: Tonson, 1700. 2nd edn. 8vo. Fldg
map & plate. Water stain in lower marg. 19th
c half calf, t.e.g., jnt cracked, headband
defective.   *(Hannas)* £160 [≈ $307]

Waller, Edmond
- Poems, &c. written upon several Occasions ...
Fourth Edition, with several Additions ...
London: for Henry Herringman, 1682. 8vo.
[xii],289 pp. Errata. R8 cancelled. 2 port
frontises. Orig calf. Wing W.516.
(Vanbrugh) £125 [≈ $239]

Wallis, George
- The Art of Preventing Diseases, and
Restoring Health ... London: Robinson,
1793. 8vo. xx,850,[12] pp. Tree calf, front jnt
cracked.   *(Goodrich)* $145 [≈ £75]

Walpole, Horace
- The Castle of Otranto ... The Second Edition.
London: for William Bathoe, & Thomas
Lownds, 1765. 12mo. xvi,200 pp. Contemp
half, worn. Anon.   *(Finch)* £185 [≈ $355]
- The Castle of Otranto ... Fourth Edition.
London: Dodsley, 1782. Half-title. Contemp

calf, hd of spine sl rubbed.
(Jarndyce) **£80 [≃ $153]**
- The Castle of Otranto, A Gothic Story. Translated by William Marshal ... From the Original Italian of Onuphrio Muralto ... Sixth Edition. London: Dodsley, 1791. 200 pp. Orig calf, gilt dec spine, rubbed, front hinge pulling but firm. Anon.
(Limestone Hills) **$85 [≃ £44]**
- A Catalogue of the Royal and Noble Authors of England, with Lists of their Works. The Second Edition Corrected and Enlarged. London: Dodsley & Graham, 1759. 2 vols. 252; 258 pp. Orig or contemp calf, inner hinges wearing but firm.
(Limestone Hills) **£180 [≃ £93]**
- A Catalogue of the Royal and Noble Authors ... Third Edition, Corrected and Enlarged. Dublin: for Faulkner & Bradley, 1759. 1st Irish edn. 2 vols in one. 12mo. Continuous pagination. Calf, sl rubbed.
(Jarndyce) **£48 [≃ $92]**
- Fugitive Pieces in Verse and Prose. Strawberry-Hill: 1758. 1st edn. 8vo. Inserted leaf after p 216 not present as often. Traces of b'plate removal. Blue mor gilt, t.e.g., by Stikeman, v sl rubbed. Anon.
(Ximenes) **$400 [≃ £208]**
- Historic Doubts on the Life and Reign of King Richard III ... Dublin: for G. Faulkner ..., 1768. 1st Dublin edn. 8vo. xvi,166,[1 directions] pp. 2 fldg plates. Contemp lightly speckled calf, label. *(Young's)* **£110 [≃ $211]**
- The Mysterious Mother; A Tragedy. Dublin: for John Archer, 1791. 1st Dublin edn (?). 8vo. x,102 pp. Unbound, rear wrapper present. Anon. *(Young's)* **£50 [≃ $95]**

Walsh, Peter
- A Prospect of the State of Ireland, from the Year of the World 1756. To the Year of Christ 1652. Written by P.W. London: Johanna Broom, 1682. Only edn. 8vo. [lxviii], 3-504, [vi] pp. Contemp calf, sl worn. Wing W.640. *(Clark)* **£285 [≃ $547]**
- A Prospect of the State of Ireland, from the Year of the World 1756 To the Year of Christ 1652. London: for Johanna Broom, 1682. [66], 504,[6] pp. Title sl browned & trifle torn in gutter. Few ff sl browned. Early 19th c half mor gilt, rubbed. Wing W.640.
(Hollett) **£85 [≃ $163]**

Walsh, William
- Ode for Thanksgiving Day. London: Tonson, 1706. Folio. Mod wraps. Anon.

(Waterfield's) **£150 [≃ $287]**

Walter, Richard
- A Voyage round the World in 1740-44 by George Anson ... London: 1748. 3rd edn. 8vo. [xxiv], 548 pp. 3 fldg charts. Contemp calf, traces of repr. *(Lewis)* **£165 [≃ $316]**
- A Voyage round the World ... see also Anson, George.

Walton, Izaak & Cotton, Charles
- The Complete Angler ... Lives of the Authors ... Notes ... London: for Thomas Hope ..., 1760. 1st Hawkins edn. 8vo. lvi,xxii, 303, [i]; xlviii,iv, ii,iv,128, [viii] pp. Sep title to Part 2. Frontis, 14 plates. Contemp calf, rubbed, 1 jnt cracked but firm, spine ends worn.
(Finch) **£175 [≃ $335]**

Warburton, William
- Tracts by Warburton and a Warburtonian [ie Richard Hurd] not admitted into the Collections of their respective Works. London: Dilly, 1789. 8vo. Mod qtr calf.
(Waterfield's) **£100 [≃ $191]**

Ward, Edward
- The School of Politicks: or, the Humours of a Coffee-House. A Poem. London: Baldwin, 1690. 4to. [iv],24 pp. Intl advt leaf. Lib stamp title verso. Outer ff sl dusty. Disbound, backstrip reinforced. Wing W.753A. Anon.
(Clark) **£350 [≃ $671]**

Ward, John
- The Young Mathematician's Guide. Being a Plain and Easy Introduction to the Mathematicks ... The Fourth Edition, Carefully Corrected ... London: 1724. [8],456 pp. Frontis port, text diags. Orig panelled calf, spine with a lacquer-like coat.
(Karmiole) **$225 [≃ £117]**
- The Young Mathematician's Guide: being a Plain and Easy Introduction to the Mathematicks. London: 1734. 6th edn. viii,456 pp. Frontis port. A few pp stained at edges, some browned. Panelled calf, rebacked. *(Whitehart)* **£50 [≃ $95]**

Ward, Seth
- An Apology for the Mysteries of the Gospel. being a Sermon Preached at White-Hall, Feb. 16, 1672/3. London: Andrew Clark, 1673. 4to. [ii],46 pp. Outer ff dusty. Lib stamp on title verso. Disbound. Wing W.814. Anon.
(Clark) **£20 [≃ $38]**

- Vindiciae Academiarum containing Some brief Animadversions upon Mr. Webster's Book ... With an Appendix ... Oxford: Leonard Lichfield for Thomas Robinson, 1654. 4to. [2], 65 pp. Sl dusty. Lib stamp. Stained at 1 crnr. Disbound. Wing W.832. Anon.   *(Jarndyce)* £85 [≈ $163]

Ward, William

- An Essay on Grammar, as it may be applied to the English Language ... London: for Robert Horsfield, 1765. 1st edn. 4to. Advt leaf at end. Occas sl foxing. Contemp calf, gilt spine, sl worn.   *(Ximenes)* $450 [≈ £234]

Ware, Sir James

- De Hibernia et Antiquitatibus ejus. London: 1654. 1st edn. 8vo. 2 full page engvd maps, red & black title. Contemp calf, jnts cracked. Wing W.843.   *(Robertshaw)* £95 [≈ $182]
- The History and Antiquities of Ireland ... Revised ... by Walter Harris. Dublin: Bell & Fleming, 1764. Folio. [6], 363,[5] pp. 22 plates, num tables. Mod elab gilt calf & bds.
                              (Karmiole) $450 [≈ £234]

Warner, Richard

- Hampshire Extracted from Domes-Day Book, with an Accurate English Translation, a Preface and an Introduction. London: R. Faulder ..., 1789. 1st edn. 4to. xviii, xlvi, 320, 8 pp. Contemp calf, rebacked.
                          (Lloyd-Roberts) £85 [≈ $163]

Warton, Thomas

- Observations on the Fairy Queen of Spenser ... London: Dodsley, 1762. 2nd edn. 8vo. xx, 228; 270 pp. Contemp calf, 2 sm cracks in jnts, hd of 1 spine worn.
                              (Young's) £150 [≈ $287]
- The Poems on Various Subjects ... Now First Collected. London: for G.G.J. & J. Robinson, 1791. 1st edn. 8vo. Early 19th c straight grained mor gilt, spine faded, sl rubbed.
                              (Ximenes) $175 [≈ £91]

Washington, George

- A Collection of the Speeches of the President of the United States to Both Houses of Congress, at the Opening of Every Session, with Their Answers ... Boston: 1796. 282,advt pp. Occas heavy foxing. Contemp calf, hinges reprd.   *(Reese)* $350 [≈ £182]
- A Message of the President ... to Congress, enclosing Three Letters from the Minister Plenipotentiary ... in London .... Phila: 1794. 15 pp. Foxed. Later half calf, front hinge

broken.   *(Reese)* $200 [≈ £104]
- Official Letters to the Honorable American Congress, written during the War between the American Colonies and Great britain ... London: 1795. 1st British edn. 2 vols in one. viii, 364; 384 pp. Occas fox marks. No frontis (found in some copies). Mod cloth.
                              (Reese) $225 [≈ £117]

Waterland, Daniel

- A Critical History of the Athanasian Creed ... Second Edition, Corrected and Improv'd. Cambridge: UP, 1728. Sm worm hole through lower marg of 2nd half of book. 19th c half calf, rubbed.
                          (Waterfield's) £65 [≈ $124]
- The Importance of the Doctrine of the Holy Trinity asserted in reply to some late Pamphlets ... Second Edition corrected. London: Innys & Manby, 1734. 8vo. Contemp calf, rubbed, front jnt cracked but sound, sl worn. *(Waterfield's)* £55 [≈ $105]
- The Nature, Obligation, and Efficacy of the Christian Sacraments considered; in reply to a Pamphlet intituled An Answer to the remarks ... London: 1730. Half-title. Disbound. Anon.   *(Waterfield's)* £25 [≈ $47]
- Remarks upon Doctor Clarke's Exposition of the Church Catechism. The Second Edition. London: for John Crownfield & sold by Cornelius Crownfield, Cambridge, 1730. Disbound. Anon. *(Waterfield's)* £25 [≈ $47]
- A Vindication of Christ's Divinity ... Third Edition. Cambridge: Corn. Crownfield, 1710. 8vo. Lacks f.e.p. Contemp panelled calf, mor label.   *(Waterfield's)* £50 [≈ $95]

Watson, Richard

- An Address to the People of Great Britain ... London: for R. Faulder ..., 1798. 1st edn. 8vo. [iv],42,[1 advt] pp. Half-title. Sm marg stain on 2 ff. Disbound.
                              (Young's) £45 [≈ $86]
- An Address to Young Persons after Confirmation ... London: for Thomas Evans, 1792. 4th edn. 8vo. 49 pp. Disbound.
                              (Young's) £25 [≈ $47]
- An Answer to the Disquisition on Government and Civil Liberty ... London: Debrett, 1782. 1st edn. 8vo. [iv],49,2 advt pp. New contemp style calf. Anon.
                              (Young's) £80 [≈ $153]
- Chemical Essays ... Third Edition. London: for T. Evans, 1784-87. Vols 1-3 3rd edn, 4 & 5 1st edn. 5 vols. 8vo. Contemp calf, red & green mor labels.

(Waterfield's) **£300 [≃$575]**

- The Principles of the Revolution vindicated in a Sermon preached before the University of Cambridge on Wednesday May 19 1776. Cambridge: Archdeacon ..., 1776. 4to. Disbound. *(Waterfield's)* **£40 [≃$76]**
- A Sermon preached before the Stewards of the Westminster Dispensary at their Anniversary Meeting in Charlotte Street Chapel April 1785, with an Appendix. London: Cadell, 1793. Disbound. *(Waterfield's)* **£35 [≃$67]**

Watson, Robert

- The History of the Reign of Philip the Third, King of Spain ... London: Robinson, 1793. 3rd edn. 2 vols. 8vo. [iv],460; [ii], 389, [18] pp. Contemp calf, rehinged. *(Young's)* **£58 [≃$111]**

Watson, William

- The Clergy-Man's Law: or, the Complete Incumbent ... The Third Edition, with large Additions. London: Nutt, Gosling ..., 1725. Folio. 4,[viii], 652,[62] pp. Minor damp staining of early ff. Contemp calf, jnts cracked but firm, minor wear to extremities, label chipped. *(Clark)* **£75 [≃$143]**

Watts, Isaac

- A Defense against the Temptation to Self-Murther ... London: for J. Clark & R. Hett ..., 1726. Sm 8vo. xi,[i],142 pp, advt leaf. Old calf, reprd, rebacked, new endpapers. *(Hollett)* **£150 [≃$287]**
- An Essay toward the Proof of a Separate State of Souls between Death and the Resurrection ... London: for Richard Hett, 1732. 1st edn. Mod wraps. Anon. *(Waterfield's)* **£90 [≃$172]**
- Evangelical Discourses on Several Subjects. To which is added, An Essay on the Powers and Contests of Flesh and Spirit. London: Oswald, Buckland, 1747. 1st edn. 8vo. Contemp calf, rubbed, backstrip sl defective. *(Waterfield's)* **£65 [≃$124]**
- A Guide to Prayer ... London: for E. Matthews, 1722. 3rd edn, crrctd. Cr 8vo. End ff soiled. Contemp calf. *(Stewart)* **£35 [≃$67]**
- The Knowledge of the Heavens and the Earth made easy; or, the First Principles of Astronomy and Geography explain'd by the Use of Globes and Maps ... London: 1728. 2nd edn. xi, 222 pp. 6 fldg plates. Contemp calf, rebacked, edges sl worn. *(Whitehart)* **£85 [≃$163]**

- The Knowledge of the Heavens and the Earth made easy ... The fourth edition, corrected. London: for T. Longman ..., 1744. 8vo. xiii, [i], 222,[12] pp. 30 figs on 6 fldg engvd plates. Contemp calf, gilt ruled sides & spine, mor label. *(Gaskell)* **£125 [≃$239]**
- Logick ... Fourth Edition, Corrected. London: 1731. 8vo. [vi],365,[v] pp. Orig calf. *(Bickersteth)* **£48 [≃$92]**
- Philosophical Essays on Various Subjects ... By I.W. London: for Richard Ford, & Richard Hett, 1733. 1st edn. 8vo. Contemp calf, gilt spine, rather worn, jnts weak. *(Ximenes)* **£450 [≃£234]**
- The Psalms of David Imitated in the Language of the New Testament ... London: for J. Clark, R. Ford, R. Cruttenden, 1719. 1st edn. 12mo. Final advt leaf. 1st & last few ff v sl damp marked. Contemp gilt-ruled calf, rebacked, crnrs sl worn. *(Sanders)* **£480 [≃$921]**

Watts, Robert

- Two Letters to the Right Honourable Viscount Townshend: shewing the Seditious Tendency of several late Pamphlets ... By a Presbyter of the Church of England. London: R. Burleigh, 1714. 8vo. 40 pp. Disbound. Anon. *(Bickersteth)* **£20 [≃$38]**

Webb, Daniel

- An Inquiry into the Beauties of Painting; and into the Merits of the Most Celebrated Painters, Ancient and Modern. London: Dodsley, 1760. 1st edn. 8vo. xvi,200 pp. Contemp calf, front hinge cracked. *(Bookpress)* **$425 [≃£221]**
- An Inquiry into the Beauties of Painting; and into the Merits of the Most Celebrated Painters, Ancient and Modern. London: Dodsley, 1761. 2nd edn. Sm 8vo. Contemp calf, lower spine rubbed. *(Bernett)* **$100 [≃£52]**
- An Inquiry into the Beauties of Poetry ... [Bound with the same author's] An Inquiry into the Beauties of Painting ... Dublin: Sarah Cotter, 1764. 2 works in one vol. 12mo. Both with final blank leaf. Contemp calf, spine sl chipped at hd. *(Georges)* **£90 [≃$172]**
- Observations on the Correspondence between Poetry and Music. By the Author of an Enquiry into the Beauties of Painting. London: Dodsley, 1769. 8vo. Half-title. 4 advt pp. Contemp calf, gilt spine, brown label. Anon. *(Jarndyce)* **£140 [≃$268]**

Webber, Samuel
- An Account of a Scheme for preventing the Exportation of our Wool ... London: for T. Cooper, 1740. 1st edn, 2nd issue. 8vo. [ii], 37, [1] pp. Fldg table. Disbound.
(Pickering) **$200 [≈ £104]**

Webster, --, of Christ-Church (pseud.)
- The Stage ... see Reynardson, Francis.

Webster, Alexander
- Calculations with the Principles and Data on which they are instituted: relative to a late Act of Parliament ... Edinburgh: Thomas Lumisden ..., 1748. 1st edn. Folio. [x],5-45 pp. Contemp calf, hd of spine bumped, extremities rubbed. Anon.
(Pickering) **$650 [≈ £338]**

Webster, Charles
- Facts tending to show the Connection of the Stomach with Life, Disease, and Recovery. London: Murray, 1793. 59 pp. Rec wraps.
(C.R. Johnson) **£85 [≈ $163]**

Webster, John
- Metallographia; or an History of Metals ... London: A.C. for Walter Kettilby, 1671. Only edn. 4to. 388, 2 advt pp.
(C.R. Johnson) **£550 [≈ $1,055]**

Wedgwood, Josiah
- Catalogue of Cameos, Intaglios, Medals, Bas-reliefs, Busts and Small Statues ... The Sixth Edition, with Additions. Etruria: 1787. 8vo. vi,[1]-44, 45*-46*, 45-48, *45-48*, 49-73, [1] pp. 2 plates, 1 text ill. Orig mrbld wraps, no backstrip, v sl wear.
(Georges) **£1,500 [≈ $2,879]**

Weems, The Rev. Mr.
- The Philanthropist. Dumfries: M.L. Weems, (1799). 8vo. [ii],30 pp. Self-wraps.
(Bookpress) **$600 [≈ £312]**

Weever, John
- Ancient Funerall Monuments ... London: Thomas Harper, 1631. 1st edn. Folio. [xvi], 871,[xiv index] pp. Port, addtnl engvd title. With the index (which was issued later). Later calf, rebacked. *(Lamb)* **£450 [≈ $863]**
- Ancient Funerall Monuments ... London: Tho. Harper, 1631. 1st edn. Sm folio. [16], 872 pp. Port, addtnl engvd title. Without the index. Mod mor & cloth. STC 25223.
(Karmiole) **$475 [≈ £247]**

- Ancient Funerall Monuments ... London: Tho. Harper, 1631. 1st edn. Sm folio. [16], 872 pp. Addtnl engvd title. Lacks frontis & without the index. Contemp calf, rebacked. STC 25223. *(Karmiole)* **$350 [≈ £182]**

Weld, Isaac
- Travels through the States of North America, and the Provinces of Upper and Lower Canada ... London: 1799. 4to. xxiv,464,advt pp. 16 maps (1 fldg) & plates. Occas foxing, mostly to plates. Later three qtr calf, some wear to extremities. *(Reese)* **$1,250 [≈ £651]**

Welde, Thomas
- A Short History of the Rise, Reign, and Ruin of the Antinomians, Familists & Libertines, that Infected the Churches of Nevv-England ... London: 1644. 3rd edn. Sm 4to. Title, [16], 66 pp (misnumbered). Some marks, some margs (inc title) shaved. Later three qtr calf. Anon *(Reese)* **$1,500 [≈ £781]**

Wells, Edward
- The Young Gentleman's Astronomy, Chronology, and Dialling ... Third Edition, Revised, and Corrected, with Additions. London: Knapton, 1725. 8vo. [viii],148, [viii], 85, [viii],43 pp. 27 plates. Marg piece torn from 1 title. Orig calf, rubbed, label defective. *(Bickersteth)* **£110 [≈ $211]**
- The Young Gentleman's Astronomy, Chronology, and Dialling ... Fourth Edition, Revised, and Corrected, with Additions. London: Knapton, 1736. 8vo. [viii],148, [viii], 86, [viii], 54 pp. 25 plates. Sl foxing on plates. Contemp calf gilt, cracks to jnts.
(Rankin) **£75 [≈ $143]**

Welsted, Leonard
- The Dissembled Wanton; or, My Son Get Money. A Comedy ... London: for John Watts, 1727. 1st edn. 8vo. [xii],72,[2] pp. half-title. Disbound. *(Young's)* **£38 [≈ $72]**

Welwood, James
- Memoirs of the Most Material Transactions in England, for the last Hundred Years preceding the Revolution in 1688. London: 1702. 4th edn. 405 pp. Contemp panelled calf, red label. *(Robertshaw)* **£40 [≈ $76]**

Wendeborn, G.F.A.
- A View of England towards the Close of the Eighteenth Century ... Translated from the Original German by the Author himself. Dublin: William Sleater, 1791. 2 vols.

Contemp calf, red & green labels.
(C.R. Johnson) **£280 [≈ $537]**

Wesley, John
- The Beauties of Methodism. Selected from the Works of the Reverend John Wesley. London: for J. Fielding, J. Scatcherd & J. Whitaker, & Willm. Lane, [ca 1785]. 1st edn. 12mo. Engvd title with port vignette. Contemp sheep, upper jnt cracked, cords just holding *(Sanders)* **£100 [≈ $191]**
- A Calm Address to our American Colonies. London: R. Hawes ... & sold at the Poultry, [1775]. 23 pp. Disbound.
(C.R. Johnson) **£150 [≈ $287]**
- The Complete English Dictionary ... By a Lover of Good English and Common Sense ... The Second Edition, with Additions. Bristol: William Pine ..., 1764. 12mo. Some staining. Contemp sheep, rubbed, sm reprs to crnrs & hd of spine. *(Jarndyce)* **£1,100 [≈ $2,111]**
- Explanatory Notes upon the New Testament ... Second Edition. London: printed in the year, 1757. 8vo. Port frontis. Contemp calf, rebacked, crnrs reprd.
(Waterfield's) **£185 [≈ $355]**

West, Benjamin
- Miscellaneous Poems, Translations and Imitations ... Northampton: for the author by Thomas Dicey ..., 1780. Half-title, xxxxii, 149, [3] pp. Contemp calf, crack in upper hinge. *(C.R. Johnson)* **£280 [≈ $537]**

West, Gilbert
- Observations on the History and Evidences of the Resurrection of Jesus Christ. Third Edition. London: Dodsley, 1747. xvi,457 pp. Calf, label on rear bd. *(Gage)* **£20 [≈ $38]**
- Odes of Pindar, with several Other Pieces in Prose and Verse, translated from the Greek. To which is prefixed a Dissertation on the Olympick Games. London: Dodsley, 1749. 1st edn. 4to. ccvi,315,[3] pp. Red & black title. Contemp calf, hinges broken but holding. *(Claude Cox)* **£75 [≈ $143]**

West, Richard, D.D.
- A Sermon Preached before the Honourable House of Commons ... Being the Anniversary of the Martyrdom of King Charles I. London: for J. Churchill, 1710. 1st edn. 8vo. 30 pp. Wraps. *(Young's)* **£35 [≈ $67]**

West, Richard, Lord Chancellor of Ireland
- An Enquiry into the Origin and Manner of

Creating Peers. London: T. Evans, 1782. 74 pp. Disbound. *(C.R. Johnson)* **£25 [≈ $47]**

West, Thomas
- The Antiquities of Furness ... London: for the author, by T. Spilsbury ..., 1774. 1st edn. 4to. [xx],lvi,288, 3A-3R4 pp. Fldg plan, 3 plates. Contemp calf gilt, edges rubbed, hinges cracked. *(Hollett)* **£220 [≈ $422]**
- The Antiquities of Furness ... London: for the author, 1784. 3rd edn. Lacks frontis map & all before title. Old half calf, rather defective, front jnt cracked.
(Hollett) **£60 [≈ $115]**
- A Guide to the Lakes, in Cumberland, Westmorland, and Lancashire. By the Author of the Antiquities of Furness. The Third Edition, revised ... London: for B. Law ..., 1784. 8vo. Half-title. 1 page advts. Frontis (offsetting), fldg map. Contemp half calf. Anon. *(Jarndyce)* **£120 [≈ $230]**

Weston, Edward
- The Country Gentleman's Advice to his Neighbours ... London: E. Owen, 1756. 3rd edn, enlgd. 8vo. 40 pp. New wraps.
(Young's) **£45 [≈ $86]**

Weston, James
- Stenography Compleated, Or the Art of Short-Hand brought to Perfection ... London: for the author, 1727. 1st edn. 8vo. [x],192, [ii], 16 pp. Port frontis, 3 engvd frontis, 3 text vignettes. Period calf gilt, sl worn.
(Rankin) **£350 [≈ $671]**

Weston, Richard
- The English Flora [with] The Supplement to the English Flora. London: 1775-80. 2 vols in one. 8vo. [xvi],259; [xii],120 pp. Contemp calf. *(Wheldon & Wesley)* **£80 [≈ $153]**
- The Gardner's and Planter's Calendar ... Second Edition, corrected and enlarged. London: for T. Carnan, 1778. Lge 12mo. [12], 336 pp. Contemp calf bds, rebacked.
(Beech) **£65 [≈ $124]**

Weston, William
- An Enquiry into the Rejection of the Christian Miracles by the Heathens ... Cambridge: J. Bentham ..., 1746. 1st edn. [2], xvi,[14], 418 pp. Contemp panelled calf, hd of spine sl chipped. *(Karmiole)* **£200 [≈ £104]**

Whately, Thomas
- Observations on Modern Gardening,

illustrated by Descriptions. London: for T. Payne, 1770. 1st edn. 8vo. V sl marg worm. Contemp calf, label v sl chipped. Anon.
(Georges) **£650 [≈ $1,247]**
- Observations on Modern Gardening. Illustrated by Descriptions. Fifth Edition. London: T. Payne, 1793. 8vo. [8],263 pp. Orig glazed green cloth, paper label, uncut, some sl wear, label a little indistinct.
(Spelman) **£95 [≈ $182]**

Wheler, George
- A Journey into Greece ... in Company of Dr. Spon of Lyons. In Six Books ... London: Cademan ..., 1682. 1st edn. Sm folio. Title, [xii], 483 pp (usual jump from 80 to 177). 3 plates, 4 pp coins, text ills. Lacks map. Browning. Later calf, jnts weak.
(Frew Mackenzie) **£295 [≈ $566]**

Whiston, William
- Historical Memoirs of the Life of Dr. Samuel Clarke ... Second Edition Corrected. London: sold by Fletcher Gyles & J. Roberts, 1750. Disbound.   *(Waterfield's)* **£60 [≈ $115]**
- Memoirs of the Life and Writings Containing Memoirs of several of his Friends also. Written by himself ... London: for the author, 1749. 1st edn. 8vo. 662,22, 40,16 pp. Fldg chart. Rebound in half calf.
(Young's) **£100 [≈ $191]**
- A Short View of the Chronology of the Old Testament, and of the Harmony of the Four Evangelists. Cambridge: UP for B. Tooke, 1702. 1st edn. 4to. [viii],543,[2],[1 blank], [1 errata] pp. 4 engvd tables. Occas sl browning. Contemp calf, minor worm tracks on sides.
(Gaskell) **£155 [≈ $297]**

Whitaker, John
- The Course of Hannibal Over the Alps Ascertained. London: for John Stockdale, 1794. 1st edn. 2 vols. 8vo. [ii],386; [ii], 284 pp. Occas spotting. Contemp green half mor, elab gilt spines. Slipcase.
(Gough) **£395 [≈ $758]**
- The Origin of Arianism Disclosed. London: for John Stockdale, 1791. 1st edn. 8vo. Final errata / advt leaf. New half calf. Inscrbd "From the Author". *(Georges)* **£100 [≈ $191]**

Whitby, Daniel
- [Greek title, then] or, the Last Thought of Dr. Whitby containing his Correction of Several Passages in his Commentary on the New Testament ... Second Edition. London: Knapton, 1728. Disbound.

(Waterfield's) **£20 [≈ $38]**
- A Paraphrase and Commentary on the New Testament. London: for J. Brotherton ..., 1744. 6th edn. 2 vols. Folio. Port frontis. Lacks map from vol 2. Marg worm holes vol 1. Contemp calf, jnts sl cracked.
(Lloyd-Roberts) **£65 [≈ $124]**

White, Charles
- Cases in Surgery, with Remarks. Part the First [all published] ... added, An Essay on the Ligature of Arteries, by J. Aiken. London: 1770. 1st edn. 8vo. xv,198,[4] pp. 7 fldg plates. Contemp calf, extremities v sl bumped, sm splits in jnt.
(Hemlock) **$875 [≈ £455]**
- A Treatise on the Management of Pregnancy and Lying-in Women ... with some Directions concerning the Delivery of the Child ... Third Edition, revised and enlarged. London: Dilly, 1785. 3rd edn. 8vo. xix,475 pp. 2 plates. Sl browning. Rec bds. *(Hemlock)* **$400 [≈ £208]**

White, Francis
- A Replie to Iesuit Fishers answere to certain questions propounded by his most gratious Ma[jes]tie King James. London: Islip, 1624. 1st edn. 2 parts in one. 4to. [xxx], 592,[iv]; [iv],74 pp. Engvd title, port frontis. 1 crnr torn away (sl loss). Contemp calf, rebacked. STC 25382.   *(Sotheran's)* **£185 [≈ $355]**

White, John, of Eccles
- The Way of the True Church ... London: for John Bill & William Barrett, 1608. 4to. Lacks *1 (blank). Name cut from title. Contemp panelled calf, upper jnt cracked, new label.
(Stewart) **£100 [≈ $191]**

White, Joseph
- A Statement of Dr. White's Literary Obligations to the late Rev. Mr. Samuel Badcock, and the Rev. Samuel Parr, L.L.D. Oxford: sold by D. Prince & J. Cooke ..., 1790. 1st edn. 8vo. Half-title. Corrigenda leaf at end. Disbound.   *(Ximenes)* **£125 [≈ £65]**

White, Stephen
- Collateral Bee-Boxes; or, a New, Easy and Advantageous Method of Managing Bees ... Third Edition improved. London: Davis & Reyners, 1764. 8vo. ix,47 pp. Plate. Marg reprs to plate & last leaf not affecting text. Mod qtr mor.   *(Lamb)* **£75 [≈ $143]**

Whitehead, William
- Ann Boleyn to Henry the Eighth. An Epistle.

London: for R. Dodsley, sold by M. Cooper, 1743. Folio. Disbound.
(Waterfield's) £125 [≈ $239]
- An Hymn to the Nymph of Bristol Spring. London: ptd by R. Dodsley, sold by M. Cooper, 1751. 4to. Title vignette, 1 head-piece, 1 tail-piece. Mod wraps.
(Waterfield's) £135 [≈ $259]
- On Nobility: an Epistle to the Right Honble the Earl of ******. London: for R. Dodsley, sold by M. Cooper, 1744. Folio. Advt leaf after title. Disbound.
(Waterfield's) £150 [≈ $287]
- Variety. A Tale for Married People. London: Dodsley, 1776. 5th edn. 4to. 24 pp. Disbound. *(Young's)* £15 [≈ $28]

Whitehurst, John
- An Inquiry into the Original State and Formation of the Earth ... London: for the author by J. Cooper, 1778. 1st edn. 4to. [xii], ii,[ii], 199 pp. 9 plates on 4 ff (2 fldg). B'plate removed. Contemp polished calf gilt, edges sl worn & scraped, upper hinge cracked.
(Hollett) £375 [≈ $719]

Whitelocke, Bulstrode
- Memorials of the English Affairs ... Publish'd ... by William Penn ... London: for E. Curll ..., 1709. 1st edn. Folio. Licence leaf before title. Contemp calf gilt, gilt spine sl rubbed.
(Ximenes) $600 [≈ £312]

Whittel, John
- Constantinus Redivivus: or, a Full Account of the Wonderful Providences and Unparallell'd [sic] Successes ... William the 3d, now King of Great Britain ... London: Harbin, 1693. Only edn. [xxviii],199,[i] pp. Wear & tear. Contemp sheep, worn. Wing W.2040.
(Clark) £75 [≈ $143]

Whitworth, Charles
- An Account of Russia as it was in the Year 1710. Strawberry-Hill: 1758. 1st edn. 8vo. Title device. Some browning at edges. Orig calf, rebacked. One of 700.
(Rostenberg & Stern) $425 [≈ £221]
- A Collection of the Supplies, and Ways, and Means; from the Revolution to the Present Time. The Second Edition. London: R. Davis, 1765. 181,6 pp. Fldg table. Contemp calf, hinge weak.
(C.R. Johnson) £70 [≈ $134]

Whole ...
- The Whole Art of Painting in Water-Colours ... see Bowles, Carington.
- The Whole Duty of Man ... see Allestree, Richard.

The Widow of the Wood ...
- See Victor, Benjamin.

Wight, Alexander
- A Treatise on the Laws concerning the Election of the different Representatives sent from Scotland to the Parliament of Great Britain ... Edinburgh: Balfour & Smellie, 1773. 1st edn. Some damp staining. Contemp calf, sl rubbed. *(Jarndyce)* £80 [≈ $153]

Wight, Thomas & Rutty, John
- A History of the Rise and Progress of the People called Quakers in Ireland ... Dublin: Jackson, 1751. Sm 4to. 484, index pp. Contemp calf. *(Emerald Isle)* £75 [≈ $143]

Wilberforce, William
- Practical View of the Prevailing Religious System of Professed Christians ... contrasted with Real Christianity. London: Cadell & Davies, 1797. 1st edn. 8vo. Orig bds, uncut, paper spine worn. *(Stewart)* £175 [≈ $335]
- A Practical View of the Prevailing Religious System of Professed Christians ... contrasted with Real Christianity. London: Cadell, 1797. 2nd edn. 8vo. [iv],491,[13] pp. Occas sl spotting. Contemp half calf.
(Young's) £36 [≈ $69]

Wildman, Thomas
- A Treatise on the Management of Bees ... London: for the author, & sold by T. Cadell, 1768. 1st edn. 4to. xx,169 pp. 3 fldg plates. Title trifle foxed. Near contemp qtr calf, unsophisticated copy. *(Gough)* £395 [≈ $758]
- A Treatise on the Management of Bees ... London: 1778. 3rd edn. xx,325,16 pp. 3 fldg plates. Occas foxing. Mod leather backed bds.
(Whitehart) £140 [≈ $268]

Wilkes, John
- A Letter to A Noble Member of the Club in Albemarle-Street, from John Wilkes, Esq; at Paris. London: W. Nicoll, 1764. 4to. Half-title, 19 pp. Disbound.
(C.R. Johnson) £125 [≈ $239]

Wilkes, Wetenhall
- A Letter of Genteel and Moral Advice to a

Young Lady; Being a System of Rules and Informations ... The Eighth Edition, carefully revised, Corrected, and enlarged by the Author. London: Hawes, Clarke & Collins, 1766. 223 pp. Frontis. Contemp calf.
(C.R. Johnson) £55 [≈ $105]

Wilkie, William

- The Epigoniad. A Poem ... Second Edition ... To which is added, A Dream, in the Manner of Spencer. London: for A. Millar, 1759. 8vo. xlviii, 228 pp. Some staining to 4 ff. Contemp calf, jnts sl cracked but firm.
(Rankin) £75 [≈ $143]
- Fables. London: Dilly, 1768. 1st edn. 8vo. 140 pp. Frontis, plates. Contemp half calf, some rubbing.   *(Chapel Hill)* $275 [≈ £143]
- Fables. London: Edward & Charles Dilly, 1768. 1st edn. [12],140 pp. Half-title. 18 engvd plates. Contemp calf, rubbed, outer hinges reprd with glue.   *(Karmiole)* $150 [≈ £78]

Wilkins, Charles (translator)

- The Heetopades of Veeshnoo-Sarma, in a Series of Connected Fables ... With Explanatory Notes ... Bath: R. Cruttwell ..., 1787. 1st English translation. 8vo. xx,334 pp. Contemp calf, sides rubbed, rebacked.
(Burmester) £120 [≈ $230]

Wilkins, John

- A Discourse Concerning the Gift of Prayer ... added Ecclesiastes or a Discourse concerning the Gift of Preaching ... London: for E. Gellibrand, 1678-79. 8vo. [6],232, [14], 204, [12] pp. Sm hole in index. Contemp calf, rebacked & recrnrd. Wing W.2183.
(Humber) £85 [≈ $163]
- A Discovery of a New World ... Fourth Edition corrected and amended. London: T.M. & J.A. for John Gillibrand, 1684. 2 parts in 1 vol. 8vo. [13],96, 93 (bis)-187, [8],184 pp, advt leaf. Addtnl engvd title, 17 text w'cuts. Contemp calf, worn but sound. Wing W.2186.   *(Fenning)* £225 [≈ $431]
- Mathematicall Magick ... London: M.F. for Sa: Gellibrand, 1648. 1st edn, 1st issue. 8vo. [xiv], 295 pp. Lacks A1 blank. 33 text w'cut figs, 8 engvd plates in text. Title sl browned, sm marg tear. Calf antique. Wing W.2198.
(Bickersteth) £550 [≈ $1,055]

Wilkinson, Edward

- Wisdom, A Poem. New York: Isaac Collins, 1797. 12mo. 21 pp. Sl marg damp stain few ff. Contemp wraps. Anon.
(Bookpress) $110 [≈ £57]

Willes, Thomas

- A Word in Season, for Warning to England ... London: Ratcliff for Underhill, 1659. 1st edn. [ii 'Votum Authoris'], [xii], 430, [xx] pp. Engvd frontis. Near contemp straight grained mor gilt, a.e.g., sl rubbed, hd of spine sl defective. Wing W.2308.
(Hollett) £120 [≈ $230]

Williams, Daniel

- The Advancement of Christs Interests the governing End of a Christians Life. A Second Sermon Preached ... January the 9th 1687/8. London: for J. Robinson, 1688. Only edn. 4to. [vi], 36 pp. Calf backed bds. Wing W.2644.   *(Young's)* £120 [≈ $230]

Williams, Griffith

- The Best Religion wherein is explained the Summe and Principal Heads of the Gospel ... London: George Miller for Stephens & Meredith, 1636. Sm folio. [8], 1106, [34] pp. Engvd title. Minor defects, v sl browned. New half calf. STC 25718.
(Humber) £135 [≈ $259]
- The True Church Shewed to all Men that Desire to be Members of the Same in Six Books ... London: for N. Butter, 1629. Sm thick folio. [10],933,24 pp. Engvd title. Marg water stain with some discolouration. Contemp calf. STC 25721.
(Humber) £125 [≈ $239]
- The True Church: shewed to all Men, that desire to be Members of the same ... London: John Haviland for Nathaniel Butter, 1629. Folio. Engvd border to title. Trace of marg worm in a few ff. Orig rough calf, crnrs worn. STC 25721.   *(Stewart)* £150 [≈ $287]

Williams, Helen Maria

- Letters containing a Sketch of the Scenes which passed in Various Departments of France during the Tyranny of Robespierre ... Phila: Snowden & M'Corkle, 1796. 12mo. Sl foxing. Contemp tree sheep, gilt spine a little worn.   *(Ximenes)* $175 [≈ £91]
- Letters written in France, in the Summer of 1790 ... London: for T. Cadell, 1790. 1st edn. 12mo. Sl worm in lower marg. Contemp half calf, sl chipped, hinges cracking.
(Jarndyce) £120 [≈ $230]
- Letters written in France; containing a great Variety of Original Information concerning the most important Events ... Dublin: J. Chambers, 1794. 8vo. A few spots. Contemp tree calf, red & green labels.
(Jarndyce) £150 [≈ $287]

- A Tour in Switzerland ... London: for G.G. & J. Robinson, 1798. 1st edn. 2 vols. 8vo. [xiv], 354; viii, 352 pp. Half-title crrctly in vol 1 only. 1 sm marg repr. Contemp calf, rubbed, jnts reprd, new labels.
(Burmester) **£150 [≈ $287]**
- A Tour in Switzerland ... London: for G.G. & J. Robinson, 1798. 1st edn & 2nd edn. 2 vols. 8vo. xii, 354; viii, 352 pp. Contemp calf, edges rubbed, rebacked.
(Young's) **£85 [≈ $163]**
- A Tour in Switzerland ... Dublin: for T. Byrne, 1798. 1st Irish edn. 2 vols. 12mo. Fldg map. Lower crnr of last 2 ff in vol 1 sl gnawed affecting 2 words. Contemp half calf, gilt spines, sl rubbed. *(Ximenes)* **$250 [≈ £130]**

Williams, John, Bishop of Chichester
- An Apology for the Pulpits ... London: for Dorman Newman, 1688. 4to. [2],58 pp. Sl dusty & spotted. Disbound. Wing W.2681. Anon. *(Jarndyce)* **£20 [≈ $38]**

Williams, John, Esq.
- The Rise, Progress, and Present State of the Northern Governments ... made during a Tour of Five Years ... London: Becket, 1777. 1st edn. 2 vols. 4to. Vol 2 ends with 'Finis' p 659. Mod qtr mor, unopened.
(Hannas) **£250 [≈ $479]**
- The Rise, Progress, and Present State of the Northern Governments ... made during a Tour of Five Years ... London: Becket, 1777. 1st edn. 2 vols. 4to. Vol 2 has addtnl 16 pp Index & advt after 'Finis' p 659. Contemp calf, jnts cracked. *(Hannas)* **£110 [≈ $211]**

Williams, John ('Anthony Pasquin')
- A Crying Epistle from Britannia to Colonel Mack, including a Naked Portrait of the King, Queen, and Prince, with Notes ... New Edition ... [Shrove Tuesday, a Satiric Rhapsody] ... London: (1794). 2 parts. 24, 36 pp. Half-title. Disbound.
(Jarndyce) **£50 [≈ $95]**
- The Eccentricities of John Edwin, Comedian ... Arranged ... by Anthony Pasquin. Dublin: Zachariah Jackson, 1791. Contemp calf, red & green labels. *(C.R. Johnson)* **£220 [≈ $422]**
- Legislative Biography; or, An Attempt to ascertain the Merits and Principles of the most Admired Orators of the British Senate ... London: for H.D. Symonds, 1795. 64 pp. Half-title. Disbound. *(Jarndyce)* **£25 [≈ $47]**
- A Looking-Glass for the Royal Family: with Documents for British Ladies, and all

Foreigners residing in London. By John Williams. London: Symonds & Bellamy, 1797. 36 pp. Half-title. Frontis (sl browned). Disbound. *(Jarndyce)* **£38 [≈ $72]**
- The New Brighton Guide; involving a Complete, Authentic, and Honorable Solution of the Recent Mysteries of Carlton House. The Sixth Edition, with Momentous Alterations and Additions. London: Symonds & Bellamy, 1796. Half-title. Disbound.
(Jarndyce) **£35 [≈ $67]**

Willich, A.F.M.
- Lectures on Diet and Regimen: being a Systematic Inquiry into the most Rational Means of preserving Health and Prolonging Life. London: Longman, 1799. 1st edn. 643 pp. Contemp blue straight grain mor, gilt spine. *(C.R. Johnson)* **£150 [≈ $287]**
- Lectures on Diet and Regimen ... chiefly for the Use of Families ... Second Edition, improved and enlarged ... London: Longman & Rees, 1799. 8vo. [iv],708 pp, 2 advt ff. Orig bds, uncut, new paper spine.
(Bickersteth) **£160 [≈ $307]**

Willis, Browne
- Notitia Parliamentaria: or An History of the Counties, Cities and Boroughs in England & Wales. The Second Edition with Additions. London: 1730. 8vo. [xii],xliv, 212,[32] pp. Contemp calf. *(Lamb)* **£45 [≈ $86]**
- A Survey of the Cathedral-Church of Llandaff ... London: for R. Gosling, 1719. 1st edn. 228 pp. 2 fldg plates, fldg plan. Rec qtr calf. *(Lloyd-Roberts)* **£70 [≈ $134]**
- A Survey of the Cathedral-Church of St. Asaph and the Edifices belonging to it ... London: for R. Gosling, 1720. 1st edn. [x], 308 pp. 2 fldg plates. Contemp calf, hinges cracked. *(Lloyd-Roberts)* **£65 [≈ $124]**

Willis, Thomas
- The London Practice of Physic ... London: for Thomas Basset & William Crooke, 1685. 1st edn. 8vo. [x],672,[16] pp. Errata leaf. Port frontis. Sl browning, some edges a bit ragged. New qtr calf. *(Goodrich)* **$1,750 [≈ £911]**

Willock, John
- The Voyages and Adventures of John Willock, Mariner ... Phila: for George Gibson, by Hogan & M'Elroy, 1798. 1st Amer edn. 12mo. 8 pp subscribers. Frontis. Rec half calf gilt. *(Ximenes)* **$550 [≈ £286]**

Willymott, William
- The Peculiar Use and Signification of certain Words in the Latin Tongue ... The Eighth Edition Revised. Eton: T. Pote, 1790. 8vo. Contemp speckled calf, red label.
(Jarndyce) **£50 [≈ $95]**

Wilson, Captain James
- A Missionary Voyage to the Southern Pacific Ocean in 1796-98 in the Ship "Duff" compiled from the Journals of the Officers ... Appendix on the State of Otaheite. London: 1799. 1st edn. 4to. c, 395 pp. Subscribers. 7 charts, 6 plates. Mod half calf.
(Lewis) **£390 [≈ $748]**

Wilson, Samuel
- An Account of the Province of Carolina in America ... London: G. Larkin, for Francis Smith, 1682. 1st edn. 2nd issue, with pp 25, 26 & 27 misnumbered. Sm 4to. Lacks map (not always present). Sl foxing. 19th c half calf, hinges reinforced. Anon.
(Chapel Hill) **$6,000 [≈ £3,125]**

Wilson, Thomas
- Distilled Spirituous Liquors the Bane of the Nation ... London: J. Roberts, 1736. Stabbed as issued. Anon.   *(Jarndyce)* **£160 [≈ $307]**

Wilson, Thomas, Bishop of Sodor & Man
- The Many Advantages of a Good Language to any Nation: with an Examination of the Present State of our own ... London: for J. Knapton ..., 1724. 1st edn. 8vo. 96 pp. Sl browned. Old wraps. Anon.
(Burmester) **£150 [≈ $287]**

Wilson, William, Chief Mate of the Ship Duff
- A Missionary Voyage to the Southern Pacific Ocean, performed in the years 1796, 1797, 1798, in the Ship Duff ... London: 1799. 1st edn. c, 395, subscribers pp. 7 fldg maps, 6 plates. Few tears reprd. Mod half leather.
(Parmer) **$650 [≈ £338]**

Winckelmann, Johann Joachim
- Critical Account of the Situation and Destruction by the First Eruptions of Mount Vesuvius, of Herculaneum, Pompeii, and Stavia ... Illustrated with Notes ... London: Carnan & Newbery, 1771. 1st edn in English. 8vo. Contemp wraps, uncut.
(Ximenes) **$600 [≈ £312]**

Wingate, Edmund
- Mr. Wingate's Arithmetick ... Revised by J. Kersey. London: 1699. [xii],544 pp. Occas foxing. Contemp mottled Cambridge calf, sl worn, sm old lib label on spine.
(Whitehart) **£95 [≈ $182]**
- Mr. Wingate's Arithmetick ... With New Supplement ... by George Shelley. London: for J. Phillips & J. & J. Knapton, 1726. 15th edn. 8vo. A few marg stains. New cloth.
(Stewart) **£120 [≈ $230]**

Winnington, Thomas
- An Apology for the Conduct of a late celebrated second-rate Minister, from the year 1729 ... till ... 1746 ... London: for W. Webb ..., [1747]. Disbound. Anon.
(Waterfield's) **£40 [≈ $76]**

Winstanley, William
- England's Worthies. Select Lives of the most Eminent Persons of the English Nation ... London: J.C. & F.C. for Obadiah Blagrave, 1684. 2nd edn. 8vo. [xxxii],661,3 advt pp. Frontis. Occas sl dust or browning. Contemp calf, backstrip relaid. Wing W.3059.
(Vanbrugh) **£125 [≈ $239]**
- The Lives of the Most famous English Poets, or the Honour of Parnassus ... London: Samuel Manship, 1687. 1st edn. [xii],221 pp. Frontis.   *(Bookpress)* **£650 [≈ £338]**

Winter Evening Conference ...
- See Goodman, John.

Winterbotham, William
- An Historical, Geographical, and Philosophical View of the American United States, and of the European Settlements in America and the West-Indies. London: J. Ridgway, 1795. 1st edn. 4 vols. 8vo. 22 plates. Lacks 10 maps & plans. Later cloth.
(Bookpress) **$225 [≈ £117]**

Wisdom, A Poem ...
- See Wilkinson, Edward.

Wise, John
- A Vindication of the Government of New-England Churches. Boston: 1772. 2nd edn. 12mo. 271, [12] pp. Browned. Orig calf, spine reprd.   *(Reese)* **$500 [≈ £260]**

Wiseman, Richard
- Severall Chirurgicall Treatises. London: 1686. 2nd edn. Folio. [xvi], 577, [13] pp.

Inner marg of title & dedic leaf remargd. Rec half mor, new endpapers.
(Fye) **$1,000 [≈ £520]**

Withers, Philip

- History of the Royal Malady, with Variety of Entertaining Anecdotes, to which are added Strictures on the Declaration of Horne Tooke ... By a Page of the Presence. London: the author, 1789. 4to. Rec calf.
(Jarndyce) **£150 [≈ $287]**

Withers, Thomas

- Observations on Chronic Weakness. York: Ward, 1777. 8vo. ix,[1],169 pp. Rec contemp style bds. *(Goodrich)* **$165 [≈ £85]**

Wollaston, William

- The Religion of Nature Delineated ... London: ptd by Samuel Palmer ..., 1726. 4th edn. 4to. 219,11 pp. Contemp calf, sl rubbed, front jnt partly cracked. Anon. *(Young's)* **£75 [≈ $143]**
- The Religion of Nature Delineated ... Sixth Edition, to which is added a Preface containing a general Account of the Life, Character, and Writings of the Author. London: Knapton, 1738. 8vo. Frontis. Contemp calf, sl rubbed, jnts cracking.
(Waterfield's) **£80 [≈ $153]**
- The Religion of Nature Delineated. The Seventh Edition. To which is added, A Preface containing a general Account of the Life, Character, and Writings of the Author ... London: Knapton, 1750. 8vo. Frontis. Contemp calf gilt, some wear, jnts cracked.
(Sanders) **£45 [≈ $86]**

Wollstonecraft, Mary

- Letters Written during a Short Residence in Sweden, Norway, and Denmark ... London: for J. Johnson, 1796. 1st edn. 8vo. [iv], 262, [vi] pp. Final advt leaf. Contemp half calf.
(Finch) **£575 [≈ $1,103]**
- Letters Written during a Short Residence in Sweden, Norway, and Denmark. London: for J. Johnson, 1796. 1st edn. 8vo. Final advt leaf. Mod half calf. *(Hannas)* **£350 [≈ $671]**
- Original Stories from Real Life ... London: J. Johnson, 1791. 1st illust edn. 12mo. 3 advt pp. Frontis & 5 plates by William Blake. Contemp tree calf, gilt spine, maroon label, sl rubbed. *(Jarndyce)* **£1,500 [≈ $2,879]**
- A Vindication of the Rights of Woman. London: Johnson, 1792. 1st edn. Tall 8vo. Sl foxing. Orig mrbld bds, uncut, rebacked with paper (damaged), front cvr detached. Slipcase.

A.E. Newton - Clements copy.
(Rostenberg & Stern) **$1,750 [≈ £911]**
- A Vindication of the Rights of Woman. Boston: Edes for Thomas & Andrews, 1792. 2nd Amer edn. 8vo. Sm ink mark in title marg. Lib stamp. Cloth.
(Rostenberg & Stern) **$425 [≈ £221]**
- A Vindication of the Rights of Woman ... Second Edition. London: for J. Johnson, 1792. 8vo. Contemp mottled calf, rebacked.
(Waterfield's) **£400 [≈ $767]**
- A Vindication of the Rights of Men, in a letter to the Rt. Hon. Edmund Burke ... London: J. Johnson, 1790. 2nd edn. Rebound in half calf.
(Jarndyce) **£220 [≈ $422]**

Womock, Laurence

- The Proselyte of Rome Call'd Back to the Communion of the Church of England ... London: for R. Clavell, 1679. 1st edn. 4to. [iv], 27 pp. Imprimatur leaf. Hole in 1st 2 ff (no loss). Disbound, uncut & unopened. Wing W.3346A. Anon. *(Young's)* **£55 [≈ $105]**

Wood, Anthony

- Athenae Oxonienses. An Exact History of all the Writers and Bishops who have had their Education in ... Oxford from ... 1500, to ... 1690 ... London: 1691-92. 1st edn. 2 vols in one. Folio. Sl used. Contemp calf, rebacked, sl worn. Wing W.3382, 3383A.
(Clark) **£300 [≈ $575]**

Wood, John

- The Origin of Building: or, the Plagiarism of the Heathens Detected ... Bath: J. Leake, 1741. Only edn. Folio. [6],235,[1] pp,errata leaf. 25 plates (numbered 1-36, 11 dble page carrying 2 numbers). Lib perf on title. Half calf. *(Sotheran's)* **£900 [≈ $1,727]**

Wood, John, the younger

- A Series of Plans for Cottages or Habitations of the Labourer ... New Edition. London: J. & J. Taylor, 1792. 2nd edn. Folio. [2], 38 pp. 28 + 2 engvd plates. Orig bds.
(Sotheran's) **£1,450 [≈ $2,783]**

Wood, Robert

- An Essay on the Original Genius and Writings of Homer: with a Comparative View of the Ancient and Present State of the Troade. London: 1775. 1st edn. 4to. xv,[1],342 pp. Frontis, fldg map, 3 plates, 2 engvs in text. Contemp calf, hinges broken but cords holding.
(Claude Cox) **£100 [≈ $191]**

Wood, William
- Sermons on Social Life. London: J. Johnston, 1775. 1st edn. 8vo. [14],236 pp. Early calf, jnts cracked.   *(Humber)* **£35 [≈$67]**

Woodward, Henry
- A Letter from Henry Woodward, Comedian, the Meanest of All Characters, to Dr John Hill, Inspector-General of Great Britain, the Greatest of All Characters. The Third Edition. London: M. Cooper, 1752. Mod wraps.   *(C.R. Johnson)* **£135 [≈$259]**

Woodward, John
- An Essay Toward a Natural History of the Earth and Terrestrial Bodies. London: Wilkin, 1695. 1st edn. 8vo. [xvi],277,[2] pp. Contemp calf, lacks free endpapers.
        (Bookpress) **$475 [≈£247]**

Woodward, Josiah
- Some Thoughts concerning the Stage in a Latter to a Lady. London: J. Nutt, 1704. 13 pp, final blank. Mod sheep. Anon.
        (C.R. Johnson) **£350 [≈$671]**

The World Unmask'd ...
- See Huber, Marie.

Worlidge, John
- Vinetum Britannicum: or a Treatise of Cider, and other Wines and Drinks extracted from Fruits growing in this Kingdom ... Third impression, much enlarged. London: for Thomas Dring, 1691. 8vo. 2 frontis, 3 plates. Contemp sheep, spine sl rubbed. Wing W.3610.   *(Ximenes)* **$1,250 [≈£651]**

Wotton, Henry
- The Elements of Architecture, Collected by Henry Wotton Knight, from the best Authors and Examples. London: John Bill, 1624. 1st edn. Sm 4to. Dusty at ends, ink stains on last leaf. Rec calf. STC 26011.
        (Georges) **£1,000 [≈$1,919]**

Wotton, Sir Henry
- Reliquiae Wottonianae: or, A Collection of Lives, Letters, Poems ... The Fourth Edition, with Additions ... London: 1685. 8vo. [lxxxviii], 713, [1 blank] pp. Usual mispagination. 4 ports. Some browning. Old calf, worn, rebacked. Wing W.3651.
        (Bow Windows) **£205 [≈$393]**

Wotton, Sir Henry (stated author)
- The State of Christendom: or, A most Exact and Curious Discovery of many Secret Passages, and Hidden Mysteries of the Times ... London: Moseley, 1657. 1st edn. Folio. [viii], 262, blank, [ii],32,[12] pp. Port. Table misbound at front. Orig calf, spine worn. Wing W.3654.   *(Vanbrugh)* **£395 [≈$758]**
- The State of Christendome ... London: Peter Parker, 1679. Folio. [xx], 262, blank, [ii], 32 pp. Contemp speckled sheep, v sl damage to headcap & lower front hinge. Wing W.3655B.
        (Vanbrugh) **£175 [≈$335]**

Wotton, William
- Reflections upon Ancient and Modern Learning ... Third Edition Corrected. London: for Tim. Goodwin, 1705. 8vo. 3 advt pp at end. New endpapers. Contemp Cambridge calf, rebacked, crnrs worn.
        (Sanders) **£85 [≈$163]**

Woty, William
- The Shrubs of Parnassus. Consisting of a Variety of Poetical Essays, Moral and Comic. By J. Copywell, of Lincoln's-Inn, Esq; ... London: for the author, & sold by J. Newbery, 1760. 1st edn. 12mo. 24, 154, [ii blank] pp. Contemp calf, sl worn, lacks label.
        (Finch) **£250 [≈$479]**

Wrangham, Francis
- The Restoration of the Jews: A Poem. Cambridge: J. Archdeacon & J. Burges, 1795. 4to. 14 pp. Rec wraps.
        (C.R. Johnson) **£450 [≈$863]**

Wraxall, Sir Nathaniel William
- The Correspondence between a Traveller and a Minister of State ... London: for J. Debrett, (1796). Contemp half calf, hinges sl split.
        (Jarndyce) **£120 [≈$230]**
- A Tour through Some of the Northern Parts of Europe ... Second Edition, Corrected. London: Cadell, 1775. 8vo. Fldg map. Contemp calf, gilt spine, sl rubbed.
        (Jarndyce) **£150 [≈$287]**
- A Tour through Some of the Northern Parts of Europe ... Second Edition, Corrected. London: Cadell, 1775. 8vo. 411 pp. Fldg map. Contemp calf, gilt dec spine. The Downes copy.   *(Gough)* **£70 [≈$134]**
- A Tour through Some of the Northern Parts of Europe ... Second Edition, Corrected. London: Cadell, 1775. 8vo. Fldg map. Contemp calf, rebacked.

(Hannas) £75 [≈ $143]

Wray, Mary (probable author)
- The Ladies' Library. Written by a Lady. Published by Mr. Steele. London: Tonson, 1714. 1st edn. 3 vols. 12mo. 3 frontis. Orig panelled calf, red labels, extremities sl rubbed. Anon. *(Karmiole)* $650 [≈ £338]

Wright, Thomas
- The Antiquities of the Town of Halifax in Yorkshire ... Leeds: ptd by James Lister, for James Hodgson ..., 1738. 1st edn. 8vo. vi,207 pp. Rec contemp style half calf.
(Young's) £85 [≈ $163]

Wycherley, William
- Love in a Wood, or, St. James's Park. A Comedy ... London: for Henry Herringman, 1694. 3rd edn. 4to. Later crushed half mor, some rubbing to extremities. Wing W.3747.
(Dramatis Personae) £125 [≈ £65]
- The Plain-Dealer. A Comedy ... The Fifth Edition. London: for R. Bentley, 1691. Sm 4to. Some browning. Epilogue cropped at ft. Disbound. *(Dramatis Personae)* $65 [≈ £33]

Wynne, William
- The Life of Sir Leoline Jenkins ... London: Joseph Downing ..., 1724. 2 vols. Folio. xx,civ,552; [4],792 pp. Port. Contemp calf, rather worn, spines chipped, later labels.
(Karmiole) $250 [≈ £130]

Wyvill, Christopher
- A State of the Representation of the People of England, on the Principles of Mr Pitt in 1785 ... Second Edition. York: W. Blanchard, 1794. Half-title, 55 pp. Disbound.
(C.R. Johnson) £75 [≈ $143]

Wilkes, Thomas
- A General View of the Stage. London: for J. Coote & W. Whetstone, 1759. 1st edn. viii, 335 pp. Engvd title vignette. Mod half calf gilt. *(Hollett)* £165 [≈ $316]

Xenophon
- Memoirs of Socrates. London: Millar & Cadell, 1767. Translated by Sarah Fielding. 2nd edn. 8vo. [2],vi,360 pp. Contemp calf, front hinge cracked.
(Bookpress) $225 [≈ £117]
- Xenophon's History of the Affairs of Greece ... Translated ... by John Newman. London: for William Freeman, 1685. 1st edn of this translation. 8vo. [1],352, 351-459, [3] pp.

Blank leaf before title. Contemp calf, rebacked, crnrs worn. Wing X.19.
(Clark) £100 [≈ $191]
- See also Bradley, Richard.

Yarranton, Andrew
- England's Improvement by Sea and Land ... London: R. Everingham for the author, 1677. 4to. Licence leaf. 8 fldg maps & plans. A few margs dusty. New cloth. Wing Y.13.
(Stewart) £150 [≈ $287]

Yates, William & Maclean, Charles
- A View of the Science of Life; on the Principles established in the Elements of Medicine, of the late celebrated John Brown ... Phila: 1797. 8vo. 232 pp. Foxing. Old bds, rebacked. *(Goodrich)* $75 [≈ £39]

Yearsley, Ann
- Earl Goodwin, an Historical Play. London: Robinson, 1791. 4to. 89,[3] pp. Disbound.
(C.R. Johnson) £250 [≈ $479]

Yorke, Charles
- Some Considerations on the Law of Forfeiture for High Treason. London: Rivington, 1748. 3rd edn. 8vo. Some foxing & dusting. Contemp calf, worn, new label. Author's pres copy. Anon.
(Meyer Boswell) $275 [≈ £143]

Youle, Joseph
- An Inaugural Dissertation on Respiration ... New York: T. & J. Swords, 1793. 8vo. 39, [1] pp. Mod qtr calf. *(Hemlock)* $175 [≈ £91]

Young, Arthur
- The Farmer's Guide in Hiring and Stocking Farms ... By the Author of the Farmer's Letters. London: for W. Strahan ..., 1770. 1st edn. 2 vols. 8vo. Advt leaf at end of vol 1. 10 plates in vol 2. Orig bds, uncut, new paper spines & labels. Anon.
(Bickersteth) £220 [≈ $422]
- General View of the Agriculture of the County of Sussex; with Observations on the Means of its Improvement. London: 1793. 4to. 97 pp. Fldg hand cold map, 2 hand cold plates (cropped with some loss of text). Mor backed bds. *(Henly)* £110 [≈ $211]
- Rural Oeconomy. London: for T. Becket, 1770. 1st edn. Demy 8vo. [ii],520 pp. Sl browning. Contemp calf, armorial device, rebacked. Anon. *(Ash)* £200 [≈ $383]

Young, David, of Perth
- National Improvements upon Agriculture in Twenty-Seven Essays. Edinburgh: for the author, & John Bell, 1785. 403 pp. 3 plates. Contemp sheep, brown label.
(C.R. Johnson) **£135 [≃ $259]**

Young, Edward
- The Centaur not Fabulous ... London: for A. Millar, 1755. 2nd edn. 8vo. xvi,384 pp. Frontis. Rec period style qtr calf, uncut.
(Young's) **£45 [≃ $86]**
- The Complaint: or, Night-Thoughts ... Revised and Corrected by himself. Dublin: for Peter Wilson, 1766. 12mo. 324 pp. Contemp speckled calf.
(Burmester) **£60 [≃ $115]**
- The Complaint: or, Night Thoughts on Life, Death and Immortality. Glasgow: Robert & Andrew Foulis, 1771. 3 vols. 12mo. Frontis in vol 1. Contemp calf, lacks 1 label.
(Waterfield's) **£135 [≃ $259]**
- Love of Fame, the Universal Passion. In Seven Characteristical Satires. The Second Edition Corrected, and Alter'd. London: for J. Tonson, 1728. 8vo. [xii],175 pp. Contemp calf, gilt spine chipped at ends, jnt ends just cracking. Anon.
(Finch) **£85 [≃ $163]**
- Love of Fame, the Universal Passion. In Seven Characteristical Satires. Second Edition, corrected and alter'd. London: for J. Tonson, 1728. 8vo. Endpapers spotted. Contemp calf, rec rebacked. Anon.
(Stewart) **£120 [≃ $230]**
- Night Thoughts on Life Death and Immortality ... added The Life of the Author ... by G. Wright. London: Rivington ..., 1777. 12mo. Engvd frontis & title. Contemp calf, gilt spine, olive label, sl worn, upper jnt cracked.
(Sanders) **£32 [≃ $61]**

- A Poem on the Last Day. Oxford: ptd at the Theatre, 1713. Browned. Erased sgntr on title. Disbound.
(Waterfield's) **£40 [≃ $76]**
- The Poetical Works. London: Curll, Tonson, Walthoe ..., 1741. 2nd coll edn. 2 vols. 8vo. Frontis in vol 1, 3 plates. Sl spotting. Orig calf, rubbed, jnts cracked.
(Bickersteth) **£60 [≃ $115]**
- The Revenge A Tragedy ... London: for Chetwood, 1721. 1st edn. 8vo. [xvi],63 pp. Half-title. 1st & last ff sl soiled. Disbound.
(Young's) **£35 [≃ $67]**
- The Works in Prose ... Now First Collected into One Volume ... London: Brown, Hill & Payne, 1765. 1st coll edn. 8vo. Lacks free endpapers. Contemp calf, worn.
(Buccleuch) **£45 [≃ $86]**

Y-Worth, William
- The Britannian Magazine: or, a New Art of making above Twenty Sorts of English Wines ... London: for N. Bodington, [1700?]. 3rd edn, with addtns. 12mo. Sm marg reprs to title, few sl stains. Calf antique. Wing Y.215.
(Ximenes) **$850 [≃ £442]**

Zimmerman, J.G.
- Essay on National Pride. To which are added Memoirs of the Author's Life and Writings. Translated by S.H. Wilcocke. London: 1797. xlii, 260, [23] pp. Paper cvrd bds, paper label.
(Whitehart) **£60 [≃ $115]**

Zimmermann, Eberhardt
- A Political Survey of the Present State of Europe ... London: 1787. 1st edn. 8vo. Contemp tree calf, gilt spine.
(Jarndyce) **£65 [≃ $124]**

Catalogue Booksellers Contributing to IRBP

The booksellers who have provided catalogues during 1990 specifically for the purpose of compiling the various titles in the *IRBP* series, and from whose catalogues books have been selected, are listed below in alphabetical order of the abbreviation employed for each. This listing is therefore a complete key to the booksellers contributing to the series as a whole; only a proportion of the listed names is represented in this particular subject volume.

The majority of these booksellers issue periodic catalogues free, on request, to potential customers. Sufficient indication of the type of book handled by each bookseller can be gleaned from the individual book entries set out in the main body of this work and in the companion titles in the series.

Agvent	=	Charles Agvent, R.D.2, Box 377A, Mertztown, PA 19539, U.S.A. (215 682 4750)
Alphabet	=	Alphabet Bookshop, 145 Main Street West, Port Colborne, Ontario L3K 3V3, Canada (416 834 5323)
Antic Hay	=	Antic Hay Rare Books, P.O. Box 2185, Asbury Park, NJ 07712, U.S.A. (201 774 4590)
Any Amount	=	Any Amount of Books, 62 Charing Cross Road, London WC2H 0BB, England (071 240 8140)
Ars Artis	=	Ars Artis, 31 Abberbury Road, Oxford OX4 4ET, England (0865 770714)
Ars Libri	=	Ars Libri, Ltd., 560 Harrison Avenue, Boston, Massachusetts 02118, U.S.A. (617 357 5212)
Ash	=	Ash Rare Books, 25 Royal Exchange, London EC3V 3LP, England (071 626 2665)
Baldwin	=	Stuart A. Baldwin, Fossil Hall, Boars Tye Road, Silver End, Witham, Essex CM8 3QA, England (0376 83502)
Bates & Hindmarch	=	Bates and Hindmarch, Antiquarian Bookseller, Fishergate, Boroughbridge, North Yorkshire Y05 9AL, England (0423 324258)
Beech	=	John Beech Rare Books, 63 Station Road, Histon, Cambridge CB4 4LQ, England (0223 232210)
Bell	=	Peter Bell, Bookseller & Publisher, 4 Brandon Street, Edinburgh EH3 5DX, Scotland (031 556 2198)
Bernett	=	F.A. Bernett Inc., 2001 Palmer Avenue, Larchmont, N.Y. 10538, U.S.A. (914 834 3026)
Between the Covers	=	Between the Covers, 575 Collings Avenue, Collingswood, NJ 08107, U.S.A. (609 869 0512)
Bickersteth	=	David Bickersteth, 4 South End, Bassingbourn, Royston, Hertfordshire SG8 5NG, England (0763 45619)
Black Sun	=	Black Sun Books, P.O. Box 7916 - F.D.R. Sta., New York, New York 10150-1915, U.S.A. (212 688 6622)
Blakeney	=	Adam Blakeney, Apartment 8, 59 Devonshire Street, London W1N 1LT, England (071 323 0937)
Book Block	=	The Book Block, 8 Loughlin Avenue, Cos Cob, Connecticut 06807, U.S.A. (203 629 2990)
Bookline	=	Bookline, 35 Farranfad Road, Downpatrick BT30 8NH, Northern Ireland (039687 712)
Bookmark	=	Bookmark, Children's Books, Fortnight, Wick Down, Broad Hinton, Swindon, Wiltshire SN4 9NR, England (0793 731693)
Bookpress	=	The Bookpress Ltd., Post Office Box KP, Williamsburg, Virginia 23187, U.S.A. (804 229 1260)

Boswell	=	Boswell Books and Prints, 44 Great Russell Street, London WC1B 3PA, England (071 580 7200)
		or Boswell Books and Prints, 2261 Market Street, Suite 288, San Francisco, CA 94114, U.S.A. (415 431 3021)
Bow Windows	=	Bow Windows Book Shop, 128 High Street, Lewes, East Sussex BN7 1XL, England (0273 480780)
Bromer	=	Bromer Booksellers, 607 Boylston Street, at Copley Square, Boston, MA 02116, U.S.A. (617 247 2818)
Paul Brown	=	Paul Brown, 3 Melbourne Terrace, Melbourne Grove, London SE22 8RE, England (081 299 4195)
Buccleuch	=	Buccleuch Books, 40 Buccleuch Street, Edinburgh EH8 9LP, Scotland (031 6681353)
Buckley	=	Brian & Margaret Buckley, 11 Convent Close, Kenilworth, Warwickshire CV8 2FQ, England (0926 55223)
Burmester	=	James Burmester, Manor House Farmhouse, North Stoke, Bath BA1 9AT, England (0272 327265)
Central Africana	=	Central Africana, The Coach House, Serpentine Road, Sevenoaks TN13 3XP, England (071 242 3131)
Chapel Hill	=	Chapel Hill Rare Books, P.O. Box 456, Carrboro, NC 27510, U.S.A. (919 929 8351)
Clark	=	Robert Clark, 6a King Street, Jericho, Oxford OX2 6DF, England (0865 52154)
Clearwater	=	Clearwater Books, 19 Matlock Road, Ferndown, Wimborne, Dorset BH22 8QT, England (0202 893263)
Claude Cox	=	Claude Cox, The White House, Kelsale, Saxmundham, Suffolk IP17 2PQ, England (0728 602786)
Dalian	=	Dalian Books, David P. Williams, 81 Albion Drive, London Fields, London E8 4LT, England (071 249 1587)
de Beaumont	=	Robin de Beaumont, 25 Park Walk, Chelsea, London SW10 0AJ, England (071 352 3440)
Dermont	=	Joseph A. Dermont, 13 Arthur Street, P.O. Box 654, Onset, MA 02558, U.S.A. (508 295 4760)
Dramatis Personae	=	Dramatis Personae, 71 Lexington Avenue, New York, New York 10010, U.S.A. (212 679 3705)
Dyke	=	Martin Dyke, 4 Gordon Road, Clifton, Bristol BS8 1AP, England (0272 742090)
Edrich	=	I.D. Edrich, 17 Selsdon Road, London E11 2QF, England (081 989 9541)
Egret	=	Egret Books, 6 Priory Place, Wells, Somerset BA5 1SP, England (0749 679312)
Ellis	=	Peter Ellis, 31 Museum Street, London WC1A 1LH, England (071 637 5862)
Emerald Isle	=	Emerald Isle Books, 539 Antrim Road, Belfast BT15 3BU, Northern Ireland (0232 370798)
Fenning	=	James Fenning, 12 Glenview, Rochestown Avenue, Dun Laoghaire, County Dublin, Eire (01 857855)
Finch	=	Simon Finch Rare Books, Clifford Chambers, 10 New Bond Street, London W1Y 9PF, England (071 499 0974)
First Issues	=	First Issues Ltd, 17 Alfoxton Avenue, London N15 3DD, England (081 881 6931)
Frew Mackenzie	=	Frew Mackenzie plc, 106 Great Russell Street, London WC1B 3NA, England (071 580 2311)
Fye	=	W. Bruce Fye, Antiquarian Medical Books, 1607 North Wood Avenue, Marshfield, Wisconsin 54449, U.S.A. (715 384 8128)
Gage	=	Gage Postal Books, P.O. Box 105, Westcliff-on-Sea, Essex SS0 8EQ, England (0702 715133)

Gaskell	=	Roger Gaskell, 17 Ramsey Road, Warboys, Cambridgeshire PE17 2RW, England (0487 823059)
Gemmary	=	The Gemmary, Inc, PO Box 816, Redondo Beach, CA 90277, U.S.A. (213 372 5969)
Georges	=	Georges, 52 Park Street, Bristol BS1 5JN, England (0272 276602)
Glyn's	=	Glyn's Books, 4 Bryn Draw Terrace, Wrexham, Clwyd LL13 7DF, Wales (0978 364473)
Goodrich	=	James Tait Goodrich, Antiquarian Books & Manuscripts, 214 Everett Place, Englewood, New Jersey 07631, U.S.A. (201 567 0199)
Gough	=	Simon Gough Books, 5 Fish Hill, Holt, Norfolk, England (026371 2650)
Grayling	=	David A.H. Grayling, Lyvennet, Crosby Ravensworth, Penrith, Cumbria CA10 3JP, England (09315 282)
Green Meadow	=	Green Meadow Books, Kinoulton, Nottingham NG12 3EN, England (0949 81723)
Gretton	=	John R. Gretton, 5 Quebec Road, Dereham, Norfolk NR19 2DP, England (0362 692707)
Hadley	=	Peter J. Hadley, 20th Century Books, 132 Corve Street. Ludlow, Shropshire SY8 2PG, England (0584 874441)
Halsey	=	Alan Halsey, The Poetry Bookshop, 22 Broad Street, Hay-on-Wye, Via Hereford HR3 5DB, England (0497 820 305)
Hannas	=	Torgrim Hannas, 29a Canon Street, Winchester, Hampshire SO23 9JJ, England (0962 862730)
Hatchwell	=	Richard Hatchwell, The Old Rectory, Little Somerford, Chippenham, Wiltshire SN15 5JW, England (0666 823261)
Hazeldene	=	Hazeldene Bookshop, A.H. & L.G. Elliot, 61 Renshaw Street, Liverpool L1 2SJ, England (051 708 8780)
Hemlock	=	Hemlock Books, 170 Beach 145th Street, Neponsit, New York 11694, U.S.A. (718 318 0737)
Henly	=	John Henly, Bookseller, Brooklands, Walderton, Chichester, West Sussex PO18 9EE, England (0705 631426)
Heritage	=	Heritage Book Shop, Inc., 8540 Melrose Avenue, Los Angeles, California 90069, U.S.A. (213 659 3674)
High Latitude	=	High Latitude, P.O. Box 11254, Bainbridge Island, WA 98110, U.S.A. (206 598 3454)
Hollett	=	R.F.G. Hollett and Son, 6 Finkle Street, Sedbergh, Cumbria LA10 5BZ, England (05396 20298)
Holmes	=	David J. Holmes, 230 South Broad Street, Third Floor, Philadelphia, Pennsylvania 19102, U.S.A. (215 735 1083)
Horowitz	=	Glenn Horowitz, 141 East 44th Street, Suite 808, New York, New York 10017, U.S.A. (212 557 1381)
Houle	=	George Houle, 7260 Beverly Boulevard, Los Angeles, California 90036, U.S.A. (213 937 5858)
Humber	=	Humber Books, 688 Beverley Road, Hull, North Humberside HU6 7JH, England (0482 802239)
James	=	Marjorie James, The Old School, Oving, Chichester, West Sussex PO20 6DG, England (0243 781354)
Janus	=	Janus Books, Post Office Box 40787, Tucson, Arizona 85717, U.S.A. (602 881 8192)
Jarndyce	=	Jarndyce, Antiquarian Booksellers, 46 Great Russell Street, Bloomsbury, London WC1B 3PA, England (071 631 4220)
C.R. Johnson	=	C.R. Johnson, 21 Charlton Place, London N1 8AQ, England (071 354 1077)
Michael Johnson	=	Michael Johnson Books, Oak Lodge, Kingsway, Portishead, Bristol BS20 8HW, England (0272 843798)

Karmiole	=	Kenneth Karmiole, Bookseller, 1225 Santa Monica Mall, Santa Monica, California 90401, U.S.A. (213 451 4342)
King	=	John K. King, P.O. Box 33363, Detroit, Michigan 48232-5363, U.S.A. (313 961 0622)
Lamb	=	R.W. & C.R. Lamb, Talbot House, 158 Denmark Rd., Lowestoft, Suffolk NR32 2EL, England (0502 564306)
Larkhill	=	Larkhill Books, Larkhill House, Tetbury, Gloucestershire GL8 8SY, England (0666 502343)
Lewis	=	John Lewis, 35 Stoneham Street, Coggeshall, Essex CO6 1UH, England (0376 561518)
Lewton	=	L.J. Lewton, Old Station House, Freshford, Bath BA3 6EQ, England (0225 723351)
Limestone Hills	=	Limestone Hills Book Shop, P.O. Box 1125, Glen Rose, Texas 76043, U.S.A. (817 897 4991)
Lloyd-Roberts	=	Tom Lloyd-Roberts, Old Court House, Caerwys, Mold, Clwyd CH7 5BB, Wales (0352 720276)
Lopez	=	Ken Lopez, Bookseller, 51 Huntington Road, Hadley, MA 01035, U.S.A. (413 584 4827)
McBlain	=	McBlain Books, P.O. Box 5062 Hamden, CT 06518, U.S.A. (203 281 0400)
McCann	=	Joey McCann, 76 Oliver Road, Cowley, Oxford OX4 2JF, England (0865 715001)
MacDonnell	=	MacDonnell Rare Books, 9307 Glenlake Drive, Austin, Texas 78730, U.S.A. (512 345 4139)
McGilvery	=	Laurence McGilvery, Post Office Box 852, La Jolla, California 92038, U.S.A. (619 454 4443)
Marlborough B'Shop	=	Marlborough Bookshop, 6 Kingsbury Street, Marlborough, Wiltshire, England (0672 514074)
Mendelsohn	=	H.L. Mendelsohn, Fine European Books, P.O. Box 317, Belmont, Massachusetts 02178, U.S.A. (617 484 7362)
Meyer Boswell	=	Meyer Boswell Books, Inc., 982 Hayes Street, San Francisco, CA 94117, U.S.A. (415 346 1839)
Moon	=	Michael Moon, Antiquarian, Booksellers & Publishers, 41, 42 & 43 Roper Street, Whitehaven, Cumbria CA28 7BS, England (0946 62936)
Moorhouse	=	Hartley Moorhouse Books, 142 Petersham Road, Richmond, Surrey TW10 6UX, England (081 948 7742)
Mordida	=	Mordida Books, P.O. Box 79322, Houston, Texas 77279, U.S.A. (713 467 4280)
Newnham	=	Anthony Newnham, 72 Dundas Street, Edinburgh EH3 6QZ, Scotland (031 556 3705)
New Wireless	=	New Wireless Pioneers, Box 398, Elma N.Y. 14059, U.S.A. (716 681 3186)
Nouveau	=	Nouveau Rare Books, Steve Silberman, P.O. Box 12471, 5005 Meadow Oaks Park Drive, Jackson, Mississippi 39211, U.S.A. (601 956 9950)
Oak Knoll	=	Oak Knoll Books, 414 Delaware Street, New Castle, Delaware 19720, U.S.A. (302 328 7232)
Offenbacher	=	Emile Offenbacher, 84-50 Austin Street, P.O. Box 96, Kew Gardens, New York 11415, U.S.A. (718 849 5834)
Parmer	=	J. Parmer, Booksellers, 7644 Forrestal Road, San Diego, CA 92120, U.S.A. (619 287 0693)
Patterson	=	Ian Patterson, 21 Bateman Street, Cambridge CB2 1NB, England (0223 321658)
Petrilla	=	R. & A. Petrilla, Roosevelt, NJ 08555-0306, U.S.A. (609 426 4999)
Pettler & Liebermann	=	Pettler & Liebermann, 8033 Sunsett Blvd. #977, Los Angeles, CA 90046, U.S.A. (213 474 2479)

Phillips	=	Phillips of Hitchin, (Antiques) Ltd., The Manor House, Hitchin, Hertfordshire, England (0462 432067)
Pickering	=	Pickering & Chatto, 17 Pall Mall, London SW1Y 5NB, England (071 930 8627)
Polyanthos	=	Polyanthos Park Avenue Books, P.O. Box 343, Huntington, NY 11743, U.S.A. (516 271 5558)
Rankin	=	Alan Rankin, 72 Dundas Street, Edinburgh EH3 6QZ, Scotland, Scotland (031 556 3705)
Reese	=	William Reese Company, 409 Temple Street, New Haven, Connecticut 06511, U.S.A. (203 789 8081)
David Rees	=	David Rees, 18A Prentis Road, London SW16 1QD, England (081 769 2453)
Reference Works	=	Reference Works, 12 Commercial Road, Dorset BH19 1DF, England (0929 424423)
Respess	=	L. & T. Respess Books, PO Box 236, Bristol, RI 02809, U.S.A. (401 253 1639)
Roberts	=	John Roberts Bookshop, 43 Triangle West, Clifton, Bristol BS8 1ES, Scotland (2 268568)
Robertshaw	=	John Robertshaw, 5 Fellowes Drive, Ramsey, Huntingdon, Cambridgeshire PE17 1BE, England (0487 813330)
Rootenberg	=	B. & L. Rootenberg, P.O. Box 5049, Sherman Oaks, California 91403-5049, U.S.A. (818 788 7765)
Rostenberg & Stern	=	Leona Rostenberg and Madeleine, Stern, Rare Books, 40 East 88 Street, New York, N.Y. 10128., U.S.A. (212 831 6628)
Sanders	=	Sanders of Oxford Ltd., 104 High Street, Oxford OX1 4BW, England (0865 242590)
Savona	=	Savona Books, 9 Wilton Road, Hornsea, North Humberside HU18 1QU, England (0964 535195)
Schoyer	=	Schoyer's Books, 1404 South Negley Avenue, Pittsburgh, PA 15217, U.S.A. (412 521 8464)
Sclanders	=	Andrew Sclanders, 73 Duckett Road, London N4 1BL, England (081 340 6843)
Sklaroff	=	L.J. Sklaroff, The Totland Bookshop, The Broadway, Totland, Isle of Wight PO39 0BW, England (0983 754960)
Sotheran's	=	Henry Sotheran Ltd., 2 Sackville Street, Piccadilly, London W1X 2DP, England (071 439 6151)
Spelman	=	Ken Spelman, 70 Micklegate, York YO1 1LF, England (0904 624414)
Stewart	=	Andrew Stewart, 11 High Street, Helpringham, Sleaford, Lincolnshire NG34 9RA, England (052 921 617)
Sumner & Stillman	=	Sumner & Stillman, P.O. Box 225, Yarmouth, ME 04096, U.S.A. (207 846 6070)
Michael Taylor	=	Michael Taylor Rare Books, The Gables, 8 Mendham Lane, Harleston, Norfolk IP20 9DE, England (0379 853889)
Peter Taylor	=	Peter Taylor, 4A Ye Corner, Aldenham Road, Watford, Hertfordshire WD1 4BS, England (0923 50342)
Temple	=	Robert Temple, 65 Mildmay Road, London N1 4PU, England (071 254 3674)
Terramedia	=	Terramedia Books, 19 Homestead Road, Wellesley, MA 02181, U.S.A. (617 237 6485)
Tiger Books	=	Tiger Books, Yew Tree Cottage, Westbere, Canterbury, Kent CT2 0HH, England (0227 710030)
Trophy Room Books	=	Trophy Room Books, Box 3041, Agoura, CA 91301, U.S.A. (818 889 2469)
Vanbrugh	=	Vanbrugh Rare Books, Pied Bull Yard, Bury Place, Bloomsbury, London EC1A 2JR, England (071 404 0733)

Virgo	=	Virgo Books, Little Court, South Wraxall, Bradford-on-Avon, Wiltshire BA15 2SE, England (02216 2040)
Walcot	=	Patrick Walcot, 60 Sunnybank Road, Sutton Coldfield, West Midlands B73 5RJ, England (021 382 6381)
Washton	=	Andrew D. Washton, 411 East 83rd Street, New York, New York 10028, U.S.A. (212 751 7027)
Waterfield's	=	Waterfield's, 36 Park End Street, Oxford OX1 1HJ, England (0865 721809)
West Side	=	West Side Books, 113 W. Liberty, Ann Arbor, MI 48103, U.S.A. (313 995 1891)
Wheldon & Wesley	=	Wheldon & Wesley Ltd., Lytton Lodge, Codicote, Hitchin, Hertfordshire SG4 8TE, England (0438 820370)
Whitehart	=	F.E. Whitehart, Rare Books, 40 Priestfield Road, Forest Hill, London SE23 2RS, England (081 699 3225)
Whiteson	=	Edna Whiteson, 66 Belmont Avenue, Cockfosters, Hertfordshire EN4 9LA, England (081 449 8860)
Willow	=	Willow House Books, 58-60 Chapel Street, Chorley, Lancashire PR7 1BS, England (02572 69280)
Woolmer	=	J. Howard Woolmer, Revere, Pennsylvania 18953, U.S.A. (215 847 5074)
Words Etcetera	=	Words Etcetera, Julian Nangle, Hod House, Child Okeford, Dorset DT11 8EH, England (0258 73338)
Worldwide	=	Worldwide Antiquarian, Post Office Box 391, Cambridge, MA 02141, U.S.A. (617 876 6220)
Wreden	=	William P. Wreden, 206 Hamilton Avenue, P.O. Box 56, Palo Alto, CA 94302-0056, U.S.A. (415 325 6851)
Ximenes	=	Ximenes: Rare Books, Inc., 19 East 69th Street, New York, NY 10021, U.S.A. (212 744 0226)
Young's	=	Young's Antiquarian Books, Tillingham, Essex CM0 7ST, England (062187 8187)
Zwisohn	=	Jane Zwisohn Books, 524 Solano Drive N.E., Albuquerque, New Mexico 87108, U.S.A. (505 255 4080)